TREES OF SEATTLE

SECOND EDITION

Madrona for mary

arth de Jain

TREES
OF SEATTLE

SECOND EDITION

ARTHUR LEE JACOBSON

First printing, January 2006; printed in the United States of America

ISBN: 0-9622918-4-6

Cover design by Keala Hagmann
Design&Typesetting by Arthur Lee Jacobson, Steve Herold, Keala Hagmann
Photo cropping, arrangement and color management by Steve Herold of Books A to Z, assisted by Emenke

All photographs by Arthur Lee Jacobson except Canyon Live Oak by Brian Carter, and the following by Garth K. Ferber: Douglas Fir, Black Cottonwood (Poplar), Coast Redwood

Bark Photographs: *Front cover, clockwise:* Pacific Yew, Daimyo Oak, Plum-fruited Yew, Common Stewartia, Veitch Fir, 'Marina' Hybrid Madrona, Monterey Cypress, Silver Maple, Black Locust, Madrona.
Back cover, top to bottom: Oregon White Oak, American Sycamore, Sycamore Maple, Common Quince Tree, Cluster Pine, Incense Cedar.
Cover Madrona Drawing: *Arbutus Menziesii;* from Charles Sprague Sargent's *The Silva of North America,* 14 volumes, 1891–1902; *this* from volume 5, 1893.

Map of Washington Park Arboretum © Lacia Lynne Bailey

Publisher:
Arthur Lee Jacobson
2215 E. Howe Street
Seattle, WA 98112
(206) 328-TREE (8733)
alj@consultant.com
www.ArthurLeeJ.com

Other titles from Arthur Lee Jacobson:
Trees of Green Lake
Trees of the Bloedel Reserve
Purpleleaf Plums
Frank Brockman Memorial U.W. Campus Tree Tour
North American Landscape Trees
Wild Plants of Greater Seattle

CONTENTS

ACKNOWLEDGEMENTS

In a sense, I've been updating this book for 16 years—continuously since the first edition came out in February 1990. During these years, various friends, colleagues, and acquaintances helped by giving advice, answering questions, or locating and identifying specimens. The book is better for having had such assistance. Also I have benefited from both emotional and financial support. However difficult, I shall limit my thanking to this *one* page; it's a *big* book.

People who reviewed the draft of this edition, and made helpful suggestions despite being given insufficient time, are Ron Brightman, Walt Bubelis, Keala Hagmann, Michael Lee, Brent Schmidt, Kathy Sutalo and Robert Van Pelt. Since I had no editor, that these patient folks caught most of my slips, made for a much cleaner book. I am to blame, not they, for the *inconsistencies* in the book. Inconsistency does not bother me much; blind adherence to standards or rules is a yoke that I eschew.

The following generous patrons all donated at least $100 toward the cause, thereby enabling me to spend more time hunting trees and writing the book, and less time fretting about bills: Anonymous, Lacia Lynne Bailey, John Dixon, Rich Ellison, Steve & Jeannie Hale, Mark Herkert, Julie Hill, Larry Glickman, Nancy M, Little Mann, Rick McGuire, Mark & Sharon, Lynn Moser, Lee Neff, Debra Prinzing, Gwen Rosseau, David Slotnick, Urban Forestry Services, Fred Weinmann, Madeleine Wilde, and Phil Wood. To the people who hired my services, and thus *indirectly* supported the writing of this book, I am also indebted and grateful.

When I was running out of time, and had too many trees to see, a couple of friends spent much time helping, even to the detriment of their own business: Lacia Lynne Bailey and Ron Brightman. Both are very generous with their time and skills. Steve Herold and Keala Hagmann also saved me from disaster.

That this book is so full of measurements is due much to the consideration of my friend Robert Van Pelt, with the University of Washington College of Forest Resources, who enabled me to borrow a laser range finder I could not afford to buy.

If Don Gordon had not passed away, he would have played a major role. Back in 1996 and 1997 he was keenly eager to help me update the book—but I was not ready then. By the time I was ready in 2004, Don had died.

Less direct, indefinite, yet very real support from many lovable and loving well-wishers, fans, friends and family has enabled me to focus acutely, during most of 2005, while not wearing out, nor degenerating into a hopelessly unbalanced slave to work. To *all*—listed by name, and the many more unlisted—I am grateful and feel blessed to be so rich in friends.

INTRODUCTION

Seattle has more different kinds of trees than any other city, and this book is your guide to learning about them and all their wonders.

Trees are vitally important to us. They hold soil against erosion; their leaves condense valuable moisture from the atmosphere; and their roots help hold fresh water in aquifers. They shade us, protect us from winds, keep our houses, yards, streets and parks cooler in summer and warmer in winter; they harbor beneficial wildlife and create microclimates essential to the health of other plants. They also yield fruit and nuts, enliven the landscape with colorful, bold or dainty flowers, foliage and branch patterns—and where else would songbirds nest? Beyond all this there is something in huge old trees that is profoundly soothing to the human psyche.

If we turn to books to learn what experts can tell us about trees, we find that they sometimes disagree among themselves. University-trained specialists are often ineffective at bridging the gap between specialized learning and the simpler needs of the rest of us. There is clearly a need for an *accessible but comprehensive local guidebook.* The rewards of an acquaintance with trees outnumber the difficulties: initial puzzlement is soon replaced with long-lasting satisfaction and joy.

About Seattle

Seattle is large, young, and unusually varied. Taking population and square miles together, it ranks foremost among Pacific Northwest cities:

	2000 census:	Approx. sq. miles
Portland, Oregon	529,121	100
Seattle, Washington	563,374	84
Vancouver, British Columbia	545,671	44

In everyday speech some people confine "Seattle" to the central business district: "Downtown." Some consider "Seattle" to be a much larger area, including such adjacent communities as Mercer Island, Bellevue and the like. In this book, "Seattle" is that entity legally incorporated and defined by the city limits: very few trees are cited outside of its legal boundaries.

Seattle's climate is without great extremes of hot or cold. Prolonged summer heat or deep winter freezes become the talk of the town when they occur. One result of this moderate climate is that we can grow many more kinds of trees here than can be grown in most other places in the northern temperate zone. A drawback is that certain trees, which need or prefer a climate with strongly contrasting seasons, do poorly here.

Seattle has hills, valleys, wet ravines, swampy marshes, dry bluffs, meadows, lakes, the Duwamish River and the Puget Sound shoreline. Its soils are equally diverse—from peat to sand to heavy clay. Over 30 species of trees are *native* here, meaning that their natural range includes our city, and wild specimens are currently growing here.

Seattle is so large and varied that it has significantly diverse microhabitats. For example, one yard—sunny, high and dry—may be ideal for apricot trees; another may be suitable only for trees tolerant of wet soil and considerable shade.

Sometimes several unusually cold winters follow one another, killing many weak trees and even some strong ones. But when mild winters succeed one another, we can grow even subtropical plants outdoors until eventual freezes put an end to them. One fortunate Seattleite actually had a banana tree ripen fruit here, outdoors!

About This Guide

Most plants a person might call a tree are treated in this guide as long as at least one established specimen is known within the city limits, except for:

1) trees known *only* at the Washington Park Arboretum;
2) certain extremely rare species known only as very young specimens;
3) certain cultivars.

This book's first edition described and cited specific examples of an impressive 740 different kinds of trees known within the city limits. Now, close to 600 additional trees have been added to this second edition, so even with the loss of some 30 kinds cited in the first edition, over 1,300 kinds of trees are treated here in the text, notes and appendices.

Entries focus on those qualities and characteristics that make each kind of tree interesting and valuable to us. Some people will be introduced to kinds of trees they have never known before, while others may use this guide to resolve a question of identification. Still others may wish to paint or photograph a particular kind of tree, or to acquire material for propagation, while a prospective purchaser may wish to observe mature examples of various trees.

Naturally enough, individual trees are cited here only if they are known to the writer, though in so large a city some significant examples inevitably escape notice. Whenever possible, those chosen for inclusion (all else being equal), are big rather than small, old rather than young, healthy rather than sickly, attractive rather than ugly, and on public rather than private land. Naturally, rarer sorts of trees are usually listed regardless of how ugly, unhealthy, scrawny or moribund they may be.

Preferential treatment is given to examples at the Ballard Locks and on the U.W. campus. In both places even poor examples are sometimes mentioned because of the great variety of trees that can be seen in one place, which makes observation that much more convenient.

Please understand that some neighborhoods are richer in trees than others, and are mentioned much more often. This imbalance is due to the presence or absence of noteworthy trees, not to any favoritism on the author's part.

How to Identify Trees

One person may rest content knowing that the big tree in a neighbor's yard is a maple. Another person may insist on knowing what *kind* of maple it is, and may also be curious as to the identities of less prominent trees. Most people are pleased to know the common names of our more numerous or conspicuous trees; a few are not satisfied until they can produce the scientific binomial for every tree they see. Whatever the level of sophistication, the general procedure for learning tree names is essentially the same, and there are just a few ways to go about it.

First and easiest, *ask* someone who is likely to know. Anyone with an unusual or professional interest in trees is worth asking: nursery workers, gardeners, landscape architects, foresters, tree-surgeons or botanists would all be likely sources.

Second, *check a library*. The answer will be in a book—but which book will have the information we need? There are so many books! The best tree identification guide for Seattle is *The Collins Tree Guide*, by Owen Johnson and David More, published in 2004. For trees in Seattle, it is much superior to any other identification guide.

A third way to identify trees is to *visit labeled collections*. In Seattle, that means going to the Arboretum, or to labeled portions of the U.W. campus, or to the gardens at the Locks. Of course, nurseries that sell trees are a good place also, though mature trees are seldom seen in that context.

A fourth way is to *join a class, lecture or tour* designed to acquaint participants with trees.

Once the name of a tree is known, books such as this one, as well as the internet, can be used to tell us more about the tree in question.

Since this is not a plant-identification treatise, words such as *berry, cone, flower, fruit, nut* and *seed,* which are given a strict scientific sense in botanical texts, are intended here in their ordinary non-technical sense. To avoid confusion, scientific nomenclature is carefully differentiated from vernacular names.

About the Arrangement of This Guide

Most tree guides arrange entries according to scientific affinity, beginning with primitive kinds followed by those more evolved, all carefully placed in related groups. Other tree guides are arranged alphabetically by scientific names. The entries in this guide are arranged alphabetically by vernacular names.

In some cases foreign names have been adopted into English usage, for example the Japanese "Katsura" for *Cercidiphyllum.* A few trees have neither an English name nor any non-English vernacular name worth using, so there is scarcely any choice but to list them by their scientific names. Accordingly, you will find *Eucryphia, Idesia* and *Maackia* alphabetized with Alder, Dogwood, Pine and Willow. On the other hand, certain trees have become well-known by their scientific appellations, so that their name of common usage is their scientific generic name. The perfect example is Magnolia. A *common name,* then, is one in common usage, whether it be vernacular or scientific in origin, though usually it is the former.

A *vernacular name* is given informally, by anyone, with no rules governing its usage. It may belong to a specific tree or to a group of similar trees, or even to quite different ones. A vernacular name may be a folk name, a local name, a medicinal or culinary name; it may come from nurserymen or gardeners, from children's rhymes or classical literature. A vernacular name is any name other than the scientific name.

A *scientific name*, in contrast, is a plant's formal, "validly published" binomial designation (for example *Alnus rubra*). Its usage is precisely regulated by internationally accepted rules which are voluntarily followed by most scientists and educated laymen the world over.

Ideally there is one and only one correct scientific name for each kind of tree. In fact scientists do not always agree—one scientist's species is frequently another's "varietas" or "forma" or "subspecies." Furthermore, rules change over the years and new findings appear continually, so synonyms are necessary in order to ensure understanding and coordination of information. This guide supplies most major synonyms, listed beneath the preferred scientific name and indicated with an equal sign (=). The main use is to facilitate cross-referencing with other books, particularly older ones. (See Appendix, page 416.)

Alphabetizing by English names has meant that some genera (*Chamæcyparis, Prunus* and *Thuja*) are split and will be found in disjunct sections of the book. This will only be disturbing to the scientist or experienced tree enthusiast who will, in any case, know vernacular names as well as scientific ones.

A problem arose in trying to add so many new kinds of trees to this second edition: not enough room. Thus many rare, young trees are relegated to small print, footnote status. The 113 crabapples are the most obvious example. To have treated them as full-size entries would have taken too much space.

Still more new trees have been for sale at local garden centers and nurseries in the 1990s and into this millennium. Yet for some I was unable to cite any examples in Seattle. Readers can help the book's *next* edition by telling me about examples of any tree that you find not included.

About Cultivars

This book cites Seatttle examples of 550 cultivars. Cultivars are probably in the majority among trees sold and planted in Seattle. Sometimes the natural or unselected kind of a tree species is rare here while certain of its cultivars are common. It will be useful then to go into some detail about the nature of cultivars.

The term "cultivar" (abbreviated *cv.*) is recent, and its application is not uniform. Some writers confuse cultivars with the botanical categories *forma*, (abbreviated *f.*) and *varietas* (abbreviated *var.*). Few books use these categories consistently and rigorously according to the international rules. To clarify, then:

Cultivars are cultivated varieties of a species or a hybrid. For example, the common apple tree (*Malus domestica* Borkh.) has over 7,000 cultivars, such as 'Red Delicious' and 'Gravenstein'.

Cultivars can differ slightly or greatly from the original tree. Cultivars of deciduous trees usually resemble the original tree recognizably. But those of certain conifers often differ bewilderingly: Lawson Cypress for example is a single species that has given rise to dozens of strikingly distinct cultivars.

Cultivars arise as chance seedlings or branch sports, or are simply chosen from among mature trees. A cultivar can be obtained from any kind of tree, but some kinds are more likely to vary in distinctive and desirable ways than are others.

Cultivars are selected for particular features such as rate of growth, shape, hardiness, disease resistance, coloring—for any feature of flower, fruit, form or health considered desirable.

Cultivars are propagated almost solely by vegetative methods such as cuttings, layering or grafting because the distinctive characteristics of a cultivar can rarely be consistently reproduced from seed. Some cultivars do not even produce seed.

Thus, *cultivars are usually clones,* at least for all practical purposes. Yet not all clonal trees are cultivars, unless they are *named and cultivated* as such.

Cultivars are often grafted onto ordinary seedlings, and this root-stock directly influences the growth rate, health and size of the cultivar grafted onto it. Thus we may obtain dwarf, semi-dwarf or standard sized apple trees of the same cultivar.

Some major wholesale nurseries also are increasingly using trademark (™) or registered-trademark names (*). The usage of such names is legally controlled. This trend, ballooning since the early 1980s, is maddening, but legal unfortunately. Before 1982, plant patents did not require a cultivar name. Plants, not their names, are patented. Patents last only 17 years, but trademarked names last indefinitely. A wholesale nursery, by making an obnoxious cultivar name and an attractive trademark name, gains financially: it can demand that other wholesalers or retailers pay a fee if they wish to use the trademark name for sales—those who do not pay can use only the repellent cultivar name. This book usually indicates *both* names but gives preferential treatment to the better known trademark names.

On the Measurement of Trees

This guide includes an unusually large number of measurements. For most kinds of trees mentioned, the maximum size ever recorded anywhere is noted. This is not to be regarded as the eventual size to be expected in Seattle, nor is it necessarily the maximum *possible* size. If you find the figures cited unbelievably large, please note that in general, the maximum dimensions of both the height and the trunk size of any given tree may be fully twice as much as its average mature size. Measurements are cited height × trunk girth (circumference), with the branch-spread or width of the tree an optional figure, usually supplied only when the tree is wider than tall. Thus for example, Seattle's largest Red Oak is 91' (tall) × 15'3" (trunk girth) × 112½' wide. The great majority of Seattle tree measurements included in this guide date from 2004 and 2005; any that date from earlier than 2003 are noted. The Locks' tree measurements are all 2003.

Private Property and Public Propriety

Some private property is treated for all practical purposes as public: cemeteries, church landscapes, office building plazas, private schoolgrounds, hospital grounds, and so on. In such places ordinary civil strolling and tree-watching is acceptable behavior. However, this book also cites trees on front lawns or in the back yards of private residences. Please do not get carried away in your enthusiasm to the point of trespassing! And rest assured that the trees on private property cited in this book can all be seen quite adequately from sidewalks, streets or alleys.

Remember, owners come and go: any one of them can at the merest whim order one or all of their trees cut down. Though over-burdened with building codes and work-safety regulations, our society does *nothing* to guard against the destruction of outstanding trees! It is legally possible to buy a residence in Seattle, and while waiting for the building permit needed to put up a garage, chop down with no need of permission a tree that may be the last of its kind on earth—or the largest of its kind, or a historic landmark, a nesting site, *etc.* Yard trees in Seattle have no rights, regardless of how remarkable or singularly important they may be. Architects have succeeded in giving first-class old buildings certain protection, but a comparable concern for and protection of our special trees simply does not exist.

Seattle does have a modest **Heritage Tree** program. It was started and is run by the nonprofit **PlantAmnesty**, with assistance from the City of Seattle through the SeaTran Urban Forestry office. Since 1996 about 30 Seattle trees have been designated Heritage. They can be celebrated; they can be loved; but the program is voluntary. A tree designated Heritage gains no official protection thereby. Nor am I arguing that it should. The best protection of trees is for them to be appreciated by many people surrounding them—not just to have a small committee deem them special and worthy of special status. The Heritage Tree program, along with this book, Arbor Day, tree stewards, and other activities, helps people get informed and inspires passion about trees.

THE MAJOR VIEWING-PLACES

Seattle Parks

The City of Seattle Department of Parks and Recreation calls most of the facilities it cares for "parks," but it is also responsible for playgrounds, playfields, viewpoints, boulevards, golf courses, look-outs, pools, camps, pathways and so forth. These vary greatly in size and in the nature of their trees. Divided into districts, the major *tree* parks are:

1) Best for *variety* of kinds & non-natives:

NORTHEAST
Cowen Park
Laurelhurst Playfield
Matthews Beach Park
NORTHWEST
Green Lake (205 kinds)
Woodland Park Zoo
CENTRAL
Lake Washington Boulevard
Leschi Park
Volunteer Park (175 kinds)
QUEEN ANNE–MAGNOLIA
Kinnear Park
Rodgers Park
Queen Anne Boulevard
SOUTHEAST
Jefferson Park Golf Course
Kubota Garden Park (169 kinds)
Mt Baker Park & Boulevard
SOUTHWEST
Hiawatha Playfield
Lincoln Park (100 kinds)
W Seattle Golf Course & Camp Long

2) Best for *native* woods in quantity:

NORTHEAST
O.O. Denny Park
Ravenna Park
NORTHWEST
Carkeek Park
Golden Gardens Park
CENTRAL
Boren & Interlaken Park
Frink Park

QUEEN ANNE–MAGNOLIA
Discovery Park

SOUTHEAST
Lakeridge Park (Dead-horse Canyon)
Seward Park

SOUTHWEST
Fauntleroy Park
Schmitz Park

In recent years Parks and Recreation staff have let die many valuable rare trees, and have removed many others—even unique specimens—either without knowing or without caring. Though hazardous trees must be addressed, it is wrong to destroy those unique in the city—until propagated. In fall 2005, at Ravenna Park the city's finest collection of Japanese Hill Cherries, along with three Korean Hill Cherries, an Oshima Cherry and a Higan Cherry were taken out. A fresh bare lawn replaced them. They had been planted in the 1930s or about 1940. If we desire to grow long-lived Japanese Flowering Cherry cultivars, we must graft them on Japanese seedlings rather than European seedlings. Now the city has lost a great source for such seeds.

Also in fall 2005, in Volunteer Park, the city's tallest (31') Black Elder tree *(Sambucus nigra)* was cut down, along with the largest (51') of extremely few

15

Dragon Spruces in the park system, and one of the park's only two 'Ukon' Japanese Flowering Cherries.

One wonders if the horticulture staff, senior gardeners, landscape architects, forester and tree crew talk with one another. Do any of them *know* that one-of-a-kind trees in the parks are dying or are being killed from either neglect or ignorance? That there are special trees in the system that ought to be propagated and replanted for the future? Do not count on it.

The Carl S. English, Jr. Gardens

Whenever a tree in this guide is cited by "**Locks** bed #" it is to be understood as growing in one of the numbered beds of the 7½ acres of gardens found on the Hiram M. Chittenden Locks property in the Ballard neighborhood. This facility, including the canal, locks and fish ladder as well as the ornamental gardens, is managed by the Seattle District of the U.S. Army Corps of Engineers.

The gardens were named after the person most responsible for developing their distinctive character, Carl S. English, Jr. (1904–76), who worked in them for decades. Thanks largely to his efforts, and to his successor Michael Fleming, the variety of trees present is amazing: 209 kinds are cited in this guide (over 280 exist). With the accompanying *map* (supplied for this guide through the courtesy of the Corps of Engineers), finding the trees cited there is usually easy—though in some beds many kinds of plants are crowded remarkably close together, making for a display at once richly beautiful and bewildering.

Visitors are welcome on the grounds daily from 7:00 A.M. to 9:00 P.M. The address is 3015 NW 54th St (98107). The Visitor Center (783-7059) is open 10:00 A.M. to 4:00 P.M. daily (closed Tuesday and Wednesday). For more information, see the *Arboretum Bulletin*, Spring 1977, pp. 24–28.

The Zoo's Trees

Woodland Park Zoological Garden is located west of Aurora Avenue North, in upper Woodland Park. The zoo proper is fenced but accessible by payment of an admission fee. Surrounding it are borders of vegetation, parking lots, a rose garden, picnic areas and a playground.

This guide cites examples of 116 different kinds of trees present either in the zoo or elsewhere in upper Woodland Park west of Aurora Avenue. The trees include both old ornamentals which were intended to please spectators, and relatively recent plantings designed for animal exhibits, to help the animals feel more at home. When feasible, trees native to the animals' homelands are planted in the appropriate exhibits. Failing this ideal, substitutes are used to create a similar effect. This plan ensures a richer, more rewarding place for animals and visiting humans alike. Because of the lush, diverse plantings, it would still be a wonderful place to visit—even if there were no animals.

Some of the more noteworthy trees: 1) very *large* for their kind in Seattle: European

Beech, Sweet Birch, Black Cherry, English Holly, Kobus Magnolia, Pin Oak, Scarlet Oak, Cluster Pine, Ponderosa Pine, and English Yew; 2) some trees relatively *rare* in Seattle: Cornish Elm, varied *Eucalyptus*, Maackia, Magnolia relatives, Chinese Phellodendron; 3) a few *conspicuous* trees: 'Shirotae' Japanese Flowering Cherry by the north restrooms, the Deodar Cedar by the south gate, and the Black Locusts on the African Savanna.

The Good Shepherd Center's Trees

The Good Shepherd Center crowns the hill of the Wallingford neighborhood (4649 Sunnyside Ave N). The grounds feature almost 150 different kinds of trees. Include adjacent Meridian Park plus Seattle Tilth's demonstration gardens and the number goes higher. Overall, this area is a veritable plant mecca. This book cites 61 kinds of trees from the site. Six are known nowhere else in Seattle: Myrtle Southern-Beech, Evergreen Hawthorn, Syrian Maple, Hybrid Cork Oak, Post Oak, weeping Gray Poplar. Nine extremely rare trees include the Armenian Oak, Mexican Oaks *(Quercus mexicana* and *Q. obtusata)*, *Photinia Beauverdiana* var. *notabilis*, Mountain Pittosporum *(Pittosporum Colensoi)*, 'Citation' "Plum" (a patented purpleleaf peach × plum cross), 'Nancy Saunders' Purple Osier (Willow), Winter's Bark, and Prince Albert's Yew.

South Seattle Community College Trees

SSCC is actually in West Seattle, 6000 16th Ave SW. The campus proper is not remarkably planted with trees, yet to its north end there is an arboretum, and immediately adjacent is the Seattle Chinese Garden, still under construction.

Every year the collection grows. Adding to the existing Milton Sutton Conifer Garden, in 2005 the superb Cœnosium Rock Garden was opened. This is a large, splendid collection of conifer cultivars and some companion species, many of them dwarf, many extremely rare. As these crowded specimens mature over the years, the larger growing trees will cause trouble for the low and slow sorts, and it is to be hoped that the staff, patrons and volunteers will be up to the task of managing them.

Children's Hospital Trees

Children's Hospital is in Laurelhurst neighborhood (4800 Sand Point Way NE). As part of its holistic approach to helping sick children, the staff sees to it that the grounds are beautifully landscaped. There is concentrated and rich plant diversity. Many rare trees were obtained originally from the Arboretum. The collection is well cataloged. The only problem is the seemingly constant *construction*, and the attendant shuffling around of plants and trees. If ever the "dust settles," the next edition of this book can include far more than the 25 tree kinds cited currently.

Notably rare trees are: 'Lutea' Monterey Cypress, Canary Island Juniper, Camphor Laurel, Canary Island Laurel, 'Picture' Saucer Magnolia, the new

Winter Lightning Box-elder (Maple), some currently unidentified Mountain Ashes *(Sorbus)*, the new Green Pillar™ Pin Oak, a young Rocky Mountain White Oak, Chinese Phellodendron, *Sycopsis*, and Rosemary Willow. Seattle's largest known specimens of the following are present: weeping Katsura, Hungarian Oak, variegated Osmanthus, and perhaps Fraser Fir—a 39' tall tree at the "giraffe" garage's SW corner awaits an exact i.d. confirmation.

Cemetery Trees

Cemeteries can be good places for trees and for tree enthusiasts. Insofar as (most) cemeteries are intended to be permanent, their trees are often planted with ample space between them which allows them to attain full size—unlike trees in typical yards, which are generally much crowded and cut back. Some cemeteries in older parts of this country and in Europe are treated much as valued parks for passive recreation such as strolling and picnicking. Too often they are treated in Seattle as places to avoid: most Seattleites visit cemeteries only to bury their departed or to pay quiet respects to them on selected Holy Days. But to walk amiably through a cemetery admiring the trees, taking in the views and curiously reading occasional inscriptions, is a peaceful and quite commendable form of relaxation. People particularly interested in trees find visiting cemeteries a pleasurable necessity; to willfully avoid cemeteries is to miss some of the best trees in existence. Each of our cemeteries is unique:

Acacia (15000 Bothell Way NE) lacks an Acacia tree, and though outside of Seattle's City limits, it is very close by and full of noteworthy trees. In fact, due to the absence of varied gravestones and upright monuments, it would be a dull place except for its trees. Conifers dominate as they do in no other local cemetery: about 35 kinds share the place with only about 17 non-coniferous kinds. Several specimens stand as large or larger than any of their kind found in Seattle. Cited in this book are:

Hiba Arborvitæ, Atlas Cedar, blue Atlas Cedar, 'Zebrina' Western Red Cedar, 'Shogetsu' Japanese Flowering Cherry, Arizona Cypress, Sawara Cypress, thread Sawara Cypress, plume Sawara Cypress, moss Sawara Cypress, White Fir, Piñon Pine, Whitebark Pine, Sierra Redwood, blue Colorado Spruce, and Norway Spruce.

Calvary (5041 35th Ave NE) commands the hillside above the University Village shopping center. Eight plume Sawara Cypresses line the entrance drive. Within are many kinds of trees and shrubs, along with diverse stone monuments. The enormous Paper Birches are impressive enough to make this cemetery worth a visit on their account alone. Other kinds cited in this guide are:

Golden Desert™ European Ash, 'Youngii' White Birch, 'Aurea' Southern Catalpa, 'Sekkan-Sugi' Japanese Cedar, Arizona Cypress, 'Erecta Viridis' & 'Westermannii' Lawson Cypress, Plume Sawara Cypress, Hardy Rubber-Tree, Eastern Hemlock, Monkey Tree, Bastard Service-Tree (Mt. Ash), weeping White Mulberry, Dwarf Alberta White Spruce, *Viburnum Lentago*, and the 'Weeping Sally' Pussy Willow.

Crown Hill (8712 12th Ave NW) was established in 1903, and many native Bigleaf Maples were planted in it. Few trees in this small cemetery rate a second glance; none are mentioned in this guide except White Poplar.

Evergreen Park / Washelli complex of several cemeteries (11111 Aurora Ave N) has greater acreage than any of the others, and is well planted with trees. The long rows of Lombardy (Black) Poplars are well known landmarks. Other trees cited in this guide are:

EVERGREEN PARK:
Hiba Arborvitæ
weeping Beech (both green and purple)
'Rohanii' Beech
'Zebrina' Western Red Cedar
'Autumnalis' Higan Cherry
'Kwanzan' Japanese Flw. Cherry
'Shiro-fugen' Japanese Flw. Cherry
'Ukon' Japanese Flw. Cherry
'Plena' Mazzard Cherry
'Erecta Glaucescens' Lawson Cypress
'Fraseri' Lawson Cypress
thread Sawara Cypress
American Elm
blue Douglas Fir
Hybrid Goldenchain Tree
Dawson Magnolia
Umbrella Tree Magnolia
'Crimson King' Norway Maple
fastigiate English Oak
Kwantung Pine
'Newport' Plum
Aspen (Poplar)
weeping Sierra Redwood
Hondo (Yeddo) Spruce
Common Stewartia
Umbrella Pine

WASHELLI:
'Fastigiata' Arborvitæ
blue Atlas Cedar
'Whitcombii' Higan Cherry
'Amanogawa' Japanese Cherry
'Allumii' Lawson Cypress
Norway Maple
Paperbark Maple
Common Mountain Ash
Austrian Pine
Ponderosa Pine
Dwarf Alberta White Spruce

BOTH:
Downy Birch
Weeping Cherry
Sawara Cypress
moss Sawara Cypress
plume Sawara Cypress
Western White Pine

(Montrepose) Forest Lawn (6701 30th Ave SW) is spacious and formal, but little planted with trees, being far more lawn than forest.

Fort Lawton (at Discovery Park) is small, with little except native Bigleaf Maples. But the Douglas Pyramidal Arborvitæ and 'Wilsonii' Highclere Holly are handsome enough to get cited in this guide.

G.A.R.—Grand Army of the Republic—(north of Lake View Cemetery) is a small park/cemetery with some very important trees. On the north side stand nine different kinds of elms! And a tenth is to the west. On the south side, the only tree mentioned in this guide is Colorado Spruce.

Lake View (1554 15th Ave E) is the large cemetery adjoining Volunteer Park on Capitol Hill. It has over 80 different kinds of trees, some of them labeled in

1999. It is rich with bold stone markers, tombs and statues. Trees found there mentioned in this guide are:

European Beech, copper European Beech, River Birch, 'Crispa' White Birch, Hybrid and Northern Catalpa, blue Atlas Cedar, Mazzard Cherry, 'Pendula Rubra' Weeping Cherry, 'Akebono' Yoshino Cherry, three cultivars of Lawson Cypress and three of Sawara Cypress, Camperdown Elm, Japanese Maple, Jack Pine, Cherry Plum, 'Moseri' Plum, White Poplar, Norway and Sitka Spruces, and White Willow.

Mt Pleasant / Hills of Eternity (700 W Raye St) is the large cemetery on north Queen Anne Hill. Its south side is bordered by large, old Crimean Lindens; its west border has a stout Black Cherry. Both the lindens and cherry are really Queen Anne Boulevard trees rather than cemetery trees, but they're immediately adjacent to the cemetery proper. Inside are many good trees and stones. It's a great place if you like hollies. Those trees mentioned in this guide are:

Oriental Arborvitæ, hybrid Bitter Cherry, 'Pink Perfection' Japanese Flowering Cherry, 'Hopa' Crabapple, 'Fraseri' Lawson Cypress, Nikko Fir, weeping Japanese Larch, a variegated Sycamore Maple, Mugo Pine, and Irish Yew.

Old Comet Lodge / Oddfellows (23rd Ave S & S Graham St) is small and long abandoned, with mostly native Bigleaf Maples.

Downtown Trees

The last original tree standing on Seattle's central waterfront got logged in 1879. Now our downtown or central business district is full of steel skyscrapers and cold gray concrete, with planted trees stuck here and there to enliven the dreary harshness. The oldest surviving tree is said to be a cherry near the Pike Place Market.

Compared to most big-city urban cores, ours is unusually rich in diversity of trees, albeit most are young specimens of common sorts and a large number are planted in containers. They consist of street-trees, park trees, plaza and courtyard trees—even rooftop-garden trees. The most concentrated collection of different varieties is at Freeway Park. London Planetrees line the monorail; they're also Pioneer Square's theme tree. Perhaps Downtown's best known "Christmas tree" is the Sierra Redwood 100' tall by Macy's (the former Bon Marché).

Superior examples of every kind can be found elsewhere in Seattle, but Downtown trees have many friends and admirers due to their prominent location. They need all the encouragement and appreciation they can get because with Downtown's ceaseless development, trees there lead a precarious existence.

The Arboretum

Most Seattleites think that the Washington Park Arboretum is scarcely more than another park. A *park* is usually intended to be aesthetically pleasing and functional for varied recreational activities. Certainly an arboretum also can gratify the eye and prove ideal for passive recreation—but its primary purpose is to educate. What a library does by way of books, or a zoo with animals, an arboretum does with its collection of trees.

Toward that noble goal, the ideal is to grow as many kinds of trees and shrubs as possible. With over 170 acres of space, our Arboretum has room enough for a representative of every kind of tree this climate can support, and once accepted specimens freely. Beauty, great rarity, scientific interest or economic value were secondary considerations for acceptance here, not necessities. Ideally, no kind of tree should be denied, and each ought to be planted in the most suitable available location, correctly labeled, and carefully tended. But in recent years the staff have become highly selective about what new trees are admitted, and many new garden trees that the public may desire to see are not present, though there always seems to be room to add foreign rarities that may or may not end up being desirable.

The *location* of our Arboretum is a mixed blessing. On the whole it is too low, wet, cold, shady and poorly drained. The site was the result of convenience and politics. Because the site is so abnormal, certain trees are exceptionally big and healthy there, and others sadly stunted.

Much of the space currently supports *native* vegetation. Instead of acres of lawn with trees here and there, as in most cemeteries and many parks, our Arboretum was intended to grow trees in conditions more or less like those found in undisturbed nature. This results in outstanding success for many trees and shrubs, for example magnolias and rhododendrons. But it has its problems, the chief one being the subtle, gradual suppression of many non-native plantings by the better-adapted wild natives. Where the average old-fashioned arboretum shows open-grown oaks exulting in their own peculiar shapes, our Arboretum has a forest of tall, slender oak trunks fighting each other for sunlight and space.

It is obviously a mistake to exclude peach trees and spreading live oaks because there is an overabundance of mediocre native cedars, maples and alders. But this is what is happening. The noteworthy and valuable native specimens ought be singled out and sedulously preserved; the rest should be gradually replaced with more non-native kinds.

To help you use the Arboretum effectively, here are a few suggestions:

Buy a copy of the catalog of its trees and shrubs: *The Woody Plant Collection in the Washington Park Arboretum*, published in 1994. It needs updating, but is still worth its modest price ($4.95). The catalog's fold-out *map* is not reprinted in this guide, yet a similar rendition was created especially for this book. This map shows the general grid system used by the Arboretum and followed in this book. It is a pity that the Arboretum grid system and map are neither user-friendly nor complete. But if you seek a tree in the Arboretum, and look for it or ask about it, use the **accession number** and the **grid location**. Some planted trees are unlabeled, partly labeled or mislabeled. Feel free to inquire of the staff about these, or about trees you seek but cannot find (whether or not listed in the catalog). When possible, supply the tree's accession number (*e.g.*, #358–62) so that the staff can answer your request readily. The last two digits of the accession number indicate the *year* the tree was acquired—1962 in this case. You will not know whether the tree arrived as a seed in 1962, or as a full-grown tree moved in with a crane; but it is a safe bet that most specimens were obtained as seeds or small whips. Remember, only a few of the more conspicuous *native* trees are labeled; over 20 species of Seattle native trees grow wild in the arboretum.

The 4-acre *Japanese Garden* is now run by the Park Department but once was part of the Arboretum proper. It has a few trees not found elsewhere in the Arboretum, and some better examples of others such as the largest Bamboo-leaf Oak and Serbian Spruce. Though it is an ornamental garden rather than part of the collection, and an admission fee is charged, it should be visited by students of trees.

Lake Washington Boulevard and the Washington Park Playfield are also lined by planted trees that largely pre-date the late 1930s Arboretum. These trees are not always—or even usually—cataloged and labeled. But in the future, perhaps, the deserving trees will be included in the records—as they are in this book.

Overall, keep in mind that the Arboretum's collection is *not* representative of the regular Seattle tree population, in that it has many rare and even unique kinds, lacks some common ones, and grows them in conditions frequently much different from what average Seattle yards offer.

University of Washington Campus Trees

Vast in acreage, decorated with many different kinds of trees, the U.W. campus deserves a separate tree guide. No such thing exists or is likely to in the near future, so *this* book includes many of the campus trees. Over 525 kinds exist on campus. This book mentions over 350, only over 20 of which are known nowhere else in Seattle. Close to 40 kinds are known nowhere else in Seattle except at the Arboretum; and a great many campus trees are noteworthy for their exceptional size or general rarity. Mere quantity makes some common trees worth noting; although no theme tree unifies the varied campus (blue Atlas Cedar comes close), a few especially noteworthy *groups* are:

–Deodar Cedar: over 40 shade the southeast part of Stevens Way.
–Yoshino Cherry: the Liberal Arts Quadrangle trees.
–Crabapple trees: about 20 kinds by Drumheller Fountain and the Rose Garden.
–Horse Chestnut: Skagit Lane is lined with massive specimens.
–London Plane: Memorial Way consists of two rows of these trees.
–Ghost (Black) Poplar: by Portage Bay, northwest of the "Montlake Cut" canal.

C. Frank Brockman, late Professor of Forest Resources, wrote five articles about campus trees for the *Arboretum Bulletin* (Fall 1979 to Fall 1980). A separate campus tree-tour of 8 large pages covering 81 trees was also published, first in the *U.W. Report*, afterwards on its own. It was updated and published in 1998 as the C. Frank Brockman Memorial Campus Tree Tour; it is online now.

U.W. Medicinal Herb Garden Trees

The Medicinal Herb Garden, has over 100 different kinds of trees, over 40 specimens of which are cited in this guide. Its plants are fully cataloged and many are labeled. It covers about 2½ acres, from Rainier Vista on the east to Benson Hall on the west, and south of Stevens Way from Garfield Lane on the east to the Botany Greenhouse on the west. Some of its more noteworthy trees include:

VERY LARGE FOR THEIR KIND IN SEATTLE:

Crape-Myrtle	Cucumber Tree (Magnolia)
Eastern Dogwood	'Hollywood' Plum
Siberian Elm	Plum Yew

RELATIVELY RARE IN SEATTLE:

Mahaleb Cherry	Medlar Tree
Chinese Cornelian-Cherry (Dogwood)	Oriental White Oak
European Silver Fir	Osage Orange
Hardy Rubber-Tree	Pawpaw
Frosted Hawthorn	Chinese Quince
Scarlet Hawthorn	Plum-fruited Yew

Contact Friends of the Medicinal Herb Garden to join their support of the garden—c/o Botany Department, University of Washington, Box 355325, Seattle 98195; (206) 543-1126.

U.W. Friendship Grove

Autumn 2005 marked the 45th anniversary of the International Friendship Grove of trees, located on NE Campus Parkway between Brooklyn Avenue and Roosevelt Way. The grove was an ambitious attempt to commemorate the 5th World Forestry Congress, held here that summer, via a living, permanent symbol, and to provide a down-to-earth demonstration of the friendship and unity among the 65 countries represented at the congress. Even as memories of the congress gradually fade away, the trees themselves take on an increasingly valuable role as a miniature arboretum.

Some trees died and were replaced with other kinds; some died and have not been replaced; most are currently unlabeled, others mislabeled; and the western end is an overgrown mess. But in general, the grove has proved a success.

The following listing of the trees is arranged as they exist going from east to west, with a loop around the western end where the dense *Escallonia* shrubbery is. A tree representing a certain country is not necessarily native to that country. Asterisks refer to notes at the end of the list (p. 25).

23

European BEECH
Fagus sylvatica
Germany

Montpelier MAPLE
Acer monspessulanum
Italy

Western LARCH
Larix occidentalis
The Union of South Africa

Cork Tree (OAK)
Quercus Suber
Spain

Hybrid GOLDENCHAIN TREE
Laburnum × Watereri 'Vossii'
Switzerland

European Hop HORNBEAM
Ostrya carpinifolia
Greece

White BIRCH
Betula pendula
Finland

Engelmann SPRUCE
Picea Engelmannii
Uruguay

Deodar CEDAR
Cedrus Deodara
India

Douglas FIR
Pseudotsuga Menziesii
The United States of America

Polish LARCH
Larix decidua var. *polonica*
Poland

MADRONA
Arbutus Menziesii
Thailand

Goldtwig White WILLOW[3]
Salix alba var. *vitellina*
Ireland

Common MOUNTAIN ASH
Sorbus aucuparia
Czechoslovakia

Red OAK
Quercus rubra
Denmark

Oriental HORNBEAM
Carpinus orientalis
Israel

Eastern HEMLOCK
Tsuga canadensis
Venezuela

Eastern White PINE
Pinus Strobus
Guatemala

Scots PINE
Pinus sylvestris
Sweden

CHINA-FIR
Cunninghamia lanceolata
China

English OAK
Quercus robur
The United Kingdom

Littleleaf LINDEN
Tilia cordata
The Netherlands

Sycamore MAPLE
Acer Pseudoplatanus
France

Siberian LARCH
Larix sibirica
The Soviet Union

Arizona Black WALNUT[1]
Juglans major
Cameroon

Amur MAPLE[2]
Acer tataricum ssp. *Ginnala*
Bulgaria

Norway MAPLE
Acer platanoides
Belgium

Boxleaf AZARA
Azara microphylla
Peru

24

Lodgepole PINE
Pinus contorta
Malagasy

Oriental ARBORVITÆ
Platycladus (Thuja) orientalis
Burma

Montezuma PINE[4]
Pinus Montezumæ
Mexico

Macedonian PINE
Pinus Peuce
Romania

Sugar MAPLE[5]
Acer saccharum
Canada

Limber PINE
Pinus flexilis
Honduras

European HACKBERRY
Celtis australis
Hungary

Western Red CEDAR
Thuja plicata
The Philippines

Manna ASH
Fraxinus Ornus
Iran

Dragon SPRUCE[6]
Picea asperata
Yugoslavia

Chestnut OAK
Quercus Prinus
Gabon

Italian CYPRESS[7]
Cupressus sempervirens
Jordan

Roblé Southern-BEECH
Nothofagus obliqua
Argentina

Sakhalin SPRUCE
Picea Glehnii
Vietnam

Himalayan SPRUCE
Picea Smithiana
Nepal

Red SPRUCE
Picea rubens
Liberia

SWEETGUM
Liquidambar Styraciflua
Haiti

Turkish OAK
Quercus Cerris
Turkey

Portugal LAUREL
Prunus lusitanica
Portugal

Blue Atlas CEDAR[8]
Cedrus atlantica f. *glauca*
Lebanon

Algerian FIR
Abies numidica
Tunisia

MONKEY TREE[9]
Araucaria araucana
Brazil

Bigleaf MAPLE
Acer macrophyllum
Ghana

[1] Originally listed as *Juglans Hindsii*, then as *J. microcarpa*.
[2] Intended to be Tatarian Maple, *Acer tataricum*.
[3] Intended to be Whitebeam, *Sorbus Aria*.
[4] Intended to be Jelecote Pine, *Pinus patula*.
[5] Either the *Scheckii* or *nigrum* subspecies.
[6] Intended to be Serbian Spruce, *Picea Omorika*.

[7] Originally listed as *Cupressus Lindleyi*, a name synonymous with *C. lusitanica*.
[8] Intended to be Cedar of Lebanon, *Cedrus libani*.
[9] Originally listed as *Eucalyptus Johnstonii*.

For more information, consult these articles:

American Forests, November 1960: "Many Nations, One Goal" pp. 10–15, 40–47.
American Forests, June 1966: "Seattle's Trees For Peace" pp. 34–37.
Arboretum Bulletin, Winter 1960: "The Arboretum and the Fifth World Forestry Congress" pp. 33–34.
Arboretum Bulletin, Winter 1964: "A Further Report on the International Friendship Grove" pp. 82–85, 113.
Arboretum Bulletin, Summer 1985: "The Friendship Grove Revisited 25 Years Later" pp. 20–26.

U.W. Center for Urban Horticulture

Abbreviated as CUH, this facility is a relative newcomer, located on the far east part of the campus close to Laurelhurst neighborhood. It presents a multifaceted approach: public outreach, research, teaching, and plant growing. The Elisabeth C. Miller Horticultural Library is a gem. The Otis Douglas Hyde Herbarium has a strong collection of pressed plant specimens, and staff to help the public with identification.

The director oversees both the Center and the Washington Park Arboretum. Therefore plants and trees pass freely back and forth, and you will see the same kind of plastic labels and accession numbers on CUH trees as on Arboretum trees. The umbrella name *University of Washington Botanic Gardens* embraces the whole sweep. This book cites 24 kinds of trees at CUH.

The City Street-Tree Program

The Seattle Transportation Department, among its many other duties, is partly responsible for the planting and care of street-trees. These are seen along arterial roads, on some residential streets, in traffic triangles and circles, and so forth—on city-owned land other than property administered by the Parks Department.

Thousands of trees—dozens of different kinds—were planted in the 1970s and 80s, giving us an unusually diverse collection of municipal street-trees. Thus a busy street in Seattle is often seen lined by trees of approximately the same kind, age, and size. The dramatic difference between streets with trees and those without them is well known: most people prefer the trees.

Information about the City street-tree program can be obtained from the office of the City Arborist (at 700 5th Avenue, room 3900, 98104; (206) 684-7649).

SEATTLE'S HISTORIC, OLD AND BIG TREES

Many individual Seattle trees are dearly beloved by certain groups of people, but none possess regional or long-standing renown. These trees can claim some fame, some connection with an historic event, or were planted on some special occasion; but alas, no single tree is important enough to be featured on post cards or in bus-tours of the city.

Rows of plane trees were planted in 1920 to commemorate U.W. alumni who died in World War I. They shade and give name to the "Memorial Way" on campus.

The P.T.A., the D.A.R. and other civic groups planted trees in 1932 to commemorate the bicentennial of George Washington's birth. Some of those trees are now truly handsome memorials indeed; they include cedars, elms, and oaks.

Some Seattle trees were given us from foreign countries or from our "Sister Cities." Throughout the city are anonymous trees that possess a hidden history, a connection with the past, that if known, would make people view them in a more appreciative manner. Any tree is enhanced in human eyes when it serves to conjoin human and natural history. A certain personification envelops such a tree, helping us to view it as a friendly relic, rather than merely another big green thing. Although this guide is sorely deficient (for lack of space) in documenting such trees, the work is well worth doing.

Trees far larger than any known today were logged decades ago, sometimes merely for firewood. Sections of huge, ancient logs and stumps, packed with many close rings, are kept displayed at the U.W. College of Forest Resources, at the Seattle Museum of History and Industry, at the Pacific Science Center, and elsewhere. Trees nearly as big still stand in some Seattle parks, and often receive fewer visitors. Scattered, isolated old-growth trees are found fairly easily in Seattle. Concentrated preserves are at Schmitz, Seward and O.O. Denny Parks.

But what is Seattle's oldest tree of all? Who can be certain when hollow trunks yield inconclusive evidence? Still surviving are some cedars and Douglas firs that stood towering and mature as the first settlers arrived in the area during the early 1850s. For various reasons spared the axe and not having succumbed to natural causes, these ancient trees may be 300–500 years old. A few of our yews and hemlocks as well as some enormous madronas and oaks may also be 300 years old. Our very oldest maples may approach the three-century mark.

These seven kinds of native trees are probably the only ones here with representatives 250 years old or more: cedars and Douglas firs present the safest claim to such antiquity. Perhaps the 5½-foot-thick Grand fir that snapped in 1990 in Schmitz Park was also 250 years old—yet this species is exceedingly fast-growing and not long-lived.

An interesting project for a local historian would be to find our oldest *non-native* tree—maybe a pear or walnut tree in one of the pioneer areas of south or central Seattle? A safe general rule is: extremely few exotics—planted non-natives—date from before 1890, and it is unlikely *any* date from before 1868!

As far as *size* is concerned, Seattle's largest and by far our tallest trees are Douglas firs, containing more wood per individual than do any others. Although very few Grand firs may presently be near 200' tall in the city, only Douglas firs are definitely known to be that tall, or up to 235'!

The tallest *exotics* measured in Seattle during 2004 or 2005 are as follows:

165½'	Coast Redwood	155'	Sierra Redwood
141'	Lombardy (Black) Poplar	132'	Ghost (Black) Poplar
127½'	Bolleana White Poplar	127'	European Beech
126½'	Ponderosa Pine	126½'	Atlas Cedar
123'	'Eugenei' Hybrid Poplar	122'	Tulip Tree
120'	Norway Spruce	118½'	Turkish Oak
118'	English Elm	115½'	Eastern White Pine
114½'	Deodar Cedar	112'	Incense Cedar
111½'	Sugar Pine	111½'	Red Oak
110½'	White Birch	109½'	'Marilandica' Hybrid Poplar
109½'	Bigcone Pine	109'	Bald Cypress
107½'	Dawn Redwood	106½'	Scots Pine

Some trees have actually attained larger measurements in Seattle than have been reported anywhere else. The following pages document them, along with many other valuable trees.

ABBREVIATIONS

Few are used, but some are vital.

ca.   means *circa*—about—usually to indicate an estimated rather than measured tree height, or an estimated planting year.

E   means east or eastern.

ex   is used between a botanist who *proposes* a scientific name and the botanist who validly *publishes* the name.

hort.   means *hortulanorum*—used for tree names from gardeners, nurseries or horticulture as opposed to botanic science.

N   means north or northern.

non   means not; used when botanists or horticulturists have *misapplied* tree names.

pl.   means planted, to tell you what year a tree was planted in Seattle.

®   means registered trademark, its used controlled by the owner.

S   means south or southern.

s.l.   means *sensu lato*—in a wide sense; adopting a broad rather than narrow interpretation of a species or genus or family

™   means trademark, registered or not.

W   means west or western.

±   means more or less.

×   (1) indicates "times" or "by" in size measurements; (2) also used in tree names to indicate a sexual hybrid (most crosses are of this kind).

+   (1) indicates "plus" (2) also used in a very *few* tree names to indicate a graft hybrid (such as Chimæric Goldenchain Tree).

'   indicates feet.

"   indicates inches.

♂   indicates male.

♀   indicates female.

ACACIA

Acacia melanoxylon R. Br.
LEGUMINOSÆ
From SE Australia, Tasmania.

Australian Blackwood
Tasmanian Blackwood
Black *or* Blackwood Acacia

A broadleaf evergreen forest tree to 120' × 13'. The extraordinarily valuable wood is used in diverse ways. Blackwood acacia has been much planted in parts of California. In Seattle, it and all *Acacia* species are extremely rare. Perhaps two dozen species (of over 1,200!) of *Acacia* have been tried here over the years, chiefly at the Arboretum and U.W. campus. Though they grow rapidly, very cold winters here kill them, so they seldom attain much size—but some resprout from their roots. For other, far more common trees sometimes known as acacia, see the LOCUSTS and SILK TREE.

– Arboretum: two #291-89 in 21-3E, are 25' and 31' tall
– U.W.: one 16' tall W of Bloedel Hall on a bank above the Burke-Gilman Trail; some with *A. longifolia* trees S of the West Campus parking garage, the tallest 22'

[**Bailey Acacia. Cootamundra Wattle**—*A. Baileyana* F.v. Muell.—from the Cootamundra and Wagga districts of New South Wales. It has ferny, dusty-blue foliage and brilliant, fragrant, golden-yellow flowers in late winter or earliest spring. A *purpleleaf* one W of 3728 SW Ida St is 17' tall, *pl.* 2001. Two *purpleleaf* trees in front of 2305 NW 100th St.]

[**Silver Wattle**—*A. dealbata* Link—from E New South Wales, Victoria, and Tasmania. Like Bailey acacia, but much larger, hardier, bigger-leaved, longer-lived. One *pl.* in Oct. 2002 at 9329 Lima Terrace S is now 22' tall.]

[**Sydney Golden Wattle**—*A. longifolia* (Andrews) Muhl. *ex* Willd.—from SE Australia. The "leaves" (phyllodes) are up to 5" long by over 1" wide. The flowers are lemon-yellow. At the U.W. campus some are mixed with Blackwoods S of the West Campus parking garage. The tallest are 26'. They are darker and bear wider "leaves" (phyllodes) (no ferny foliage) than the Blackwoods. (The i.d. of these specimens as this species is *tentative.*)]

[**Screwpod Acacia. Ovens Wattle**—*A. pravissima* F.v. Muell. *ex* Benth.—from NE Victoria and New South Wales. A small tree with slender whiplike twigs bearing highly distinctive sage-green, dull, dryish-feeling tiny (half-inch) "leaves" (phyllodes) of broadly *triangular* shape. The branches are partly pendulous. Bright clear yellow flowers in February–March. A few in Seattle yards: 122 17th Ave E (17½' tall; S side of front yard). 4340 NE 55th St (15' tall in SE corner of the yard). 8517 8th Ave NE. 11222 1st Ave NW.]

[**Everblooming Acacia. Wirilda. Swamp Wattle**—*A. retinodes* Schltdl. *(rhetinodes)*—from Tasmania, Victoria, and S Australia. A shrub or small open-crowned tree up to 33' tall, with *long*, pale to dark green, very *narrow* "leaves" (phyllodes) 5–9" long by ½" or much less. Pale yellow flowers appear mostly in summer and fall. One several years old is on Beacon Hill in a back yard, not yet visible from the street. 3240 NE 96th St has a youngster.]

[**Red-leaf** or **Red-stemmed Wattle**—*A. rubida* A. Cunn.—from SE Australia. The twigs are often reddish; the "leaves" (phyllodes) 2–8" long, at most 1" wide. A bit of ferny pinnate foliage is present. The flowers are light golden. At 9329 Lima Terrace S, one 17' tall is just N of the larger *A. dealbata*. One in a Seattle garden was producing self-sown seedlings, but was cut down.]

European ALDER

Alnus glutinosa (L.) Gaertn.   (not our) Common Alder
BETULACEÆ   Black Alder
From Europe, N Africa, W Asia, Siberia.

The original "Alder" recalls our native Red alder, but has thinner, glossier, more rounded leaves with fewer veins. It can attain 115' × 17½'. It is extremely rare here. It has proved short-lived. Wild offspring have been noted around Union Bay. The cutleaf cultivar 'Imperialis' (Royal Alder) is occasionally offered by specialty nurseries; it makes a small narrow tree bearing elegant, ferny foliage.

- Arboretum: best of three #411-64 in 15-1W are 75½' × 6'3" and 74' × 7'1¼"; #379-57 in 16-1W is 55' × 6'5¼"; #104-46 on Foster Island is small & rotten; an 'Imperialis' #1355-50 was cut down in April 2005 (at its prime it measured 40' × 2'8"); a #591-50 'Pyramidalis' is 40' tall in 12-1W
- 3519 West Laurelhurst Dr NE: an 'Imperialis' 47' × 3'3" in a lovely garden is visible from 43rd Ave NE, east of where 42nd Ave NE intersects with 43rd

Italian ALDER

A. cordata (Loisel.) Desf.   Neapolitan Alder
From Italy, Corsica.   Italian: Lontano, Alno *or* Ontano

A desirable ornamental alder, more glossy and prim than our native one—indeed it looks a bit like the common pear tree. It is also smaller than our native alder, though capable of growing as large as 100' × 16¼' with a narrow spire-like crown. Its cones are notably plump. Although perfectly hardy, and readily available from California nurseries, it is extremely rare in Seattle.

- Arboretum: the best is 87' × 6'1½" (#56-51 in 13-2E); 16-1W has one 70½' × 5'4"
- Locks #23 has one
- Genesee Park: 8, *pl.* during the 1970s near 43rd Ave S & S Adams St, tallest 54½'; two more in the NE part of the park
- NSCC: one 53½' × 3'3" is near the north end of a row of 26 Blue Atlas Cedars east of the parking lot

Red ALDER

A. rubra Bong., *non* Marsh.   (our) Common Alder
=*A. oregona* Nutt.   (our) Native Alder
Native here; from SE Alaska to S California.   Oregon *or* Western Alder

Seattle's second most abundant tree, in sheer numbers surpassed only by the ubiquitous Bigleaf Maple. Grows rapidly, but is not long-lived. Few in the city are taller than 120' or have trunks over 8' around, but one at Golden Gardens Park measured 86' × 15' × 81' wide—cut down in 1996 by Burlington Northern. The stoutest trunks currently known in Seattle parks range from 10' to 14'3½" around. The largest dimensions ever recorded anywhere are 143' × 20½'.

It is especially adapted (*via* symbiotic nitrogen fixation) to pioneering after landslides, fires, floods, logging or other such disturbances. Parks and greenbelts frequently have dense stands of tall, slender specimens easily uprooted or shifted by erosion and storms. Being such a common tree, without floral beauty, without autumn color, without moderation in its reproduction, and often infested with ugly tent caterpillars—it is often despised. Nevertheless, dull or little esteemed as the tree may be, it is important ecologically and yields valuable wood.

[**Cutleaf Red Alder**—*A. rubra* f. *pinnatisecta* (T.J. Starker) Rehd.—has leaves deeply lobed in cutleaf fashion. Extremely rare in Seattle. Arboretum has two #580-51 in 16-2W, the larger is 46' × 5'5½"; a 3rd in 28-4W is 64½' × 2'7¼". One at Kruckeberg Botanic Garden is 50' × 4'6½". Three street-trees are at 5631 3rd Ave NW.]

[**Sitka Alder**—*A. sinuata* (Reg.) Rydb.—is a shrubby species from NW North America and NE Asia. It *is* a Seattle native but is far less rare just north of the city, as well as on Vashon Island and on gravelly soil in Bellevue. Few specimens reach *ca.* 40' × 3'0".]

ALERCE

Fitzroya cupressoides (Mol.) I.M. Johnson   Alerze
CUPRESSACEÆ   Patagonian Cypress
From S Chile & SW Argentina rainforests.

It can live 3,600 years and its wood is choice. Its foliage is scaly. Extremely rare here. Scarcely found, and only *young*, outside the Arboretum: #535-90 is 8' tall by GVC parking lot; #537-90 is 7½' tall in 8-3E; #279-91A is 4' tall in 38-4W.

ALMOND TREE

Prunus dulcis (Mill.) D.A. Webb
=*P. Amygdalus* Batsch
=*Amygdalus communis* L.
ROSACEÆ
From N Africa to Syria.

A close cousin of the peach tree, grown not for its dry and thin fruit, but for the kernel, the well known almond. In the Language of Flowers, almond signifies "indiscretion; heedlessness; stupidity,"—or "promise." Take your choice!

In Seattle, uncommon. Various cultivars exist in the nursery trade (*e.g.,* 'Non Pareil,' 'Mission', 'Ne Plus Ultra'). So-called "Flowering Almonds" are shrubs grown for floral display, not for nut production. At any rate almond trees *are* attractive ornamentals: March finds them laden with big, beautiful, white or palest pink flowers. Almond trees tend to grow to about 20' × 3½' at most, but may eventually reach 40' in height. Usually they are wider than tall.

— 503 S Brandon St: *pl. ca.* 1947, our largest specimen, 41' × 7'6" × 48' wide
— 2804 NW 67th St: a street-tree, under wires
— Sycamore Ave NW & NW 72nd St: NW corner yard has 2 good trees
— 16th Ave S, south of S King St: many young street-trees

- 6773 Division Ave NW
- 7019 Palatine Ave N: 2 street-trees
- 28th Ave NE, south of NE 62nd St: a street-tree, west side, 31' tall
- 6521 27th Ave NE: a street-tree 29½' tall
- U.W.: a street-tree 18' × 2'7½" on NE Boat St just west of 15th Ave NE
- NW 62nd St, east of 2nd Ave NW: a street-tree, north side, under wires, not large
- Newton St, east of 4th Ave N: a street-tree, south side

Hybrid ALMOND TREE

P. × *persicoides* Dalla Torre & Sarnth.
=*P.* × *Amygdalo-persica* (West.) Rehd.
=*Amygdalus Amygdalo-persica* West.
=*A. hybrida* Poit. & Turp.

A hybrid between the almond and peach trees. Different races are grown variously for floral beauty or for nuts. In general they resemble the almond parent more, though they have self-fertile, pink flowers. The best known cultivar is 'Hall's Hardy' which is grown for nuts. 'Pollardii' originated in Australia *ca.* 1864 and is grown for ornament: it bears large, pale pink flowers in late March–early April, and its nuts ripen enough for the squirrels from mid-August to mid-September. The nuts are encased in thin, green, fuzzy husks, are difficult to crack, and taste slightly bitter. A few can be eaten with impunity but large amounts may be toxic, at least if eaten raw.

In Seattle, rare. Purebred almond trees can be difficult to distinguish from hybrids; those cited below are certainly hybrids and feature pink flowers, later in spring, and larger leaves.

- Arboretum: a 'Pollardii' 25' × 6½' north of the Lynn St parking lot was the city's largest almond tree of any kind, until it tipped over in Dec. 1990, aged 40 years
- 25th Ave E & E McGraw St: NW corner yard has a 'Pollardii' near McGraw
- 260 NE 43rd St (east of Thackeray Pl NE): a street-tree
- 4226 6th Ave NW: 2 in yard
- 17th Ave NW & NW 87th St: NE corner
- 2846 NW 61st St: in front yard, east of steps
- 8310 Stone Ave N: a street-tree

Japanese ANGELICA TREE

Aralia elata (Miq.) Seem.   Japanese: Tara-no-ki タラノキ
=*A. japonica* hort., *non* Thunb.   Onidara
=*A. chinensis* L. var. *mandshurica* (Ruprecht & Maxim.) Rehd.
ARALIACEÆ
From Manchuria, E Siberia, Sakhalin, Korea, Japan, the S Kuriles.

A small, almost invariably spiny tree, generally suckering from the base or even from the roots. The appellation Angelica Tree comes from its bold compound-leaf foliage, reminiscent of the herb Angelica. Tiny white flowers in enormous spreading clusters, August–October, gradually grow showier as the flower-stems turn purplish-red and the little berries ripen black. In parts of its homeland the tender young shoots and very young leaves are cooked as vegetables. Short-lived; recorded to 45' × 3'6" in the wild. The largest *here* measured 22' × 2'9½" × 24½' wide before dying.

In Seattle, common. Only shrubby specimens are known on public land.

– 13th Ave NW & NW 100th St: NW corner yard (short, broad, S of driveway)
– Zoo: many, some 18' tall
– 9838 60th Ave S: a two-trunked tree by front yard steps is 19' tall
– 3602 E Pike St: treelike, S of house
– 14322 Roslyn Pl N: 2 with long single trunks
– Arboretum: W of Lynn St parking lot (40-3W) is a 21' tall thicket #78-68
– Locks #114, 306

[Variegated Angelica-Tree—*A. elata* 'Aureo-variegata' (gold-variegated), 'Silver Umbrella' and 'Variegata' (silver-variegated)—are, in Seattle, extremely rare, known only young and shrub-sized. At S.U. a gold one is with 2 Italian cypresses south of the Lynn Bldg.; a 7' tall silver one is by the pond W of Loyola Hall.]

[Devil's Walking-Stick, or Hercules' Club—*A. spinosa* L.—is a taller, more slender tree from the SE United States. Exceedingly rarely cultivated in the West. It can be compared side by side with the common Asiatic species in the moss garden at The Bloedel Reserve on Bainbridge Island. In 2000 one was planted at the U.W. Medicinal Herb Garden.]

[Prickly Castor-oil Tree, or Castor Aralia—*Kalopanax septemlobus* (Th. *ex* J.A. Murr.) Koidz. (= *K. pictus* Nakai)—Leaf maple-like, large (to 14" wide); fall color unspectacular dull yellowish or reddish in October. The leaf resembles that of the castor bean *(Ricinus communis)* while the trunk and branches are *prickly* with short stout spines, hence its English names. Flowers creamy-white, minute yet abundant and showy in late July and August. Berries tiny, reddish-black on whitish stalks. A large shade tree performing best in moist soil, it is bold and unconventional with a primitive aura. Recorded to 100' × 20'0" in the wild. Extremely rare in Seattle. The Arboretum has one 53' × four-trunked #919-52 leaning to north in 28-4W; 24' to the east is smaller #363-53; largest of all is #950-48 in 15-1W: 55' × 7'2¾". The zoo has 3 youngsters at the Tropical Asian Elephant Forest entrance, the tallest 21'. The Good Shepherd Center has a 10' youngster.]

APPLE TREE

Malus domestica Borkh., *non* Poir.   Cultivated Apple
=*M. pumila* auct. p.p., *non* Mill.   Common Apple
=*M. communis* Poir., in part   Orchard Apple
=*Pyrus Malus* L., in part   Edible Apple
ROSACEÆ
From Eurasia, of ancient hybrid origin.

The most important fruit tree of the northern part of the globe. The apple itself, far more than the tree that bears it, is of far-ranging importance in our culture, both economically and symbolically. The tree can grow to 70' × 15¼'. Flowering time ranges from late March to mid-May. Thousands of cultivars exist.

In Seattle, very common. It comes up wild from seed here and there.

– Meridian Park: a large number of old orchard trees, plus different cultivars bordering the Seattle Tilth Demonstration Garden and Good Shepherd Center
– Carkeek Park: an old pioneer orchard here is kept up by volunteers
– 6th Ave W by W Emerson St: one, 32' × 5½'
– 118 N 58th St: 20' × 6'10½" × 30' wide
– 1402 N 100th St: 40' tall × nearly 50' wide
– Martha Washington Park: old orchard trees in NE lawn area
– Maplewood Playground (Corson Ave S & S Angeline St): 4 NW of baseball area

APRICOT TREE

Prunus Armeniaca L.   Chinese: Hsing *or* Xing
=*Armeniaca vulgaris* Lam.
ROSACEÆ
From China (E Manchuria), Korea.

A close relative of the Peach tree, but stouter, with *round* rather than long and slender leaves. Lætrile is extracted from apricot kernels. If situated on well-drained sandy soil in a warm and sunny location, an apricot tree can bear many pounds of fruit despite our soggy, gray climate. The flowers, (late February) March–April, are extremely pale pink: a healthy specimen in full bloom may be aptly described as smothered in blossoms. If not consistently and carefully pruned, it grows miserably stunted, full of ugly dead twigs and bears few flowers and fewer if any fruit. However, the extra pains needed to produce apricots here are well repaid when the harvest is ripe and ready. Our most common cultivar is 'Puget Gold'.

In Seattle, common. Most are less than 15' × 4'.

– Woodlawn Ave N & N 39th St: NE corner yard has a giant about 39' × 6'
– NW Bowdoin Pl, W of Leary Way (& the Burke-Gilman Trail): a street-tree, S side
– 702 11th Ave E: a young street-tree
– U.W.: N of Winkenwerder Hall dumpster; NW corner of Gerberding Hall has an 18' tall *wild* tree that by & by will be swallowed by a wild Shumard Red Oak
– E Republican St, W of 11th Ave E: 27' tall (S of a Cherry tree) between 2 driveways
– 12th Ave NE & NE 61st St: NE corner yard has one E of a blue Colorado Spruce

Japanese APRICOT

P. Mume (Sieb.) S.& Z.   Japanese Flowering-Apricot
From China, Korea, Taiwan.   Japanese "Plum" Tree
                                                        Japanese: Ume ウメ
                                                              Chinese: Mei

Smaller than the common apricot tree, this species has slenderer twigs which bear smaller leaves. Its flowers vary greatly in color, form, fragrance and bloom time. The apricots are 1–1½" wide, ripen mid- to late July, and have bland to somewhat bitter, clinging flesh. The green fruit, specially preserved in salt, forms a staple condiment in the traditional Japanese diet. Many cultivars exist: most with beautiful flowers, others featuring various fruit qualities. The tree is February's Floral Emblem in Japan. In Seattle the trees are rare. The most common ornamental kinds have pink, doubled flowers ('Dawn', 'Peggy Clarke').

- 1902 E Blaine St (with a Yulan Magnolia): a 'Dawn' 21' × 3'¼" × 27' wide
- St Peter's (1610 S King St): one 24½' tall on the N side, seen from S Jackson Pl
- 2171 38th Ave E: a 'Dawn' south of the driveway
- 4721 Lake Washington Blvd S: topped; neon pink in bloom (?'Matsubara Red')
- Seattle Chinese Garden's Song Mei Pavilion; *pl. ca.* 1999: 2 'Dawn'
- Arboretum: the Japanese Garden's orchard has it
- Locks #214 has a 'Peggy Clarke'
- 8250 Ashworth Ave N: a front yard tree, under the wires
- 1911 NE 117th St: a young tree east of the driveway has reddish flowers
- 9700 41st Ave S (south of S Burns St): a tall specimen at house's NW corner
- 3503 S Graham St: one at house's NE corner

ARBORVITÆ

Thuja occidentalis L.   Northern White Cedar
(Thuya, Thuia)   Eastern White Cedar
CUPRESSACEÆ   American Arborvitæ
From eastern N America.   Tree of Life

In 1535–36, Jacques Cartier's expeditionary forces were dying of scurvy. A friendly Canadian native informed them that this tree afforded "a singular remedie agaynst that disease." The desperate men tested it:

After thys medicine was founde and proved to be true, there was such strife aboute it, who shoulde be first to take of it, that they were readye to kill one another; that a tree as bigge as anye Oake in *Fraunce*, was spoyled and lopped bare, and occupied all in five or sixe dayes, and wroughte so well, that if all the Phisitions of *Montpelier,* and of *Louaine,* hadde beene there with all the drugges of *Alexandria,* they woulde not have done so muche in one yeare, as that tree dydde in five dayes. . . . (Cartier, p. 68)

The recovered explorers returned to France, bringing seeds and young plants of the tree to King Francis I, who named it "d'Arbor Vitæ" for its life-preserving qualities and its fragrant evergreen foliage. Its name and fame spread throughout civilized Europe.

This illustrious evergreen is a small, compact, slow-growing cousin of our native cedar (*i.e.,* the Western Red), similar in bark, foliage and cones. In nature it may reach 125' × 18'. In Seattle most are less than 30' tall, and many mere shrubs. Very commonly grown here (mostly cv. 'Fastigiata'), it is used extensively as a foundation planting, for accent, for screens and hedges—rarely is it seen as a single, open-grown specimen. It usually turns bronze-colored in winter.

- Lincoln Park: W of Rose St are 5 multitrunked trees, the largest 56½' × 3'3" (it was tilted by the December 1990 storm)
- Ravenna Park: one on the S side, east of the 15th Ave NE bridge 28' × 4'1¼"
- U.W.: 32' × 1'5¼" in the pine grove W of Anderson Hall; 45' × 2'2½" E of the

Medicinal Herb Garden nursery by Garfield Lane; N-1 parking lot
- Loyal Heights School: one 32' × 3'1" W of flagpole; 2nd one N of bldg. to west
- 1109 N 47th St (west of Midvale Ave N): a street-tree, 24' × 3'2"
- 3707 47th Pl NE: a 3-trunked three 32½' tall (in same yard is a 'Fastigiata')

cv. 'Aureospicata'
='Semperaurea' or 'Semperaurescens'

A dense, narrow, coarse tree, whose young growth is a bit yellowish. Very rare in Seattle; by far the strongest kind of *T. occidentalis* grown here.

- Volunteer Park: NE corner has one 57½' × 5'11½"
- Evergreen Park Cemetery: 44½' × 5'10"—50' south of a sundial
- Zoo: 5 trees in Australasia, from N to S: 32½' tall; 42' × 4'7½"; 40½' × 5'11¾" (below forking); 37' tall; 43' tall
- Magnuson Park: two along Sand Point Way NE, N of NE 65th St, the taller 35'

cv. 'Douglasii Pyramidalis'   Douglas Pyramidal Arborvitæ

A dense, narrow-pyramidal tree with crowded, twisted and frond-like foliage on short upswept branches. Bronzy in winter. Few cones. A strong grower, handsome in foliage and form, it can surpass 50' in height. It originated in an Illinois nursery before 1855. Apparently cv. 'Spiralis' is either the same as this one or may be a slightly improved version from ≤1888.

In Seattle, common. Often mistaken for the abundant cv. 'Fastigiata'.

- Arboretum: 5 #1426-50 are N of the viaduct footbridge (39-2W), the tallest 41' × 3'5¼"; of 3 #1426-50 in 41-1W the largest is 41' × 2'7¾"
- 14th Ave E & Delmar Dr E: a screen planting by the sidewalk
- Fort Lawton Cemetery: 4 in a triangle by entrance, the tallest 34'
- U.W. Medicinal Herb Garden: by the big blue Atlas Cedar north of section A

cv. 'Fastigiata'   Pyramidal Arborvitæ
=*Thuja pyramidalis* hort.   Pyramidalalis
='Pyramidalis'
='Columnaris'
='Stricta'

Columnar or *very* narrow-pyramidal with very short branches bearing dense foliage and many cones. Turns brownish in winter.

In Seattle, one of the most abundant and well-known trees; nearly every block in the city has some. Often like a row of soldiers standing at attention.

- Washelli Cemetery: 31½' × 4'6½" larger of two multitrunked splayed old trees
- 13th Ave S, north of S Albro Pl: 2 in a yard, W side; tallest 35'
- Good Shepherd Center: 4 in Seattle Tilth Children's Garden, the tallest 34½'
- 40th Ave NE & NE 70th St: the NW corner yard has one 31½' tall by the driveway
- Summit Ave & Spring St: NW corner parking lot has typical screening rows
- St. Demetrios Church (2100 Boyer Ave E): 9 on Boyer, the tallest 26'
- Evanston Ave N & N 110th St: 2 broad ones in the NW corner yard, the taller 19½'

cv. 'Lutea'   George Peabody Arborvitæ
='George Peabody'

A dense, vigorous, yellowish, narrowly pyramidal, bright and widely acclaimed tree that originated in Geneva, New York, about 1870. Some are over 65' tall. It's very rare in Seattle. But our winters would be better if we used more of these colorful trees instead of the dark 'Fastigiata'. A newer cv. is 'Yellow Ribbon'.

– U.W.: 34' tall multitrunked at the NW corner of Clark Hall

cv. 'Smaragd'   Emerald Green Arborvitæ

From Denmark. Bright emerald green, compact, pointy-topped, and replacing 'Fastigiata'. Planted in Seattle primarily since the late 1980s.

– U.W.: 6 by the Penthouse Theatre
– SSCC Arboretum: a row NW of the rose garden; tallest 17'
– 4400 Fremont Ave N: 7 W of bldg. and 3 older bigger 'Fastigiata' are S of the bldg.

[**Korean Arborvitæ**—*T. koraiensis* Nakai—From NE China as well as Korea. Shrubby or a small tree. Undersides of the young foliage strikingly *whitish*. Extremely rare in Seattle. Arboretum #317-69A is a sprawling specimen 14¾' tall in 42-5W, and #83-96 is in the nursery. Roanoke Park's SW corner has a 4' tall youngster.]

Hiba ARBORVITÆ

Thujopsis dolabrata (Th. *ex* L. fil.) S.& Z.   Hiba *or* Deerhorn Cedar
(*Thuyopsis*)   Lizard Tree *or* Battle-axe Cedar
From Japan.   Japanese: Hiba; Ate; Asunaro アスナロ

Though attaining in nature 100' × 9½' at most, in cultivation the Hiba is slow-growing, generally multitrunked, occasionally a mere shrub. It is sometimes treated as a clipped hedge or bush. It is very densely foliated when grown in the open, so the trunk is invisible. Its aspect is quiet, unassuming and inconspicuous, perhaps the reason it is often called rare. In fact only large specimens are uncommon. Its *substantial* foliage differs strikingly from that of its relatives in the *Thuja* genus. The "white-splashed" cultivar '**Variegata**' is hardly any different and has a tendency to revert to pure green.

– Leschi Park: a 6-trunked one is 56½' tall
– Acacia Cemetery: a multitrunked specimen 50½' tall
– Evergreen Park Cemetery: a 3-trunked one 48' × 3'10½" (its largest trunk)
– NE 55th St, at 18th Ave NE: a 50½' tall street-tree (and a plume Sawara Cypress)
– Arboretum: the larger of a pair (#1259-37 in 0-B) north of the Japanese Garden parking lot is 46' × 3'½"
– 2152 E Shelby St: 43½' tall, by sidewalk & alley

Oriental ARBORVITÆ

Platycladus orientalis L.   Chinese Arborvitæ
=*Biota orientalis* (L.) Endl.   Chinese Thuya

= *Thuja orientalis* (L.) Franco   Chinese: Ce Bai
CUPRESSACEÆ
From NE China and adjacent Korea and Russia.

This species is easily identified by its strongly vertical foliage bearing unusual "fleshy" cones which bear relatively large, unwinged seeds. In China it grows up to 80' × 16' and is regarded as an emblem of chastity.

In Seattle, common. Far more often grown in tightly compact cultivars, of which dozens exist, than in its wild tree form. Nearly all are multitrunked.

– 2206 E Crescent Dr: 40½' tall, three-trunked
– Arboretum: besides cultivars and smaller examples, four #239-53 in 33-2W were raised from seeds received from Korea in 1953, the tallest 41'
– U.W.: 2 behind Hutchinson Hall (flanking 2 'Zebrina' Western Red Cedars), the taller 38' × 3'7¼"; one in *front* of Hutchinson Hall is 32' tall
– Cowen Park: one 35' tall (crowded by a Plane tree) is N of the formal entrance
– Broadway E & E Allison St: NW corner, by driveway, 33½' tall
– 46th Ave SW & SW Oregon St: NE corner has one 31½' tall E of a Monkey Tree
– 14th Ave E & E Olive St: NW corner has one 24' tall

cv. **'Sanderi'**

A dwarf conifer, not treelike except after decades. Rare in Seattle. Foliage wholly juvenile, fluffy and coneless. At 905 NW 103rd St, a relatively big one 13½' tall, east of the 1948 house is believed to be this cultivar.

European ASH

Fraxinus excelsior L.   (not our) Common Ash
OLEACEÆ   English Ash
From Europe and Asia Minor.

This is the ash tree of history and legend among northern Europeans. The tough, elastic wood is valued for its many different uses—it even burns well when green. In Scandinavian myth, ash is the World Tree, Yggdrasill or Igdrasil, a complex symbol of the entire universe.

On a lesser scale, ash features in domestic folklore of the British Isles. It is said to heal certain illnesses in children, and to have an unhappy propensity for being struck by lightning: "Avoid the ash, it courts the flash!" After oak was crowned King of the Forest, beech Mother of the Forest, and birch Lady of the Woods, Gilpin called ash "Venus of the Woods"—upon which Cobbett commented:

It is well known that the Ash grows to a very great height, and that it will, if left to grow, become a very large tree. It is also well known, that it is a beautiful tree. GILPIN calls it the Venus of the woods. It has, however, one great disadvantage: that is, that it puts on its leaves later in the spring, and loses them earlier in the fall, than any other English tree. But perhaps GILPIN was thinking of a *naked* Venus, and then, indeed, the ASH claims the pre-eminence in our woods. Laying aside this nonsense, however, of poets and painters, we have no tree of such various and extensive use as the ASH (Cobbett, paragraph 104)

This "Venus" can, like most of its *Fraxinus* kin, be male, female or bisexual, and can live for over 250 years. The largest specimens have reached 150' × 33' so in size as well as in value and reputation, it is altogether a tree of the foremost magnitude. In the Language of Flowers it means, appropriately, "grandeur." It is uncommon here.

– Volunteer Park: a female 78' × 5'0" southwest of the upper tennis courts
– Lakeview Park: a female 77' × 5'9½"
– Jefferson Park: one 73' × 7'10"
– Arboretum: #X-329A in 23-3W is a male 72½' × 5'8¾"
– Madrona Park: one 71½' × 8'4" by the picnic shelter (north of it are a Manna ash and 2 Green ashes; further south are 2 Manna and 4 Green ashes)
– U.W.: N of the annex east of the Plant Lab, a male 70' × 5'1½"
– 7510 Earl Ave NW: a 47½' tall male in the back yard near the alley
– NE 52nd St, west of 19th Ave NE: 3 street-trees, N side, under wires
– Thackeray Pl NE, south of NE 45th St: an old 6'3" street-tree, W side (S of a European White Elm and a Honey Locust—all 3 trees under wires)

cv. 'Jaspidea'   Golden Desert™ Ash
=*F. oxycarpa* Golden Desert™ *or* 'Aureafolia'

Bark mustard orange; leaves pale yellow-green early in summer, pale green in summer, finally bright yellow in October. Seeds produced. Rare; most young.

– Arboretum: #313-64 in 25-3W is a female 52½' × 3'8½"; 70' SE of it is #139-82
– Lakeside Ave, S of Lake Washington Blvd: 6 street-trees *pl.* in 2004 on west side; also 6 uphill on Lake Wash. Blvd; (older 'Flame' Narrowleaf ashes also nearby)
– Melrose Ave, E side, between Pike & Pine St: 5 street-trees (*pl.* in 2000)
– Calvary Cemetery: one in the SE part (12' tall as of April 2005)

cv. 'Kimberly Blue'   Kimberly Blue Ash
=?'Rancho Roundhead'

Small and compact; round-headed or oval; *dark* green; seedless. Very rare.

– Pike St, from Minor Ave to Madison St: 15 City street-trees (with 'Armstrong' Freeman Maples and various other trees); the largest 35' × 5'¼"; the *original* 1970s planting had many more ashes, but poor performance led to their replacement
– 4th Ave NW, just S of NW 55th St: 4 (+ a smaller Green ash), largest 32' × 3'2"

Green ASH

F. pennsylvanica Marsh.   Red Ash
=*F. lanceolata* Borkh.
=*F. viridis* Michx. fil., *non* Bosc
=*F. pubescens* Lam.
From central & eastern N America.

So similar to our native species (the Oregon Ash) that the two have been treated as subspecies rather than separate species by one scientist who studied their characteristics. Common in Seattle, Green Ashes here can usually be distinguished from Oregon Ashes (see Oregon Ash for differences). Green Ash reaches up to 145' × 20¼'. It is represented in the nursery trade by such cultivars as 'Marshall', 'Emerald', 'Summit' and 'Patmore'—frequently used as street-trees.

– The Washington Park neighborhood near 34th E & 36th E, from E Madison to Mercer St, locally famous for its elm-lined streets, also has our best Green Ashes. They are usually set back on lawns rather than in the planting strips. The largest of over a dozen is 89' × 11'7" × 79' wide (1988)
– 13th Ave E, south of E John St: 5 ♂ and 2 ♀ street-trees, tallest 86½', stoutest 10'6"
– Madrona Park: 6, plus 1 European and 3 Manna Ashes
– '**Marshall Seedless**' City street-trees on NE 125th St, from 25th Ave NE to Roosevelt Way NE; and on 22nd Ave S, north of S Jackson St
– '**Summit**' (broad-crowned, shaggy-barked, with narrow leaflets) City street-trees on Fairview Ave N, from Denny Way to N Mercer St
– **Leprechaun**™ = 'Johnson' (a dwarf, top-grafted clone, patented in 1995) 13 street-trees *pl.* in 2000 on 24th Ave W, north of W Manor Pl.

Manna ASH

F. Ornus L. Flowering Ash
From S Europe, SW Asia.

This differs from most of its *Fraxinus* cousins in several ways: it bears creamy white fragrant flowers in (April) May–June (July), has unusually smooth bark, is less tolerant of shade and wet soils, and grows smaller than most species in the genus. It can attain 85' × 11'. From its bark can be obtained a dried exudate, one of the better known of various substances called "manna," useful as a laxative and for similar medicinal applications. In Seattle, common; females reseed weedily.

– Volunteer Park: several, the largest 55' × 8'7½" by the #10 bus-stop near an Eastern White Pine 88' tall at the SE corner of the park
– 224 14th Ave E (south of E Thomas St): a street-tree under wires, 29½' × 7'8¼"
– Madrona Park: 2 by the picnic shelter, the larger 5'4½" around
– U.W. Friendship Grove, representing Iran
– Locks in beds #30, 201 & 314; also *wild* here and there (*e.g.,* beds #4, 15, 17, 213)
– North Transfer Station (Dump), N 34th St & Carr Pl N: many
– NW 64th St, east of 20th Ave NW: 5 street-trees, S side, tallest 35½', stoutest 6'9"
– Fauntleroy Way SW & SW Juneau St: 3 City street-trees in the triangle here

Narrowleaf ASH

F. angustifolia Vahl Caucasian Ash
=*F. angustifolia* Vahl ssp. *oxycarpa* (M. Bieb. *ex* Willd.) Franco & Alf.
=*F. oxycarpa* M. Bieb. *ex* Willd.
From SW Europe & N Africa to the Caucasus.

Compared to most ashes, this has delicately elegant foliage and is further unusual in that some of the compound leaves are borne in whorls of three around the twig, rather than in opposite pairs. Moreover, a runt in wet soil, it can thrive in drier sites. It can grow to 100' × 16¼'.

In Seattle, common and popular ever since introduced in the 1970s. Though an ordinary seedling of the species may turn yellow in autumn and may set many seeds, 99% of the trees planted here are more or less seedless cultivars turning a pleasing bronzy-purple in October. These are 'Raywood' (a.k.a. the Claret ash) that originated in Australia; and 'Flame'—a 1965 patented U.S. selection a bit darker than 'Raywood'. Most often these are seen as street-trees; few are in parks or elsewhere. Although *sold* as seedless, some make seeds. There are also a few street-tree plantings from the 1970s of 'Dr. Pirone' that turns clear yellow in fall. Most of the plantings cited below are *mixed*. A street originally planted with 'Flame' will usually have replacement trees of 'Raywood', and even more recent replacements of White ash cultivars. The replacements are, in each case, an effort to improve on the previous choice.

— Arboretum: #308-62 in 49-1E is 75' × 6'6" (♀); #7-61 in 24-3W is 69' × 4'5" (♀)
— Arboretum: a 'Raywood' in 47-3E is 78½' × 4'9½" #479-69 (leans eastward)
— 6th Ave W, W McGraw to W Galer St: 'Raywood' City street-trees *pl.* in 1995
— 35th Ave NE, from NE 84th to NE 137th: 'Flame' City street-trees *pl.* in 1972, the largest (@ 10532) 70' × 8'5¼" × 73' wide
— N 45th St in Wallingford, from I-5 to Midvale Ave N: 'Flame' City street-trees
— Broadway, from Madison St to Jefferson, and Howell St to Roy: 'Flame' City street-trees but with some 'Summit' Green ashes
— S Dearborn St, east of 28th Ave S: 'Dr. Pirone' City street-trees
— 27th Ave, south of E Cherry St: many 'Dr. Pirone' City street-trees
— Midvale Ave N, just S of 45th St: a 'Dr. Pirone' City street-tree, E side, 43½' × 5'3"
— Arboretum: a 'Dr. Pirone' 55' × 4'9" #840-59 (♂ & ♀ flowers) is on the road to Foster Island N of the golf course fence
— Twin Ponds Park: a 'Scanlon Pyramid' is 76' × 5'3¾"
— Arboretum: a 'Scanlon Pyramid' in 26-2W is 64½' × 4'9½" (#821-59)

Oregon ASH

F. latifolia Benth.   (our) Native Ash
=*F. oregona* Nutt.
=*F. pennsylvanica* ssp. *oregona* (Nutt.) G.N. Mill.

This resembles Green ash closely. Both turn yellow in October; both species consist of either seedless males or seed-bearing females. It attains up to 150' × 22'.

Green ash:	Oregon ash
- bark of old trees *usually* hard, tight, not easily flaked off	- bark of old trees easily flaked from the trunk
- leaflets usually 9	- leaflets usually 7
- leaflets slightly, or not at all hairy	- leaflets very hairy except on seedlings and suckers
- leaflets narrower & pointed	- leaflets rounded & broad
- leaflets usually disease-free	- leaflets often diseased
- seeds narrower	- seeds broader

- planted non-native; rarely reseeds   - wild, native; rarely planted

In Seattle, common. Most abundant and largest in moist, low-lying places near lakes. It can be seen nearly everywhere but was rarely *planted* 'til lately.

- South Park Playground (8th Ave S & S Sullivan St): one on the E side 86' × 12'4½" was cut down in 2005
- Arboretum (the prime location for Oregon ash): in the north part specimens reach 105' × 9'5" and 93' × 9'6"; Foster Island has hundreds
- Beer Sheva/Atlantic City Park (Seward Park Ave S & S Henderson St): many
- U.W.: some by the waterfront NE of the Montlake Bridge
- U.W. Medicinal Herb Garden: a male southwest of section G, 4'7½" around
- Lake Washington Blvd E by E Republican St: one 96' tall
- 2nd Ave W, south of W Prospect St: 6 street-trees, west side

White ASH

F. americana L.   American Ash
From the eastern half of the U.S., and S Ontario.

An important timber tree, of grand size (to 175' × 29'), great value and nobility of appearance. Especially attractive in autumn when it turns rosy purple. Its wood has been used for baseball bats, hockey sticks, oars, paddles, and many other things. In Seattle, uncommon; only young trees are known.

- Arboretum: in 47-3E is a '**Rosehill**' #299-68A 55' × 4'2½" (droopy crown, leans eastward); and a '**Skyline**' #208-81A 63' × 4'1½" (ascending crown)
- Amy Lee Tennis Center (2000 Martin Luther King, Jr. Way S): 4 west of 2 Manna ashes S of the entrance; across the street are street-tree White ashes *pl.* in 1991 or '92
- Loyal Heights School: 2 street-trees on 26th Ave NW, N of Dawn Redwoods
- N 43rd St, west of Midvale Ave N: four street-trees, N side
- Densmore Ave N, near N 49th St: '**Autumn Applause**' street-trees *pl.* 1996–97
- 12th Ave, just north of Yesler Way: an '**Empire**' street-tree *pl.* 2004, E side
- NW 80th St, by 26th–27th Ave NW: 6 **Urbanite**® = 'Urbdell' street-trees *pl.* 1992

AZARA

Azara microphylla Hook. fil.   Boxleaf Azara
From Chile and Argentina.   Chilean (Mapuche): Chinchin
FLACOURTIACEÆ

Named after Félix de Azara (1742–1821), Spanish geographer and naturalist who did fieldwork in South America. Petite, dark and very shiny evergreen leaves hide inconspicuous yellow flowers, strongly vanilla- or chocolate-scented in late winter. The fruit is a tiny one-seeded berry ¼" long, ripening in June or July. A cold-tender, shrubby tree of fine texture. In Seattle, uncommon.

- Arboretum: 40' tall #131-73B in 35-B; nearby are #131-73C and #376-74; #1245-56 in 33-1E is small despite being far older
- 4049 NE 58th St: one 30½' tall at house's NW corner (with a Nymans Eucryphia)
- U.W.: the Friendship Grove, representing Peru, has an old tree 25½' × 2'5"; a younger tree is S of Hansee Hall

- 2702 10th Ave W: 26' tall
- 1941 8th Ave W: 26' tall
- Good Shepherd Center: front side has one 19' tall (to the S), one 20' tall (to the N)
- 1623 E Republican St: E of house
- 2244 E Blaine St: at corner of house
- 7554 44th Ave NE: a 25' tall 'Variegata' (leaves cheerfully creamy & yellowish-variegated) in the back yard, but visible from the street
- Children's Hospital: a 'Variegata' 15½' tall by the emergency services patient's door
- 6214 36th Ave NE: a young 'Variegata' N of front door
- 707 E Prospect St: 2 young 'Variegata'

[**Whiteberry Azara**—*A. serrata* Ruiz & Pav.—Leaf broad, to 2¾" long × 1½" wide. Showy yellow flowers in April or May; porcelain-white berries in late August. Shrubby. Extremely rare in Seattle. 7519 22nd Ave NW has one 9½' tall by the driveway. 2125 N 90th St also has one 9½' tall.]

[**Narrowleaf Azara**—*A. lanceolata* Hook. fil.—Leaf slender, to 2½" long. Flowers showy yellow in April. Shrubby. Extremely rare here. Locks beds #204, 305, 306 have it, the tallest 20'. The Arboretum has #191-88 labeled *A. microphylla* (four in 13-8E & two in 12-8E). S.U. campus has a leaning 8½' tall tree in Campion Hall's Zen Garden. The Good Shepherd Center has one 4½' tall, in the NE area, *pl.* 2005.]

American BEECH

Fagus grandifolia Ehrh.
=*F. americana* Sweet
=*F. ferruginea* Ait.
FAGACEÆ
From eastern N America, NE Mexico.

Very rare in Seattle compared to the European Beech, and without variants or cultivars. The American Beech resembles a refined hornbeam tree more than it does the massive European Beech. Its sharply toothed leaves have 14–15 pairs of veins. It sometimes suckers, forks into its crown much lower than does European Beech, and grows slowly enough so that it does not soon outgrow a typical Seattle yard. In October it turns a pretty yellow-orange. It can grow to 161' × 28½'.

In April the young leaves are edible raw. They have a fresh, tangy, astringent taste. The tiny nuts, infrequently borne here, are also edible, as are the seedlings. In its native lands, its nuts (called "mast") were the favorite food of foraging hogs and the now extinct Passenger Pigeons:

. . . when the beech-nuts are ripe, they fly 200 miles to dinner, in immense flocks, hiding the sun and darkening the air like a thick passing cloud. They thus travel 400 miles daily. They roost on the high forest trees, which they cover in the same manner as bees in swarms cover a bush, being piled one on the other, from the lowest to the topmost boughs, which so laden, are seen continually breaking and falling with their crashing weight, and presenting a scene of confusion and destruction, too strange to describe, and too dangerous to be approached by either man or beast. While the living birds are gone to their distant dinner, it is common for man and animals to gather up or devour the dead, then found in cartloads. (Faux, pp. 248–249)

- U.W.: N of the Music Building 44½' × 4'1¼"
- Arboretum: largest of nine is 64' × 4'9" #321-42B
- 20th Ave, E Cherry to E Union St: 18 street-trees (+4 European beeches), tallest 38'
- Locks bed #21
- Fairview School: on NE 78th St, west of Roosevelt Way NE, are 5 European (e) and 3 American (a) beeches. From west to east: e a e e e e a a, the largest American 31' × 4'8"
- Fauntleroy Way SW & SW Director St: NE corner yard has one 26½' tall
- 1661 Shenandoah Dr E

European BEECH

F. sylvatica L.   Common Beech
From Europe and E as far as the Black Sea.

Mother of the Forest and symbol of prosperity, a beloved tree with a great dense head of foliage, supported by a sturdy, light-colored, smooth-barked trunk. In Europe, people often choose beech trunks to carve upon; in Seattle, Red Alders are more commonly so abused, yet many of our beeches bear carving scars. Beech nuts are mostly hollow duds: sound ones are edible, at least in small amounts or if cooked. Natural beech forests exert a somber influence and cast a dark shadow beneath which little grows, yet the best truffles and morel mushrooms grow in such places. The tree can attain enormous dimensions, up to 164' × 31¾'.

In Seattle, common. Some cited below date from the 1890s or early 1900s.

- Zoo: the largest of 14 between the Savanna and Family Farm is 84' × 15'4"
- Arboretum: a boulevard tree west of the sidewalk in 3S-6E is a lofty 127' × 6'11"
- Volunteer Park: tallest of many is 113' × 11'10½" by a Western Red Cedar across the road S of the play area; the stoutest trunk is behind the museum, 12'9½" around
- Lake View Cemetery: one in the NW part is 78½' × 12'3"
- 815 18th Ave (south of E Marion St): a street-tree 84½' × 11'9"
- 39th Ave, south of E Howell St: a street-tree, W side 83½' × 13'1"
- U.W.: 93½' × 8'5" on Parrington Hall lawn; 58' × 6'2½" SW of Anderson Hall

cv. 'Aspleniifolia'   Cutleaf *or* Fernleaf Beech

Smaller and more refined than regular beech. Different cut-leaved cultivars exist; 'Aspleniifolia' has been confused with them and sometimes has been miscalled by their names: 'Heterophylla', 'Incisa' and 'Laciniata'. It is very rare in Seattle.

- 122 Lake Washington Blvd E: Seattle's largest, behind the concrete wall, 75' tall
- 140 Lake Washington Blvd E: one at NW corner of house
- Arboretum: 63' × 4'½" #1142-49 in 41-1E
- Kubota Garden Park: by 55th Ave S service gate 47½' × 3'3¾"; also a larger 5-trunked specimen in the park to the NW
- 1310 E John St: 55½' tall
- U.W.: 2 on the lawn W of Odegaard Library

cv. 'Dawyck'   Columnar *or* Fastigiate Beech

Columnar in form after the fashion of Lombardy (Black) Poplar. The original tree from which all Dawyck Beeches have been cloned grows in Scotland. The tree is uncommon in Seattle.

– Arboretum: 86' × 3'1¼" #490-57 in 40-1E
– Bagley School (7821 Stone Ave N): 2 at front entrance, bigger 66' × 4'3¼"
– Lincoln High School: 54½' × 6'½" (below branching), on Woodlawn Ave N
– St Anne Church (1st Ave W & W Lee St): 6 street-trees interplanted with 9 'Eddie's White Wonder' Dogwoods on 1st Ave W
– Columbia School (3528 S Ferdinand St): one at the SE corner
– Substation at NE corner of 34th Ave SW & SW Roxbury St: two, the taller 56½'

cv. 'Dawyck Purple'   Purple Dawyck Beech

Raised in Holland in 1969; not sold in Seattle until 1990s. *Purple*-leaved and columnar. ('Dawyck Gold' is also a brand new tree you may find here.)

– 35th Ave NW & NW 70th St: NW corner, 26½' tall against the chimney
– 7056 9th Ave NW: a yard tree
– 1614 36th Ave: a street-tree south of a purpleleaf Smoke Tree
– 615 34th Ave E

f. *pendula* (Loud.) Scheele   Weeping Beech

Common in Seattle, and eye-catching, this *drooping* tree is easily recognized even in winter, from a distance—but see 'Purple Fountain' below.

– Evergreen Park Cemetery: 54' × 5'2¼" × 58½' wide
– 27th Place W & W Manor Place: SE corner 56½' tall
– Arboretum: 52' × 2'10½" #169-66A in 37-2E
– 8th Ave & Columbia St: one 49' tall seems to be coming out of the top of the building on the NE corner
– U.W.: 45' × 3'7¾" and 48' × 3'2¼" against Wilcox Hall
– 30th Ave NE & NE 110th St: NW corner yard, 48' tall
– 3164 NE 83rd St: 47' tall
– 45th Ave NE & NE 74th St: SW corner yard has a broad one 43½' tall
– S.U.: NW corner of Lemieux Library has 3, the taller 38', the stouter 35' × 3'7¾"; also near the bookstore, Campion Residence Hall, and elsewhere.
– 2640 39th Ave W

cv. 'Purple Fountain'   Purple Fountain Weeping Beech

Raised in Holland as a seedling of 'Purpurea Pendula'; not sold in Seattle until 1990s. Purple-leaved and narrowly upright, unlike its squat shrubby parent.

– 2015 Airport Way S: two; the taller 31½'
– S.P.U.: Emerson Park triangle has one 26' × 1'9½"; a smaller one 160' away at the NE corner of Demaray Hall
– 21st Ave NW & NW 65th St: NW corner has two, the taller 32'
– 33rd Ave NE & NE 73rd St: NE corner has one 30' tall S of house
– Evergreen Park Cemetery: two, 18' and 21' tall

f. *purpurea* (Ait.) Schneid.   Copper *or* Purple Beech

Every bit as big as the regular kind, these differ only in their bronzy to dark purplish leaves. Some are seed-grown trees, others are grafted cultivars.Various names used for them include 'Atropunicea', 'Atropurpurea', 'Cuprea', 'Purpurea', 'Riversii' and 'Spaethii'. It is common here.

- Volunteer Park: one north of the museum is 96' × 15'4¼"
- Lake View Cemetery: 69½' × 15'3¼" on high ground by the road, on the S side
- Queen Anne Playfield (1st Ave W & W Howe St): one 72' × 14'5½"
- Kinnear Park: 72½' × 12'8½" (by a bench) & 140' to the east: 53½' × 11'0"
- 36th Ave & E Pike St: NW corner yard, 80' tall
- Leschi Park: 91' × 9'10½"
- U.W.: 62½' × 7'0" NW of Anderson Hall; another SE of the Art bldg.
- Lincoln High School (Interlake Ave N & N 43rd St): 8 in a row in front

cv. 'Purpurea Pendula'   Squat Purple Weeping Beech

A purple weeping shrub-sized tree scarcely ever found even 10' tall. Rare; being replaced by its tall seedling 'Purple Fountain'.

- Kubota Garden Park: two, the taller 10' × 1'8½"
- 4026 NE 55th St: at SW corner, 9½' tall
- 318 N 76th St: 2 street-trees
- 3533 46th Ave NE: 6½' tall by sidewalk at head of driveway with a Hinoki Cypress
- 2421 Montavista Pl W: specimen by a bigger 'Youngii' European White Birch
- 322 17th Ave E
- S.U.: Pigott Building courtyard; 7' tall near main entrance of Connolly Center

cv. 'Purpurea Tricolor'   Purple Tricolor Beech
='Roseo-marginata'   Rose-pink Beech

Purplish leaves with *pinkish* variegation. In summer the purple fades badly to bronzy-green. Uncommon in Seattle; all relatively young and small.

- Kubota Garden Park: 56½' × 5'3"
- 5821 Oakhurst Rd S: 55' tall
- Seattle Center: NE part of the fountain lawn has one 45½' × 4'2½"
- 3401 NE 81st St: 47½' tall
- U.W.: one at 15th Ave NE & NE 43rd St in a rectangular bed by the stairs
- S.U.: 36' tall E of Bannan Center

cv. 'Rohanii'   Purple Cutleaf *or* Oakleaf Beech

Besides having purple, "oaklike" leaves, this tree is narrower than the regular kind, at least when young. It is uncommon in Seattle.

- Arboretum: 72' × 3'8¼" #382-50A is in 42-1E
- Kruckeberg Botanic Garden: 50' × 4'4½" × 35½' wide
- 7346 20th Ave NE: a stout, broad tree 35' tall
- Evergreen Park Cemetery(N end): 33' × 5'1¼" and unusually broad at 32' wide
- 1905 E Lynn St: 44' tall
- 36th Ave SW & SW Hanford St: NE corner has one 39' tall

- S.U.: one 25' tall at SE corner of 10th & Spring St, with a shorter *Stewartia monadelpha* N of it
- 5511 8th Ave NE: one crowded between a Birch and a Sweetgum
- 5026 18th Ave NE

cv. '**Zlatia**'   Golden Beech
='Aurea'

Yellowish foliage, especially in spring on the sunny side of the tree. From Serbia; *zlato* is the Serbo / Croatian name for gold. It is extremely rare in Seattle.

- Arboretum: 65½' × 4'5¾" #655-54A in 43-1E
- 5544 29th Ave NE: a street-tree 51' tall

Southern-BEECHES in general

Of the 35–40 species in the genus *Nothofagus* only five are known in Seattle outside of the Arboretum. Related to our familiar beeches, and in their native Southern Hemisphere perhaps resembling them—as grown in Seattle so far they don't look much like beeches, especially in foliage. The Arboretum is the best place to see and learn about them. (See the *Arboretum Bulletin*, Spring 1978). Their native names are supplied below.

Antarctic (Southern-) BEECH

Nothofagus antarctica (Forst. fil.) Oerst   Ñirre
From Chile, Argentina, Tierra del Fuego.   Guindo

Capable of growing as tall as 115', this tree from South America has small, glossy deciduous leaves, of crinkly nature and smelling like beeswax or cinnamon when crushed. Although rare in Seattle, the other Southern-Beeches are still rarer. The Arboretum trees were named cv. 'Puget Pillar' in 1990.

- Arboretum: largest is 52' × 5'7½" #101-51 in 49-2E; two #827-76 in 49-2E are 56' × 4'0" & 55' × 4'3"; two younger #270-92 are in 9-3E
- Zoo: Llama Exhibit
- 18th Ave NW & NW 95th St: NW corner has one (& 2 David Stripebark Maples)
- U.W.: 2 *pl.* 1992 east of Henderson Hall, the taller 31'
- 39th Ave E & E Lee St: NE corner yard has 3 on its south border
- 1822 N 55th St: 4 street-trees

Black (Southern-) BEECH

N. Solandri (Hook. fil.) Oerst.   Maori: Tawhai Rauriki
From New Zealand.

An airy, slender tree whose dainty dark evergreen leaves suggest *Azara microphylla* in foliage texture and the arrangement of its leaves in neat rows. Leaves ¼–¾" long, holly-green above, sage-green beneath. It hates dryness, wind, or soggy soils. Recorded to 84' × 15¾'. Extremely rare in Seattle.

var. *Cliffortioides*, the Mountain Beech, has smaller, thicker, pointier leaves, buckled with their edges rolled under. It is apt to be less cold-tender here.

– Arboretum: #219-95 is small, bronzy, in 10-2E and in 9-2E by the lookout (a dry, brutally exposed site with horrible soil); var. *Cliffortioides:* #13-91 is 46' × 2'4" in 48-2E; #447-90 is smaller; #28-92 is in 36-2W; #447-90A in 8-4E is 28½' × 1'5¼"; #447-90C in 8-4E is 37' × 1'1½"
– 4340 NE 55th St: in the back yard, not visible from the street, one *ca.* 20' tall

[**Myrtle (Southern-) Beech**—*N. Cunninghamii* (Hook.) Oerst.—From Tasmania and S Australia rainforests. Looks similar to *N. Solandri.* The north end of the front of the Good Shepherd Center has one 17' tall (31' south of a 20' tall *Azara microphylla*).]

Dombey (Southern-) BEECH

N. Dombeyi (Mirb.) Bl.   Coigüe
From Chile, Argentina.   Coihue

A broadleaf evergreen tree that can reach 165' × 40' and is usually judged one of the most ornamental of the genus. Leaves intense dark shiny green, ½–1⅜" long. It's very rare here.

– Arboretum: largest is 93' × 5'½" #797-49A in 41-1W
– Kruckeberg Botanic Garden: 57' × 5'8½"
– 4311 / 4319 43rd Ave NE: a street-tree
– 5715 63rd Ave NE
– 5717 NE 57th St

Roble (Southern-) BEECH

N. obliqua (Mirb.) Bl.   Roble (Pellín)
From Chile, W Argentina.   Coyan *or* Hualle

A *deciduous* species that can grow as large as 160' × 20½'. Leaves dull, raggedly toothed, 1½–3½" long, late to show fall color. Extremely rare in Seattle.

– Arboretum: two reseeding #1249-56 in 49-2E, the larger 69½' × 6'1"; 79½' × 4'2½" #658-48A in 42-B; 57' × 3'7¾" #601-50A in 42-B; #158-94A in 9-3E
– Locks #201 has one 39' tall, and behind it a shrubby *N. antarctica*
– U.W. Friendship Grove, representing Argentina: cut in April 1991, now shrubby

[**Raoul** *or* **Raulí (Southern-) Beech**—*N. procera* (Poepp. & Endl.) Oerst.—From Chile & W Argentina. Sold at local nurseries since 1990 but the only specimen known at this writing is in the Arboretum: #668-60A, 34½' × 1'1" in 41-B. Leaves bold, to 4¾" long.]

Chinese Redbark BIRCH

Betula albo-sinensis Burk.
From central China.
BETULACEÆ

Chinese Paper Birch
Chinese: Hong Hua

Though in the Arboretum for decades, none of these were planted *elsewhere* in Seattle until the 1990s. They are still rare. Greatly prized for their lovely bark: red, coppery to gray-pink. In the wild this species has attained 100' × 16¼'.

– Arboretum: 16; the largest 66½' × 3'2½" (#710-60 in ash tree area 22-3W); 43½' × 3'3½" (E of Azalea Way in 17-B); 41' × 3'4" (#581-63B in 17-B); 43½' × 2'9¼" (#820-59 in 16-1E)
– U.W.: CHDD South building has 3 W of a Persian Ironwood, largest 30' × 1'6"
– S.U.: one 23½' tall E of Broadway & Columbia garage, NW of Loyola Hall
– 7737 16th Ave NW: a yard tree
– Bagley Ave N, north of N 40th St: 2 street-trees, E side
– Good Shepherd Center: 2 NW of main parking lot, the taller 18'
– Magnuson Park: 3 *pl.* 2004 in *Geometric Garden in Red* W of Community Garden

Downy BIRCH

B. pubescens Ehrh.
From Europe, far N Africa.

Much like White birch, but less attractive. It varies from ugly scrubby trees (the norm) to admirable giants. The name Downy birch refers to its twigs—more or less felty hairy. However, White birch seedlings and sometimes suckers are similarly downy. Downy birch leaves are lighter green, duller, shaped differently and stay green longer in autumn.

In Seattle, common, mostly in older parts of the city. Due to hybrids with White birch (such hybrids are known as *B.* × *aurata* Borkh.) the city has a confusingly variable population. Some trees cited below are certainly hybrids, others are not, and some are uncertain. All have at least lightly hairy twigs.

– Evergreen Park Cemetery: the largest is 66½' × 9'3" × 60' wide
– Washelli Cemetery: a 3-forked trunk measured below forking is 65' × 13'11¾"
– Madrona Park: taller of a pair N of concession bldg. is 73' × 6'½"
– 119 W Boston St: a street-tree 54½' × 11'2½"
– Seward Park: tallest of several in the woods at the peninsula tip is 97' × 4'½"
– Rodgers Park: 7 Downy & 3 White; NE of restrooms is a poor one 65' × 5'2" near a bigger White birch
– Cal Anderson Park: one at the N end is 53' × 7'10"
– Arboretum: literally hundreds are wild in the cattail marshes on and near Foster Island, along with some White birches
– 43rd Ave NE & NE 75th St: NE corner has one 49' × 10½' × 74½' wide (1989)

Gray BIRCH

B. populifolia Marsh.
From northeastern North America.

White *or* Old Field Birch
Wire *or* Fire Birch

Gray Birch is dirty white, often crooked and twiggy. The leaves bear distinctive drawn-out tips and fall early in autumn. Though many specimens are dull-barked, small, graceless trees difficult to admire, the finest are ghostly white slender trunks 80' tall quivering with attractively fluttering leaves. It is the birch featured in poems by Robert Frost, James Russel Lowell and other New England bards. It is uncommon in Seattle. Before learning better, I used to think our specimens represented a dwarfish, poor race of White birch.

– E Calhoun St between 16th and 18th Avenues E: 10 street-trees (+ 2 White birches), the stoutest trunk 5'3¼" around (at 1611); the tallest 63' (at 1627)
– 48th Ave NE & NE 45th St: NE corner yard has 2 big ones, tallest 60'+
– LDS Church (8th Ave NE & NE 57th St): 2-trunked, just north of the entrance
– U.W.: 3 on lawn N of Pend Oreille Rd, E of Burke-Gilman Trail
– 39th Ave S & S Burns St: NE corner yard has a 3-trunked tree in poor condition
– 5207 29th Ave NE: a multitrunked one in the yard's SE corner
– 7908–7910 Ashworth Ave N: 2

Jacquemont BIRCH

B. utilis D. Don ssp. *Jacquemontii* (Spach) Kit.   Kashmir Birch
=*B. Jacquemontii* Spach   Whitebark Himalayan Birch
From the W Himalayas.

If not Seattle's only white-barked Asiatic birch, certainly our only common one. Nurseries have stocked other species, however. All the Jacquemont Birches cited below (except those at the Arboretum) are young, grafted trees with exceptionally pretty, very white bark. At least 10 clones have been named in Europe, including 'Grayswood Ghost' and 'Jermyns'; some have been sold here.

– Arboretum: largest of three #647-50 east of Azalea Way in 19-B is 79' × 4'9"
– Zoo: some by Snow Leopard exhibit
– 316 Lake Washington Blvd S: three
– 6010–6012 27th Ave NE: 4 street-trees
– 28th Ave E & E Ward St: 2 in the traffic circle
– U.W.: 6 youngsters northwest of parking lot E-3

Paper BIRCH

B. papyrifera Marsh.   American White Birch
From Alaska, Canada, and   Paperbark Birch
the northern U.S.   Canoe Birch

In the *Song of Hiawatha*, in paintings by Tom Thompson and other artists, and in collective memory, this white-wrapped tree features vividly. A valued and beautiful friend of humankind, in earlier times it supplied hunters, traders, trappers and explorers with chalky white bark for canoes, tents, roofs, wigwam coverings, baskets and tinder.

Geographic races of Paper birch and some hybrids exist. Some are not even white-barked. The largest yield useful wood, and may grow to 120' × 16'.

In Seattle, common. Possibly a rare native here—but barely known in a wild state at present. More than one race has been planted. Easily told from the far more common White birch by its larger leaves, papery and peelable (rather than deeply furrowed) mature bark, upright (non-weeping) habit, and stoutness.

– Calvary Cemetery: 2 outstanding trees of superior size and character, 180' apart; the S-most 43½' × 10'3" × 57' wide; the N-most 57½' × 9'6½" × 68½' wide
– Arboretum: 88' × 7'1¾" (untagged) in 42-4W
– Green Lake: 69½' × 8'7" but dying W of the wading pool; on the SE shore by Kirkwood Pl is one 54½' × 8'2"; west of 63rd St is one 42½' × 7'9½"
– 748 17th Ave E (@ E Aloha St): 4 old street-trees, E side, largest 70½' × 5'10½"
– U.W.: Medicinal Herb Garden N of Cascara Circle 66' × 4'10½"; one E of the Physical Plant office bldg. 58½' × 5'2"; one S of Thomson Hall 47' × 4'5½"
– Camp Long: largest of several is SW of the main building, 59' × 6'11½"
– Seward Park: a *wild* tree between the road and Lake Washington is 50' × 6'5"
– 24th Ave S & S Brandon St: NE corner yard has a 3-trunked specimen 53½' tall

River BIRCH

B. nigra L.   Red Birch
=*B. rubra* Michx.
From the eastern U.S.

A birch with a densely foliated, glossy aspect all its own. The bark of older trees is extremely hard, deeply furrowed and *dark* gray. Young trees in the Arboretum have scaly, reddish bark. It can grow to 120' × 15½' and doesn't need riverside sites to do so. Rare in Seattle; aside from those at the Arboretum few older trees are known. But *numerous* young specimens exist of **Heritage**™ (cv. 'Cully')—a pale-barked version that was found as a chance seedling in 1968.

– Arboretum: best are two #265-64 in 12-1W, 76½' × 8'5" & 72½' × 8'9¼"
– Lake View Cemetery: one 58' × 8'10¼" × 62½' wide stands about in the center
– 6034 40th Ave NE: N of driveway, 50½' × three-trunked
– E Spring St, west of 16th Ave: 2 street-trees, N side
– Green Lake: 50 **Heritage**™ by December 2001, most *pl.* 1997 or so
– 2811 NW 62nd St: **Heritage**™
– U.W.: 2 **Heritage**™ north of the Academic Computer Center
– 37th Ave W & W Dravus St: one S of the stairway east of this intersection

Sweet BIRCH

B. lenta L.   Mahogany Birch
From the eastern United States,   Black *or* Cherry Birch
extreme S Ontario and Québec.   Sugar *or* Spice Birch

This tree was named "Cherry birch" for its resemblance to the American Black Cherry. Though Yellow birch twigs possess the same delicious wintergreen flavor, the concentration is greater in Sweet birch. Sweet birch may grow to be 117' × 19' and has been employed medicinally by herbalists. Euell Gibbons devotes a chapter to it in *Stalking the Wild Asparagus*. It is rare here.

- Zoo: east of the Rose Garden, one 55' × 7'3" × 60'+ wide
- Volunteer Park: SE of the upper tennis courts, 58' × 5'7¼"
- Seward School: in a mixture of 7 Sweet and 3 Yellow birches, the largest of the former is by the chessboards, 5'6¼" around
- 13th Ave, north of E Marion St: 2 street-trees, W side, the larger 5'5½" around
- Salmon Bay Park: one SW of the restrooms is 51½' × 5'6¾" (2 Yellow birches are also in the park: 1 N of the play area; one 200' south of the Sweet birch)
- McDonald School: 3 street-trees on Latona Ave NE, north of NE 54th St
- Dayton Ave N & N 127th St: NE corner yard

White BIRCH

B. pendula Roth — European White Birch
=*B. verrucosa* Ehrh. — Common Birch
=*B. alba* L., in part — Warty Birch
From Europe, Asia Minor, N Africa. — Silver Birch

The best known, most abundant white-barked tree, it is the original "Birch." In European domestic history it gained renown for its picturesque presence in the landscape as well as for supplying useful bark, timber, sap for beverages or shampoo, twigs for brooms and rods for reprimand. It yellows in autumn. A Michigan specimen measured 110' × 12½' in 1983.

In Seattle, very common, popular nearly everywhere and much planted—fully naturalized, too. It tends to suffer severely from aphid honeydew drip. Not long-lived, many older ones are now senescent and decaying. Only a few of the very largest or tallest are cited below.

- Interlaken Park: ravine below the #12 bus turnaround has one 110½' × 4'8¾"
- Volunteer Park: the largest is on the east border, 84' × 7'1½"
- Ravenna Park: some in the ravine, the tallest 95' × 5'3¼"
- 5808 17th Ave NE: one 81' × 8½'
- 19th Ave E & E Harrison St: the SW corner church has one 8'+ around

cv. '**Crispa**' — Cutleaf Weeping Birch
= 'Dalecarlica' hort. — Swedish Birch

This Scandinavian is the most abundant and prized of various cutleaf, weeping clones. Slenderer than the regular form, its trunk less commonly forked, the bark smoother and unfissured except at the base of the oldest specimens; the leaves are long-stalked and *deeply jagged*.

In Seattle, common. Usually called 'Dalecarlica'—but incorrectly.

- Mt. Baker Park: one with 14 young Jacquemont birches is 95' × 4'5½"
- Denny-Blaine Park: the largest of 4 is 71½' × 6'1½"
- 34th Ave E, south of E Valley St: 2 street-trees, E side; the larger 72½' × 6'2¼"
- 46th Ave SW & SW Holgate St: NW corner has 6 street-trees; the best 68½' × 6'2"
- Good Shepherd Center: one W of the building is 62' × 6'0"
- Lake View Cemetery: one 68' × 5'4" at the extreme S end, about in the middle
- U.W.: one 58' tall with 4 Pacific Dogwoods in front of Physical Plant office bldg.
- NE 33rd St, west of W Laurelhurst Dr NE: 11 street-trees, S side, tallest 65' × 4'6"

cv. 'Fastigiata'   Pyramidal White Birch

Branches grow wavily upward with the trunk, forming a narrow congested spire of a tree, smaller than the regular form. Common in Seattle.

— Arboretum: N of the road to Foster Island, #557-57 is 70½' × 4'6"; one on Azalea Way in 11-B is 65½' × 4'7¼"
— Rainier Beach High School: tallest of 9 in front is 58' × 3'10"
— 28th Ave W & W McGraw St: NE corner, 2 by the school's SW corner
— U.W.: 48½' × 2'9¼" E of the salmon homing pond

cv. 'Purpurea'   Purple Birch

Purplish young foliage, gradually turning murky dark green. Rare in Seattle, probably because most people think it ugly. The trees cited below may consist of varied clones such as 'Burgundy Wine', 'Crimson Frost' (a hybrid), and Purple Rain™. They grow much smaller than the regular green-leaved kind.

— 10715 39th Ave NE: exceptional size, though topped in 2005
— City Light facility at Interlake Ave N & N 97th St: a 3-trunk one with a Hinoki Cypress on the S side east of the gate; a 2-trunked one on the N side east of the gate
— NW 67th St & 21st Ave NW: NE corner, one 30' tall S of the house
— Bradner Gardens Park: a young specimen 29½' tall
— 51st Pl S & S Graham St: NW corner yard
— 2619 39th Ave SW: two street-trees

cv. 'Tristis'   Weeping White Birch

A pendulous tree of regular size (not a mop-head dwarf like 'Youngii'). Leaf normal. It has straight branches with notably long slender branchlets and twigs swaying attractively. In Latin *tristis* means sad or mournful. Trees fitting this description are common in Seattle, but are not of merely *one* grafted clone.

— U.W.: with an Eastern White Pine behind the Music bldg., 50' × 4'5"
— Volunteer Park: above lower tennis courts 55½' × 5'6¼"
— Green Lake: about half a dozen on the SE shore, between the asphalt path and the lake. Many ordinary White birches keep them company

cv. 'Youngii'   Young's Weeping White Birch

A common bush-sized mop-head weeper. The smallest birch tree. Snake-trunk versions have been made—the trunk curves in and out like a slithering snake.

— Calvary Cemetery: near a huge Paper birch is a 'Youngii' 20½' × 3'7½" × 29' wide
— Arboretum: 27½' × 2'2¼" #167-66A in the Woodland Garden (32-1E); #167-66B in 11-B on Azalea Way is 16' × 2'11¼" × 31' wide
— 815 NW 116th St: 22½' × 3'5" × 22' wide is one of 4
— Seward Park: entrance circle has one 22½' × 3'1"
— Blaine School (2550 34th Ave W): SW of the bldg.
— Fauntleroy Way SW & 37th Ave SW: 4 conspicuous ones on the NW corner
— 51st Ave SW & SW Dakota St: NE corner has a snake-trunk specimen
— 2027 23rd Ave E: 2 snake-trunk street-trees

Yellow BIRCH

B. alleghaniensis Britt. Curly Birch
= *B. lutea* Michx. fil. Hard Birch
From eastern N America. Gold Birch

This and the similar Sweet birch are unlike familiar white-bark birches: in bark, form, and leaf they look more like cherry trees. Their twigs when chewed release a gratifying wintergreen flavor. Uncommon in Seattle, Yellow birch is sometimes found with Sweet birch, possibly because young nursery trees were mistaken for one another: they are much alike. Yellow birch is larger (in nature it reaches up to 114' × 22') and does better here than the relatively rare Sweet birch. It consistently turns a bright, pure yellow every October—but its name does not refer to fall color (which most birches share) so much as to its yellowish-gray bark.

– U.W.: Denny Hall lawn has 3, the larger 72½' × 8'6¾" NE & 64½' × 9'10" SW
– Interlaken Park: where 19th Ave E enters the park above Boyer Ave E, the larger of two is 74½' tall (*pl. ca.* 1928 to 1934)
– Volunteer Park: the largest is in the SE corner, 57' × 6'6"
– Phinney Neighborhood Center: largest of 4 street-trees is 52' × 6'8¾"
– Seward School & Playground, by children's play area: 3 Yellow and 7 Sweet; at the SW end of the playing field are 2 Yellow birches, the largest 5'0" around
– Lake Wash. Blvd: from the Arboretum to Seward Park, Yellow birches are scattered as street-trees or in adjacent parks; one 6'3½" around is at Denny Blaine Park
– Day School & Playground: 11 street-trees
– Queen Anne Blvd: 35 on 8th Ave W near Mt Pleasant Cemetery

[**Avalanche Birch**—*B.* Avalanche* = 'Avalzam'—An east Asian hybrid introduced to commerce in the 1990s. Vigorous; leaves large and thick. Not definitely known in Seattle; a *possible* specimen is 37½' tall at 3220 Conkling Pl W.]

[**Water Birch**—*B. occidentalis* Hook., *non* Sarg.—From eastern WA and the Rockies. Usually in clumps less than 30' tall; bark gray; leaf broad. Not prized usually; extremely rare in Seattle. The Arboretum #383-61 in 28-4W consists of three clumps, the tallest 35'. The Zoo's Northern Trail exhibit has youngsters (along with shrub birches), the tallest 23'. Much larger & older trees are at Bellevue's Bellefields Nature Park.]

Mount Ætna BROOM

Genista ætnensis (Biv.) DC.
LEGUMINOSÆ (FABACEÆ)
From Sardinia and Sicily.

A treelike Scotch broom relative. It has yellow flowers in June. Scarcely found in Seattle, and only *young*, outside the Arboretum: #172-82 in 16-6E and 14-7E. 2308 E Lee St has one 13' tall by the front door, with a 'Swane's Golden' Italian Cypress. 6029 27th Ave NE has a front yard tree SE of a Sweetgum. The garden at 12th Ave S & S Hanford St has a 2-trunked specimen 19' tall on Hanford, west of the telephone pole.

New Zealand CABBAGE TREE

Cordyline australis (Forst. fil.) Hook. fil.　　　　　　Grass *or* Dracena Palm
AGAVACEÆ, DRACÆNACEÆ, or LOMANDRACEÆ　　　　　　Palm Lily
From New Zealand.　　　　　　　　　　　　　　　Maori: Ti Kouka

Seedlings start like a tuft of grass, then look like a Yucca. Old specimens develop
swollen, corky, gray trunks and well-forked crowns of evergreen foliage. The early
settlers ate its younger tender heads, cabbage style. The leaves are sword like, to
3' long × 2½" wide. Fragrant, creamy white flowers in large clusters appear in
May or June (autumn). Its maximum recorded size is 64½' × 69½'.

In Seattle, common, but all are young—dating from the 1990s or onward.
Most are less than 12' tall and few are treelike yet. Many people who plant
them have no idea that cabbage trees can grow large eventually. Nonetheless, an
old-fashioned winter will kill them to the ground though many will resprout.
Bronze- or *purple-leaved* cultivars exist here, but none are presently known large
enough to cite below.

 – U.W.: the largest at the CUH is 17' tall
 – 2854 NW 58th St: about 6 in the front yard
 – 4018 NE 73rd St: 2 street-trees
 – Nordic Heritage Museum (3014 NW 67th St): one by the 61' tall fastigiate Locust

[**Mountain** *or* **Broadleaf CABBAGE TREE**. Toi—*C. indivisa* (Forst. fil.) Steud.—a species
with immense leaves (to 6' × 8") is extremely rare here. Frequently, however, its name is
misapplied by nurseries to specimens of *C. australis*. For almost 10 years one grew in a
pot downtown; 4 tiny ones are at the Arboretum (#155-99 in 8-4E).]

[**Forest CABBAGE TREE**. Ti Ngahere—*C. Banksii* Hook. fil.—Though some were
planted at the U.W. in 1986, they were killed in a cold winter. At the Locks in bed #8 by
the restrooms, 2 graceful, crowded, shrubby examples exist and bloom. They froze to the
ground in 1989-90 but resprouted. This species is less treelike than the previous two.]

CASCARA

Rhamnus Purshiana DC.　　　　　　　Cascara Buckthorn *or* Cáscara Sagrada
RHAMNACEÆ　　　　　　　　　　　　　　　　Chittam *or* Chittim
=*Frangula Purshiana* (DC.) Cooper　　　　　　　　Oregon Bearwood
Native here; from British Columbia　　　　　　　　Sacred Bark Tree
to Montana to California.　　　　　　　　　Bitterbark / Coffeetree

Though little known in the landscape, this tree is economically significant for
commercial harvesters and processors of its bark, which is famous for its tonic
and laxative properties. Rendered all but extinct in some heavily harvested
areas, it is saved by an ability to sprout from the stump when felled, and its
extraordinary ability to thrive in dense shade. Generally small and short-lived,
its maximum recorded size is 70' × 9½'.

In Seattle, common yet inconspicuous and unremarkable, going unnoticed
among the larger, more abundant Red Alders and Pacific Dogwoods. It is only
easily spotted in native woods when it turns yellow in autumn. Although less

common, specimens growing in the open often assume other autumnal tints, while seedlings and saplings are essentially evergreen. Most are less than 30' tall. The leaves, commonly 4" × 1½" but as large as 8" × 3", are distinctive, with 10–17 pairs of parallel veins. Edible berries ripen late August–October; they are black, coffee-flavored, about ½" wide and have 2 or 3 big seeds.

– Arboretum: the largest of many is 48' × 3'10½" in the NW corner of 12-6E
– Carkeek Park: the largest of many is 36' × 1'3"; a slender tree is 48' tall
– Volunteer Park: one on E border S of Highland Dr is 28' × 2'5"
– U.W. Medicinal Herb Garden: youngsters ring "Cascara Circle" and others are under the blue Atlas Cedar nearby (the largest was 25' × 2'9" but died)
– Camp Long, Discovery, Interlaken, Lincoln, O.O. Denny, and Seward Parks (among others) all have specimens in native woods
– Laurelhurst church on NE 50th St by 49th Ave has one 28½' tall + a Bigleaf Maple
– 3012 NW 62nd St: 29½' tall; + a small old rosybloom Crabapple and a Camellia

[**Alder Buckthorn**—*Rhamnus Frangula* L.—of W Eurasia, is grown here mainly in its cv. '**Asplenifolia**' that features elegantly narrow, almost thread-like leaves, to 6¼" × ⅜". It is usually a mere shrub; a slender *tree* 12' tall is at 4547 S Lucile St. There are shrubby specimens as the U.W. Medicinal Herb Garden, near the bus stop / shelter / shed.]

[**Eurasian Buckthorn**—*Rhamnus cathartica* L.—known here only at the Arboretum (two #961-37 in 6-B; taller 25') and on the U.W. campus: one 25' × 2'7" stood S of the Bagley Hall annexes until it was displaced by the Chemistry building in 1992. One 10' tall tree remains 35' E of the overpass to the Health Sciences complex. In parts of the United States this species is very weedy, but has reseeded only sparingly in Seattle.]

[**Italian** *or* **Mediterranean Buckthorn**—*Rhamnus Alaternus* L.—is a dark green, glossy evergreen shrub or slender tree; rare here and mostly young. Ten are south of the Good Shepherd Center parking lot, the tallest 24½'. The Green Lake PCC Natural Market (7504 Aurora Ave N) parking lot has some in the NE corner (with Black Locust), the tallest *ca.* 17½'. SSCC Arboretum has some, up to 22' tall. The cheerful white variegated cv. '**Argenteo-variegata**' is 13½' tall south of the S.U. Sullivan Hall/School of Law bldg, E of the basalt sculpture.]

CATALPAS in general

Catalpas leaf out very late, but make up for their tardiness by bearing inordinately large leaves. They're chiefly treasured for showy white "popcorn" flower displays in summer, followed by slender, bean-like seedpods. They turn dull yellow in fall. They grow rapidly, and unfortunately tend to get rotten trunks all too soon. Sometimes they produce fascinating "canopy" or "ærial" roots such as are rarely seen except in the tropics. Distinguishing the various catalpas is difficult for beginners: although every single detail is distinctive, the trees as a whole are remarkably alike. The most easily confused are Hybrid and Southern catalpas. The Empress Tree *(Paulownia)* too is vaguely similar in appearance but even in winter its smooth bark is distinctive.

Hybrid CATALPA

Catalpa × *erubescens* Carr.   Teas' Hybrid Catalpa
=*C. hybrida* hort. *ex* Späth
=*C. Teasiana* Dode, *C. Teasii* Penh.
(*C. bignonioides* × *C. ovata*)
BIGNONIACEÆ

These are a cross between Southern catalpa and Yellow catalpa. Various clones exist. In general they resemble Southern catalpa more, but the leaves are often lobed and are less fuzzy on the undersides; and the flowers are smaller, more abundant and persist later into August. The largest specimens can reach 78' × 11¼'. They are uncommon here.

– Ballard Playground: 5, along with 5 Yellow catalpas and 3 Southern catalpas. The largest of all, just S of 61st St, is a hybrid: 35' × 7'½"
– U.W.: one 50' × 7'4" northwest of Benson Hall
– 2nd Ave W, north of W Galer St: a street-tree, W side, 39½' × 9'6¼" × 53' wide
– Volunteer Park: one 46' × 5'5" south of 2 smaller Yellow catalpas on the E border
– Arboretum: #269-51B in 14-B is 48½' × 5'11½"; and #269-51A in 13-B is 53' × 5'9"
– Lake View Cemetery: one in the S part is 40' × 7'4¼"
– 19th Ave E, north of E Aloha St: a street-tree, W side
– S.U.: a street-tree on E Columbia St across the lawn from Lemieux Library
– Leschi Park: two young '**Purpurea**' on the slope below the tennis courts; taller 25'

Northern CATALPA

C. speciosa Warder *ex* Engelm.   Western Catalpa
From S Illinois, SW Indiana, SE Missouri,   Hardy Catalpa
NE Arkansas, W Tennessee, W Kentucky.

The largest Catalpa in every respect: largest size (up to 150' × 22'), largest leaves (relatively weakly scented), largest flowers (though fewer per cluster), which are first to bloom (late June–early July), and seedpods up to 23" long! The bark is dark and deeply furrowed rather than scaly. It is a valuable timber tree with very durable wood. In Seattle, common.

– 37th Ave E, south of E Madison St: a street-tree, 83½' × 13'0"
– 3218 Conkling Pl W: one 60' tall
– 19th Ave, south of E Union St: a street-tree, E side (house #1124), 48' × 11'11¼"
– Flo Ware Park (28th Ave S & S Jackson St): one 9'11¼" around
– Lake View Cemetery: the best of 2 in north part is 51½' × 10'8½"
– NW 51st St, just west of 6th Ave NW: a street-tree, S side, under wires, 45' tall
– 4625 50th Ave S (near S Alaska St): leaning severely, 63½' tall
– U.W.: one NE of Architecture Hall; 2 south of the basketball court near the canal west of the Montlake Bridge, the larger 40' × 9'10¼"
– Green Lake: one at the SE part, NW of the ballfields & Sunnyside, 54' × 8'5¾"
– Locks #203 has a slender specimen
– 37th Ave SW, north of SW Hanford St: 4 street-trees, E side, the tallest 58' (plus a smaller Southern catalpa)
– 2nd Ave W, between W Olympic Pl & W Kinnear Pl: 2 street-trees, E side

Southern CATALPA

C. bignonioides Walt.
=*C. syringæfolia* Sims
=*C. cordifolia* Moench
=*C. Catalpa* Karst.
=*Bignonia Catalpa* L.
From SW Georgia, NW Florida,
Alabama, Mississippi.

Common Catalpa, Catalfa *or* Catawba
(Indian) Cigar Tree
Smoke Bean Tree
Indian Bean Tree
Pencil-pod Tree
Caterpillar Tree
Candle Tree

The first catalpa known to science and the most familiar and widely grown. The leaves have a reputation for stinking when crushed, but this is subjective and may not be a reliable characteristic. The *twigs,* especially in spring, are also quite odorous. The flowers appear July–August, and are smaller than Northern catalpa's but bigger than those of the Hybrid and Yellow catalpas. The seedpods measure up to 16" long. The scaly-barked trunks frequently lean and are crooked. Dimensions can surpass 90' × 22'. In the Language of Flowers it means "beware of the coquette." In Seattle, common.

– 11265 Marine View Dr SW: an immense local landmark 51' tall—far wider
– Warren Ave N, south of Galer St: a street-tree, E side, 43½' × 9'8" × 63½' wide
– U.W.: one 50' × 7'8" in Sylvan Grove Theatre
– Franklin High School Playfield: 7 on the east bank, the largest 45½' × 6'6½"
– Zoo: by Primate Islands, South America exhibit, and elsewhere
– Lincoln Park: 3 not far from SW Rose St
– Seward Park: 6
– Bitter Lake Playground (Linden Ave N & N 130th St): 4 by the play area
– Waters Ave S & S Roxbury St: SE corner yard has 2

cv. 'Aurea'   Golden Catalpa

A smaller tree whose leaves are bright yellowish at first, becoming greenish by September. Uncommon; all known in Seattle date from the 1990s or later.

– S.U.: 13' tall NE of Garrand bldg (2 Hollywood Chinese Junipers by it)
– Calvary Cemetery: 9½' tall youngster 100' W & S of mausoleum
– NW 84th St, east of 3rd Ave NW: a street-tree, S side
– Summit Ave E, north of E Harrison St, a yard on the west side
– 520 17th Ave E
– 6751 40th Ave SW (at SW Willow St)

cv. 'Nana'   Umbrella Catalpa
=*C. Bungei* hort., *non* C.A. Meyer   Broom Catalpa

A grafted, flowerless little tree 10–15' tall, almost always with a conspicuously angled, often rotting trunk very rarely seen over a foot thick, supporting a dense rounded head of foliage, usually severely pruned back each year. The leaves are small and slightly hairy, unlike regular Southern catalpa leaves. It's common as a street-tree in older residential neighborhoods.

– 12th Ave S & S Sullivan St: many old street-trees, the stoutest trunks 5'3" around

- 33rd Ave S & S Lander St: NW corner has 11 street-trees
- 47th Ave NE & NE 50th St: NE corner yard has a big unpruned specimen, and a large Wisteria vine in a Ponderosa Pine
- 3274 Walnut Ave SW (north of SW Hinds St): a stout one

Yellow CATALPA

C. ovata G. Don	Japanese Catalpa
=*C. Kaempferi* Sieb.	Chinese Catalpa
=*C. Henryi* Dode	
From China.	Chinese: Zi *or* Tzu; Ch'iu-Shu

Distinguished from other catalpas by its small, yellowish flowers, and relatively slender seedpods (up to 12" long). In China, it grows as large as 100' × 12½', and both the flowers and young seedpods are sometimes eaten.

In Seattle, very rare and small. All known are presumed to be cv. '**Flavescens**' which has markedly small, yellow flowers.

- Ballard Playground: 5 along with 3 Southern and 5 Hybrid catlapas, the largest Yellow (under the wires near 28th Ave NW & NW 61st St) only 38' × 5'5"
- Jefferson Park: one 60' × 3'10¼" SE of the pond
- Volunteer Park: two on the east border 51' × 4'8¼"and 49' × 4'9¼" (not far N of a larger Hybrid catalpa)
- Arboretum: two #597-57 in 23-4W, the larger 38½' × 2'1½"

[*C. Fargesii* Bureau f. ***Duclouxii*** (Dode) Gilmour is a Chinese species remarkable for having small, hairless leaves, extremely slender seedpods, and blooming well before the other kinds. Moreover, the flowers are *pinkish*—the background petal color is white but *profusely* speckled with violet. *One* old tree is known in the city, 1900 Shenandoah Dr E. The Arboretum #82-96 in 13-3E is 15' tall.]

CEDARS in general

For ages the word "cedar" and its cognates in European languages have referred to trees with very fragrant, durable and lightweight wood. In the northern hemisphere these have usually been conifers, but in the tropics and southern hemisphere this is not always so. Neither "cedar" nor the similarly-used common name "cypress" refers to any *one* genus of trees. The pedantic dictum that there are but few *true* cedars among a lot of trees wrongly bearing the name is an inappropriate quibble over common usage.

Alaska CEDAR

Cupressus nootkatensis D. Don	(Alaska) Yellow Cedar
=*Chamæcyparis nootkatensis* (D. Don) Spach	Stinking Cypress
=*Xanthocyparis nootkatensis* (D. Don) Farjon & D.K. Harder	Nootka Cypress
=*Callitropsis nootkatensis* (D. Don) Örsted	Yellow Cypress
CUPRESSACEÆ	Sitka Cypress

From S Alaska to N California, mostly in higher elevations.

In the Olympic Mountains and similar high-elevation locations where it is native in Washington State, this cedar can attain 200' × 37½' and live 3,500 if not 4,000 years, making choice timber.

Common in Seattle, it is grown for its unique ornamental silhouette: most here are especially slender, gaunt, and strongly weeping, presenting such a wilted "Dr. Seuss" aspect that mistaking them for any other kind of tree (except weeping Lawson Cypress) is impossible. Such trees have been sold as 'Pendula', 'Strict Weeping', 'Green Arrow', 'Van den Akker' and the like. Alaska cedar is recognizable by smell alone, as the bruised foliage emits a strong, distinctive odor. It produces few cones, up to ½" wide.

- 49th Ave SW & SW Brandon St: a group of several in a yard; the tallest 65'
- 4215 E Lee St: 86' tall
- Arboretum: at least 15, the tallest (#X-332H in 39-2W) 63½' × 4'6½"; also 3 'Glauca' #111-52 in 36-5E (barely glaucous, non-pendulous); and a 'Lutea' #142-62A in 38-4W
- U.W.: a compact, heavily-foliated and squat 60' tall tree SE of Benson Hall
- Locks #26, 101 (three), 211 (56' tall), 315A (the latter pair unusually weepy, 49' tall)
- The Polyclinic (1200 Harvard Ave): one 57½' tall S of a Leyland Cypress
- 29th Ave E & E Aloha St: NW corner has a 54' multitrunked tree *mostly* weeping
- Mt Baker Park: two 'Variegata' (largest 26' × 1'1½") with a reverted 3rd, in the shadow of a 75' tall English Oak
- 613 W Lee St: a 'Nana' (4-trunked, *ca.* 20' tall × 20' wide) about 60' S of Lee St; the house was built in 1909, so this *dwarf* cv. had a long time to grow tree-sized

Atlantic White CEDAR

Chamæcyparis thyoides (L.) B.S.P.   White Cypress
=*C. sphæroidea* Spach   Coast White Cedar
=*Cupressus thyoides* L.   Southern White Cedar
From the Atlantic Coastal Plain of   Swamp Cedar
the eastern U.S., Maine to Mississippi.

A swamp-dwelling cedar with an interesting, if fleeting, role in history. Growing as large as 120' × 18½', it produced ideal wood for 19th century Atlantic coast whaling boats, such as those so well described in *Moby Dick*. Moreover, the groundwater obtained from cedar swamps possessed a superior flavor and remained fresh and drinkable longer than ordinary water, so it was taken aboard ships for drinking at sea. A real life preserver of a tree for whalers!

In Seattle, rare. As everywhere, scarcely planted except in shrubby cultivars. Has a reputation of homeliness compared to its cousins, and grows very slowly. Easily identified by its freely borne tiny round cones, only ⅛" wide, perhaps the smallest of all tree cones (unless we adopt an artificial definition of "cone" that includes what most people call juniper berries).

- Ravenna Park: largest of 4 east of the 15th Ave Bridge is 44' × 2'6½"
- Arboretum: four #590-63, tallest 28' (in 28-3W); shade-stunted #157-44 in 38-2W;

an '**Andelyensis**' 17½' tall in 1S-6E
- 6306 East Green Lake Way N: 20'+ tall at house's NW corner
- 3852 Surber Dr NE: one east of garage
- 1425 41st Ave E: right by the gate
- SSCC Arboretum: Cœnosium Rock Garden has some small cv. '**Variegata**' with foliage green and yellow or golden variegated
- 1921 E Lynn St: an '**Ericoides**' 16' tall *dwarf* cv. with delicately soft, gray-green juvenile foliage that turns plum purplish-bown in winter

Atlas CEDAR

Cedrus atlantica (Endl.) Manetti *ex* Carr.	North African Cedar
=*C. libani* ssp. *atlantica* (Endl.) Battand. & Trab.	Mount Atlas Cedar
PINACEÆ	Algerian Cedar
From the Atlas Mountains of Algeria and Morocco.	African Cedar

By far the most abundant of the very few African trees grown in Seattle. Information about its behavior in nature is scarce, but heights exceeding 160' and trunks up to 62' around are recorded. Under cultivation in climates such as ours it outgrows most other cedars, on average. In fact, it can outgrow its own optimal rate, exuberantly forming lush, weak growth that falls easy prey to windstorms and snowloads.

Though mostly grown, known and admired in its decidedly powder-bluish or silvery forms, it also comes in a bewildering variety of colors and habits of growth. Aside from natural seedling differences, and variations due to environment, there are distinctive cloned and named cultivars. And nearly every so-called Cedar of Lebanon in Seattle is really an Atlas cedar—or Deodar cedar.

- 3109 West Laurelhurst Drive NE: a bluish one is *ca.* 80' × 16'
- 5827 16th Ave NE: a green one 101' × 15'10¾"× 87' wide
- Holy Names Academy (728 21st Ave E): a green one *pl. ca.* 1910 is 95' × 15'6½"
- Laurelhurst Playfield: a gray-green one NW of the building is 80' × 13'10½"
- U.W.: one quite green NW of the HUB is 101' × 13'7" with 2 branches at least 60' long; 4 behind Lewis Hall are bluish, the largest 96½' × 11'9"
- Acacia Cemetery: 85' × 13'7"× 92½' wide, and 83' × 13'8½"× 74' wide
- 8326 19th Ave NW: 69' tall
- The Bush School (405 36th Ave E): a bluish one on the S end of the upper campus grounds is 94½' tall
- Brighton School (45th Ave S & S Holly St): a gray one 78' × 13'6¾"× 71' wide
- Locks #2 has a spidery grayish one 79' tall

cv. '**Aurea**' *and / or* '**Aurea Robusta**'	Gold Atlas Cedar

Yellowish-blue needles on a smaller-growing tree. Uncommon in Seattle, and all are relatively young.
- Kubota Garden Park: one 69' × 4'7¾"
- S.U.: 59' × 4'0" by a 15' tall weeping Sierra Redwood @ SW corner of Pigott bldg.
- Bagley School (7821 Stone Ave N): one 56½' tall on the front side, to the south
- Beacon Hill School (2025 14th Ave S): one 49' at the south end

- Blaine School (2550 34th Ave W): 48' tall south of the bldg.
- Arboretum: 30½' tall (#157-74 in 42-6W—conifer meadow opposite McGraw St)
- Woodlawn Ave N, opposite N 44th St: an extra bright, bushy specimen

cv. 'Glauca'   Blue (Atlas) *or* Silver Cedar

Atlas cedar seedlings can be green, gray or blue. Examples of each have already been cited. A distinctive clone with bluish foliage and arching, upright branching, has been grafted and widely sold in our area over the decades. The examples cited below are presumed to be identical. *Seedling* Atlas cedars of a definite bluish color, similar to yet genetically this clone, are given the proper name **f.** *glauca* Beissn.

- Lincoln Park: 126½' × 7'2¼" and 125' × 9'¼" are tallest of 8 among Incense cedars
- Seward Park: 123' × __'___" in old fish hatchery site
- former Colman School (1515 24th Ave S): one *pl.* by the P.T.A. in 1932 at the S end
- Lake View Cemetery: one tilting a tombstone in the S part is 79' × 14'4"
- Me-kwa-mooks Park: one 84' × 12'4½"
- Acacia Cemetery: one in the SE part is 15'7" around × 78' wide
- Washelli Cemetery: one just N of Edmond Meany memorial pool is 77' × 12'1¾"
- U.W. Medicinal Herb Garden: one north of Cascara Circle, 9'5" around

cv. 'Glauca Fastigiata'   Sentinel *or* Fastigiate Atlas Cedar

Bluish foliage on upswept branches making a narrow, almost columnar tree. But ultimately it grows broader. Rare in Seattle.

- Arboretum: #701-66 in 42-4E very near the road is 56' × 6'6"
- 18th Ave E & E Aloha St: SW corner, 88½' tall
- 22nd Ave E & E Highland Dr: NW corner, 74' tall
- McGilvra Blvd E & E Lee St: SW corner has at least 5 youngsters

cv. 'Glauca Pendula'   Weeping Atlas Cedar

Baby-blue foliage, absolutely dripping, a curtain of limp tresses. Common in yards but extremely rare on public property. Nearly all are rather young and shrub-sized.

- Kubota Garden Park: many, including Seattle's largest, 11' × 5'4" × 32' wide
- S.U.: SE corner of 11th Ave & E Columbia St has one, too crowded
- 18th Ave NW & NW 73rd St: NE corner yard has a splendid one by the driveway
- N 48th St, west of Evanston Ave N: 3 yards on the S side have specimens
- 8236 30th Ave NE
- 3510 NE 86th St: a gorgeous specimen
- 4921 NE 70th St: a heavily pruned specimen
- 5th Ave N & Garfield St: NW corner

Deodar CEDAR

*C. **Deodara*** (D. Don) G. Don fil.   Himalayan *or* Indian Cedar
From the Himalayas.   Deodar

The Himalayan equivalent of our Douglas Fir—the largest and most important of timber trees. Living sometimes nearly 1,000 years, it can reach 250' × 50' and was greatly venerated by the natives. Its Sanskrit name Devadaru loosely translates to "Tree of the Gods." When Great Britain built railroads in India, vast forests of stately trees were felled for railroad ties and fuel, for bridges and buildings, for furniture and firewood. Today, Deodars grace British estates, parks and gardens, where they unite an elegant habit with carefree gigantism. They are either male, female, or both. Males produce pollen, shed October–December. Females make squat cones, first pale green (rarely reddish), turning brown as they ripen and fall to pieces. Seedlings are common here.

– Leschi Park: close by Lakeside Ave S is one 86½' × 13'4¾" (*pl. ca.* 1890)
– 1859 Boyer Ave E (opposite E Howe St): one of a pair is 114½' tall
– Zoo: a limby, purple-coned tree 70' × 12'7" × 69' wide N of the Education Center
– Lakeview Park: one 113' × 10'11¼"
– Volunteer Park: many; one S of museum is 104½' × 11'4"
– U.W.: 39 lining Stevens Way, the tallest 103' × 10'10½"
– hundreds along I-5 (*pl.* 1968–69) and in Freeway Park
– Locks #26, 28 (two; tallest 91'), 115 (88' tall), 207 (large), 208 (two)
– 32nd Ave NW & NW 57th St: a big 80½' tall twin-trunked tree on the SW corner
– Wallingford Center (1815 N 45th St): a landmark specimen
– 2068 Interlaken Pl E: a large one at the corner by 21st Ave E

cv. '**Aurea**'   Gold Deodar Cedar

Young needles yellowish. Uncommon in Seattle.

– 5809 Ann Arbor Ave NE: 73' tall
– Seattle Yacht Club (1807 E Hamlin St): 69' × 7'7", flat-topped
– 8443 34th Ave SW: three, the tallest 51'
– 1516 Magnolia Blvd W: a stout, broad tree 50' tall

                                                          Weeping Deodar Cedar

A confusing lot. Since the '90s, three or more Deodar clones have been sold *wrongly* as weeping cedars of Lebanon. One is a bluish, squat shrub or low tree. A second makes sparse branches on a full-sized tree—the kind listed below. A third clone is small, narrow, upright tree, its branches drooping strongly—one 22' tall is by the steps on the NE corner of 1st Ave NW & N 42nd St. The trees sold as *C. libani* 'Beacon Hill' or 'Pendula Victoria' or *C. Deodara* 'Miles High' are just renamings of one first called 'Repandens' ≤1930.

– Fremont Ave N & N 49th St: NE corner, 54' tall
– 1612 SW Massachusetts St: one 50' tall
– 7803 West Green Lake Dr N
– 6319 24th Ave NW
– 3713 W Ruffner ST: a street-tree by the driveway, east of a Sweetgum

64

Incense CEDAR

Calocedrus decurrens (Torr.) Florin
=*Libocedrus decurrens* Torr.
CUPRESSACEÆ
From Oregon, California, Lake Tahoe in Nevada, and N Baja California.

Incense cedar in nature grows as large as 229' × 39' and furnishes both valuable wood and sawdust said to be slug-repellent. It is common in Seattle and reseeds freely. It grows compact, dense, notably columnar (whether broad or narrow), with rich green foliage sweeping up from a cinnamon-brown trunk. The cones are narrow, like duck bills, ½–1" long.

– Ravenna Park: 40 in a grove in the ravine; tallest 110½' × 8'6½" & 112' × 9'11½"
– Bagley School (7821 Stone Ave N): SW corner, one 91½' × 11'11½"× 44' wide
– Lincoln Park: many; the largest is in a grove S of the tennis courts, 83' × 10'5"; tallest is 104' × 6'11"
– Seward Park: many at the far south end, none very large yet
– U.W. Medicinal Herb Garden: one 99' × 6'4½" north of Cascara Circle
– 36th Ave & E Cherry St: SE corner yard has 3, the tallest 75'
– Camp Long: many
– Locks #6, 29 (76' tall), 205 (three)
– 20th Ave NW & NW 67th St: NW corner yard has a stout one 53' tall
– SSCC Arboretum: a young cv. **Berrima Gold** (bright gold) on the east side of the Cœnosium Rock Garden is 4½' tall

Chilean Incense CEDAR

Austrocedrus chilensis (D. Don) Pic. Serm. & Bizzarri   Chilean Cedar
=*Libocedrus chilensis* (D. Don) Endl.
From Chile, Argentina.

A cousin of the common Incense cedar. Where native, it is called Ciprés or Cedro, can live 1,000+ years and grows as large as 80' × 20½'. In Seattle it's extremely rare, slow-growing and coneless so far, but handsome withal.

– Locks bed #30 has one 19' tall
– Arboretum: #650-48 in 17-6E is 30½' (6-trunked); #682-60 in 17-6E is 30' × 2'2¼"; #682-60B in 35-3W is 22½' tall; #682-60C is smaller

Japanese CEDAR

Cryptomeria japonica (Th. *ex* L. fil.) D. Don
CUPRESSACEÆ (formerly TAXODIACEÆ)
From Japan; *long* cultivated in China.

Japanese Red Cedar
Peacock-Pine
Japanese: Sugi スギ

Japan's most important lumber tree, growing to 210' × 66' at best and supplying wood used for everything from matchboxes to shipbuilding. This tree and its cultivars figure prominently in Japanese gardens. The bark is reddish and fibrous similar to that of our native (Western Red) cedar, while the foliage is prickly like that of Sierra Redwood; the cones are round, spiky and ½–1" in diameter.

In Seattle, common, in various forms, including bushy cultivars.

– Denny-Blaine Park: two; the larger southernmost, 94' × 9'7"
– Leschi Park: one by the restrooms is 98½' × 8'0"
– Lincoln Park: a multi-trunk tree at extreme N end, 90½' × 5'10" (largest trunk)
– Mt Baker Park: the best of 10 is at the north end, 80' × 7'11"
– Volunteer Park: largest of many is east of the museum, 84' × 7'8½"
– 3642 W Lawton St: 75½' tall
– Locks bed #5 (four), #22 (W end), #122, #202 (in shade of #203's Yellow Buckeye)

cv. 'Black Dragon'   ブラックドラゴン

Growth slow and dense, extra dark. In Seattle, rare. All are young.

– 7519 22nd Ave NW: a street-tree 8½' tall, N of a 'Frisia' Black Locust

cv. 'Cristata'

Crested *or* Cockscomb Japanese Cedar
Japanese: Sekka Sugi クリスタタ

A certain percentage of branch tips and twigs are tightly "glued" together to truly monstrous effect. The congested twig bunches are warped and twisted. It is slow growing and rare.

– Arboretum: south of the gate to the Japanese Garden (1-B) one is 42' × 2'1"
– Children's Hospital: one 8½' tall across the road S of the "giraffe" parking garage
– 6th Ave NW & NW 89th St: NW corner yard: a young 11' tall tree in the yard
– 13500 Northshire Road NW: a young specimen
– 3708 Cascadia Ave S: a young specimen in the yard's NW corner

cv. 'Elegans'

Plume Cedar *or* Plume Japanese Cedar
Japanese: Yawara Sugi ヤワラスギ

Much smaller than average, even bushy, though one in New Zealand is over 70' × 13'. Very distinct in its ferny, fluffy, *soft* nature. So dense that its trunk is rarely visible, unless its lower branches are removed. Nearly always coneless. It turns an eye-catching *purplish-brown* color in winter—though variants called 'Elegans Aurea' or 'Elegans Viridis' remain yellow-green or green all year.

In Seattle, uncommon. Most are less than 20' tall.

– north of Yesler Way, E of a walkway, between 8th Ave & Broadway: 38' tall
– U.W: 33' tall S of the Allen Library, towards the E end
– Children's Hospital: one 29' tall N of the "giraffe" parking garage

– 3041 NW 72nd St: two-trunked and 28' tall
– California Ave SW & SW Southern St: NE corner has one 27½' tall
– SSCC Arboretum: a very wide one 19' tall in the Milton Sutton conifer garden

cv. 'Lobbii'

Twigs more slender than average and densely concentrated at the branch tips. A darker, tighter tree as big as the regular kind. It is uncommon in Seattle.

– 6th Ave NW & NW 67th St: the NW corner yard has a 57' tall twin-trunked one (between a plume Sawara Cypress and a moss Sawara Cypress)
– Cascadia Ave S & S Ferris Pl: SW corner has one 65½' tall
– Hiawatha Playfield: the south side has a 3-trunked one, partly rotten
– 1212 Minor Ave: 2
– 6734 34th Ave NW: over sidewalk, S of a Deodar Cedar; this—or a 'Compacta'

cv. 'Sekkan-Sugi' (Sekhan-Sugi; セッカンスギ)   Golden Japanese Cedar

Growth slow and dense with foliage creamy-tipped to bright yellow-golden. In Seattle, once very rare, now uncommon; all are young; most are less than 12' tall. It is becoming widely planted.

– Calvary Cemetery: 14½' tall
– 38th Ave E & E Howe St: NW corner yard has two, the taller 17½'
– S.U.: 8' tall N of the Pigott building, at the E end
– 509 21st Ave E: 15' tall at N fence of front yard

[**Taiwan Cedar** or **Formosan Redwood**—*Taiwania cryptomerioides* Hay.—is related, and looks similar. It is from mountainous Taiwan, SW China, NE Myanmar, N Vietnam. Extremely rare in Seattle. Scarcely found, and only *young*, outside the Arboretum, where the largest of 9 is #465-74 in 19-4E: 41½' × 2'11".]

[**Smooth Tasmanian Cedar** or **Pencil Pine**—*Athrotaxis cupressoides* D. Don—is related, from mountainous Tasmania. Extremely rare in Seattle; known as a few youngsters such as one 7' tall at Kubota Garden Park, 68' west of the long Poplar row.]

CEDAR of Lebanon

Cedrus libani A. Rich.   Lebanon Cedar

PINACEÆ

From Lebanon, Turkey, Syria.

Strong and incorruptible, the cedar of Lebanon, most famous of all cedars, owes its fame largely to its ancient associations and history, but also to a certain intrinsic quality more easily experienced in the presence of the tree than described. Had it no other merit, its role in the Bible alone would have been sufficient to ensure its popularity for eternity.

> Behold, the Assyrian was a cedar in Lebanon
> with fair branches, and with a shadowing shroud,
> and of a high stature; and his top was among the
> thick boughs.

The waters made him great, the deep set him
up on high with her rivers running around his
plants, and sent out her little rivers unto all
the trees of the field.

Therefore his height was exalted above all
the trees of the field, and his boughs were
multiplied, and his branches became long because
of the multitude of the waters, when he shot forth.

All the fowls of heaven made their nests in
his boughs, and under his branches did all the the
beasts of the field bring forth their young, and
under his shadow dwelt all great nations.

Thus was he fair in his greatness, in the
length of his branches: for his root was by
great waters.

The cedars in the garden of God could not
hide him: the fir trees were not like his boughs
and the chestnut trees were not like his branches
nor any tree in the garden of God was like unto
him in his beauty.

I have made him fair by the multitude of his
branches: so that all the trees of Eden, that were
in the garden of God, envied him.

Ezekiel 31:3-9

The Lebanese groves in particular have been for centuries the goal of eager pil-
grims; the tree is the official symbol of that republic—seen on its flag, coins and
postage stamps. Heights up to 150' and trunks up to 47' around are recorded.

In Seattle, unfortunately uncommon, scarcely to be seen compared to its close
cousins the Atlas and Deodar cedars. Of course the city is seemingly alive with
Atlas cedars masquerading under its proud name. Its rarity here is partly due
to difficulties of propagation. Large, older trees are scarce; most examples cited
below are young. Trees *sold* as weeping Cedar of Lebanon are Deodars.

- Green Lake: 6 with 4 Eastern White Pines W of the west-side tennis courts; the
  tallest 97½' × 10'7½"; the largest 11'5" around
- Arboretum: #1048-37A is 83½' × 5'7¼" in 39-5W; #46-50 is 70' × 7'6¼" in 19-5E
- U.W.: one 86' × 10'10½" S of the Art Building; one SE of Hansee Hall by a big
  sickly golden plume Sawara Cypress
- 18th Ave E & E Aloha St: SW corner yard, only 47' tall—yet stout, old and massive
- McClure School: at 2nd Ave W & W Crockett St, 50½' × 8'8¾" (above a low fork)
- 2nd Ave NE & NE 91st St: SE corner has a *bluish* immense specimen 78' tall but it
  may be an Atlas cedar; its appearance is ambiguous
- Madison School (3429 45th Ave SW): 3 with 2 bigger Silver Maples in the SE area
- High Point Playfield: 47' tall by a Black Locust E of 32nd Ave SW & SW Myrtle St

[**Cyprus** *or* **Cyprian Cedar**—*C. libani* ssp. *brevifolia* (Hook. fil.) Meikle—is from Cyprus. A
narrow, open tree; *short* needles. Extremely rare in Seattle. Scarcely found, and only *young*,
outside the Arboretum, where the largest of 4 is #541-64 in 19-4E, 53' × 5'4¾".]

Western Red CEDAR

Thuja plicata Donn *ex* D. Don (our) Native Cedar
= *T. Menziesii* Dougl. *ex* Endl. Pacific Red Cedar
= *T. gigantea* Nutt., *non* Carr. Giant Arborvitæ
(*Thuya, Thuia*) Shingle Cedar
CUPRESSACEÆ Canoe Cedar
Native here; from S Alaska to N California, E to Montana. Giant Cedar

Seattle has only one native cedar, but what a tree! Big, abundant, well known, valuable, it's a living monument to firm, unyielding resolve: deeply anchored in earth, strongly ascending towards heaven, mocking the might of the wind, resistant to rot, vigorously enduring for untold centuries.

It stands unrivaled in size by any other cedar on earth, capable of attaining dimensions of 277' × 78½' or even more. The wood is so famous for its durability that certain scoundrels make an illegal living by "cedar rustling" much as their criminal counterparts in the East poach Empress Tree and Black Walnut trees. To the Indians of this area it was by far the most important tree.

It can be seen everywhere in Seattle, both wild and planted. Its irregularly fluted, swollen base, and fibrous, reddish bark are distinctive. Very old specimens are generally hollow, frequently with elbowy, forking crowns, surmounted by dead, gray snag tips. Off the beaten path in Seward Park is a titan hundreds of years old, fire-hollowed so that a person can walk in one side and out the other. The wood decays so slowly that many parks have huge old stumps remaining from the pioneer logging era, such as one in Carkeek Park 25'3" around.

– O.O. Denny Park: the largest 173' × 24'6" (dead-topped leaner by the creek)
– Schmitz Park: at least one over 20' around, and the tallest over 160'
– Seward Park: some are over 175' tall but the largest trunks are only 16' around
– Lakeridge Park (68th Ave S & S Ryan St): the largest is 170' × 16'10"
– Lincoln Park: the largest 14'10¼" around; N end; leaning at bottom of zig-zag trail
– Frink Park: the largest 15'2" around

cv. 'Zebrina' Zebra *or* Variegated Cedar

Foliage variegated creamy-yellow or gold and dark green. Form of growth and intensity of color both vary. Called *Thuya Lobbii* in older books. One of over 20 cultivars of this cedar but the only one here both strikingly distinctive and very common. It is frequently misidentified as a cultivar of Arborvitæ (*Thuja occidentalis*). It can grow to be enormous—over 80' tall × 65' wide.

– Lakeview Park: one 77' tall by the road
– Acacia Cemetery: large specimens, one in SE part 71' × 15'4" × 59' wide
– Evergreen Park Cemetery: one 63' tall × 48' wide
– Locks #122, 123 (59' tall)
– Pacific Medical Center (1200 12th Ave S): many
– U.W.: a close-spaced row of 22 behind Raitt Hall, and elsewhere
– Arboretum: by the boulevard next to Japanese Garden parking-lot

Accolade CHERRY

Prunus 'Accolade'   Accolade Cherry
ROSACEÆ
(=(?) *P. Sargentii* × *P. subhirtella*)

This tree, a supposed hybrid between Sargent and Higan cherries, originated about 1945 in an English nursery. Its virtues were quickly noticed, and it was in the nursery trade soon. Dark pink buds open to soft pink flowers 1–1½"wide, of 12–15 petals, in March–April. Almost no cherries are produced. The habit is broad and low, an open airy crown of long slender twigs that droop gently. It resembles the 'Whitcomb' Higan cherry cultivar but, thankfully, lacks the *brownish* cast of summer foliage. In Seattle, very popular.

– Arboretum: #519-63 is 26' × 3'4" (W) and 42' × 2'9" (E) in 13-2E; #513-63 is smaller and to the west; two #514-80 are in 39-1E
– 2nd Ave N & Crockett St: 7 on the southeast corner
– W Blaine St, east of 7th Ave W: 2 street-trees, S side
– 38th Ave E & E Denny Way: the SW corner has one with a smaller 'Autumnalis' Higan cherry
– E Aloha St between 19th Ave E & 18th Ave E: street-trees *pl.* spring 2002
– 1417 N 48th St: 2 street-trees
– 711 McGilvra Blvd E
– 2507 30th Ave W: 2 street-trees
– 5605 NE Windermere Rd: three large specimens
– 345 NW 48th St: 2 street-trees

Birchbark CHERRY

P. serrula Franch.   Redbark *or* Cellophane-bark Cherry
From W China, Tibet.   Tibetan Cherry

A cherry tree grown not for floral display or fruit production, but for its splendid bark: bright reddish-brown, glossy and peeling, absolutely unmistakable. In advanced age the tree can surpass 60' in height but its trunk loses the heart-warming beauty of youth. Its flowers are small and plain and its cherries worthless.

In Seattle, uncommon. None very large or old yet. The 'Hally Jolivette' cherry (and occasionally other kinds) is sometimes grafted onto Birchbark trunks. The graft line is so glaring that misidentification is easily avoided.

– Arboretum: 25' × 3'9½" on Azalea Way (#170-55 in 15-B) have had some of their brilliant bark peeled off by admirers possessing more curiosity than conscience
– 1017 Minor Ave (Gainsborough Condo.): two in front, the taller 38'
– 336 NW 48th St: street-tree
– 3140 East Laurelhurst Drive NE: 2
– 6727 27th Ave NW: a stout old street-tree 27' tall, wider still
– 8018 28th Ave NW: 2 street-trees

Bird CHERRY

P. Padus L.	European Bird-Cherry
=*P. racemosa* Lam.	Harbinger Cherry
=*Padus racemosa* (Lam.) Gilib.	Mayday Tree
=*Cerasus Padus* DC.	Hackberry
From Eurasia.	Hagberry

During late March–May this brightens the landscape while perfuming the air with long clusters of pure white blossoms. Its cherries taste vile except to birds. Compared to most cherry trees it has unusual bark and foliage. Generally small, it can reach 88' × 6¼'. About a dozen cultivars exist. It is uncommon here.

– S Southern St between 7th & Dallas Avenues S: City street-trees of cv. 'Spæthii' (tallest 44' × 3'4") were *pl.* in the 1970s—almost all are gone now
– 5512–5516 17th Ave NW: 3 City street-trees
– 28th Ave NW & NW 65th St: NW corner yard has one 33' tall in its SW corner
– Fire Station #9 (Linden Ave N, south of N 39th St)
– Bell St, west of 1st Ave: 4 street-trees, N side
– Zoo: about half a dozen in Rain Forest Loop
– 2221 2nd Ave W: one SE of the house

Bitter CHERRY

P. emarginata (Dougl. *ex* Hook.) Eaton	(our) Native Cherry
=*P. prunifolia* (Greene) Schafer	Quinine Cherry
=*Cerasus emarginata* Dougl. *ex* Hook.	Fire Cherry
=*C. mollis* Dougl. *ex* Hook.	

Native here; from British Columbia to New Mexico.

Seattle's native cherry is little known though abundant. The striking thing about it is surely its extreme skinniness: no other cherry tree in Seattle and hardly any other native tree can match it in this respect. Trunk and twig are both extraordinarily slender. It grows fast but doesn't live long and is easily toppled in storms. Tiny, bright, almost translucent cherries, ripening late August–October are bitter enough to make one grimace in agony, but become barely palatable after being nipped by frost. The small, soft leaves turn to a pale yellow in late September–October.

It grows up to 104' × 9½' despite being described in book after book as scrub rarely reaching half that size. Most well-wooded Seattle parks contain examples at least 75' × 4½'. This is a weak, short-lived tree with nondescript flowers, bitter fruit, mediocre wood value and pale autumn color; yet, a sunlit forest scene beset with its silvery-bronzy shafts towering over 50' without taper or twig, surmounted by an elegant, shapely crown of uncommonly light foliage, is a satisfying, even beautiful sight. This is a tree for artists and poets to notice and trace, sketch, paint and reflect upon.

– Discovery Park: many large ones were west of the Ft Lawton Cemetery—the largest reached over 90' × 5'7" but blew down; now the biggest may be 66' × 4'11½"

- Seward Park: the tallest of many was 103' × 4'10¾" in 2000—when it fell over
- Arboretum: E of service road, S of the *Berberis* intersection (20-1E) 90½' × 3'9¾"
- Lake View Cemetery: an old, decrepit one was 7'10" around, but died in 1989
- O.O. Denny Park: 74' × 5'7¾" × 37¼' wide; on bank, east of the road
- Paramount Park in Shoreline: 79' × 5'8" × 35' wide—but ready to fall
- 19th Ave NE & NE 107th St: SE corner has a 5-trunked tree 80' tall
- 5th Ave W & W Raye St: SE corner has specimens in yard and in planting-strip
- 2235 NW 63rd St: front yard has a small one, awkwardly close to the house

hybrid Bitter CHERRY

P. emarginata × *P. avium*

Seattle's native cherry crosses with the introduced Mazzard cherry. Such hybrids have been seen between S Vancouver Island and Tacoma. To commemorate the hybrid's locality and its presently known center of distribution, Peter Zika and I propose to name it after Puget Sound.

These hybrid trees appear intermediate between the two parents. In general, the hybrid is too robust and large in its leaves and flowers to be called Bitter cherry; it is too slender and hairy to be called Mazzard. It is very full-appearing while in flower, making a more showy display than that of Bitter cherry. Yet the flowers mostly set no fruit; most fruit set aborts; and though it can set some seemingly viable seeds, seedlings from the hybrid are not known to us. Hence, the hybrid seems not the least bit likely to prove invasive or weedy.

In Seattle, rare.

- Carkeek Park: N meadow hillclimb over 100' N of rock; by a Hemlock; 89' × 5'0"
- Mt Pleasant Cemetery: one 77' × 3'5" on the E side, in the forested middle border
- Frink Park: one with larger Mazzards is 66½' × 2'9½"
- U.W.: one N of the Penthouse Theatre is 54½' × 2'11¾"
- Boyer Ave E, west side, north of SR 520: a topped thicket

Black CHERRY

P. serotina Ehrh.
From central & eastern N America,
Mexico, Guatemala.

Wild Black Cherry
Rum Cherry

The giant of its genus and even of its entire family: trees are known 146' tall, over 23½' trunk circumference and over 120' wide. Imagine a cherry tree so gigantic! A strong and handsome trunk, roughly plated with bark, supports a head of dark glossy foliage that turns yellow in autumn. Its wood is highly valuable and has been used for making much of the prized American cherry-wood furniture. A foul odor results if the twigs are bruised. Small white flowers adorn the tree mid-May through June. Small black cherries are bitter but edible after about mid-August. A commercial flavoring is extracted from the pits.

In Seattle, common—represented mostly by park trees (planted 60–90 years ago) and their continually increasing wild offspring.

- Queen Anne Blvd: 8th Ave W near Mt Pleasant Cemetery, by W Fulton St, has a stout old dying wreck 9'6" around, now only 13' tall
- Jefferson Park Golf Course: the largest is 92' × 8'3" × 52' wide
- Volunteer Park: southwest of the upper level tennis courts is a very pendulous one 78½' × 8'7½"
- Zoo: SW of Zoomazium the larger of two is 70' × 8'6" (note its self-grafted limbs)
- U.W. Medicinal Herb Garden: near Island Lane in section F is one 69' × 7'4½"
- Ravenna Park: over a dozen on the N border east of the 20th Ave bridge; many *wild*

Choke CHERRY

P. virginiana L.   Common Chokecherry
From most of North America.

A slender shrub or small tree, much like Bird cherry *(P. Padus)* but smaller, with smaller, duller flowers later in spring, shiny or *less dull* leaves, and usually it root suckers. Also its fruit is more often edible. Recorded to 73' × 5'9".
   In Seattle, extremely rare except in its purpleleaf cultivars.

- Kruckeberg Botanic Garden: 51' × 4'10" × 44' wide
- 3017 NW 67th St: 48½' × 4'1½" × 38½' wide
- Arboretum: #141-62 clump 33½' in 16-1W; *ca.* 5 with Hollies in the old lath-house area (in or near 38-5E), tallest 26½'
- U.W.: CUH Soundscape Garden has one 16½' tall that suckers much and is relatively open and gaunt (50' SE of a 19' tall Bird cherry that barely suckers)

cv. 'Schubert' and 'Canada Red'   Purpleleaf Chokecherry

Uncommon in Seattle; young. Leaves green at first, then dark purple all summer. Lawrence Schubert discovered this and it was first sold in 1943 in North Dakota. Since 1979 'Canada Red' has mostly replaced the original clone.

- 4017 Woodlawn Ave N: 2 street-trees, taller 27½'
- Arboretum: #46-73 is 32' tall in 33-B
- 18th Ave E, north of E Lynn St: 2 street-trees, W side
- Zion Academy (4730 32nd Ave S): 2 in SW part of property
- 2901 W Elmore St: a young street-tree
- 6528 27th Ave NE: a young street-tree
- 3216 NW 65th St: 2 street-trees
- 1950 6th Ave W: in front yard

Dream Catcher CHERRY

P. 'Dream Catcher'

An Okamé cherry seedling from the U.S. National Arboretum. Early, deep pink single flowers. Bronzy, hairless young foliage. Yellow-orange fall color. Sold locally since ≤2001. Extremely rare in Seattle; all known are these youngsters:

- U.W.: CUH has four #173-97, the tallest 18½'
- Arboretum: #7-01A at N end of Azalea Way on W side (42-3E); #7-01B on W side of Azalea Way, in 20-1W

Formosan CHERRY

P. campanulata Maxim.
From S China,
Taiwan, and the Ryukyus.

Bell-flowered Cherry
Crimson Cherry
Taiwan Cherry

Deep pink flowers very early in spring. Leaves high-gloss. It can reach 33' × 6'.
It's extremely rare in Seattle, and severe winters may kill specimens.

– 5256 37th Ave NE: a top-grafted, shaded street-tree *pl.* ≤2001

Goldbark CHERRY

P. Maackii Rupr.
From Manchuria, Korea,
northeastern U.S.S.R.

Mongolian Goldbark Bird-Cherry
Amur *or* Goldbark Chokecherry
Manchurian Cherry

Attractive honey-brown bark is this tree's claim to attention. But for all that, it
is ornamentally inferior to many other trees we grow here, so is little planted,
though landscapes in severely cold climates requiring very hardy trees are the
better for it. It can reach 50' in height. The flowers begin in late March. Tiny,
shiny, black, bitter cherries ripen in June. It's extremely rare in Seattle.

– Seattle Buddhist Church Wisteria Plaza: five on a grassy knoll W of the parking lot,
  the largest 27' × 2'9" but dying
– Ballard Playground vicinity (NW 60th & NW 62nd between 26th & 28th Avenues
  NW): City street-trees, only 7 left, the largest (2607 NW 60th St) 25' × 3'9¼"
– Arboretum: a small, slender #828-58 is 25½' × 1'5" leaning strongly in 30-3W
– 26th Ave & E Columbia St: NE corner brick houses/apartments have 12
– Hugo House / New City Theatre (1634 11th Ave): 2 *pl.* in 1991

Hally Jolivette CHERRY

P. 'Hally Jolivette'
? (P. subhirtella × P. apetala)

Dr. Karl Sax of the Arnold Arboretum in Massachusetts raised this hybrid in
1941, giving it his wife's maiden name. Flowers white, double (15–24 petals) in
(January) March (May). Bushy; usually grafted onto Birchbark cherry trunks;
definitely the tiniest of all cherry trees. Twigs very slender; leaves 1–2¼" long,
deeply toothed, lightly hairy on both sides. It is uncommon but conspicuous
in Seattle.

– Seattle Buddhist Church Wisteria Plaza: many (among other kinds)
– 2nd Ave NW & NW 52nd St: NW corner has 6 street-trees
– Interlake Ave N & N 38th St: the NE corner has 2 street-trees
– 1809 5th Ave W: two in the yard
– 1639 21st Ave E: 3 street-trees
– 2015 42nd Ave E: 2 street-trees
– 6513 40th Ave NE: 3 street-trees

Higan CHERRY

P. × *subhirtella* Miq.   Spring Cherry
From China, Korea, Japan.   Rosebud Cherry
(P. pendula var. *ascendens* × *P. incisa)*   Ko-higan-zakura コヒガンザクラ

A hybrid unknown in the wild, but cultivated because of its elegant, dainty look. Pale pink buds open in March to white, single flowers, to 1½" wide. The fruit is *ca.* ⅓" long, shiny black, sparse and bitter. The twigs are slender and hairy. Trunks vary according to whether grafted or not, and upon what stock.

In Seattle, rare—represented by old trees in parks; it has long been out of commerce except its cultivars. (For other cultivars see Weeping cherry.)

– Green Lake: 16, mixed with many more Yoshino cherries; the tallest 25' and stoutest trunk only 4'6½" around
– Arboretum: 17-1W has a 1955 tree 26' × 3'11"; larger of two in 13-3W is 14' × 2'8¼"
– Volunteer Park: one 17½' × 1'7¼" across the street NW of the water tower
– View Ridge Playfield: a broad short one in planter by the restrooms; 5'7½" around
– 1518 N 40th St: 12' tall
– Denny Park: 3 in the middle, the largest 21½' × 2'3¾"
– Mapleleaf Playground: two on the border west of play area

cv. 'Autumnalis Rosea'   Autumn-flowering Cherry
='Jugatsu-zakura' ジュウガツザクラ   Winter-flowering Cherry

This, the very popular and distinctive Autumn cherry, has semi-double flowers, pale pink. A few blossoms can be seen in almost any month, but most appear from November–April. In the Language of Flowers it aptly signifies "deceit." Slender of trunk, it can reach 30' in height and is usually wider than tall. It is common, and universally called 'Autumnalis'—a name that properly belongs to a *white*-flowered tree never encountered here.

– Evergreen Park Cemetery: 22½' × 5'5" × 36' wide is largest of six in the NE part
– U.W.: 1 N and 4 E of Benson Hall, the tallest 28' × 2'5"
– Seattle Center: 4 in courtyard of Intiman Theatre, tallest 29'
– Beacon Ave S: many planted *ca.* 1993–94
– Locks #106
– 41st Ave E & E Highland Dr: NW corner has 6 street-trees
– 6026 41st Ave NE: one 29' × 5'6" × 39½' wide (1990)
– 13th Ave NW & NW 90th St: SW corner has a stout specimen
– Fourth and Blanchard building: 2 on S side

cv. 'Whitcombii'   Whitcomb Cherry

A sport of *P.* × *subhirtella* 'Rosea' originally planted *ca.* 1913 in David Whitcomb's garden, in Woodway Park, northwest of Seattle; propagated *ca.* 1925–1930. This has long *replaced* 'Rosea'—a later-blooming, less vigorous clone.

Single (or with a few semi-double) deep pink flowers, in February–March. Leaf finely toothed, not coarsely as in 'Autumnalis Rosea'. In Seattle, very popular and common, but in recent years its disease susceptibility has rendered it far less appealing and many trees are being cut down.

- Washelli Cemetery: 26' × 7'4" × 48½' (NE) and 23½' × 8'10½" × 45' (S) of 7
- Arboretum: at least four on Azalea Way, in 38-2E, 30-2W, 21-1W; and one #424-58 in 12-1E is 28' × 4'6"
- U.W.: 3 south of Mechanical Engineering bldg. & north of More Hall
- Locks #110, 325 (two, young, to east)
- 913 18th Ave E: 35' tall
- Montavista Pl W & Westmont Way W: NW corner yard
- 28th Ave W & W Blaine St: SE corner (Christian Science Church)
- 4038 NE 85th St: one 32' × 6'10" × 48' wide (1988)—not as wide now
- Belvedere Park (SW Admiral Way & SW Olga St): one 27' and 40' wide

Japanese Flowering CHERRIES

Miscellaneous cultivars & hybrids often but wrongly attributed to *P. serrulata*

The Japanese call these "Sato-zakura"—domestic, garden, or village cherries grown for floral display. The trees have been extensively bred for several hundred years. A multitude which differ in form, flowers, fragrance and vigor. Entire books attempt to sort out, name, illustrate and tell a bit about the origin and history of them. April in Japan is Cherry Blossom month and the highlight of spring; flowering cherry trees are little short of being the Japanese national symbol.

The various cultivars bloom at different times from early March through late May, with large petals pure white to creamy yellow and all shades of pink, usually semi-double or double-flowered and usually scentless. The twigs are stout, leaves large, and branches few, usually arranged in broadly arching, spreading crowns. Some kinds are slightly weeping, a few are strongly vertical, and in mature size they vary from about 8' to 40' tall. The emerging leaves are more often than not bronze rather than pure green in color.

In Seattle these trees are well known. Twenty different cultivars are treated in this guide. Probably 90% of the whole population consists of the ubiquitous 'Kwanzan'—the pink-flowered, gaudy cotton-candy cherry tree planted by the thousands here. Nearly all specimens were and are propagated by grafting on Mazzard cherry rootstock, though a few of our oldest specimens originated as cuttings and so are on their own roots. Some in recent years have been grafted on Birchbark cherry trunks. Own-root trees live longer.

Learning to recognize *all* kinds is formidable, but any tree-enthusiast should be able to identify the 6 or 7 most common ones. The Arboretum collection, though well-stocked (17 kinds), is not representative of Seattle as a whole.

cv. 'Amanogawa'   White-Column Cherry

Fastigiate, its stout knobby twigs and branches all grow straight upward after the fashion of Lombardy (Black) Poplar. However, it rarely reaches 25' in height. Its shape alone makes it quite unmistakable—among cherry trees, only 'Spire' and some of the narrowest forms of Sargent cherry closely match it. Flowers slightly fragrant, semi-double or single, (6) 9 (15) petals, very pale pink or practically white. Young foliage slightly yellowish-bronze. Ama-no-gawa アマノガワ means

"Milky Way" or "River of Heaven" or "Celestial River." In Seattle, common. Few old or large examples.

- Washelli Cemetery: an old one 36½' × 5'4" × 32' wide is 175' NW of the new mausoleum; smaller, narrower specimens are present elsewhere here
- 1916 E Blaine St
- Seattle Buddhist Church Wisteria Plaza: 18, among other flowering cherries
- Malden Ave E & E Mercer St: SW corner has 12 (+ a bigger Mazzard cherry)
- 57th Ave NE & NE 65th St: SW corner has one with *Osmanthus* in the back yard

cv. Cascade Snow™
='Berry'

Named and introduced in 1994 in Oregon. Possibly its Japanese name is 'Shira-yuki' シラユキ. Pale pink buds open to pure single white flowers, weakly fragrant, to 1½–1¾" wide in short-stemmed clusters of (2) 3 (4); the individual flower-stems lightly *hairy*, the sepals slightly toothed. Young foliage bronzy, contrasting prettily with the white flowers. Becoming common in Seattle.

- U.W.: CUH has one #172-97
- Arboretum: #336-01A in 33-2W and #336-01B in 32-2W, the taller 16'
- W McGraw St, near 29th and 30th Ave W: many street-trees
- 42nd Ave SW, south of SW Genesee St: street-trees, W side

cv. 'Choshu-hisakura'   チョウシュウヒザクラ
=*P. serrulata* f. *splendens* Miyoshi

Name means "red-" or "pink-cherry of Choshu." An upright, vigorous tree. Purple-red buds open to deep rosy-pink flowers, nearly single, 5–7 (9) petals, early-blooming, in loose clusters on long stalks. Young foliage reddish-brown or coppery-red. In Seattle, extremely rare.

- Arboretum: #1-40G 33½' × 4'3" W of Azalea Way in 28-2W; #53-66 15' × 1'9¼" E of pond in 13-2E
- U.W.: between the Administration Building and Suzzallo Library are 4 east and 5 west of the steps; tallest 28½' × 4'5½" (south of them are some 'Kwanzan')

cv. 'Fugenzo'   フゲンゾウ
='Kofugen'
='James (H.) Veitch'

A moderately strong, broadly rounded tree. Flowers double, (16) 25–30 (50) petals, pale pink, usually with 2 (rarely only 1) tiny leaflike organs in the middle. Young foliage with a hint of bronze. Among the last to bloom in spring. The name means "Fugen elephant" (the petal tips are curved like an elephant nose) or "Goddess on a white elephant." It is extremely rare in Seattle.

- Locks bed #211 (two small yet old trees)

cv. 'Hokusai' ホクサイ

A strong, wide tree. Flowers double, (7) 15–17 (20) orbicular petals, pale pink, in loose, long-stemmed clusters of (3) 4–6. Young foliage a faint bronze. The 1925 name refers to a famous Japanese artist Hokusai Katsushuka (1760–1849). In Seattle, only two trees known. But Tacoma's Point Defiance Park has one 24' × 6'11" × 57' wide (as of 1990).

– 942 18th Ave E: 22' tall in front yard (2 'Kwanzan' street-trees)
– Arboretum: 28-1W has #51-66 measuring 25' × 2'9½" (received as 'Sumizone'; then labeled 'Oshokun' in 1987)

cv. 'Horinji' ホウリンジ
=*P. serrulata* f. *decora* Miyoshi

Name is of an ancient Buddhist temple in Kyoto. A strong, broadly rounded, compact tree (our form)—or a weak little tree (the "book" form previously extremely rare, and now not known here). Mauve-pink buds open to double flowers, (10) 15 (20) petals, pale pink, becoming noticeably darker in the middle when fading; in large, drooping clusters of 2–6. Young foliage a faint bronze.

In Seattle, rare. 'Hokusai' is similar but has broad petals that are not delicately nicked or fringed at their tips. 'Tanko-shinju' has broad petals, broad and always untoothed sepals, and blooms earlier.

– Arboretum: 4 as follows: 24-1W has #7-40 34' × 5'2" (at base); 11-3E has #7-40G 47½' × 5'5¾"; 18-1W has #13-55 2'10¾" around; 10-B has #13-55 1'6¼" around
– Montlake Playfield (16th Ave E & E Calhoun St): one 30' × 5'0"south of the tennis courts; 2 'Kwanzan' east of it and a Yoshino cherry west of it
– Green Lake: a 3-trunked one 19' × 4'6½" is southernmost in the bed west of the Bathhouse Theatre
– 29th Ave W, just north of W Galer St: a street-tree, W side
– Hiawatha Playfield: a 3-trunked tree 31' tall west of the wading pool

cv. 'Hosokawa-nioi' ('Hosokawa') ホソカワニオイ

Named after Lord Hosokawa, a Japanese noble. Faint pink buds open to pure white flowers, single or nearly so, cupped, richly *fragrant*, to 1½" wide in long-stemmed clusters of 3–7. The sepals are sharply toothed. Young foliage weak yellowish-bronze but soon green. In Seattle, rare. It has never been sold under its true name, but rather as 'Shirotae'—or who knows what else.

– 14th Ave NE, from NE 65th St to 6314 and 6317 14th Ave NE: street-trees, with 1 'Shirotae' at 6322; tallest 26½' at 6314 (all topworked on Mazzard cherry)
– SW Stevens St, west of Fairmount Ave SW: 2 street-trees W of 3 'Shirotae' (N side)
– 367 N 48th St: a street-tree W of a 'Shirotae'
– 3205 13th Ave W (Fire Station No. 20): two, with a larger 'Shirotae'
– 3243 NW 59th St
– 7348 20th Ave NW
– 4th Ave N & Galer St: NW corner
– 39th Ave W, west of Altavista Place W: 4 relatively young street-trees
– N 44th St, W of Sunnyside Ave N: 2 street-trees, N side, w of a stunted Yoshino c.

cv. 'Kiku-shidare-zakura'　　　　　　　　　キクシダレザクラ
='Cheal's Weeping Cherry'
=*P. serrulata* 'Pendula'
=*P. Jamasakura* Sieb. *ex* Koidz. cv. 'Plena Pendula'

The name means "Weeping Chrysanthemum Cherry." Arching and more or less weeping from a topgraft—unlike the others. Tends to be gawky and thinly furnished. Flowers *very* double, 50–90 petals, dark pink. Young foliage faintly bronze but very soon turns quite green. Leaves dark, narrower than those of most Sato-zakura, and exceptionally glossy; prominently edged with incised teeth; stem rich red.

In Seattle, common and easily recognized any time of year. It has a clumsy beauty when in bloom, but is sparse and gawky in winter.

– SW Stevens St, W of Fairmount Ave SW: 8 trees, S side, E of a Chinese Chestnut
– 836 S Cloverdale St: in back yard visible from the alley, 13' tall
– 6th Ave W & W Dravus St (NW corner yard): 12½' tall (with birdnest Spruces and blue Colorado Spruce)
– 2755 S Washington St (east of Martin Luther King, Jr. Way S): a 10½' tall street-tree (with a Mazzard cherry and W of 3 'Profusion' Crabapple trees)

cv. 'Kwanzan' ('Kanzan' *or* 'Kansan')　　　　　　カンザン
='Ohnanden'
='Sekiyama'

Both the 'Kwanzan' and 'Sekiyama' names refer to the same sacred mountain in China. Strongest-growing and most massive of all, this overplanted tree can surpass 50' in height. Flowers double, 20–30 (40) petals, dark rosy pink becoming paler in time. Young foliage dark bronzy red. Leaves very large. This cultivar vastly outnumbers the rest. Thousands exist here and more are being planted. You can scarcely turn in a circle in Seattle during April without seeing one.

– Arboretum: at least 12, in 40-2E, 39-2E, 38-1E, 33-B, 31-1W, 29-1W, 28-2W; the tallest 53' × 3'9¼" (#1117-49 W of drinking fountain in 40-2E); the stoutest 5'5"
– Evergreen Park Cemetery: 35½' × 8'2" × 57½' wide
– Green Lake: 81
– Roosevelt High School: a stout old specimen in front is 31' tall
– Locks #107B, 202, 203 (to east), 313 (two), 320 (two; big); 322 (three)
– Volunteer Park: north of museum (with a Yoshino cherry) and elsewhere
– U.W.: Rainier Vista is lined by 30
– Condon Way W is planted with more than 40

cv. 'Mikuruma-gaeshi'　　　　　　　　　　ミクルマガエシ
='Kirigayatsu'

Flowers single or semi-double, 5–7 (10) petals, pink and rather early in spring, in short-stemmed clusters. Young growth bronzy-green. The name means "the royal carriage returns" (so the riders could see whether this beautiful tree's flowers were single or not!). Seattle has but *one*, 21½' × 2'9½" at Green Lake, in a bed of 8 kinds of cherry trees west of the Bathhouse Theatre.

cv. 'Ojochin'   オオジョウチン
='Bullata'
='Morni-jigare'

Tree strong, up to 30' tall or more, broadly spreading or rounded. Flowers weakly fragrant, single or slightly semi-double, 5–10 (13) large wrinkled petals, whitish with a faint hint of pink, up to 8 per cluster. Each flower is quite large, up to 2¼" wide, much like those of 'Tai Haku'. Young foliage bronzy green, many leaves *rounded* instead of long-tipped. The name means "Large paper lantern." In Seattle, very rare.

– Green Lake: one leaning, propped, 21' × 3'6¾" approximately in the middle (W side) of a bed of eight kinds of cherry trees west of the Bathhouse Theatre
– E Olive St & Evergreen Pl: two large old street-trees, the taller 23½'
– Arboretum: #45-66 is 25½' × 1'10" in 14-2E north of the pond

cv. 'Pink Perfection'

A hybrid from England raised in 1935: 'Shogetsu' × 'Kwanzan'. Flowers double, *ca.* 30 petals, pink. Young foliage pale bronzy. Extremely rare in Seattle.

– Arboretum: #43-66 is 21' × 2'4" in 8-1W
– 4800 Fauntleroy Way SW: 4 with 2 'Kwanzan' and 8 Sargent cherries—all topped
– Mt Pleasant Cemetery: 10' tall in southeast area, 150' north of the mausoleum wall

cv. 'Royal Burgundy'

A 'Kwanzan' mutation discovered in Oregon; patented in 1989. Young foliage *purplish-black*; paler in summer; reddish-orange in fall. Common.

– Volunteer Park: one *pl. ca.* 1999 NE of the water tower
– Arboretum: #8-01A in 11-B
– U.W.: CUH has one #174-97
– E Alder St, east of 20th Ave: 5 street-trees
– 4120 Meridian Ave N: a street-tree with a Kousa Dogwood

cv. 'Shiro-fugen'   シロフゲン
=*P. serrulata* f. *albo-rosea* Wils., *non* Mak.

A broad and strong tree with slender twigs. Flowers double, 20–36 petals; deep pink buds open soft pink, then white, then age to pink-cerise. Two (or as many as five) tiny leaflike organs in the middle. Late-blooming compared to most. Young foliage coppery red. The name means "White god" or "White red" and indeed the contrast between the whitish flowers and dark young leaves is striking.

   In Seattle, common and relatively well known. (Note: The Japanese common name for this cultivar is *Fugenzo*. If 'Shiro-fugen' *is*, as attested by certain writers, really a *synonym* of 'Fugenzo' then we need to find out the *proper* name for the few Seattle 'Fugenzo' specimens.)

– Evergreen Park Cemetery: 18½' × 5'9¾" × 49' wide and 21½' × 6'6¼" × 47' wide
– Locks #111 (top-grafted), 113, 120, 202 (by 201), 204 (to south), 325 (to northwest)
– Green Lake: 2 in the NE part near Ravenna Blvd

- 2330 Federal Ave E
- 3827 44th Ave NE: 33½' tall, up against house
- Arboretum: old specimens all died; #118-97 in 27-1W is young, only 1'9½" around;
  three even younger #94-00 are in 10-1W, 10-2W and 9-2W

cv. 'Shirotae' ('Sirotae')　　　　　　　　　　　　シロタエ
='Mount Fuji'
='Kojima'
=*P. serrulata* f. *albida* Miyoshi

Usually a very strongly spreading tree, wide and low. It may be recognized any
time of year by its flat-topped, horizontal growth. Pale pink buds open to pure
white (name means "Snow white" or "Snow flake") lightly fragrant flowers,
semi-double, 5–11 petals, appearing earliest of all: early March. Young foliage
green. Leaves edged by delicate long-fringed teeth. Common and popular in
Seattle; its stunning beauty makes people stare.

- Zoo: one 20' × 7'2" × 43' wide is east of the north lawn picnic area
- Epiphany Church (38th Ave E & E Denny Way)
- Arboretum: #10-40 is 33' × 6'2¼" W of Azalea Way in 36-1W; #112-58 is W of
  Azalea Way in 29-2W; Graham Vistor Center; Japanese Garden
- Locks #202 (small; by Douglas Fir), 204 (to the north)
- Volunteer Park: one east of the 12th Ave E exit, 19½' × 4'½"
- U.W.: an old tree S of Balmer Hall with a grove of Crabapples; 2 by McCarty Hall
- Green Lake: 2 at the N end of a bed of eight kinds of cherry trees W of the
  Bathhouse Theatre; also 6 *youngsters* (from this bed to the Community Center)
- 427 11th Ave E: an old large tree

cv. 'Shogetsu'　　　　　　　　　　　　　　　　ショウゲツ
='Superba'
='Shimidsuii' *or* 'Shimidsu (-zakura)'
='Longipes' hort., *non* Miyoshi
='Oku-miyako' Ingram, *non* Miyoshi

Weak, delicately drooping, wide-spreading in form. Apple-pink buds open to
double flowers (20–30 petals), white, with 1 or 2 tiny leaflike organs in the
middle. They are long-stemmed (to 2¾") and dangle in clusters altogether *ca.*
6" long, blooming late in spring and long persisting, fading to pale pink near
the end of their tenure. Young foliage green. The name means "Moon hanging
low by a pine" or "Fairy queen." In Seattle, common and well known. A small
tree very rarely seen with a trunk more than 1' thick.

- Acacia Cemetery: 3 west of the flagpole on the hill; largest 16' × 3'9" × 36' wide
- Arboretum: #42-80 is 13' × 1'6¾" E of Azalea Way in 30-1W; #X-98 is 15' × 2'9" E
  of Azalea Way in 20-1W; #114-58 is W of Azalea Way in 17-1W, and E in 9-1E
- Locks #27, 112, 201 (by garbage can), 206 (young), 209 (hard to see)
- Evergreen Park Cemetery: 13' × 3'4" × 22½' wide
- SW Edmunds St, east of 40th Ave SW: one on the S side

cv. 'Tai Haku'   タイハク

A strong tree, up to 40' tall. Flowers single; palest pink buds open pure white,
up to 2½" wide. Young foliage a deep copper. Leaves large, up to 9⅜" long × 4"
wide, with attractively fringed teeth on the edges. This "Great White" cherry was
nearly lost: all in Japan had died, but England had a specimen—from which all
those now alive are descended. It is very rare and little known in Seattle.

– Arboretum: #842-59 is represented by one W of Azalea Way in 24-2W; *and* two E
  of Azalea Way—25' × 2'10¼" & 28½' × 2'11½"; #745-60 is in both 9-B (smaller)
  & 7-1W (bigger); #895-65 are three in 7-1W (Azalea Way), the largest 19½' × 4'6"
– 5500 NE Penrith Rd (a 'Shogetsu' in the yard, too)
– 4331 NE 58th St: 25' tall
– 8704 Wabash Ave S (N of Beer Sheva Park): two street-trees
– 3435 Densmore Ave N: north of house
– 29th Ave NE & NE 65th St: SW corner
– 10th Ave S, just S of S Rose St: a street-tree, E side
– 8522 25th Ave NW

cv. 'Tanko-shinju'   ???しんじゅ

Mauve-pink buds open relatively early to fluffy, double flowers, 9–15 petals, pale
pink, becoming noticeably darker in the middle when fading. The petals and
sepals are *broad*. Young foliage a faint bronze. The name was given ≤1929 in the
U.S.; it was *meant* to mean "Pink Pearl" (ピンクしんじゅ) but can also be read as
"Two people commit suicide in a coal mine." Maybe this clone's proper Japanese
name is 'Fuku-rokuju' フクロクジュ (*contorta*)—or that is merely a similar tree. In
Seattle, extremely rare. Like 'Horinji' but with *broad* sepals, always untoothed;
and earlier to bloom. 'Hokusai' also has broad petals, but narrower sepals.

– Arboretum: #176-58 is 19' × 2'5¾" W of Azalea Way in 13-1E
– 316 /318 16th Ave: one 20' × 4'5" and wider than tall
– Green Lake: in NW part; one 14' × 1'6" with a Larch opposite N 76th St
– Leschi Park: one in the SE corner with 3 Naden cherries

cv. 'Temari'   テマリ
= 'Globosa'

A broadly rounded tree, usually quite wide, of moderate strength. Flowers double,
(15) 20–25 (30) petals; deep red buds open pale pink, occasionally with a tiny
leaflike organ in the middle. Young foliage tardy to appear, very faintly bronze,
essentially green. The leaves are frequently *rounded* instead of sharp-tipped.
The name means "Ball" appropriately enough, because the flower clusters are
truly compact heavy balls. Some British writers erroneously call 'Temari' a mere
synonym of 'Mikuruma-gaeshi'. A similar tree is 'Ito-kukuri' イトククリ (*fasicu-
lata*)—not known here. In Seattle, little known by name but not rare. From a
distance it looks much like 'Horinji'.

– 31st Ave NE & NE 82nd St: one in dwarf English laurel is 19½' × 5'1" × 36' wide
– U.W.: 2 south of Balmer Hall (with a 'Shirotae', a Yoshino cherry and Redvein

82

Crabapples)
- 11 NW 60th St: 25' × 4'4" × 45' wide (in 1995)
- 2812 Broadway E (south of E Shelby St): a street-tree, N of a big maple
- 2822 10th Ave E (south of E Shelby St): a street-tree, south of a Peach tree
- Green Lake: two W of Ravenna Blvd's end
- 2nd Ave NE & NE 44th St: one on NW corner (First Church of the Nazarene)
- 3252 45th Ave SW
- 4328 Bagley Ave N: 2 street-trees
- 17th Ave NW & NW 83rd St: 4 street-trees on NE corner (own root?)
- 1124 17th Ave E: in yard; not big; 2 'Kwanzan' street-trees
- Howell Park: one east of big Deodar Cedar; a 'Shirotae' on the S edge
- 4219 NE 123rd St: one N of the house, partly under overhead wires
- 1st Ave N, opposite Garfield St: 5 street-trees, W side
- 5136 S Juneau St

[Some trees look like 'Temari' except they have in every flower-center a tiny leaflike organ. The name **'Hisakura'** ヒザクラ may be applicable to these, but if their only difference from 'Temari' is one requiring close examination, it seems pointless to give them a separate name. Arboretum #206-70 is 14' × 1'3" under a Vineleaf Maple in 12-3E. It had been received as 'Shogetsu', but was relabeled 'Sumizone', then 'Ichiyo'.]

cv. **'Ukon'**   ウコン
='Yukon' of some local nurserymen!
='Asagi(e)' The "Alaska Yellow Cherry" of some nurseries!
=*P. Lannesiana* f. *grandiflora* (Wagner) Wils.

Name means "yellowish." Common. Also called the green cherry. A tall tree to 40' or more, rounded and strong. Flowers semi-double, 5–14 petals, at first creamy-white or pale yellow with green tones, fading to red in the center. Young foliage light bronzy green. Because the other flowering cherry trees bear white or pink flowers, the yellowish ones of this tree make it conspicuous. Also its fall color is usually superior. It is common and well known in Seattle.
- Arboretum: #273-91 in 40-3E; #48-66 is 25½' × 3'3" in 13-2E; #402-67 in 10-B
- Evergreen Park Cemetery: of 5 in the N end the largest is 27½' × 6'7" × 47' wide
- Volunteer Park: on the east side north of E Highland Dr
- Green Lake: 10 in the northern half, from the NW parking lot to Ravenna Blvd
- Locks #111 (low graft; by 112), 203 (to west), 205 (two), 206 (old)
- Cowen Park: one 32' tall by the formal Ravenna Blvd entrance; maybe *pl.* 1928
- 6956 57th Ave NE: a splendid specimen north of the driveway
- Ingraham High School: one 25½' tall at SE corner of the student parking lot

Japanese Hill-CHERRY

P. Jamasakura Sieb. *ex* Koidz.   Yama-zakura ヤマザクラ
=*P. serrulata* var. *spontanea* (Maxim.) Wils.
=*P. Sargentii* ssp. *Jamasakura* (Sieb.) Ohwi
=*P. mutabilis* Miyoshi
From the S half of Japan.

An elegant species revered in its native Japan, but scarcely known in the West. It is very rare in Seattle. The twigs, winter buds, and leaves are *slender*. The leaves, pale beneath, devoid of hairs, are edged with very tiny teeth. It flowers markedly *early* in spring; pink buds open to pale pink or white blossoms, showy against the bronze or coppery young foliage. Fall color is pastels of yellow, orange and red, the *pale* undersides of the fallen leaves afford a lively contrast. Recorded in the wild to 82' × 24'.

– Arboretum: #2488-40A is 60' × 7'2¾" W of Azalea Way in 22-2W
– NW Roundhill Circle has 3 *pl.* 1930s with 2 Yoshino; largest 26' × 7'1" × 62' wide
– Interlaken Park: one 26' × 5'9" east of 24th Ave E, smaller than a Korean Hill-cherry 25' east of it; two 'Kwanzan' are west of it
– Ravenna Park: until the Park Dep't killed them all in fall 2005, 5 graced the hillside W of ballfield; tallest 50' and stoutest 7'1½" around (also killed were 3 Korean Hill-cherries, an Oshima and a Higan cherry)
– Loyal Heights CC: 2 W of a Pissard Plum S of bldg. (behind 1st base of softball)
– Volunteer Park: one NW of N pond is 33½' × 2'7½"
– Colman Park: 8 or more (+ at least 2 Korean Hill-cherries)

Korean Hill-CHERRY

P. verecunda (Koidz.) Koehne   Kasumi-zakura カスミザクラ
=*P. serrulata* var. *pubescens* (Nakai) Wils.   Ke-yama-zakura ケヤマザクラ
=*P. Leveilleana* Koehne
From China, Korea, Japan.

The Korean Hill (or Mountain) cherry is a large tree closely related to Sargent cherry. It differs in its leaves and flowers when closely examined but is very similar in size, form, and brilliant autumnal coloration. Overall, compared to Sargent cherry it is a less showy ornamental chiefly because instead of having early pink flowers it has later palest pink or white ones. And in our landscape the former floral effect is far more prized. Though the fruit is not choice, it is better than that of Sargent cherry. The Korean has *hairy* leaf stems and flower stems. It is rare in Seattle.

– W Seattle Golf Course: of 7 "street-trees," tallest is 42' and stoutest 8'4"
– Interlaken Park: one 40' × 7'2" east of 24th Ave E is 27½' east of a smaller Japanese Hill-cherry; one 43' × 6'3½" west of 24th Avenue, too
– Ravenna Park: 5 (with 2 Mazzard cherries) are above the hillside W of the ballfield; the largest is 44' × 7'½"
– 17th Ave NE & NE Ravenna Blvd: one E of house
– Loyal Heights CC: one 40' × 5'3½" N of the bldg.; a second W of the bldg.
– Leschi Park: one by restrooms; 2 E of a Japanese Hill-cherry by the bridge
– Substation on Bellevue Ave E, north of E John St has one
– Denny Park: one in front of the building, N of the entrance walk
– Arboretum: one 28' × 5'9½" by Western Red Cedars on Azalea Way in 31-2W; #12-56 is 44' × 4'3½" W of Azalea Way in 26-2W; #701-57 in 25-3W is 1'8" around

Mahaleb CHERRY

P. Mahaleb L.   Perfumed Cherry
=*Cerasus Mahaleb* (L.) Mill.   St Lucie Cherry
From Europe, SW Asia.   Rock Cherry

Remarkable as the source of wood used to make cherry-wood smoking pipes. Occasionally used as a dwarfing rootstock for grafting of cultivated cherry trees, but seldom grown for its own intrinsic floral beauty. Ornamental cultivars exist, but are probably not to be found here. Its tiny, clustered white flowers truly perfume the air in (early) late April–May. Tiny, black, bitter cherries follow. The leaves remain green into November. It grows up to 50' × 8'.

In Seattle, very rare.

– W Prospect St, west of 7th Ave W: a topped tree more than 4' around, on the south side at the top of the stairs, has been fenced off by the adjacent property owner
– 1st Ave W & W Boston St: NE corner lot; by driveway, 25½' tall
– N 44th St, just east of Midvale Ave N: a 3-trunk street-tree 31½' tall
– U.W.: one on SW side of Gowen Hall is 30' × 3'1" by a Pacific Dogwood; a 16½' tall *wild* specimen in the ivy bank S of the Burke-Gilman Trail on Rainier Vista
– U.W. Medicinal Herb Garden: a leaning tree 20' × 2'0" between the compost area and Stevens Way

Mazzard CHERRY

P. avium L.   Wild Sweet Cherry
=*Cerasus avium* (L.) Moench   Merry Tree
=*C. sylvestris* Lund.   Gean
From Europe, N Africa, SW Asia.

The original "Cherry Tree" in name; also the prime parent of cultivated orchard races—see Sweet cherry. It differs from its improved progeny in being leaner and taller, with smaller, less delectable cherries. An important timber tree in Europe, reaching up to 110' × 21½' both there and on this side of the Atlantic, where it is thoroughly naturalized. Mazzard is the most frequently used rootstock for grafting of various fruiting and flowering cherry trees. Pure white flowers 1" wide appear in (mid-March) April–early May. Cherries ripen (late May) June–early August, varying in their mature color from red to black. In the woods its fall color is usually yellow, late October through mid-November; in the open it varies greatly.

In Seattle, very common; easily mistaken for a native, as it comes up wild. It also hybridizes with our native Bitter cherry—see *hybrid* Bitter cherry.

– Interlaken Park: a twin-trunked specimen 101' × 5'6" in the main ravine below 19th Ave E & E Crescent Dr
– Lake View Cemetery: larger of two in the NE part is 56' × 10'3¼" × 61½' wide
– U.W.: some on north border area from Hansee Hall to 15th Ave NE
– Ross Playground: two big double-trunked trees in middle; taller 63½', stouter 8'0"
– Arboretum: naturalized; 34-2W has one 48' × 5'2"; 11-1W has one 50' tall

cv. 'Plena'   Double-flowered Mazzard

Identical to the above except double-flowered and utterly fruitless. Grown as an ornamental. Very rare in Seattle.

- Evergreen Park Cemetery: one 60' × 8'5" × 67' wide east of the gate at N 117th St; four smaller examples also in this cemetery
- Arboretum: #1210-49 in 10-1W is 48' × 6'11½"; three smaller trees also present; best 48½' × 5'7" in 22-2W
- U.W.: one 34½' × 6'1" at the E corner, and a smaller one SW of MacKenzie Hall
- Boyer Ave E, just N of E Edgar St: a street-tree 30' × 2'½"
- 2129 NE Ravenna Blvd.: a street-tree 27' × 1'11¼"

Naden CHERRY

P. × *Sieboldii* (Carr.) Wittm.   Naden ナデン
=*P. serrulata* cv. 'Takasago'   Takasago タカサゴ
=*P. serrulata* cv. 'Naden' hort. p.p., *non* Miyoshi, *non* Makino

From Japan, a hybrid of uncertain parentage. Unknown in the wild; widely cultivated. Spreading, congested, twiggy, rarely over 25' tall. Flowers usually semi-double, some occasionally double or single, pale pink to nearly white, fragrant, in late March–April. Young foliage yellow-brown to reddish bronze, coated on both sides with persistent, fine *hairs*.

In Seattle, rare. Judging from the examples cited below, it is easy to see why. No cherry is as clumsy and heavy-looking as the Naden.

- 1002 37th Ave E: 24' × 4'6" × 40' wide (1993)
- Leschi Park: three in the SE corner with a 'Tanko-shinju' cherry, a Black Locust, a Downy Hawthorn, and two Ghost (Black) Poplars; largest 19' × 3'½" × 37' wide
- Arboretum: #1267-47 is 19½' × 3'1¼" N of Rhododendron Glen in 14-5E; #1267-47 is 22½' × 1'8½" W of Rhododendron Glen in 14-3E
- Locks #304 (one by a *Eucryphia* × *intermedia*)
- 3038 East Laurelhurst Dr NE: one hangs over sidewalk by a lightpole

Okamé CHERRY

P. 'Okamé'   オカメ
=*P.* × *incam* hort. 'Okamé'
(*P. incisa* Thunb. × *P. campanulata* Maxim.)

An English garden hybrid that originated before 1944. A small twiggy tree with very deep pink, single flowers late February–March. Only recently (1986–87) made widely available in the nursery trade; still uncommon here. Disease-prone; it may be most vigorous in warm, sunny, exposed sites.

- Arboretum: #52-50 is 21' × 2'8¾" in 31-1W; also in 20-1W
- Leary Way NW, south of NW Market St to 17th Ave NW: 39 street-trees
- 1st Ave & Vine St: the E corner has one or two in planters
- Locks #205

Oshima CHERRY

P. speciosa (Koidz.) Ingram   O-shima-zakura オオシマザクラ
=*P. Lannesiana* (Carr.) Wils. var. *speciosa* (Koidz.) Mak.
=*P. Lannesiana* f. *albida* (Mak.) Wils.
=*P. serrulata* var. *speciosa* (Koidz.) Koehne
=*P. serrulata* f. *albida* Mak.
From Japan.

Little known in the West compared to many Japanese cherry trees. It is, however, a very desirable tree. Usually fragrant, relatively large single flowers pink in the bud stage, open whitish or pale pink, in long-stalked loose clusters of 3–7. They appear with the unfolding green or bronze leaves in late March–April.

In Seattle, very rare. Some trees cited below are not this wild species but are derivations or hybrids of Japanese garden origin. These are listed here since it is clear that they're closely related to Oshima Cherry, even though they have extra petals on some flowers or differ in pubescence or habit.

– Arboretum: #290-55 is 35' × 6'11" in 42-2E; #51-61 is 29½' × 2'1¾" in 40-2E; #2488-40S is 37' × 5'5½" in 31-1W; #1-40G is pink-flowered, 4'3" around, W of Azalea Way in 28-2W; #1-40B is 47' × 2'9" in 22-2W east of Azalea Way; #1-40S is 41' × 4'9½" in 22-2W east of Azalea Way
– Roanoke Park (10th Ave E & E Roanoke St): a 3-trunked 25' one on the west side (*like* but not the same as 'Hosokawa-nioi' Japanese Flowering cherry . . . It has fuzzy veins; broader leaves; smaller flowers without such "red centers")
– Williams Place (15th Ave E & E John St): two (the W tree 35' × 8'4¾"; the E tree 31' × 7'2½") *pl. ca.* 1923 in the NE part (with 6 Zelkova trees *pl.* 1967 or later)
– Green Lake: the biggest tree (33' × 7'4½") and easternmost in the bed of cherry trees W of the Bathhouse Theatre; and two other smaller examples with pinker flowers, one north (fell over in March 2005) and the other south of it

Sargent CHERRY

P. Sargentii Rehd.   North Japanese Hill-Cherry
=*P. serrulata* var. *sachalinensis* (F. Schmidt) Wils.   Yama Cherry
From N Japan, Korea, Sakhalin.   O-yama-zakura オオヤマザクラ

A forest tree up to 80' × 12½' in the wild. Rich pink, single flowers in (early) late March–April, in clusters of 2–3. Tiny bitter black cherries. Leaves notably wide (to 6⅛" × 3¼"), abruptly pointed, pale beneath, red-stemmed. Bright reddish-orange or yellow fall color.

In Seattle, common. Narrow cultivars favored as street-trees are '**Columnaris**', '**Rancho**'—and maybe in time the very new **Pink Flair**™ (='JFS-KW58').

– Arboretum: at least 17, including #2488-40H is 40½' × 4'5" in 42-2E; #2488-40S is 33½' tall in 28-1W (in azaleas); #12-56 is 44' × 4'3½" in 26-2W
– Substation landscape on 6th Ave NE, north of NE Northlake Way: 3
– E Aloha St, west of 26th Ave E: many street-trees
– 21st Ave, north of E Alder St: City street-trees
– 15th Ave E & E Roy St: NE corner has 5 N of apt. bldg., tallest 39'

- Locks #313 has one flanked by two 'Kwanzan' cherries
- U.W.: one 32' × 2'6" at NW corner of parking lot N-5

Snow Fountains® CHERRY

P. 'Snofozam'   Snow Fountains® Weeping Cherry
Probably a Higan Cherry selection.

A new, dwarf, weeping, white-flowered tree, introduced *ca.* 1985. Very similar
to weeping Yoshino cherry, but more refined. Lovely fall color. Common.

- 5th Ave W & W Crockett St: NW corner
- 12239 8th Ave NW
- 1101 NW 62nd St: 4 street-trees
- 6038 52nd Ave NE: one N of the driveway

Snow Goose CHERRY

P. **'Snow Goose'**
(P. speciosa × *P. incisa)* Raised in Holland.

Named in 1970. A narrow-crowned tree whose pure white flowers appear with
bright green foliage. Extremely rare in Seattle; *all* known are these youngsters:

- Volunteer Park: 5 street-trees, tallest 27' (+ 1 'Akebono') across the road S of the
  wading pool; 3 more *not* street-trees to the S (with a double Weeping cherry)
- Arboretum: #17-04A on Azalea Way, W side, in 33-2W; #17-04C on Azalea Way,
  W side, in 38-1W;
- 7059 24th Ave NE: 3 street-trees on Birchbark cherry trunks

Sour CHERRY

P. Cerasus L.   Tart Cherry
=*Cerasus communis* Poit. & Turp.   Pie Cherry
=*C. vulgaris* Mill.
Presumed to be from the Near East; long naturalized in Europe.

Small, sometimes bushy and suckering. The bright red fruit borne by most
cultivars is highly pleasing to the eye as well as to the tongue. Cultivars include:
'Early Richmond', 'English Morello', 'Louis Philippe', 'Meteor', 'Montmorency',
'North Star', Surefire™ and others. Not as commonly grown in Seattle as Sweet
cherries, these are generally back yard trees, but street-trees exist.

- 1129 21st Ave E: a street-tree, 25' tall
- 4217 32nd Ave W: a street-tree
- 520 20th Ave E: a street-tree (2 Sweet cherries @522)
- 7711 Sunnyside Ave N: a street-tree, 21' tall

[**Snow Cherry**—*P.* × *Gondouinii* 'Schnee'—is a sour / sweet cherry hybrid from Germany; *schnee* means snow in German. A nearly fruitless clone grown as an ornamental. It is extremely rare in Seattle. Green Lake has one in the NW part, next to the unpaved trail that goes from the parking lot to the huge boulder near the asphalt lakeside path: 22½' × 3'6". High Point housing has some street-trees by 32nd Ave SW & SW Morgan St.]

Spire CHERRY

P. 'Spire'   Hillier Spire Cherry
=*P.* × *Hillieri* hort. 'Spire'

Raised in 1937 at Hillier nursery in England. A *narrow*-crowned tree that recalls 'Amanogawa' cherry. Flowers pale pink. Young foliage reddish. Superb fall color. Uncommon in Seattle; all are youngsters from the 1990s onward.

– U.W.: CUH has three #170-97, the tallest 19½'
– View Ridge Clubhouse (10040 15th Ave NW): 5 + 2 Zumi Crabapples
– 819 S Rose St: a street-tree (a huge Sweet cherry in the yard)
– S McClellan St, east of Martin Luther King, Jr Way S: some street-trees
– 1412 N 50th St: street-trees
– NE Naomi Pl at 19th Ave NE: 2 street-trees
– 1103 20th Ave E: 2 street-trees
– 2808 NE 60th St: a street-tree 24½' tall
– 4424 42nd Ave SW (south of SW Genesee St): 2 street-trees

[**Hillier Cherry**—*P.* 'Hillieri'—is the parent of *P.* 'Spire'. It is extremely rare in Seattle. In 1993 one measured 30' × 8'5" × 56' wide at 10709 39th Ave NE. Arboretum #602-46 in 30-2W is 30½' × 5'6½"; no others are definitely known here at this writing. But one *or* a Korean Hill-cherry may be at 1626 39th Ave E (Sargent cherries also on this street).]

Sweet CHERRY

P. avium cvs. & hybrids   Garden *or* Cultivated Cherry
=*Cerasus avium* (L.) Moench   Edible *or* Fruiting Cherry

Most fruiting cherry trees grown in Seattle are Sweet cherry cultivars. Mazzard cherry is parent to these improved fruiting kinds. Familiar here, cultivars include: 'Bing', 'Black Tartarian', 'Lambert', 'Rainier', 'Royal Anne', 'Sam', 'Stella', 'Sunburst' and many more. There *was* a street-tree almost 9½' around on the north side of NE 55th St, east of 1st Avenue NE.

– South Park neighborhood has many old, large examples
– Good Shepherd Center: Seattle Tilth Children's Garden has 'Bing', 'Hardy Giant' and 'Angel' cultivars

Weeping CHERRY

P. pendula Maxim.	Wild Weeping (Higan) Cherry
=*P.* × *subhirtella* 'Pendula'	Weeping Spring Cherry
=*P.* × *subhirtella* 'Pendula Rosea'	Single Weeping Cherry
=*P.* × *subhirtella* 'Ito-zakura' イトザクラ	Weeping Higan
=*P.* × *subhirtella* 'Shidare (Higan) Zakura' シダレ(ヒガン)ザクラ	

This is a species that grows wild in Japan, and is naturally pendulous. But in the U.S., for decades it has been called a Higan cultivar. The examples cited below are alike and distinct from the two weeping cultivars which follow. Unlike the other two weepers this is usually seen on its *own* roots and trunk, and it grows far larger—to 80' × 12½' or more in Japan. Old trees are common here but no youngsters exist; nurseries do not sell it.

- 6820 Phinney Ave N: one 30' × 7'2" × 45' wide (1988)
- 39th Ave E, north of E John St: one 41' × 7' × 37' wide (1989) in a E side yard
- 4028 Delridge Way SW: one 23' × 6'9" × 40' wide (1988)
- 9653 50th Ave SW: one 20' × 8'6" × 50'½' wide
- Locks #112
- 5230 35th Ave NE: two street-trees
- Volunteer Park: 6 by the Burke monument; tallest 29' and stoutest 5'7¾"
- Ravenna Park: 2 west and 1 north of the wading pool, the stoutest 26'½ × 8'5¾"
- Zoo: many in Family Farm, and by the old elephant barn
- Parsons Gardens Park: two E of lawn
- 9725 12th Ave NW (31' tall; more than 40' wide; 2-trunked)
- 2046 42nd Ave E: overhanging the sidewalk
- Leschi Park: one 7'½" around
- Highland Park Playground (11th SW & SW Thistle St): 9 on the W border

var. *ascendens* Mak.	Wild Spring Cherry
=*P. pendula* f. *ascendens* (Mak.) Ohwi	Equinox Cherry
=*P.* × *subhirtella* var. *ascendens* (Mak.) Wils.	Edo-higan エドヒガン

From China, Korea, and Japan. Not weeping; a tall tree recorded up to 80' × 20' in Japan. Leaves longer and narrower than those of Higan cherry. Flowers white or palest pink, small. Extremely rare; known only as follows in Seattle.

- Colman Park: one leaning by the boulevard's amazing curves, 44' × 4'7¼"
- Shilshole Ave NW at NW Vernon Place: 28' × 5'10¼" (wider than tall); a 'Whitcomb' cherry N of it, a 'Kwanzan' cherry S of it

cv. 'Fukubana'	Double Pink Higan Cherry
=*P.* × *subhirtella* 'Fukubana'	
=*P.* × *subhirtella* 'Momijigari' (misspelled 'Momijugara')	
=*P.* × *subhirtella* 'Roseo-plena'	

Double flowers, carmine-red in their bud stage, open deep rosy-pink, then fade somewhat. Last of the clan to bloom in spring, with a long display—it's a wonderful ornamental that unfortunately is extremely rare. Only one is known here: at the Locks (bed #309): 19' × 2'10" × 16½' wide.

90

cv. '**Pendula Plena Rosea**'   Double Weeping Cherry
=*P.* × *subhirtella* 'Pendula Plena Rosea'
=*P.* × *subhirtella* 'Plena Rosea'
=*P.* × *subhirtella* 'Sendai Ito-zakura'   センダイイトザクラ
=*P.* × *subhirtella* 'Yae Shidare-higan' *or* 'Yae Beni-shidare'   ヤエベニシダレ
=*P.* × *subhirtella* 'Endo-zakura'   エンドウザクラ

Darker pink and *double* flowers opening later in spring than those of the single-flowered weeping cherries. It is the most common kind now sold in nurseries and is invariably grafted up on Mazzard cherry trunks, forming a small mop of a tree. Large, old specimens are relatively rare.

- Arboretum: #1281-47 on Azalea Way, 15' × 3'9" in 38-B & 16½' × 1'11" in 23-2W
- Locks #104, 112 (close to #113)
- Volunteer Park: one SW of the William Henry Seward statue
- 3107 16th Ave S (south of S Winthrop St): one with a large male Ginkgo W of it
- 28th Ave W & W Ruffner St: SE corner by Apt. entrance (17' tall; with Scots Pines)
- Eastmont Way W & W McGraw St: SW corner yard

cv. '**Pendula Rubra**'   Pink Weeping (Higan) Cherry
=*P.* × *subhirtella* 'Pendula Rubra'   Beni-shidare-higan ベニシダレヒガン

Compared to seedling-grown *P. pendula*, this has smaller, coarser leaves and pinker flowers that open a bit later in spring. It may actually be hybrid. Always grafted high—just like 'Pendula Plena Rosea'.

- Arboretum: 27 on Azalea Way (many labeled 'Eureka Weeping'); the tallest 25' × 4'8¼" (in 37-B); the stoutest trunk 4'11½" around (in 41-2E)
- Lake View Cemetery: one 24' × 6'11" × 32½' wide is in the NW part (50' NW of an 81' tall Tulip Tree)
- Evergreen Park Cemetery: 23½' × 6'2½" × 37' wide is largest of four
- Washelli Cemetery: few
- 6515 58th Ave NE

cv. '**Stellata**'   Star-flowered Spring Cherry
=*P.* × *subhirtella* 'Stellata'
=*P.* × *subhirtella* 'Pink Star' ('Beni-hoshi')

A *non*-weeping cultivar. Dark pink buds open to pale pink, tightly *clustered* single flowers (as many as 10 per bud), with an extremely long season of bloom in spring. Scarcely known in Seattle except at the Arboretum, where 3 are on Azalea Way—the largest 28' × 6¾' (#2-40 in 18-1W; others in 33-1W & 25-1W). 64 young street-trees are from 28th Ave W & W Ruffner towards Emerson St, and along Emerson to 34th.

Yoshino CHERRY

P. × *yedoensis* Matsum.   Potomac Cherry
From Japan, a natural hybrid   Somei Yoshino ソメイヨシノ
first cultivated in Tokyo <1867.

The chief cherry tree of the Washington, D.C. tidal basin: made famous by tour companies, postage stamps, postcards and photographs. A mid-sized cherry tree; the largest may be in Maryland, 56' × 15½'× 73' wide. Slightly fragrant, pale pink or nearly white single flowers (mid-) late March–early April; the flowerstems *hairy*. Small, shiny black, bitter cherries. It is common in Seattle.

The charm of Yoshino is in its perfect *balance:* its dark rugged trunk, often burly and besprouted, makes an ideal contrast for the quintessentially delicate pink blossoms. Nor is the tree so fussy and weak as the winter-blooming Higan cherry, or so bloated and gaudy as are 'Kwanzan' and the other Sato-zakura.

- U.W.: the "Quad" (=Liberal Arts Quadrangle) is lined with about 30 large specimens, spectacular at bloom time: the largest is 40½' × 11'7"; some 50'+ wide
- Arboretum: largest of *ca.* 15 is in 11-4E, #2233-39G, 44' × 8'11¾"
- Woodland Park: 18 multi-trunked slender trees on a hillside; the tallest 57' × 1'11" (with 3 'Kwanzan' and 2 'Shogetsu' Japanese Flowering cherries)
- Lincoln Park: many; at least two among coniferous evergrerens E of the south restrooms are over 49' in height, yet are very slender
- Volunteer Park: one N of the museum (with a 'Kwanzan' cherry) and two NW of the water tower
- Montlake Playfield (16th Ave E & E Calhoun St): 3 big old ones, with 3 'Kwanzan', a 'Horinji', 11 younger 'Akebono' and 3 'Shirotae' Japanese Flowering cherries
- Laurelhurst Playfield: 4 along the south edge (with 3 'Kwanzan' and a 'Ukon' Japanese Flowering cherry)
- Locks #112 (several), 114, 201 (large), 317, 321 (two, small), 325 (southwest)
- Green Lake: 45, most in the northern part, four have trunks from 8'3" to 8'8" around; the tallest is 33'—and most are wider than tall

cv. 'Afterglow'   Afterglow Yoshino-Cherry

A new selection of the Yoshino, with better fall color. Three street-trees may be viewed in front of 3815–3819 Bagley Avenue N.

cv. 'Akebono'   Akebono Cherry
='Daybreak'   Daybreak Cherry

A popular selection of the Yoshino, originated by nurseryman W.B. Clarke of San José, about 1920. It is smaller (to 30' tall); bears larger, darker pink flowers, in full bloom a bit later in spring than Yoshino, and makes a denser display.

- Arboretum: largest of *ca.* 9 are in 10-2E
- Locks #114 has a young specimen with a Yoshino; 317
- Lake View Cemetery: many

f. *perpendens* Wils.

Weeping Yoshino-Cherry
Shidare Yoshino シダレヨシノ

A bushy little tree with pure white flowers, very few of them semi-double. Possibly a hybrid with a weeping Higan cherry. Utterly lacking the grace of weeping Higans, it has all of the heaviness of Yoshino. Very rare in Seattle; far ountnumbered by the similar Snow Fountains® cherry.

- Arboretum: 29-2W has #13-78 on the west side of Azalea Way
- 512 18th Ave E
- 1610 Warren Ave N
- 5234 Ivanhoe Pl NE: by driveway
- 55th Ave NE & NE 73rd St: NE corner yard has one SE of the house

CHESTNUT TREES (in general)

Chestnut trees can be edible-nut kinds (genus *Castanea*, here considered) and the poisonous Horse Chestnuts (found under that name; genus *Æsculus*). Any such tree is called "Chestnut" without qualifying prefixes in common usage.

American CHESTNUT TREE

Castanea dentata (Marsh.) Borkh.
=*C. americana* Raf.
FAGACEÆ
From eastern N America.

Once a dominant forest tree in parts of its range, growing as large as 140' × 37½'. Now it's essentially extinct due to an Asiatic fungal blight that arrived in New York in the late 1800s. Similar to its European cousin, the chief practical distinction is in the American's smaller, sweeter nuts. Early nut-growers hybridized the European and American species hoping to combine the size of the former and sweetness of the latter.

In Seattle, authentic specimens are extremely rare. Hybrids are less rare. The destructive blight reached the city once before and was fortunately wiped out, but it can reappear any time. Some of our oldest European chestnut trees have died; others are sorely decrepit and have slowed down greatly. But various stresses can cause such decay.

- 310 30th Ave S: an old specimen 74' × 13'4" × 78' wide (1988); the surrounding yards have a number of European Chestnut trees
- Woodland Park: 3 near soapbox derby ramp by N 50th St; largest 46' × 7'1"
- Arboretum: hybrids only, in 44-1E, 14-4W

Here is an identification aid (intermediate characteristics indicate hybridity):

AMERICAN CHESTNUT:	EUROPEAN CHESTNUT:
- (15) 20 (25) leaf-veins	- (14) 18 (22) leaf-veins
- leaves average over 3 times longer than broad, easily,	- leaves average less than 3 times longer than broad

and some are 4 times longer than broad
- leaf-bases narrowed to the stalk; never notched
- leaves never fuzzy
- leaves color earlier and brighter in autumn
- raw nuts fresh from the tree are small, delicious and eagerly sought

and some are only twice as long as broad
- leaf-bases broadly wedge-shaped, often notched
- leaves often slightly fuzzy
- leaves still green when American's are colorful
- raw nuts fresh from the tree are big and pucker one's mouth so that roasting them seems vital

Chinese CHESTNUT TREE

C. mollissima Bl.
From China, Korea.

Chinese: Li Shu
Pan Li

Resistant, but not immune to the blight. Grows up to 80' tall. Used in attempts to produce resistant hybrids. Various cultivars are available for nut-production. Most Chinese chestnut trees are recognizable because of their small, fuzzy leaves; even the twigs are often lightly coated with fuzz.

In Seattle, rare; most of our Chinese chestnuts are very young.

– Lincoln Park: 8 NW of the wading pool & nearby picnic area, the tallest 66' × 4'11" and the largest 57' × 6'8" × 72' wide
– 22nd Ave NE, N of NE 63rd St: a street-tree, W side by telephone pole, 38' × 4'9"
– 6315 21st Ave NE: 2 street-trees
– Arboretum: one #2338-37, leaning in 43-1W, is low-forking, small
– 4233 E Lee St: two street-trees

European CHESTNUT TREE

C. sativa Mill.
=*C. vesca* Gaertn.
=*C. vulgaris* Lam.
=*C. Castanea* Karst.
From S Europe, N Africa, W Asia.

Eurasian Chestnut
Spanish Chestnut
Italian Chestnut
Edible Chestnut
Sweet Chestnut

The original "Chestnut Tree" in name, this species is both economically important and rich in ancient literary history and European lore. It reaches monumental dimensions: sizes reported from Mediterranean countries seem scarcely believable (up to 167' around the trunk!), but even planted specimens in Great Britain are over 120' in height and the largest trunks 37½' around.

The nuts are starchy with carbohydrates, not fatty with oils as are most nuts. Traditionally they're roasted, used in stuffings, and so on. Most sold in the markets are imports. Harvest time in Seattle is mid-September through early October. Single, isolated trees usually bear few fertile nuts; go to groves for good yields.

In Seattle, common; wild offspring also exist.

- 3212 22nd Ave W: a wide, not particularly tall tree, over 15' around
- Queen Anne Blvd: Bigelow Ave N has 20, the stoutest trunk 14'8½" around
- Jefferson Park: larger of a pair between 15th & 17th fairways, 86½' × 13'3½"
- Dayton Ave N & N 47th St: NE corner has a street-tree 49½' × 15'11¼"
- Me-kwa-mooks Park: one 55½' × 15'3¼"
- Laurelhurst Playfield: 15, the largest 82½' × 13'2¾"
- Corliss Ave N, near Haller Lake: a row of large old trees; largest 49½' × 15'0"
- W Lee St, east of 6th Ave W: two street-trees; larger 69' × 12'7½"
- U.W.: a relatively small one N of Bagley Hall, *pl.* in 1963, 50' × 5'2¼"
- Roosevelt Way NE & NE 90th St: NW corner

CHINABERRY

Melia Azedarach L.
=*M. australis* Sweet
MELIACEÆ
From N India to central China,
the Ryukyus, Taiwan and Australia.

Pride of India
China Tree
Bead Tree

A tree much known and grown in the southern U.S. Extremely rare in Seattle. Glossy, handsome large doubly-compound leaves. In May or June sweetly fragrant lilac flowers bloom, giving rise to toxic, persistent, yellow-green, small-marble-sized berries. Recorded to 147½' tall in Australia.

- 915 30th Ave S (*pl. ca.* 1970; cut way back if not killed in 2004)
- U.W. Medicinal Herb Garden: north of section B has one 13½' tall; too close to a sugar maple; *pl. ca.* 1997; stays green into late Nov. or early Dec.

[**Chinese Toon, Chinese Cedar, Chop Suey Tree, Stir-Fry Tree**—*Toona sinensis* (A. Juss.) M. Roem. = *Cedrela sinensis* A. Juss.—from Pakistan across Asia to Malaysia, is an extremely rare cousin. It has edible, onion-flavored compound leaves of 10–32 leaflets. The Arboretum's conifer meadow (44 and 45-6W) has three #4-86; largest (A) 28' × 1'7¼"; #229-57 in 5-1E is 22' tall. 6811 20th Ave NE has 2 young street-trees, under wires. Meadowbrook Park's edible arboretum has one 18' tall, *pl.* 2000.]

CHINA-FIR

Cunninghamia lanceolata (Lamb.) Hook.
=*C. sinensis* R. Br. *ex* Rich.
=*Belis lanceolata* Sweet
CUPRESSACEÆ (formerly TAXODIACEÆ)
From China, Laos, Vietnam.

Chinese-Fir
Chinese: Shan Mu Shu
Sha Shu

An important timber tree up to 150' × 18' in its homeland. The wood is also made into coffins, gunpowder-charcoal, and is used in decoction for certain medicinal applications. The tree is often multitrunked or forking, suckering from its base, with reddish-brown fibrous bark like that of Seattle's native (Western Red) Cedar. In moist soil it is lush. In drier sites a narrow crown of gaunt, irregular branches is topped by a rounded rather than sharply spired apex. The needles are broad, flat, fiercely sharp, and the cones are squat, 1–2" long, prickly, often growing in clusters and falling while still attached to large twigs.

In Seattle, common yet often called rare because it's so little known.

- 2218 32nd Ave S: one 84½' tall
- Interlaken Park: one 84' × 5'6½" where 19th Ave E enters the park from Boyer E
- 4012 3rd Ave NW: 81' tall
- 8304 34th Ave NE: 77' tall, multitrunked
- 1st Ave NE & NE 64th St: SE corner, 71½' tall
- 524 NE 94th St: one 63' tall
- Bagley Ave N & N 37th St: SE corner has one 57' tall
- 8th Ave NW & NW 87th St: SE corner has one 53½' tall
- U.W. Friendship Grove: one in poor condition is representing China
- 6808 Ravenna Ave NE: 56' tall, multitrunked

cv. 'Glauca'   Blue China-Fir

Some China-fir seedlings are more or less powder blue. The most attractive are propagated and sold by nurseries. They are very rare in Seattle.

- 8009 18th Ave NE: 74½' tall
- U.W.: NW corner of Bloedel Hall has a 3-trunked tree 56½' tall—compare with green versions at the W end of Anderson Hall and S of that building at its E end
- Arboretum: by viaduct footbridge in 39-4W are 3 #532-64 raised *via* seeds from Taiwan (largest 40' × 2'8")—compare with the standard China-Firs in 33-5W
- Zoo: five in Conservation Aviary

CHINESE SCHOLAR-TREE

Sophora japonica L.   (Japanese) Pagoda-Tree
=*Styphnolobium japonicum* Schott   Chinese: Huai Shu
LEGUMINOSÆ (FABACEÆ)   Japanese: Enju エンジュ
From China, Korea, Vietnam.

The tree traditionally planted on the graves of Chinese scholars. It fixes nitrogen through rhizobial symbiosis, so can thrive on sterile soils. The tree is an excellent source of the bioflavinoid *rutin*. The twigs are greenish and stink when bruised. Its seeds are constricted in pods and are probably poisonous: only in times of famine have they been eaten. Dimensions up to 100' × 18¼' are recorded.

In Seattle, uncommon. A little-known, trouble-free shade tree unfortunately shy-blooming: ideally, it produces white flowers in late summer, but most years our trees are inhibited by youthfulness, are sparing in adulthood or frigidly refuse to flower at all. Truly a rare, lovely sight when they do happen to flower fully. In general it looks like a less languid, more perky Black Locust. The two trees are cousins, but as far as flowers and reproduction here are concerned, one is a nun and the other a wanton. (Cultivars such as 'Pendula' and 'Regent' exist, but are extremely rare here.)

- Cal Anderson Park (Broadway Reservoir): in NW corner, 55½' × 10'11" × 66' wide
- 12th Ave NE, north of NE 41st St: a street-tree, W side, 40½' × 8'3¼"

- 10th Ave E & E Harrison St: SW corner has one 54' tall
- Seattle Center: W and SW of Key Arena (the former Coliseum)
- Locks #204 has one 49' tall
- 3627 42nd Ave NE: by driveway
- 1414 Lake Washington Blvd S
- U.W.: 5 S and W of Mercer Hall
- 10011 Bayard Ave NW: one 48' tall south of the house
- 50th Ave NE & NE 73rd St: two east of the NE corner house
- 1500 Ravenna Blvd. NE: a 'Pendula' is 21' tall

[*S. microphylla* Ait., from New Zealand (where its Maori name is Köwhai and it is the National Flower), and also from Chile(!). Extremely rare. It bears petite evergreen leaflets, has bright yellow spring flowers, and is hurt by hard freezes. Locks bed #313 has one 21' tall. The Arboretum has 8 in 15-6E, 15-7E, 16-7E: #127-88, 63-89, 540-90, & 200-91. All died to the ground in the 2000–2001 winter; the tallest is now 23' and stoutest 1'1". A 9th (#540-90) is in 9-4E, 21' tall. The Zoo has two in the Australasia / North Meadow border, the larger 14' × 11¾".]

[*S. tetraptera* J.F. Mill., is even rarer. Large-leaved, North Island *or* Taupo Köwhai. The Arboretum has two #124-88 in 18-5E & 16-6E. Both died to the ground in the 2000–2001 winter; the tallest is now 13'. The U.W. has one (#124-88) 8' tall in the shadow of 3 Red Oaks by Brooklyn Ave NE & Boat St.]

CHINQUAPINS & kin

Chinquapin, also spelled Chinkapin or Chincapin, an eastern North American Indian name for a chestnut, is used loosely to denote various close cousins of oaks and chestnuts. Five such species are treated below, all broadleaf evergreens. Only one is uncommon in Seattle—the rest are *rare* and are likely to remain so despite their merits. More information is in the *Arboretum Bulletin* Summer 1983.

Castanopsis cuspidata (Thunb.) Schott.   Japanese Chinquapin
=*Quercus cuspidata* Thunb.   Japanese: Tsubara-Jii ツブラジイ
FAGACEÆ
From China, Korea, Japan, the Ryukyus.

A tree up to 150' × 29¾' in the wild but shrubby in cultivation. Leaves very dark green above, silvery-bronze beneath; to 4½" long. Extremely rare in Seattle.

- Arboretum: #2073-38 is 21½' × 1'6" in 43-2E; and #462-80 is 13' tall in 41-B
- Locks #17 has a shrubby one about 7' tall [var. *Sieboldii* (Mak.) Nakai]

Chrysolepis chrysophylla (Dougl. *ex* Hook.) Hjelm.   Golden Chinquapin
=*Castanopsis chrysophylla* (Dougl. *ex* Hook.) A. DC.   Giant Chinquapin
From Washington to California.   Golden Chestnut

A giant forest tree to 150' × 31½' or a shrub in some places. Hard to establish in a garden: many admirers cannot grow it. Though it may sprout in sunny exposed spots in the wild, shady sites seem to suit young cultivated ones best. Leaf dark green above, warm gold beneath. Extremely rare in Seattle.

- 4315 NE 60th St: in back yard, growing 1½' yearly
- Arboretum: #183-90A is 4½' tall, wider still, east of viaduct footbridge in 39-1W

Lithocarpus densiflorus (H.& A.) Rehd.　　　　　Tanbark Oak
=_Quercus densiflora_ H.& A.　　　　　　　　　　　Tan Oak
From SW Oregon, California.　　　　　　　　　　Tanoak

A strong timber tree (up to 208' × 28½') or a bush, depending on conditions. Sudden Oak Death has killed many since 1995. Uncommon but easily grown here; the large acorns are abundant at the Locks and often sprout into seedlings.

- 853 NW Elford Dr: 68' tall two-trunked; with Japanese Red Pine
- Kruckeberg Botanic Garden: 64' × 6'1" and 61' × 6'10"
- 8546 30th Ave NW: 56' tall
- Locks: over a dozen, largest 35' × 5'6" (in bed #7); also in #22, 23, 23A, 24, 25, 101
- Arboretum: 39-B has two #503-61, and so does 14-5E
- 4625 Eastern Ave N: visible from the alley west of the yard, 41' tall
- Sherman Rd NW & NW 137th St: SE corner, 40' tall (under wires)
- 4207 Woodlawn Ave N: 2 in yard

f. **_attenuato-dentatus_** J. Tucker, Sundahl & D.O. Hall　　　Cutleaf Tanoak

An open, airy tree, its leaves deeply lobed and attenuated. It blooms rarely and may be sterile. In 1971 Art and Mareen Kruckeberg raised two from cuttings, in Shoreline, N of Seattle (now Kruckeberg Botanic Garden). In 2003 the larger was 48' × 4'6¾". Locks bed #114 has one. No others are known in Seattle.

L. edulis (Mak.) Nakai　　　　　Japanese: Mateba-Shii マテバシイ
=_Pasania edulis_ Mak.
From Japan, the Ryukyus.

A tree up to 65' × 9½'. Leaf bright green above, pale bronzy-green and minutely hairy beneath; to 8¼" × 2⅞". Extremely rare in Seattle.

- Locks #17 has one 19' tall immediately north of a shrubby _Castanopsis cuspidata_

L. Henryi (Seem.) Rehd. & Wils.　　　　　Longleaf Chinquapin
From China.　　　　　　　　　　　Chinese: Hui Ke; Mien Chu

A tree up to 65' × 9¾', with laurel-like, narrow, glossy leaves to 13" × 2⅞". Extremely rare in Seattle.

- Arboretum: in 39-1W #62-65B is 22' × 1'2¼"; in 24-B #609-67 is 23½' × 1'2½"
- Locks # 110 (near the fence) has a two-trunked tree 19' tall

CHITALPA

× **_Chitalpa tashkentensis_** Elias & Wisura
(_Catalpa bignonioides_ × _Chilopsis linearis_)
BIGNONIACEÆ

98

Hybridized in the early 1960s at Tashkent, Uzbekistan. The leaves are slender, to 6⅝" × 1⅔" and fall yellow-green in late October. Showy pink or white flowers in large clusters appear all summer. It can grow 30' tall and is wider than tall. In Seattle, uncommon; all date from the 1990s onward.

– U.W.: CUH has three #115-91, the tallest 23½'
– 614 12th Ave E (south of E Aloha St): one 23' tall
– 1119 NW 60th St: two big street-trees, taller 21'
– 1612 N 35th St: 16' tall
– NE 47th St, east of 35th Ave NE: a street-tree, N side
– 813 NW 57th St: two street-trees
– 828 NE 56th St: a street-tree
– 6507 2nd Ave NW: a street-tree
– 2030 42nd Ave E
– 5704 39th Ave NE
– Palm Ave SW, east of 1728 California Ave SW: a street-tree, N side

[**Desert** *or* **Flowering Willow**—*Chilopsis linearis* (Cav.) Sweet—is a SW U.S. / N Mexico native shrub or small tree with willow-like leaves and lovely fragrant summer flowers. In Seattle, none known except *ca.* 6 at the U.W. east of the W Campus parking garage.]

CRABAPPLES in general

Crabapple trees are shortchanged in most tree books, this one included. There are *too many kinds*. In Seattle there are 140+ different kinds of crabapples, surpassing such large groups as the oaks and pines. In this book only Seattle's native species of crabapple is singled out for *full attention*. Concerning the rest, tiny print and thumbnail remarks must do. In growth and overall appearance at maturity, most are comparable to the common apple tree, though a few are strongly weeping in form and some are very narrow and upright. They are small, rarely seen over 25' tall. Most are grown for ornament though a few are grown because their fruit are tart, edible delicacies. The foliage is green or (especially in spring) bronzy-purplish. The flowers are often red or pink in the bud, opening white though some are pure white, pink or purplish. They bloom mostly March through May. Very fragrant flowers, as well as doubled ones, are relatively rare. Typically each flower has 5 petals; semi-double or doubled flowers bear extra petals. The fruits range from pea- to golfball-size, in color from green to yellow and red to purple. They are rarely worth eating raw, due to runty size or excessive astringency, but they're often highly ornamental and attractive to birds. Whether the calyx (leftover sepals) remains at the bottom of the fruit, or drops away, is a detail that helps make identification precise.

Seattle's best collection is at the U.W. by the roses around the fountain: these old trees were moved from the Arboretum. Though the 20 pages following detail 111 kinds, still *more* exist in Seattle but were not identified in time for this book's deadline. Also the Arboretum has 29 kinds not known elsewhere in the city.

Pacific CRABAPPLE

M. fusca (Raf.) Schneid.   (our) Native Crabapple
=*M. rivularis* (Dougl. *ex* Hook.) Roem.   Western Crabapple
=*Pyrus diversifolia* Bong.   Oregon Crabapple
=*P. fusca* Raf.
Native here; from S Alaska to N California.

Little known, usually small and inconspicuous. The white or faintly pink flowers are borne some time mid-April through May and are succeeded by ½" long, oblong, dark-yellowish crabapples: ripe, tart and edible from mid-August until frosts soften, acidify and discolor them. It is not cultivated here because many non-native kinds are more attractive in blossom, or bear larger, more colorful (if not tastier) fruit. Autumn color varies from a conspicuous red, of much beauty, to dull yellowish. It is readily distinguished from non-native crabapple trees by its often *lobed* leaves (rare in crabapple trees) and its tiny, *oblong* (rather than the usual round) yellow fruit. Unlike many of its cousins, this species handles very wet, mucky soil. Tallest recorded is 79'; some trunks are over 8½' around.

In Seattle, common—in scattered places. See also *M.* × *Dawsoniana* below.

– Arboretum: N end has big trees—tallest 52' × 3'8½" (45-1W) and 49' × 4'½" (NW of the Lynn St parking lot); the stoutest (in 39-1E) is 45' × 6'8¼" × 70' wide
– Lincoln Park: the S half has both wild and planted ones, the largest 41' × 6'0" east of picnic shelter #3, with a leaning spiralled trunk full of sapsucker holes
– Seward Park, Discovery Park, Carkeek Park and Camp Long all have some, none so large as the foregoing

[*M.* 'Adams'—Originated *ca.* 1947. A rosybloom crabapple introduced <1952. Rare in Seattle; one at Children's Hospital N of Whale garage. Tree to 20' tall & wide, broadly rounded; sparse and very open, or eventually dense. Red buds open to pink flowers, 1½" wide. Leaves tinged reddish in spring, turn green in summer; orange-red in fall. Fruit glossy carmine-red to dark red, ½–¾" long, with small calyx scars; abundant; persistent.]

[*M.* 'Adirondack'—Released in 1987 by the U.S. National Arboretum. Common in Seattle; street-trees on NW corner of 23rd Ave NW & NW 77th St. Compact, *strongly upright habit*. Red buds open to waxy-white 1¾–2¼" wide flowers, with traces of carmine, and heavily-textured petals. Leaf dark green, hairy at first, becoming hairless; sharply toothed. Fruit ⅝" long; stem to 1⅝" long; yellow-pink mostly blushed with red, becoming brilliant orange-red and enduring until December.]

[*M.* 'Almey'—Named in 1945 in Manitoba. A famous, once widely planted rosybloom clone, but disease-prone; no longer sold. Rare in Seattle: 2 street-trees @ 4134 42nd Ave NE; SW corner of 39th Ave E & E Howe St has 4 street-trees. Compared to the ubiquitous and similar *Malus* 'Hopa', it is smaller and more open. Its flowers are darker red, larger (1¾–2⅝" wide), with distinct white petal bases, on long flowerstems (to 1⅜" long), in clusters of 5–8 instead of 4–5. Leaves purplish when very young but very quickly green; sharply toothed, albeit indistinctly so. The fruit are fewer, harder, ribbed, orange covered with carmine or crimson, ⅞" long, persisting instead of dropping when ripe; the calyx almost always drops away; the pulp is yellow-golden, firm, and foul-tasting.]

[*M.* × *arnoldiana* (Rehd.) Sarg. *ex* Dunbar—Originated in 1883 at the Arnold Arboretum; named in 1908. Common and long popular, but weak and disease-prone, so going extinct commercially. Rare in Seattle: NW corner of 5th Ave W & W Comstock St; NE corner of 14th Ave E & E Howe St. Like a larger-flowered, larger-fruited, but smaller-sized *M.* × *floribunda*. Bushy, 6–10' (28') tall, compact and graceful; with somewhat zigzag twigs. Buds bright red, shaped like snowdrop flowers, held on wirelike flowerstems up to 2–3" long. Flowers in clusters of 4–6, shell-pink, aging almost white; to 1⅞" wide; sometimes semi-double. Fruit ½–⅝" long, yellow, butterscotch blushed, large-scarred, on stems to 2½" long. When profuse and glossy the fruit is lovely.]

[*M.* × *atrosanguinea* (Späth) Schneid.—Carmine *or* Red Japanese crabapple. Originated <1889. In the nursery trade by 1898. Rare in Seattle: U.W. has 4 (+ 3 *M.* × *floribunda*) by Architecture Hall and 3 (+ 1 *M.* × *floribunda*) S of Cunningham Hall. Like a pink flowered *M.* × *floribunda* but smaller (usually low and mushroom-shaped, rarely to 20'), with an airier, less dense crown; its leaves larger, darker, glossier, less hairy, more frequently lobed, coarser toothed, and bearing prominent stipules. Blood-red buds open to pink flowers that do not fade to white; ¾" wide. Fruit few, ¼–½" long, not ornamental; yellowish.]

[*M. baccata* (L.) Borkh.—Siberian crabapple. From much of Asia. Introduced to Western cultivation in 1784. Though the book name Siberian crabapple is applied to this species, in practice the name has been used often for *M. baccata* hybrids. Rare in Seattle: U.W. has 4 between the Rose Garden and Bagley Hall; largest 41' × 6'3" × 47' wide (1992). Flowers white, 1–1½" wide. Fruit usually pea-sized (⅓–⅝"), yellowish, yellow-brown or red, usually longer than wide, the calyx wholly dropping off leaving a smooth scar.]

[*M. baccata* 'Aspiration'—A seedling raised in 1946 at the Seattle Arboretum. Named *ca.* 1957, for its aspiring branches of fastigiate habit. Extremely rare in Seattle: U.W. has one between the Rose Garden and Guggenheim Hall 42' × 4'6" × 37' wide (1992). Flowers like those of *M. baccata* 'Columnaris', early in spring—although it flushes a bit later than 'Columnaris'; pure white, 1¾" wide. Calyx and flowerstems hairy, not nearly hairless as 'Columnaris'. Fruit differs in being pear- or rosehip-shaped, not round, and twice as large (⅞" long), but has the same yellow and red coloration when seen in mid-September, and the same slender 1⅜" stem. In November the fruit can become dark red. The tree has all the shape and scab of 'Columnaris' and looks nothing like its reputed parent—the healthy, scabfree, round-berried *M. baccata* var. *himalaica*.]

[*M. baccata* 'Columnaris' = *M. baccata* 'Pyramidalis'—Columnar Siberian crabapple. Named and introduced in 1940; still sold. Uncommon in Seattle: McClure School's W side has 3; the largest of 3 in the Arboretum is #828-58B in 14-2W, 43' × 4'6½". Narrowly upright when young, it splays out in age. Creamy-white buds open to early, pure white flowers 1½–1⅔" wide. Fruit sometimes sparse; round; yellow or yellow with a red cheek; pea size (some larger than ½"); pitted where the calyx was.]

[*M. baccata* var. *himalaica* (Maxim.) Schneid. = *M. baccata* var. *ellipsoidea* Yü—Himalayan crabapple. From Kashmir to Bhutan. Poorly understood; needs research. It has mostly circulated only among botanic gardens and arboreta. Extremely rare in Seattle. Locks bed #121 has one 43' tall × 45' wide, its wild offspring in #212 and elsewhere. Blooms later than most *M. baccata* cultivars, has very hairy flowerstems and calyces. Scabfree, dense, healthy; astonishing vigor. Fruit profuse; pure red, becoming gooey by late October or in November; ⅜–½" long and wide; stems to 2⅛" long.]

[*M. baccata* 'Jackii'—Jack crabapple. In 1905, John George Jack (1861–1949), sent scions from Seoul to the U.S. This cultivar was named after him in 1915. Extremely rare in Seattle: 5414 3rd Ave NE has a street-tree (with *M.* × *domestica*). Vigorous; upright, broadly rounded, to 30–40' tall. Likely a good street-tree. Large, milk-white or slightly pink buds open to pure white 1½" wide flowers (larger than most forms of Siberian crabapples). A cloud of solid white in bloom. Leaves barely toothed, dark above, strikingly paler below. Fruit firm at first, soft & dropping in early September; to ⅝" long, shiny, dark red-purple, with tiny scars; stem to 2⅜" long.]

[*M. baccata* var. *mandshurica* (Maxim.) Schneid.—Manchurian crabapple. Despite the name, this is widely distributed in NE Asia. The northernmost crabapple, it varies from a bush to nearly 100' tall. Extremely rare in Seattle: U.W. has one between the Rose Garden and Guggenheim Hall 38' × 4'2" × 41' wide (1992). It vies with *M.* × *micromalus* to be the first crabapple to flower in spring, with pure white, notably fragrant flowers 1½" wide. Sepals hairy—unlike those of typical *M. baccata*. Leaves broad, sharp-toothed and hairier than most *M. baccata* forms. Goes bare early in fall. Fruit usually red, sometimes yellow, ripens early; to ⅝" on a 1" stem. A broadly rounded, sturdy tree.]

[*M.* 'Baskatong' (*M.* 'Simcoe' × *M.* 'Meach')—Raised in Ottawa. A rosybloom crabapple introduced <1948. Rare in Seattle: one at Children's Hospital. Grows to 30' tall and wide, spreading much like *M.* × *floribunda*. Leaves deep purple, changing to dark bronzy-green all summer, reddish in fall. Buds attractive, highly colored maroon-red; flowers in clusters of 3–6, dark-red fading to light purplish-red, the petals with white claws; 1¾" wide. Fruit dark reddish-purple with russet marks, 1", edible.]

[*M.* 'Beauty'—Originated in South Dakota, from seeds obtained from St. Petersburg in 1919. Introduced *ca.* 1929. Rare in Seattle: NE corner yard of 48th Ave NE & NE 42nd St has one, and to the W is a *M. spectabilis*. Tree fastigiate when young. Flowers like those of *M.* × *domestica* (orchard apple) pure white, 1¾–2" wide, fragrant, from ivory or pink-tinged buds; sepals remarkably long. The *M.* × *domestica* influence shows in the broad leaves, white hairs, and short flowerstems—usually <1" long, rarely to 1⅜" long. Fruit abundant, pinkish red to brilliant red, quarter-dollar sized (to 1½" wide), flattened, with a large brown pit where the calyx was; handsome, earning its cultivar name, though harshly disappointing to taste. Ripe and falling from mid-September to early November. An alternate-year bearer.]

M. 'Bechtel'—see *M. ioensis* 'Bechtel'

[*M.* 'Beverly'—Parentage not known except one parent was likely *M.* × *floribunda*. Introduced *ca.* 1940. Extremely rare in Seattle: U.W. has one 26½' tall *pl.* 1993 behind Hutchinson Hall. Tree upright spreading, becoming rounded. Dark red buds open to clear white flowers, to 1⅜" wide (like those of *Prunus cerasifera*), on long, slender slightly hairy stems. Leaves small, fine textured. Fruit profuse, showy, bright red, roundish, ½–⅝" (¾"); calyx usually drops, leaving small scars.]

[*M.* 'Blanche Ames'—Selected at the Arnold Arboretum; named in 1955. Extremely rare in Seattle: U.W. has one between the Rose Garden and Guggenheim Hall 30' × 6'3" × 41' wide (1992). Its leaves and buds are similar to those of *M.* × *Hartwigii* 'Katherine' but the fruits, flowers and tree habits differ. Buds half pink. Flowers white; small, to 1½" wide; double, with 13–19 (23) narrow petals; delicately pretty. An enchanting sight, the tree partly weeps; its branches slender and light enough to sway gently in the breeze. Alas, by early May the tree is ugly with scab. Can be fecund or practically fruitless. Fruit pea-sized, to ½"; yellow mostly covered in red, conspicuously shiny; either elliptic or wider than long; with very large calyx scars (usually with a protruding tip).]

[*M*. **Brandywine*** = *M*. 'Branzam'—Named and introduced <1979. Uncommon in Seattle: 1202 McGilvra Blvd. E has a street-tree S of a *M. floribunda;* 1804 6th Ave W has 2 street-trees. Tree to 25' tall and 20' wide, vase-shaped, then rounded; rapid growing. Flowers double, fragrant, deep rose. Leaves large, green with a distinct burgundy overcast; fall color attractive deep purple or reddish-brown. Fruit yellow-green (some with a pink or orange blush), to 1½" wide, stem to 1⅜" long; drops in October.]

M. Candied Apple*—see *M*. Weeping Candied Apple*

[*M*. **'Candymint'** PP 6606 (1989) = *M. Sargentii* 'Candymint'—A rosybloom-like Sargent crabapple seedling featuring picturesque, horizontal, very low, wide, vigorous growth. Extremely rare in Seattle: 3 at Woodland Park, just N of 50th St, and 3 SW of Shelter #5. Twigs dark purple. Leaves purplish and white-hairy when young, then dark green; thick and bold; very sharply toothed, with some strong lobes. Some leaves as large as 4½" × 4". Carmine buds open to flowers with pink petals edged red; effective over a long period. Fruit dark purple, ¼–½" wide, quickly eaten by birds.]

[*M*. **'Centennial'** (*M*. 'Dolgo' × *M*. 'Wealthy')—From Excelsior, MN. An intentional cross, 1931; selected in 1940; introduced in 1957. Grown mainly for its edible fruit. Uncommon in Seattle: at Meadowbrook Park's edible Arboretum. Pink buds open to white flowers. Fruit egg-shaped, red-striped over yellow-orange, 1¾–2" wide; stem long and slender; calyx persists; ripe and delicious from late August through early September. Large, thin leaves with sharp teeth.]

[*M*. **Centurion***—A rosybloom introduced in 1979. Uncommon in Seattle: Nordic Heritage museum has 8 by parking lot; 28th Ave E at E Ward St has 5 street-trees. Narrow upright columnar form, growing rapidly to 30' tall and 15' wide, gradually widening to a broad vaselike or rounded crown. Red buds open to dark pink flowers, 1½–2" wide. Fruit cherry-red, becoming glossy, showy for 2 months or more, ½–⅝" long, faintly ribbed, with small calyx scars; pulp amber-colored. Leaves purple when young, aging to glossy bronzy-green in summer. Good fall color.]

[*M*. **Coralburst**™ PP 2983 (1970) = *M*. 'Coralcole' ('Coral Burst')—Raised *ca*. 1954 as a seedling; introduced in 1968 by Cole nursery of Painesville, OH. Uncommon in Seattle: 4710 4th Ave NE has 2 street-trees; NE 71st St, just E of 8th Ave NE has 3 street-trees, S side (with 2 Norway Maples). A rounded, slow-growing bushy dwarf, often topgrafted at 2½–3½'. Coral-pink buds open to single or semi-double rose-pink flowers, ½–¾" wide. Leaves small, dull dark grayish-green, very hairy, sharply toothed, <2" × ⅞". Fruit sparse, tiny and dull, to ⅜" wide, yellow-green with brown speckles; stem hairy, to ⅝" long.]

[*M. coronaria* (L.) Mill.—American, Garland *or* Wild sweet crabapple. From the Midwest and eastern U.S., and S Ontario. Related to the Prairie crabapple *(M. ioensis)*. Extremely rare in Seattle: Arboretum #1403-46 is 60½' × 3'0" in 33-2E; U.W. has one between the Rose Garden and Guggenheim Hall 37' × 3'9" (1992). Pink buds open to white flowers 1½–2" wide, sweetly fragrant. Leaves hairless. Fruit green or yellow-green, hard and waxy, ¾–1⅝" wide.]

[*M. coronaria* var. *dasycalyx* Rehd. 'Klehm's Improved Bechtel' = *M. ioensis* 'Klehm's (Improved) Bechtel'—Selected by nurseryman Clyde Klehm in a Chicago park; in commerce ≤1953. A tree of great value for sweet-scented, lovely flowers, and rich orange fall color. Uncommon in Seattle: many street-trees on 37th Ave S, south of S Hanford St. E Marion St, east of 17th Ave, has 3 street-trees, N side; west of 17th Ave are 2 street-trees, S side. So much better than the original Bechtel crabapple (*M. ioensis* 'Plena') that nurseries stopped selling the original, and instead offer Klehm's under the old name. Klehm's is far more disease-resistant. Flowers 1⅝–2⅛" (2½") wide, of *ca.* 18 (26) petals; short, broad downy sepals. It fruits regularly.]

[*M.* 'Cowichan'—An open-pollinated seedling of *M. Sieversii* 'Niedzwetzkyana'. Raised in 1920 in Ottawa. An original rosybloom crabapple selected in 1928; named in 1930. Very rare in Seattle: 7224 Palatine Ave N has a street-tree; 108 Galer St has a street-tree. Pale red buds open to pink flowers which fade to pale pink or nearly white, 1¾" wide, profuse. Fruit 1½" wide; bright crimson to reddish-purple with some pale yellow or ivory; pulp pink; good for jelly. Good fall leaf color. Tree vigorous, to 30' tall; habit spreading.]

[*M. dasyphylla* Borkh. 'Plena' = *M. pumila* 'Plena', = *M. pumila* 'Translucens', = *M. spectabilis* 'Alba Plena', = *M. spectabilis* f. *albi-plena* Schelle, = *M. sylvestris* 'Flore Plena', = *M. sylvestris* 'Plena'—Doubleflowered Danube crabapple. The Danube crabapple is wild in E Europe's Danube River basin and N Balkan region. Its cultivar 'Plena' (with double flowers), has been grown in Europe since <1770. Extremely rare in Seattle: 6257 Vassar Ave NE has one. Pinkish buds open to white flowers, double (13–15 petals), to 1½" wide, in very dense clusters completely covering the tree. Leaves thick, broad, very downy and veiny. Tree slow growing. Fruit sparse, ripe in early September, edible but not delectable apples, yellow and red, to 1¾" wide, on a stout stem.]

[*M.* 'David'—Named in 1957 after a grandson of A. den Boer of Des Moines, IA. Very rare in Seattle: 1608 N 35th St; Greenwood Ave N, N of N 50th St has 3 street-trees, W side. Light pink buds open to white flowers, 1½" wide. Fruit ⅜–⅝" wide, shiny scarlet, with large scars, and crisp yellow pulp; persistent. A compact rounded tree to 12'. A few sucker leaves are lobed a bit.]

[*M.* × *Dawsoniana* Rehd.—A hybrid between our native species (*M. fusca*) and the orchard apple tree. Only two big specimens are known in Seattle. At Discovery Park, just off the Loop Trail, not far N of the Visitor Center, one stood in a grove of natives: Red Alder, Bitter Cherry, Western Hemlock, Bigleaf Maple. It was 80' × 4'5" in 1993, *fell* in 1998–99, yet is still *alive*. Sapsuckers have drilled much of its trunk. The apples are up to *ca.* 1½" long, oblong, yellow with a red blush. The tree seems well worth propagating on account of its rarity, great vigor and tasty fruit. Green Lake's Pitch n' Putt golf course 3rd hole tee has a specimen 40' × 5'8" that makes larger fruit than the Discovery Park tree.]

[*M.* 'Dolgo'—A *Malus* × *robusta* seedling imported from Russia in 1897 to South Dakota. Introduced in 1917. Originally named 'Dolga' (meaning "long" in Russian), nurseries were miscalling it 'Dolgo' ≤1926 and the corruption stuck. Common in Seattle: Arboretum #332-52B is 43½' × 3'1¼" in 36-4E; U.W. has 4 between the Rose Garden and Guggenheim Hall. Slightly pink buds open to early, pure white, abundant, fragrant flowers, 1½–2" wide. Fruit oval, yellow and deep red, 1¼" long, delicious for eating in late July and August; usually drops by mid-September. An alternate-year bearer.]

[*M.* 'Donald Wyman'—A chance seedling that arose <1950 at the Arnold Arboretum; named in 1970. Common in Seattle: NW corner of 1st Ave NE & NE 51st St has 5 street-trees; S.U. has one W of the Pigott bldg. Carmine buds open to white flowers 1¾" wide, appearing quite like those of *M. baccata*. Essentially hairless parts. A great crop of ½" long red fruit persists well. Although some fruit is a bit big for typical *M. baccata*, the cultivar in most respects fits the description; the leaves are broad, and bluntly toothed.]

[*M.* 'Doubloons' PP 7216 (1990)—Bred by J.L. Fiala of Ohio; named in 1968, introduced in 1988. Rare in Seattle: 7020 20th Ave NE has a street-tree; 7342 18th Ave NE has a street-tree to the north (then a big Serviceberry, then a possible *M.* 'David'). A small, refined, rounded tree, bushy at first. Bright red buds open relatively late in spring to white, double (10–15 petals) flowers, 1¼–1½" wide. Fruit ⅜–⅝"; roundish; yellow-gold turning deeper gold or beige or yellow with butterscotch blush; calyx drops. Twigs purple. Leaves dark, heavy-textured, like those of 'Red Delicious' apple, but strong shoots bear some lobed leaves.]

[*M.* 'Echtermeyer' ('Echtermayer') = *M.* 'Oekonomierat Echtermeyer', = *M.* ×*purpurea* 'Pendula', = *M.* ×*gloriosa* 'Oekonomierat Echtermeyer', = *M.* 'Pink Weeper' —Weeping Purple crabapple. Introduced in 1914 in Germany. Origin disputed; likely *M. Sieversii* 'Niedzwetzkyana' × *M.* 'Exzellenz Thiel'. A many-named weeping rosybloom crabapple. Common in Seattle: 4 at the church on 8th Ave NE @ NE 57th St; 3 by I-5 Freeway at NE 50th St (+ a *M. Sieversii* 'Niedzwetzkyana'). Habit *weepy*—more than *M.* 'Red Jade'. Flowers purplish-red fading to pale pink. Leaves purplish in spring, dark green by late summer. Fruit ¾–1¼" long, purplish-red, oblong, sparse to abundant; calyx stays.]

[*M.* × *Eleyi* (Bean) Hesse = *M.* 'Jay Darling', = *M.* ×*purpurea* 'Eleyi', = *M. floribunda atropurpurea* hort. (*cf. M.* ×*purpurea*)—Eley crabapple. Jay Darling crabapple. History confusing. Originally known ≤1904 as *Malus atropurpurea* in France. Imported to the U.S. <1915. An apparent offspring of the same parentage arose in England, and was described officially in 1920 as *M.* × *Eleyi*. The French strain was named *Malus* 'Jay Darling' in 1943. A famous and widely planted rosybloom crabapple by any name. Common in Seattle: Sand Point/Magnuson Park has many, such as 18 N of the 74th St entrance; Locks bed #208; U.W. has 3 N of Academic Computer Center. Dark red-purple buds open to red flowers 1¼–1¾" wide, on thin stems to 2⅜" long. Fruit deep purple, bewilderingly variable in size and shape; always ½–1"+ long or wide, and usually retaining the calyx. Disease-prone, often looks terrible except when in bloom. An alternate-year bearer. The trunk is characteristically short and burly, with sprouts of reddish leaves.]

[*M.* 'Elise Rathke' ('Eva Rathke', 'Elisa Rathke', 'Elsie Rathke') = *M. pumila* 'Pendula', —A *weeping* version of an ordinary orchard apple, originated *ca.* 1874 in Germany. Extremely rare in Seattle: 5033 21st Ave NE has a street-tree. Red buds open to pinkish-white flowers, 1¾" wide. Fruit to 2¾", green with a purplish-red cheek, of fair quality.]

[*M.* 'Evereste'—Introduced ≤1980 in Europe; in North American commerce ≤1987. Common in Seattle: 6545 27th Ave NE has 3 street-trees; 3002 NW 62nd St has a street-tree, + 2 *M.* 'Prairifire' E of it. Red buds open to white flowers, 2" wide. Leaves dark green, heavy like those of *M.* × *domestica* (orchard apple). Fruit profuse, cherry size (less than 1" wide); yellow becoming orange or red; calyx stays and becomes fleshy, or drops away, leaving a pit; flavor acceptable. Tree small and conical.]

[*M.* 'Flame'—A chance seedling from Minnesota, selected in 1920, introduced in 1934. Extremely rare in Seattle: 2208 E Miller St has an old tree. Pink buds open to white flowers 1½" wide. Fruit to ¾"+ long, deep red on sunny side, yellowish on shaded side; hairy; calyx usually persistent; pulp well flavored; stem to ⅝" long, hairy.]

[*M.* ***florentina*** (Zucc.) Schneid. = × *Malosorbus florentina* (Zucc.) Browicz—Hawthorn-leaf, Italian, *or* Balkan crabapple. From Italy, the Balkan Peninsula, & N Turkey. Introduced to North America *ca.* 1897. Extremely rare in Seattle—known only in the Arboretum: two #41-72 in 42-4W, two in 42-1W, one #1424-50 in 17-5W, and one 26½' tall 210' SW of Washington Park's ballfield. Pale pink buds open in May to white flowers, ⅝–1⅜" wide. By late August or early September, the tree has a hawthorn aspect—profuse pea-size fruit against small, jaggedly-lobed leaves (to 4" long). Fruit lightly hairy; has a strong red side facing the sun, otherwise is green—very sun-responsive; the calyx drops away leaving a hole. The best specimens are full of lipstick-red fruit, lovely in October. Fruit turns brown, soft and rotten in late October and is totally gone by early November.]

[*M.* × ***floribunda*** Sieb. *ex* van Houtte—Japanese *or* Showy crabapple. From Japan; not known wild. Sent to the U.S. in 1862. *Very* common in Seattle: SE corner of 10th Ave E & E Galer St has one 33' × 4'8" × 44' wide (1993); Locks bed #210; 44th Ave NE between NE 62nd & 65th Sts has 20 (+ a *M. Sieversii* 'Niedzwetzkyana'). Tree rounded or wider than tall. Red buds open to profuse pink flowers which fade to white, 1–1½" wide. Fruit ¼–½" wide or long, yellowish with a reddish blush; usually not showy.]

[*M.* **'Golden Hornet'** = *M.* × *Zumi* 'Golden Hornet'—Originated <1949 in England; introduced to the U.S. in 1955. Extremely rare in Seattle: 301 31st Ave E has one south of house; 3800 block of 46th Ave NE has one on W side. Pink buds open to white 1½" flowers in the manner of the *M.* × *robusta* group. Fruit the most showy of all: roundish, abundant, yellow, then gold, large (⅝–1" long, on 1" stems); calyx usually drops away, sometimes stays. An outstanding small tree for winter ornament.]

[*M.* ***Halliana*** **'Parkmanii'**—Parkman crabapple. Not known in the wild in Japan; called Yae-kaido. Introduced from Japan to the U.S. in 1861. Very common until the 1980s. Named after historian Francis Parkman. Rare in Seattle: 1947 5th Ave W has 3 street-trees; Locks bed #15; SW corner of 30th Ave S & S King St. Shrubby or a small tree; green and leafy into November. Flowers single & semi-double (5–16 petals); clear deep pink; 1¼–1¾" wide; on very long (to 2⅛"), blood-red, wire-like stems. Leaves dark, leathery, narrow, glossy, hairless with short, winged reddish stems. Fruit sparse; to ⅓" wide; red, dark purple on sunny side, green on shady side; on long slender stems.]

[*M.* × ***Hartwigii*** Koehne (*M. baccata* × *M. Halliana*)—From Germany <1906. A vigorous tree. Extremely rare in Seattle: Arboretum has three #155-52 in 5S-9E; U.W. has one W of parking lot E-2. Pink buds open to white, early, flowers; single or semi-double, 5–15 petals; 1½" (2") wide, as many as 8 per cluster. Flowerstems hairless, to 1⅝" long; calyx tube lightly hairy on the outside, clearly so inside. Fruit sparse, red or purplish-red, ½–⅝" wide, with a large scar where the calyx was.]

[*M.* × ***Hartwigii*** **'Katherine'** = *M.* 'Katherine'—Found *ca.* 1928 in Rochester, NY. Named and distributed in 1943. A small, weak, dense tree. Rare in Seattle: Arboretum has #952-48 in 8S-9E, 21½' × 1'10" × 24' wide (1994); 1400 Boren Ave has one. Profuse pink buds open to light pink flowers, fading to white; large (to 2⅛" wide), double (20–26 petals), with narrow petals. Compared to *M.* 'Blanche Ames' it has earlier, larger, fewer flowers with more petals. Leaves narrow, hairless, finely and sharply toothed. Few fruit set: ⅓" wide, yellow, sometimes with a tawny reddish blush, hard and somewhat shiny, faintly ribbed, with a big calyx scar, on stems to 1⅝" long. An alternate-year bearer.]

[*M*. 'Henrietta Crosby'—Originated in 1939; introduced in 1947; named in 1955. A rosybloom crabapple. Extremely rare in Seattle: vacant lot N of 9822 62nd Ave S has one; one at 5233 Kensington Pl N. (Neither of these trees is a *certain* i.d.) Flowers deep magenta, fading to pink; like those of *M*. × *Eleyi* but the petals a bit darker. The leaves are narrower, less hairy; leaf teeth sharp. Fruit profuse; roundish but usually longer, ≤1⅛"; dark red, bloomy; calyx nippled; skin with indented dots. Pulp bright pink, harsh tasting.]

[*M*. 'Henry Kohankie'—Almost certainly a *Malus* × *robusta*. Raised in 1930s at Henry Kohankie & Son nursery of Ohio; registered in 1965. Rare in Seattle: at 5268 15th Ave NE, in back by the alley one is N of a *M*. 'Irene'; NE corner of 12th Ave E & E Lynn St has one. Pink buds open to white flowers 1⅓–1⅞" (in the manner of the *Malus* × *robusta* group). Fruit edible, late ripening (*i.e.,* late October), beautiful carmine-red and green-yellow, shiny, 'Dolgo'-like, to 1½" long on 1¼" long hairy stems; calyx persists.]

[*M*. 'Hopa' (*M. baccata* × *M. Sieversii* 'Niedzwetzkyana')—Hopa crabapple. From South Dakota. Not an intentional cross. Introduced in 1920. *Hopa* means beautiful in the Sioux language. The most common rosybloom crabapple in Seattle: Green Lake Church of 7th Day Adventists has 8; SW corner of 39th Ave NE & NE 77th St has 7 big old ones; Mt Pleasant Cemetery, on W side, in the middle, has one 25' × 3'11½" × 39½' wide. Flowers large (1⅝–1¾" wide), bright purplish-pink; petals spread widely, fade to rosy color; parts hairy; stem to 1⅛" (2") long but usually ¾" or less; sepals ⅜" long, more or less reflexed. Leaves like those of *M. Sieversii* 'Niedzwetzkyana', with teeth blunt except on shoots. Fruit roundish, ¾–1⅛" long, like tomatoes in their yellow-pink to orange-red color and shape. Calyx usually drops but can persist and turn into fleshy bumps. Pulp mealier than that of *M*. 'Almey' and pinkish, of bearable flavor; good for jelly. Fruit dropped by November. Fruit stems usually <¾"; to ⅞".]

[*M. hupehensis* (Pamp.) Rehd. = *M. theifera* Rehd.—Tea *or* Hupeh crabapple. From China, Assam, Bhutan. Named in 1910. Uncommon in Seattle: Locks #15B has 4 (+ 3 *M*. × *robusta*); 2008 E Louisa St has a street-tree, W of a 'Hopa'; SE corner of 23rd Ave NE & NE 90th St. Flowers large (2" wide), cherry-like, with broad white petals; parts essentially hairless. Flowerstems to 2⅛" long. Blooms relatively late, in mid-May. Fruits shiny, abundant, longstemmed, yellow-red to murky or pleasing red, ⅜–⅝" long or wide. Foliage healthy and attractive. Leaves reddish when young, becoming shiny, large, wide and spoonlike in shape (or narrowly tapered and not spoonlike—leaf size and shape varies considerably). In general, *Malus hupehensis* is a superior ornamental, especially strong in its dark, glossy leaf character and elongated branching habit. The trunks fork low and branches spread wide—excellent for espaliering. Can be a large shrub.]

[*M. hupehensis* f. *rosea* Rehd. = *M. theifera* 'Rosea'—Rose Tea crabapple. A natural seedling variant with *pink* flowers. Named in 1915. In North American commerce ≤1931. Rare in Seattle: Meadowbrook Playfield has *ca*. 9; 6 on the N side of S Bangor St, east of 51st Ave S, 2 on the S side; SE corner substation @36th Ave NE & NE 110th St has 3.]

[*M*. 'Hyslop'—Origin North American, but the details are lost. It was old and common by 1869; still in commerce. Grown mainly for its edible fruit. Rare in Seattle: 24th Ave NE, north of NE 47th St (Blockbuster Video) has a street-tree, E side (+ other kinds). Pink buds open to white flowers. Fruit very brilliant dark red or purplish, thickly bloomed, roundish, 1½". Ripens late in the season. An alternate-year bearer, sometimes annual.]

[*M.* 'Indian Magic' (*M. Zumi* 'Calocarpa' × *M.* 'Almey')—A rosybloom seedling raised *ca.* 1955 at Vincennes, IN. First flowered in 1958. Introduced for trial *ca.* 1969; named in 1975. Rare in Seattle: 7313 33rd Ave NE has a street-tree (+ a *M.* 'Radiant' N of it); 6544 Cleopatra Ave NW has a street-tree; 25th Ave NE, south of NE 75th St has a street-tree on the W side (+ 7 older *M.* × *moerlandsii* 'Profusion' and a *M.* 'Hopa'). Tree broadly rounded, too low and wide for ideal street-tree usage. Red buds open to showy rose-pink flowers 1½" wide. Fruit abundant; ⅝" long; with small calyx scars; glossy red changing to golden-orange, then brown; persisting and *gorgeous* August through November. Leaf purplish when young, later dark green, coarsely toothed, often lobed on shoots.]

[*M. ioensis* (Wood) Britt. = *M. coronaria* var. *ioensis* Wood—Prairie, Iowa, *or* Western crabapple. Named after Iowa, where it was first distinguished in 1860 (as a variety of *M. coronaria*). Pink buds open to white, fragrant flowers. Similar to *M. coronaria* but with narrower, less lobed, fuzzy leaves, and smaller fruit. Fruit like abundant dull green golfballs. Seattle had specimens at the U.W. and Seattle Science Center, but they were cut down—sacrificed at the altar of Progress. All we have *now* is the following cv:]

[*M. ioensis* 'Plena' = *M.* 'Bechtel'—Bechtel crabapple. Discovered *ca.* 1840; cultivated since 1888. Until about the 1970s it was the most-planted American crabapple. Its disease-susceptibility, plus the ascension of better clones such as *M. coronaria* var. *dasycalyx* 'Klehm's Improved Bechtel' caused its decline. Rare in Seattle: 1820 E McGraw St has one; Ravenna Ave NE, north of NE 73rd St has 2 street-trees, E side (a young 'Klehm's Improved Bechtel' on W side); 17th Ave, 68' N of Denny Way has a 25½' × 2'1½" street-tree, E side. A small tree, with scaly bark, blooming late in the season—late May. Flowers release a delicious sweet violet fragrance; 2–2½" wide; fully double (20–33 petals); sepals slender. Fruit few or none, 1¼" wide, green.]

[*M.* 'Irene'—A *Malus* × *Eleyi* seedling raised *ca.* 1939 in Des Moines, IA. Introduced in 1951. A low, broad and dark rosybloom crabapple. Extremely rare in Seattle: Arboretum #285-62 is 100' SE of Lake Washington Blvd & Roanoke St, 16' × 2'4¾" × 33' wide; at 5268 15th Ave NE, in back by the alley one is south of a *M.* 'Henry Kohankie'. Flowers dark red with white centers. Sparse very dark fruit to 1⅜" long, 1⅛" wide, on stems to 2½" long. Its beet-red pulp tastes delicious.]

M. 'Jay Darling'—see *M.* × *Eleyi*

[*M.* 'John Downie'—Found in 1875 in England. Introduced to the U.S. ≤1927. Grown nearly exclusively for its edible fruit. Extremely rare in Seattle: U.W. has a tree NE of the Burke Museum (i.d. tentative). Pink buds open to large white flowers. Fruit exceptionally ornamental as well as delicious, 1¼" long, orange-yellow blushed with scarlet. An alternate-year bearer.]

M. 'Katherine'—see *M.* × *Hartwigii* 'Katherine'

[*M.* 'Kelsey'—Kelsey crabapple. First flowered in 1966; introduced in 1969–70. Manitoba's official Centennial tree. A rosybloom crabapple. Extremely rare or now nonexistent in Seattle: Harvard Ave E, north of E Roy St, had 3 street-trees *cut down* ≤Aug. 2003. Flowers profuse, purplish-red, 1–2" wide, semi-double, of 10–16 petals. Leaves first reddish, then bronzy, finally green with red veins. Fruit like blueberries, small (⅜–⅝"), dark purple, and bloomed; the calyx stays, very prominently sitting atop the ribbed end of the fruit. Grows 15–20' tall, of low-branching, compact, upright-rounded habit.]

[*M.* 'Kingsmere'—An open-pollinated seedling of *M. Sieversii* 'Niedzwetzkyana'. Raised in 1920 in Ottawa. One of the original rosybloom crabapples; selected in 1930. Extremely rare in Seattle: 5563 S Holly St has one (or a similar clone; i.d. tentative) 30' × 5'0" (2002). A small tree; the habit like orchard apple (*M. × domestica*). Deep carmine buds open to purple-pink, 2⅛" wide flowers. Fruit 1⅛", crimson over purplish-brown, greenish-brown on the shady side, edible, excellent for jelly.]

[*M.* 'Kola' (*M. ioensis* 'Elk River' × 'Duchess' *or* 'Oldenburg' Russian apple)—A tetraploid from Brookings, SD; introduced in 1922. *Kola* means friend in the Sioux language. Extremely rare in Seattle: 24th Ave NE, south of NE 48th St, a street-tree, E side, (+ 5 *M.* 'Hopa', 1 *M. × domestica*, and a Blireiana Plum; 2321 NE 95th St substation has 3 (+ 2 *M. hupehensis*). Flowers 1⅞–2¼" wide, palest pink, fragrant. Among the earliest of the *M. coronaria* clan to bloom. Leaves broad and large, to 6¾" × 5¼"; weakly lobed; lightly hairy beneath at first, most hairs falling away, making leaves practically hairless by fall; stem to 2¾" (3½") long. Handsome orange fall color. Looks much like *M. coronaria*. Fruit profuse, 2⅜" wide, yellow-green, waxy, with quince-like fragrance. Fascinating.]

[*M.* Lancelot® = *M.* 'Lanzam'—Introduced in 1991. Extremely rare in Seattle: the Arboretum has two #197-93 in 40-5W; 7307 33rd Ave NE has a street-tree (S of a rosybloom crabapple). Red buds open to white flowers 1–1¼" wide. Crisp green leaves, downy when young. Fruit lasts until the New Year; ¼–½" long; yellow-green to gold; calyx drops. Tree *dwarf*, slowly reaching 10' tall and 8' wide; branching erect and foliage dense.]

M. Lemoinei—see *M. × purpurea* 'Lemoinei'

M. 'Liset'—see *M. × moerlandsii* 'Liset'

[*M.* 'Louisa'—Selected in 1962; introduced in the 1980s. Related to *M. baccata*. Rare in Seattle: Arboretum has #198-93 in 40-5W; 4545 48th Ave NE; 5512 29th Ave NE. Red buds open to pink flowers 1¼–1½" wide; petals widely spaced; stems slender and reddish. Fruit ⅜–½" long; lopsided; yellow with an orange-red blush; with a small calyx scar. Tree dwarf, to 15' tall and wide, with thin, strongly *weeping* branches that sprawl along the ground. Leaves rarely lobed; remain green long into fall.]

[*M.* 'Madonna'® PP 6672 (1989) = *M.* 'Mazam'—Bred by J.L. Fiala of Ohio. Named in 1979; introduced in 1987. Extremely rare in Seattle: 322 NW 78th St has a young street-tree to east (+ a *M. × floribunda* to west). Pink buds open to large (2½–3" wide), double, white, fragrant, flowers opening early, lasting long. Young leaves bronze. Fruit ½"; golden-yellow with red blush; a huge calyx scar with a central point. A compact upright tree to 18' tall and 10' wide.]

[*M.* 'Mary Potter' (*M. Sargentii* 'Rosea' × *M. atrosanguinea*)—Originated in 1939; named in 1955. Introduced in 1947. Rare in Seattle: Arboretum #1617-56 in 13-3W is 26' × 3'10½" × 31' wide; 30th Ave S, north of S Massachusetts St, south of S Atlantic St: 10 street-trees. Pink-red buds open to fragrant white flowers, 1" wide; the calyx, stems & sepals hairless. Fruit abundant, red, bloomed, ⅜–½", roundish; calyx drops. Tree broad, low, semi-pendulous, with a pretty branching habit. Notably flaky bark. Some leaves deeply lobed.]

[**M.** × *micromalus* Mak. = *M. Kaido* (Sieb. *ex* Wenz.) Pardé 1906, *non* Dipp. 1893—Kaido *or* Midget crabapple. Known only in cultivation; probably a *M. spectabilis* hybrid. Introduced from Japan to Europe; named in 1856. According to T. Makino, it was formerly called Kaido in Japan, a name now applied to *M. Halliana* and likely also to *M.* × *floribunda*. Common in Seattle but only as old trees; NW 62nd St, W of 32nd Ave NW has 3 street-trees, S side; the Arboretum has #411-53 in 2S-6E; U.W. has 6 S of Loew Hall (+ 3 *M.* × *floribunda*). Tree leafy, with long, slender dark leaves. Bark pale grayish, smooth. Dark carmine buds open to palest pink flowers 1½–2" wide; *early*—one of the first to bloom. Flowerstems and calyx tube lightly hairy. Fruit abundant; roundish; ribbed; ½–⅞" wide; first green, eventually yellow, red-blushed, turning butterscotch brown as it rots—similar to that of *M.* × *Scheideckeri;* the calyx usually drops. Though the fruit is not showy, in bloom and vigor the tree excells.]

[**M.** × *moerlandsii* 'Liset' = *M.* 'Liset' *or* 'Lizette'—A rosybloom crabapple raised <1938 in The Hague, the Netherlands. Sold in North America since ≤1958. Uncommon in Seattle: McClure School has 3 big ones on the E wall; 4115 Brooklyn Ave NE has 5 N of a big Hollywood Juniper; S.U. has a street-tree on Marion St 27' × 3'7" × 35' wide (1993). Flowers similar to those of *M.* × *moerlandsii* 'Profusion' but fuller (less space between the petals), less hairy parts, longer stems—to 1⅞". Tree much smaller growing; beginning upright and sometimes nearly columnar, it broadens in age. Foliage very dark purplish in early summer, army-green by late August. Leaves numerous, large, especially wide, giving the tree a bulky look. Fruit profuse, ½" (1"), very deep purplish red, at first thinly bloomed, with a conspicuous pale pit or "eye" where the calyx was. By November, the fruit is hideously dark, shiny, and not pretty.]

[**M.** × *moerlandsii* 'Profusion' = *M.* 'Profusion'—A rosybloom crabapple in North American commerce ≤1956. The name refers to the numerous flowers relative to those of *M.* × *purpurea*. The fruit, too, can be profuse. Common in Seattle: 1552 NW 52nd St has a street-tree; 11th Ave NW, north of NW 53rd St has 6 (+ 4 *M.* × *Scheideckerii* 'Hillieri'); 29th & 30th Aves, E Cherry St to Yesler Way: many City street-trees. Deep red buds open to violet-red flowers, fade to violet-pink; ≤1½" wide. A rich spectacle in full April bloom, then paler in May. Leaves reddish-purple when young, then (if not destroyed by scab) becoming bronzy-greenish, finally green changing to amber in October; midrib and stem remain purplish. Some sucker leaves are lobed at the middle. Spur leaves subtly toothed, almost untoothed except at the apex. Fruit deep red or purple with a few pale speckles near the stem, ⅜–½" wide, calyx scar usually small; stem to 1¼" long.]

[**M. Molten Lava*** = *M.* 'Molazam'—Bred by J.L. Fiala in Ohio; registered ≤1983. Very rare in Seattle: 921 NW 105th St has one W of the house. An elegant medium-size, broad semi-weeper, 12' tall × 15' wide. Sometimes topgrafted. Red-pink buds open to white, 1½" wide flowers. Fruit profuse, shiny orange-red, with small calyx scars, like those of *M. baccata* in size and shape: ½" long. At first partly hidden by the cherry-like leaves, the fruit persists. Fall foliage bright yellow. Distinctive yellowish bark in winter.]

M. Niedzwetzkyana—see *M. Sieversii* 'Niedzwetzkyana'

M. 'Oekonomierat Echtermeyer'—see *M.* 'Echtermeyer'

[**M. 'Ormiston Roy'**—Parentage not known. Named and introduced in 1954 in Iowa. Very rare in Seattle: 3100 block of Fuhrman Ave E has 3 street-trees, W side. Rose-red buds open to pale pink flowers, fading to pure white; 1½" wide; resembling those of *M.* × *floribunda*. Fruit shiny, green, yellow, then orange-yellow with a reddish blush; reddish after frost; ½"; abundant and *persistent into winter*. Leaf sharp-toothed, like that of *M. hupehensis*. Tree vigorous, wide, to 20' tall and 25' wide or more.]

M. Parkmanii—see *M. Halliana* 'Parkmanii'

[*M.* 'Pink Beauty'—A rosybloom crabapple seedling raised <1945 in Manitoba. Named and first sold ≤1957–58. Extremely rare in Seattle: U.W. had a prominent one 24' × 4'9" × 46' wide (1992) by the Communications Bldg. until 2004; a youngster has replaced the veteran. Flowers glowing rich rose, almost magenta-free; remaining bright. Leaf bluntish-toothed, reddish when young, maturing bluish-green, the fall color pretty like the yellow-orange of pencils. Fruit ¾–⅞" wide, dark red, prominently pale-speckled; calyx persists; pulp red; stem slender, to 1¼" long.]

[*M.* **Pink Princess**™ = *M.* 'Parrsi'—A *Malus Sargentii* seedling introduced ≤1988. It can be called a rosybloom crabapple. Extremely rare in Seattle: Golden Gardens Park has two *pl.* in 1993, by the road, uphill, E of the tracks. Purple buds open to pink flowers. Fruit bloomed purple, ¼–⅜" wide; calyx drops; pulp red. Leaves purplish when young, then dark green; yellow in fall; lobed on shoots; coated on both sides with short inconspicuous white hairs. Tree low and spreading broadly; pendulous in part; to 8' tall × 12' wide.]

[*M.* 'Pink Spires'—A rosybloom crabapple from Saskatchewan. Introduced ≤1966. Extremely rare in Seattle: 32nd Ave E & E John St vicinity has street-trees; Renton Ave S near S Barton St does, too. Symmetrical and narrowly upright, at least in youth. Dark lavender buds open to pink flowers; *early*. Leaves purple-red in spring, turning to bronzy-green in summer, spectacular red-orange in fall. Fruit purplish-red, ½", persistent.]

[*M.* 'Prairie Maid' (*M. Zumi* 'Calocarpa' × *M.* 'Van Eseltine')—Introduced ≤1988 by Simpson nursery of Vincennes, IN. It can be called a rosybloom crabapple. Extremely rare in Seattle: Arboretum has #199-93 in 40-5W; U.W. had two *pl.* 2005 between the Rose Garden and Guggenheim Hall. Reddish-purple buds open to profuse flowers, 1–1½" wide, deep pink fading to whitish. Fruit up to ½" wide, orange-red; calyx drops. Leaves rusty-coppery when young, with silver hairs; lobed strongly on new growth shoots. Tree compact, forks low, *broadly* rounded, medium sized.]

[*M.* 'Prairifire'—Introduced in 1982 by the University of Illinois, Urbana. It can be called a rosybloom crabapple. Common in Seattle: 3rd Ave NW, from N 49th St to Market has many street-trees; 31st Ave W, N of W Emerson St has many street-trees with a white-flowering crabapple. Crimson buds open to dark purplish-red flowers, not fading, 1⅝" wide. Leaves mostly unlobed; sharply toothed; deep red-purple when young, maturing dark tawny green, orange in fall. Fruit ⅜–½" long, shiny purplish-red; pulp red; calyx drops, leaving prominent scars; stem slender, to 1⅓" long. Tree low, dense, broadly rounded, to 20' tall and wide, or wider than tall. Winter bark dark red and cherry-like with numerous prominent lenticels.]

[*M.* 'Professor Sprenger'—Raised <1950 in The Hague, Netherlands. Introduced to commerce ≤1958; in North America only common since the 1970s. Said to be a *M.* × *Zumi* clone, leaves and flowers scarcely different yet with *big bold orange-red fruit*. Common in Seattle: 23rd Ave NE, N of NE 73rd St has 5 street-trees, E side; U.W. E of Meany Hall has 4 *pl.* in spring 1990. Red buds open to white flowers. Fruit orange-red, ⅝–¾" long—about the size and shape of those of *Malus* 'Hopa'. Leaves dark green.]

M. 'Profusion'—see *M.* × *moerlandsii* 'Profusion'

[*M. prunifolia* (Willd.) Borkh. = *M. asiatica* Nakai—Plumleaf crabapple. Plum-leaved apple. Pear-leaf crabapple. Inu crabapple. Highly variable; probably a hybrid. From Asia; but unknown in a wild state there. Introduced in 1758 to England. To the U.S. <1831. It is naturalized in parts of eastern North America and comes up wild in Seattle meadows. Uncommon in Seattle: 5914 8th Ave NW; 16th Ave E, north of E John St has 2 street-trees, E side; NW corner of 34th Ave S & S Walker St. Pink or red buds open to white flowers flushed with pink, 1½" wide, with long and hairless sepals. Fruit red, yellow or orange, ¾–1½" long, the calyx staying, often raised & bumpy. The flowers can be ±pinkish and to 2", and the fruit to 2⅜" in the var. *Rinki* (Koidz.) Rehd. = *M. Ringo* Sieb. *ex* Dipp.—Chinese apple. Chinese pear-leaf crabapple. Ringo. Ornamentally, *M. prunifolia* is no better in bloom than an orchard apple, but has large, colorful, persistent fruit. Its fall leaf color can be beautiful. But the tree is an alternate bearer, and scabby.]

[*M.* × *purpurea* (Barbier) Rehd. = *M. floribunda atropurpurea (cf. M.* × *Eleyi) (M. Sieversii* 'Niedzwetzkyana' × *M. atrosanguinea)* —Purple crabapple. It can be called a rosybloom crabapple. Originated *ca.* 1900 in France; introduced in 1910. Widely sold for decades; now extinct in commerce. Disease problems, scanty blooms, and better cultivars have rendered it an old-fashioned eyesore. Uncommon in Seattle: Rodgers Park has at least 7; Green Lake has some, east of the wading pool; a 20' street-tree on 16th Ave E just N of E Lynn St. Flowers magenta, 1–1⅜" (1¾") wide, sometimes limited to the top of the tree; *early* in the season. Fruit are like dark, hard, red-purple cherries; *ca.* ¾–1"; with prominent persistent calyces. Leaves sharply toothed, dark purple when young, aging to green.]

[*M.* × *purpurea* 'Aldenhamensis' = *M. aldenhamensis* hort.—Aldenham crabapple. Originated *ca.* 1912 in England. Introduced to the U.S. in 1923. It can be called a rosybloom crabapple. Previously much grown in North America, Aldenham crabapple has lost favor, and since the 1980s has rarely been sold. Extremely rare in Seattle: Locks bed #210 has one; U.W. has a likely Aldenham *seedling* between the Rose Garden and Guggenheim Hall (elongated wrong fruit shape unlike typical Aldenham). Unlike typical Purple crabapple, Aldenham is *dwarfish*, 10–12' (20') tall, the flowers (1⅔–2") appear weeks later and are semi-double (5–11 petals); it often blooms again in fall. Leaf teeth closely appressed, sharply toothed. Fruit abundant, ⅝–1⅛" wide, dark red-purple becoming lovely cherry-red, ribbed at the ends, speckled with tiny whitish freckles; hefty stems to 2¾" long; persistent calyces. Flavor plain.]

M. × *purpurea* 'Eleyi'—see *M.* × *Eleyi*

[*M.* × *purpurea* 'Lemoinei' = *M. Lemoinei* hort.—Lemoine crabapple. Introduced in 1922 by Lemoine nursery in France. To the U.S. in 1925. It can be called a rosybloom crabapple. Very commonly sold during the 1950s; ±commercially extinct now. Uncommon in Seattle: U.W. has 5 (+ a *M.* × *Eleyi*) E of Graves Hall; NE corner of Eastern Ave N & N 45th St has one; the Arboretum has #209-53 in 33-6E. More than one clone goes under the name 'Lemoinei' so the following description is tailored loosely enough to fit all of the variable specimens. Compared to typical Purple crabapple, 'Lemoinei' is more robust, often with a handsome trunk. It is slow to form flowerbuds (at age 10–12 years), and scabby right from the start, yet (for the little it's worth) less scabby than typical Purple crabapple. Flowers larger (1¾–2⅛" wide) but usually fewer, sometimes semi-double, of *superior redness*—supremely showy, a beautiful, pure sight. Leaves *often lobed*, and strongly so; often very *glossy*. Fruit purple-red or red, roundish but can be either wider than long or longer than wide, ½–1", the calyx stays or drops, the pulp is pinkish like that of *M.* 'Hopa', or reddish. Stems to 1⅛" and lightly hairy.]

[*M.* 'Radiant'—A *Malus* 'Hopa' seedling selected *ca.* 1940 in Minnesota; introduced in 1957–58. It can be called a rosybloom crabapple. Its name refers to the luminous color of the deep red buds opening to pinkish-red flowers. Like *M.* × *moerlandsii* 'Profusion' but blooms earlier, with not as dark an effect. Praised elsewhere, in Seattle it is unhealthy and fruitless, or bears too few attractive fruits, and set against too ugly a foliar backdrop. Uncommon in Seattle: the Arboretum has two #528-57 in 16-2W & 17-2W, the larger 25' × 3'0"; 2582 3rd Ave W has a street-tree; 419 Malden Ave E has 2 street-trees. Leaf reddish-purple when young, maturing green; sharp-toothed. Fruits pea-sized, persisting well, mimicking *Rosa canina* hips excellently: bright red on the sunny side, yellow-pink on the shady side, to ⅞" long; harsh-tasting yellow pulp; stem to 1½" long.]

[*M.* 'Red Barron' ('Red Baron')—Originated from the Arnold Arboretum. A rosybloom crabapple introduced ≤1984. Uncommon in Seattle: NW corner of Burke Ave N & N 37th St has 6 street-trees; 19th Ave E south of E Calhoun St has 2 street-trees, W side; 4606 Bagley Ave N has a street-tree. Very dark red buds open to dark solid pink flowers, 1½–1⅞" (2") wide. Leaves bronzy-red, fading quickly to bronzy-green with purplish venation; bluntish teeth; lightly hairy. Fruit dark to bright red, to ⅝" long, ribbed; calyx drops leaving a small to medium pit-scar; stem red, weakly hairy, 1⅓" long. Pulp pink or red, harsh-flavored. Habit compact and narrowly columnar to 18' tall and 8' wide. (A 'Red Baron' *orchard apple* was raised in Minnesota as a 'Golden Delicious' hybrid in 1926, selected in 1940, and named and introduced in 1969.)]

[*M.* 'Redfield' (*M.* 'Wolf River' apple × *M. Sieversii* 'Niedzwetzkyana')—A rosybloom crabapple bred in 1924 in Geneva, NY. Introduced for trial in 1938. Very rare in Seattle: 3804 E Crockett St has a huge one (*or* a similar clone such as 'Redford'). Flowers rosy-red, 1⅝" wide, amazingly similar to those of *M. Sieversii* 'Niedzwetzkyana' and scarcely different—'Redfield' has a white-wooly calyx and narrower petals. 'Redfield' leaves are rounded at the base rather than narrowed, as well as being broader, healthier and a bit hairier. Fruit giant, up to 3¾" wide, as large as an orchard apple; red skin; a white core surrounded by *red pulp*. Plenty are borne, but they are are marred visually by a bloomy coating, and the leaves being so dark and dull result in the tree not being ornamental in fruit. Fruit ripe from mid-August, into early October, fallen by November. Edible, but primarily a novelty to use in pie baking. Tree like an orchard apple in habit and looks.]

[*M.* 'Red Jade' PP 1497 (1956)—Introduced in 1953. Uncommon in Seattle: Arboretum #346-53 at the S end of the Japanese Garden parking lot is 13½' × 2'11½" × 29½' wide; 2566 5th Ave W has 2 street-trees; 8320 21st Ave NW. Buds ivory, tinted with faded lipstick-pink, opening white, 1–2" wide, fragrant, like those of *M. baccata*. Each flower like an orchard apple blossom yet the parts and leaves are only a little hairy. Fruit ⅝" long; first yellow-green with a pink blush, turning orange-red and then bright red; persistent—classic *M. baccata* type, as are the leaves. Tree a *weeper*. Not a vulgar mop like *Malus* 'Echtermeyer', 'Red Jade' grows broader.]

[*M.* Red Jewel™ PP 3267 (1972) = *M.* 'Jewelcole'—Introduced by Cole nursery of OH. Registered ≤1975. Common in Seattle: Green Lake has 36 *pl.* in 1997 SW of the Bathhouse Theatre; the SW & NW corners of 18th Ave E & E Prospect St have 5 street-trees. Pink buds open to pure white flowers, small, 1" wide or less. Fruit brilliant red ⅜–½"; persists and looks like holly berries; stem to 1¼" long. Flushes *early*, the bright green spring leaves contrast prettily with the persisting red fruit. Looks like a *M. Sieboldii* offspring; it may be a *M.* × *Zumi* offspring, with harder, longer-lasting fruit. Leaf persistently hairy on both sides, sometimes lobed. Habit upright pyramidal to 18' tall and 12' wide, with horizontal branching.]

113

[*M.* 'Red Siberian' = *M.* × *robusta* 'Red Siberian'—Originated in France. Described in 1803. In North American commerce since <1831. Uncommon in Seattle: U.W. has 3 fruitful and 2 fruitless trees (largest 48' × 5'6" × 47' wide 1992) between the Rose Garden and Guggenheim Hall. Fruit decidedly ornamental, borne in clusters, red, ¾–1" diameter; calyx stays or drops. '**Large Red Siberian**' is a vigorous, hardy tree, alternate-bearing, with larger fruit (to 1½"). Both of these, doubtless representing various clones, were formerly commonly grown for their edible fruit, but are now commercially extinct. A variation on the theme is *Malus* '**Yellow Siberian**'.]

[*M.* '**Red Silver**' (*M. baccata* × *M. Sieversii* 'Niedzwetzkyana')—A rosybloom crabapple bred in 1928 in South Dakota. Rare in Seattle: NE 40th St, opposite 48th Pl NE has 5 street-trees, N side; E Newton St, W of 23rd Ave E has a street-tree; SE corner of 30th Ave S & S King St has one, shade-stunted. Flowers deep red to china-rose, 1¼–1½" wide; petals narrow. Foliage reddish-bronze with *silvery* white hairs in spring, then dingy bronzy-green in summer. Leaf sharp-toothed; lobed on suckers. Fruit dark purplish-red, to ¾" long, calyx usually stays and can become fleshy; stem to 1" long or more. Too dark to be showy, not pleasant for eating raw, the fruit can be used for jelly. Tree can be an alternate bearer. Tree to 30' tall × 15' wide, with willowy branch tips tending to droop.]

[*M.* '**Robinson**'—A rosybloom crabapple introduced in the 1980s. Common in Seattle: NW corner of 30th Ave NW & NW 61st St has 6 street-trees; SE corner of Whitman Ave N & N 107th St has 9 street-trees; Decatur School has many (+ *M.* × *floribunda*) Tree vigorous, to 25' tall or more. Hyped as the fastest-growing crabapple. Crimson buds open to deep pink flowers. Leaves dark purple when young, becoming bronzy dark green with red veins, thinly coated beneath with white hairs; some *shoot leaves remarkably large and lobed;* edged with fine, sharp teeth; fall color can be handsome. Fruit dark red, at first bloomed, becoming glossy, ⅜–⅝"; has an orange pit where the calyx was; stem to 1⅞" long; pulp red, flavor ok.]

[*M.* × *robusta* (Carr.) Rehd. = *M. cerasifera* Zab., *non* Spach *(M. baccata* × *M. prunifolia)*— Cherry *or* Orchard crabapple. First raised ≤1815 in Europe. Uncommon in Seattle: Seward Park has 3 on bank W of the boulevard, *pl.* 1932; Locks #15B has 3 (+ 4 *M. hupehensis*). Numerous clones such as *Malus* 'Red Siberian' may be placed under the *robusta* banner. Purebred Siberian crabapple *(M. baccata)* was economically little valued because of its tiny fruits. So it was crossed with *M. prunifolia* to produce larger-fruited offspring, which were then cultivated as Siberian crabapples. (Bafflingly similar offspring can result from *M. baccata* × *M. domestica*, for which the name *M.* × *adstringens* has been used.) Since many *robusta* cultivars exist, the following description is almost uselessly general: Pink buds open to white flowers, 1½–2¾" wide, on trees looking like orchard apples (*M.* × *domestica*) but slenderer; leaves comparatively thin and scantily hairy; fruit like miniature apples, yellow, red-blushed, or wholly red, ¾–1¾". The calyx sometimes drops, sometimes is retained as a swollen bumpy tip; stems ¼–2". Old specimens of the trees can be enormous, 40–50' tall & wide, and when laden with colorful fruit in late summer or fall, are breathtakingly lovely.]

M. Rockii—see *M. sikkimensis* 'Rockii'

[*M.* '**Rosseau**'—One of the original rosybloom crabapples, raised in 1920 in Ottawa. Selected in 1930 and named. Very rare; out of commerce. May not be in Seattle, but a *possible* specimen is at 5810 17th Ave NW. Maroon-red buds open to rose-red flowers 1⅝–1¾" wide; petal claws white. Foliage bronzy-green in spring, bright red in fall. Fruit annual, bright red, 1", hangs until late fall. Tree rounded, dense, to 40' tall.]

[*M.* "**Rosybloom**"—The name rosybloom crabapple is applied generally to dozens of trees, either intentional hybrids or open-pollinated seedlings or descendents of *M. Sieversii* 'Niedzwetzkyana', which retain more or less the purplish to rosy floral color, and usually feature reddish young leaves as well. The first trees so called were 33 raised in 1920–21 in Ottawa. Later on, W.R. Leslie of Manitoba raised 1,700 rosybloom seedlings and selected 8 of the best for introduction. Still other breeders and nurseries added to the rosybloom group, and not a year goes by without Mother Nature producing another somewhere. The present volume has 38 which may be called rosybloom cultivars.]

[*M.* **Royal Fountain**™ = *M.* 'Huber'—A weeping rosybloom *almost identical* to but less disease-prone than *Malus* 'Echtermeyer'. Introduced in 1992–93. Flowers rose-red to deep pink. Fruit ⅜"; deep red. Foliage purplish-bronze most of the season. Though none are known definitely in Seattle, youngsters must be here, having been in our nurseries.]

[*M.* 'Royalty'—A rosybloom seedling introduced in 1962. Common in Seattle: 212 N 52nd St has 4 street-trees; 414 N 63rd St has a street-tree; 326 NW 83rd St has a street-tree; Eckstein School has one in front. Flowers purple, large, almost like the leaf color, amazingly dark. Leaves purple, thin, hairless, shiny, sharp-toothed. Fruit bloomy, blueberry-sized (½–⅝"), too dark purple to be showy; calyx stays. The *darkest foliage of all crabapples*, passing for a Purpleleaf Plum. At best, weak scab disease resistence; can be sparse-crowned and ugly. When present, green root suckers are an eyesore.]

[*M.* 'Ruby Luster'—A rosybloom offspring introduced ≤1991. Extremely rare in Seattle: Nordic Heritage Museum has 2 against the W wall. Scarlet red flowers. Leaves lobed on shoots. Fruit sparse, dull red-brown, silver-specked, 1–1¼"; pulp crisp, blood-red, acceptably flavored or even delightful; calyx stays. Bark can be cherry-like.]

[*M. Sargentii* Rehd. = *M. Sieboldii* var. *Sargentii* Rehd.—Sargent *or* Pygmy crabapple. Introduced in 1892 to the U.S. from Japan; not known wild in Japan. Long widely planted and popular. It does not hybridize readily but breeds ±true when raised from its own seed. Common in Seattle; even some *wild* offspring here. Woodland Park Zoo Rose Garden has one 18' × 1'11" × 31' wide (1993); NW corner of 4th Ave N & Galer St has 8 street-trees; SW corner of 40th Ave E & E Boston St has 7 topgrafted street-trees. Palest pink buds open to pure white flowers, 1" wide; the roundish petals cupped around a heart of gold anthers; very fragrant. Fruits red, pea-sized (⅓"), lovely against the yellow leaves in October, turning soft early but hanging well; sweet flavored like rosehips. Leaves dark green, lobed on strong shoots, hairy above and beneath. A scab-free shrub or bushy, broad little tree. *M. Sargentii* 'Tina' = *M.* 'Tina'—Introduced ≤1974, is dwarfer than typical *M. Sargentii*, claimed to grow only 4–5' tall. Topgrafted usually.]

M. Sargentii 'Candymint'—see *M.* 'Candymint'

[*M.* × *Scheideckeri* Späth *ex* Zab. (*M. floribunda* × *M. prunifolia*)—Scheidecker crabapple. From Germany in 1887. Common in Seattle: U.W. has one 21' × 3'2" × 24' wide (1992) between the Rose Garden and Guggenheim Hall; 4710 15th Ave NE (The Wilsonian) has one; NW corner of Whitman Ave N & N 48th St has 4 street-trees. Pale red buds open to pale pink flowers, fading white, semi-double, 9–14 (20) petals; 1⅜–1¾" wide, on downy stems; calyx woolly; 5 styles. Flowers like those of *Malus* 'Blanche Ames' except hairier, with shorter stems. Leaves long, slender, sharply toothed, hairy on both sides, especially beneath. Fruit often scarce, yellow-green, finally orange-juice color, roundish, slightly ribbed, ½–¾", at most ⅞" wide; usually dropping the calyx; on a lightly hairy stem to 1⅞" long. Flavor bland. Tree small and bushy; slow.]

[*M.* × *Scheideckeri* 'Hillieri' = *M.* 'Hillieri'—In commerce ≤1942. Uncommon in Seattle: 5th Ave NW, north of NW 70th St has 7 street-trees (both sides); 11th Ave NW, north of NW 53rd St, W side has 4 street-trees (grafted on reverting *M.* × *domestica*) (+6 *M.* × *moerlandsii* 'Profusion'). Differs from *M.* × *Scheideckeri* in having less doubled flowers, and greater vigor. Deep red buds open to pink flowers which fade nearly white; single or semi-double (5–10 petals); to 1½" wide; in clusters of 5–8; calyx tube and stems hairy. Fruit ⅜–¾" wide, yellow to orange.]

[*M.* 'Selkirk'—Raised in Manitoba. A rosybloom crabapple seedling; widely tested and even sold (as 'MR 457') before being named 'Selkirk' in 1962. Uncommon in Seattle: 1902 N 46th St has 2 street-trees; 25th Ave E, north of E Lynn S has 2 street-trees, E side; 3rd Ave N, just N of Newton St has a street-tree, E side. Tree upright vase-shaped, spreading in age, rounded, to 25' tall and wide. Flowers 1½–2⅜" wide, deep purplish-pink, with rounded petals; stamens long and prominent. Leaves *glossy*, reddish-green changing to dark greenish-bronze, then dark green; leaf teeth blunt or barely sharp. Fruit very glossy, ¾–1" wide, with a prominent calyx scar; ribbed; *bright cherry-red, early, abundant, extremely attractive;* pulp pink or red, plain to good-tasting; stem to 2" long.]

[*M.* 'Sentinel'—Named in 1978. Rare in Seattle: 27 (+10 *M.* Sugar Tyme®) street-trees on W Government Way & Gilman Ave W, west of Williams Ave W. It certainly has *M. baccata* in its background. *Narrowly upright* to 20' tall × 12' wide. Red buds open to white flowers, tinged pale pink. Leaves dark green; some lobes. Fruit showy, dark red, ½" long, persistent; pulp yellow; stem short, to ⅝" long.]

[*M.* "Siberian"—Most trees called Siberian crabapples are *M. baccata*, and *M.* × *robusta* cultivars such as 'Red Siberian'.]

[*M. Sieboldii* (Reg.) Rehd. = *M. Toringo* Sieb. 1856, *non* Nakai 1916—Toringo crabapple. (In Japanese, *to-ringo* is applied to *M. prunifolia* var. *Rinki*, while *M. Sieboldii* is known as *zumi.*) From Japan. In the narrow sense, Siebold crabapple is a bushy little tree with yellow fruit, while larger-growing, more variable forms of the species are var. ***arborescens*** Rehd. (= *M. Toringo* Nakai 1916, *non* Sieb. 1856). But in a practical sense intergrading sizes and fruit colors argue for only one name—to cover shrubs or trees, with fruit variously yellow, orange or red. Rare in Seattle: U.W. has 2 SW of Husky Stadium, and 5 bordering E-2 parking lot (+*M. baccata*, *M.* × *domestica* & *M.* × *Hartwigii*). Red or reddish-pink buds open to profuse white or slightly pink flowers with downy stems and sepals. Leaves characteristically *lobed* on strong shoots (sometimes almost like those of the Amur maple), persistently hairy on both sides; usually of a tawny cast. Fruit usually yellow-orange (the color of orange juice); roundish; ¼–⅜"; calyx drops. Stems to 1" or more, hairy.]

M. Sieboldii var. *Zumi*—see *M.* × *Zumi*

[*M. Sieversii* (Ldb.) M. Roem. 'Niedzwetzkyana' = *M. pumila* var. *Niedzwetzkyana* (Dieck) Schneid. = *M. Niedzwetzkyana* Dieck—Redvein *or* Russian Purple crabapple. Turkestan apple. From Turkestan, SW Siberia. The ancestor of nearly all rosybloom and purpleleaf crabapples. In 1891 the *purplish-pigmented* clone of *M. Sieversii* was named after Julian Niedziecki (1845–1918), Austrian geologist and traveller who collected plants in Turkestan. "*M. Niedzwetzkyana*" was described and introduced to cultivation based on a garden specimen grown from seeds of a tree found in the Ili District of Central Asia. To call 'Niedzwetzkyana' a *species* stretches credibility. It is a cultivar—of what species is the only question; *M. Sieversii* itself may not be a distinctly valid species, just a mere version of another species. In any case 'Niedzwetzkyana' was much planted, but is now commercially extinct. Uncommon in Seattle: U.W. has 15 (+ 1 *M.* ×*purpurea*) between Denny and Balmer Halls; Green Lake has 9 by NW tennis courts, largest 26' × 3'7¼"; View Ridge Swim & Tennis Club by Sand Point Way & NE 77th St has 5 (+ 12 *M.* ×*floribunda*). Scabby, yet leafy withal, of a tired bronze-yellow cast. Fruit few, dull deep purple, *large*, often 2" or more (to 2¾"+). Blooms similar to those of *M.* 'Hopa' but narrower in petal, with a less bounteous display, on shorter flowerstems.]

[*M. sikkimensis* (Wenz.) Koehne *ex* Schneid. '**Rockii**' = *M. Rockii* Rehd.—Himalayan *or* Rock crabapple. From W China. Named in 1933. Extremely rare in Seattle: two Arboretum #1288-56 (979-58?) in 17-3W are old and large; a few private gardens have young trees. Pink buds open to white flowers; floral parts lightly hairy. Fruit profuse, first pale green, lightly hairy, teardrop-shaped, a pit where the calyx was, red on its sunny side by early October; much of the crop goes soft and red-brown by mid- or late-October, at which time it tastes just like applesauce.]

[*M.* '**Snowcloud**' PP 2913 (1969) ('Snow Cloud') (*M. Hartwigii* 'Katherine' × *M.* 'Almey')—Introduced in 1970. Rare in Seattle: 18th Ave E, north of E Galer St has 9 street-trees, W side (+ 1 *M.* × *Scheideckeri*); 4321 NE 58th St has 3 street-trees; 6212 45th Ave NE has 2 street-trees. Deep pink buds open to masses of pure white flowers 2–3" wide; 13–15 petals; hairy stems and calyx tube. Leaves narrow, dark green, with sharp teeth; lightly hairy while young. Twig bark exfoliates. Fruit sparse, yellow with a pink blush, ½" wide, a pit where the calyx was; stem 1¼" long, *swollen*. Tree vigorous, upright when young, broadening in age. Scabby and scale-infested.]

[*M.* '**Snowdrift**'—A chance seedling, likely a *M. baccata;* named & introduced in 1965. Uncommon in Seattle: 31st Ave S, S Jackson St to Yesler Way has many City street-trees, as does 30th Ave S, S Norman St to S Dearborn St. A straight-trunked, strong grower 15–25' tall; compact, rounded; of good street-tree form. Also used as a commercial pollenizer. Pink-red buds open to white flowers, fragrant, cupped, 1¼–1¾" wide; petals broad; stem to 2¼" long. Leaves glossy, with fine, sharp teeth; very pest resistant. Fruit abundant, persistent, glossy orange-red, ⅜–½" wide; calyx drops; stem long and slender.]

[*M. spectabilis* (Ait.) Borkh. = *M. spectabilis* 'Flore Pleno' *or* 'Plena' *or* 'Rosea Fl. Plena' = *M.* 'Frau Luise Dittmann'—Chinese crabapple. Chinese Flowering (crab-)apple. Chinese Double Flowering crabapple. Showy Chinese crabapple. Tai tang crabapple. Not known wild; long cultivated in N China—maybe the oldest ornamental crabapple. Grown in the West ≤1780. Much sold by U.S. nurseries in 1800s and earlier 1900s, but since the 1970s, ±discarded in favor of better cultivars. Rare in Seattle: SW corner of 14th Ave & E Columbia St has 2; U.W. has 2 between the Rose Garden and Bagley Hall, larger 25' × 3'2" × 29' wide (1992). Red buds open to soft pink fragrant flowers, 1⅛–2⅛" wide, double (13–16 petals), in scanty clusters against a sea of foliage. Leaves narrow, highly *glossy* above, pale lettuce-green and hairy on veins beneath; often with a yellowish tint. Fruit in mid-September is yellow, red-blushed, roundish, ¾" long or sometimes larger (to ⅞" or rarely even 1⅛"); calyx persistent; *stem thickened markedly*. An alternate-year bearer. Tardily deciduous.]

[*M.* '**Spring Snow**' PP 2667 (1966)—Introduced in 1965–66 in Hamburg, IA. Thought to be a *M.* 'Dolgo' seedling. Rare in Seattle: NW 56th St, between 32nd & 30th Ave NW has street-trees, S side; 6th Ave W & W McGraw St vicinity has street-trees. Compact habit; *branches upswept*. Flowers single, fragrant, produced in masses of pure white; *nearly sterile* (ovary usually absent). Leaves rich bright green. Fruit ¾–⅞" long; yellow with reddish blush; calyx usually drops; pulp tart and good.]

[*M*. 'Strawberry Parfait' PP 4632 (1981) *(M. hupehensis × M. atrosanguinea)*—Introduced in 1982. It can be called a rosybloom crabapple. Very rare in Seattle but apt to be more frequently planted; 814 35th Ave has 3 street-trees. A little tree, reported eventually to 25' tall; vase shaped, spreading. Flowers fragrant, pink with rose margins. Leaves reddish-purple when young, sparsely hairy; mature leaves thick, *glossy*, dark green, very finely sharp-toothed. Fruit often sparse, ½–¾" wide, yellow with red blush or glossy orange-red, with a large, shallow calyx scar.]

[*M*. **Sugar Tyme**® PP 7062 (1989) ('Sugartime') = *M*. 'Sutyzam' —From Michigan; named Sugar Tyme® ≤1983. Common in Seattle: 4132 Burke Ave N has 4 street-trees; W Boston St, east of 1st Ave W has 2 street-trees, S side; NE Ravenna Blvd, east of 21st Ave NE has 9 street-trees, S side. Tree vigorous, upright-spreading to oval (18' tall × 15' wide); good street-tree form. Pale pink buds open to white flowers, 1" wide. Leaf crisp green, slender, hairy, sharply toothed usually but some are bluntly toothed, almost never lobed. Fruit at first bloomy green with a red blush, becoming rich red ¼–½" (⅝"); persistent mid-September through January; *large* calyx scars; yellow pulp; slender red 1" stem.]

[*M*. 'Sundog'—A rosybloom crabapple from Manitoba; selected in 1939, introduced in 1947. Named for the prairie "winter rainbows" often popularly termed sundogs. Very rare in Seattle: U.W. has one between the Rose Garden and Guggenheim Hall; 2215 Lake Washington Blvd. E. has one; 5015 44th Ave NE has one; Arboretum #216-48 is in 33-5E. Tree begins life with columnar habit but ends up widely vase-shaped. Red buds open to huge, profuse, palest pink flowers. Young leaves red. Quite sumptuous in full bloom. By mid-June the *glossiness* of the fruit is striking. In September the tree has copious, gorgeous fruit, to ⅞" long, deep scarlet-red, shiny, contrasting well with the dark green leafy crown; stem to 2⅛"; the fruit falls in October. Leaves to 5" × 3"; can turn yellowish on the edges from some disorder.]

M. 'Tina'—see under *M. Sargentii*

[*M. toringoides* (Rehd.) Hughes = *M. bhutanica* (W.W. Smith) J.B. Phipps = *M. transitoria* var. *toringoides* Rehd.—Cutleaf crabapple. From W China—called by E. Wilson "the mountain fastnesses of the Chino-Thibetan borderland." To the U.S. in 1908. Its 1915 specific name means *Toringo* (see *M. Sieboldii*), and Greek *-oides*, resemblance. The 1911 *bhutanica* epithet resurrected in 1994 was first validly published, and technically must replace the familiar *toringoides* name. Extremely rare in Seattle: U.W. has 3 between the Rose Garden and Guggenheim Hall (largest 25' × 4'0" × 29' wide in 1992); Arboretum #574-48A in 13-2W is 34½' × 2'11" (+ two #35-60 cv. 'Macrocarpa' in 33-6E; fruit to 1⅛" long). Flowers *late* in the season; ≤1" wide; white; very downy parts. Shoot leaves *strongly lobed*. Attractively rugged, oak-like habit of growth, not at all dense. Foliage can be dingy appearing—looking thirsty. Fruit profuse, ⅝" long. In June it is waxy with a bloom; in mid-September, yellow-green, red-cheeked, pear shaped, often markedly narrowed to the stem; at the peak of its showy red color in late October and early November. An alternate-year bearer.]

[*M*. 'Transcendent'—Unknown history. Still in the nursery trade, it was grown as early as 1844. One of the very best eating crabapples; widely planted. Rare in Seattle: a *possible* specimen is a street-tree on 24th Ave NE, north of NE 48th St (Travelodge), E side (+ *M*. 'Hopa' *et al.*). Tree robust and broad, to 25' tall or more. Young parts downy at first. Pink buds open to white flowers, 1⅝" wide. Fruit to 1¾", red-striped on a golden-yellow background, or nearly all reddish; ripe late August through mid-September. Pulp dark yellow, hard, delicious.]

[*M. transitoria* (Batal.) Schneid. **Golden Raindrops**™ = *M.* 'Schmidtcutleaf'—Introduced in 1991–92. A highly distinctive and promising little tree; how it differs from typical Tibetan/NW China *M. transitoria* trees is unknown. Likely too bushy for ideal street-tree usage. Common in Seattle: 820 S Rose St has a street-tree 18' × 1'11"; 55th Ave S, south of Seward Park Ave S has many street-trees; 1618 N 48th St has 2 street-trees. Healthy foliage like Amur Maple; that is, red shoots bearing *glossy, lobed* leaves. Fruit profuse, clear golden-yellow, ⅜" wide.]

[*M. Tschonoskii* (Maxim.) Schneid. = *Eriolobus Tschonoskii* (Maxim.) Rehd.—Largeleaf *or* Pillar crabapple. From Japan, where it is called O-urajiro-no-ki *or* Zumi-no-ki. Introduced to the U.S. in 1892. Uncommon in Seattle: 25th Ave NE, south of NE 75th St has 6 street-trees; S Lane St, MLK Way to 32nd Ave S: many City street-trees, as does S Rose St, 7th Ave S to Dallas Ave S. A species with ho-hum flowers and worthless fruit, but of strong constitution, attractive narrow form and *flaming* fall color—burgundy to orange. Pink buds open to white flowers, 1¼" wide. Fruit usually sparse and not showy, to 1¼", yellow-green or brownish, hard and sour. Leaves up to 6" × 3½".]

[*M.* 'Van Eseltine' *(M. spectabilis* 'Plena' × *M. arnoldiana)*—Introduced in 1938 as *Malus* 'Geneva'; renamed 'Van Eseltine' in 1943. Uncommon in Seattle: SE corner of 11th Ave E & E Lynn St has 10 street-trees; 4004 Beach Dr SW (S of SW Andover St) has 6; Nordic Heritage Museum S wall has one *ca.* 30' tall. Tree begins as notably narrow, but flares out with age. Large bright mahogany-red buds open to very large rose and white flowers, 2–2⅜" wide, double, 13–20 petals; calyx *very broad;* stem 1½" long. Leaves glossy light green, slender, finely sharp-toothed, hairless; stems red. Fruit sparse, small, pear-shaped, yellow or with a red blush or entirely pale red, ¾" wide with *huge calyx scars.*]

[*M.* 'Vanguard'—A *Malus* 'Hopa' seedling selected in 1940; named and introduced in 1963. Very rare in Seattle: Qwest bldg. on 14th Ave NW between NW 63rd & 64th St has 2 street-trees (a Carrière Hawthorn between them), the taller (N) 28' & stouter (S) 3'8" around; St. Demetrios Church (2100 Boyer Ave E) has 3 in courtyard. A rosybloom crabapple, flushing relatively early. Flowers rosy-red, 1⅜–2" wide. Leaves reddish while young, very big, very lightly hairy. Fruit to ⅞" long, beautiful bright red; calyx drops; stem to 1½" long; flavor poor. Tree vase-shaped in youth, slowly growing wider.]

[*M.* **Weeping Candied Apple**® PP 4038 (1977) = *M.* Candied Apple® = *M.* 'Weepcanzam'— Introduced ≤1978. Very rare in Seattle: Blaine School (2550 34th Ave W): 5' tall S of the bldg. A 10–15' tall rosybloom branching broadly horizontally to pendulously, with an irregular pattern. Red buds open to pink flowers, 1" wide. Leaves heavy-textured, purplish when young, then dark green with an overcast of red; hairy; sharp-toothed. Fruit bright cherry-red, ⅜–⅝" wide, with a calyx pit, stem to 1⅝" long; pulp harshly astringent; persistent until February or March.]

[*M.* 'Wintergold' ('Winter Gold')—Originated in Holland. In U.S. commerce since ≤1970s. Rare in Seattle: S Thistle St, 8th to 12th Ave S has many City street-trees; E Alder St, MLK Way to 32nd Ave S has many City street-trees, as does E Jefferson St. Pink buds open relatively late in spring to white flowers, 1–1½" wide, on hairless slender stems to 1½" long. Young growth lightly hairy. Leaves can be remarkably deeply lobed; edged with sharp teeth. Fruit shiny, greenish-yellow to clear-yellow, or with an orange, beige or pink blush; ⅓–½" wide; calyx persistent or (usually) drops.]

[*M. yunnanensis* (Franch.) Schneid. var. *Veitchii* (Veitch) Rehd.—Veitch crabapple. From central China. In U.S. commerce ≤1934. Extremely rare in Seattle: Arboretum #838-49 NE of Lake Washington Blvd. & E Miller St is 30' × 3'11¾" × 41' wide; U.W. has 1 between the Rose Garden and Bagley Hall; Locks bed #9. Tree fastigiate in youth, becoming vase-shaped and ultimately broad. Fall color superb orange and scarlet. In flower and fruit it is *not* showy. In this regard it recalls *M. Tschonoskii*—denser, richer green in summer leaf color, and more sparing in fruit. *Late* to bloom. Greenish-white buds open to white *Sorbus*-like flowers in dense, flattened clusters. Each flower is ¾" wide; the petals white, then orange. Leaves large (to 7⅛" × 4¼"; stem to 2½" long), scabfree, but off-color. Fruit plentiful, dull, slightly hairy, first greenish-pink, then red on the sunny side, pale-brown dotted, round, ½–⅝" wide; pulp grainy.]

[*M. × Zumi* (Matsum.) Rehd. 'Calocarpa' = *M. calocarpa* hort. = *M. Zumi* var. *calocarpa* (Rehd.) Rehd.—Redbud crabapple. From Japan. Raised in 1890; introduced to cultivation in 1905. Common in Seattle: 17th Ave E & E Mercer St has 5; E Jefferson St, 25th Ave to MLK Way has many City street-trees, as does E Fir St. A markedly dense small tree, its branches spreading to form a crown ultimately wider than tall. Red buds open to white flowers which totally blanket the tree, 1–1⅓" (1¾") wide. Leaves tawny, especially beneath; persistently hairy on both sides, or tardily becoming nearly hairless; often lobed and obviously toothed. Profuse, bright red, showy, persistent fruit, to ½" wide on a stem to 1⅝" long.]

CRAPE-MYRTLE

Lagerstrœmia indica L. (and hybrids)   Ladies' Streamer
LYTHRACEÆ   Crêpe-Myrtle
From China, Korea, adjacent Far East Asia;
widely naturalized in India and elsewhere.

Crape-Myrtle never fails to excite admiration, and, when in bloom, joyous awe. Appropriately, it signifies "eloquence" in the Language of Flowers. They make suckering shrubs or trees, up to 60' × 9½' in the SE States. Dozens of cultivars—some of hybrid origin with *L. Fauriei*—vary in size and in flower color. Smooth, peeling, pale bark on the slender trunks is very handsome. Crape-Myrtles are uncommon in Seattle. They flower late summer–early fall, and require much summer sunshine and warmth to be at their best.

– U.W. Medicinal Herb Garden: at the west end of section D one has raspberry pink flowers, is 3-trunked and 32½' × 19½' wide; next to it is a single-trunked one about 12' tall, with pale pink flowers
– Arboretum: the specimen outside the old offices was moved to the rockrose area, and subsequently to the U.W. Center for Urban Horticulture in 1990 where it is 25' tall; a 'Powhatan' #648-67A is in the nursery
– 9th Ave & James St: NE corner, red-purple flowered, 24½' tall
– Corliss Ave N & N 36th St: NW corner yard, red-purple flowered, 22' tall
– Seattle Center: 6 white ones S of Fisher Pavilion
– 2030 42nd Ave E: a 'Natchez' (white) street-tree and a 21' tall 'Zuni' (lavender)
– 3921 W Armour St (at 40th; SE corner): 6 street-trees
– 39th Ave SW & SW 107th St: NE corner has one S of house (dark pink)
– Ellis Ave S, south of S Warsaw St: 12 pink street-trees, W side

- 36th Ave NE, N of NE 75th St: several street-trees of 'Tuscarora'
- S.P.U.: 6 east of Gwinn Commons
- S.U.: many of various colors including deep purple and dark red
- Swanson's Nursery: 5 against wall in N parking lot
- 46th Ave NE, south of NE 54th St: several street-trees of 'Tuscarora'
- 3456 41st Ave SW: a 'Pink Lace' street-tree, *pl*. 1988, flanked by 'Professor Sprenger' Crabapples

CRINODENDRON

Crinodendron Patagua Mol.	Lily-of-the-Valley Tree
=*C. dependens* (Ruiz & Pav.) Schneid.	Flowering Oak
=*Tricuspidaria dependens* R.& P.	Chilean: Patagua
ELÆOCARPACEÆ	Patahua
From Chile.	

A broadleaf evergreen up to 50' × 6¼'. Not reliably winter-hardy here; extremely rare. It has white flowers in late summer. The leaves are semi-glossy above, *very* pale whitish beneath, minutely hairy. They can be opposite *or* alternate.

- Locks #313 has an old tree 27' tall, against the building wall
- Arboretum: 9-3E has three: 20' tall #131-98A; 21' tall #131-98B; 19' tall #131-98C
- Fremont Ave N & N 83rd St: NW corner has 6 street-trees
- 5215 36th Ave NE: in back yard, with bamboo—visible from the alley only
- Good Shepherd Center: one *pl*. in 2002 is 8' tall near the NE part of the building

[**Red Lantern-Tree**—*C. Hookerianum* Gay—a red-flowered cousin, also Chilean, of perhaps greater hardiness and certainly floral beauty, but difficult to propagate, exists here only as young specimens in a few yards, not easily seen from streets.]

Arizona CYPRESS

Cupressus arizonica Greene	Smooth Arizona Cypress
(including var. *glabra* (Sudw.) Little*)	Arizona Smooth Cypress
CUPRESSACEÆ	
From the SW U.S., and Mexico.	

Appreciated for attractive peeling reddish-brown bark, resinous green to ghostly bluish-green foliage, and a shapely crown. It can grow to 84' × 14'. It is uncommon in Seattle. Various cultivars are available from nurseries.

[*Should still use the epithet *glabra*? The *Flora of North America* does not recognize it: "Although bark texture may be consistent within populations, over the species as a whole there is complete intergradation between smooth and fibrous barks."]

- Acacia Cemetery: one 54' × 7'2¼" in the SE part
- Arboretum: #194-54A in 12-8E is 58' × 4'8"
- E Madison St & E Lee St: one 63' tall (E of a 46' Box-elder Maple) on NE corner
- Children's Hospital: 3 'Silver Smoke' in the ER valet parking lot; tallest 36½'
- Arboretum: #20-89 'Blue Pyramid' pair in *Rhus glabra* grove; larger 35' × 2'9"
- 7511 23rd Ave NE: a 'Blue Pyramid' street-tree, *pl*. <1990

- Calvary Cemetery: a young 'Carolina Sapphire' 7' tall, *pl.* <2005
- 6559 55th Ave NE: a young 'Carolina Sapphire' by the garage
- 3407 NW 56th St: a young 'Golden Pyramid' 16' tall
- 3635 Woodland Park Ave N: a young 'Limelight'
- 7707 28th Ave NW: a young 'Limelight' *pl.* <2003
- SSCC Arboretum: a young cv. 'Blue Ice' in the Cœnosium Rock Garden is 9½' tall
- SSCC Arboretum: a young cv. 'Sulfurea' in the Cœnosium Rock Garden is 6' tall

[**Santa Cruz Cypress**—*C. Goveniana* var. *Abramsiana* (C.B. Wolf) Little = *C. Abramsiana* C.B. Wolf—From California. Foliage rich green, highly aromatic. Bark lovely red-brown. Apt to be far less cold-hardy. The Arboretum has #585-90C in 34-4W; it is 22' × 1'7½" (**A** & **B** are in 3-5E). One 18' tall is at 1108 NW 80th St. On S Hanford St, east of 12th Ave S, three were planted downhill south of three typical *C. Goveniana*.]

[**Mexican Cypress. Cedar of Goa**—*C. lusitanica* Mill.—An immense Mexican species that was cultivated in Portugal by 1644. Little known in U.S. cultication. The Arboretum has #340-64A in 9-7E; shade-stunted, it is 34½' × 1'11". But four #587-90 are thriving southeast of the Graham visitor center parking lot, and two #217-91 are in the pinetum (34-4W). A youngster 24½' tall is among the diverse trees and shrubs on the south side of S Hanford St, east of 12th Ave S; two Arizona cypresses are west of it.]

Bald CYPRESS

Taxodium distichum (L.) Rich.
=*Cupressus disticha* L.
CUPRESSACEÆ (formerly TAXODIACEÆ)
From the southern United States,
essentially.

Deciduous Cypress
Louisiana Cypress
Gulf *or* Southern Cypress
Marsh *or* Swamp Cypress
Sabino Tree

...in deep and sickly swamps, the haunts of fever, musquitos, moccasin snakes, alligators, and all loathsome and ferocious animals, that congegate far from the abode of man, and seem to make common cause with nature against him. The cypress loves the deepest, most gloomy, inaccessible and inundated swamps; and south of 33-degrees is generally found covered with the sable festoons of long moss, hanging, as it seems, a shroud of mourning wreaths almost to the ground. (Flint, p. 41)

Majestic denizen of Southern swamps and bayous, the Bald cypress is a huge, deciduous timber tree that can grow to 180' × 61' and live as long as 1,700 years. Sacred to certain Indians, this State Tree of Louisiana is renowned for its durable, rot-resistant wood. Peculiar conical "bumps" from the roots sometimes form and are known as cypress knees. They can reach 14' in height and apparently stabilize the tree rather than help it breathe, as had formerly been thought.

Rare in Seattle, it can be confused only with Dawn Redwood. The foliage changes to rusty-brown in November, contrasting bravely with golden-yellow cottonwoods.

- Green Lake: the tallest of *ca.* 100 is 109' × 9'9½"; a few small knees in the far western grove opposite N 68th St
- Arboretum: 21—including some with knees about 1½' high so far; largest is 89' × 7'2½" (#1216-39G in 33-3W). About 20 youngsters are on Foster Island near the 520 bridge

- Locks #212 has five, one of them 81' tall
- Holly Park Dr S, west of 35th Pl S: one 57' tall, not far from a River Birch
- U.W.: two on the lawn beneath the NE 45th St viaduct; the larger 59' × 4'11½"; a smaller one NW of the wildlife sanctuary E-5 parking lot
- Ravenna Park: 8 young trees in the ravine E of the 15th Ave bridge

[**Pond Cypress**—*T. distichum* var. *imbricatum* (Nutt.) Croom = *T. ascendens* Brongn.—a smaller tree with shorter needles closely held against the twigs; extremely rare here; only young trees known. CUH has a #40-90B 20½' tall; the garden on S Hanford St, east of 12th Ave S, has two, and to their west (south of the house) the cv. 'Nutans' is 15' tall.]

Hinoki CYPRESS

Chamæcyparis obtusa (S.& Z.) Endl.
=*Cupressus obtusa* (S.&Z.) K. Koch
=*Retinispora obtusa* S.& Z.
CUPRESSACEÆ
From Japan, Taiwan.

Its Japanese name Hi-no-ki (ヒノキ) translates as Fire Tree. It attains up to 150' × 31½' in nature, yet is the slowest-growing cypress cultivated here (except dwarf bushy cultivars and Arboretum rarities). Dark green, scaly foliage has conspicuous white lines on the underside. Richly colored eye-catching round cones are about ⅓" wide. Hinoki grows broader than its associate the Sawara cypress. The tree is common in Seattle. Many cultivars exist.

- 1160 20th Ave E: one by 20th Ave sidewalk is *ca.* 53' × 5'0"
- alley off 33rd Ave E & E Valley St: 51' tall, S of a Sawara cypress
- Arboretum: four #42-55 are 40' to 49½' tall
- Parsons Gardens Park: a multitrunked 46' tree in the NW part (+Sawara cypresses)
- 815 NW 116th St: 42' tall, two-trunked, near a Fire Tree
- Salmon Bay School (formerly James Monroe School) 1810 NW 65th St: one 41' × 3'9" at the SW corner
- Zoo: quite a few in the Family Farm; largest 38½' × 4'2½"
- Washelli Cemetery: 32' × 5'8½" 70' west of a *Pinus nigra*, 70' N of a *P. ponderosa*
- Ravenna Park: two south of the lower level restrooms, the eastern much larger
- U.W.: 18 youngsters around The Bank of America Executive Education Center

cvs. '**Aurea**' & '**Crippsii**' *et al.*   Gold Hinoki Cypress

Yellowish-colored Hinokis are commonly seen in Seattle. Examples cited below show the range of variation and represent more than one clone. They grow more slowly and stay smaller than regular Hinoki, yet in the long run can exceed 60' in height. Few in Seattle are even 25' tall so far.

- 4257 NE 73rd St: one 39½' tall
- W Seattle Library (2306 42nd Ave SW): two in front, the taller 35½'
- an Apt. Bldg. on the S side of Valley St, east of 3rd Ave N, has two, the taller 34½'
- 28th Ave NE & NE 82nd St: NE corner, one 34½' tall just E of a green Hinoki
- 102 NW 43rd St: one 33' tall by the sidewalk
- 39th Ave W & W Bertona St: NE corner yard has one 32½' tall W of the house

- 43rd Ave NE & NE 80th St: NW corner yard has one 31½' tall
- 6343 Hampton Rd S: one 30' tall by the driveway
- 58th Ave NE & NE 65th St: NW corner yard has one 28' tall
- 20th Ave E & E Prospect St: NW corner lot has one S of house
- 46th Ave S & S Willow St: SW corner lot has one SE of house

['**Coralliformis**' is very rare, semi-dwarf. Dark, wet-looking foliage of irregularly gently twisted cordlike sprays and little cockscomb fasciations suggest coral. Green Lake has one by Kirkwood Place N. Arboretum #83-65B is 14' tall in 36-2W. On S.U. campus one is 13' tall south of the west entrance to University Services bldg. One 11' tall at 6549 Fauntleroy Way SW.]

['**Filicoides**' is rare, semi-dwarf. Extenuated branches bear dark green, densely congested short side-sprays; individual twigs fernlike. S side of Seattle Center's Key Arena. 415 Summit Ave E. 7743 38th Ave NE. 550 N 83rd St.]

Italian CYPRESS

Cupressus sempervirens L.
CUPRESSACEÆ
From SE Europe, N
Africa, W Asia.

(not our) Common Cypress
European *or* Mediterranean Cypress
Roman *or* Classical Cypress
Funereal Cypress

Ancient of name and fame, and rich in associations, this cypress was once prominent to a degree difficult for us to imagine, surfeited as we are with coniferous evergreens. But to most people in Mediterranean countries, this was one of the few common and large coniferous evergreens: its dark crown was a conspicuous feature of the landscape.

Symbolizing mourning, despair, death and eternal sorrow, this cypress was frequently planted in graveyards and used in funereal wreaths. It stood quiet, exceptionally dense, dark, evergreen and long-lived. The durable wood was used for chests and shipbuilding. Some people claim the "Gopherwood" used to construct Noah's Ark was actually cypress wood. More certainly, the wood was used for the Parthenon at Athens, the statue of Jupiter in the Roman Capitol that existed over 600 years, and the hallowed doors of St Peter's Church in Rome from the time of Constantine to Pope Eugene IV—over 1,100 years! The doors were replaced not because they were worn out, but because *brass* gates were desired.

It grows to a maximum size of 164' × 36' and is either flame-shaped (the form preferred for planting) or widely spreading (the usual natural or wild form). It can live 2,200 years. Roundish woody cones up to 1⅓" long render it distinct from similar trees except Monterey cypress.

In Seattle, common. All are flame-shaped; almost all are markedly dense, narrow spires ('**Stricta**'). It is a favorite in formal residential landscaping. The bluish-green '**Glauca Stricta**' and yellowish '**Swane's Golden**' are now in nurseries.

- U.W.: one 49' × 5'8" × 18' wide was moved in spring 1988 from the HUB lawn, and then died; the front of Anderson Hall was flanked by smaller specimens, the larger 41' × 2'1" when cut down in 2005

- Harvard Ave E & E Gwinn Pl: tallest of 5 in the SE corner yard (with 4 Dawn Redwoods and a blue Atlas Cedar) is *ca.* 50'
- 2703 E Yesler Way: 37½' tall
- Bellevue Ave E & E Harrison St: NE corner has one 30' tall
- Arboretum: tallest of six is #647-58A in the conifer meadow (44-5W), 22½'
- U.W. Friendship Grove, representing Jordan, a non-fastigiate specimen

cv. 'Swane's Golden' — Gold Italian Cypress

Like ordinary narrow Italian cypress in shape, yet gold-colored; smaller. It is uncommon in Seattle and all date from the 1990s onward.

- 3114 Lakewood Ave S: a whole hedgerow of them
- 35th Ave, just north of E Olive St: 2 street-trees with 3 regular green ones
- 2040 42nd Ave E: a street-tree
- 2636 10th Ave E: at house's NW corner
- 114 NW 51st St: 3

Lawson CYPRESS

Chamæcyparis Lawsoniana (A. Murr.) Parl.   Port Orford Cedar
=*Cupressus Lawsoniana* A. Murr.   Oregon Cedar
From SW Oregon, NW California.   White Cedar
Ginger Pine

The natural range of this remarkable tree is limited to the small area where it is a dominant forest tree. There, the largest specimens measured as much as 245' × 50' with bark up to 10" thick. Cultivated since the second half of the 19th century, it possesses an astonishing variability: over 200 cultivars are known, ranging from dwarf bushes to tall, graceful trees.

In Seattle, common. It thrives here and has been much planted. Alas, it is unusually prone to being uprooted or split by violent windstorms, and is being killed by easily transmitted, incurable root rots *(Pythium* and *Phytophthora).* However, some cultivars are far sturdier and more disease-resistant than others. The examples immediately following are seedlings; following them is a sampling of our more common and/or distinctive tree-sized cultivars—18 kinds. Since the 1st edition of this book, Seattle has lost some extremely rare clones (*e.g.,* 'Filifera' and 'Filiformis'), and some new ones have been discovered. Several other kinds present here are impossible to assign names to.

- U.W.: many, such as on Rainier Vista east of Anderson Hall
- Interlaken Park: a grove of 33 by 20th Ave E & E Crescent Dr
- Woodland Park: many, *e.g.*, a grove by Lombardy poplars SW of the N restrooms
- Arboretum: 38-3E, 37-1W
- Lincoln Park: many at the S end north of the parking lot; many by the park maintenance facility in the north end
- Ravenna Blvd NE: 86' × 6'6" & 77' × 5'11" (+12 English Maples) by 15th Ave NE

cv. 'Albovariegata'   Variegated Cypress
and cv. 'Aureovariegata' *and* cv. 'Versicolor'   Cream Cypress

Seattle has at least two Lawson cypress clones with creamy-white or yellowish variegation. Authors so disagree on names for these that it is impossible to know precisely which names are correct. The trees are uncommon, slow-growing, and bear few cones. They brighten a dark location and are cheerful.

- 4620 Sunnyside Ave N: one 49' tall in the back yard (see from alley)
- Baker Park (8347 14th Ave NW): one 31' tall on the W side of the park
- NE 52nd St, west of 18th Ave NE: a 30' tall street-tree, S side
- 1st Ave NW & NW 50th St: SE corner, 28' tall
- 824 NW 60th St: 26' tall
- Parsons Gardens Park: in NE corner, 25½' tall

cv. 'Alumii' (Allumii)   Scarab Cypress

Likely the most common form in Seattle. Narrow and flame-shaped when young, it ages to a wide bushy base topped by a narrower spire. It has upswept vertical bluish sprays of foliage and bears few cones until it is quite large. One in Scotland was 98' tall in 1981.

- Volunteer Park: a massive old one 70½' tall near 4 broad Western Red Cedars between the bandstand and the conservatory
- Washelli Cemetery: 80½' × 16'7" (below a dozen verticals); 75' N of S end fence
- Palatine Pl N & N 57th St: one 76' tall on the NE corner
- 25th Ave NE & NE 125th St: SW corner has one 67½' tall
- U.W.: two by the south entrance of Savery Hall; by Denny Hall; the tallest 64'
- Hiawatha Playfield: one south of the tennis courts
- 55th Ave SW & SW Dakota St: NE corner has one 51½' tall NW of the house

cv. 'Ellwoodii'

Most recent of the cultivars mentioned here, this originated in 1925 and soon skyrocketed in popularity. It is very common in Seattle. A narrow oval in shape, it has exceedingly dense, prickly foliage of a bluish color and grows to 40' tall here. It never makes cones. Its dark blue density and juniper-like foliage make it unmistakable—'Fletcheri' is a poor lookalike far less common here.

- 1743 26th Ave E (north of Boyer Ave E): a pair, the taller 42'
- 916 20th Ave E: 42' tall
- 6843 43rd Ave NE: one by the driveway is 40' tall
- 5718 29th Ave NE: 38' tall
- S.P.U.: 37½' tall with a 'Zebrina' Western Red Cedar W of Beegle Hall
- 938 NW 97th St: a broad stout tree by the fire hydrant
- 17th Ave NE & NE 136th St: SE corner, 31' tall, at house's NE corner

cv. 'Erecta Glaucescens'   Blue Column Cypress

Very rare in Seattle, this looks somewhat like 'Alumii' and somewhat like a glaucous, less tightly compact 'Erecta Viridis.'

- Lake View Cemetery: one 60' × 6'7¼" in the SE part, south of the south road; one

62' × 7'½" on the cemetery's high point of ground, by a 'Moseri' purpleleaf Plum
 – Evergreen Park Cemetery: largest of 3 is 48' × 4'7¼" in the NW part (about opposite 120th St) near 4 f. *glauca* and 3 'Erecta Viridis'

cv. 'Erecta Viridis'
Green Column Cypress
Green Pyramid

This originated around 1855, so is among the very oldest of Lawson cypress cultivars. It has rich grass-green foliage held compactly in flat vertical sprays and grows flame-shaped, from narrow to broad (not columnar as some sources maintain). Few cones are produced. Common in Seattle, it reaches 30–70' here, though the tallest in the British Isles is 115'.

 – Lake View Cemetery: 2 on the E side, toward S end; the taller 71' × 8'8"
 – Calvary Cemetery: one 70' × 11'½" in the SW part
 – U.W.: one 52' tall and 32' wide, densely branched to the ground on the lawn NE of the Montlake Bridge

cv. 'Fletcheri'

'Fletcheri' is traditionally compared to the similar 'Ellwoodii.' In Seattle there are perhaps 25 to 50 'Ellwoodii' for every 'Fletcheri.' The latter is an older clone (originated <1913), broadly flame-shaped and bushy at the base rather than a narrow oval, and sometimes bears a few cones near the top, whereas the former produces none. Furthermore, the foliage is less "juvenile" than is that of 'Ellwoodii' and is gray-green touched with bronze in winter rather than silvery-blue all year round. Though most writers say 'Fletcheri' grows larger than 'Ellwoodii,' the two are actually very similar in rate of growth and size attained.

 – Sand Point Way NE & NE 115th St: NW corner at house's SE corner, 41' tall
 – Beacon Ave S & S Graham St: NE corner (Bethany Church) 37' tall
 – U.W.: one with other kinds of Lawson cypresses against the Administration Building by the parking lot; one 34½' tall with a larger 'Wissellii' at the SW entrance of Hutchinson Hall
 – Durland Ave NE & NE 107th St: NE corner (by telephone pole) 32' tall
 – 2915 NE 52nd St: a 42½' tall *bluish* one at the NW corner

cv. 'Fraseri'

A dark, dusky bluish and especially *narrow* tree that grows to about 90' tall, bearing many cones. Common only in older neighborhoods.

 – Evergreen Park Cemetery: one 84' × 7'½" a second 72' × 7'3"
 – 18th Ave E & E Aloha St: a pair on the NE corner, the taller 82'
 – Lincoln Park: by the N end ladies' room, 78' tall
 – 2158 E Shelby St: one 75½' tall
 – Hiawatha Playfield: one on the W side, 73' tall, two-trunked
 – Mt Pleasant Cemetery: one 68½' × 5'2½" in the southwest part
 – 23rd Ave E & E Aloha St: one on the NE corner, 67'

f. *glauca* Beissn.   Blue Lawson Cypress

Any bluish colored but otherwise ordinary Lawson cypress seedlings may be called f. *glauca*. To be sure, some especially vivid blue seedlings have been grafted and much planted, under other names: 'Triomf van Boskoop' is a very blue and beautifully proportioned example. These trees are common in Seattle.

 – 35th Ave NE, from NE 80th to NE 84th: mostly f. *glauca* on the west side, along with 'Erecta Viridis', plume Sawara cypresses and various other *Chamæcyparis* and *Thuja* manifestations (root rot has begun killing the blue Lawson cypresses)
 – Green Lake: regular and blue Lawson cypresses by restrooms at NE 72nd St
 – 5750 36th Ave NE: two dissimilar trees on the S edge of the yard
 – 32nd Ave S, south of S Atlantic St: a yard, E side, has two *ca.* 60' tall
 – 1902 Bigelow Ave N: two, the taller 62½'; at 1502-1504 one is 67' tall

cv. 'Golden Showers'

A compact small tree sold since 1972 (sometimes incorrectly as Golden King'). Uncommon. Foliage tips golden. The name *showers* suggest droopiness but the clone isn't so. 11717 19th Ave NE has one 31' tall in the yard's SE corner.

cv. 'Hillieri'

Foliage yellow, small, in hard, often parallel upright sprays; cones small. Rare.

 – 938 18th Ave E: 50' tall
 – S.U.: 45' tall, 3-trunked, across Spring St south of the Fine Arts bldg.
 – Montlake Blvd E, south of E Hamlin St: a yard, W side, has one 41½' tall
 – 2502 1st Ave W (@W Smith St): one 41' tall
 – 7725 16th Ave NW: 40' tall

cv. 'Intertexta'   Intertexta Weeping Lawson Cypress

A slender weeping tree of dark, hard, sparse foliage. It originated in 1869 at Lawson's Edinburgh nursery. The oldest specimens have grown to 80' × 6'. It is extremely rare in Seattle.

 – Green Lake: the larger of two near the children's play area northeast of Evans Pool is 74' × 5'4"
 – Laurelhurst Playfield: one 49' × 4'6½"on the south side, west of the driveway

cv. 'Lutea'   Weeping Yellow Lawson Cypress

Bright yellow, narrow and strongly *weeping* in form, 'Lutea' is greatly outnumbered here by the golden 'Stewartii' but not because it is a less lovely tree. More likely, it is a weaker clone and so was planted less and had a higher mortality rate.

 – 27th Ave NE & NE 136th St: SW corner yard
 – 42nd Ave W & W Barrett St: one 41½' tall east of the house on the NW corner
 – 2212 Morley Pl W: 37' tall

[A similar clone, name unknown, of *yellow-bluish* foliage is 70' tall on the NE corner of 17th Pl NE & NE 85th St. One 48' tall is by the driveway at 4338 SW Trenton St.]

cv. 'Lycopodioides'

An upright small dense tree with gray-green contorted foliage. Known only:
- Arboretum: #124-67A is 17' tall
- Good Shepherd Center: one less than 6' tall is W of the NE parking lot

cv. 'Oregon Blue'

Silver blue foliage. Sold much since the 1980s. May resist the deadly root rot.
- S.U.: 6 N of Broadway & Columbia Garage
- Seattle Center: W side of Key Arena (with a weeping Eastern White Pine)
- Green Lake: one 19½' tall by a bench in the SW area below Woodland Park

f. *pendula* (Beissn.) Beissn.   Weeping Lawson Cypress

Many Lawson cypresses strongly droop with great limp tresses of foliage. There are greenish and bluish and weakly golden-green ones, all capable of reaching 100' or more and coning profusely. Any such weeper may be called *pendula* but the name **'Pendula Vera'** is reserved for the far less common trees whose main branches droop markedly, thereby forming a narrow and very floppy crown. The weeping Alaska Cedars look similar to these from a distance and sometimes even in proximity.
- Lincoln Park: extreme N edge has a splendid example 89' × 7'5½"
- Discovery Park: 94½' × 6'8½" is the tallest of 6 by Vermont Ave & Texas Way
- Volunteer Park: one in a grove across the street E of water tower is 85½' × 5'3¾"
- 36th Ave W & W Emerson St: SE corner yard has one 79' tall
- Lake View Cemetery: a pair S of the entrance driveway, the larger 74' × 7'8"
- between 2215 & 2219 E Howe St: 60' tall
- U.W.: a row of varied Lawson cypresses on NE Pacific St northeast of the hospital includes several weepers (*also* an Alaska Cedar, blue Atlas Cedar, & Incense Cedar)

cv. 'Stewartii'   Golden Lawson Cypress

Our common yellowish Lawson cypress. Its young spring growth is especially bright. The shady side of the tree is greenish, so it has been called "The Sunshine Tree." With age it grows greener and droopier. It is usually seen 20–50' tall here and produces many cones. It dates from the 1890s.
- Arboretum: four #1245-47 in 30-1W east of Azalea Way
- 8216 Linden Ave N
- 3rd Ave W & W Galer St: S side; 51½' tall
- Burke Ave N & N 43rd St: one 66' tall at NW of the NW corner house

cv. 'Westermannii'

An old clone, narrow or broad, more or less pendulous; foliage gold when young but greenish by winter. After decades the tree shows only a weak hint of gold in spring on the tree's sunny side. Rare in Seattle.
- 4026 NE 55th St: 74' tall
- Calvary Cemetery: 68' × 8'11½"

- Volunteer Park: 70' × 4'8½" SE of art museum
- Belmont Place E & E Prospect St: one 56' tall
- 1618 34th Ave
- E Spruce St, between 16th & 17th Ave: 4 street-trees, N side

cv. 'Wisselii'

Short twisted sprays of very dark-bluish twigs in congested tufts borne on a slender tree with a *jagged* silhouette. It makes many cones. Very strange and distinctive. It is common.

- 303 36th Ave E: two about 80' tall
- 47th Ave NE & East Laurelhurst Dr NE: one 75' tall (across the street is a 'Glauca')
- Lincoln Park: one by the sidewalk in the extreme NE corner, 64½' × 5'7"; one to the west in the park is 65' × 4'6¼"
- Eastern Ave N & N 44th St: 62' tall in SW corner yard (with a 27½' Irish Yew)
- 1831 23rd Ave E (south of E Newton St): 60' tall
- Sunnyside Ave N & N 40th St: SW corner has one 52' tall
- 18th Ave & E Spring St: SW corner: 50' tall
- U.W.: 1 with a smaller 'Fletcheri' at the SW entrance of Hutchinson Hall

Leyland CYPRESS

Cupressus × Leylandii Dall. & Jacks.
= × *Cupressocyparis Leylandii* (Dall. & Jacks.) Dall.
= × *Cuprocyparis Leylandii* (Dall. & Jacks.) Farjon
(*Cupressus macrocarpa* × *Cupressus nootkatensis*)

Monterey Cypress/Alaska Cedar crosses originated in the United Kingdom in the late 1800s. These hybrid cypresses boom in vigor and rapid growth. They're popular and available in such cultivars as: 'Castlewellan', 'Haggerston Grey', 'Leighton Green', 'Naylor's Blue', 'Robinson's Gold' and 'Silver Dust'. The little round cones are rarely produced so the tree's energy is free to be spent on growth. The tallest Leyland cypresses are so far over 120' and trunks over 12' around have been measured. Many Seattleites have planted specimens on their property, but the tree quickly grows so large that its use in residential landscaping calls for restraint. *Coryneum* fungus can strike older specimens. Only a *few* older examples on public property are cited below.

- Arboretum: the largest of many are (#421-50) 90½' × 8'6", in pinetum E of service road 37-3W; 89' × 8'10", S-most of 8 lining the road in 37-4E; 80' × 10'6", larger of a roadside pair in 0-5E. Cultivars: 1 'Castlewellan Gold', 5 'Haggerston Grey', 4 'Naylor's Blue', and 2 'Silver Dust' (46' tall in 42-6W)
- Colman Park: one 85' × 9'9½" by the blvd, below the p-patch

cv. 'Castlewellan'   Golden Leyland Cypress

Foliage tinted with yellow. Growth smaller than the regular green form. Other "gold" foliage cultivars may be in Seattle—but are relatively rare and young.

- Arboretum: #372-77 in 41-6W (conifer meadow) 42' tall

– 20th Ave E & E Mercer St: NE corner (above a Fraser Photinia), 51' tall

cv. 'Picturesque'   Contorted Leyland Cypress

Branches and foliage *twisted*. It is also called 'Contorta'. Growth smaller than normal. Only one known here, 30' tall, flanked by 2 Scots Pines, by the sidewalk, NW of the house on the SE corner of 39th Ave W & W Ruffner St.

[*C.* × *Ovensii* (A.F. Mitch.) stat. nov. = × *Cupressocyparis Ovensii* A.F. Mitch. was raised in 1962 in Wales by Howard Ovens. "Mom" was a Mexican species *C. lusitanica* Mill., and "dad" an Alaska Cedar. The foliage is glaucous and not as coarse as that of Leyland cypress. The Arboretum has two: 46½' × 2'3¾" (#88-91 in 40-5W) and 43' × 2'1¼" (#88-91B in 36-3W). A very young tree is known in a private garden; others may exist here.]

Monterey CYPRESS

Cupressus macrocarpa Hartw. *ex* Gord.
=*C. Lambertiana* Gord.
From Monterey, California: a grove at Point Lobos;
another at Cypress Point, north of Carmel.

Monterey cypress is famous and picturesque. A rumor conjectured this Californian tree to be of ancient Chinese origin! It grows to only 80' × 21' in nature but is much larger in cultivation: 156' tall (New Zealand), trunks up to 32' around (Oregon), 39' around (Ireland) and 43½' (San Mateo County, CA), branches spreading as much as 110' wide.

In Seattle, rare. It can be hurt by our occasional severe winters (at least while it's young and in less than ideal sites), and may also be susceptible to *Coryneum* fungus attacks. Its foliage is lemon-scented, bright green; its cones are a bit larger than those of Italian cypress, to 1½". Seattleites interested in seeing superb specimens of Monterey cypress should visit Point Defiance Park in Tacoma (one there is 87' tall); Long Beach Peninsula in SW Washington; Port Townsend on the Olympic Peninsula; or Victoria, Vancouver Island. Three *gold*-foliaged cultivars are cited below, and others also exist, but sorting their proper names is hard.

– 4424 48th Ave S (north of S Oregon St): one in the back yard is *ca.* 75' tall
– 30th Ave W & W Barrett St: SW corner yard has one 57½' tall
– 909 E Fir St (between Broadway & 10th Ave): one 52½' × 8'8½"
– 3936 SW Ida St: a gold-foliaged cultivar (name unknown; likely 'Aurea' or 'Donard Gold'), 24½' tall in yard's SW corner, west of a weeping Eastern White Pine
– Children's Hospital: a gold-foliaged cultivar (name unknown; likely 'Lutea'), 14½' tall in Whale Garage's SE corner; originally obtained *ca.* 1997

cv. 'Conybearii Aurea'   Golden Weeping Cypress
= 'Saligna Aurea' *or* 'Aurea Saligna'

From Australia; not sold here until *ca.* 1987. Yellow, fine drooping foliage on an open tree. Extremely rare. At least one Seattle garden has a specimen but it is being kept shrubby by pruning, and is not visible from the street.

cv. 'Fine Gold'

A yellowish compact tree introduced in 1994 from New Zealand. Very rare.

– 2211 E Newton St: one 20' tall *pl.* ≤1999

cv. 'Goldcrest'   Goldcrest Cypress

A bright yellow-green, juvenile foliaged semidwarf tree very popular in this new millenium as a potted plant. Likely to be killed or hurt in severe cold. The similar **'Wilma'** is also here; the two are not distinguished below.

– 3040 11th Ave W: five
– 32nd Ave NE & NE 92nd St: NE corner has three
– 518 Federal Ave E: four less than 6' tall right by the sidewalk
– 1942 E Blaine St: one less than 8' tall
– 36th Ave NE & NE 55th St: SE corner yard has 6 in a row *pl.* 2005
– NW 73rd St & 24th Ave NW: SE corner has 3 on the N side

Sawara CYPRESS

Chamæcyparis pisifera (S.& Z.) Endl.   Japanese: Sa-wa-ra サワラ
=*Cupressus pisifera* (S.& Z.) K. Koch
=*Retinispora pisifera* S.& Z.
From Japan.

The Sawara resembles our native cedar more than it does any other common tree here: a person can walk by these and easily fail to observe that they are not mere slender aberrations of our familiar native. It attains 164' × 21' at most; so far, half that size here. The round cones are about ¼" wide.

Three distinct sets of garden varieties, less gaunt and far more imposing ornamentally, are more common than is the natural type. The examples cited immediately below include both the typical version and the very similar, scarcely worth distinguishing cv. **'Aurea'** (spring growth yellowish).

– McGilvra School (1617 38th Ave E): one 79½' × 9'4½" is the largest of 3
– Interlaken Park: one 75½' × 5'5½" is S of the boulevard, half a block W of 24th E
– Locks bed #121–122, 124—the largest 66' × 7'3"
– Acacia Cemetery: the largest 67' × 7'0", 73½' × 8'¼" (half broken), 69½' × 8'2½"
– Washelli Cemetery: the largest is 60' × 8'4¼" in the NE part
– Evergreen Park Cemetery: an **'Aurea'** is 72½' × 8'6" (*one* of its two trunks)
– Lincoln Park: largest (NW of south parking lot) is 57½' × 6'2"
– Volunteer Park: across the street E of the water tower, and elsewhere, such as one 76' × 5'1" on the W border ±opposite a huge Red Oak street-tree; two **'Aurea'** are 200' N of bandstand, growing into a silver maple (2 bigger typical Sawara cypresses are *ca.* 40' east of them)
– Leschi Park: a 5-trunked tree with some yellow foliage is by the sidewalk
– U.W.: each end of the front of Anderson Hall, the W one 70½' × 4'11½"

f. *filifera* (Sén.) Voss   Thread-branch (Sawara) Cypress
                                                String (Sawara) Cypress

This bears the same relation to the natural type as spaghetti to macaroni, or sauerkraut to whole cabbage. In a word, it's stringy and quite unmistakable due to its extraordinarily elongated, slender, cord-like drooping twigs. It varies from green to yellow and from bushy to over 80' tall. Several clones are included in the group. Usually the most stringy are small, and those specimens less stringy (and more like the regular Sawara) are larger. Common in Seattle.

– Evergreen Park Cemetery: a scarcely stringy one 72½' × 6'11½" by a roadside garbage receptacle NE of N 115th St; and 268' NE of it across the road in a hollow is a far more stringy specimen 34' tall, low and shrubby
– Seward Park: the stoutest of 6 at the entrance circle is 5'1" around, the tallest 60'
– Acacia Cemetery: the largest is 52' × 7'3½"
– Lake View Cemetery: the largest, in the SE part, is 37' × 6'4"
– U.W.: 4 are N and 10 W of Denny Hall; the tallest is 52'
– Parsons Gardens Park: several
– 3720 E John St (west of Madrona Pl E): 2 by sidewalk, bright yellow, taller 36'

f. *plumosa* (Carr.) Beissn.   Plume Sawara Cypress
                                     Japanese: Shinobu-hiba

Dense, large and vigorous—in effect the natural type writ **boldface**; strongest growing and largest of the Sawara clan. Very common in older neighborhoods but is far less often grown in recent times—perhaps because people found that these trees do not age gracefully: year after year the foliage *thins*. Most specimens here are essentially green ('Plumosa' or 'Plumosa Viridis') or yellow-tinged ('Plumosa Aurescens'). The various cultivars may be divided as follows:

1. 'Plumosa' *or* 'Plumosa *Viridis*' is the standard green form.

2. 'Plumosa *Aurescens*' has young foliage somewhat yellowish-tinged in spring and early summer, gradually turning greener as winter approaches.

3. 'Plumosa *Aurea*' has unvarying bright yellowish color all year.

4. 'Plumosa *Argentea*' is dark green with splashes of white variegation.

5. 'Plumosa *Albo-picta*' is like #4 but a dwarf bush—however until very recently writers used this name for #4!

Intermediates exist in these plume Sawara trees and the gradual reversion of the colored forms back to rich green is common and almost inevitable. The various clonal names are for convenience only.

– Leschi Park: one 106' × 11'3" and with it the natural type as well as '**Aurescens**' and the moss Sawara cypress
– Lake View Cemetery: the largest '**Viridis**' is 77' × 9'1" (on the west border, N of the middle); the largest '**Aurescens**' is 68' tall (on the west border, S of the middle); an '**Aurea**' in the NE part is 52' × 6'2½"
– Columbia Library (4721 Rainier Ave S): 6 '**Viridis**', the tallest 72'
– Queen Anne Library (400 W Garfield St): 2 natural types flank the steps, and a '**Viridis**' is to the W; an '**Aurea/Aurescens**' in the SE is south of 2 '**Viridis**'

- Washelli Cemetery: of 2 'Aurescens' in the SE part, the larger is 76' × 11'4", the taller 78½' × 10'8¾"
- Evergreen Park Cemetery: largest 'Aurea' is 76' × 11'4", the taller 79½' × 11'6¼"
- Acacia Cemetery: largest of many—72½' × 12'¼" (green) & 74½' × 9'9½" (gold)
- Calvary Cemetery: 8 'Viridis' at the entrance, the tallest 62' × 6'6¼"
- Zoo: 4 partly-reverted 'Aurescens' W of the S parking lot; tallest 64'
- U.W.: a sickly 63½' × 6'4½" 'Aurescens' at the SE corner of Hansee Hall (with a Cedar of Lebanon); a twin-trunked 63' 'Viridis' by King Lane W of Raitt Hall (near a holly-like *Osmanthus heterophyllus*)
- Volunteer Park: one 84' × 6'11¼" on the W border
- E Blaine St, east of 22nd Ave E: an 'Aurea' (and a Moss Sawara) in a yard, N side
- Locks bed #10 (62' tall), 121–122
- W Seattle Golf Course: by holes #15-17 are several 'Argentea'—most of their upper crowns have reverted; largest that is still obvious is by 17 tee, 54' × 6'8"
- 30th Ave NE & NE 65th St: SW corner has an 'Argentea'
- one house south of 5103 46th Ave NE has an 'Argentea'
- 8025 20th Ave NW: a bright though not big 'Aurea' in yard's SE corner

f. *squarrosa* (Zucc.) Beissn. & Hochst.

Moss Sawara Cypress
The Brown-junk Tree
Japanese: Hi-muro ヒムロ

Not a bit like the other Sawaras, this one seems to take after some junipers in appearance, with prickly, bluish-gray fluffy masses of juvenile foliage. Partial maturation into a fertile, cone-bearing state seldom occurs. It can reach 90' in height. Anyone who has had to garden in proximity to one knows well about the "brown junk" of its cast off dead twigs.

In Seattle, common. Frequently seen pruned in a "formal Japanese" manner into smooth stylized mounds or surrealistic tree forms—jokingly called lollipop, mum or afro trees.

- Evergreen Park Cemetery: many & large; one 70' × 11'6½" (below where it forks)
- Washelli Cemetery: the largest is 70' × 12'8¼" (below where it forks)
- Lake Park Dr S, just north of S McClellan St: one on the E side is 85' × 5'5½"
- Lakeview Park: two 80' × 4'11" and 76½' × 5'4" in a grove with typical Sawara and 'Plumosa'
- Acacia Cemetery: the largest is 70' × 8'9"
- Lincoln Park: extreme north end has 2 big ones flanking an 84' tall Birch, the largest 66' × 5'11" (larger of 2 trunks)
- Zoo: Rose Garden has formally pruned "mum" trees & sheared 'Plumosa Viridis'
- Locks #121–122, 203A (two)
- Jones Ave NW, south of NW 73rd St: a street-tree, E side
- 5610 20th Ave NE: a 42' tall street-tree of the *almost* identical 'Squarrosa Veitchii'

['Squarrosa Intermedia' is an extremely rare freak. When young, and pinched yearly, this is a lovely bluish dwarf with small juvenile foliage. But planted and ignored it grows to a straggly tree of mixed congested bluish juvenile foliage and long whiplike shoots of adult foliage. The Arboretum has 4, the largest 39' × 3'7" in 37-1W. The U.W. has 13 above Pend Oreille Rd, 220' N of the gatehouse, but some are reverting; the tallest is 52½' and stoutest 3'9½".]

cv. '**Boulevard**'   Boulevard Moss Cypress
='Cyanoviridis'

A brighter blue, "new and improved version" of the Moss Sawara, this is smaller, denser, and is nowhere near as common. It does best in partial shade and moist, acidic soil, as the fully exposed and open-grown ones can "sunburn."

- 4548 NE Tulane Pl (north of NE 55th St): 41½' tall
- 2144 38th Ave E: one S of the driveway is 41½' tall, 2-trunked
- 4411 31st Ave W: 31' tall (with a pink Weeping Cherry)
- 9024 1st Ave NW: 31' tall
- 3247 NW 59th St: 28' tall in yard right next to sidewalk
- Greenwood Ave N & N 95th St: SE corner apartment bldg. has 2 N of it
- Arboretum: #857-50A in dwarf conifer bed (37-1W) is 16' tall
- 5026 9th Ave NE: two
- 40th Ave SW & SW Manning St: two on the SW corner rockery

DAPHNIPHYLLUM

Daphniphyllum macropodum Miq.   Japanese: Yuzuri-ha ユズリハ
=*D. glaucescens* hort., *non* Bl.   Chinese: Jiao Rang Mu
=*D. himalense* (Benth.) Müll.-Arg. ssp. *macropodum* (Miq.) Huang
DAPHNIPHYLLACEÆ
From China, Korea, and Japan.

A broadleaf evergreen shrub or small tree to 50' tall. Lush rhododendron-like foliage—but *dinky* flowers. From Greek *daphne* (bay laurel; named after the Greek nymph and daughter of the earth goddess Gea), and *phyllon*, a leaf. Leaf 3–8" long; its stout red stem to 1¾" long. Flowers April–June, ♂ and ♀ on separate trees. Females are like clusters of glaucous radish seeds, each topped by purple-black stigmas. Males are more showy, reddish anthers. Fertilized females make powder-blue berries. A conversation piece, *Daphniphyllum* is very rare here.

- Volunteer Park: a ♂ in the huge ♂ English Holly SE of the museum is 32' × 2'6"
- Arboretum: 7-2E has #585-77 (three ♀), tallest 26' and 21½'; #205-82 (two ♂)
- U.W. Medicinal Herb Garden: a 14½' tall ♀ under a Katsura Tree in section F

Cornelian-Cherry (DOGWOOD)

Cornus mas L.   Cherry Dogwood
CORNACEÆ   Long Cherry Tree
From Europe, W Asia.   Male Dogwood

This bids goodbye to winter with a sunny display of tiny yellow flowers on dark bare twigs, in (late January) February–March, then leafs out. Its fruit ripens to red in late summer or fall. Unless eaten when *dark* red, soft and juicy, these are unpleasantly astringent; even when fully ripe they are "an acquired taste."

The tree is shrubby, with maximum recorded dimensions 45' × 7¼'—trees even half that large are scarce in Seattle, where the species is common.

- U.W.: one 27' tall at NW corner of Hall Health; one 26' tall on the Denny Hall lawn, south and a bit west of the building; many others on campus, such as one 23½' tall by the road N of Clark Hall; CUH has a grove of 42 *pl.* in 1984
- Volunteer Park: one of 3 NW of the N lily pond is 32½' × 3'3½"
- Parsons Gardens Park: on west side
- Locks bed #16 (26' tall), 112, 207, 214; bed #313 has a closely related California shrub **Miner's Dogwood** (*C. sessilis* Torr. *ex* Durand) which ripens black fruit
- SW Orchard St, east of 39th Ave SW: many
- 5510 Kenwood Pl N: a '**Variegata**' *ca.* 7' tall S of the house

[*C. officinalis* S.&Z. Chinese *or* Japanese Cornelian-Cherry. From Japan, Korea, and China. Like Cornelian-Cherry but larger, better ornamentally; not in fruit edibility. Extremely rare. Arboretum #286-80 is 8½' tall and wider, just west of Azalea Way in 20-2W. The SE corner of the U.W. Medicinal Herb Garden section G has two that first flowered in 1986—they were severely pruned in 2005.]

Eastern DOGWOOD

C. florida L.   Flowering Dogwood
From the eastern U.S., S Ontario, NE Mexico.   American Boxwood

Common in Seattle; closely related to our native Pacific dogwood but far smaller and more often than not grown in *pink*-flowered forms. In its native home Eastern Dogwood is as popular and beloved as ours here: it is the State Tree of Missouri, State Tree and Flower of Virginia, and State Flower of North Carolina. Often shrub-sized, at most it attains 55' × 8½' with dense twiggy crowns, checkered bark resembling alligator hide, white or pink flowers (late April) mid- to late May. Some Indians used the peeled twigs as toothbrushes. The very hard, very heavy wood is difficult to split and prone to much shrinking and checking, but is valuable for items such as golf club heads and piano keys.

Cultivars exist, such as 'Cloud 9', 'Cherokee Princess', and 'White Cloud'. Only a few more common or distinctive kinds grown here are singled out below.

- U.W.: one 28½' × 3'11½" S of Burke Museum
- Volunteer Park: SW of the conservatory, 39½' × 3'6½"
- Arboretum: the Mexican semi-evergreen var. *urbiniana* [Rose] Wang. is lofty at 62' × 2'1½" (#865-48 in 23-B); and stouter 37' × 2'10¾" (#865-48 in 14-8E)

cv. **Rainbow**® *et al.*   Rainbow Dogwood

Rainbow®, patented in 1967, has leaves variegated with yellowish stripes. Similar clones include '**First Lady**' patented in 1969 (leaves variegated green & yellow); '**Golden Nugget**' introduced ≤1987 (leaves variegated green & gold); '**Hohman's Golden**' introduced ≤1963 (leaves variegated green & gold). With *pink* flowers and leaves variegated green & yellow, patented in 1988, is **Cherokee Sunset**™.

- 3721 Densmore Ave N: a Rainbow® 23' tall
- Arboretum: 37-B has a Rainbow® #363-67 and a 'First Lady' #89-68
- 11921 Exeter Ave NE
- NE corner of Nob Hill Ave N & Crockett St: a Rainbow®

– 1st Ave NW & NW 132nd St: the NE corner church has 4 in a row in NW corner

f. *rubra* (West.) Schelle   Pink *or* Red Dogwood

Most common of all. This name includes pink- and red-flowering cultivars such as Cherokee Brave®, 'Cherokee Chief', 'Royal Red' and 'Sweetwater Red'. Very well known here. Usually less than 20' tall with trunks rarely a foot thick. Good examples on public property are those at the arboretum (many); several at Parsons Gardens Park; one by Denny Hall on the U.W. campus that is 29' × 3'4" × 32' wide; one at the U.W. Medicinal Herb Garden 27' × 3'2".

cv. 'Welchii'   Tricolor Dogwood

An old clone, common and eye-catching as a shrub or small tree grown for its green, creamy white, rosy pink variegated foliage.

– 1412 36th Ave: 23' tall in N part of yard
– 8454 40th Ave SW: 21½' tall
– 2707 45th Ave SW: a street-tree 18' tall
– 7045 18th Ave NW: a yard tree

Eddie's White Wonder DOGWOOD

(C. Nuttallii × C. florida)   Hybrid Pacific Dogwood

Common in Seattle, this hybrid originated *ca.* 1945 in B.C. and was first sold 10 years later. Compared to Pacific dogwood it is smaller, denser, somewhat weeping—a dumpling of a dogwood; it also is more disease resistant. Its 4 (5) white flower "petals" surround an especially *tiny* center button; it is infertile and almost never blooms in autumn. Its fall color is heartwarming.

– 1819 2nd Ave N: 31' tall
– 28th Ave NW & NW 83rd St: 30½' tall in NE corner yard
– St Anne's Church (1st Ave W & W Lee St): 9 street-trees interplanted with 6 'Dawyck' Beeches on 1st Ave W; the tallest 29' × 2'5"
– 815 NE Ravenna Blvd: 28' tall
– Zoo: one 24½' tall in Our Backyard exhibit—labeled *C. Nuttallii*
– 2220 22nd Ave E: a street-tree 20½' tall
– Arboretum: 16' × 1'7½" #672-70 on Azalea Way (35-1W)
– Interlaken Park: 5 near 19th Ave E & E Galer St
– Seward Park Environmental Learning Center: 2—labeled *C. Nuttallii*

Evergreen DOGWOOD

C. capitata Wall. *ex* Roxb.   Himalayan Strawberry-tree
From the Himalayas to Indochina.   Bentham's Cornel

A semi-hardy, ±evergreen small tree with yellow flowers and edible strawberry-like fruit. Very rare; specimens at the Arboretum and Locks died in cold winters. Some trees dating from 1987 or later are:

– Good Shepherd Center: one 18' × 1'9½" east of the Tilth Children's Garden; a 2nd

is 20' tall @ the NE corner of the building, north of a little courtyard
- Arboretum: #15-00 is 15' tall, and #333-94 is 14½' tall in 24-1W
- NE 88th St, west of 15th Ave NE: a yard, N side
- N 38th St, west of Carr Place N: a street-tree, S side
- U.W.: CUH has a 10' tree NE of NHS Hall labeled #167-89 *C. Kousa* var *angustata*
- 23rd Ave NW & NW 77th St: SW corner
- 53rd Ave SW & SW Admiral Way: SW corner has one 12½' tall leaning from shade
- 42nd Ave SW, south of SW Juneau St: 9 young street-trees, W side

C. capitata ssp. *emeiensis* (Fang & Hsieh) Q.Y. Xing **Summer Passion**™

Since ≤1993 nurseries have sold *seedlings* under this trademark. From Mt. Omei of China's Szechwan province. Like an evergreen Kousa Dogwood with copper-colored spring growth. Many have been planted in Seattle, but few have survived. The best specimens may be two at S.U., flanking a fernleaf Full Moon Maple on the N side of the Pigott building's west entrance. The taller is 17'.

Giant DOGWOOD

C. controversa Hemsl.	Table Dogwood
From the Himalayas & E Asia.	Pagoda Dogwood

Normally in the wild as well as in cultivation this scarcely earns the name Giant dogwood, being no more than 70' × 6'—but in Taiwan it reaches up to 100' tall, rivaling our native Pacific dogwood for being the largest of dogwoods. A Chinese name [Deng Tai Shu](Shui Mu) means "Wood of Good Omen!" It and *C. alternifolia* are both called Pagoda dogwood. Both of these dogwoods are unusual, bearing their leaves in alternation instead of in opposite pairs.

In Seattle, uncommon; being planted far more *now* than in earlier decades.
- 39th Ave E & E Blaine St: an old one 39' tall on the SW corner yard
- 39th Ave E: 3rd yard on the west side north of E Blaine St has a sapling offspring from the bigger tree half a block south
- Arboretum: head of Rhododendron Glen has one 47' × 1'11¾" (#98-89) & 38½' × 1'6" (#239-89); south of Loderi Valley (27-1W) is one 26' × 2'1½" (#136-83)
- 7064 35th Ave NE: largest of several old trees is 26½' tall
- U.W.: 2 by Thompson Hall *pl.* 2001; also a youngster on the Quad. by Miller Hall
- Burke Ave N & N 43rd St: NE corner, northwest of the house has a broad one
- 6722 23rd Ave NW: 2 street-trees

cv. **'Variegata'**   Variegated Giant Dogwood

Less vigorous. Leaves smaller, often misshapen, and edged creamy-white. Has been called the *wedding cake tree* in England. Very rare in Seattle. (The yellow-green variegated cv. **'Janine'** likely also exists here as young trees.)
- 1619 E Republican St: one east of the house
- 3314 43rd Ave NE: one NW of the house
- 12th Ave S & S Hanford St: garden here has one 14' tall, visible from Hanford St
- 1st Ave W & W Prospect St: SW corner graden has one

– Roanoke Park: SE corner has a young specimen

Kousa DOGWOOD

C. Kousa (Buerg. *ex* Miq.) Hance   Japanese Dogwood
From China, Korea,   Korean Dogwood
Japan, the Ryukyus.   Japanese: Kousa; Yama-boshi ヤマボウシ

Seattle's only common Asiatic dogwood. Shrubby or a small tree at most over 40'
tall. It blossoms from June to mid-July (occasionally lingering into late August)
following the Eastern dogwood's prime time, even as that species in turn follows
the Pacific dogwood in bloom. On rare occasions a second bloom occurs in autumn. The fall color is gorgeous at best, and the fruit resembles dull raspberries
of austere flavor and unpleasant texture. In recent years a *flood* of cultivars have
been introduced. It is, alas, too early to account for them in this book.

– Laurelhurst Playfield: one at the S end of the building is 31' × 7'4" (around a base
  that divides into 7 forks) × 48½' wide
– Arboretum: 33½' × 5'5½" #89-41 south of Rhododendron Glen in 12-4E
– Fauntleroy Way SW & SW Henderson St: NE corner yard has one 41½' tall
– Volunteer Park: by water tower, and S & W of the reservoir
– Locks bed #24, 120, 205, 207 (sickly), 214, 302
– Epiphany Church (38th Ave & E Denny Way)
– 1829 N 57th St: 2 street-trees of the white-variegated cv. '**Wolf Eyes**'
– 7713 20th Ave NW: a pink-flowered cv. such as '**Satomi**' or '**Radiant Rose**'
– 8331 20th Ave NW: a pink-flowered cv. such as '**Satomi**' or '**Radiant Rose**'
– 11915 Exeter Ave NE: a pink-flowered cv. such as '**Satomi**' or '**Radiant Rose**'

Pacific DOGWOOD

C. Nuttallii Audub.   Western Dogwood
Native here; from B.C. through California.

Well known, much admired; acclaimed as our premier native flowering tree.
British Columbia's Provincial Floral Emblem. Largest of the dogwoods, up to
100' tall in the woods; trunks to over 14' around. Creamy-white flowers (early
April) mid-April to mid-May (an exceptional few into late July!). A second bloom
often from (mid-) late August to early (late) October. Anthracnose fungal disease
hurts or kills our old and weaker specimens; young vigorous individuals *endure*
the debilitating annoyance but their foliage may look hideous.

In Seattle, common. Most well-wooded parks have examples.

– 6925 37th Ave SW: a broad 45' tall tree, its trunk 11'4½" around (in 2000)
– 5703 Palatine Ave N: one is 57' × 12'9" × 43' wide
– Woodland Park: NE of shelter #5 one is 63' × 7'4"; a second to the SE is 77' ×
  6'11"; a third to the N is 81½' × 4'3"
– 9222 30th Ave NE: one is 56' × 6'½" × 66½' wide
– Laurelhurst Playfield: 13 on the west side; largest is N of the fire pit, 77' × 6'11"
– Salmon Bay Park: one S of the restrooms is 49' × 7'5"

cv. '**Eddiei**'   Goldspot *or* Variegated Pacific Dogwood

Leaves splashed and dotted with yellow. This clone originated in 1919 near Chilliwack, B.C. and, like the normal Pacific dogwood, often blooms again in late summer. No very old or large examples are known here, and smaller ones are uncommon. Kubota Garden Park has a 19' tall, leggy multitrunked tree. One is at 3182 NE 84th St. It does best in a sunny location.

[Other cultivars are 'Barrick', 'Boyd's Hardy', 'Colrigo Giant', 'North Star' and 'Pilgrim'. All are extremely rare or not grown at all here except '**Colrigo Giant**'—a selection with *large* leaves and flowers: one 45' × 1'9" is in the Arboretum nursery (#869-65).]

Pagoda DOGWOOD

C. alternifolia L. fil.   Blue (fruited) Dogwood
From central & E North America.   Pigeonberry *or* Green Osier

Its branches being tier-like and horizontal suggest the name Pagoda dogwood. Only this and Giant dogwood bear their leaves alternately; all other *Cornus* bear leaves in opposite pairs. A shrubby small tree; recorded to 48' × 5¾'. Flowers small, creamy-white, in clusters 1½–2½" wide in May or June, giving rise to a dark bluish-black berry on attractive red stems. Rare in Seattle.

– Arboretum: of 3 #1244-50 in 28-1W, largest 27½' × 3'0"; #300-53 is small in 15-7E
– 2152 E Shelby St: one west of the front door
– 4015 E Lee St: one 13' tall with a Smoke Tree by the entry gate
– Washelli Cemetery: a youngster 80' west of the new mausoleum

cv. '**Argentea**'   Variegated Pagoda Dogwood

Leaves small, silver-variegated; growth shrubby. Very rare in Seattle.

– 5660 NE Windermere Rd: one was 24' × 2'4" in 1995—but is gone
– Arboretum: #283-88 is 13' tall by the pond in 14-4E

Stellar Hybrid DOGWOODS

(*C. florida* × *C. Kousa*)   Rutgers' Hybrid Dogwood
=*C.* × *rutgersensis* hort.

Intentional hybrids from Rutgers University of New Jersey. Six cultivars were named and released in 1991–92: Aurora®, Constellation®, Galaxy® (renamed Celestial® ≤1995), Ruth Ellen®, Stardust®, and Stellar Pink®. All six have been sold in Pacific Northwest nurseries. If you see a relatively young dogwood in Seattle and it looks *intermediate* between the two parent species, it is one of these.

– 7721 Earl Ave NW: 2 street-trees
– S.P.U.: one with a Japanese Maple in a triangular bed SE of the SUB
– 11th Ave SW, south of SW Holden St, street-trees of **Stellar Pink**® *pl.* 2002
– 12th Ave NE, south of NE 92nd St, a street-tree **Aurora**® on the W side

[New *C. Kousa* × *C. Nuttallii* cultivars are **Venus**® ('KN30-8'); **Starlight**® ('KN4-43').]

DOVE TREE

Davidia involucrata Baill.   (Pocket) Handkerchief Tree
DAVIDIACEÆ (*or* NYSSACEÆ *or* CORNACEÆ)   Kleenex *or* Laundry Tree
From China.   Ghost Tree

In Chinese it is Gong tong. Its English names refer to conspicuous dangling white floral bracts in late April–late May. Seen from afar the tree in bloom is less effective ornamentally than it is when viewed close up. When not in bloom it is plain. It has reached 82' × 7½' in England and does best in part shade. Its fruits are like round underripe pears up to 1¼" across, borne singly or in pairs on 2–3" stalks. Astringent flesh surrounds hard, sharp kernels resembling a peach pit. Crack these kernels and sprout the enclosed seeds to grow a Dove tree.

In Seattle, uncommon but conspicuous when in bloom. Specimens with leaves fuzzy on the underside are considered "typical" Dove trees; those devoid of fuzz are the var. *Vilmoriniana* (Dode) Wanger.—the latter is more common and probably hardier. Its fall color may be prettier too.

- 7140 55th Ave S: one 52½' tall
- Arboretum: four older trees, the largest 47' × 5'0" (#2416-40 var. *Vilmoriniana*) in 16-6E; the tallest is 53½' × 2'3" (#2009-45) in 23-2E
- Volunteer Park: E of the museum is a 5-trunked 53' tall one; N of the bandstand, by the road, is a 42' × 5'4¼" var. *Vilmoriniana* above *Pieris* shrubs
- U.W.: N of Hutchinson Hall (with tree peonies); near Communications Bldg.
- 4625 Eastern Ave N: 38' tall
- yard of 2nd house (on S side) from bottom of stairway above Lakeview Blvd E, west of E Howe St, has a 44' tall, very broad specimen
- 179 Lake Washington Blvd E: three
- 23rd Ave NE & NE 117th St: SE corner: one by the driveway
- 3427 Beacon Ave S: one 43½' tall by the alley/driveway

Largeleaf EHRETIA

Ehretia Dicksonii Hance
=*E. macrophylla* hort., *sensu auct.* Japon, *non* Wall.
BORAGINACEÆ (EHRETIACEÆ *or* CORDIACEÆ)
From China, Taiwan, Vietnam, Japan, the Ryukyus.

Named after George Dionysius Ehret (1708–70), German-English botanical artist. A gawky large shrub or bold tree up to 65' × 7⅓'. Bark corky; twigs stout. Leaves thick and large, to 8" × 4¾" (sucker leaves to 13" × 7½"); rough-hairy on both sides, especially beneath; green *late* into fall. Flowers white or slightly yellowish, *fragrant*, in 2–4" terminal panicles in June. Extremely rare in Seattle; other than the two below, only 1 young tree is known here, in a back yard.

- Arboretum: 37½' × 1'10" (#454-90) in 15-1E
- Locks bed #327: one *pl.* in the 1990s was cut to the ground in 2003, but regrew

ELMS in general

Our area is one of few in the temperate northern hemisphere lacking native elms. But Seattle has over 20 distinct non-native kinds: the exact number is uncertain because no genus of trees here is more difficult to sort. In fact it is impossible to name every particular kind. Elm classification is not only unsettled, it is hotly disputed with no resolution in sight.

Dutch Elm Disease, from Asia, was noted in Holland about 1919 (hence the name *Dutch* Elm Disease—ominously abbreviated D.E.D). It reached North America about 1930 and has killed millions of trees. It did not reach Seattle until the 1990s. Elms were not especially important economically but as landscape trees had become extraordinarily enshrined, as it were, in the hearts of Europeans and Americans. Thus the combined cost in dollars needed to remove destroyed trees, and in the shock of shattered landscapes, proved keenly painful. Now, Seattle elm owners must hire licensed pesticide applicators to treat their elms preventively, or risk fatal infection.

American ELM

Ulmus americana L.   White Elm
=*U. alba* Raf.   Water Elm
ULMACEÆ   Gray Elm
From central & eastern N America.   Soft Elm

That a tiny bug carrying a few bits of microbial dust can fatally infect such an embodiment of ideal health as this, the greatest and most beloved of elms, is one of the woeful wonders of the world.

Its symmetrical towering presence as the foremost ornamental shade tree in New England, generously giving at once a tranquilizing and an invigorating influence, helped mold in a beneficial way the national character of the youthful Union. It became an unofficial natural symbol of patriotism, the distinguishing verdure of home to millions who dwelt under its graceful influence. The largest specimens attained up to 180' × 41'.

In Seattle, common. Below are cited some of our largest.

– Ravenna Blvd NE, east of 15th Ave NE: one 88½' × 14'10½" × 111½' wide
– E Columbia St, east of 25th Ave: S side has one 79½' × 14'5½" × 88½' wide
– 4th Ave W & W Comstock St: the NW corner has one 85' × 13'3½"
– 16th Ave E, south of E John St: a street-tree, W side, 85' tall
– 923 16th Ave E (north of E Aloha St): a street-tree 66' × 12'7"
– Harvard Ave E, north of E Aloha St: largest of 7 on the W side is 12'6½" around
– E Denny Way, west of 14th Ave E: one on the S side is 71' × 12'4½"
– U.W.: parking-lot W-3 has one 71' × 12'4"
– 10th Ave E, north of E Galer St: one on the W side is 71½' × 11'11½"

[The Washington Elm—Under an elm at Cambridge, Massachusetts, General George Washington took command of the Revolutionary Army on July 3, 1775. Clones of that tree exist in Seattle. U.W.: 64' × 8'4" between Communications Bldg. and Clark Hall.

Evergreen Park Cemetery: 75' × 8'7". Arboretum #2166-37 is 59' × 5'0" west of the road in 35-4E. The largest of all is 70' × 11'4" on Ravenna Ave NE, south of NE 98th St.]

Camperdown ELM

U. glabra Mill. cv. '**Camperdownii**'   Upside-down Elm
=*U.* 'Camperdownii'   Tabletop *or* Umbrella Elm
A famous clone. It originated as a hybrid seedling in Scotland <1850. Grafted on Wych elm trunks, its branches *strongly weep* in *mop-head* fashion; in aspect and general size, only the weeping White Mulberry tree is similar. A slow-growing tree, the largest on record measure 30' × 10'. It is common in Seattle.

– Lake View Cemetery: the largest of 3 measures 18' × 6'7" × 28' wide
– Leschi Park: one 19½' × 4'¼"
– 41st Ave SW & SW Holgate St: SE corner yard has one 16½' tall, much wider
– Kubota Garden Park: several, largest 16' × 5'3" (+ weeping White Mulberry trees)
– Arboretum: the best of a pair W of the road in 34-4E, is 15' × 4'4"
– Volunteer Park: one 13' × 3'11"on the west side, shaded by a Horse Chestnut
– Ravenna Park: one in the SW part is 12½' × 4'1½" × 23' wide

Chinese ELM

U. parvifolia Jacq.   Lacebark Elm
=*U. chinensis* Pers.   Japanese: Aki-nire; Aki-nira アキニレ
From China, Korea, Japan, Taiwan.   Chinese: Lang Yu

The "official" Chinese elm (for what millions of Americans call Chinese elm, see Siberian elm). One of its Chinese names (Wen-shu) translates as Mosquito Tree. It is a small-leaved tardily deciduous to semi-evergreen tree, often with very attractive bark, and can grow as large as 95' × 15½'. It differs from most elms in flowering from mid- to late September instead of in late winter or spring.

     In Seattle, rare.

– Sand Point/Magnuson Park: 2 along the fence on Sand Point Way NE, just north of NE 65th St; a 3rd, just N of 74th St entrance is 60½' × 7'0"
– Burke Ave N & N 40th St: 3 in the SW corner yard; tallest 35½'
– 3910 Whitman Ave N has 2
– Arboretum: an ugly, limby #120-49 in 36-2E little resembles those previously cited; a 34½' tall var. *coreana* is #69-86A in 30-5E—north of the nursery

Cornish ELM

U. minor Mill., s.l. var. *cornubiensis* (West.) Richens
=*U. angustifolia* (West.) West. var. *cornubiensis* (West.) Melv.
=*U. carpinifolia* Gledit. var. *cornubiensis* (West.) Rehd.
From Cornwall, W Devonshire and S Dorset, England.

Despite disagreement over which of its forbidding scientific names is correct, this has always been uniformly called Cornish elm. It reaches at most about

121' × 26', is characterized by a gaunt *narrow* silhouette and is among the last of elms to leaf out in spring. It is very rare in Seattle.

- U.W.: of 21 elms N & NW of Parrington Hall most are Cornish; largest 96' × 7'10"
- Hiawatha Playfield: two NW of the running track, the taller 80' × 7'3"
- Zoo: 2 in the Asian Tropical Forest; the tallest is 84'
- G.A.R. Cemetery/Park: the 2nd from the west in the row of 9 elms on N border
- 17th Ave E, south of E Aloha St: 6 street-trees on the W side, tallest (@727) 84' × 9'6" yet also it is broadest and its bark differs, so it is apt to be a hybrid

English ELM

U. minor Mill., s.l. var. *vulgaris* (Ait.) Richens   Hedgerow Elm
= *U. campestris* L., pro parte
= *U. procera* Salisb.
From England—but really an ancient introduction
from Europe to S England in the latter Bronze Age.

The English counterpart (a Briton might say "prototype") of the American elm. Attaining up to 165' × 28' they long stood majestic, dignified, thriving and dearly beloved; but lately have died, are deeply missed and fondly remembered.

Tiny purplish flowers in March produce copious winged seeds resembling miniature fried eggs, maturing in April–May: they're edible while young and tender, and are infertile. English elm reproduces only from root-suckers: sizable specimens have grown up *inside* European churches from such suckers! Although not every English elm suckers, the majority do. Since its suckers and twigs are often corky-ridged, English elm is frequently called "Cork elm" here. But another elm (not present in Seattle) is the Cork elm of books.

In Seattle, our most common elm, and the hardest hit by elm leaf miner, a pest who chews the guts out of leaves, often skeletonizing entire trees.

- Midvale Ave N, north of N 40th St: a street-tree, E side, 97' × 15'11"—wider still
- S.P.U.: the tallest tree on campus, 118' × 13'10¼"
- Zoo: the largest of 4 in and east of the butterflies is 94' × 12'10½"
- Washington Park neighborhood: of 89 English elms on 34th Ave E & 36th Ave E, the stoutest is 12'6¼" around (at 36th Ave E & E Prospect St); near these are 20 American elms, on 37th, and on 36th north of E Valley St
- U.W.: many, the largest is on Denny Hall lawn, 105' × 12'6"; a street-tree 104' × 11'10" stands west of Hall Health
- Beacon Hill Playground (14th Ave S & S Holgate): N of restrooms, 12'5½" around
- Arboretum: one in 30-4E north of the nursery is 98' × 10'8½"
- 46th Ave SW & SW Atlantic St: 4 street-trees
- 1610 9th Ave W: 76' tall

European White ELM

U. lævis Pall.   Fluttering Elm
= *U. effusa* Willd.   Spreading Elm
From C & SE Europe, W Asia.   Russian Elm

Among the most densely leaved of elms, its branches and fluted, burly trunk are heavily feathered with twigs. It usually sets large crops of tiny seeds, year after year, whereas the closely related American elm (in Seattle at least) is sparing in seed-production. It can surpass 113' × 23'—and be over 100' wide. Although unknown even to most tree experts, this species is common in Seattle; it is the most resistant of our commoner elms to leaf miner damage.

– Martha Washington Park: 2 (SW of 4 American elms), the taller (north one) 95' and the stouter (south one) 11'11" around
– Leschi Park: the largest of two is 90½' × 11'2"
– W Fulton St, E of 9th Ave W: 10 street-trees, the largest 11'0" around
– S.P.U.: one south of the Student Union Building is 90½' × 10'10¾"
– Volunteer Park: 93' × 9'9" on S border, W of 15th Ave; a second is 82½' × 9'6" in the middle of an open grove of trees north of the bandstand
– U.W.: Denny Hall lawn has one 83' × 9'11"; Lewis Hall lawn has one 70' × 9'7"
– Arboretum: the best is #351-38, by the road in 34-4E, only 61' × 5'7"

Guernsey ELM

U. minor Mill., s.l. var. *sarniensis* (Loud.) Druce　　　　Wheatley Elm
=*U. carpinifolia* Gledit. f. *sarniensis* (Lodd.) Rehd.　　　　Jersey Elm
=*U.* × *sarniensis* (Loud.) H. Bancr.
=*U.* 'Sarniensis'
From the Channel Islands.

An especially distinctive and unusual elm. Scientific names vary from book to book but the English ones are fairly constant. *Narrow*, like a pointy-topped conifer in outline, it can attain up to 125' × 18'. Extremely rare in Seattle.

– Harvard Exit (SE corner of Harvard Ave E & E Roy St): a 2-trunked one 64½' × 7'2½" that was possibly planted when the building was erected in 1925, sets much seed and throws up some suckers
– Jefferson Park: 103½' × 11'3" × 64½' by tee #5
– Arboretum: #343-68 in 36-2E is 41½' × 1'6¼"

Hybrid ELMS

U. × *hollandica* Mill.　　　　　　　　　　　　　　Dutch Elms
(mostly *U. glabra* × *U. minor*)
From Europe.

There are an indeterminate number of hybrids (cultivated, named clones and a grab-bag of seedlings), some more distinct from one another, others less. Their ancestry is so baffling, nomenclature so confused and variations so many, that naming them is an exercise in futility. They vary so much that generalizations about them must be minimal. The Huntingdon (=Chichester) elm is in a class by itself, in being largest (a giant one at Oxford that blew down in 1911 was 143' × 28'3" and had 2,787 cubic feet of wood!), least similar to the rest (being far closer to Wych elm), and is one of the less rare clones in Seattle. The rest

145

look more like English or Smoothleaf elms. Hybrid elms are rare in Seattle. The locations cited below are outstanding for the variety of different elms (not necessarily all hybrids) growing together.

- G.A.R. Cemetery/Park: a row of 9 different kinds of elms! Plus an isolated 10th! Quite an elm arboretum! None of the ten except one Cornish and 1 September elm are *typical* representative species such as are alphabetically treated in this guide; most seem to be hybrids—but perhaps a few are Smoothleaf elm forms or even extremely rare east Asiatic species.
- S.P.U.: besides American, English, European White and Wych elms on the main campus, there are 14 elms (most hybrids) and a Birch in a street-triangle
- Harvard Ave E & E Mercer St: NE corner has 8 street-trees of Seattle's best Huntingdon elms, the largest 90' × 9'0"
- Volunteer Park: one 88' × 10'3½" east of the wading pool
- Jefferson Park: one 71' × 9'3½"
- U.W.: Denny Hall lawn and the lawn NW of Parrington Hall have various elms, including hybrids; four cv. 'Pioneer' street-trees south of Schmitz Hall
- Green Lake: one 58' × 8'2½" on a hill by the NW parking-lot; five cv. 'Pioneer' were planted in a row near the boat rental bldg. in the late 1990s

[Accolade™ Elm—*U.* 'Morton' *(U. japonica* × *U. Wilsoniana)*—was raised in 1924, selected at the Morton Arboretum, named in 1986 and has been sold since the 1990s. It resists DED, leaf miners and beetles, plus has a graceful habit and glossy foliage. The U.W. has 5 *pl.* in 2005 south of Suzzallo Library.]

September ELM

U. serotina Sarg.   Southern Red Elm
From the southeastern U.S.

Odd in flowering in September–October: the only other elm to do so (here) is the Chinese. September elm can reach 150' × 9½'. The only specimens known in Seattle are one N of 3 Winged elms on Denny Park's W border, 54½' × 5'4½"; and one in the G.A.R. Cemetery/Park, off to the W by itself, 38' × 3'1".

Siberian ELM

U. pumila L.   Manchurian Elm
From central and E Asia.   Chinese Elm

Though millions of midwestern Americans, including many nurserymen, call this Chinese elm, writers on trees persist in calling it Siberian elm. Others, current evidence to the contrary (so far in this country, it has exceeded 120' × 19'), still refer to it as "Dwarf Asiatic elm"! The name *pumila* (*i.e.,* "dwarf") is unfortunate. Its *leaves* are relatively small, to 2½" × 1¼".

In Seattle it is common. In appearance it can be more reminiscent of our common White Birch than of other elms. It can sucker, but rarely does here, and never so much as English elm. It reseeds far more than any other elm. Overall it behaves better here than in many parts of North America, and can become a

146

handsome shade tree if it has enough room and sunlight to satisfy its powerful appetite. Still, if an elm is desired, most any other kind is a superior choice.

- Lowell School Playground (1058 E Mercer St): one 61½' × 14'5" × 74' wide
- U.W. Medicinal Herb Garden: one 72' × 7'11½" in the nursery area (section G)
- Fremont Ave N & N 90th St: SE corner has one 47½' tall but much wider
- 2040 McGilvra Blvd E: a cabled specimen 58½' tall
- N of W Raye St, on the median where 12th Ave W turns: 3-forked, 54' tall
- 31st Ave SW & SW Holly St: the SE corner has 2, the larger 10' around
- Arboretum: #344-38 in 36-3E (3-forked, 70' tall); and #368-59 in 22-4W
- 5532 27th Ave NE: a 47' tall pendulous tree between two Black Pines
- 8th Ave & Alder St: three south of this intersection

Smoothleaf ELM

U. minor Mill., s.l.   European Field Elm
= *U. carpinifolia* Gledit.   Narrowleaf Elm
= *U. foliacea* Gilib.   Feathered Elm
= *U. nitens* Moench   Smooth Elm
From Europe, N Africa, SW Asia.

A highly varied, poorly understood species. The largest are reported to be over 140' × 28⅓'. The leaves are not necessarily smooth, nor narrow. Uncommon in Seattle, few trees here seem to fit its description exactly, but hybrids between it and Wych Elm are relatively common.

- Interlaken Park: a grove of 7 in the woods near the dead-end of 22nd Ave E off Boyer Ave E, the tallest 90' and stoutest 5'6½"
- Hiawatha Playfield: 2 Smoothleaf (largest 78' × 10'5½" SE of track), 2 Cornish (NW of track), and one Hybrid elm (SW of track, with a Smoothleaf elm)
- Green Lake: one 50' × 7'8" (& 4 American elms) SW of the Bathhouse Theatre
- Volunteer Park: one 76' × 6'4¾" is not far away from a larger Hybrid elm
- U.W.: a 34' × 5'9¾" tree S of the Conibear Shellhouse flushes very early and may really be some other species (such as *U. japonica*) or hybrid
- S.P.U.: 2 in the street triangle with various Hybrid elms and a White Birch
- Miller Park (20th Ave E, S of E Republican St): 63' × 8'11" (N) and 61' × 7'5" (S)
- 22nd Ave, *ca.* 75' N of E Pine St: one 72' tall on E side (by street-tree White Birch)

cv. 'Gracilis'   Tornado Tree

A compact, twiggy small tree, extremely rarely setting seed. Known here only as follows:

- Arboretum: five #602-39 in 37-2E & 38-3E, the tallest 47'; of *ca.* 14 in an irregular row in 9-3W, 10-3W & 11-3W, the tallest is 50'
- U.W.: 3 at S corner of Allen Library, the tallest 43½'
- NSCC: one 23' tall by the N end of 26 blue Atlas Cedars E of the parking-lot

Winged ELM

U. alata Michx.
From the southeastern U.S.

Cork Elm
Wahoo

Its twigs are often corky with two wide thin *wings*. It can reach 118' × 15½'. The only specimens known in Seattle are 3 (S of a September elm) on Denny Park's W border, the stoutest 44½' × 5'4" & tallest 56' × 4'9".

Wych ELM

U. glabra Huds.
=*U. scabra* Mill.
=*U. montana* Stokes
=*U. campestris* L., in part
From Europe, N and W Asia.

Broad-leaved Elm
Mountain Elm
Scotch Elm

A massive elm in every respect; easily distinguished from the others except the Huntingdon Hybrid elm. It grows to 164' × 25'. The peculiar name Wych is likely akin to Old English *wican*—to yield or bend—in reference to the pliant branches of this or any of several other trees. Extremely rare in Seattle.

– S.P.U.: 3 are S and SE of the Student Union Building, 103' × 10'6½", 100' × 12'2", and 84' × 11'11¾"
– Seward Park: one 67½' × 6'7" is by the far SW parking-lot

EMMENOPTERYS

Emmenopterys Henryi Oliv.
RUBIIACEÆ
From China.

From Greek *emmenes*, enduring, and *pteron*, a wing or feather, as a portion of the flower enlarges into a showy, leaflike wing. Named after Augustine Henry (1857–1930), Irish doctor, botanical explorer in China, forestry professor and author. Recorded to 100' × 13'0" in the wild, it is a heat-loving, cold-tender tree remarkable for being so rarely blooming in cultivation. Branching bold and horizontal. Leaves large (to 15" × 6¾"), new growth attractively reddish fading to bronze color; stem wine-red. Flowers white, spectacular in June or July, with bracts that persist and turn pink. It first flowered in Western cultivation in 1971, from a tree planted in 1937 in Italy. After 40 years of biding its time, a New Zealand specimen decided to flower in 1987. It first flowered in England in 1987, in America in 1994. Seattle nurseries have stocked it recently, and at least one garden has a youngster, not visible from the street.

EMPRESS TREE

Paulownia tomentosa (Thunb.) S.& Z. *ex* Steud. Royal Paulownia
=*P. imperialis* S.& Z. Blue *or* Purple Catalpa
SCROPHULARIACEÆ Princess Tree *or* Foxglove Tree
From China, Korea. Chinese: Mao Pao Tong

In general appearance, Empress tree is similar to a Catalpa, yet *smooth*-barked and lavender-flowered in spring rather than rough-barked and white-flowered in summer. Grown in this country since 1834; naturalized in many warmer areas including parts of the South where it is called "Cottonwood" or "Cotton Tree" since its seedpods look like cotton balls. In the Language of Flowers it signifies "a foreigner," possibly because it is so exotic in appearance: taut smooth gray bark; enormous bold thick leaves; large fragrant bluish-purple flowers in April or May. The Japanese so prize the Empress tree's wood (they call it Kiri キリ) that trees from the U.S. have been logged, legally and otherwise, for export: sad irony when ornamental non-native trees are mistreated as commercial commodities! The largest dimensions recorded: 105' × 21¾'.

Extremely rare in Seattle—but see cv. '**Lilacina**'.

- West Viewmont Way & W Ruffner St: NE corner has one 33½' tall
- Kubota Garden Park: 7 very old trees, the tallest only 36' and stoutest 6'6"
- 2542 36th Ave W

cv. '**Lilacina**'

Common. Flowers paler, larger, and unspotted. More cold-hardy. Reseeds.

- Arboretum: several, including #565-48 that is 79' × 9'2¾" in 45-5E
- 10314 Sand Point Way NE: 47' tall
- U.W.: one 40½' × 4'6¾" north of Benson Hall; 3 youngsters N of Music Bldg.
- Locks bed #24 (by stairs), 122
- Zoo: many; one 40' × 6'11¾" between the Snow Leopard exhibit and the felines
- Seola Greenbelt (11617 Marine View Dr SW): one 43½' × 8'4¼"
- 5655 NE Ambleside Rd: one with a huge limb over the driveway

Fragrant EPAULETTE TREE

Pterostyrax hispida S.& Z. (*hispidus*) Wisteria Tree
STYRACACEÆ Japanese: Oba-Asagara オオバアサガラ
From Japan.

A rarely cultivated relative of the Silverbell Tree. It grows 50' tall and has corky-barked trunks, often suckering from the base. Pretty, fragrant, white flowers hang in long clusters late May–early June. In Japan its wood is used to make chopsticks. It is very rare in Seattle.

- Arboretum: at least 4, the tallest 50' × 4'3½" (of 4 trunks), #44-48 in 10-7E
- 1264 NW Norcross Way: a youngster W of a Silk Tree
- U.W.: CUH by the library

Smoothbark EPAULETTE TREE

P. corymbosa S.& Z. *(corymbosus)*   Japanese: Asagara アサガラ
From China, Japan.   Chinese: Xiao Ye Bai Xin Shu

Bark smooth rather than corky; the flowers appear at the same time or a bit earlier but differ in appearance, smell like soap. Also very rare in Seattle.

- Arboretum: five, the largest pair in 10-6E: 70' × 3'10¼" (#73-57E, to SW) and 66½' × 4'½" (#73-57A, to NE); smaller trees in 10-5E, 20-2W & 36-B
- Locks bed #214 has a multitrunked 24' tall one (with two Red Horse Chestnuts)
- S.U.: one 34½' tall east of Loyola Hall
- 2061 Interlaken Pl: a young one by the driveway
- 18th Ave NE, north of NE 80th St: a young street-tree is on the E side

[Smoothleaf Epaulette Tree—*P. psilophylla* Diels *ex* Perk.—from China, is nearly identical in habit and foliage; its seedpods differ. The Arboretum has #236-83 in 12-8E (thriving) & 8-5E (ill). Local nurseries have sold some since the 1990s.]

EUCALYPTS in general

Standing out strongly no matter where planted in Seattle, these world famous trees add great impact to our landscape with their characteristic bluish-gray color and airy, elegant crowns. Nearly all eucalypts (*ca.* 800 species) are native to Australia. All broadleaf evergreens, they vary in size from sprawling shrubs called "mallees" to the tallest tree recorded in history: a *Eucalyptus regnans* F. Muell. that in 1872 measured 435' to its 3'-thick broken top. Another had a 97' trunk girth! The tallest at present is 317'. California's first eucalypts were planted in 1856; currently, the tallest there are over 200' and at least one trunk measures over 48' around! Some species are now naturalized weedily there.

Seattleites interested in eucalypts must note four things. First, the trees here are still in an experimental stage and are a gamble; at least three dozen kinds have been tried; many others are worth testing. Second, the limiting factor is freezing—our occasional severe winters hurt or kill the less hardy majority. Third, their growth is usually rapid, sometimes astonishingly so. Fourth, most bear both juvenile and adult foliage—the former typically bluish and often rounded, used in dried arrangements. Both juvenile and adult leaves are fragrant.

Below are treated, first, three species relatively well known and much grown for decades in Seattle, then, 23 lesser known species. Others also have been tried in the city, and some exist here currently. Colvos Creek nursery on Vashon Island has sold more than 50 species since the 1990s! Virtually all of those that may have been planted in Seattle will date from 1991–92 or later, and when the next big freeze occurs, we will observe its effects on the hardy, the tender, and the intermediate among the lot. Some specimens here defy efforts to identify them, and are either hybrids or otherwise baffling (for example a tree at the Locks in bed #23). Thanks to Ian Barclay for much help with this eucalypt section.

Eucalyptus Gunnii Hook. fil.   Cider Gum
MYRTACEÆ

From Tasmania. Sage-green (sometimes silvery) adult foliage. Gray-green to pale brown bark. Can grow to over 120' × 19¾'. It was first tested in Seattle decades ago. Its alpine phase, *E. Gunnii* ssp. *Archeri* (M.& B.) L. Johnson & D. Blaxell, is smaller, usually not so bluish, and likely hardier than most *Gunnii*—it has been grown here since the mid 1980s. I cannot reliably distinguish the two, so both are mixed in these examples—though most trees cited are likely *Gunnii*. Trees sold as *E. Gunnii* var. *divaricata* may prove hardiest of all.

- 5428 49th Ave SW: one *pl.* in 1991 is 76' tall
- 7526 11th Ave NW: one 72' tall
- Arboretum: 69½' × 2'9½" (#1295-56A in 8-5E); #127-92A is smaller, in 8-4E
- Phinney Ave N & N 40th St: NW corner has a 4-trunked tree 69' tall NE of the telephone pole; the same yard also has an *E. pauciflora* and some other eucalypts
- SSCC: an immense specimen east of the cafeteria
- 3514 Woodlawn Ave N: one 57½' tall
- 323 N 84th St: a large 3-trunked tree is 54' tall
- Locks bed #313 has one 53½' tall
- 839 NE 84th St: one 52½' tall
- 7519 22nd Ave NW: one *pl.* 1996 is 51' tall (+ a 20' *E. pauciflora*)—see from alley
- Good Shepherd Center: a *Gunnii* 45' tall at N end of parking lot, by entrance drive, just W of a smaller *E. stellulata*; an *Archeri* 32' tall at NE part of grounds; a stout 16½' tall *E. pauciflora* NW of the main parking lot
- 4228 Eastern Ave N: a street-tree 48½' tall
- 8517 8th Ave NE: a *Gunnii* 48' tall, an *Archeri* 35' tall, an *E. Nicholii* 29' tall
- 5104 26th Ave NE: a street-tree
- S.P.U.: one 44½' × 3'7½"
- U.W.: Stevens Court student housing, south of M, has two *pl.* 1993, the taller 35½'
- Zoo: Australasia has at least 1 *Archeri* and 9 typical *Gunnii*
- 6281 Ellis Ave S
- 7737 32nd Ave NW: a multitrunked one S of the house
- 1st Ave NE & N 57th St: NW corner (sort of) street-tree
- 906 20th Ave E: an 18' tall var. *divaricata* by the sidewalk W of telephone pole

E. pauciflora Sieber *ex* Spreng.   Snow Gum

In nature, it varies from a small tree to 100' tall; in western cultivation some are over 82' × 5½'. Lovely bark. *Thick* leaves of relatively weak fragrance. Slower than most eucalypts; extremely cold-hardy. Seattle has the typical species, *and*

ssp. *Debeuzevillei* (Maiden) L. Johnson & D. Blaxell   Jounama Snow Gum
ssp. *niphophila* (M.& B.) L. Johnson & D. Blaxell   Alpine Snow Gum

- Arboretum: the largest eucalypt, by the visitor center parking lot, was 50' × 4'8" but died in 1987; a #106-91B multitrunked tree is in 9-3E (by *Pittosporum*); two (#304-90 & #305-90) shade-stunted *Debeuzevillei* trees in *Hypericum* bed of 8-5E
- 46th Ave NE & NE 97th St: SW corner yard has one 41' tall
- 42nd Ave SW & SW Andover St: ssp. *pauciflora*, 37' tall SW of house
- 8520 and 8521 Latona Ave NE: 3 street-trees, tallest 33'; plus an *E. MacArthurii*
- U.W.: CUH has three #106-91, the tallest 30½'

- 1528 Martin Luther King, Jr Way
- 2014 E Calhoun St: 33' tall; *pl.* 1995
- 19th Ave S, north of S Stevens St: a *Debeuzevillei* street-tree, W side
- by I-5, on E side, just S of the NE 50th St bridge; *pl.* 1989
- Green Lake: one *pl.* fall 2001 along Aurora, S of N 68th St
- Zoo: Australasia has at least 4 *Debeuzevillei* and 4 *niphophila*
- 322 N 104th St: a greenleaf, red-twigged tree
- 1811 20th Ave (north of E Madison): a *Debeuzevillei* street-tree 33½' tall (in wires)
- 10th Ave E & E Hamlin St: NW corner has two *Debeuzevillei* against the house; also *E. Gunnii*
- 7746 18th Ave. NE: one 32' tall with a wider spread

E. Perriniana F. Muell. *ex* Rodway — Spinning Gum / Round-leaved Snow Gum

This usually grows to 30' tall, over 60' at most. Its common names refer to the rounded juvenile leaves that *spin* on the twigs after dying and turning brown. Adult leaves are long, slender and darker than juvenile leaves. In Seattle, many of our larger and older eucalypts are of this kind, and reseeding has occurred. A Bainbridge Island specimen dates from 1955—as old as any eucalypt known hereabouts.

- 45th Ave NE & NE 58th St: SW corner yard, 42' tall
- Arboretum: #502-66 is N of N-bound SR-520 offramp is 45' × 2'11¾" (4-trunked)
- Seola Greenbelt (11617 Marine View Dr SW): one 43½' tall
- 938 NW 52nd St: one 41' tall behind the house, visible from the park to the north
- 6128 S Pilgrim St: one 34' tall
- 4006 Latona Ave NE
- Zoo: one in Australasia
- 2366 Boyer Ave E: a youngster right by the sidewalk; apt to get into the wires

[**Red River Gum. Long-beak Eucalypt**—*E. camaldulensis* Dehnh.—Australia's most widespread eucalypt; grown in the SW U.S. but *not* hardy in Seattle. It can reach 171' × 23'0". Twigs red. Leaves slender, curved, pale green, 5–8" long. Arboretum "*E. subcrenulata*" #508-90 in 1S-4E is this. Locks bed #313 has one. Both keep freezing to the ground.]

[**Silver Dollar Gum. Argyle Apple**—*E. cinerea* F.v. Muell. *ex* Benth.—A small tree (30–60' tall) whose long-retained silvery juvenile foliage contrasts prettily with its dark beige bark. Much grown for the florist trade, and commonly planted here, but not reliably cold-hardy. One 41' tall by the sidewalk at 8840 Burke Ave N. 1704 S Hanford St. One 33' tall at 3516 SW Charlestown St. A slender one 35' tall east of a Corkscrew Willow at 4518 SW Director St. One by the driveway on the NW corner of 1st Ave NW & NW 116th St. One 33½' tall on the NE corner of 6th Ave NW & NW 74th St. One 23½' tall under a Deodar Cedar on the SW corner of 24th Ave E & E Crescent Dr. The Zoo has one in Australasia.]

[**Tasmanian Snow Gum. Mt. Wellington Peppermint**—*E. coccifera* Hook. fil.—Twigs of seedlings at least are conspicuously *warty* with red glands. Juvenile leaves to 2⅜" × 1¾"; adult leaves 1–4" × ½–¾"; less fragrant than most. Color varies from grayish-green to wholly dark green, usually dull but can be glossy. Bark shed in long strips, leaving a smooth white trunk, blotched or streaked gray and red. Has been likened to an evergreen White Birch in stature and shape. Arboretum has one 40' × 3'8½" (#501-90A SE of GVC parking lot—it may be a hybrid with Silver Peppermint, *E. tenuiramis* Miq.) 9808 35th Ave SW has a young tree 21' tall by the road (other species there as well).]

[**Buxton Silver Gum**—*E. crenulata* Blakely & de Beuzev.—A small tree, endangered in the wild. It keeps its silvery juvenile foliage. U.W. has two, one 26½' tall next to a *E. neglecta* by Bloedel Hall: one 41' tall by the Burke-Gilman Trail E of 9 Incense Cedars.]

[**Mountain Gum. Broad-leaved Ribbon Gum**—*E. Dalrympleana* Maiden—Juvenile leaves 1⅓–4¾" × ¾–2¾"; adult leaves 3½–10¼" × ½–1⅜"; usually green and semi-glossy, sometimes dull gray-green. Twigs usually reddish. Trunk whitish and smooth. A huge tree, its foliage willowy in heavy tresses. One *pl.* 1992 is 72½' × 2'7½" by a massive Western White Pine on E Blaine St, 160' E of 22nd Ave E. 7206 29th Ave NE has a 4-trunked 62½' tall tree N of a small *E. Moorei*. 224 30th Ave. E: one 60' tall against N fence, flanked by 2 smaller *E. Gunnii*. Two at 5829 16th Ave S, the taller 36½'. The Zoo has five in Australasia.]

[**Alpine Ash. Gum-topped Stringybark. Woollybutt**—*E. delegatensis* R.T. Bak.—One of Australia's most important commercial lumber trees; too big for ornamental use in restricted sites; the largest cold-hardy eucalypt. Juvenile leaves 3¼–10" × 2–4"; adult leaves 3–14" × ¾–1½" (2"); green and glossy, sometimes gray-green and dull. Bark of lower trunk dark brown, fibrous; bark above shed in ribbons, leaving branches smooth and creamy. SW corner of 33rd Ave NE & NE 75th St has one 40' tall *pl.* 2000.]

[**Tingiringi (Tingaringy) Gum**—*E. glaucescens* Maiden & Blakely—Branchlets and juvenile leaves strikingly silvery-glaucescent. Juvenile leaves ¾–2¾" × 1⅝–3¼"; adult leaves 2¾–6" × ½–1¼"; green or less commonly grayish-green and dull (like culinary sage leaves). Extremely variable in habit. Bark rough, stringy, beige. 53rd Ave NE, just south of NE 65th St: a street-tree, east side 51' × 4'0". 615 NE 77th St: one 39½' tall in yard's NW corner (a street-tree *E. Nicholii*). The Zoo has one in Australasia. McGilvra School (1617 38th Ave E): one 33' tall NW of the vegetable garden.]

[**Blue Gum**—*E. globulus* Labill.—Earth's most widely planted species; *not* hardy in Seattle. It can reach 250' × 35'5". Its weediness, messiness and flammability in California has unfairly given the whole genus a bad name. For a similar-looking hardy species see *E. nitens*. One 43½' tall is at 1137 NW 60th St right at the house's NE corner. Two behind 2006 42nd Ave E, visible from the alley, the taller 40½'. One 25½' tall is W of 2707-2709 E Marion St.]

[**Wolgan Snow Gum**—*E. Gregsoniana* L. Johnson & D. Blaxell—Trunk handsome whitish-gray, smooth. Twigs orange to deep blood-red. Flowers creamy. Leaf notably thick, green or somewhat glaucous, to 5" × ⅞". Grows as a mallee 7–23' tall. For a snow gum, not exceptionally hardy; but it resprouts readily if winter-killed. The Zoo has one in Australasia. S.U. has one with a Peanut-Butter Tree by the parking lot near 11th & Marion.]

[**Weeping Snow Gum. Weeping Sally**—*E. lacrimans* L. Johnson & K. Hill.—Usually sold as *E. pauciflora* 'Pendula'. Gray-green juvenile leaves up to 9½" × 4⅛" yield to slender green adult leaves 3–6" × ⅓–¾" borne on white twigs. It can reach 50' tall and is *very* pendulous. Bradner Gardens Park has one 13½' tall by the S gate. One 11' tall by the sidewalk at 2141 N 130th St.]

[**Camden Woollybutt. Paddy's River Box**—*E. MacArthurii* Deane & Maiden—Not well known. Leaves narrow, dull green. Bark fibrous, persistent. One with two *E. pauciflora* street-trees at 8521 Latona Ave NE.]

153

[Mt. Buffalo Sallee. Weeping Sally—*E. Mitchelliana* Cambage—Rare in the wild. A small tree at most 70' tall. Bark smooth, gray or white tinged yellowish. Leaves notably slender and willowy, 3–6" long × ½", green to pale gray-green. One *ca.* 22' tall—with *E. coccifera, E. glaucescens, E. Gunnii,* and two *E. pauciflora*—at 9808 35th Ave. SW.]

[Narrowleaf Sally (Sallee)—*E. Moorei* Maiden & Cambage—Shrubby species with slender leaves. Not well known. One behind the house at 5428 49th Ave SW is 21½' tall. 7206 29th Ave NE has a small street-tree south of a 4-trunked 62½' tall *E. Dalrympleana.*]

[Omeo (round-leaved) Gum—*E. neglecta* Maiden—Twigs often *square.* Leaves distinctively *broad, very dark* bluish-green (color of collard greens) with a stout red midrib, to 6" × 5" when juvenile. Adult leaves still broad but smaller (to *ca.* 5" × 2"). A shrubby tree 25–40' tall. Bark shreddy-flaky, dark gray-brown, recalling that of Common Hawthorn. The U.W. has one 22' tall at the corner of Bloedel Hall (+ a *E. crenulata*). 746 N 74th St has 2 east of the house, the best 28' tall. 6202 9th Ave NW has one 19½' tall S of the house.]

[Peppermint Gum. Willow-leaved Peppermint—*E. Nicholii* Maiden & Blakely—Not hardy but still grown; fun while it lasts. Twigs red; leaves remarkably *slender.* A 25½' tall street-tree @ 615 NE 77th St. 1st Ave NW & NW 95th St: NE corner yard has one 22' tall SW of the house. One at 5722 25th Ave NE. The Zoo has two in Australasia. 8517 8th Ave. NE has one 29' tall near the telephone pole.]

[Shining Gum. Silver *or* Shiny Top—*E. nitens* Maiden—Much like a ±cold-hardy version of the Blue Gum *(E. globulus)* so common in California. A giant. 4019 2nd Ave. NE has a massive tree 61' tall. Three at 9329 Lima Terrace S *pl.* in 2001, the tallest now 33½'.]

[Swamp *or* Black Gum—*E. ovata* Labill.—A tree to 100' tall. Adult leaves greenish, to *ca.* 6" × 1¼". The Zoo has one in Australasia.]

[Small-leaved Gum—*E. parvula* L. Johnson & K. Hill (= *E. parvifolia* Cambage 1909, *non* Newberry 1895)—Twigs red on sunny side. Leaves up to 4¼" × ¾", dark blue-green, highly fragrant. A small to medium, broad tree of fine texture and dark aspect. Bark tan, sloughing off to leave a smooth grayish trunk. One 26' tall on NE corner of 24th Ave E & Boyer Ave E. 2301 N 65th St: behind house, 45' tall. 3112 E Union St has 2. The Zoo has two in Australasia.]

[Silver-leaved Mountain Gum. Powdered Gum—*E. pulverulenta* Sims—Heart-shaped, thick, *pale silvery* leaves on a smooth-barked tree. 2014 E Calhoun St has one 33' tall; *pl.* 1995. U.W.: Bloedel Hall has a 10' tall *sideways* one—27' wide. The Zoo has one in Australasia. 2112 E Republican St. 9329 Lima Terrace S has a small one poking over the fence under some *Acacia* trees.]

[Black Sally. Muzzlewood—*E. stellulata* Sieb. *ex* DC.—*Stellulata* means resembling small stars—in reference to the small, pointed bright yellow buds in clusters of as many as 16. Leaf dark sage-green, slender and small, exceptionally to 5⅞" × 1". Seedpods or urns are tiny, like peppercorns. Bark peely on young trees but eventually close and scaly, very dark if not black. A small to medium-sized tree. The Zoo has seven in Australasia. The Good Shepherd Center has one 29½' tall in the parking lot, leaning E of a larger *E. Gunnii.*]

[Alpine Yellow Gum—*E. subcrenulata* Maiden & Blakely—Foliage *greenish.* A tree to 60'. A street-tree 34½' tall at 1419 E John Ct. A street-tree *pl.* 2004 @ 2014 E Calhoun St. The Zoo has one in Australasia. One north of 6849 46th Ave NE.]

[**Urn Gum. Urn-pod Gum. Urn-fruited Gum**—*E. urnigera* Hook. fil.—Foliage amazingly variable. Juvenile leaves ¾–3¼" × ½–3½"; adult leaves 2–6" × ¾–2"; dark green to silvery glaucous (from hardier, higher-altitude trees). Flowers white, more showy than those of the other cold-hardy species. Seedpods perfect little urns. Bark peely, smooth, pale gray or blotched greenish-yellow; often ribbed and pale brown near the base of the trunk. Usually a small tree. The Zoo has four in Australasia.]

[**Manna Gum. Ribbon Gum**—*E. viminalis* Labill.—The chief food of the koala. Up to 165 × 23'6". Trunk creamy white. Twigs dark red. Leaves 4–7" long. Flowers in trios. 6204 9th Ave NW has a multitrunked one 37' tall by the garage (+ a small *E. neglecta* S of the house). On the north side of E Marion St east of 27th Ave, two are just W of the alley.]

EUCRYPHIA

Eucryphia spp.
EUCRYPHIACEÆ

As cultivated here, these are slender, usually multitrunked shrubs or small trees, bearing white flowers (June) July–August (September). Only one is deciduous. They're little known and rare, or at most uncommon here; few exist on public property. All 5–7 species are from the southern hemisphere. The best way to get acquainted with the various kinds of *Eucryphia* is to visit the Arboretum.

E. glutinosa (Poepp. & Endl.) Baill.   Hardy *or* Deciduous Eucryphia
From Chile; very rare in the wild state.

Deciduous, semi-evergreen or fully evergreen. Fall color yellow to orange-red or crimson. Leaves consist of 3–5 leaflets, in shape and size reminiscent of those of the common Mountain-Ash, except dark and shiny. Flowers are the largest of the genus (2–2¾" wide) and the first to appear (beginning late June or early July). They are slightly almond-scented and resemble single white roses or Rose of Sharon *(Hypericum calycinum)*, with lovely bunches of greenish-white or rarely red stamens. Highly variable from seed. Some have more or less double flowers. Usually an 8–20' shrub; can be trained into tree form. Recorded to 44' tall in the British Isles. The most cold-hardy *Eurcryphia*.

– Kruckeberg Botanic Garden: 26' × 1'6½"
– Arboretum: largest of 7 in 7-3E, 8-2E & 8-3E is 22½' tall (#130-47); others include one 19½' tall (#528-58), 16' tall (#130-47C), and 10' tall (#556-42)
– 1150 19th Ave E: 18' tall
– Dunn Gardens: one 15' tall
– Denny Park: two youngsters SE of the formal center bed, the taller 10½'
– Locks bed #327 has a small specimen by the building

E. × *intermedia* Bausch.
(*E. glutinosa* × *E. lucida*)

A cross of a hardy Chilean and a tender Tasmanian species. The original form of the cross ('**Rostrevor**') is a natural garden hybrid from Rostrevor House, County

155

Down, Ireland. Leaves glossy, toothless or barely-toothed above the middle, usually simple (to 3" × 1¼"), sometimes trifoliate. Blooms fully in August, then sporadically in September, October, November, even through January in mild winters. More free-flowering than *E. glutinosa*. Flowers 1½" wide, fragrant.

– Arboretum: larger of two in 7-3E is 33' × 1'1"; largest of 3 north of Rhododendron Glen (15-5E) is 30½' tall; a 6th is 21½' tall in 8-3E (all six are #369-56)
– Zoo: tallest of at least two W of Day & Night Exhibits is 12'
– Children's Hospital: one 18½' tall uphill not far from the smoker's shelter
– Locks bed #304 has an old yet small specimen by the building corner
– 8034 Fairway Dr NE: one north of the driveway

E. lucida (Labill.) Baill.   Leatherwood

A cold-tender Tasmanian species; to 100' tall in the wild. Leaves simple (to 3" × ⅝"), dark green on top, satiny white beneath. Cupped white flowers 1–2" wide in June or July; a good honey plant. 'Pink Cloud' is pink flowered.

– Arboretum: of three (#188-90) in 8-3E, A is 12' tall, B is dead, and C is 15' tall
– Zoo: Australasia has at least 15; tallest 15'
– 2422 NW 58th St: possibly 'Pink Cloud'
– 3425 West Laurelhurst Drive NE: a 'Pink Cloud' *pl.* 2004 right against the house, *ca.* 6' tall; between the front door and a *Distylium racemosum*

E. × *nymansensis* Bausch.   Nymans Hybrid Eucryphia
(*E. glutinosa* × *E. cordifolia*)

The original form of the cross ('Nymansay') is a natural garden hybrid from Sussex, England. Leaves usually consist of 3–5 extremely dark green, shiny, sharply toothed leaflets. Foliage can turn brown in a severe winter, then recover to flower perfectly in summer. Flowers in August–September, 2–2½" wide (larger than those of *E.* × *intermedia*), honey-scented, milk-white petals surrounding yellow, pink or teracotta anthers. Nymans eucryphia is easily raised, vigorous, and as beautiful as any we can grow. Old English specimens measure at most 75' × 6⅓'. It is Seattle's most common eucryphia. Growth rapid: it can reach nearly 40' in 15 years. But the tops often die in severe freezes, so it begins growing anew from lower down. Dense narrow habit.

– 2030 42nd Ave E: 25' tall
– 1906 14th Ave E (in back yard; visible from alley): 27' tall
– Arboretum: largest of 2 north of Rhododendron Glen (15-5E) is 24' tall (#970-49); three more (also #970-49) are in 7-3E
– 633 NW 116th St: 23½' tall, by street just west of a purple Smoke Tree
– U.W.: three NW of the HUB, the tallest 23'
– 6021 Wellesley Way NE: one *pl.* 1994 by the driveway is 23' tall
– 3609 42nd Ave NE: 22' tall; W of driveway
– 33rd Ave S & S Atlantic St: NE corner yard has five, the tallest 20½'

[*E.* × *nymansensis* 'Mt. Usher' is of garden origin, from Mt. Usher, Ashford, County Wicklow, Ireland. Leaves predominately *simple*. Flowers 2" wide, often double. The Arboretum has two #970-49 in 7-3E, the larger 25' tall.]

[*E.* × *Hillieri* Ivens *(E. lucida* × *E. Moorei)* is of garden origin, from England. Known in Seattle only as a tree *pl.* 2004 in a private garden.]

Hardy EUODIA

Tetradium Daniellii (Benn.) Hartley
=*Euodia Daniellii, E. Delavayi, E. Henryi, E. hupehensis, E. velutina, E. vestita*
(*Evodia*)
RUTACEÆ
From China and Korea.

In 1981 six *Euodia* species were switched to *Tetradium Daniellii*. There is no English name, but "BeeBee Tree" has been coined, as the tiny shiny black seeds look like pygmy BB pellets. Hardy Euodia has reached over 80' × 10½' in cultivation. It has smooth gray bark like a beech or holly. Its leaves are compound and vary from 5 glossy dark green leaflets to 13 dull narrow ones; tardily deciduous in autumn. Wide clusters of tiny white flowers mid- to late July, make powerfully odorous seed-clusters. Other than two #348-71 in the Arboretum (50½' × 2'9¾" in 8-6E and 52½' × 4'10½" in 9-6E), the only tree known in Seattle is one 56½' × 6'7" (and far wider) in Volunteer Park, in a grove of mixed trees midway between the bandstand and conservatory. It rubs elbows with a Kentucky Coffee Tree, and is reseeding. The seed from which this tree grew came from Fenghsien, Shensi, China, and had been collected by Frank Meyer, who reported that the native people called the tree "Shan La Tzu Shu" or mountain pepper-tree.

FIG TREE

Ficus Carica L.   Common Fig
MORACEÆ   Edible Fig
From SW Asia.

Fig trees are common here, and abound in some older neighborhoods of south-central Seattle. Most Seattle fig trees are in effect fig-less shrubs: neither ripening fruit fully, nor growing as trees. They are not to blame, for of the 700–800 species in their genus precious few survive outdoors at all here, and our coldest winters turn the thick branch-tips black. The few that do ripen fruit tend to be select cultivars, or happy trees in congenial spots (they hate shade) during extra-warm summers. If one desires a fig crop here it pays to contain the tree's roots, to prune, but mostly to plant adapted cultivars such as 'Brown Turkey', 'Gillette', '(Desert) King', 'Lattarula' (=Italian Honey). That done, beware of feasting yellowjackets, birds and squirrels. A fig tree in a warm, sunny location bears yearly here. As a mere ornamental, it is easy to grow: few plants are so undemanding. It can be kept bushy or allowed to reach 30' × 6'—even taller when trained up a wall! It responds well to pruning and tolerates most soils.

To see a fig leaf pictured, look at a painting of Adam & Eve: apparently these two archetypal gardeners grew figs in Eden, since they're usually represented with such foliage. In the Language of Flowers, the fig tree signifies "prolific" and the fig fruit "argument" or "I would keep my secret."

— 33rd Ave S & Mt Baker Blvd S: the NW corner has one over 40' tall and wider still
— U.W. Medicinal Herb Garden: section B has a handsome, large tree that very rarely ripens fruit; one S of the Plant Lab does ripen fruit; one 26' tall west of Harris Lab
— 13th Ave & E Denny Way: SW corner apartment building has one at its SE corner
— Green Lake: one *pl.* in 1991 on the NE shore near Meridian Ave
— 4024 42nd Ave S
— 4333 SW Concord St: one 25' tall

Algerian FIR

Abies numidica De Lann. *ex* Carr.
PINACEÆ
From mountainous NE Algeria.

This fir is an associate of the Atlas Cedar in its native land. In the British Isles and Ireland it has attained 115' × 12¼' so far. It is extremely rare in Seattle, but thriving and handsome. The following specimens are reseeding.

— Arboretum: 66' × 4'6" (#319-59 in 17-3E); 56' × 3'3½" (#319-59 in 17-4E); #449-52 trees may be really *A. Pinsapo* ssp. *marocana* (Trab.) Emb. & Maire; #X-275 in 21-1E, labeled *A. alba*, is likely *A. numidica*, and lofty at 84' × 6'3"
— U.W. Friendship Grove, representing Tunisia; 59' × 3'9½"

Alpine FIR

A. lasiocarpa (Hook.) Nutt.   Western Balsam Fir
From western North American mountains.   Sub-Alpine Fir

In the wild, up to 175' × 21' but as cultivated *here,* short-lived, and rarely reaching 60' × 5', usually nowhere near that. Popular and widely planted in Seattle landscapes, often with bark mulch and boulders. Most are transplanted from mountains, a few are nursery-grown; great variation in appearance and performance. In general, our Alpine firs are bluish rather than greenish, narrow, slow-growing, stunted, swollen-twigged and aphid-infested, and make few or no cones. Most die before or soon after reaching 30' in height; few trunks 1' thick exist.

— Arboretum: the largest in 16-4E: 51' × 3'¼" (#512-37C) & 28½' × 2'3½" (#451-53)
— 3634 Woodlawn Ave N: one 47' tall by fire hydrant
— Kubota Garden Park: NE part has four, the tallest 43' and stoutest 4'4¾"
— 2608 4th Ave N: huge trunked, 28' tall
— 3507 47th Ave NE: 43' tall
— 5403 NE 54th St: 39' tall

var. *arizonica* (Merriam) Lemm.   Arizona *or* Corkbark Fir

With very attractive whitish, corky bark and bluer-than-typical foliage. Rare here; most are very young, compact forms.

- Arboretum: of three in 6-1E, *pl.* 1958, the best measured 30' × 1'9"—but died
- Woodland Park: one reached 30' × 1'6" before dying in 1987
- 16th Ave S & S Jackson St: NW corner
- 31st Ave W & W Armour St: NE corner yard has one by the sidewalk on Armour
- SSCC Arboretum: a 10' tall one in the Milton Sutton Conifer Garden

[*A. bifolia* A. Murr. is, in the recent *Flora of North America*, treated as a distinct species, the **Rocky Mountain Alpine Fir**. Slightly shorter needles and chemical differences support this view. But by just gazing at Alpine firs planted in Seattle one cannot tell if an individual is a *lasiocarpa* or *bifolia*. The Corkbark fir would be an example of *A. bifolia*.]

Balsam FIR

A. balsamea (L.) Mill.   Balm of Gilead Fir
From a vast range in the NE part of the continent.   Balsam

Narrowest of firs, it grows to 125' × 11¼' at most, but is usually a small tree. What it lacks in size is amply made up for in quantity and beauty: it is valued as a pulp source, Christmas tree and general purpose ornamental. Its fragrant resin, "Canada Balsam" or "Balm of Gilead" was used medicinally, to make a varnish, to seal birchbark canoe seams, to glue microscope slide coverslips, *etc.*

In Seattle, rare. It relishes moist soil and grows slowly. Short-lived; it reaches 20–30' tall and 5–10" trunk diameter, then dies. Like Alpine fir, but slenderer, not as dense, and shorter-lived.

- school at 1st Ave W & W Florentia St: one 32' × 2'0" at the N end +Douglas firs
- Arboretum: one 37' × 1'7" died; #665-70 is 28' × 2'3" in 41-5W (conifer meadow)
- Montlake Playfield (16th Ave E & E Calhoun St): two NE of the Tudor building; the tallest 27½' and the stoutest 2'6½"

Caucasian FIR

A. Nordmanniana (Stev.) Spach   Nordmann Fir
From the Caucasus area east of the Black Sea.

This tree has endeared itself to Russian foresters because it is one of their few big timber producers, growing up to 225' × 20½' and capable of living 700 years. Uncommon here. Nearly all are on park land.

- Volunteer Park: of 5, the best is immediately behind the museum, 94½' × 6'0"
- Rodgers Park: the larger of two W of the play area is 83' × 4'8"
- Zoo: the Family Farm has 3; two (and 3 blue Colorado Spruces and a Deodar Cedar) are south of N 59th St, east of Evanston Ave N; two are also NE of the north gate (with Norway Spruces), the larger 84½' × 4'1¼"
- Green Lake: best of 3 E of the Aqua Theatre 73' × 3'10½" (+ a Greek fir); one 67½' × 4'¼" by a Colorado Spruce near the #48 bus-stop by Sunnyside Ave N
- Lincoln Park: the extreme N part has one 58' × 3'5¾"
- U.W.: one 40½' tall between Sieg Hall and Allen Library

Douglas FIR

Pseudotsuga Menziesii (Mirb.) Franco   (our) Common Fir
=*P. mucronata* (Raf.) Sudw.   Coast Douglas Fir
=*P. taxifolia* (Poir.) Britt. *ex* Sudw.
=*P. Douglasii* (Lindl.) Carr.
Native here; from British Columbia to Mexico.

Seattle owed its early economic health to this tree. Settlers were met by a dense unbroken evergreen forest composed mostly of fir. Clearing the fir-clad hills gave Seattle the room to expand, as well as wood to build with and to export. This is still our most abundant conifer, largest tree, and a contender for the title of oldest as well. Douglas fir is the most important timber tree in the U.S. and the most extensively planted tree in Europe. Uses for its wood seem to be endless—even its bark is now a well known feature of the urban landscape. No other species has such a hold on the commercial Christmas tree market. Not surprisingly, it is the State Tree of Oregon. The greatest dimensions on record for this tree are 415' × 56½'! Though 1,350 is a conservative maximum age, the oldest may live for as long as 1,500–2,000 years, with bark over 20" thick! Coast Redwoods of greater girth abound, and some might have grown taller, but no records exist to that effect.

In Seattle, very common. A few old growth specimens are preserved in parks, and second-growth stands are abundant. Douglas fir is as popular a landscape tree now as it has always been. Local strains and imported races are both planted, but few cultivars are planted here, even though over 50 exist.

O.O. Denny Park had a Douglas fir 255' × 27'0" but it broke off at 91'. The tallest specimen alive there now is 235', the stoutest 21'8". Trunks over 21' around are also at Lincoln, and Seward Parks, and on Blake Island; Carkeek Park's largest trunk is over 18¼' around; Schmitz Park's largest living trunk is 18' around, and the stoutest at Golden Gardens Park is 14¼'. Heights of 160–180' are easily found but the number of trees near or over 200' is small, though many were once taller before windstorms or lightning broke their towering tops.

cv. 'Pendula'   Weeping Douglas Fir

Many Douglas firs weep a bit—those below distinctly *flop* and raise eyebrows. The first trees cited are not in the city limits, yet are *very* near Seattle and are larger than any known in the city—the cultivar is very rare here.
 – NE 155th St skateboard park opposite 9th Ave NE: the largest of 5 is 50' × 3'9½"
 – 58th Ave SW between SW Spokane & Hillcrest: one by a Jap. maple on a rockery
 – Kubota Garden Park: one trained into an arch, its trunk 2'5½"

160

Bigcone Douglas FIR

P. macrocarpa (Torr.) Mayr   Largecone Douglas Fir
From S California mountains.   Bigcone Spruce

Compared to the regular Douglas fir, this cousin has longer, sharper, and more curved dark green glossy needles of weaker scent, and cones 4–7½" long (rather than 2–4½"). It can attain 173' × 21½' or more, but is usually much smaller. Very few trees are as drought tolerant. It is extremely rare in Seattle.

– Arboretum: 3, the largest (#503-48) in 6-2E, 46½' × 3'2" & in 20-2E, 42' × 2'8¾"
– U.W.: a slender youngster 26' × 1'1½" under a Ponderosa Pine west of Bloedel Hall

Rocky Mountain Douglas FIR

P. Menziesii ssp. *glauca* (Beissn.) E. Murr.   Interior *or* Inland Douglas Fir
From mountainous, inland areas.   Blue *or* Colorado Douglas Fir

Compared to regular Douglas Fir, this kind is more cold-hardy, the needles are bluer, the cone bracts longer & bent, the tree stouter, and bark more corky. It can attain 209' × 24½'—so is smaller. It is rare in Seattle, but a good ornamental.

– Evergreen Park Cemetery: one 64½' × 5'10"
– U.W.: one 61' × 4'11" is 25' from a coast Douglas Fir behind Bloedel Hall
– Keystone Pl N & N 52nd St: a 62½' tall street-tree with *Yucca* by the fire hydrant
– 2847 NW 74th St: a 39½' tall tree, previously topped
– Green Lake: two youngsters not far from the Pitch 'n Putt golf course
– I-5 Freeway: many northward from Northgate

[In 1988 a small *Pseudotsuga Wilsoniana* Hayata was planted at the Locks in bed #201 (near #202). It is still there, in the shade. This species is native to Taiwan, so may be called Taiwan Douglas fir. The Arboretum has four #115-96 in the nursery.]

European Silver FIR

Abies alba Mill.   (not our) Common Silver Fir
=*A. pectinata* (Lam.) Lam. & DC.
From mountainous Europe.

The original "Silver fir", which is the largest conifer of Europe, up to 225' × 31½'; previously very important as a timber tree. Extremely rare in Seattle. Highly susceptible to aphid harm and not proving as attractive as most firs here. A floppy little weeping cultivar ('Pendula') is in the nursery trade.

– Arboretum: 43-6W has one 34' tall (#104-66) with cv. 'Pendula' (#261-64) 16½' tall by it; 40-5W has one 30½' tall; 17-4E has one 70' × 4'11" (#150-67); 16-5E has one 90' × 6'10¼" (#344-59); 12-4E has one 58½' × 4'9½" (#344-59); 8-2E has #97-66 holding some needles green as long as 21 years
– U.W. Medicinal Herb Garden: one north of Cascara Circle is 65' × 3'6"
– NE corner of 12th Ave W & W Ruffner St has a '**Pendula**'

Fraser FIR

A. Fraseri (Pursh) Poir.
From the S Appalachians in
Virginia, Tennessee, and North Carolina.

Mountain Balsam Fir
Southern Balsam Fir
She Balsam

Fraser fir grows on Mt Mitchell of North Carolina, the tallest peak east of the Mississippi River (6,684'). An imported European insect pest and acid rain are seriously hurting the population. The largest dimensions noted are 100' × 10'.

In Seattle, uncommon. Sold by some nurseries as living Christmas trees, these are occasionally planted in yards. Dark green, strong and handsome when young, they unfortunately prove short-lived here, in this respect quite like Balsam fir, a close cousin. Small, attractive and distinctive cones are often freely borne.

— S.U.: one 31' × 2'10" S of the Lynn Bldg.
— Arboretum: 16-3E has one 23' × 1'3½" (#1005-47); '**Prostrata**' in 37-1W (#184-59)
— 17th Ave NW & NW 87th St: SW corner has one 14½' tall
— U.W.: one *pl.* 2004 on NE Campus Parkway, W of University Way
— Children's Hospital: a 39' tall tree at the SW corner of the "giraffe" garage may be this species but its i.d. remains uncertain

Grand FIR

A. grandis (Dougl. *ex* D. Don) Lindl.
Native here; from S British Columbia
to coastal N California, essentially in
lowlands rather than mountains.

Lowland White Fir
Giant (Silver) Fir
Vancouver Fir
Yellow Fir

Outdoorsmen and loggers frequently call this "White fir" and many Seattleites are surprised to learn that it's native in the city. Strong *tangerine* odor exudes from the crushed needles. It is widely grown in Europe for timber and ornament and is their fastest-growing introduced conifer, at up to 5 feet per year. Planted trees in the British Isles have reached 206' × 24' so far. In nature, the tallest on record were 300' but no trunks any stouter than 23' have been reported: it tends to rot and die before it can grow so large.

In Seattle, common both wild and planted. Its *narrow* habit and the rounded nest-like top of mature specimens is distinctive. The tallest is 188' × 13½' at O.O. Denny Park. The tallest at Schmitz Park is 170' and the stoutest 14½'; at Kubota Garden Park 13½'; at Discovery Park 12½'; at Carkeek Park 12⅓'; at Lincoln Park 12'+; at Golden Gardens Park 12'; at the Arboretum 12'; at Woodland Park 10½'.

Greek FIR

A. cephalonica Loud.
(incl. var. *Apollinis* (Link) Beissn.)
From mountains of Greece, S Yugoslavia,
S Albania, and the isles of the Aegean Sea.

Black Mountain Fir
Cephalonian Fir
Mt Enos Fir

A close relative of Spanish fir, but broader, with fiercely sharp needles (usually). It has grown up to 136' × 18' in the United Kingdom; one in Tacoma's Point Defiance Park may be the largest in the U.S., in 1993: 116' × 15'2" × 75' wide! It is very rare in Seattle.

– W Parkmont Pl & Crestmont Pl W: one about 68' × 8'
– 2000 NW 61st St: one 75' tall
– Locks #28 has one over 63' tall
– Green Lake: one 72' × 5'3½" (+ 3 smaller Caucasian Firs) E of the Aqua Theatre
– Zoo: one 64½' × 6'1" by the sidewalk NW of the Phinney (west) entrance
– Arboretum: the trees died from too much shade

Hybrid FIR

A. × *insignis* Carr. *ex* Bailly
(*A. Pinsapo* × *A. Nordmanniana*)

From France *ca.* 1850, this hybrid between the Spanish and Caucasian Firs is closer to the latter in appearance, growing thicker and wider but not necessarily as tall. Dimensions over 125' × 15' are on record. The cones are conspicuous, long and narrow, greenish, up to 8¼" × 2" wide. This tree is extremely rare here.

– Camp Long: two SW of cabin #8, the best 86½' × 7'9¼"; smaller ones N of there
– Arboretum: the largest #597-44 in 38-5W is 77' × 5'3¼"; two still larger, 6½'
  around in 1984, grew ill and were cut down
– 39th Ave NE & NE 68th St: SE corner has one 40½' tall

[Other Mediterranean hybrid firs exist in Seattle outside the Arboretum. Since the 1990s local nurseries have sold trees called *A. Bornmuelleriana*, and *A. Pardei.* Whether such trees are really hybrids to begin with is disputed—let alone if the trees so-called in local nurseries are truly named. Arboretum trees labeled #370-54 *A. Pardei* are likely *A.* × *Vilmorinii* Mast. (*A. Pinsapo* × *A. cephalonica*). Arboretum trees labeled *A. Bornmuelleriana* vary, but some, if not most, are true-to-name; the tallest is 34' (#629-64C in 40-5W). One 23' tall was *pl.* in 2004 at Cal Anderson Park.]

Korean FIR

A. koreana Wils.
From Korea, largely in alpine areas.

A *dwarf* tree of stubby needles and many cute bluish-purple cones with fringe-like bracts at first pale green, then red-brown. In nature it grows up to 75' tall. It is rare in Seattle, and those cited below are both young and small.

– 4025 NE 110th St: one *pl. ca.* 1992 N of the house is *vigorous* and 18' tall
– SSCC Arboretum: a 10' tall one in the Cœnosium Rock Garden
– 8th Ave NE & NE 83rd St: NE corner yard has one S of the house by the sidewalk
– Seattle Center: east of Allen Family Pavilion
– 1100 38th Ave E
– Locks bed #316 but only *ca.* 2' tall
– 30th Ave NE & NE 57th St, NW corner yard: a youngster in yard's NE corner
– 2424 35th Ave W: one by the sidewalk

Manchurian FIR

A. *holophylla* Maxim.   Needle Fir
From Korea, SE Manchuria and adjacent Russia.

A seldom cultivated species with sharp needles 1–1¾" long, flushing early in
spring. In nature it grows up to 150' × 12'. It is extremely rare in Seattle.

– Arboretum: Foster Island has at least two (larger #395-37 is 47' × 2'2"); #941-50 in
  16-4E is 3'6½" around; *possibly* an untagged tree 1'6½" around in 21-1E
– Locks #24, 25, 26 & 28 have six, the tallest 61'

Momi FIR

A. *firma* S.& Z.   Japanese Fir
From Japan.   Japanese: Momi モミ

Of all Japanese firs, this is most widely distributed, the most important timber
producer, the largest (to 150' × 20'), and to many the most beautiful.

In Seattle, rare. About a dozen are known on private property. During the
Depression it was one of the trees extensively planted in parks, often with two
other Japanese firs—Veitch and Nikko.

– U.W.: one NW of the stadium was 65' × 6'0" × 48' wide, but was so hurt by nearby
  construction that it died; one behind Anderson Hall is 43' × 3'5"
– 49th Ave NE & NE 39th St: SW corner yard, one 74' tall S of a Japanese Red Pine
– Mt Baker Park: two, the larger 74' × 5'1½"
– 6910 56th Ave NE: one 71' tall in the back yard
– Dayton Ave N & N 40th St: NW corner yard has one 68' tall
– Arboretum: 40-5W has one mislabled *A. concolor* #206-63A; 20-5E has two 67½' ×
  4'7" & 65' × 4'10¼"(#41-55); 19-1E has one 44' × 2'6"; 17-4E has one 54½' × 5'2"
  (#447-50); ten are west of the Japanese Garden, the tallest 70' and stoutest 4'9¼"
– Golden Gardens Park: 18 N of dog area (+11 Nikko firs and a Veitch fir)

Nikko FIR

A. *homolepis* S.& Z.   Japanese: Urajiro Momi ウラジロモミ
From Japan.   Dake Momi *or* Nikko Momi

In nature, not as abundant as Momi Fir, with which it can hybridize. It grows
to 130' × 16' and its cones are purple, not green, and smaller (3–4¾" long).
Both Nikko and Momi Firs have the same broad-spreading silhouette. Though
uncommon overall in Seattle, many are in the park system.

– W Seattle Stadium (35th Ave SW & SW Snoqualmie St): 19, largest 83½' × 6'5"
– Lake Washington Blvd S & S Atlantic St: best of 3 E of 4 Deodars is 59½' × 6'5½"
– Ravenna Park: 25, the tallest 88' × 5'3¼"
– Mt Pleasant Cemetery: one, in the N part in the middle, is 54½' × 5'6½"
– Dayton Ave N & N 125th St: SW corner yard has a 56' tall twin-trunked tree
– Volunteer Park: one 67½' × 4'8" across the street SE of the wading pool
– Woodland Park: far N part, by Aurora Ave N, has many dozens
– Arboretum: two, 2'8½" around (#849-50 in 20-2E); 2'10½" (#161-51 in 16-3E)

- Camp Long: over three dozen
- Lincoln Park: 13
- Rodgers Park: 19

[*A. Forrestii* Coltm.-Rog. = *A. Delavayi* var. *Forrestii* (Coltm.-Rog.) A.B. Jacks.—Forrest's Fir is a W Chinese species; as with most Chinese firs, its identity and attributes are disputed. Needles notched; dark green above, lovely whitish beneath. Arboretum #977-58 in 17-4E is 19' tall and 21' wide under a Momi fir among tree peonies. #48-67A measures 24' × 1'3" in 9-2E. A grafted one was *pl.* in 1998 west of the tennis courts at Twin Ponds Park.]

Noble FIR

A. procera Rehd.   Oregon Larch
=*A. nobilis* (Dougl. & Lamb.) Lindl.
From the Cascades and coastal mountains of Washington and Oregon.

Largest of firs except Douglas; noted up to 325' × 28½'. In Seattle, common in yards, very rare in parks. When bearing its heavy, fringed cones (6–10" × 3–4" wide) it's highly ornamental and nearly unmistakable (but see Shasta Fir).

- Arboretum: the largest of at least 7 are in 16-3E, 98½' × 6'5¾" and 62' × 3'7½"
- Kubota Garden Park: NE part has one 72' × 6'1½"; a second is 80' × 7'1"
- 5717 28th Ave NE: one 57' tall is north of a Douglas Fir
- Children's Hospital: one 56' tall on the east border (45th Ave NE)

Pacific Silver FIR

A. amabilis Dougl. *ex* Forbes   Lovely *or* Beautiful Fir
From mountains, extreme SE Alaska   Cascades Fir
to extreme NW California.   Red Fir

Up to 268' × 26¼' in nature. In Seattle, uncommon. Its youthful beauty is soon followed by decline, not due to natural antipathy to our climate or soils so much as to being planted in warm dry yards rather than cool moist park ravines. While it lasts it makes a notably dark, dense spire.

- Arboretum: best are 59' × 3'¼" (#1419-46 in 4-1E); 55½' × 3'0" (#518-37 in 16-3E)
- 25th Ave NE & NE 143rd St: NW corner yard has one 58' tall
- 45th Ave SW & SW Spokane St: NE corner yard has one 52' tall
- Dahl Playfield (25th Ave NE & NE 77th): 7 on E side +Scots pines; 42½' × 3'3¾"
- 133 NE 133rd St

Pindrow FIR

A. Pindrow (Lamb.) Royle   West-Himalayan Fir
From the Himalayas.

A tree up to 250' × 26' with long needles for a fir (some over 2½"). The epithet *Pindrow* is of obscure origin, likely a name in India referring to the growth being tall and cylindrical. The tree grows well here, but is rare in Seattle.

- 13th Ave S & S Holgate St: a stout one on the NW corner

- U.W.: two north of Sieg Hall, the larger 70' × 5'2½"
- 434 McGilvra Blvd E: 64' tall
- Viewlands School: E of play equipment is one 54' × 4'6¼"
- Arboretum: one 51' × 1'10" in 21-B (#1896-39)
- Locks bed #202 has a small one in the shadow of a Douglas fir
- Seward Park Ave S & S Othello St: one 54' tall on the SW corner
- Seward Park Ave S & S Willow St: NW corner yard has one 54' tall
- 4321 S Holly St: 2, the larger 54' tall

Sakhalin FIR

A. sachalinensis (Schmidt) Mast.   Sachalin *or* Saghalin Fir
From Sakhalin, N Japan, S Kuriles.   Japanese: Aka-todo-matsu トドマツ

A plain sort of fir, in nature up to 130' × 11'. Extremely rare in Seattle: likely the only examples are several at the Arboretum (best is #631-57 in 17-4E: 51' × 2'7¾") and a small, heavily shaded one at the Locks in bed #27.

Santa Lucia FIR

A. bracteata (D. Don) D. Don *ex* Poit.   Bristlecone Fir
=*A. venusta* (Dougl.) K. Koch
From the Santa Lucia mountains of California.

A tree up to 182' × 16' with sharp, large, stiff needles and attractively *bristly* cones. Extremely rare in Seattle. Three thriving Arboretum specimens are in 6-B and 6-1E, the tallest 87' × 5'7" (#961-56). Two youngsters planted at the Locks died in 1985. At least one Seattle yard has a young specimen. Twin Ponds Park just north of the city has one 7½' tall on the east border, south of the restrooms.

Shasta FIR

A. magnifica A. Murr. var. *shastensis* Lemm.   Shasta Red Fir
=*A.* × *shastensis* Lemm., *emend.* Liu
From Lassen Peak (N California) to Crater Lake (SW Oregon.) The Red fir species as a whole ranges southward to central California and W Nevada.

This tree has long confused foresters. Some think it a hybrid of California Red fir (*Abies magnifica* in the strict sense) and Noble fir. Its pretty cones look like those of Noble fir. But its ecology differs notably. It can reach 250' × 27' and is notably *narrow*. In Seattle, very rare. Seen as living Christmas trees in yards. It may perform better than does the similar-looking Noble fir.

- Arboretum: 19-2E (shade-stunted), 17-3E and 16-3E have the largest 81' × 7'10" & 75½' × 6'3" (they have been mislabeled *A. magnifica* or *A. procera* for decades)
- 42nd Ave SW & SW Bradford St: NW corner yard has one 42' tall
- 2125 N 133rd St: the front yard has one 44' tall next to a Scots Pine
- Twin Ponds Park: one NW of the tennis courts is 24' tall (Grand fir nearby)

Spanish FIR

A. Pinsapo Boiss.   Bottlebrush *or* Hedgehog Fir
From S Spain (& N Morocco   Spanish: Abeto de España
according to broader views of the species).   Pinsapo

This looks vaguely like a blue Colorado Spruce. But it has *blunt* needles where the spruce has sharp ones. In Spain the largest trunks are over 20½' around. In climates such as ours it thrives and may reach up to 108' × 13' in time. It is common in Seattle, successful and very distinctive. Most are on private property.

– Acacia Cemetery: one with a trunk over 7' around (in 1983) fell down
– Arboretum: the largest of at least 6 is in 6-1E, 78½' × 4'3½" (#749-49)
– 3601 47th Ave NE: one 76' tall
– 6004 34th Ave NE: 70½' tall
– 4505 35th Ave W: 62' tall
– 7523 22nd Ave NW has a small street-tree of cv. '**Aurea**'—golden foliage
– Mayfair Park (2nd Ave N & Raye St): a 2-trunked tree 59½' tall in NW corner
– 38th Ave SW & SW Lander St: SE corner has a muliple-topped one 53' tall

Veitch FIR

A. Veitchii Lindl.   Veitch Silver Fir
From Japan.   Japanese: Shirabiso シラベ (Shirabe)

In nature, the equivalent of our Alpine fir, growing up to 100' × 9½'. It is rare in Seattle. Virtually our entire stock consists of trees planted on public property during the Depression. It has not fared as well as Momi or Nikko firs, being weaker. No fir here is more beautiful than a happily grown Veitch. The contrast between its shiny dark green needle-tops and vividly white undersides is a rich and delightful sight. Of *ca.* 75 specimens cited in this book's first edition, *all but a dozen* have since died; most cited below will *soon* die. Our tallest had reached 84' and stoutest 5'5".

– Golden Gardens Park: one north of dog area is 70' × 2'10"
– Green Lake: 2, (55½' × 4'5½" and 22' × 2'9¼"), near NW tennis courts
– 5723 Palatine Ave N: one 57' × 4'7" (1993)
– Arboretum: 40-5W has #653-39C mislabeled *A. koreana;* 43-6W has #1290-49A, 32½' × 2'2½" (grafted on Nikko fir roots); 42-3W has two #220-80, the larger 40½' × 2'0"; 21-1E has one 65' × 2'8¼" mislabeled *A. alba* #171-49; 19-4E has one 31½' × 2'8" mislabeled *A. amabilis*
– W Seattle Golf Course: 2, the largest 38' × 3'9" and 51' × 2'6½" (dying)
– Rodgers Park: one by a Western Red Cedar E of the kid's play area is 43' × 3'5¾"
– Leschi boat moorage by E Terrace St: 2, the larger 3'1" around, the other dying
– Lincoln Park: one 2'9¾" around

White FIR

A. concolor (Gord. & Glend.) Lindl. *ex* Hildebr.   Colorado Fir
From much of western N America; but not in Washington.

White fir is common and widely planted here and worldwide; it's easily grown and very pretty in its *bluish-gray* foliage, akin in color to blue Atlas Cedar and blue Colorado Spruce. Of various kinds grown few are notably *greenish*—the Pacific, Sierra or California White fir, called ssp. *Lowiana* (Gord.) E. Murr. It can reach 250' × 28'.

 − Acacia Cemetery: the largest is 82½' × 8'5¾"
 − Arboretum: best are in 16-6E and 16-7E (three #2233-38), the largest 91' × 8'0"
 − Lakeview Park: one 96' × 6'1" (two-forked)
 − Zoo: the largest of 4 near N Meadow stage is 80' × 7'6½"
 − U.W.: SW of the stadium is a broadly triangular one 65' × 8'11" × 54½' wide; of five tall slender ones nearby the tallest is 83' × 5'5"
 − W Seattle Golf Course: one 76½' × 6'10"
 − Green Lake: the largest is in the east parking lot (+ 3 Pin Oaks), 75' × 6'6½"
 − Colman Park: one 82' × 5'10¼"
 − Volunteer Park: 79½' × 7'3½" SW of conservatory; smaller by the water tower with Caucasian Firs; one on the W border is 81½' × 3'7½"
 − 43rd Ave NE, north of NE 41st St: a yard, W side, has one 76' tall
 − 2708 Nob Hill Ave N has a 49' tall ssp. *Lowiana* right by the telephone pole
 − Corliss Ave N & N 133rd St: NW corner has a 57½' tall ssp. *Lowiana*—or maybe this specimen is a hybrid between Grand fir and White fir
 − 4015 NE 70th St: an especially striking powder blue young one 13' tall

Chilean FIRE-TREE

Embothrium coccineum J.R. & J.G. Forst.   Flame Tree
=*E. longifolium* hort., *non* Poir.
=*E. lanceolatum* Ruiz & Pav.
PROTEACEÆ
From Chile, Argentina.

A broadleaf evergreen or semi-deciduous shrub or tree up to 65' tall, with scarlet flowers of great brilliance in (April) May–June, attracting hummingbirds. No other tree here equals its stunning show of *tropical color*. It is narrow in form, can sucker, and can be hurt in our occasional severe winters. It is uncommon.

 − 815 NW 116th St: one 52' × 4'3¼" (below forking) on W edge of lot, *pl.* 1955
 − Arboretum: 44½' × 2'7¼" #264-81A in 8-4E
 − 8538 30th Ave NW: in front yard 33½' tall
 − 904 21st Ave E: in back yard 32' tall
 − 2244 E Blaine St: 24½' tall
 − 2820 W Dravus St (29th & Dravus NE corner yard): by alley
 − S.U.: 3 (tallest 15½') in a bed in the NW part of The Green
 − Zoo: here and there, such as 14½' tall in Conservation Aviary; 3 (+ a Antarctic Southern-Beech) NE of Food Pavilion; older yet short in Prairie Dog/Llama exhibit
 − 3240 NE 96th St: in front yard 27' tall

- 1708 NW 63rd St: one west of the house
- 7327 23rd Ave NW: one by the sidewalk
- 5707 29th Ave NE: one in yard's NE corner
- 35th Ave S & S Massachusetts St: SE corner yard has one 27½' tall, NE of house
- 12018 15th Ave NE: 27½' tall, right by the sidewalk

FRANKLIN TREE

Franklinia alatamaha Bart. *ex* Marsh.

THEACEÆ

From the Altamaha River of SE Georgia.

Named after Benjamin Franklin. A shrubby tree grown for its beautiful white flowers against brilliant leaves from late July into September–October. Some of its popularity also stems from its name and fate in the wild: discovered in 1765, it was rare and has not been found wild since 1803. Very susceptible to root-rot, it needs well-drained soil. Leaves 5–10½" long, shiny; orange or scarlet in fall. Flowers fragrant, 3–4" wide, consisting of an orange heart cupped by 5 (6) plump white petals; borne in late summer and fall. Recorded to: 52' × 6'6".

In Seattle, rare. Many get planted but mortality is high. It is barely treelike.

- Arboretum: #89-43 by the road in 11-6E is cabled, 3-trunked 17' tall; #89-43 on Azalea Way in 38-B is 13' tall
- Zoo: 13' tall east of N-most restrooms; one smaller is SE of the Food Pavilion
- S.U.: one 9½' tall W of of Loyola Hall

Chinese FRINGE TREE

Chionanthus retusus Lindl. & Paxt.   Chinese: Liu Su Shu

OLEACEÆ

From China, Korea, Japan, and Taiwan.

Very rare in Seattle; only sold here since the 1990s. It bears opposite pairs of oval leaves 1–4" long and elegant, white summer flowers. It can attain 90' × 7' yet may remain *small* in Seattle due to our low summer tempeatures.

- S.U.: 3 west of Loyola Hall; tallest 13½'
- Zoo: 3 north of the N picnic shelter
- 707 15th Ave (just north of E Cherry St): one in the front yard
- 6th Ave NW & NW 89th St: NW corner yard has one

[**Fringe Tree**—*C. virginicus* L.—from the S & E United States, is more common yet also more shrubby. It has heavier foliage and earlier, drooping flowers (♂ & ♀ on separate trees). Its maximum size is 41' × 4½'. Some parks have specimens decades old yet still shrubby. Tallest is a 20' female at the Arboretum (#49-42 in 20-4W).]

GINKGO

Ginkgo biloba L.
=*Salisburia adiantifolia* Sm.
GINKGOACEÆ
From E China.

Golden Fossil-Tree
Maidenhair Tree
Chinese: Yin Hsing, Pai Kuo *or* Ya Chiao
Japanese: Icho イチヨウ

The odd leaf of this tree is unparalled and in outline reminded Englishmen of their beloved fern called the Maidenhair. Less poetically, in this country kids have christened it Stink-bomb Tree because its ripe fruits (late September–October) are so disgustingly fetid. Plum-like orange-colored fruit is borne only by mature female trees in the presence of males; the large seeds are edible. In China certain Ginkgo cultivars selected for superior seed production are grown in orchards. In the U.S. selected Ginkgo cultivars are also grown, but only in the male sex and solely for ornament. The tree can surpass 200' × 52½' and live more than 1,000 years. Grown in this country since 1784, the largest are now over 135' tall and up to 22½' around. It thrives in many environments, is troublefree and attractive. The leaves turn pure yellow consistently in November.

Many of us have visited the Ginkgo petrified forest in central Washington, seeing rock-hard evidence that Ginkgos once grew over a great territory. Called Golden Fossil Tree, it is earth's most primitive tree, having remained essentially unchanged for over 200 million years! Aside from its ornamental and nut-tree roles, various medical discoveries have been made with it. One of the most promising, an extract from the leaves, is used for treating senility.

In Seattle, common. Virtually all larger specimens are on private property. None here can compare in size with far older and larger examples to the south in Puyallup, Tacoma, and Portland (up to 86' × 12'0" or more).

– 13th Ave & E Columbia St: a ♂ 63' × 8'3¼" on the NW corner
– 800 block S Sullivan St: in back yard by alley a 70' tall ♂
– Volunteer Park: S side, W of 14th Ave, has 2 ♀; the taller 69' × 3'2¾"
– 11330 Sand Point Way NE has a ♀ "street-tree" 61½' tall
– 1912 38th Ave E: a ♂ 58½' tall
– Roosevelt High School: a ♂ 56' × 5'6" at the SE corner
– Locks bed #122 (slender; bent), 202 (slender; in yellowwood's shade), 302 (56' tall)
– 2624 West Viewmont Way W: 55' tall
– 1756 S Spokane St (west of Beacon Ave S): a ♀ street-tree, 53' × 6'½"
– 603 Malden Ave E: a ♀ 51' tall
– 6708 Fremont Ave N: a 2-trunked ♂ 50' tall
– 3330 Lakewood Ave S: a ♀ 50' tall is SE of the house
– E Miller St, east of Broadway E: a ♂ street-tree, S side, 49½' × 5'2½"
– a broad ♀ in alley W of 18th Ave E between E McGraw & E Lynn is 44½' × 5'2"
– 1032 S Cloverdale St: a stout, wide ♂ 37½' tall
– 5813 McKinley Pl N (north of Kenwood Pl N): 2 street-trees (one of each sex), the ♀ 46½' × 4'8¾", the ♂ 42½' × 3'5¼" (below forking)
– 1500 Lakeside Ave S: ♂ and ♀ street-trees, the southernmost ♀

GOLDENCHAIN TREE

Laburnum anagyroides Med.
=*L. vulgare* Bercht. & Presl
=*Cytisus Laburnum* L.
LEGUMINOSÆ (FABACEÆ)
From Europe.

Common Laburnum
Bean Trefoil Tree
Pea *or* Bean Tree
Golden Rain Tree
French Ash

This nitrogen-fixing tree produces basal suckers, reseeds freely and is relatively short-lived. The clover-like leaves fold up at night. Though rarely growing to more than 25' tall, it has on occasion been measured at over 40', with trunks more than 5' around. Cultivars exist but are apparently not present in Seattle.

Five inconsistencies stand out: 1) It is a shrub and a tree at the same time: few other plants are so ambiguous in form and size. 2) Its beautiful mien in bloom, gracefully weighed down by large clusters of cheerful yellow flowers from mid-April all the way into June, deteriorates thereafter until autumn, when unsightly dull brown seedpods mar its otherwise bland appearance. 3) Its trunks are coated with notably soft, weak bark—yet the aged wood within is so heavy, hard and tough that it is called False Ebony in Europe. 4) Its seedpods, though closely resembling edible bean or pea pods, are poisonous. 5) Though universally called Goldenchain in modern American books, it is called "Golden Rain" in nearly all European countries and often in England too. On the other hand American writers apply the name "Golden Rain" to quite another tree, which has almost nothing in common with this one except the color of its flowers.

It is pleasing to close a list of contradictions on a harmonious note: in the Language of Flowers, Goldenchain Tree signifies "forsaken" or "pensive beauty"! One of the most abundant of Seattle trees. But none stand out as remarkable examples. The Arboretum, north of E Madison St, along the road, has many.

Alpine GOLDENCHAIN TREE

L. alpinum (Mill.) Bercht. & Presl
From Europe.

Alpine Laburnum
Scotch Laburnum

A close cousin of the preceding, Alpine Goldenchain flowers later in spring, is more treelike, with smaller flowers. It is extremely rare in Seattle.

– Green Lake: on the SE side, between N 65th & N 66th, is an extra stout specimen 23' × 5'5½"—but doomed by the shady embrace of a young Plane Tree
– Arboretum: #307-41 pair in 19-4E and 19-3E; larger 28½' × 3'3½"

cv. 'Pendulum'

Weeping Goldenchain *or* Laburnum

Uncommon here, all are dense, small (5–7' tall), very weepy mounds scarcely to be termed trees, and not very floriferous.

– 6040 30th Ave NE: 2 street-trees, the taller 7'
– Dayton Ave N, north of N 71st St: 3 street-trees, E side

Chimæric GOLDENCHAIN TREE

+ *Laburnocytisus Adamii* (Poit.) Schneid.   Adam's Laburnum
=*Laburnum Adamii* (Poit.) Kirchn.   Pink Laburnum
=*Cytisus Adamii* Poit.

Of French origin in 1825 when Monsieur Adam, a nurseryman, grafted a Dwarf
Purple Broom (*Cytisus purpureus* Scop.) onto a Goldenchain. This fascinating
freak is an example of a rare phenomenon called a chimæra or graft-hybrid. The
tree grows overall like plain Goldenchain, but bears some Purple Broom flowers,
some Goldenchain ones, and some intermediate ones. Extremely rare here.

– Arboretum: #1285-47 in 19-4E is 28' × 2'4¼"; one in 17-5E is 31' × 3'3¼"
– 1135 19th Ave E: a street-tree 18' × 1'8¾"
– 606 20th Ave E : a yard tree 31' tall

Hybrid GOLDENCHAIN TREE

L. × *Watereri* (Wettst.) Dipp.   Hybrid Laburnum
=*L. Vossii* hort., in part   Voss's Laburnum
(*L. anagyroides* × *L. alpinum*)

This hybrid truly combines the better traits of each parent, making it preferable
to either as an ornamental, and increasingly popular for planting in yards or for
use as a small street-tree in residential neighborhoods. Common Goldenchain
still vastly outnumbers it.

– Arboretum: 17-5E has one (#1059-57) cabled together, 34' × 5'6¾"
– Evergreen Park Cemetery: one in the S end is 24½' × 6'7½" × 28' wide
– Bellevue Ave E & E Mercer St: SW corner bldg., 32½' tall S of Apt. bldg.
– 6252 38th Ave NE: a stout old specimen
– 8903 35th Ave NE: one 31½' tall NW of driveway
– 1221 Minor Ave: 29' tall
– U.W. Friendship Grove, representing Switzerland, 26' × 5'4¼"
– 10th Ave E & E Thomas St: NW corner has 3 street-trees, tallest 26'
– Queen Anne Ave N, north of W Smith St: many young street-trees

GOLDEN RAIN TREE

Koelreuteria paniculata Laxm.   Pride of India
SAPINDACEÆ   Shower Tree *or* Varnish Tree
From China, Korea.   Gate Tree *or* China Tree

In China, called Luan-hua (Ruan Shu) and used medicinally, gastronomically
and materially. In the West, this small tree with a crooked, often leaning trunk is
grown ornamentally. Its compound leaves emerge pinkish-bronze; bright yellow
flowers adorn the crown July–August (some as late as early October) and are
followed by bladdery "Chinese Lantern" seedpods that set off its warm autumn
color. Considered troublefree, except that it is hurt by shade, and its seedlings
are weedy. The largest reach 87' × 8'; most trees grow half as large.

It is common in Seattle.

- Green Lake: the largest of about a dozen by the NW parking lot is 41' × 6'½"
- E Madison St at Woodrow Pl E: the largest known on private property
- Locks bed #122 (42' tall), 328
- 3321 E Valley St: one 20' tall at house's NW corner
- E Denny Way, west of 34th Ave E: a street tree, N side, under wires
- Zoo: near the Hippos
- 1141 22nd Ave E
- 3228 64th Ave SW: a street-tree
- Queen Anne Ave N, south of Aloha St: 2 street-trees, E side

[*K. bipinnata* Franch.—Chinese Flame-Tree. Chinese Lantern Tree—is also from China (Fu Yu Ye Ruan Shu). Very rare here. It grows larger, its foliage is more luxurious, flowers less showy, but its seedpods more so. Arboretum #636-64A in 35-4E is 30' × 2'11½". S.U. has a 24' tall 4-trunked one on the S side of the W entrance to the Pigott Bldg. Three are in the 600 block of 1st Ave W. 6822 30th Ave NE has a young street-tree.]

HACKBERRY

Celtis occidentalis L.
ULMACEÆ
From much of the U.S.
& extreme S Canada.

Common *or* Northern Hackberry
Pompion Berry/ Sugarberry/ One Berry
Hack Tree/ Nettle Tree/ Unknown Tree
Hoop Ash/ Beaverwood
False *or* Bastard Elm

Even where native, this has been called the Unknown Tree. Far more so here! Aside from a gray, distinctively *warty* bark, it is nondescript and easily passed by. Its fall color is soft yellow. In winter its thin-fleshed berries are sweet-flavored. The tree can attain up to 134' × 19½'. In Seattle it is very rare, slow-growing.

- Jefferson Park Golf Course: one on the west side about in the middle, S of the sand bins, is 43½' × 4'4¾" × 48' wide
- Day School/Playground: the best of four west of N 40th St is 33½' × 3'9¼"
- Arboretum: 37-1E, 38-1E, 11-3W (#258-51 is 37' × 3'0"), 11-4W
- Zoo: by Dayton Ave N & N 50th St, the larger of two is 35' × 2'9"
- Seattle Buddhist Church Wisteria Plaza: a leaning one by a 23' Downy Hawthorn and 5 Jack Pines is 18' × 4'3¼"; a 2nd in the NW part by a driveway is 27' × 4'4"
- Lake Washington Blvd E opposite E Republican St: one 24½' × 1'4" is far too shaded by an Oregon Ash, Plane trees & Norway Maples

Chinese HACKBERRY

C. sinensis Pers.
=*C. labilis* Schneid.
From China, Korea, Taiwan and Japan.

Chinese: Po Shu

Very tardily deciduous, with somewhat rough brown bark, and tiny orange berries. It can grow to 100' × 16½'. Extremely rare in Seattle.

- U.W.: a very old tree 37½' × 2'10¾" S of Lewis Hall by Stevens Way Pin Oaks
- Arboretum: #294-58 in 30-4E (N of the nursery), 62' × 2'7¾"

European HACKBERRY

C. australis L.
From S Europe,
N Africa, SW Asia.

European Nettle-Tree
Southern Nettle-Tree
Lote Tree

About the same size (up to 131' × 20'), this differs from Common hackberry in its *smooth* bark, larger berries on longer stems, and longer, darker, narrower, rougher and hairier leaves. It has sometimes been put forth as a candidate for the Lotus of the Lotus-Eaters in *The Odyssey*. But that Lotus was fabulous—an example of Homer's poetic license and not an actual entity. In the Language of Flowers this tree signifies "conceit"! It is a successful ornamental shade tree in California and is worth further trial in Seattle, where it is extremely rare.

– U.W. Friendship Grove, representing Hungary: 37½' × 3'9½"
– Arboretum: #242-68A in nursery is 45' × 1'11½" but has rough corky bark so is something else; it came from Yugoslavia

[**Caucasian Hackberry** *or* **Nettle Tree**—*C. caucasica* Willd.—from SE Europe to the Himalayas, is closely related to *C. australis*. Known in Seattle only at the Zoo (19' tall on the Rain Forest Loop) and Arboretum #720-60 in 38-1E (20½' × 2'5½" in a salmonberry clump).]

[**Netleaf** *or* **Western Hackberry**—*C. reticulata* Torr.—from the west U.S. and Mexico, recorded to 74' × 15', is known in Seattle only at the Locks in bed #329 (an old small tree) and #30 (a very young, leaning specimen). An Arboretum tree labeled *C. reticulata* #X-640 in 37-1E is *not* so, but likely *C. lævigata* Willd.]

HARDY RUBBER-TREE

Eucommia ulmoides Oliv.
EUCOMMIACEÆ
From China.

Chinese Thread Tree
Stone-Cotton Tree
Gutta-Percha Tree

A unique tree with no close relatives. It may no longer be wild in China, but has long been cultivated there (called Tu-chung *or* Du Zhong Shu) for its medicinally valuable bark; the young leaves are also eaten. It is small (the largest recorded is only 98' × 6½'), and tends to fork low. Male and female flowers are both petty, and are usually borne on separate trees. A tree can be ♂ one year and ♀ the next! The dark and shiny leaves fall dull yellowish-green or green late October–early November. If either leaf, bark or winged seed is gently torn, the sap congeals into delicate rubbery strands. Dogwoods, and *Weigela* (shrubs), make similar but weaker strands.

In Seattle, rare. The name Gutta-Percha is more commonly applied to at least two other trees of warmer climates (not hardy here).

– U.W. Medicinal Herb Garden: section G (nursery area) has 3, largest 55' × 4'9½"
– Arboretum: a ♂ #130-43A is 56½' × 3'0" by north fence S of a Paper Birch, W of a tall maple in 37-5E; in 8-5E a ♀#130-43 is 44½' × 2'5 (best of several trunks)
– Lincoln Park: tallest of 29 NE of the wading pool is 51'; the stoutest 3'1" around
– Mt Baker Park: 2 N of restrooms, shaded by 2 native cedars, the largest 41' × 4'5½"

- Zoo: Australasia has 5 youngsters
- Calvary Cemetery: a young ♀

HAWTHORNS in general

Over 200 species of these crabapple cousins exist, most in east North America. Most are thorny little trees with small jaggedly lobed leaves, white flowers in May–June, and red, more or less edible "haws" ½" long. Rugged, twisting, widely spreading branches form dense heads. They loathe shade.

In Seattle, Black Hawthorn is native, but is overshadowed by 5 common non-native species; another 3 compete for attention but are uncommon; 16 are *rare*. And 2 species are known to be *so* rare, young, and hard to see, that the following account excludes them even though specimens exist here: Chocolate Hawthorn (*Cratægus erythropoda* Ashe), and Mayhaw (*C. opaca* H. & A.).

'Autumn Glory' HAWTHORN

Cratægus 'Autumn Glory'
ROSACEÆ

A chance hybrid that originated near San Francisco in the early 1940s and was first sold by nurseryman W.B. Clarke in his Garden Aristocrats catalog under the name 'Crimson Glory'. One parent of the hybrid was a European hawthorn *(C. lævigata);* the other a Mexican *(C. mexicana* Moc. & Sessé.). The tree bears few thorns; it has reached 39' tall in California. Its single white flowers make 1" haws, late to color red but glossy and "glorious" to behold by early winter. The foliage stays green late into autumn. It is uncommon in Seattle.

- Zoo: the north Primate Island has some—Squirrel Monkeys eat all the fruit unripe
- 19th Ave E & E Mercer St: the SW corner has 6
- N Pacific St, west of 1st Ave NE: 4 street-trees, N side (+3 Carrière hawthorns)
- Burke-Gilman Trail: in Fremont, east of 3rd Ave NW has 11 (+6 Wash. hawthorns)
- 29th Ave W & W Tilden St: NE corner yard
- 11th Ave E, south of E Prospect St: a 16' tall street-tree, W side (+a Wash. haw.)

Azarole HAWTHORN

C. Azarolus L.   Mediterranean Medlar
=*C. Aronia* (Willd.) Bosc *ex* DC.   Neapolitan Medlar
From SE Europe, N Africa, SW Asia.   Azarole

Some of this species' varied forms are cultivated for their edible yellow or red haws. It can reach 30' in height. Only *one* specimen is known in Seattle:

- U.W.: west of the Burke-Gilman Trail bridge over Rainier Vista, a row of trees south of the trail includes: a Smooth Sumach; 2 Downy hawthorns; a red-fruited Azarole (23' × 2'8½"); a Dotted hawthorn; a smaller Downy hawthorn; a big Black Cottonwood (Poplar); many Eastern Dogwoods

Black HAWTHORN

C. Douglasii Lindl.
Native here; from Alaska to
Texas, and around Lake Superior.

Western (Black) Hawthorn
(our) Native Hawthorn
Black Thornberry *or* Thornapple

One of Seattle's least known, rarest native trees. Distinct from other hawthorns in its *black*, juicy fruit, ripe for eating (mid-) late July through mid- (late) August. Birds eagerly devour them far more readily than they do other hawthorn fruit here. The tree has shreddy, pale bark; the roots can sucker. Once rare in Seattle, it has been much planted in habitat enhancement projects since the 1990s.

- Arboretum: one *pl.* in 1948 in 16-2W was 47' × 5'3½" when cut down in 2005; an old multitrunked tree by the lakeside 40' N of SR-520 is 27' tall and 44' wide
- U.W.: Stevens Way across from Anderson Hall, one 28' × 3'10" × 37' wide; east of it are 2 Cockspur haws & a Common haw; west are 2 Scarlet and a Frosted haw
- Discovery Park: many planted near the West Point treatment plant
- Seward Park and nearby Martha Washington Park have wild ones
- S Othello St, just east of Bowlyn Pl S: a street-tree, S side, 4'2¼" around (so over-pruned that its exact i.d. is uncertain—it may be a *Shortspine* Black Hawthorn)

Shortspine Black HAWTHORN

C. Suksdorfii (Sarg.) Kruschke
=*C. Douglasii* var. *Suksdorfii* Sarg.
=*c. brevispina* Heller
Native here; from Alaska into California.

Like the preceding, but: *short* spines (± ½" rather than up to 1"); blooms earlier; has 20 (not 10) stamens; smaller, less deeply-lobed leaves with larger stipules; rounder berries. It is a diploid and crosses with Common hawthorn. Very rare; almost never *planted* here. It grows as large as 51' × 7½'; its roots don't sucker.

- 30th Ave W & W Dravus St: a relatively big specimen 26' tall under wires
- U.W.: one 15' tall under the Water Oak & Deodar Cedar SW of Architecture Hall
- Discovery Park: by the tennis courts and children's play area
- Seward Park: both it and Black hawthorn are wild here, near the lakeshore
- Camp Long: in front of the lodge is a 19' tall 2-trunked, planted variant with *big hairy leaves*, thought to be from the Portland, Oregon area

Carrière HAWTHORN

C. × Lavallei Hérincq *ex* Lav. cv. 'Carrierei'
=*C. × Carrierei* Vauv. *ex* Carr.

Hybrid Cockspur Hawthorn
Lavallé Hawthorn

This hybrid between a Mexican species and the Cockspur hawthorn originated in France about 1870. It doesn't resemble other hawthorns so much as an evergreen crabapple tree: it holds its thick, dark, glossy, scarcely lobed leaves *late* into winter on scarcely thorny twigs (young nursery stock *is* very thorny), and bears ¾" long orange-red fruit. Common in Seattle, popular, often planted. Narrow in youth, wide in older age; one of the stronger and larger hawthorns.

- 3020 Magnolia Blvd W (*see* from 44th Ave W): one 36' × 6'10" × 49' wide (1993)
- Arboretum: #1543-45 in 31-3E is 41' × 6'7½" × 50' wide
- U.W.: one 36' × 5'5" at the W end of Anderson Hall
- Volunteer Park: the lawn across the road SW of the conservatory has one 25' × 6'4¼" (by a 79½' tall White Fir)
- 55th Ave NE & NE 65th St: NW corner has one one 26' tall south of the house

Cockspur HAWTHORN

C. crus-galli L.   Newcastle Hawthorn
From eastern N America.   Hog-Apple

Glossy, dense, flat-topped, spreading and fiercely thorny—its thorns up to 4–6" long and branched. A nickname is *Pin hawthorn*. The flowers appear late May into June, and are malodorous. Haws ⅓–⅞" wide, dull red. It's easily recognized at any season. It may reach 44' × 6½'. Common in Seattle.

- 11th Ave W & W Wheeler St mini-park: about a dozen large old specimens
- Volunteer Park: 4 S of the stairway across the road W of the reservoir, the tallest 30½' × 3'11½" just S of the stairs
- Green Lake: about a dozen by the ballfields; 17 at the north part of the lake
- U.W.: 2 across Stevens Way from Anderson Hall; the larger 24½' × 4'6¼"
- Arboretum: #421-53 in 12-2W is 32' × 2'8¼"

var. *inermis* Lange   Thornless Cockspur Hawthorn

Since the 1990s this has been the only kind planted in Seattle. A Cockspur Hawthorn without thorns is like a lion without claws or fangs.

- 3 on island-median east or uphill of 1st Ave NW & N 43rd St—Seattle's oldest
- 1st Ave W & W Garfield St: street-trees
- 3rd Ave NW, from NW Market St to NW 56th St: many street-trees
- S Southern St, east of 8th Ave S: street-trees (with a few Washington hawthorns)

[*C. Canbyi* Sarg. is now considered a mere variation of Cockspur hawthorn, but it is distinct—flushing first, with flowers earlier in spring; shorter and fewer thorns; leaves less dark, less glossy and persisting longer in autumn; and larger haws with a shiny skin, red (not yellow) fleshed and juicy. It is extremely rare in Seattle. Volunteer Park has 2 north of the 4 typical Cockspur hawthorns, and one 29' × 3'1" across the road W of the museum, by a metal bench. The U.W. campus has a forked-trunk one 17' tall × 27' wide E of the Burke-Gilman Trail bridge over Rainier Vista.]

Broadleaf Cockspur HAWTHORN

C. ×*persimilis* Sarg.   Plumleaf Hawthorn
=*C.* ×*prunifolia* Pers.
=*C. crus-galli* var. *prunifolia* T. & G.
From New York and E Ontario near Niagara Falls.
Possibly a hybrid of *C. crus-galli* with *C. macracantha* or *C. succulenta*.

Cultivated since the late 1700s; more than one clone exists. Branching less layered than on regular Cockspur hawthorn, leaves broader. Twigs hairless, purple-brown, thorns 1" or so. Leaves 1½–3"; hairy on the veins beneath. Thorns few to numerous, purple, ¾–3". Blooms *earlier* than regular Cockspur hawthorn, and the flower-clusters are *hairy*. Haws ⅓–⅝" long, rich red, dropping in late October or early November with the leaves. Known here only as follows:

– Alki Bathouse /Art Studio (2701 Ave SW) has 3 NE of it, the largest 25' × 3'10"; a few others northward along Alki Beach Park
– Volunteer Park: a shrubby one 17' tall is 90' east of E Highland Drive's N sidewalk

Common HAWTHORN

C. monogyna Jacq. Oneseed *or* English Hawthorn
=*C. Oxyacantha* L. var. *monogyna* Loud. Quickthorn / White Thorn
From Europe, N Africa, W Asia. May (Tree)

Best known of the clan, this is the original "Hawthorn." It is abundant and fully naturalized here. Unlike the American species, it is shade tolerant, and thus competes well in woods. Country children in Britain used to eat the newly emerged shoots and leaves, calling them "bread and cheese" or "God's meat." And the tender mild-flavored young leaves were once used in salads. The haws are generally ripe enough to eat by late September, and remain on the tree much of the winter. Herbalists recommend hawthorn flowers and fruit for healthy hearts. In the Language of Flowers, the tree stands for "hope." The Common Hawthorn can attain uncommon size: to 69' × 14½'.

– Volunteer Park: one 69' × 5'8" by a Red Maple across the street west of the bandstand is the tallest recorded hawthorn *of any kind*
– Washington Park Playfield (Lake Washington Blvd E & E Madison St): the slope below E Madison St has three, the tallest 43'
– U.W. Medicinal Herb Garden: one in section E (2 Cockspur hawthorns W of it)
– Locks bed #208 has a wild specimen close to #209
– 539 29th Ave S (just north of S Lane St): a *pink*-flowered street-tree 25½' × 2'6½"
– Green Lake: dozens

f. *pendula* (Loud.) Rehd. Weeping Hawthorn

A percentage of hawthorns raised as seedlings display a weeping form to some degree. Those having the trait most strongly are called by this name. These gracefully weeping individuals are uncommon.

– 16th Ave E, south of E Roy St: a street-tree, W side, 25' × 3'1½"
– Midvale Ave N & N 43rd St: SE corner yard has one 25½' tall
– Minor Ave E, just north of E Boston St: a street-tree, E side, 21' tall

f. *stricta* (Loud.) Zab. Pyramidal Hawthorn

Uncommon here; sometimes sold by nurseries as Columnar hawthorn. Though strictly upright and tightly narrow in youth, it widens in age.

– University Heights (5031 University Way NE): 26 street-trees (+Carrière haws)
– Arboretum: 46-8E (two #961-58), 7S-9E (one 37' tall #961-58)

Dotted HAWTHORN

C. punctata Jacq.
From eastern North America.

Called "Dotted" because its haws have dots—though many hawthorns do. This species somewhat resembles the *Canby* Cockspur hawthorn, but yellows and loses it leaves and fruit earlier than any of our other kinds. It is extremely rare here, and shows no sign of growing to its maximum reported size of 40' × 8'.

– Arboretum: #1245-50B is 31' × 4'1"× 48' wide in 14-2W
– U.W.: a multitrunked 27' tall one N of Hansee Hall stays green into November unlike the rest; one by the Burke-Gilman Trail—see Azarole hawthorn
– Hiawatha Playfield: one 19½' tall at the north stairs, one 17½' tall at the west stairs
– 3803 42nd Ave NE: a yellow-fruited tree S of house is 20' × 3'10"× 32' wide (1992)
– NE 88th St, opposite 12th Ave NE: big and old, by the sidewalk; puzzlingly unique

Downy HAWTHORN

C. mollis (T. & G.) Scheele Summer Hawthorn
=*C. coccinea* L. var. *mollis* T. & G. Red Hawthorn
From eastern North America. Turkey-Apple

Large leaves and haws, both more or less downy-hairy, identify this hawthorn. In size it rivals our native Black hawthorn for being the largest North American species: one in Michigan was 52' × 8'9" × 62' wide in 1972. It is the State Flower of Missouri. The haws can be 1" wide and are among the best for eating, available in October. Uncommon in Seattle and little known; only *old* trees are here.

– Leschi Park: one 37' × 4'3½" in the SE corner
– 2109 N 41st St: one NW of the house is only 26½' tall yet *very* stout-trunked
– Volunteer Park: one 45' × 3'3" by E Prospect St, east of 14th Ave E
– Queen Anne Blvd: 1st Ave W/W Smith St/W McGraw Pl has two, both 23' × 3'9"
– U.W. Medicinal Herb Garden: 35½' × 2'1" SW of Cascara Circle, by a pink-flowered Eastern Dogwood; also by the Burke-Gilman Trail—see Azarole hawthorn
– Hiawatha Playfield: one in the NE corner
– Locks bed #25: an atypical form, very hazel-like in aspect; 32' tall
– Arboretum: an old tree by the lakeside N of SR-520 is (like the preceding trees) really *C. submollis* Sarg. Narrowly-defined *C. mollis* is known in Seattle *only* as 2 trees in 13- or 14-4W on the W side of Interlaken Blvd. Shaded by maples, the taller is 23' and stouter 1'8¾". They are far more hairy, and make larger leaves (to 6⅝").

Evergreen HAWTHORN

C. × *grignonensis* Mouillef.   Hybrid Mexican Hawthorn
(C. mexicana × *C. ?monogyna?)*   Grignon Hawthorn

A hybrid that originated in France ≤1873. Tardily deciduous or partly evergreen leaves, variably shaped, dark and glossy above, coated lightly with rough-feeling hairs; paler and notably hairy beneath. Few thorns to nearly thornless. It blooms later than many hawthorns (mid-May to early June), and the flowers can fade to pink. Haws large, good to eat, to ⅞" long, 1–2 seeded, red, *very* shiny and persistent. Even as it blooms in spring, the rich red fruit and glossy green leaves of last year are still largely present. Extremely rare in Seattle.

– Good Shepherd Center: NE part of grounds has one 22½' tall just east of the only Syrian Maple known in Seattle

Frosted HAWTHORN

C. pruinosa (H.L. Wendl.) K. Koch   Waxy-fruited Hawthorn
From eastern North America.

A small, little grown species, not especially showy—notable for its "bloomy" or "frosted" haws. Known here only as follows:

– U.W.: two E of parking lot W-6, the larger 17' × 2'2"; one on Stevens Way opposite Anderson Hall west of 2 Scarlet hawthorns; one west of Bloedel Hall by a Bay Laurel; one among the pines west of the overpass to the Health Sciences complex

Green HAWTHORN

C. viridis L.   Southern Hawthorn
From the SE United States.   Tall Hawthorn

A nearly thornless tree with handsome bark. Leaves shallowly lobed, 1–4" long, dull yellow in autumn. Flowers in many-flowered clusters, making—at least *here*—few haws, to ⅓" wide or long, orange-red; usually 5-seeded. The largest recorded specimen: 40' × 5'1" × 45' wide in Marlinton, WV (1981). Rare in Seattle; some of the following may be cv. '**Winter King**'—a prettier clone.

– 4325 Densmore Ave N: a street-tree 32' × 4'2¼"
– Montlake School: 4 (best 27' × 2'7") on E McGraw St +8 Washington hawthorns
– 928 E Allison St: young street-trees
– 506 18th Ave E: a young street-tree

Hupeh HAWTHORN

C. hupehensis Sarg.   Chinese: Hubei Shan Zha
From much of C & NE China.

A small tree grown in China for its edible fruit. Extremely rare here. Leaves to 4" long, edged with glandular, incurved teeth; 3–4 lobed towards the tip. Flowers few, big. Haws dark red, to 1" wide, edible, 5-seeded. Thorns *ca.* ⅝" long.

– 6837 30th Ave NE: one 17½' tall, decades old, among common hydrangea shrubs

[*C. pinnatifida* Bge.—Chinese Bigleaf Hawthorn—is NE Asian, also grown for big edible fruit; also extremely rare here. 7519 22nd Ave NW has a youngster 11' tall in the back, visible from the alley. Unlike Hupeh Haw, its leaves are *strongly* lobed, fruit *hairy*.]

Oriental HAWTHORN

C. orientalis Pallas *ex* Bieb.   Silver Hawthorn
=*C. laciniata* auct., *non* Ucria   Blue Hawthorn
From SE Europe and SW Asia.

A nearly thornless small tree. Leaves "frosty" bluish-gray, very hairy, deeply lobed into slender segments, notably short-stemmed. Flowers ⅝–¾" wide, opening later than those of most hawthorns, in early June. Haws lovely, edible, succulent, ½–1", brick- to coral-red or yellowish-orange. Extremely rare in Seattle.

– Arboretum: one *pl.* in 1945 by the road in 15-2W was 19' × 1'8½" in 1994; cut down and replaced by #39-95 west of boulevard in 15-3W
– Meadowbrook Park's edible arboretum has cv. '**Blanco**' (*pl.* 1997)

Pink HAWTHORN

C. lævigata (Poir.) DC.
=*C. Oxyacantha* L., *emend. Jacq.*
=*C. oxyacanthoides* Thuill.
From Europe, N Africa.

In nature, similar to its very close cousin the Common hawthorn, with which it readily hybridizes. It is smaller, flowers earlier, is strongly scented, has less-lobed leaves, and has 2–3 seeds (not one) per haw. In cultivation it is usually grown in pink/red, often double-flowered cultivars. The double flowers make few haws, if any, and these are usually flattened in shape.

In Seattle, one common (the DOUBLE RED Paul's Scarlet) and 7 rare kinds, as cited below. Some are really hybrids with Common hawthorn. Such hybrids are called *C.* × *media* Bechst.—but to simplify matters, writers describe the cultivars under the parent of their choice. Authoritative books of American, English, Dutch and German origin don't fully agree on Pink hawthorn cultivar names or descriptions, so the names given below are only good guesses.

—SINGLE WHITE: the typical state of the species *C. lævigata* is unknown in Seattle, but with 54 DOUBLE REDS on E Gwinn Pl (cited below) is a single white hybrid at the far west end of the street on the north side (house 812)
—SINGLE PALE PINK (f. *rosea* [Willd.] Rehd.): a street-tree on the south side of NE 51st St, east of Latona Ave NE (with some DOUBLE REDS); a street-tree on the east side of 18th Ave, north of E Spring St (with Common hawthorns, a Box-Elder Maple and a Siberian Elm)
—SINGLE RED (cv. **Crimson Cloud**™ = 'Superba'): 6 young street-trees at 1938 Franklin Ave E (south of E Newton St)

—SINGLE DARK PINK (cv. 'Bicolor'): 607 18th Ave E has one that was 31' × 4'11" × 45' in 1993, but then was topped; it has regrown, but has been much thinned

—SINGLE RED (cv. 'Punicea'): Green Lake has *ca.* a dozen in the north part, from Bagley Ave N to N 77th St; 6 street-trees on the west side of 15th Ave NE, north of NE 42nd St

—DOUBLE WHITE FADING TO PINK (cv. 'Plena'): 3rd Ave W, just S of W Newell St: 2 street-trees: 34½' × 5'5" (below fork) and 32½' × 3'3½"; a street-tree (S of a DOUBLE RED) on Latona Ave NE, just N of 52nd St, E side; 3520 NE 110th St: a street-tree with 3 DOUBLE RED

—DOUBLE RED (cv. 'Paul's Scarlet' or 'Paulii'): abundant here, ubiquitous as a street-tree in older residential neighborhoods but less often seen in yards and parks than Common hawthorn. It comes from the nurseries nearly a real red color, but with age many branches or entire trees begin making merely deep pink flowers. People often prune it into a lollipop-headed monstrosity in vain attempts to check the extent of aphid honeydew drip. *Very* disease prone unlike *any* of the others. On E Gwinn Pl, west of Fuhrman Ave E, are 54 old street-trees (with 2 Common hawthorns and 1 SINGLE WHITE hybrid); Volunteer Park has one 40' × 4'½" across the street SW of the wading pool; St James Cathedral has one by Cathedral Book Store 37½' × 4'9"; old street-trees on 40th Ave SW, south of SW Oregon St; 31st Ave S, south of S Ferdinand St: 6 street-trees, W side

—DOUBLE SCARLET CONTORTED-BRANCHED (cv. 'Pink Corkscrew'): a shrub-size, thornless 'Paul's Scarlet' that has contorted zig-zag branches—distinguished any day of the year. Some nurserymen call it *Cratægus contorta*. Very rare in Seattle; the largest of 8 specimens known is at S.U., across the street E of Lemieux Library, NW of Student Center Pavilion, 24' tall in a crowded corner planting that includes a weeping blue Atlas Cedar. A big one at 10561 15th Ave NW.

Piper HAWTHORN

C. chrysocarpa Ashe var. *Piperi* (Britt.) Kruschke   Columbia Hawthorn
From NW North America.

A little tree armed with slender thorns. In February, 1995 10 were planted at the U.W. Medicinal Herb Garden, along with 1 Longspine hawthorn (*C. macracantha* Lodd. *ex* Loud.) and 1 Castlegar hawthorn (*C. castlegarensis* Phipps & O'Kennon). The seeds from which all 3 species were raised are thought to have been from E Washington, but no one is *sure*. These 3 species are known nowhere else in Seattle—except a Longspine hawthorn at the U.W. CUH Soundscape Garden, and a Castlegar hawthorn at Discovery Park.

Scarlet HAWTHORN

C. coccinea L.
=*C. pedicellata* Sarg.
From eastern North America.

Extremely rare here. Leaves hairless, very sharply toothed, 2–4" long. Thorns 1½–2". Flowers ½–⅞" wide; anthers pink or red, 5–10. Haws scarlet, ½–⅝" long; 2–5 seeded. The tree's shape is compact and pleasingly narrow.

– U.W.: Stevens Way has 2 opposite Anderson Hall (tallest 23'; to the west is a Frosted Hawthorn; to the east are a Black, 2 Cockspur, and a Common hawthorn)

Shining HAWTHORN

C. × *nitida* (Engelm.) Sarg.   Glossy Hawthorn

Possibly a hybrid between the Cockspur and Green hawthorns. This splendid ornamental is a broad-crowned tree of few thorns. At its best in October with orange leaves and red haws. Unfortunately it is extremely rare in Seattle.

– U.W.: one 19½' × 4'7¼" × 31' wide is SW of Parrington Hall—it had been *moved* here. In 1947 the Arboretum got a seed from Massachusetts; a seedling was raised, then planted in 1951. Ousted by SR-520, it was moved to the U.W. in 1962. To make way for a new building, it was moved again to its current site in March 1992.
– Arboretum: #106-94 in 15-2W and 12-2W; the tree cataloged and labeled #187-47 in 18-3W is something else—it never flowers or fruits so its i.d. remains shrouded

Siberian HAWTHORN

C. sanguinea Pall.
From Russia, Mongolia, N China.

A species scarcely known in the West. It is extremely rare in Seattle, and the specimens cited *differ;* their positive identification is tentative.

– Volunteer Park: a very old multitrunked tree 38½' tall, wider still, by the road, N of the bandstand (firmer, oblong, 3-seeded haws)
– Arboretum: #783-46, an old tree by the lakeside 100' N of SR-520 is 22½' tall (soft, round, 5-seeded haws)

Toba HAWTHORN

C. × *mordenensis* Boom cv. 'Toba'

There is some dispute involved, but this is said to be a hybrid between a Pink Hawthorn and the Fleshy hawthorn (*C. succulenta* Schrad.) that originated in Morden, Manitoba in 1935. It is a small, slow-growing tree. It flushes green *early* then has double white flowers, aging to deep pink like those of 'Paul's Scarlet' Pink hawthorn. The haws are red, shiny, like little 'Red Delicious' apples about ½" wide, sparsely borne, persisting long on the branches.

    In Seattle, uncommon. Only relatively young ones are here.

– NE 75th St, east of 35th Ave NE: 9 street-trees (SAFEWAY)
– 39th Ave NE, north of NE 55th St: a street-tree 21' tall, W side, S of a Goldenchain
– Elliott (Goodyear) Tire & Service, 4441 Fauntleroy Way SW: 4 street-trees
– Burke-Gilman Trail: 5 ±opposite the Wallingford transfer station
– Jefferson Recreation Center (3801 Beacon Ave S): 1 in front

Washington HAWTHORN

C. Phænopyrum (L. fil.) Med.   Virginia Hawthorn
=*C. cordata* (Mill.) Ait.
From the eastern U.S.

Named neither for the State nor the first President, but for Washington, D.C., because it was first commercially grown on a large scale by a Georgetown nurseryman in the late 1700s. The slenderest of our hawthorns, reaching 40' or more in height but rarely seen with a trunk a full 1' thick. Of all hawthorns, it is least shade tolerant and makes the tiniest haws (¼–⅜") wide. It flowers later than usual too, from early June into July.

In Seattle, our most common eastern North American haw; much in favor.

– Ravenna Park: 4 N & W of the wading pool; largest 34' × 3'0"
– Arboretum: the largest of 3 in 11-2W and 12-2W is 31' × 2'11¾"
– 34th Ave E & E Mercer St: a large one in the NW corner yard, E of garage
– U.W.: by the road N of Clark Hall (a Cornelian-Cherry Dogwood W of it); also 21 are S of Henry Art Gallery

Turkish HAZEL

Corylus Colurna L.   Constantinople Hazel
CORYLACEÆ (BETULACEÆ / CUPULIFERÆ of some)   Balkan Hazel
From SE Europe, Asia Minor.   Tree Hazel

A tree with *corky* bark, recorded up to 100' × 13'. Its nuts, enclosed in clusters of boldly armed husks, are small and hard-shelled but well flavored: available mid-August through September. Turkish hazels are uncommon in Seattle.

– Volunteer Park: one 62' × 4'10¼" NW of E Highland Dr by the N–S gravel path makes duds or blanks yearly since it lacks a cross-pollinator companion
– Arboretum: two #2184-37 in 45-7E (the best 43' × 4'6¼") make sound nuts yearly
– U.W.: one by Ponderosa Pines behind Winkenwerder Hall is 49' × 3'9½"
– Locks bed #24 has a generally nutless tree 42' tall right next to the path
– NW 80th St, west of 20th and east of 24th Ave NW: street-trees *pl.* Oct. 1992
– 14th Ave, south of E Spring St: 8 street-trees on W side
– Burke-Gilman Trail has 9 youngsters ±opposite the Wallingford transfer station

[*European* Hazel—*C. Avellana* L.—Also called Cob Nut. The original hazel; from Europe, W Asia & N Africa. Its hybrids are the cultivated filberts. Pioneers grew it in orchards, now it's naturalized here. Still planted. A larger version of our native hazel (*C. cornuta* Marsh. var. *californica* (DC.) Sharp). A huge shrub unless pruned to tree form. 9629 14th Ave NW: stout single-trunked. U.W.: 32½' tall multitrunked S of Hansee Hall.]

[*Chilean* Hazel—*Gevuina Avellana* Mol.—PROTEACEÆ. Also called Chile Nut, Hardy Macadamia; in Spanish *Avellano*. A cold-tender Chilean/Argentinian small tree. Leaves *compound, evergreen*. Flowers small; in fall. Fruit looks cherry-like; seeds edible roasted. Extremely rare here; all known *pl.* 1980s or onward. Arboretum #60-89 is 14' tall in 8-4E. One that I *pl.* in 1986 froze to the ground in 1990; now is 18' tall—not easily viewed.]

[*Witch* **Hazel**—*Hamamelis virginiana* L.—HAMAMELIDACEÆ. An east N American shrub or small tree up to 45' tall. Leaves lopsided. Flowers small; in fall. Seeds ejected from bumpy pods. Common (like its more showy winter-blooming E Asia kin) only as *shrubs;* but at Green Lake W of the Bathouse Theatre one of 3 is 17' × 2'6½"; tallest is 19½'.]

HEMLOCK TREES in general

The original "Hemlock" is a deadly poisonous, fetid, biennial weed (*Conium maculatum* L.), a product of the Old World naturalized throughout much of the habitable part of the planet. Socrates placidly ended his life with a cup of hemlock tea. It is also called Poison or Deadly Hemlock and in Seattle can reach 12' tall with a taproot 3½' deep!

When English settlers arrived in the New World they were greeted by many new kinds of trees, including one they came to call variously the Hemlock Spruce, Hemlock Pine, Hemlock Fir—finally Hemlock Tree, probably because its growth habit resembled that of the poisonous weed—horizontal branches characteristically ending in branchlets with a slight, graceful droop. Botanists ended up calling these trees by the Japanese vernacular "Tsuga." All 9–11 (14) species in the genus are lacy, graceful evergreen conifers: they are *not* poisonous.

Eastern HEMLOCK

Tsuga canadensis (L.) Carr.   (not our) Common Hemlock
PINACEÆ   Canada Hemlock
From eastern North America.   Hemlock Spruce

This, the State Tree of Pennsylvania, was long valued more for its bark's use in tanning than for its wood, which was considered coarse, cheap and poor. In gardens it earned a better reputation: many attractive cultivars exist. It can attain up to 176½' × 20'. Its needles and cones are smaller than those of most hemlock trees. In the Language of Flowers its meaning is "honor."

In Seattle, common. Compared to our native species, it is stout, dense, less graceful and lush, and of a less healthy, duller hue. Especially stodgy and slow-growing in sunny, dry locations; best and most attractive in shaded, moist places. Bush-sized, strongly weeping or spreading cultivars, wide as high, are relatively rare here, but do well. Variegated and golden-leaved cultivars are sold, but as yet most such Seattle specimens are *young.*

– Calvary Cemetery: the largest of 17 measures 66' × 9'8"
– Volunteer Park: many, scattered, the stoutest 6'11½" around; the tallest 87' × 5'3"— one of 10 in a grove by the road W of the reservoir
– U.W. Friendship Grove, representing Venezuela
– 13340 3rd Ave NE: 5
– E Denny Way near 14th Ave E: a 10' tall weeping specimen
– 309 22nd Ave E: an 8' tall weeping specimen

(Northern) Japanese HEMLOCK

T. diversifolia (Maxim.) Mast.   Japanese: Kome-tsuga ツガ
From central and N Japan.

A tree up to 100' × 9½'. Very rare here.

– Arboretum: at least 4; the largest 33½' × 2'8" (#1226-37 south of the Japanese
  Garden in 1-1W), 29' × 1'5½" (#383-48 in 30-2E), and 26½' × 1'4½" (#42-52 in
  30-1E); #42-52 in 30-2E is tiny
– 4th Ave W & W Crockett St: NE corner yard, one 32' tall S of garage (+ a Walnut)
– 508 Randolph Ave (@ Wellington Ave intersection): one 27' tall
– S.U.: 14' tall at SE corner of 10th & Spring, just E of a Mountain hemlock
– Green Lake: three youngsters N of the golf course; tallest 15'

(Southern) Japanese HEMLOCK

T. Sieboldii Carr.   Japanese: Tsuga *or* Toga コメツガ
From S Japan, Korea.

A tree up to 100' × 9½'. Very dark green. Extremely rare here.

– Arboretum: the largest of 2 in 30-2E is 56½' tall with twin 2'1" trunks (#1412-41)
– U.W.: one 27' × 2'¼" is east of the Burke-Gilman Trail, south of the 45th St
  viaduct, among White Birches, and 9 pines
– Good Shepherd Center: a youngster east of the building, near the N end, 7½' tall

Mountain HEMLOCK

T. Mertensiana (Bong.) Carr.   Alpine Hemlock
From mountains, S Alaska to central California.

Unlike the other species, Mountain Hemlock has features suggesting a spruce; its
needles *whorl* all around the twigs rather than parting evenly in two flat ranks,
and its 1½–3" long cones are much larger than the others. It grows as large as
200' × 23¼' in nature, yet in Seattle this common tree is markedly slow, sometimes downright bushy: a good choice for a tub tree. Most of our specimens are
bluish, some are green. Few make cones yet.

– Arboretum: largest is 57½' × 3'9¼" (#1612-37 S of Rhododendron Glen in 12-4E)
– 13th Ave NW & NW 90th St: NE corner has one 39½' tall
– Locks: several; at least one 37' tall in bed #118 produces cones
– 1118 Federal Ave E: 38' tall
– 8222 39th Ave NE: 38' tall
– 3002 36th Ave SW: one 36' tall north of a larger blue Atlas Cedar
– 6020 27th Ave NE: by front door
– 851 NE 59th St: 3 street-trees
– U.W.: 15½' tall in front of the Burke Museum, to the south (by *Myrica californica*)
– 54th Ave NE & NE 44th St: NE corner has both color forms; squat from pruning
– Ingraham High School: faculty and visitor parking lot has 2, + 1 Western hemlock

Western HEMLOCK

T. heterophylla (Raf.) Sarg.   (our) Common Hemlock
= *T. Albertiana* (A. Murr.) Sénécl.   (our) Native Hemlock
= *T. Mertensiana* auct., *non* (Bong.) Carr.   West-Coast Hemlock
Native here; from S Alaska to N California   Pacific Hemlock
W of the Cascades, and the N Rocky Mountains.

Our State Tree, this is the largest hemlock, reaching a maximum of 259' × 31½'. Slender of trunk and limb, it is elegant in appearance and easily climbed; it produces high quality wood, tolerates much shade and reseeds effectively therein. Certain Northwest Indians ate the soft inner bark, not as a famine food but as a tasty delicacy equaling potatoes nutritionally. No native tree of Seattle is as pleasant to meditate under: something about its soft carpet of needles and sturdy bole proves peaceful, comforting and strengthening, as if it were an arboreal embodiment of the very spirit of Mother Earth.

Mistletoe proper doesn't occur in Seattle, but Dwarf Mistletoe (*Arceuthobium tsugense* [Rosend.] G.N. Jones) parasitizes some of our hemlocks. It forms dense little thickets or assumes tree-like growths to 5" tall. Enjoying sunshine, it is mostly found high in the tree. No leaves are present, but it has bone-like jointed stems with 3–5 branches per node. It is best observed by a climb into an infected tree. Failing that, search under a tree after a windstorm to find pieces on the ground. The effect of the parasite on the host is to slow growth, cause "witches'-brooms," lessen seed production, lower wood quality and can eventually so deform and weaken the tree that it dies standing or blows down. Another pest is an insect that covers the twigs with a powdered-sugar / artificial snow substance.

The tree is common here. The tallest specimens are over 150' and every park listed below has trunks over 9' around; some trunks are 11–12' around. Seward Park certainly has Seattle's best collection of vigorous, large, handsome hemlocks; the largest there is 153' × 11'9½". Below are other parks, largest trees noted.

—O.O. Denny Park: 156' × 12'4"   —Discovery Park: 80½' × 11'5¼"
—Arboretum: 129½' × 10'10½"   —Lincoln Park: 10'9½"
—Viretta Park: 9'11½"   —Schmitz Park: 10'9"
—Golden Gardens Park: 9'9½"   —Woodland Park: 9'5½"

Tree HIBISCUS

Hibiscus Syriacus L.   Shrub *or* Shrubby Althea
MALVACEÆ   Rose of Sharon
From E Asia.

A familar garden shrub of Seattle yards. Now and then trained into a mini tree. These days whole streets have been planted. Beloved for showy late-summer flowers in a rainbow of colors. Leaves three-lobed. Recorded to 20' tall.

– NW 58th St, west of 11th NW: 8 street-trees *pl.* 1999 (most white-flowered), S side
– 1406 NW 59th St: a stout specimen; double white flowers

- Minor Ave & Virgina St: the south corner has an old specimen on a lawn
- Roanoke Park: the east side, towards the south end, has cv. 'Blushing Bride'
- 5628 Fauntleroy Way SW: one with double, lavender flowers in NW corner of yard
- Locks bed #26 (by #28), 304 (N of flagpole)

[*Hoheria sexstylosa* Col.—Lacebark—a Hibiscus relative from New Zealand. Maori: *houhere;* its inner bark prettily patterned and useful for cordage. An elegant broadleaf evergreen, fine textured tree to 50' tall, hurt severely or killed in hard winters. It exists as youngsters at most 14' tall so far, in a few gardens—one on Vashon Island is far larger. It grows rapidly and blooms while young. Bright glossy green leaves are sharply toothed. White ¾–1" flowers are borne in summer. Cultivars such as '**Snowflurry**' and the hybrid '**Glory of Amlwch**' exist here. *H. populnea* A. Cunn. is similar to *H. sexstylosa*, but more cold-tender, grows larger, and only one is known here, 6' tall in a back yard.]

Shagbark HICKORY

Carya ovata (Mill.) K. Koch   Little Shellbark Hickory
=*C. alba* Nutt., *non* (Mill.) K. Koch   Scalybark Hickory
=*Hicoria ovata* (Mill.) Britt.   Upland Hickory
JUGLANDACEÆ
From eastern North America.

Derived from an Indian name, "Hickory" designates *Carya* species growing in the central and eastern United States (except the Pecan, *Carya illinoensis*). They're relatives of walnut trees. The easily husked nuts are hard to crack. Hickory signifies "glory" in the Language of Flowers. The Shagbark is the hickory of common acquaintance. It grows over a vast range and is sometimes planted for its excellent nuts or brilliant yellow fall color. As the name indicates, it has at maturity a loose, shredding bark. Hickory wood is famous for strength, toughness and elasticity, used for axe handles and drumsticks, among other things. It is first-class fuel wood too, and is especially valued for smoking meats. The tree can attain 153' × 13½'. It is very rare in Seattle.

- Arboretum: two (#347-69), the largest 67½' × 2'10½" in 29 or 30-2W; and three (#500-57), the largest 74' × 4'3½" in 31-3W
- U.W.: 2 by the Burke-Gilman Trail SE of Winkenwerder Hall; larger 41' × 1'10¾"
- Carkeek Park: three youngsters in Piper's Orchard with the many fruit trees

[*C. glabra* (Mill.) Sweet—Pignut Hickory; Sweet Pignut—from C & E North America, is known here only at the U.W.: one 67½' × 4'10¼" NE of Denny Hall makes small infertile nuts yearly. It is puzzling and may be a hybrid or something else.]

Shellbark HICKORY

C. laciniosa (Michx. fil.) Loud.   Thick *or* Big Shellbark Hickory
=*C. sulcata* Nutt.   Bottomland *or* Big Shagbark Hickory
From eastern N America.   Kingnut / Bigleaf Shagbark

Compared to Shagbark hickory, Shellbark has larger nuts, 7 (not 5) thicker, larger, darker leaflets. The tree can attain 145' × 14½'. It's extremely rare here.

- Federal Ave E, north of E Newton St: a street-tree, E side, is 58½' × 6'0"
- U.W.: one SW of Bloedel Hall is 39' × 2'8"

Pecan Tree (HICKORY)

C. illinoiensis (Wang.) K. Koch
=*C. Pecan* (Marsh.) Engl. & Graebn., *non* (Walt.) Nutt.
=*Hicoria Pecan* (Marsh.) Britt.
From the south-central U.S. and parts of Mexico.

The most important and largest North American nut tree, up to 200' × 30'! It is the State Tree of Texas, where there is an immense pecan industry. Its wood is comparatively poor, unlike the very valuable wood of the related hickory and walnut trees. Its pollen aggravates hay fever. In Seattle, very rare. Distinct from hickories in that its leaves have (9) 13–15 (19) narrow leaflets, which stay green *very* late into fall.

- Arboretum: larger of two #2210-41 in 31-2W is 86½' × 5'2"; sets some nuts but none ripen fully; larger of two #570-49 in 30-2W is 88½' × 4'1"
- Midvale Ave N & N 43rd St: the NE corner yard has one 61' tall by a grapevine-covered carport (a Black Walnut is also present in the south part of the yard)
- U.W.: a shrubby, atypical one immediately west of the overpass to the Health Sciences complex, is overshadowed by a Pitch Pine

HOLLIES in general

Most kinds of hollies (genus *Ilex*) and virtually all those grown here are small broadleaf evergreen trees or shrubs. Usually individual specimens are essentially male or female. Only females and bisexuals produce the tiny to large pea-sized berries which are usually reddish. Not every member of *Ilex* fits our traditional notion of "holly-like" appearance, while other genera have very "holly-like" species—such as some *Osmanthus* and evergreen oaks.

In Seattle, over 90% of our hollies are English holly and its hybrids. The best place to get acquainted with our rare and shrubbier kinds is the Arboretum, where the collection is superb—though as the new Madrona Terrace complex is built, the holly collection is going to be variously altered, moved, and ruined.

American HOLLY

Ilex opaca Ait.
AQUIFOLIACEÆ
From the eastern U.S.

Delaware's State Tree. Rendered nearly extinct in some areas near big cities due to over-harvesting by holiday enthusiasts. It can reach 100' × 13⅓'. An excellent article on American holly appeared in *American Forests*, December 1966.

In Seattle, very rare. Almost impossible to locate outside of the Arboretum. Differs from English holly in having its flowers and berries on the *current* year's shoot rather than on last year's; the leaves are usually duller and more yellow-green in color. And it almost never reseeds in Seattle.

– Arboretum: 28 in 6-4E, 5-4E, 4-4E, 4-3E; the tallest: #535-45 is 43' × 2'8¼";
#420-48 is a '**Maxwell Point**' 40' × 2'9"; and #412-48 is a '**Hampton**' 38½' × 2'11"
– 14th Ave E & E Valley St: SE corner yard has one 23' tall on its very NE corner

[*I.* × *attenuata* Ashe *(I. Cassine* × *I. opaca)*—**Topel Holly**—found wild first in Florida; cultivated since the 1930s; over a dozen cultivars now exist. But in Seattle *rarely* grown. The Arboretum's tallest are #556-44, 47½' × 2'2" in 4-3E; and a '**Hume**' #415-46, 22' tall in 5-4E. 2010 Franklin Ave E has 2 '**Hume**'—the taller 25'.]

Asian HOLLIES

All Asian hollies present in Seattle are either *shrubby*, or if tree-like, *rare*. Below is a succinct account of Seattle's 13 Asian hollies (*more* exist at the Arboretum):

– *I.* × *aquipernyi* Gable *ex* W.B. Clarke. (Hybrid Perny Holly) is much like Perny holly yet has larger leaves (to 2½" × 1¼" *vs.* 1½" × ¾") and grows more treelike. A 5-trunked ♂ 31' × 1'1¾" is at the U.W. behind Hutchinson Hall (by it are a yellow-berry English holly and a Highclere hybrid). The Arboretum's tallest are #394-48, a ♂ 29' × 1'6" in 5 or 6-3E, and the stoutest is #355-45, a ♂ 23' × 1'7½" in 4-3E.

– *I. Buergeri* Miq. is nearly *nonexistent* in Seattle. One died at the Locks in bed #16, and spindly shrubs dating from 1964 died at the Arboretum—but cuttings survive.

– *I. cornuta* Lindl. & Paxt. (Chinese *or* Horned Holly) is an uncommon shrub featuring thick trapezoid-like leaves armed with 3–5 huge spines. The Arboretum's tallest is #108-42B, a ♂ 18' × 11½" in 5-3E. One 14' × 4-trunked is at the U.W. Medicinal Herb Garden SW of Cascara Circle. One 14' tall, *very* wide, is on the NE corner of Linden Ave N & N 74th St.

– *I. crenata* Thunb. *ex* J.A. Murr. (Japanese *or* Box-leaved Holly) is a common shrub that *looks like boxwood*, with dark tiny leaves and *black* berries. The Arboretum's tallest: #1251-50 is a '**Mariesii**' 21½' × 1'3" in 4-3E; #723-60 is a '**Snowflake**' 21' × 1'½" in 4-3E. U.W. Mechanical Engineering Bldg's N end has 4, the tallest 19'.

– *I. Fargesii* Franch. (Farges' Holly) is a shrub or tree, extremely rare here. Slender leaves, to 5" × ⅞" wide, are *barely* toothed. Red berries. Arboretum #124-81A is 7½' tall in 6-3E. Two nearly as big but far younger are known in a private garden.

– *I. integra* Thunb. *ex* J.A. Murr. (Mochi Tree; モチノキ) is admittedly a real tree, but only 2 specimens are known outside of the Arboretum. Its leaves are spineless and blunt-tipped, its berries big and pale. The Arboretum's tallest: #2799-40 is a ♂ 26½' tall in 5-3E, and the tallest ♀ is 22½' tall in 4-3E.

– *I. latifolia* Thunb. *ex* J.A. Murr. (Tarajo Holly; タラヨウ) is a tree, very rare here, easily told by its *huge* leaves, up to 9¾" × 3⅞" wide! It has salmon-pink berries. The Arboretum's tallest of 10 is #1926-41, 29' × 1'8¾" in 4-3E. One 19' × 1'6¼" is across the path east of the park maintenance yard at the N end of Lincoln Park.

– *I.* '**Mary Nell**' is an *I. latifolia* cross named in 1981 in Alabama. Leaves *glossy*, to 4" × 1¾"; long-lasting clustered red berries to ⅜" wide. The Arboretum's largest is #336-81 in 5-3E, 21½' × 1'1". The Seattle Center has one 12' tall NE of Key Arena.

- *I.* 'Nellie R. Stevens' is *I. Aquifolium* × *I. cornuta*, found in Maryland and sold since the 1950s. Leaves *puckery*, to 3⅜" × 1⅝" with several big spines; berries to ½" long, bright orange-red. The Arboretum's largest is #783-59 in 5-3E, 23½' × 1'4". None known elsewhere are near as large. One 10' tall is at 1249 NE 88th St.

- *I. pedunculosa* Miq. (Longstalk Holly) is a small floppy tree, extremely rare here. Thin, wavy, untoothed leaves. Berries on thin stalks up to 2⅛" long. One 19' tall is at the Locks in bed #119 (in the shadow of an *Osmanthus*). The Arboretum specimens of #633-37 died, or if still alive are poor, the largest 20' × 1'1¼" in 4-3E.

- *I. Pernyi* Franch. (Perny Holly) is a *small*-leaved, uncommon slender, scrawny shrub or gaunt little tree. Kubota Garden Park has a 23' tall ♀ (under a Black Locust east of N-most pond). The zoo has a 20' tall ♀ (on Rain Forest Loop E of black & white Colobus). The Arboretum's tallest is #1958-45, a leaning ♀ 15½' tall in 5-3E.

- *I. purpurea* Haask. (Kashi Holly) is very rare here; a *tall tree*, with narrow, thin and glossy leaves, to 5¾" × 2", not the *least* bit spiny. The Arboretum's tallest of 6 over 40' is #1383-41C, a ♂ 49' × 3'¼" in 4-4E. The Good Shepherd Center has a youngster 13' tall, by a Loquat tree. Roanoke Park has one 11½' tall.

- *I.* 'September Gem' is *I. ciliospinosa* × *I. aquipernyi*, a shrubby hybrid from the U.S. National Arboretum, released in 1978. Leaves to 4¼" × ¾" with 3 spines per side; berries to ⅜" wide, red by early September. The Arboretum's largest is #27-86 in 5-3E, only 9' tall. 11 are at the U.W. Center for Urban Horticulture, the tallest 11'+.

English HOLLY

I. Aquifolium L.   Common *or* Christmas Holly
From Europe, N Africa, W Asia.   Holm / Hulver

Scarcely any Seattle non-native tree is so well known, abundant and variable. Variations grown here include: yellow-berried; spineless; extra-spiny; more or less weeping; big-leaved; small-leaved; and leaves splashed, edged or blotched with yellow or creamy white. The species can attain 80' × 15½' but is rarely over 40' × 4½' here, where it's weedily naturalized.

- Volunteer Park: a 'Laurifolia' SE of the museum is colossal: 57½' tall, it fills a circle over 160' around! It is a sparingly spiny ♂ of multiple trunks and largely envelopes a Daphniphyllum tree; also a large 24' tall ♂ 'Angustifolia' is on the park's E edge
- Zoo: one not far W of the restrooms by the Primate Islands is a 'Laurifolia' 50' × 6'7"; a 2nd 'Laurifolia' also 50' tall is E of the Rose Garden
- Jefferson Park: 54½' × 6'0" is largest of many hollies; a ♂
- between 2215–2219 E Howe St (see from Blaine St): 51' × 3'7"—Seattle's tallest ♀
- U.W.: behind Hutchinson Hall is a 19½' tall yellow-berry English holly, a much larger Highclere holly 38' × 2'9", and an Asian Hybrid Perny holly 31' tall; W of Guthrie Hall are many ♀ 'Angustifolia', the tallest 16'
- Arboretum: 36 different cultivars! But all of the females are going to get axed
- 4586 34th Ave W: an 'Argentea Marginata' *ca.* 35' tall, with a Western Red Cedar
- Mt Pleasant Cemetery: a 'Ferox Argentea' 18' × 2'½" in south part, in the middle

Highclere HOLLY

I. × *altaclerensis* (hort. *ex* Loud.) Dallim.   Hybrid English Holly
(I. Aquifolium × *I. Perado)*

The name derives from Alta Clera, the medieval Latin name for Highclere, in north Hampshire, England, where this hybrid was first raised in the early 1800s. Similar to English hollies yet *larger* in leaf, flower, berry and often in overall size—but less spiny. While not rare here, they're vastly outnumbered by English hollies. Cultivars include: 'Camelliifolia', 'Hendersonii', 'Hodginsii' and 'Wilsonii'. They rarely or do not at all reseed in Seattle.

- 908 14th Ave E: tallest of some '**Camelliifolia**' is 52'
- U.W.: behind Hutchinson Hall is a 19½' tall yellow-berry English holly, a much larger '**Camelliifolia**' 38' × 2'9", and an Asian Hybrid Perny holly 31' tall; 6 '**Camelliifolia**' to 35' tall are SE of Johnson Hall & SW of Mary Gates Hall
- Arboretum: '**Camelliifolia**' #1918-41C in 5-3E is 36' × 1'9½"
- Arboretum: '**Wilsonii**' #858-54 in 6-2E is 35' × 1'10"
- Discovery Park: Ft. Lawton Cemetery has '**Wilsonii**' in the corner by the shed
- Parsons Gardens Park: a ♀ 31' tall—but neither 'Camelliifolia' nor 'Wilsonii'
- 1515 2nd Ave W: a 'Camelliifolia' NE of the house

HOP TREE

Ptelea trifoliata L.   Wafer *or* Stinking Ash
RUTACEÆ   Shrubby *or* Tree Trefoil
From much of N America.   Potato-chip Tree / Skunk Bush

Leaves trifoliate like a bean plant, aromatic; yellow in fall. Pale greenish-white flowers in dense clusters May–July, give rise to winged seeds that were used as *hop* substitutes. A shrubby tree, at most up to 45' × 4'. In Seattle, rare.

- 4025 NE 110th St: a leaning, two-trunked one 21½' × 1'4½"
- Interlaken Park: one 18' tall by the roadside in the section closed to vehicles
- Zoo: several; at least one 14' tall by elephant barn

[**Hop Bush**—*Dodonæa viscosa* Jacq.—(SAPINDACEÆ) A *widely* distributed willow-like broadleaf-evergreen foliage shrub or small tree. Grows from sea level to 11,800' in the Andes; in the Old World, New World, N and S hemispheres, in tropical, subtropical and nearly temperate climates. Hopbush, Hopseed bush or Native Hops names were given because its seedpods were used to flavor beer. Scarcely found in Seattle, and only *young*. The tallest of many *purplish*-leaved ones at the U.W. is 13'—S of Guthrie Annex #1.]

HORNBEAMS in general

These cousins of alders and birches are so little known that if they all vanished suddenly, they would hardly be missed by most of us. It is due not to their faults (few or none) but to their plainness: they are thought to lack any notable value or beauty, so they tend to be overlooked. They are conventional to a fault. It is all the more ironic that in the Language of Flowers their meaning is "ornament."

One European Hornbeam cultivar is widely planted here. The other hornbeams are all rare. The Arboretum collection is excellent.

American HORNBEAM

Carpinus caroliniana Walt.   Blue *or* Water Beech
=*C. americana* Mich. (in part)   Muscle Tree
CARPINACEÆ (BETULACEÆ)   Ironwood
From C & E North America and S Mexico to Honduras.

Compared to European hornbeam, this has brighter green leaves that are far more colorful in fall. It also branches *very* low and often grows much wider than tall. Recorded to 69' × 9¾'. In Seattle it is known only as old trees in the Arboretum plus a few street-trees planted since the 1990s.

– Arboretum: at least 5, including: #180-46A in 46-7E is 24½' tall × 2-trunked, #2178-37A in 45-6E is 24' × 3'7¼", and #480-45A in 46-7E is 21' tall × 4'2"
– 5th Ave W, n of W Smith St: 6 young street-trees with 10 old European hornbeams
– 1527 31st Ave: a street-tree

European HORNBEAM

C. Betulus L.   Common Hornbeam
From Europe, SW Asia.   Yoke-Elm *or* Hornbeech

Aside from its ornamental role, the chief human value of this tree is in its wood: exceptionally difficult to work with, hard and heavy as the *horn* names indicate. The tree can attain 131' × 20¾'; its crown is broad and its shadow heavy; its strongly fluted trunk is wrapped in tight gray bark. The leaves turn yellow in November. On young trees many leaves often persist, brown and withered, through the winter. The singular thing about hornbeam is its seed-clusters: each tiny seed is attached to a peculiar three-pronged wing 1½–2" long.

Common here. Old ones in parks and boulevards; few on private property. Naturalized in some wild areas, reproducing via seedlings and root-suckers.

– Kinnear Park: some by the tennis courts, the largest 73' × 6'9½" × 77' wide
– U.W.: one 79½' × 5'3½" NE of Allen Library
– NW 56th St, below Phinney Ave N, east of 2nd Ave NW: 25 street-trees *pl.* 1915, the largest 8'7" around
– Lakeview Park: 3; 16 on Lake Wash. Blvd E below the park, the best 74½' × 7'0"
– Camp Long: many
– Roanoke Park: two in the S part; 59' × 7'5½" (to SW) and 57½' × 7'7¼" (to NE)
– Keystone Pl N & N 50th St: 7

cv. 'Fastigiata'   Pyramidal Hornbeam

Planted by the thousands here during the 1970s and 80s, largely as a street-tree and in apartment building landscapes, this has become common in a hurry. It starts life skinny but becomes *rotund* in age. The tidy, predictable and handsome shape of this clone endear it to lovers of the ordinary and uniform: those who prefer picturesque individuality may be bored by it. Compared to regular hornbeams it colors darker in the fall and bears few seed-clusters. As for ultimate size: one planted in England in 1902 was 85' tall by 1984. A more slender version from Holland, sold since the 1990s, is **Frans Fontaine**'.

– Arboretum: N of the road to Foster Island, #64-53 is 54½' × 6'0"
– 2701 3rd Ave W: the taller of a pair is 67' × 5'9"
– McDonald School (144 NE 54th St): one 52' × 3'1" by a Japanese White Pine
– U.W.: three east of Kincaid Hall
– 35th Ave SW: many street-trees from SW Southern St to Roxbury St
– 19th Ave E: 149 street-trees from E Madison to E Galer St

cv. **'Globosa'**   Globe Hornbeam

A quite wonderfully *round* crown results when this clone is top-grafted. The only planting known in Seattle is at the U.W., where 15 are on the brick plaza of the HUB along Stevens Way; largest 28' × 2'7¾" (by the fire hydrant).

cv. **'Incisa'**   Cutleaf Hornbeam

A curiosity with very deeply jagged leaves, this is extremely rare in Seattle.

– 26th Ave NW between NW 56th & 57th Sts: 7 as street-trees along with a regular hornbeam and two European Hop-Hornbeams
– Arboretum: N of the road to Foster Island, #684-57 is 32½' × 3'1"
– 19th Ave, between E Cherry & E Columbia Sts: 10 street-trees (+5 'Fastigiata')

cv. **'Pendula'**   Weeping Hornbeam

Floppy and dwarf. The only tree known in Seattle is a street-tree at 6843 17th Ave NE. Being young, its future is unknown; maybe it will grow impressively large eventually.

Japanese HORNBEAM

C. japonica Bl.   Japanese: Kuma-shide クマシデ
=*Distegocarpus Carpinus* Sieb.
From Japan.

A tree up to 50' × 6¼'—but mostly *shrubby* here—with dark, slender, many-veined leaves of poor yellow-brown fall color; and large, greenish buds. Until the 1990s it was extremely rare in Seattle; now, just uncommon.

– Arboretum: of six, #1615-56 in 50-2E is 26' × 3'8½", #665-68A in 46-7E is 28' × 3'1¼", and #482-45A in 45-7E is 31½' tall × 3-trunked; also in Japanese Garden
– U.W.: 2 N of Hall Health Center, tallest 27½' (+ a Looseflower hornbeam); 4 were *pl.* 2004 in courtyard of Paul Allen Center for Computer Science & Engineering
– Rainier Playfield: 9 along S Alaska St, west of 38th Ave S
– Magnuson Park: two on north side of NE 74th Street entrance
– NE 110th St, west of 35th Ave NE: many street-trees *pl.* in 2005 on S side

Looseflower HORNBEAM

C. laxiflora (S.& Z.) Bl.   Japanese: Aka-shide アカシデ
From China, Korea, Japan.

Up to 50' × 9½', with dainty and elegant foliage coloring pumpkin orange and yellow in October. Extremely rare in Seattle.

– U.W.: one 25½' × 4'3¾" NE of Savery Hall; one 26½' × 4'3¾" SE of Raitt Hall; a low-forking one 27½' × 1'9¼" N of Hall Health Center with 2 Japanese hornbeams against the building
– Arboretum: two in 45-6E, the larger (#292-68A) is 19' × 1'11½" and broad crowned

Oriental HORNBEAM

C. orientalis Mill.   Eastern Hornbeam
=*C. duinensis* Scop.
From SE Europe, SW Asia.

A drought-tolerant little tree, at most over 50' tall. Extremely rare.

– Arboretum: 45-6E has one 38' × 4'6¾" (#395-53A), and in the nursery
– U.W. Friendship Grove, representing Israel, 18' × 2'5¼"

American HOP HORNBEAM

Ostrya virginiana (Mill.) K. Koch   Eastern (U.S.) Hop-Hornbeam
=*O. virginica* Willd.   Beetlewood
=*Carpinus Ostrya* L. (in part)   Stonewood
=*Carpinus virginiana* Mill.   Leverwood
CARPINACEÆ (BETULACEÆ)   Ironwood
From central and eastern N America.   Hardtack

Hop Hornbeams are told from hornbeams by their rough, shaggy, dark bark (instead of smooth, taut, light-colored bark) and by having their seeds encased in papery "bladders", "husks" or "sacks"—hence the name **Hop** hornbeam, because they are reminiscent of hop seed-clusters. American hop hornbeam is generally a small tree, but like the European, can surpass 75' × 9½'. Unlike the European, it colors earlier and brighter in autumn. It is rare here.

– Lincoln Park: one in the NE part, drawn up by adjacent Douglas Firs & Norway Spruces, is 60½' × 2'8¼"
– Arboretum: #373-56 is 36½' × 2'8" in 19-3W; #36-56 is surrounded by *Viburnum* shrubs in 24-4W and is 38' × 1'11"
– Meridian Park (Meridian Ave N & N 50th): 6 by circular path at the NW corner

European HOP HORNBEAM

O. carpinifolia Scop.
=*O. vulgaris* Willd.
=*Carpinus Ostrya* L.
From S Europe, Asia Minor, the Caucasus.

This differs from its American relation in small details. On a practical note, it is larger (to 80' × 15¾'), and colors poorer and later in fall. It's very rare.

- Arboretum: #60-75 in 50-1E is 63' × 4'9"; #336-53A in 46-7E is 65½' × 5'9¼"
- U.W.: a low-branching one 37' × 2'11¼" S of Padelford parking garage, N of stairs
- U.W. Friendship Grove, representing Greece, 36' × 2'2"
- 26th Ave NW between NW 56th & 57th Sts: two street-trees, E side, the N-most and S-most (among cutleaf European hornbeams)
- Zoo: one 22½' tall by the Demoiselle Crane
- Delridge Way SW & SW Andover St: 8 street-trees *pl.* 2004 on SE corner

HORSE CHESTNUTS (& Buckeyes) in general

Although these are all the same to scientists, who naturally view them as various species of *Æsculus*, Americans call our native *Æsculus* "Buckeye" and follow Europeans in calling the Old World one "Horse Chestnut." Similarly, we have European "Linden" and American "Basswood"; European "Judas Tree" and American "Redbud"; European "Plane tree" and American "Sycamore"; or European "Poplar" and American "Cottonwood." This book sometimes departs from strict alphabetical order, tending to keep such groups united under the better known and more common appellations from Seattle's point of view. Four Horse Chestnuts and three Buckeyes are known in Seattle.

The American name refers to the split nut-husks of autumn revealing shiny nuts looking like deer eyes. Buckeye and Horse Chestnut *nuts* are poisonous raw: only processing can render them safely edible.

Common HORSE CHESTNUT

Æsculus Hippocastanum L.   Horse Chestnut Tree
HIPPOCASTANACEÆ   White Chestnut
From Greece, Albania, & nearby areas.

As mentioned in the CHESTNUT TREE account, these are often called "chestnut trees" without prefix, as in Longfellow's lines:

> Under a spreading chestnut-tree
> The village smithy stands;
> The smith, a mighty man is he,
> With large and sinewy hands;
> And the muscles of his brawny arms
> Are strong as iron bands.
>
> (from "The Village Blacksmith")

These lines firmly apply to the tree as well as the smith. Few trees are so tough and tolerant of the vicissitudes of modern urban residence. In brief, it is VIGOR writ large. Dimensions of 134' × 22' are on record.

The qualifying "Horse" was given long ago for reasons now uncertain, although possibilities are: the overall shape of the compound leaf is like the outline of a hoof; the leafstalk scars on the twigs are shaped like horseshoes; the nuts were said to be given to cure broken-winded horses, or were considered unfit for any but horses! Long after its introduction to western Europe (*ca.* 1550–1615), the tree was believed to be a native of India, and in several European languages came to be called the Chestnut of India.

In Seattle it is very common, well known and naturalizing.

– 922 28th Ave S: an old goliath 15'2½" around grew sick, so was cut down in 2004
– Volunteer Park: largest of many is 77½' × 12'6¼"
– Mt Baker Blvd, south of S McClellan St: the largest of 3 is 85' × 12'6"
– 17th Ave NE, from NE 45th St to Ravenna Blvd: 184, (+2 Redflower horse chestnuts & 3 Yellow buckeyes); the largest over 70' × 10'0"
– U.W: the largest of many is 83' × 11'1" on Denny Hall lawn
– Cowen Park: one 88½' × 10'2½"

cv. 'Baumannii'   Doubleflower Horse Chestnut

Has doubled flowers of large size in very dense clusters, that produce no (or very few) nuts. The tree tends to be narrower too. Too bad it is so rare here.

– 722 28th Ave S: one 79' × 15'2" × 62' wide (1987)
– Arboretum: #683-57 in 22-4W is 63' × 6'7½"
– E Highland Dr, west of Federal Ave E: 2 street-trees, S side, both 74'; stouter 10'3"
– Summit Ave, north of Seneca St: the W side has 8 street-trees, one of which is a 'Baumannii' 46½' × 3'3¾" (by steps/entry of Cascade Court) and in another of which (4th from Seneca) the *south* half is Redflowering and the *north* half regular horse chestnut; the remaining 6 trees are regular horse chestnuts

Himalayan HORSE CHESTNUT

Æ. indica (Camb.) Hook.   Indian Horse Chestnut
From the Himalayas, Nepal westward.

A huge tree, up to 150' × 25'. It is somewhat slenderer and more glittery than Common horse chestnut, and flowers later in the year than the late April–May of most. It is extremely rare in Seattle, and is cold-tender.

– Locks bed #11 (two), the larger 44' × 7'5"
– 8546 30th Ave NW
– U.W.: a youngster 12½' tall N of Mary Gates Hall

Japanese HORSE CHESTNUT

Æ. turbinata Bl.   Japanese: Tochi-no-ki トチノキ
From Japan.

To 130' × 31½'. Like Common horse chestnut, but husks without prickles; the leaves usually are larger, bluer beneath & fuzzier. Extremely rare in Seattle.

- E Jefferson St, W of 22nd Ave: a street-tree, N side, under wires, is 34' × 6'11"
- Arboretum: the Japanese Garden has one 47½' tall; 8-3W has #178-85B, 30½' × 3'5", and #293-57S, 29½' × 3'2½"

Redflower HORSE CHESTNUT

Æ. × *carnea* Hayne   Ruby Horse Chestnut
=*Æ. rubicunda* Loisel.   Red Horse Chestnut

This hybrid between Common horse chestnut and Red buckeye originated in Europe early in the 19th century. It is smaller than Common horse chestnut (to 90' × 11'), has smaller, darker leaves, less prickly nuthusks, and dark pink to scarlet flowers. Unfortunately it often develops an ugly, warty trunk. Cultivars such as '**Briotii**' have better flowers.

It is common in Seattle, and produces some seedlings here.

- Me-kwa-mooks Park: one 70' × 8'7½" not far S of the huge Yellow buckeye
- Volunteer Park: one 68½' × 5'9½" on the west border below the lower tennis courts; two more conspicuous ones are S of the upper tennis courts
- E Galer St, west of 16th Ave E: 4 street-trees, N side, the largest 54½' × 6'6"
- Harvard Ave E & E Hamlin St: SE corner has 4 old street-trees with particularly obvious graft divisions visible; largest 40½' × 5'2¼"
- Locks: many '**Briotii**' (#215)

California Buckeye (HORSE CHESTNUT)

Æ. californica (Spach) Nutt.
From California.

This is often bushy and wider than tall: the largest recorded was 48' × 14'6" × 78' wide. The bark is white or rusty-pink and very attractive.

In Seattle, rare. It flowers any time from late June through mid-August. Unlike most Californian specimens, Seattle's don't lose their leaves in *early* summer.

- Locks bed #126: two white-barked trees, the larger 44' × 8'3" × 52' wide
- Arboretum: three #883-58 in 6-1W to 5-B, largest 24½' × 2'9½" and 22½' × 3'6"
- 5608 SW Admiral Way
- 8546 30th Ave NW
- 2854 NW 58th St: 3 street-trees
- Sunnyside Ave N, south of N 43rd St: a street-tree, W side

Red Buckeye (HORSE CHESTNUT)

Æ. Pavia L.   Red-flowering Buckeye
=*Æ. discolor* Pursh   Scarlet *or* Woolly Buckeye
=*Æ. splendens* Sarg.   Fire-cracker Plant
From the southeastern U.S.   Fish-poison Bush

A shrub or tree to 40' × 4' with *slender deep red* flowers. Very rare in Seattle.

 – Locks bed #209: a fork-trunked one 19' × 2'2" × 26½' wide under a Deodar Cedar
 – 3252 10th Ave W
 – 3706 NE 75th St: one 20' tall with a larger Yellow buckeye
 – Arboretum: 10, in 8-B, 7-2W, 6-1W, 6-B, 2-1E, 1-1E
 – alley N of E Newton St, east of 42nd Ave E: one 30' N of sidewalk is 17½' tall
 – 2438 NW Blue Ridge Drive

Yellow Buckeye (HORSE CHESTNUT)

Æ. octandra Marsh.   Sweet Buckeye
=*Æ. flava* Soland.   Big Buckeye
From the eastern U.S.

A tree as large as 152' × 18' having wood that is difficult to split, too soft and too easily decayed but still used for specialty items including artificial limbs. The nuts can be made into a book-binding paste disliked by worms.

In Seattle, uncommon. Most on public property. Brilliant autumn color in mid- to late September, brighter, prettier and earlier than that of Common horse chestnut (mid- to late October). The flowers are slender and yellowish (or somewhat pink—we may have some hybrids). It reseeds readily.

 – Me-kwa-mooks Park: one 74' × 10'3" north of a smaller Redflower horse chestnut
 – Arboretum: in 37-3E #2616-40H is 77' × 4'11" & I is 75½' × 5'5¾"
 – Ravenna Blvd NE: 4 (largest 68' × 7'5¼") mixed with 42 Common horse chestnuts and 2 Redflower horse chestnuts, east of 15th Ave NE
 – 14320 19th Ave NE: 67' tall
 – Queen Anne Blvd: W Wheeler St, east of 9th Ave W, 61' × 6'8"
 – Zoo: 61' tall not far west of the restrooms by the Primate Islands; two (and a Redflower horse chestnut) on Phinney Ave N, between N Argyle Pl & N 56th St
 – 1st Ave NW & NW 49th St: NE corner has 5 street-trees (one with *pink* flowers)
 – Locks bed #202 (64' tall), and two in bed #327 (taller 54')
 – 3706 NE 75th St: one with a smaller Red buckeye
 – Green Lake: 46½' × 7'0" (+ a Redflower horse chestnut) NE of the golf course
 – 5260 12th Ave NE: 2 street-trees

[*Æ.* × *neglecta* Lindl. '**Erythroblastos**' (*Æ. octandra* × *Æ. sylvatica*)—**Sunrise Horse Chestnut**—found in Europe; sold since 1912. But in Seattle *one* known, 39' × 2'2" in 1992 in a private garden. Youngsters may exist here. Bright shrimp-pink new foliage, then pale green.]

IDESIA

Idesia polycarpa Maxim.　　　　　　Japanese: Iigiri イイギリ
FLACOURTIACEÆ　　　　　　　　　　Chinese: Shan Tong Zi
From China, Korea, Japan, the Ryukyus, Taiwan.

A large-leaved tree to 65' × 7½'. Individual trees are usually either male or female. A little-used English name it shares with the Castor Bean plant is "the Wonder Tree." Females produce conspicuous clusters of seedy red or orange berries if males are also present. The crushed berries are malodorous like *Clerodendrum*, and bitter. In late October the leaves turn yellow. Idesia is very rare here.

– Locks bed #305 has two multitrunked trees, the larger 39' × 3'2" × 45' wide
– Arboretum: a ♀ 27½' × 2'3" #169-88 south of Loderi Valley, east of Azalea Way; one NE of the Graham Visitor Center
– Zoo: one *ca.* 20' tall on Tropical Rain Forest Loop; smaller ones elsewhere
– U.W.: 7 (+3 *Styrax Obassia*) N & W of Fisheries Teaching and Research Center

Catalina IRONWOOD

Lyonothamnus floribundus Gray　　　　　　　　　　　　Lyon Tree
ROSACEÆ
From islands off S California.

Named for William S. Lyon who found it in 1884 on Santa Catalina Island. A cold-tender broadleaf evergreen slender shrub or tree to 55' tall. The bark is fibrous, dark rusty red and gray. Broad clusters of creamy white flowers in June-July give rise to unsightly brown seeds. We grow the "fernleaf" *(aspleniifolius)* form with leaves elegantly divided into 3–9 slender, toothed leaflets, dark glossy green above, hairy beneath. Extremely rare in Seattle. One 33' tall at 11420 37th Ave SW; one 23' tall in another Seattle yard is not visible from the street.

JAPANESE BLUEBERRY TREE

Elæocarpus sylvestris (Lour.) Poir.　　Japanese: Horuto-no-ki ホルトノキ
=*E. decipiens* Hemsl. *ex* Forbes & Hemsl.　　Chinese: Du Ying
=*E. ellipticus* (Th.) Mak. 1904, *non* Smith 1809
ELÆOCARPACEÆ
From India to E Asia.

A broadleaf evergreen tree, sold here since 1995; still very rare. Leaves to 5" long, bronzy-red when young, dark green in summer; red before they fall. Flowers yellowish-white in dense little clusters in summer. Fruit a bluish-black berry. Recorded to 45' tall but often, if not usually, wider than tall.

– Zoo: at least 5 in Australasia, tallest 14½'
– 6200 block of Ellis Ave S (between 6281 & 6273): a street-tree 11' tall
– NW 70th St, east of 16th Ave NW: 3 street-trees in 2000—one *ca.* 6' tall by 2005
– 1941 8th Ave W: one *ca.* 8' tall next to the driveway

JAPANESE RAISIN-TREE

Hovenia dulcis Th.   Honey Tree
=*H. acerba* Lindl.   Japanese: Kenponashi ケンポナシ
RHAMNACEÆ   Chinese: Chih-chü (Zhi Qu)
From China, Korea, and Japan.

Named after David ten Hoven (1724–87), Amsterdam senator, botany patron.
A heat-loving tree of poor performance in cool-summer regions. Recorded to
15' × 13' in the wild. Leaves with three main veins from the base; to 8¾" × 6",
stem to 3½"; pale yellow fall color. Flowers tiny, fragrant; white, yellowish-white
or greenish-white, in late June to late July; much liked by bees. Fruit a 3-seeded
black, shiny dry capsule, borne on a contorted fleshy *peduncle* that is sweet and
edible. Color russet to ruby red, pulp yellowish, chewy, rasin flavored. Ripe in
October. In Seattle, very rare. An old Arboretum tree has never thrived: #213-46
in 6-2E, only 44' × 1'9". A young one 25' tall is west of a Silk Tree on the SE
corner of 19th Ave NW & NW 77th St.

JUJUBE

Ziziphus Zizyphus (L.) Karst.   Chinese Date
=*Z. Jujuba* Mill., *non* Lam.   Chinese: Tsao (Zǎo)
=*Z. vulgaris* Lam.
RHAMNACEÆ
From SE Europe and much of Asia.

A shrubbly little tree (maximum 50' × 10') of hot dry places, grown for its edible
'datelike' fruit. Many cultivars exist. The leaves are dark *shiny* green, ¾–3" long,
with 3 main veins. Tiny flowers smell of grape soda. In Seattle a few backyard
growers have grown Jujube trees for decades. The *only* public specimen I know
is a young street-tree at 4514 3rd Ave NW, north of a Chestnut tree.

JUNIPERS in general

Cultivated junipers are difficult to sort and name because there are so many.
Most are shrubs, so it is fairly easy to learn the tree kinds. Full sunshine and well-
drained (even dry) soil suit them best. Many are prickly or strongly fragrant. All
species make berries, but many individual plants are berry-less males. The berries
tend to be unpalatable though a few are more or less edible. In the Language of
Flowers, junipers signify: "protection," "asylum" or "succor."

Chinese JUNIPER

Juniperus chinensis L.   Chinese: Yuan Bai
CUPRESSACEÆ
From China, Mongolia, Japan, *etc.*

Notably variable, especially in cultivation; ranging from sprawling groundcover mats to stout trees 80' × 17'! First cited below (before the cultivars) are examples of the natural type—or cultivars mercilessly similar. These are uncommon.

- 3711 48th Ave NE: a 54' tall mostly ♀ bisexual in extreme S part of yard
- Lincoln Park: the central part (S of the tennis courts) has 2 forms: a floppy, gaunt ♂ 30' tall; and a tight, upright ♀ 37' × 2'7" with mostly juvenile foliage
- Arboretum: #362-53 is a 30' tall lush ♂ in 31-7E, and a 28½' tall ♂ in 38-4W
- 9638 47th Ave SW: an 18' tall ♂ (just N of a thread Sawara Cypress)

cv. 'Keteleerii'   Keteleer (Chinese) Juniper

A popular, distinctive, very dark green and emphatically tree-like female with profuse, big, light-blue berries. Common.

- Arboretum: 22; best 53' × 5'6" & 50' × 5'10" SE of Lake Wash. Blvd. & E Roanoke
- Bobby Morris Playfield (11th Ave & E Olive St): larger of 2 is 52½' × 5'4½"
- U.W. Medicinal Herb Garden: one 45' × 4'¼" behind Cascara Circle
- Van Asselt Playground (Beacon Ave S & S Myrtle St): 5 in the SW part
- Highland Park Playground (11th Ave SW & SW Cloverdale St): two N of tennis courts, the taller 40'

cv. 'Oblonga'

The best way to describe 'Oblonga' is to compare it to the well known and far more common Hollywood Chinese juniper (i.e., var. torulosa). The two have similar color, foliage and berries, but 'Oblonga' is more conservative in growth, not wildly zig-zaggy and irregular. The names 'Corymbosa', 'Fœmina', 'Reeves' or 'Reevesiana' and 'Sylvestris' have been used inconsistently and in conflicting fashion by various authors and by nurseries—in any given book one of these names applies to the juniper in question.

- Seward Park: one 32½' × 2'11" N of the entrance circle (by a blue Atlas Cedar)
- U.W.: one 23' tall with a large Bigleaf Maple south of Hansee Hall
- Arboretum: #1002-48 in 3S-7E (SE of stone cottage) is 27' × 1'11"
- 3806 W Parkmont Pl: one W of the house, above the alley
- 4216 6th Ave NW: in STUFF yard
- 6821 39th Ave NE

var. *pendula* Franch.   Weeping Chinese Juniper

More or less pendulous or droopy trees have been called by this name. Rare.

- 10332 Ravenna Ave NE has a drooping specimen by the front door; topped in 2005

var. *pyramidalis* (Carr.) Beissn.   Spiny Greek Juniper

A gray-green, prickly, tightly vertical bush, only tree-sized after decades, as is one 18' tall on the SE corner of 19th Ave NW & NW 77th St (N of a 30' tall 'Keteleerii'). Typical shrubby examples are occasional in yards, e.g., one 14½' tall at 3831 NE 96th St; 6807 28th Ave NE; 2 street-trees at 4430 Baker Ave NW.

cv. 'Robusta Green'

Dull sea-green foliage on a broad, informal rugged tree. Berries freely borne, but also some male pollen. It grows slowly to 12–18' tall or more. Some of the following may be *similar* clones—or seedlings that resemble it. Uncommon.

– 29th Ave SW & SW Holden St: NE corner has one 25½' tall SW of the house
– 3046 18th Ave S: one 24' tall
– 9743 45th Ave NE: one 24' tall (in front of a Corkscrew Willow)
– 2241 40th Ave E: a street-tree 15½' tall south of the driveway
– Woodlawn Ave N & N 46th St: NE corner has a topped one <10' tall S of house
– 7340 20th Ave NE: two in the yard's SW corner

var. *torulosa* (Eastwood) Bailey   Hollywood (Chinese) Juniper
= cv. 'Kaizuka'   Twisted (Chinese) Juniper

A widely planted and very well known grass-green female of wildly irregular, twisted, compact form, eventually assuming tree size: 45' tall and 37' wide in California; to at least 35' tall here. Its berries sometimes give rise to seedlings here, but the plant is grown from cuttings or is grafted.

– Tyee Apartments, 4115 Brooklyn Ave NE: one 28½' × 3'7" with Seattle's largest specimen of the holly-like *Osmanthus × Fortunei*
– 4218 55th Ave NE: one 30' tall and wider still
– Orca at Columbia School (3528 S Ferdinand St): 3 in front
– S.U.: two E of the Garrand Building (tallest 28½') and elsewhere
– 4522 Purdue Ave NE

var. *torulosa* cv. 'Variegata'   Variegated Chinese Juniper

Creamy, yellowish and green mixed on the foliage. Slow; small. Rare.

– 2305 N 44th St: once more than 30' tall, it was topped in 1993; now 23' tall

Common JUNIPER

J. communis L.   Dwarf Juniper
From much of the Northern Hemisphere: Ground Cedar
no other conifer species is so widely distributed.

The original "Juniper." This species is the chief source of berries used for flavoring gin; oil is extracted from its berries for medicinal use all over the world. Though a shrub (rarely a small tree up to 40' tall), and relatively uncommon in Seattle, it merits inclusion here. Most in Seattle are tight columns of prickly gray-blue foliage, usually called **Irish** or **Swedish junipers**. They are seen as yard trees or foundation-plantings and are sometimes tied with wire or string to keep their shape. Do not confuse the 'Ellwoodii' Lawson Cypress with Common juniper.

– 7044 20th Ave NE: 21' tall
– 3539 Wallingford Ave N: 14' tall, by a rhodie
– 3310 S Massachusetts St: by sidewalk, 13½' tall
– 32nd Ave NE & NE 62nd St: 4 south of the bldg. on the NE corner; tallest 12½'

- Arboretum: two #651-60 in 1S-4E, not treelike; most listed in the 1994 catalog *died*
- SSCC Arboretum: a cv. '**Compressa**' in the Milton Sutton Conifer Garden is 6' tall

[*J. Cedrus* Webb & Berthel.—Canary Island Juniper—is rare in the wild and almost unknown in gardens, though is now in commerce locally. It is a tree to 100' × 10' and bears bluntish short needles in trios around *whitish* twigs. In Seattle an 11½' tall tree (*pl.* 2002) is with many older Incense Cedars by the "giraffe" garage of Children's Hospital.]

Eastern Red Cedar (JUNIPER)

J. virginiana L.   Pencil Cedar
From the E half of the U.S., and S Ontario and Québec.   Red Juniper

This is known simply as "Red Cedar" where it is native, to distinguish it from the white cedars; in books of broad scope it is designated **Eastern** Red Cedar because other trees elsewhere are also called Red Cedar, with qualifying prefixes such as Southern or Western. The Cedar Waxwing bird was named because of its fondness for this tree, and Baton Rouge was so named because this tree was common there. Its maximum recorded dimensions are 120' × 17½'. It means "think of me" in the Language of Flowers.

In Seattle, uncommon. A slow-growing tree much like its close cousin the Rocky Mountain juniper, but with finer, less aromatic foliage and berries that ripen in one year instead of two.

- Brooklyn Ave NE & NE 52nd St: NE corner yard has one 40½' tall that is pale bluish-gray (such color forms can be called f. *glauca* [Carr.] Beissn.)
- U.W.: a ♀ 35½' × 4'4½" is SE of the Physical Plant Office Building
- 2821 E Ward St: 3 ♂ and 2 ♀ street-trees, the tallest 24½'
- 10035 36th Ave NE: a broad, 26' tall ♂
- 3717 31st Ave W (south of W Emerson St): a broad shrubby ♂ by the sidewalk
- 13th Ave E, south of E John St: apartment building on the E side has a ♀ 27' tall
- 725 16th Ave: 2 street-trees

Meyer JUNIPER

J. squamata Buch.-Ham. *ex* D. Don cv. '**Meyeri**'   Fishback Juniper
From China, of garden origin.   Fishtail Juniper

This juniper is a prickly, silvery-blue shrub or small tree of flaring, open form, about 15–25' tall with a trunk over 1' thick. It is distinctive and very common as a shrub but is rarely seen as a tree.

- Nordic Heritage Museum: one 23' tall × 33' wide south of the building
- Viewlands School: a pair at the far south end by 105th St, the taller 21'
- 2207 12th Ave W: one SW of the building
- the old Fauntleroy School (9131 California Ave SW): one 16½' tall by The Hall

Needle JUNIPER

J. rigida S.& Z.   Temple Juniper
From China, N Korea, Russian Far East, Japan.   Chinese: Du Song

A shrub or tree (to 56' × 5½') of soft looking but very prickly pendulous "needled" twigs. Much cultivated in Japanese temple gardens. Though most attractive, it is very rare in Seattle. The best example was hidden in a back yard, but got cut. The Arboretum has #136-50 in 20-1E; #136-50 in 3S-8E is only 8' tall but 24' wide; and of four #143-50 in 6S-9E the best is 24½' × 1'6". SSCC Arboretum's Cœnosium Rock Garden has one 11' tall west of the shelter. A young tree can be found at 2125 N 90th St.

Rocky Mountain JUNIPER

J. scopulorum Sarg.   Rocky Mountain Red Cedar
=*J. virginiana* var. *scopulorum* (Sarg.) Lemm.   Colorado Juniper
From much of western North America.

A tree up to 78' × 20½'; that can live 1,888 years. Over 40 cultivars exist, a few being: 'Blue Heaven' (miscalled 'Blue Haven'), 'Cologreen', 'Gray Gleam', 'Moffettii', 'Pathfinder', 'Platinum', 'Skyrocket', 'Spartan' (miscalled a *J. chinensis* cv.), 'Tolleson's (Blue) Weeping', 'Welchii' and 'Wichita Blue'.

Some are green, others palest blue, some brownish; some are narrow spires, others broad pyramids, some horizontal or weeping; some are pollen-producing males, others berry-making females. The foliage is (usually) finer than that of *J. chinensis*, coarser than that of *J. virginiana*, and more fragrant than either. Both the 'Burkii' and 'Skyrocket' cultivars are Rocky Mountain junipers despite being listed in most books and nursery catalogs as *J. virginiana* cultivars.

In Seattle, common as a whole, in various manifestations:

- Arboretum: various kinds ('Big Blue', 'Blue Pillar', 'Fulgens', 'Gracilis', 'Pathfinder', 'Platinum'), in 44-6W, 43-6W, 42-6W, 34-4W, 1S-4E, 1S-5E, 2S-5E. . . . tallest 29'
- 2912 1st Ave W: narrow and silvery, 26' tall
- Seattle Center: SW of Key Arena
- Brighton Playfield (42nd Ave S & S Juneau St): a pendulous green ♂ 29' × 2'9¼" at the north end in a bed of shrubs and trees
- 10032 35th Ave NE: 2 silvery-blue females (with Pyramidal Arborvitæs)
- 63rd Ave NE & NE 60th St: SW corner has many slender, silvery specimens
- U.W.: 9 '**Skyrocket**' were *pl.* in 2003 NE of 15th Ave NE & NE 42nd St
- Children's Hospital: some '**Wichita Blue**' west of parking lot 4
- 2116 N 60th St (just west of Kensington Pl N): a silvery, topped male under wires
- 6th Ave NW, south of NW 90th St: an 18½' tall ♂ street-tree, east side
- 44th Ave SW & SW Fletcher St: the NE corner has a green 27' ♂ and shorter ♀
- 7747 18th Ave NE: 8 '**Tolleson's Blue Weeping**' in back yard—see from alley
- 5707 28th Ave NE: '**Tolleson's Blue Weeping**' 17' tall
- 8533 2nd Ave NE: a '**Tolleson's Blue Weeping**' with a weeping blue Atlas Cedar
- 3011 NW 60th St: '**Tolleson's Blue Weeping**' west of a Leyland Cypress

Weeping JUNIPER

J. squamata Buch.-Ham. *ex* D. Don var. *Fargesii* (Komar.) Rehd. & Wils. *ex* Sarg.
=*J. Lemeeana* Lévl. & Blin
From W China, Tibet.   Chinese: Chang Ye Gao Shan Bai

In nature this is a tree up to 90' × 22'. In cultivation it is a small, very prickly medium-green tree of graceful weeping habit—one of the "weeping junipers." It makes inconspicuous 1-seeded black berries *ca.* ¼" long. It is extremely rare here. [Its retention at varietal level *(Fargesii)* is denied by A. Farjon in his 2005 *Cupressaceæ* monograph, but is maintained in the *Flora of China.*]

— Golden Gardens Park: one 41' × 6'0" is 3-trunked above a common base, easily seen from the road near the bottom of the hillside below the upper-level restrooms
— Arboretum: of seven #1118-37 in the pinetum (35-5W), the tallest is 27½'
— Seward Park: the fish hatchery has one by the stream
— Lincoln Park: two (taller 27') by the stream as it cascades down over rocks on the steep hillside at the south end of the park (with bamboo and 3 Scots Pines)

[*J. recurva* Buch.-Ham. *ex* D. Don—Drooping Juniper—is a widespread E Asian shrub or tree to 130' that is closely related and similar to the preceding. In Seattle a young 5' tall tree is by the driveway at 7519 22nd Ave NW.]

Western JUNIPER

J. occidentalis Hook. fil.   Western Red Cedar
From central Washington to S California.   Sierra Juniper

A scrubby bush, or at the other extreme a giant up to 86' × 40'0" and *ca.* 4,000 years old! In any case its stout gray-blue foliage is the most resinous and aromatic of all the junipers mentioned in this guide. Every twig is coated with white crusted exudations; on some summer days a liquid flow of fragrant resin coats the foliage. If you relish strongly fragrant plants *smell this*. It thrives on perfect drainage and much sunshine. Too bad it is extremely rare in Seattle.

— Arboretum: #5-75 in conifer meadow (44-6W) 22' tall; #582-56 '**Glauca**' by lookout (11-2E) 25½' × 1'10"; #1026-56 both by lookout 23' × 2'1", and the rockery (1S-4E); #775-58 in the rockery came from Bend, Oregon, and is the most resinous, most open in habit, 31' × 1'8½"
— 11037 Sand Point Way NE: a ♀ 20½' tall by the mailbox

KATSURA

Cercidiphyllum japonicum S. & Z. *ex* Hoffm. & Schultes
CERCIDIPHYLLACEÆ
From China, Japan.

Called Katsura (カツラ) in Japanese, it is neither closely related to, nor does it much resemble any Western tree. Where native, it is a forest tree up to 130' × 63' yielding valuable wood. Roundish leaves emerge bronzy-green in March and light up into bright yellows and oranges—or smoky purple—in late September–October. A curious cotton-candy or wild strawberry fragrance sometimes accompanies the fall color. In Seattle, common, popular; nearly all are relatively young. It is attractive, strong, troublefree—though *thirsty*. For more information see the *Arboretum Bulletin*, Fall 1982.

– 1900 Shenandoah Dr E: one 84' × 10'11" × 63' wide (1993)
– Arboretum: 2 #409-38 in 30-2E (90' × 6'1½" & 86' × 7'2½") and 2 #X-328 in 13-7E (102' × 6'3½" ♀ & 94' × 5'11" ♂) are tall due to the woodland setting
– Volunteer Park: 3 ♀ and 2 ♂ W of the wading pool, the largest 55½' × 8'4¾" and the tallest 65' × 7'8"
– 34th Ave E, north of E Mercer St: 6 street-trees, E side
– Seattle Center: some by the Mural Amphitheatre
– U.W.: W of Padelford Hall are 5 with 8 Scots Pines
– Locks #25 (tiny), 204 (two), 304A

cv. 'Pendulum'   Weeping Katsura

More or less pendulous or droopy trees have been called by this name. All known in Seattle are relatively young, and most are topgrafted mop-head weepers that will remain short and broad. A few clones will eventually grow tall.

– 10829 11th Ave NE: one 13½' tall in yard's SE corner
– Children's Hospital: two relatively large, old trees N of the building, the taller 13'
– Warren Ave N, just north of Garfield St: a street-tree, W side
– 10516 8th Ave NW (at NW 106th St): a prominent yard specimen
– S.U.: courtyard of Xavier Hall
– 5031 Ivanhoe Place NE
– 4511 48th Ave NE: by a Hollywood Juniper at telephone-pole base
– Arboretum: #34-87 is 8' tall in 32-2E (the Woodland Garden)

[*C. magnificum* (Nakai) Nakai, from mountains of Japan, called "Hiro-ha-katsura," is smaller, has wider and larger leaves; a short, usually single and less fluted trunk covered with smooth rather than fibrous and furrowed bark. Aside from the old one (#764-46 41' × 6'0") at the Arboretum, few are in Seattle, such as @1123 16th Ave E: 2 ♀ street-trees and one 25' tall ♂ in the yard; both N & S on the planting strip are *regular* Katsura trees.]

[**Spur Leaf**—*Tetracentron sinense* Oliv.—TETRACENTRONACEÆ—is an E Asian relative recorded to 131' × 19¾'. It has *veiny* leaves borne on obvious *spurs*, dreadful fall color, and smooth bark. Scarcely found in Seattle, and only *young*, outside the Arboretum, where the largest of 5 is 36' × 3'9¼" (#385-62 in 30-3E). 5643 3rd Ave NW has 2 in the yard by the walkway. The Good Shepherd Center has one 8½' tall NE of the building. Locks bed #26 has a 3-trunked youngster.]

KENTUCKY COFFEE-TREE

Gymnocladus dioicus (L.) K. Koch   Kentucky Mahogany
=*G. canadensis* Lam.   Coffee-nut Tree
=*Guilandia dioica* L.   (K)nicker Tree
LEGUMINOSÆ (FABACEÆ)   Stump Tree
From the central and eastern   Luck Bean
U.S. and extreme S Ontario.   Chicot

Strong, striking, rough and bold enough to usurp the official designation of Kentucky's State Tree from the Tulip Tree (Yellow Poplar). Many call it coarse and clumsy, and in this respect it is admittedly more akin to the Dodo Bird than to the Eagle, yet withal it is a tree of truly distinctive character. Lovers of the extraordinary and outlandish may complacently admire it. It can attain 135' × 17¾' and is essentially a poisonous tree, but its large seeds, well roasted, have been rendered safe to eat as nuts or to be ground and used as a coffee substitute. Some specimens make seeds, others don't. Alas, it is rare in Seattle.

– Volunteer Park: one 61' × 4'7½" in a grove of mixed trees midway between the bandstand and conservatory (nearby is the massive Euodia tree)
– Arboretum: #865-57B is 57' × 3'5" (40-3W); smaller ones in 20-4E & 19-5E
– U.W. Medicinal Herb Garden: one suckering N of the Plant Lab is 46½' × 3'2¼"
– SW 106th St, west of 35th Ave SW: 2 street-trees, S side

LARCHES in general

Of those anomalies, the deciduous conifers, larches are the most widely distributed and best known; others include Bald Cypress and Dawn Redwood. All of these, apparently unhandicapped by their deciduous habit, produce large, ornamental and commercially valuable trees. "Tamarack," derived from an Indian name, is often used for species of *Larix* in North America. When their needles yellow in autumn, larches look like dying trees. When naked in late winter, especially when encrusted with gray lichens, they appear quite dead. But the resurrecting beauty of their spring greenery is one of the most refreshing sights in all nature. For reasons unknown but presumably appropriate, in the Language of Flowers Larch represents "boldness" or "audacity."

European LARCH

Larix decidua Mill.   Common Larch
=*L. europæa* DC. *ex* Lamb. & DC.
PINACEÆ
From the Alps of Europe.

Growing as large as 180' × 28' and producing a tough, strong, durable timber of many uses, this larch has been employed extensively in European forestry. There it is grown in cycles on plantations and periodically logged. As an ornamental tree it enjoys a chance (however remote) of reaching its full stature, and a possible lifespan of over 2,000 years.

In Seattle, it is common: our most abundant larch. It makes cones up to 1¾" (2⅛") long, that persist on the twigs. Reseeding occurs sparingly.

– Green Lake Pitch n' Putt Golf Course: a large-limbed one 45' × 9'¼" × 63' wide!
– Green Lake: largest is 73½' × 7'6½" (SW of restrooms @Meridian Ave & 64th St)
– U.W.: 77' × 5'1" south of law building; 5 NE of tennis courts by Hutchinson Hall
– Volunteer Park: one 85' × 4'7" on the north border by the wading pool; another south of the lower tennis courts is 77' × 6'1½"

- Jefferson Park Golf Course: largest of 10 at the N end by the pond is 6'10¼" around
- Zoo: 7 by the Snow Leopard exhibit, the tallest 81' × 4'9"
- Locks beds #23, 24: one at the top of the stairs, one below

var. *polonica* (Racib.) Ostenf. & Syr.-Lars.　　　　　　　Polish Larch
From SE Poland, NW Ukraine, N Czechoslovakia.

Known in Seattle only at the Arboretum (6, the largest 71' × 5'8" #133-59 in 18-2W) and one 48' × 3'9" with a distinctively swollen base at the U.W. Friendship Grove (north of a smaller Siberian larch), representing Poland.

Golden LARCH

Pseudolarix amabilis (Nels.) Rehd.　　　　　Chinese: Jin Qian Song
=*Chrysolarix amabilis* (Nels.) H.E. Moore
=*Larix amabilis* Nels.
From E China.

Unlike other larches, the Golden larch has 2–3" long cones that *break up* when ripe. Its needles are unusually wide, 1¼–2½" long, and turn golden in fall. In nature it may attain 150' × 10'. In Seattle it is very rare, slow-growing and so beautiful that it deserves to be much better known.

- Locks bed #16 has one 28' × 4'11"
- Kubota Garden Park: two *pl.* here in 1990 when over 25 years old, 27½' × 2'5½" (uphill) and 26½' × 2'5" (downhill)
- Arboretum: the south end of Azalea Way (9-1W) has #280-77 that is 14½' tall
- Twin Ponds Park: SE of tennis courts one is 9½' tall
- 2801 NW 63rd St: a street-tree under wires
- U.W.: behind forestry buildings, by Burke-Gilman Trail, one *ca.* 6' tall

Japanese LARCH

L. Kaempferi (Lamb.) Sarg., *non* Carr.　　　Japanese: Kara-matsu カラマツ
=*L. leptolepis* (S.& Z.) Sieb. *ex* G. Gord.
From Japan.

Like European Larch but with wider needles more blue than pure green, borne on conspicuously pink-red twigs (not yellowish-tan ones), and having cones more squat, with recurved scales. It can exceed 130' × 12½'. Rare in Seattle: a few in parks or yards, but far outnumbered by the European larch.

- Ravenna Park: 13 mixed with Norway Spruces in the ravine, the tallest 93' × 5'1"
- Camp Long: tallest of four by the lodge is 73' × 4'5¾"
- Arboretum: the largest of 24 is 73' × 5'2¼" (in 9-2W)
- Green Lake: 51½' × 5'10½" is best of a grove of 6 +2 Europeans near the middle of the NW parking lot; (in the same area of Green Lake are many Europeans)
- 3201 Magnolia Blvd (at W Dravus St): one
- 2207 E Marion St: a cv. **Blue Rabbit** 30' tall is prettily glaucous
- 1st Ave W & W Prospect St: the SW corner garden has a cv. **'Diana'** ('Diane') 21½'

tall by the driveway; it has *twisted* branches and needles

cv. 'Pendula'   Weeping Japanese Larch

A weepy dwarf tree sold either as "Weeping European" or "Weeping Japanese" larch. Albeit grafted on European roots, the clone is clearly Japanese.

– 31st Ave W & W Armour St: NE corner has one 13' tall by the alley on Armour
– 11319 17th Ave NE: one 7½' tall between an Alaska Cedar and a Katsura
– Mt Pleasant Cemetery: one 5½' tall in the middle
– 16th Ave S & S King St: one 5½' tall on E side of house on the NW corner
– U.W.: one 6' tall in grove W of Anderson Hall; overcrowded by Viburnums, *etc.*
– S.U.: one 4½' tall NE of the Pigott building, SE of The Green
– 5315 NE 74th St: made into a living archway north of the house

Siberian LARCH

L. sibirica Ledeb.
=*L. russica* (Endl.) Sabine *ex* Trautv.
From NE (European) Russia, W Siberia, N Mongolia.

Extremely rare: *one* is known here, and it may be a hybrid with Polish larch: at the U.W. Friendship Grove, representing the U.S.S.R., 20' × 3'4½".

Western LARCH

L. occidentalis Nutt.   West American Larch
From parts of British Columbia, Alberta,   Western Tamarack
Idaho, Washington, Oregon, Montana.   Montana Larch

Characteristically slender, tall, and short-branched, at most reaching 250' × 30'. Its grass-green needles are longer than those of most larches, up to 2¾"; its cones are 1–2" and have conspicuous protruding bracts. It is uncommon in Seattle yards and unknown on public property except as cited below.

– Arboretum: best of 3 in 33-4W is 67½' × 3'4"; one in 18-1W is 69' × 5'0"
– U.W. Friendship Grove, representing The Union of South Africa, 66' × 3'2¾"
– 1212 NW 105th St has one 51½' tall in yard's SE corner
– 3608–3610 Meridian Ave N: by driveway
– 11054 Fremont Ave N: by fire hydrant
– 315 N 40th St: 60' tall

[*L. laricina* (Du Roi) K. Koch.—Tamarack; Eastern *or* American Larch—from across N America in the far north; to 125' × 12'. Thin scaly bark, short bluish needles and tiny cones. In Seattle, youngsters (17½' tall) at Zoo's Northern Trail; 3 young #53-96 and 4 old #134-57 at Arboretum: best 72½' × 4'8" in 18-2W and 68' × 5'8½" in 17-1W.]

Bay LAUREL

Laurus nobilis L.

Poet's *or* Sweet *or* Apollo's Laurel

LAURACEÆ

Roman *or* Grecian Laurel

From the Mediterranean region.

Royal *or* Sweet Bay

As its names indicate, this is the bay rich in culinary, historical and literary memories. In *name* it may be confused with various other bays or laurels—trees or shrubs so named because they more or less resemble this original version. All they really have in common with it is their broadleaf evergreen habit. In *appearance* it can be confused less easily: a small Portugal laurel or an Oregon Myrtle may resemble it. In leaf fragrance it can be confused only with Oregon Myrtle.

At most 70' tall, Bay laurel *here* is a shrub or multitrunked tree rarely 40' tall. Occasionally it is seen single-trunked (and often sheared) in formal gardens or as a street-tree. It is more likely to be hurt by severe winters when sheared. Whitish-yellow flowers appear late March–early May; the two sexes are (usually) on separate trees. Nearly all of ours are males, which have showier flowers.

Compared to Oregon Myrtle it is usually multitrunked, less hardy, seldom reseeds here, has darker leaves with a translucent and often crisped margin, and has milder fragrance. In the Language of Flowers, the Bay tree means "glory" and bay wreaths are "the reward of merit."

– U.W.: N of Sieg Hall 2 multitrunked trees, the taller 45'; between the Art (44½' tall) and Music (48½' tall) buildings; NW of the fish-homing pond
– 951 17th Ave E: 36½' tall
– Lincoln Park: at the far N end is one 33' tall with 10 trunks
– Good Shepherd Center: a 17' tall female in Seattle Tilth's compost area
– 6710 23rd Ave NW: street-tree
– Dunn Gardens: a 15' tall '**Aurea**' north of the house is cheerfully *gold* leaved

[**Camphor Laurel**—*Cinnamomum Camphora* (L.) J.S. Presl—is a cousin from tropical and subtropical Asia & Malaysia. Extremely rare and inconsistently hardy in Seattle: the only *old* specimen known is in section E of the U.W. Medicinal Herb Garden. Under a Pin Oak, it has 4 slender trunks and is 23' tall. Now & then it freezes to the soil. A 2nd U.W. one was *pl.* spring 2005 east of Guthrie Annex 1. Children's Hospital has one 24' tall south of the grounds maintenance area. A small one 13' tall is at 1764 Boyer Ave E.]

[*Japanese* **Camphor Laurel**—*Cinnamomum japonicum* Sieb. *ex* Nakai—is a more cold-hardy cousin from E Asia, including Japan, where it is called Yabunikkei (ヤブニッケイ). Extremely rare in Seattle. The Zoo has at least 8 in Australasia, tallest 17'.]

[**Canary Island Laurel. Barbusano**—*Apollonias Barbujana* (Cav.) Bornm.—is from the Canary Islands. It is similar to and related closely to Bay Laurel. In April 2001 one about 10 years old was planted at Children's Hospital; others may exist in Seattle too.]

[**Silky Laurel** *or* **Japanese Silver Tree**—*Neolitsea sericea* (Bl.) Koidz.—is from E Asia; in Japanese: Shiro-damo シロダモ. Its emerging young spring leaves are *silky* with hairs. Very rare here. Arboretum #8-68 in 22-1E is 29' × 1'4"; #59-92B S of it is 7' tall. City Light's North Service bldg. has one 12' tall on Stone Ave N, opposite N 98th St (it is S of a 23' Evergreen Magnolia, N of a 19½' Tanyosho Pine. A few yards have specimens.]

[**Yunnan Laurel**—*Machilus yunnanensis* Lecomte = *Persea yunn.* (Lecomte) Kosterm.—is from W China. It has narrow willow-like leaves. In 21-1E at the Arboretum, #1374-38 is 44' × 3'0" (1 of 3 trunks) and has reseeded for decades. Its offspring are now planted elsewhere there, and in Seattle, such as one at 4322 NE 38th St, *pl.* <1990. Some botanists have questioned whether the Seattle tree is named *correctly;* time will tell.]

English LAUREL

Prunus Laurocerasus L.   Common Laurel
=*Padus Laurocerasus* (L.) Mill.   Cherry Laurel
=*Laurocerasus officinalis* Roem.   Laurel Cherry
ROSACEÆ
From SE Europe and adjacent Asia.

It may be of interest to those intimately acquainted with this plant, to learn that its flowering branch signifies "perfidy" in the Language of Flowers. Thriving in every degree of light, and most extremes of soil, it is a wonder to all who behold it freely exuberating where given ample room, but a herculean task to all who try containing it (rather like keeping an elephant in the back yard). Seattle laurels are not infrequently cut with chain-saws in desperate attempts to keep them in check. Probably more truckloads of its clippings get taken to the dump than those of any other tree. It is, in short, a jolly green giant. Not limited to troubling all who try keeping it shrubby, it is so naturalized here as to choke out native vegetation in wooded parks.

If not too closely clipped, it flowers late March–late May, producing black cherries, resembling black olives, ripe and edible (late July) August through mid-October. Spit out the poisonous pits. Shrubby cultivars such as 'Otto Luyken' and 'Zabeliana' exist. Cv. 'Magnoliæfolia' has leaves up to 12¾" × 5" wide. The tree itself can reach 50' tall in wooded areas; in the open it grows broad.

It is *very* common here. Seven huge examples follow—such trees are prone to being brutally hacked from tree-size back to stumpy shrubs.

– Seattle Center Fisher Pavilion has one 33' × 9'1½" × 52' wide
– 5825 16th Ave NE: 42' tall × 62½' wide
– Tashkent Park (Belmont Ave E, south of E Mercer St): 31' × 5'2¼" × 55' wide
– S.U.: east of the Garrand Building 26½' × 5'5¼" × 46' wide
– Louisa Boren Lookout (15th Ave E & E Garfield St): one 26' tall being strangled by a bench built too tight around its 5'6¼" trunk
– U.W.: north of Lander Hall basketball court bicycle parking

cv. '**Camelliæfolia**' ('Camelliifolia')   Curlyleaf Laurel

A shrubbier form, but still capable of attaining treehood. It has small leaves *curled* in a manner suggesting an infested plant, and is very rare in Seattle. One 27½' tall is NW of the McDonald's restaurant on First Hill (1122 Madison St)—look west of the trash containers in the parking lot.

Portugal LAUREL

P. lusitanica L.　　　　　　　　　　　　　　Portuguese: Azareiro
From Spain, Portugal, the Azores.　　　　　　Louro *or* Loureiro

This has such dark small leaves that it looks more like Bay Laurel than English. It grows so dense that unless pruned, the trunks are invisible. Very fragrant flowers in slender long clusters in late May–June. Cherries smaller than English laurel's, reddish-purple rather than black, and foully bitter. Recorded to 70' × 12½'.

In Seattle, common, including wild seedlings. Cultivars almost nonexistent; sometimes nurseries sell stock called "standards" for street-tree usage, which are pruned after the fashion of Bay laurel, Fraser Photinia and Tree Privet.

– Matthews Beach Park: *ca.* 12 old ones in a row N of children's play area; tallest 45'
– Discovery Park: one of a pair by N parking lot bus-stop is 36½' × 8'7¼" × 40' wide
– Me-kwa-mooks Park: largest of several is 30½' × 6'8"
– Leschi Park: old, large examples SE of the restrooms
– 2017 Broadway E: 2 standard street-trees
– 2561 10th Ave W: a 19' tall specimen of 'Variegata' by the sidewalk

[Carolina Laurel—*Prunus caroliniana* (Mill.) Ait.—is a cousin of the preceding two species. A dense, bright green, glossy tree. Extremely rare in Seattle. It can attain 55' × 10½'. Seattle's largest example may be one 23½' tall at 1216 E Newton St in the SE corner of the yard. 4754 22nd Ave NE: two, tallest 30'—*cut down* Nov. 2005. One behind the fence at 2316 N 50th St.]

[Hollyleaf Cherry—*Prunus ilicifolia* (Nutt. *ex* H.&A.) D. Dietr.—is a shrub or small tree from coastal California, where it is also called Islay. Leaves evergreen, holly-like. Extremely rare here; two at the Arboretum in 10-2E (#275-88, taller 9½'). Hollyleaf Cherry hybridizes with the S Californian Catalina Cherry—*P. Lyonii* (Eastw.) Sarg.—a larger species. Such a hybrid tree at the Good Shepherd Center was 20½' × 1'5¼" when the groundskeeper cut it down in April 2005 because its seedlings bothered him; he was concerned that it might end up becoming a weedy species in Seattle.]

Tree LILAC

Syringa reticulata (Bl.) Hara　　　　　　　Japanese Tree Lilac
=*S. amurensis* var. *japonica* (Maxim.) Fr. & Sav.　　Giant Tree Lilac
=*S. japonica* Maxim. *ex* Decne.　　　Japanese: Hashidoi ハシドイ
OLEACEÆ
From Japan.

Though our familar garden lilac shrub *(S. vulgaris)* exists over 20' tall in some Seattle yards, the Tree lilacs are notably dissimilar. The bark is often cherry-like, not vertically shreddy. The expanding bright greenery of *early* spring affords a lovely sight. Leaves 3–8" long, are hairy beneath, rounded or broadly wedge-shaped at the base; yellow early in fall. Flowers yellowish-white in dense 8–24" clusters from May to July; their odor powerful but not necessarily lovable. Recorded to 49' × 7'.

In Seattle, uncommon. Old trees vary, but all planted since the 1990s are cv. 'Ivory Silk'—said to be relatively compact, bearing large clusters of flowers even when young, and less prone to chlorosis.

- Stimson-Greene Mansion (1204 Minor Ave): E corner has one 24' tall
- U.W.: two by the doors in the S courtyard of Hansee Hall, tallest 22½'
- Arboretum: 13-3W has *ca*. 11 shrubs, the tallest 21' (#242-40) & 20' (#1238-56)
- 3502 43rd Ave NE: one by the driveway is 19½' tall
- Good Shepherd Center: one 18' tall is in a crowded bed under the poplars
- Volunteer Park: S border, east of 11th Ave E, has 3 old shrubby ones; tallest 15'
- 4514 46th Ave SW: an old street-tree 14½' × 2'4¾"
- 6035 32nd Ave NE: 2 'Ivory Silk' street-trees
- US Bank 1st Ave W & W Mercer St: 'Ivory Silk' *pl. ca*. 1996
- 5115 Wallingford Ave N: an 'Ivory Silk' street-tree *pl*. in 1990
- 1707 S Main St: 2 'Ivory Silk' street-trees
- NW 62nd St, just E of 34th Ave NW: 'Ivory Silk' street-tree, S side (E of a Kousa)
- Bradner Gardens Park: an 'Ivory Silk' in the SE corner

Chinese Tree LILAC

S. reticulata ssp. *pekinensis* (Rupr.) Green & Chang   Peking Lilac
= *S. pekinensis* Rupr.   Chinese: Bei Jing Ding Xiang
From N China mountains.

Some specimens have handsome cinnamon-brown bark, peeling in cherry-like strips; some have deeply corrugated bark. Leaves 2–4" long, hairless or sparsely hairy, relatively *narrowed* at the base. Flowers yellowish-white in nodding, loose 3–6" clusters in June. Usually shrubby (recorded to 45' × 5½'), graceful. Most of our trees are **Summer Charm**® (1994 patented = 'DTR 124') "Reliably upright and of pleasing tree form. Flowers well annually. Foliage relatively fine-textured."

- 1127 17th Ave E: 2 street-trees *pl*. Fall 2001
- Roanoke Park: one *pl*. Feb. 2002 by the bus-stop
- 1608 E Lynn St: 2 street-trees
- Meridian Ave N & N 44th St: SW corner has 2 street-trees
- vicinity of NW 83rd St, from 25th to 29th Ave NW: many street-trees *pl*. Nov. 2005 of a newer clone, **China Snow**® (='Morton')

LINDENS in general

Lindens, in north-central Europe, were traditionally familiar, highly esteemed and useful. They yielded fresh spring leaves for sandwiches and salads, dried mature foliage for livestock fodder, fragrant flowers for comforting summer teas and for honeybees to feed upon. The stringy bark fibers were used for paper-making and were woven into mats, ropes, baskets and fish-nets in winter. The light to medium weight, close-grained wood was used for carving, sculpting, and cooperage, and making furniture, toys, *etc*. After the story of Baucis and Philemon, the fine-proportioned trees themselves were adopted as a symbol of conjugal love and matrimony. So many German villages had either great avenues of stately lindens, or venerable landmark trees shading the greensward where the townspeople gathered, that many fondly called linden their National Tree. The Dutch, French, Swiss, English and others all enjoyed their long-lived lindens also. In England the trees are known as **limes**. The New World **basswoods** (which are related to lindens) have never achieved comparable popularity.

In Seattle, neither lindens nor basswoods are native. Few citizens know them by name; many couldn't describe one even if their lives depended on it. The European custom of planting linden avenues has endured intact, for it is noteworthy that the vast majority of our lindens line boulevards or are street-trees: very few stand as isolated specimens in parks, cemeteries or yards. These plantings, whether by design or accident, consist more often than not of a mix of at least two kinds of lindens/basswoods. Also worthy of mention is the puzzling fact that the most vigorous of lindens (*Tilia* × *europæa* L., *emend.* Sm.) is absent. Reseeding is common here but establishment and growth into saplings is virtually nil. Occasionally lindens (chiefly Bigleaf linden) reproduce by root-sucker.

Basswood (LINDEN)

Tilia spp. as cited below   American Linden *or* Linn
TILIACEÆ   Bee Tree / Wickyup / Monkeynuts Tree
From eastern North America.   Whistlewood *or* Whittlewood

"Basswood" is derived from bast-wood, referring to fibers in the bark which were once widely used and economically significant. "Basswood" is strictly an American name applied to American species of *Tilia*; Old World cousins in the genus are called "Linden" or "Lime" trees in English. The password to basswoods is "baffling." These trees are difficult to sort and classify: botanists choose either to split the various manifestations of these trees into differently named kinds; or recognize only *one* species, allowing it great variation. Seattle's specimens will key out in Rehder's *Manual of Cultivated Trees and Shrubs* to at least four species, but here, following the modern consensus, we lump them into but two:

BASSWOOD	WHITE BASSWOOD
Tilia americana L.	*Tilia heterophylla* Vent.
= *T. glabra* Vent.	= *T. monticola* Sarg.
= *T. neglecta* Spach	= *T. Michauxii* Nutt.
Tree up to 140' × 24½'	Tree up to 135' × 18½'
Leaf undersides green	Leaf undersides
and more or less hairless	densely whitish-hairy

The two extremes are distinct and easily distinguishable, but some trees with intermediate characteristics are referable to either species.

In Seattle, Basswood outnumbers White Basswood. Basswoods as a whole are uncommon here compared to their linden cousins; nor do they generally perform as well. The only basswood much planted recently is the '**Redmond**' cultivar. To distinguish a basswood from a linden, the easiest feature to use is leaf size. Linden leaves are usually no more than 5½" long and wide—at most up to 7"; but basswoods commonly bear leaves 7–12" long, and even longer on their basal suckers, or when their tops have been much pruned.

BASSWOOD:
— N 50th St, just W of Greenwood Ave N: a street-tree, S side, 60½' × 10'4¼"
— 35th Ave, south of E James St: a street-tree (with 2 Bigleaf lindens) is 73' × 9'1½"
— 62nd Ave S & S Cooper St: one 57' tall in the NE corner yard
— 16th Ave E, north of E Mercer St: a street-tree 61½' × 7'7¼"(+ 3 Bigleaf lindens)
— Zoo: extreme NW part (outside fence) by children's play area, one 55' × 6'¼"
— 1148 NW 50th St: larger of 2 street-trees is 48½' × 7'1½" (below fork)
— Belmont Pl E, at E Prospect St: two street-trees, S side
— 4006 NE 60th St: 41' tall
— NE 68th St, east of 19th Ave NE: 3 street-trees of cv. 'Redmond' on the S side
— 17th Ave NE & NE 82nd St triangle has 'Redmond' street-trees
— Benefit Park: many 'Redmond' trees, the tallest 64' and stoutest 4'2½" around

WHITE BASSWOOD:
— Arboretum: #385-52A is 68' × 6'0", B is 66' × 7'1" and C is 77½' × 6'6½"
— 4700 8th Ave NE: a street-tree 69' × 6'11"
— by John Hay School (411 Boston St) on 4th Ave N, south of Boston St: two street-trees (largest 59' × 7'5"), E side (also 20 Bigleaf and 3 Littleleaf lindens)
— W Garfield St, west of 9th Ave W: a 61' × 7'4" street-tree, S side (W of an elm and a Northern Catalpa)
— 6746 28th Ave S: 2 south of the house
— 12018 Sand Point Way NE: one 7'4½" around is pruned due to overhead wires

Bigleaf LINDEN

T. platyphyllos Scop.
= *T. grandifolia* Ehrh.
From Europe, SW Asia.

Bigleaf Lime
Broad- *or* Large-leaved L.
Summer *or* Female *or* Red-twigged L.

Called *Bigleaf* Linden (or Lime) not because its leaves are big compared to the whole genus, but merely to distinguish it from Littleleaf linden. The biggest leaves measure 5½–7" long and wide, on 2" stalks. As they emerge and unfold in late March–April, their soft green beauty contrasts handsomely with the fuzzy, dark twigs. Bigleaf linden flowers first of all, beginning in June, with perfume strong and sweet. It's also first to lose color and drop its leaves. In particular, old, stressed street-trees turn sickly, dull and yellowish, often dropping leaves infested with honeydew, sooty mold, bugle galls, or spidermites, from late July through mid-August. When fully defoliated in winter it presents an attractive silhouette. It can attain 135' × 44' or more, after centuries of patient growth.

In Seattle, edges out Littleleaf linden as the most abundant of older specimens of the genus; nowadays scarcely planted. As the following examples attest, it's generally found with other lindens, especially Littleleaf linden. Cultivars exist, but Seattle's are not very distinct, and are rare.

— Kinnear Park: a leaning one 71' × 10'1½" × 77' wide by the lower level tennis courts
— Frink Park: 5 boulevard trees, largest 103' × 6'3"

- Denny-Blaine Park: 8 (+a giant Littleleaf linden); tallest 73', stoutest 8'10½"
- Mt Baker Park: 36 street-trees (and 13 Littleleaf lindens)
- W Wheeler St & 10th Ave W have 22 street-trees (+2 Littleleaf lindens)
- John Hay School (411 Boston St): 20 street-trees (+2 White basswoods and 3 Littleleaf lindens)
- S of the Montlake Bridge: 11 Bigleafs (mostly east) & 11 Littleleafs (mostly west)
- Wallingford Center (1815 N 45th St): 10 street-trees
- Spring St, between 7th Ave & 9th Ave: vigorous young City street-trees
- Locks bed #103 (misidentified as *T. petiolaris*)
- Arboretum: '**Fastigiata**' (46-1E), '**Handsworth**' (2-trunked in 44-5E), '**Laciniata**' (45-4E), and '**Örebro**' (48-2E)
- '**Handsworth**' (yellowish-green twigs) is at Hiawatha Playfield W of tennis courts
- '**Örebro**' City street-trees: California Ave SW, from SW Walker St to SW Dakota

Crimean LINDEN

T. × *euchlora* K. Koch   Crimean Lime
(T. dasystyla × *T. cordata)*   Caucasian L.

From the Caucasia-Crimea region, grown in Europe since the mid-19th century, it is well thought of there, being as handsome as average but healthier than most lindens. The largest are about 70' × 10'. The twigs are apple-green, the leaves dark glossy green, the seeds football-shaped, fuzzy and strongly ribbed.

In Seattle it's rare: most are young street-trees. The clone sold by nurseries as cv. 'Redmond' is a basswood. Some streets lined mostly with glossy dark green Crimean lindens have some pale, large-leaved 'Redmond' basswoods.

- Queen Anne Blvd: by the cemetery on W Raye St, east of 8th Ave W, are 38 lindens—19 on each side of the road. A few are Bigleaf but most are Crimean grafted on Bigleaf rootstock; the tallest is 69½' × 5'3" and the stoutest 59' × 8'1¼"
- 15th Ave NW, from NW 47th to NW 65th St: City street-trees
- Roosevelt Way NE, from Ravenna Blvd to NE 80th St: City street-trees
- 35th Ave SW, from SW Oregon to SW Morgan St: City street-trees
- Rainier Ave S, from S Kenny to S Rose St: City street-trees
- 20th Ave S, from S Jackson St to Yesler Way: City street-trees
- U.W.: 5 street-trees (+ a Littleleaf linden) on University Way NE, n of NE Pacific St
- Harvard Ave & E Union St: 3 (+ 1 'Redmond' Basswood) street-trees

Dropmore LINDEN

T. × *flavescens* A. Br. *ex* Döll cv. '**Dropmore**'

This cultivar has been around since 1955. Said to be a cross of *T. americana* and *T. cordata*, it is nonetheless so much more like basswood than like Littleleaf linden that this parentage is questionable. At any rate, for all practical purposes the 'Dropmore' linden is a basswood. It is extremely rare in Seattle. Green Lake Way N, north of N 50th St, is lined with 22 old Littleleaf, 14 old Bigleaf, and (at the north end with 4 Norway Maples) 5 young 'Dropmore' lindens.

Littleleaf LINDEN

T. cordata Mill.
= *T. parvifolia* Ehrh. *ex* Hoffm.
From Europe, the Caucasus.

Littleleaf Lime
Small-leaved L.
Winter *or* Male L.

Littleleaf Linden has leaves less than 4" long and wide, dark green on top and pale blue-green below with orange-brown tufts of hairs at the junction of blade and stalk. It can grow to 138' × 29¾'. Common in Seattle; various cultivars used as street-trees, *e.g.*, 'Bicentennial', Rancho™, Greenspire® and others.

– Denny-Blaine Park (Lake Washington Blvd E & 40th Ave E): one 85' × 15'6½" is easily our largest *Tilia* of any kind; 8 smaller Bigleaf lindens too
– Volunteer Park: of 4 west of the bandstand, the tallest 101' × 6'6½" and the stoutest trunk 8'2½" around
– Hunter Blvd S: 39 (+ 21 Bigleaf and 3 Crimean and 10 basswoods)
– Lake Washington Blvd E, from Montlake Blvd E through the Arboretum and across E Madison St towards Lakeview Park: over 50 (and 19 Bigleaf lindens, 10 basswoods)
– E Queen Anne Playground (2nd Ave N & Howe St): one south and a Bigleaf linden north of the building
– Cowen Park: one 85½' × 7'8¼"
– Hiawatha Playfield: on SW Lander St most of the 17 lindens are Littleleaf; on the playground itself are 4 'Handsworth' Bigleaf lindens W of the tennis courts
– U.W.: two south of the observatory, the larger 62' × 6'7"; 'DeGroot' street-trees *pl.* 1995 on 15th Ave, S of Pacific St; 3 Summer Sprite™ (='Halka') were *pl.* in 2004 on Stevens Way in front of Padelford Hall
– 'Bicentennial' City street-trees: Roosevelt Way NE from 80th St to Pinehurst Way
– 'Greenspire' City street-trees: N 35th St, from Fremont Ave N to Stone Way N

Mongolian LINDEN

T. mongolica Maxim.
From N China, Mongolia, the Russian Far East.

Mongolian Lime
Chinese: Meng Duan

A distinctive linden: its leaves unfold *early* in spring and have *large bold teeth*. It can grow to 80' × 6'. Young grafted specimens are the only ones here.

– Arboretum: #23-63 is 54½' × 4'8" in 46-4E and 52' × 3'5" in 46-1E
– 10th Ave E, north of E Republican St and south of E Mercer St: 13 City street-trees
– 25th Ave NE, N of the 45th St viaduct: 41 City street-trees (+45 Littleleaf lindens)

Silver LINDEN

T. tomentosa Moench
= *T. argentea* DC.
From SE Europe, SW Asia.

Silver Lime
European White L

More uniformly healthy and vigorous than any of Seattle's other lindens. Thick, round leaves, dark green above, fuzzy white beneath. All too rare for its merits. It can reach 125' × 21' and usually has a distinctly rounded outline—like the Indian goddess Durga, of a thousand radiating arms.

- 21st Ave NE at NE 50th St: a street-tree 77½' × 14'10"—and wider than tall
- N 49th St, at Dayton Ave N: a street tree 7'10" around (under wires)
- 1610 40th Ave: a street-tree 58½' tall
- 2221 Broadway E: a pollarded street-tree 6'10" around
- 1505 N 43rd St: a street-tree under wires is 36' × 7'10¼" (with it are 3 Box-Elder Maples, an American Elm and a Bigleaf linden)
- Green Lake: 4 young trees *pl. ca.* 1997 SW of the wading pool
- 8039 26th Ave NW: 2 young street-trees—likely cv. **Sterling**® Silver and *pl.* 1992
- 3208 NW 56th St: 2 young street-trees
- Fauntleroy Way SW & SW Findlay St: SW corner yard has one 35' tall

Spectacular LINDEN

T. × *Moltkei* Späth *ex* Schneid. 'Spectabilis'   Spectacular Lime
= *T.* × *spectabilis* Dipp., *non* Host   Showy L.

Said to be a hybrid of *T. americana* × *T. tomentosa*, the Spectacular linden's identity remains a puzzle: some experts say it is an odd cultivar of *T. americana*. It has large leaves dark on top and paler gray-green below, resembling White basswood or Silver linden. It is extremely rare here.

- Kinnear Park: *pl.* 1893, a beautiful specimen 63½' × 8'1½" × 62' wide on the upper level by a bench west of where 6th Ave W meets Olympic Pl
- Eastlake Ave E, north of E Louisa St: the southernmost street-tree, 40' × 5'2"; all 30 other lindens circling the playground & school are Bigleaf, except one Littleleaf

Black LOCUST

Robinia Pseudoacacia L. *(Pseudacacia)*   Pea-flower Locust
LEGUMINOSÆ (FABACEÆ)   Yellow, White, *or* Green Locust
From parts of the central & eastern U.S.   Whya Tree / False Acacia
and naturalized widely elsewhere.   Silver Chain

Thorny, rugged-trunked, of great strength, supporting an elegant crown of foliage, it can attain 162' × 23½'. No matter what its size, it is characteristically ornamental, whether in full vigor of rapid youthful growth, or in picturesque, broken decrepitude of age. It is often confused with Honey Locust, so here:

BLACK LOCUST:	HONEY LOCUST:
- old trees abundant here	- old trees uncommon here
- wild here	- not wild here
- tiny thorns usually present	- no thorns, or huge, branched ones
- root-suckers as a rule	- rarely or never root-suckers
- medium to dark green foliage	- yellowish-green foliage
- 8–14" leaves of 9–25 leaflets	- small leaves of 14–36 leaflets
- showy white flowers	- tiny greenish flowers
- seedpods 2–5" long, abundant	- seedpods 8–20" long, scarce

Once planted far more frequently than Honey Locust, Black Locust is nowadays scarcely ever planted in Seattle, while Honey locust is much-used. Despite its declining popularity, Black locust is here to stay, having naturalized via root-suckers and seedlings. It out-performs Honey locust in health, size, rapidity of growth and ornamental quality. Honey locust is prized mainly because of its dainty foliage and low maintenance. Black locust is frowned upon since it is huge and brittle, but usually not long-lived.

The first one planted in France (in 1635) remains alive, albeit in sorrowful condition. In the mid- to late 18th century, shipbuilders happily found Black locust wood made better trenails than the Sussex-grown English Oak formerly used. The trenails (tree-nails, trunnels) of locust proved "heavier, harder, stronger, more rigid, more elastic and tougher" and so, in a word, superior. Vast quantities were made. Now their use may be altogether a thing of the past, but as recently as World War I there existed quite a demand for them. Locust wood's qualities make it seem a veritable paragon of timbers—who needs any other kind when they've got locust? It is strong, stiff, hard, tough, elastic, very durable, and very high in fuel value even when green. On the minus side, like many woods it checks, and though it's not the tree's fault, it is subject to insect borers.

In the Language of Flowers, a green locust tree signifies "affection beyond the grave." Black locust's value is not limited to timber quality. It exerts a beneficial influence on surrounding plants, much as Black Walnut trees exude a baneful one. Grass under locust trees is remarkably dark, green and lush. A good honey plant and friend of wildlife, it supplies fodder, conserves soil and fixes nitrogen. It is a pleasing ornamental, especially during full bloom of its fragrant white flowers in May–June. About edibility and toxicity, dispute reigns. According to published reports, it definitely qualifies as both edible and toxic—it *depends*.

Immediately below are cited examples of the regular kind, followed by 5 of the more distinctive cultivars.

- 2806 19th Ave S (south of S McClellan St): a street-tree 61' × 13'5"—cut in 2005
- S Orcas St, west of 3rd Ave S: a street-tree, N side, 77½' × 12'11¼"
- 1228 20th Ave E: a street-tree, cabled, 74' × 11'10¾"
- E Prospect St, west of 20th Ave E: a street-tree, N side, is 73' × 11'7"
- 10th Ave E, north of E Garfield St: a street-tree, W side, 73' × 12'½"
- Seattle Center: fountain lawn has one 44½' tall leaning at a 45° angle, propped up
- Zoo: African Savanna feature tree in the lion exhibit
- Lincoln Park: many on both the lower and upper levels
- 48th Ave SW, north of SW Raymond St: a street-tree, W side

cv. 'Frisia'   Golden Locust

Uncommon in Seattle, this stands out with yellowish-gold foliage, especially bright and appealing when emerging in spring. Not to be confused with the 'Sunburst' Honey locust.

- Kubota Garden Park: 7 in a row at the far south end; largest (W-most) 70½' × 3'3"
- 9631 58th Ave S: one 63' × 5'2" × 45' wide (1989) in the back yard
- 4828 Beach Dr SW
- 8247 Ashworth Ave N: in back yard
- 5601 Greenwood Ave N: in the back yard
- 8th Ave & John St: NE corner (The Unity Church of Truth): 43' × 5'4"

- 13239 3rd Ave NW: 48' tall; just south of a Black Pine
- 8th Ave NW & NW Elford Dr: NW corner has one 42' tall

cv. 'Pyramidalis'   Pyramidal Locust
='Fastigiata'   Fastigiate Locust
Tight and narrow like Lombardy (Black) Poplar. It produces few flowers, but
the leaves flutter pleasantly in the wind. Extremely rare in Seattle.
- Arboretum: #893-65 in 16-6E is 74½' × 5'6¾"
- Nordic Heritage Museum 3014 NW 67th St: one 61' × 4'4½"

cv. 'Rozynskiana'   Weeping Locust
An elegant clone from Poland in the 1800s. Leaf to 19½" long with 15–21 drooping, loosely held leaflets. Extremely rare in Seattle; known as *one* individual.
- 1102 E Spruce St: a street-tree 55½' × 5'11¼" (ordinary Black locusts in the vicinity)

cv. 'Tortuosa'   Twisted Locust
Contorted branches like those of the Corkscrew Hazel (a bush), but not so
extreme. It is smaller than normal, but still a tree; with age it may lose much of
its distinguishing character. Rare here; being replaced by Twisty Baby™.
- 8038 31st Ave NW: a stout one 32' tall, with a white bench beneath it
- 13203 4th Ave NW: 36' tall
- E Blaine St, east of 22nd Ave E: one 45' × 3'5" (by garage of 2209 E Howe St)
- E Lee St, at 42nd Ave E: one 42' tall behind laurel hedge
- Arboretum: #894-65 in 15-6E

cv. Twisty Baby™ ('Lace Lady')   Twisty Baby™ Dwarf Locust
Zig-zags as the preceding but *claimed* to be smaller, less floriferous. On its *own*
roots in an unirrigated site it may stay small; but *grafted* and watered it is apt to
grow big. Patented in 1996 and sold only since 1997. Becoming common.
- 2711 Boyer Ave E
- 13th Ave NW & NW 70th St: on SE corner, in front yard
- 6732 14th Ave NW
- 32nd Ave NW & NW 74th St: NW corner
- 1015 5th Ave W
- one N of 2901 11th Ave W
- Latona Ave NE, just north of NE 56th St: a street-tree, W side
- 6008 30th Ave NE: a street-tree
- 5038 48th Ave NE

cv. 'Umbraculifera'   Globe, Parasol *or* Mushroom Locust
Depending upon the graft, the pruning it gets or doesn't get, and its age, it is a
little lollipop tree after the style of the Umbrella (Southern) Catalpa, or a more
spreading (yet still compact) tree. It is flowerless and thornless. Uncommon.

- Queen Anne Apartments (2nd Ave N & Galer St): two (+13 Zelkova) on the west side, the taller 31'
- Magnolia Community Center (2550 34th Ave W): one 21½' tall east of the bldg.
- 10056 Dibble Ave NW: two unpruned street-trees
- 9th Ave NW, just north of NW 100th St: two pruned street-trees, E side
- Green Lake: one north and one south of the little building opposite N 77th St
- Arboretum: #440-54A in 17-6E is 24½' tall on its own roots, not top-grafted as are all the others cited
- 25th Ave SW, north of SW Genesee St: many street-trees, W side
- NE 80th St, just west of 19th Ave NE: 4 street-trees, N side

Black LOCUST hybrids

1) *R.* × *ambigua* Poir. *(R. Pseudoacacia* × *R. viscosa)*
2) *R.* × *Slavinii* Rehd. *(R. Pseudoacacia* × *R. hispida)*
3) *R.* × *Holdtii* Beissn. *(R. Pseudoacacia* × *R. neomexicana)*

Various hybrids differ from purebred Black Locusts in their smaller size and in having pink, rosy or purple flowers. At least ten clones exist, some old, some young, shrubby or treelike, common or rare. Sorting them is almost impossible. Below is my attempt to account for those in Seattle. Others (such as one called 'Pink Cascade' or 'Casque Rouge') may well be here, too.

cv. 'Bella-rosea'   Belle Rose Locust

Originated in 1860 in Holland. Seattle has *one* specimen that *may* be this. It is an old, 13' tall shrub at 7047 17th Ave NW. Twigs spiny. Flowers darker pink than those of 'Decaisneana', less dark than those of 'Idaho' and 'Purple Robe', scentless, 20–30 jammed together in a cluster *ca.* 2½" long. Leaflets 11–23, not notably bronzy at first. Looks like ⅔ *R. viscosa* and ⅓ *R. Pseudoacacia.*

cv. 'Decaisneana'   Pink Locust

Originated <1860 in France; named after a botanist. Seattle has very old trees only. It grows large yet has smaller and paler flowers than newer kinds that have long replaced it in the nursery trade. Leaflets 9–21. It makes seedpods.
- Monterey Pl S, *ca.* 275' east of Beacon Ave S: a yard, S side, has one 69' × 9' (1987)
- Arboretum: #348-45 in 17-6E is 75' × 6'9½"
- Volunteer Park: of 2 about halfway between the museum and the wading pool, the W one is 56½' × 6'7" and the E one (dead-topped) is 68½' × 7'1"
- 5816 Beacon Ave S (north of S Juneau St): a street-tree 35' tall, under wires
- 4442 S Morgan St (west of 46th Ave S): 63' tall, dying
- 1732 N 122nd St: 66' tall, two-trunked
- N 90th St, west of Fremont Ave N: a yard, N side
- Zoo: none present—but the Savanna has a similar clone represented by many specimens with *very* pale pink, larger flowers; the Zoo also has a 2nd clone with pinker flowers often with *fused* calyces and petals

cv. 'Idaho' — Idaho Locust

First sold in 1938 in Utah. Flowers dark pink; leaflets 9–15, lightly hairy. Few seedpods. More than one clone has gone under this name. Now seldom sold.

- Arboretum: 17-6E has #670-50 once labeled 'Idaho' (42½' × 2'6½"), and to the NW a bit 17-4E has a paler-flowered *seedling* of it (37' × 5'4")
- Kubota Garden Park: two 50½' tall; the stouter 1'11¼" below forking into two
- 38th Ave NE & NE 125th St: 3 on east side of SW corner yard, tallest <35'
- E Denny Way, east of 16th Ave E: three on the north side; largest 32' × 2'4¼"
- Zoo: 6 by African Village; 3 on board walk; the tallest 31'

cv. **Purple Robe**™ — Purple Robe Locust

An intentional cross, patented in 1964. Replacing 'Idaho'. Flowers dark pink, *early* in spring; a few later in summer. No seedpods. Leaflets 7–21, hairless, bronzy at first. It grows broader than 'Idaho'. If irrigated it grows too rank, and breaks up. Bark not as rough as that of 'Idaho'.

- Martin Luther King, Jr. Park: 13 top-grafted at 3–4', the largest 33½' × 3'1"
- ARC School of Ballet (9250 14th Ave Nw): NE corner of playground has two N of 2 Lombardy poplars, the larger 25½' × 2'4"; also one N of the bldg.
- 1st Ave W & W Comstock St: 2 street-trees on SE corner
- 8th Ave NW between Market & 60th: 24 street-trees *pl. ca.* 1996
- 11th Ave NW & NW 60th St: a 26' tall street-tree (under wires)
- Meridian Ave N & N 120th St: SW corner, 27' tall S of a 'Forest Pansy' Redbud
- Loyal Heights School: two N of bldg.
- NW 59th St, just west of 32nd Ave NW: 2 street-trees, S side

[**Bristly Locust** *or* **Rose Acacia**—*R. hispida* L.—A suckering shrub from the SE U.S. Twigs *bristly*, leaflets 7–13, flowers big and dark rosy, scentless, podless usually. Common in old neighborhoods. Some are forced into small tree form. 37th Ave NE, south of NE 48th St, 3 street-trees, E side, tallest 17'. NE 57th St, east of 37th Ave NE, 2 street-trees, S side, tallest 12'. 7269 27th Ave NE, 2-trunked, 11½' tall, wider still. A top-grafted scarcely bristly clone of it sold as '**Flowering Globe**' *is* a tree, as at NW 70th St, just east of 18th Ave NW, 2 street-trees, N side. Also 2 street-trees between 6281 & 6273 Ellis Ave S.]

[**New Mexican Locust** *or* **Southwestern Locust**—*R. neomexicana* Gray—A suckering shrub or small tree from the SW U.S. & N Mexico. *Slender* habit; almost thornless. Leaflets 5–17 (25), narrow, bronzy at first. Flowers *densely* clustered, pink. Known here only at the Arboretum (#672-54 and 678-62 shaded in 19-5E) and two (the larger 25' tall) at the Zoo, NW of the hippos, under a sickly Honey locust.]

Honey LOCUST

Gleditsia triacanthos L. — Honey Shucks Locust
(Gleditschia) — Sweet Bean Tree
LEGUMINOSÆ (FABACEÆ) — Thorny Acacia / Thorny Locust
From S Ontario & the central and east U.S. — Sweet Locust

In nature the Honey Locust is ferociously thorny, is adorned with enormous seedpods up to 2' long, and attains dimensions as large as 150' × 19½'. Pioneers made good use of its thorns, but found the thorn-embedded wood difficult to handle. Unlike many of its relatives (leguminous plants) this locust lacks nitrogen-fixing capacity.

Seattle's specimens leaf out very late (in May) and are often infested with podgall midges. When the twisty pods are produced (not often), their sweet pulp and seeds are worth eating in September–October; thereafter they gradually harden, turn dark brown, and dry until the seeds rattle within. Neither this nor Black locust are noteworthy for fall color, but this has an edge in that respect, being bright yellow. In general, Seattle's trees prove weak and slow; yet despite this lack of full vigor and health, they present a fine appearance and are certainly easy to maintain. More common, better known cultivars (± thornless, podless) include: 'Halka', 'Shademaster', and 'Skyline'.

– Volunteer Park: one 76' × 7'0" on lawn east of museum
– Arboretum: #32-46A in 15-2W is 73½' × 5'3½" and B in 17-3W is 74' × 5'7¼"
– Lake Washington Blvd E: one 61' × 4'8½" at the hairpin curve above McGilvra Blvd (by a towering Pin Oak 103' × 9'4"); a 2ⁿᵈ southward is 73' × 4'9½"
– U.W.: one 60' × 5'9" west of Johnson Hall's north end
– 14th Ave, north of Pine St: largest of 4 street-trees on W side 48' × 6'10"
– 1520 7th Ave W (south of W Garfield St): a street-tree 50' × 6'1½" N of a Zelkova
– Seattle Center: many of middling size
– 3rd Ave, from Denny Way to Virginia St: City street-trees

cv. 'Elegantissima'   Globe Honey Locust

A small, truly elegant vase-shaped tree; dwarf, thornless, podless, with smaller leaflets. Highly ornamental yet hard to propagate and extremely rare in Seattle. One 33' tall on the U.W. campus NW of Benson Hall. One 28½' tall just W of a yellowberry Holly on the N side of S Ferris Place west of Cascadia Ave S.

cv. Sunburst® ('Suncole')   Golden Honey Locust

Young leaves bright cheerful yellowish. Also thornless and podless. Common.

– Arboretum: two #346-61 in 16-7E are 46' × 3'6¾" (taller) and 3'8" (stouter)
– Hearthstone (6720 Sunnyside Ave N): 19 street-trees
– 3706 47th Pl NE
– 32nd Ave S, north of S McClellan St: 11 street-trees

LOQUAT

Eriobotrya japonica (Thunb.) Lindl.   Chinese: Pe Pah, Pi Ba *or* P'i-p'a
ROSACEÆ   Japanese: Biwa ビワ
From China, Japan.

A broadleaf evergreen shrub or tree to 40' tall, of bold aspect. Leathery, firm, wrinkled leaves fuzzy beneath, up to 16½" × 5½" wide. Fragrant white flowers appear anytime from August through January, according to the tree, the situation, and the weather. Yellow-orange edible fruit 1½–3" long, usually ripens in late spring or early summer. Cultivars for fruit production exist.

In Seattle, uncommon: most are young.

– 612 NW 56th St: one with a tree house built around it is *about* 33' × 4'0"
– U.W.: two S of Benson Hall; one 24' tall north of Kincaid Hall
– Ponderay Apartments (5625 15th Ave NE): 22' tall, at N end, by a Japanese Maple
– 611 8th Ave S: two, *pl. ca.* 1961
– 6108 9th Ave NE: in back yard by alley
– 12th Ave S & S McClellan St: SE corner
– 1622 40th Ave (by E Olive St)
– 2352 17th Ave S: one by the front door; not large

[*Bronze* **Loquat**—*Eriobotrya deflexa* (Hemsl.) Nakai—is far more cold-tender, and from Taiwan. Leaves *bronzy-red* when young. Flowers in spring are *sweet, white and showy.* Fruit ⅝" or less, not prized. A broad, large shrub or small tree. Very rare here; all known *pl.* 1990s or onward. The Zoo has at one 10' tall by the jaguars. 12525 9th Ave NW has one *pl.* 2003. 3305 43rd Ave NE: one E of the door on backside (faces SW) of house.]

[*Hybrid* **Loquat/Rhaphiolepis**—*Eriobotrya deflexa* × *Rhaphiolepis indica*—A large shrub or small tree; sold as the patented *Rhaphiolepis* **Majestic Beauty**™ ('Montic'). Flowers in spring are *sweet* and *pink.* Leaves 3–6" long, sharply toothed, beige felty while young. Rare here; none known as *trees.* Locks bed #211 has one by the iron gate.]

MAACKIA

Maackia chinensis Takeda   Chinese Maackia
=*M. hupehensis* Takeda   Chinese: Ma An Shu
LEGUMINOSÆ (FABACEÆ)
From China.

Maackia is related to the Chinese Scholar Tree, the Yellow-wood, and more distantly, to Black Locust. It has 9–17 pleasingly fragrant leaflets, that are densely silvery with hairs in late April or early May as they unfold. White flowers in tall clusters July–August give rise to seedpods 1–2 (3⅝)" long, 1–2 (5) seeded. It can grow 75' × 7'. Known here only as cited:

– Arboretum: 40½' × 6'6" (#2595-40 in 17-5E) and 41½' × 5'5" (#426-53 in 16-6E)
– Zoo: the largest of three in the Family Farm is 37' × 5'6½" east of Bug World, near Walk-through Stump; two smaller ones by Tunnels, Mounds & Burrows
– Lake Washington Blvd & Howell St: SE corner yard has one 52' × 5'5" (1995)

[**Manchurian Maackia**—*M. amurensis* Rupr. & Maxim.—From Manchuria, Korea, Ussuri, the Kuriles, and Japan. Leaflets 7–9 (13), broad, untoothed, essentially hairless or hairy beneath in var. *Buergeri* (Maxim.) Schneid. Poor fall color of green, yellow and brown (if not bare) in late October, when *M. chinensis* is still green. Flowers dull whitish, in summer in 4–8" clusters. Seattle's only large old examples are at the Arboretum: 50½' × 3-trunked (#2594-40 in 17-5E) and 36½' × 3'3¼" (#2593-40 in 16-5E). A youngster 7' tall is at SSCC Arboretum.]

MADRONA

Arbutus Menziesii Pursh   Pacific *or* Coast Madrona
ERICACEÆ   Madrone
Native here; from B.C. to S California.   Spanish: Madroño

Smooth reddish, peely bark makes this the most distinctive of our native trees; it is also the only broadleaf evergreen among them. It drops leaves, bark and berries, but is a beautiful and impressive tree despite its messy habit. It grows largest of a clan including such well known cousins as azaleas, rhododendrons, blueberries, heathers and salal. A Californian titan of long fame measured 96' × 34' × 113' wide in 1984. One planted in New Zealand attained 85' × 20'8". The tallest ever recorded was over 130'. Happiest on well-drained soil, in Seattle it is characteristically coastal, living not far from salt water. Like many trees in such austere habitats, it assumes in advanced age an imposing aspect of gnarled, windblasted fortitude; the rind of the ancient madrona grows thick and crusty, wrapping in tatters round the swollen, leaning trunk. One by one, mighty branches die, shrink, bleach gray and harden. Native and non-native fungal pathogens have hurt or killed many of our madronas in recent decades.

In Seattle, Laurelhurst, Magnolia and Madrona neighborhoods were named for this tree. Its snaky, crooked, climbable trunks are easily found. The berries, ripe and red by early October, hang in grape-like clusters until as late as February, if not eaten. They taste good, but their texture and tiny seeds are annoying.

– Seward Park: forest-grown trees tower to 118' × 10½"; cliff-perched specimens reveal clinging, spreading root systems of much interest; many trunks are encased in poison-oak; and the largest tree measures 95' × 20'10" × 84' wide!
– Volunteer Park: one NE of the museum is 96' × 15'10½"
– Lincoln Park: on the south bluff is a colorful colonnade of specimens
– Magnolia Blvd W: many—though far fewer than in years past
– 10054 Stone Ave N: a broad stout tree N of the house

[**Arizona Madrona**—*A. arizonica* (Gray) Sarg.—has been grown at the Arboretum and Locks—but at present only *one* is known in a garden here—invisible from the street.]

[**Hybrid Madrona**—*A.* 'Marina'—A hybrid from San Francisco; in Seattle since the 1990s; uncommon. Like our madrona, but with smaller leaves, pink autumnal flowers, bigger berries. A tree in San Francisco, dating from 1942, was 46½' × 8'5" × 45½' wide in 1994. 8th Ave NW between 70th & 60th has many street-trees. Green Lake has 1 planted along Aurora. U.W. has two NE of Allen Library.]

[**Texas Madrona**—*A. texana* Buckl.—From the SW U.S. through Mexico to Guatemala. Known here *only* as a floppy shrub in Locks bed #327.]

[**Strawberry Tree**—*A. Unedo* L.—From Ireland, and the Mediterranean. A common shrub here that seldom unites tree form and stature. 1415 NW 52nd St (Seattle Sports): 23' × 3'6¾" and 23' × 3'5¼". 539 McGilvra Blvd. E: one 30' tall S of chimney. 27' tall on the SW corner of 16th Ave E & Denny Way.]

[**Summer Holly**—*Comarostaphylis diversifolia* (Parry) Greene—is a S Californian and Mexican native shrub or small tree; extremely rare here. At the Locks, on a west-facing building wall (bed #319), is a 16' tall thriving tree, *pl*. 1992. Despite its name, it is not a member of the Holly Family. Like Strawberry Tree *above* yet with tiny, profuse berries. The leaves are thick, evergreen, 1⅓–5" long, and usually edged with fine sharp teeth. The top is rich green and glossy; the underside is usually gray or whitish with felty hairs.]

MAGNOLIAS in general

There are 80–215 nicely varied species of *Magnolia*. At their finest in rich woodland, they range from skinny shrubs to large trees. Most are valued for their highly ornamental flowers, some for their bold foliage or their wood, and a few for incidental medicinal or culinary uses. Though dull in autumn when other trees often blaze in bright display, their winter aspect is sometimes highlighted by an array of big, fuzzy buds. The fallen leaves often skeletonize attractively. These are primitive, pest- and pollution-resistant trees whose splendid floral display means "magnificence," "peerless and proud" and "love of nature" in the Language of Flowers. Seattleites are fortunate to have such an admirable collection of them at the Arboretum. Thanks to Ron Brightman for much help with this Magnolia section.

Anhwei MAGNOLIA

Magnolia cylindrica Wils.   Chinese: Huang Shan Mu Lan
MAGNOLIACEÆ
From the Chinese provinces of S Anhwei and N Fukien.

A small tree, extremely rare and little known. White flowers appear in March before the leaves expand. Some trees sold under its name over the years are now thought hybrids with Yulan *(M. denudata)*. A close look at the trees cited below will show that they differ in details. Will the *real* McCoy please stand?

– Arboretum: the tallest is 39' × 1'5" (#47-81B in the nursery), and the stoutest trunk 28½' × 3'6½" (below the fork; #741-49 in 25-B); #78-97 is 11½' tall in 26-1W
– 6451 NE Windermere Rd
– Locks bed #30 has a two-trunked youngster 3½' tall
– Miller Community Center: 2 youngsters at the S end of the building *may* be this

Anise MAGNOLIA

M. salicifolia (S.& Z.) Maxim.   Willowleaf Magnolia
From Japan.   Japanese: Tamu-shiba タムシバ

In addition to fragrant flowers, many magnolias have pleasingly perfumed leaves and twigs. Anise magnolia, a prime example, has a sweet scent of anise in its leaves, and delightfully lemony twigs. People may respond differently when asked what the scent reminds them of, but all agree that a charmingly beautiful tree

227

so rich in fragrance deserves wider cultivation. It grows to 60' × 5' and displays pure white flowers before the leaves emerge. It is rare here.

- Arboretum: 8; stoutest #96-49 is 50' × 3'7¾" (26-2E); tallest is 52' × 2'1¼" (22-1E)
- 10017 38th Ave NE: one east of the house
- Locks bed #16 has one 36' tall near the top of the stairs
- 328 21st Ave E: a street-tree *ca.* 20' tall
- 808 36th Ave E: north end of house north of the driveway
- 5500 NE Penrith Rd: one by the driveway
- 8328 29th Ave NW: NW corner of yard, above sidewalk

Bigleaf MAGNOLIA

M. macrophylla Michx.   Great-leaved *or* Large-leaved Magnolia
From the southeastern U.S.   Elephant Ear

No tree hardy here has larger leaves, except for compound ones of many small leaflets, and Empress Tree sucker-shoots. This, with the fact that its overall floral display is relatively plain for a magnolia, makes it an ideal foliage plant for sheltered spots needing a tropical accent. The leaves measure 1–3½' long. Borne June–July, the giant white flowers are 10–20" wide and awe-inspiring up close—but are sparsely produced, high on the tree and hard enough to see, let alone smell. The tree has been recorded to 105' × 8¾'. In Seattle, rare. The Umbrella Tree (Magnolia), a cousin, is uncommon and may be mistaken for it.

- Arboretum: 3; best 59' × 2'11" (#907-40; 22-1E) 52½' × 1'11½" (#2602-40; 24-1E)
- 625 34th Ave E: one 54' × 5'3" × 40' wide (1993)
- Central Area Senior Center (30th Ave S & S King St): one in back
- Zoo: a young one 33' tall W of the Gorilla exhibit
- 100 39th Ave E: one south of a clipped hedge at the north end of the yard
- Harvard Ave E & Prospect St: SE corner has one 35' tall, 3-trunked
- 4432 Kenyon Pl SW: one 34½' tall
- S.U.: a relatively young one is S of the Quad
- Burke Ave N & N 122nd St: SW corner yard

[Ashe *or* Dwarf Bigleaf Magnolia—*M. macrophylla* var. *Ashei* (Weatherby) D. Johnson—is like Bigleaf magnolia, but a precocious bloomer with smaller leaves and flowers. Much better suited to urban residential landscape needs than its enormous, clumsy peer. Leaf to 19" × 9". Flowers 5–12" wide, sometimes doubled. Very rare in Seattle. Arboretum: one 18' tall #465-62 in Loderi Valley (29-2E). The Good Shepherd Center has one 8½' tall on the west side of the building.]

Brooklyn MAGNOLIA

M. × *brooklynensis* Kalmb.
(*M. liliiflora* × *M. acuminata*)

An intentional cross from the Brooklyn Botanic Garden. Named in 1972. The following cultivars exist here, but are extremely rare.

- 'Hattie Carthan' was introduced in 1984. Named after Hattie Carthan (1901–84), who founded the Magnolia Tree Earth Center in 1973. Flowers light yellow with magenta-rose veins extending from the base halfway up the center. At 1424 41st Ave E, a street-tree was *pl.* Oct 2001 (N of a 'Sun Ray' Yellow Magnolia).
- 'Woodsman' was bred by J.C. McDaniel of Urbana, IL. Introduced ≤1975. Leaves glossy. Flowers multicolored—greenish-yellow, pink and purple. The NE corner bldg. of Summit Ave E & E Harrison St has one on its W side 16½' tall.

Campbell MAGNOLIA

M. Campbellii Hook. fil. & Thoms.   Pink Tulip-Tree
From the Himalayas.   Pink Magnolia

An aristocratic magnolia, this is the first to bloom in spring, bearing 10" wide pink or white flowers. In nature it has reached 150'× 20'; even in cultivation it has grown to 88½' × 15¾' so far. An array of scientific and horticultural varieties exist, all beautiful—the best, splendid: visit the Arboretum to get acquainted with them—and such acquaintance is *well* worth seeking. Very rare in Seattle.

- Arboretum: 2 in Loderi Valley; 7 S of Rhododendron Glen; tallest 64½' × 2'8½" (#1206-47 var. *mollicomota* in 13-5E) and stoutest 56' × 6'6" (#296-58A in 12-6E)
- 615 W Highland Dr: one 37' × 5'11" (1993)
- 8644 Fauntleroy Pl SW: a large old white-flowered tree east of the house
- Locks bed #314 has a suppressed specimen

Cucumber Tree (MAGNOLIA)

M. acuminata (L.) L.   Cucumber *or* Mountain Magnolia
From the eastern U.S. and extreme S Ontario.   Indian-bitter

A rugged straight-trunked forest tree, up to 141' × 24½', the Cucumber Tree may provide sound timber, or make a stately long-lived shade tree. It differs from most magnolias in that its bark is rough, flaky and brownish, instead of the usual smooth, gray rind; and its flowers are modest: 2–4" long, yellowish-green or blue-tinted, appearing with foliage of similar color during May. The 2–4" long seedpods, colorful red when ripe, are too small and too few here to make a show. The green, tender, unripe seedpods were pickled by some pioneers as cucumber substitutes, hence the tree's common name, or, at any rate, the unripe fruits *resembled* a young or small cucumber. More than one geographic race has been named, but only the best known (**Yellow Cucumber-Tree**) is treated below.
In Seattle, uncommon.

- Dunn Gardens: one 92½' × 9'¼" on the Great Lawn; *pl. ca.* 1920
- U.W.: the largest, on Rainier Vista by the Medicinal Herb Garden, is 82' × 7'5½"
- Kinnear Park: one on the upper level (with a Colorado Spruce) is 61' × 6'5½"
- Arboretum: the tallest of 7 is #2604-40, 75' × 4'10¾" (in 22-B)
- Hiawatha Playfield: 3 west of the tennis courts; tallest 54', stoutest 5'4"
- 29th Ave W, near Condon Way & W Blaine St: a street-tree 47' tall
- 8062 30th Ave NE: 45' tall

- 50th Ave S & S Hudson St: NE corner yard has a topped specimen in back

var. *subcordata* (Spach) Dandy   Yellow Cucumber-Tree
=*M. acuminata* var. *cordata* (Michx.) Sarg.

Smaller (recorded to 102' × 13') with smaller, less hairy leaves; less furrowed bark; and especially distinct, delightfully bright canary yellow flowers that may appear not only in spring but also in August–September. Very rare here.

- 37th Ave E & E Ward St: one 36' tall
- Locks bed #17
- Good Shepherd Center: one S of the bldg., east of the Children's Garden brick wall
- Arboretum: not present except a runty 13' tall #370-69A in the nursery's N end

Dawson MAGNOLIA

M. Dawsoniana Rehd. & Wils.   Chinese: Guang Ye Mu Lan
From W China.

Recalls Sargent magnolia. The flowers, in March or April on bare twigs, face sideways, 10" wide, pale purple. Leaves to 6" × 3", nearly or quite hairless. It is uncommon here and does so well that more ought to be planted.

- Arboretum: 6, the tallest #3-51, is 72½' × 4'0" (in Loderi Valley 28-1E); the stoutest is #347-53, 53½' × 5'1½" (in Loderi Valley 28-1E)
- 1900 Shenandoah Dr E: 58' × 4'5" × 45' wide (1990)
- 6925 56th Ave S: one 46½' tall in the yard's NE corner
- 6823 32nd Ave NE: 44' tall
- 410 Federal Ave E
- Evergreen Park Cemetery: 32' × 5'8" (below forking) of two on the east border
- Zoo: Tropical Asia (Elephant Barn) has 4 by entrance, 3 of these in close grouping behind bench

Evergreen MAGNOLIA

M. grandiflora L.   Southern *or* Great-flowered Magnolia
=*M. fœtida* (L.) Sarg.   (Great) Laurel Magnolia
From the southeastern U.S.   Loblolly Magnolia / Bull Bay

The most spectacular and most admired of North American magnolias, and the one best known by that name. A broadleaf evergreen, up to 147' × 22' and bearing exquisitely fragrant flowers 6–14" wide, appearing (here) from late May to October. Over 150 cultivars exist: over a dozen are represented in Seattle—only a *few* are cited below. It is the State Flower of Louisiana, and both State Flower and State Tree of Mississippi, the Magnolia State. Signifying "dignity" in the Language of Flowers, it's one of the characteristic Southern trees, along with the Live Oak and Bald Cypress. Like them, it is both a beloved ornamental and a useful timber tree. It is abundant in Seattle. None on public property match those cited below for size.

- 3710 E Howell St (Epiphany School)—one 46½' tall, N of a 33' Chinese Photinia
- 4181 42nd Ave NE: 46' tall
- 3964 Dayton Ave N: 46' tall
- 5011 9th Ave NE: one 45' tall
- 2557 28th Ave W (just north of W Halladay St): one 42½' tall
- 5816 Vassar Ave NE: a very stout one 41' tall
- 4524 East Laurel Dr NE: 41' tall
- McGilvra Blvd E & E Lee St: SW corner has one 40' tall
- 2706 Mt St Helens Pl S: SW part of yard
- Locks beds #16, 318, 319
- 1520 35th Ave S: one 38' tall

cv. **Blanchard**™ ('D.D. Blanchard') Compact pyramidal habit. Leaves very dark glossy green above, intense with copper fuzz beneath. Flowers typical.

- 2033 E Newton St: 3 street-trees *pl.* Dec. 2000; tallest 16½'
- Swanson's Nursery has 2 in the N parking lot, 1 in the E parking lot
- Willard Ave W, south of W Highland Dr: 2 street-trees, E side

cv. **'Little Gem'** Habit compact and narrowly upright. Flowers (to 8¾" wide) and leaves (to 7½" × 2½") smaller than usual. Becoming very popular lately.

- 18th Ave E & E Prospect St: NW corner
- 3820 E McGilvra St: one against house, west of front door is 27½' tall
- 7015 2nd Ave NW: a good-sized healthy tree
- 3rd Ave NW & NW 83rd St: 3 street-trees on SW corner
- 400 Harvard Ave E: two up against the bldg. by the entrance

cv. **Majestic Beauty**™ ('Monlia') Leaves light-green, broad, like paddles, with little fuzz beneath; recall those of the rubber plant *Ficus elastica*. Tree branches readily break from wet snow loads. Flowers gigantic, 12" wide.

- S.U.: 4 west of Gene E. Lynn bldg.
- 22nd Ave E, just north of E Highland Dr: 4 street-trees, E side
- Roanoke Park: 3 *pl.* Feb 2002 in the SE part, N of 3 older White Birches

cv. **Russet**™ Leaf small (to 6½" × 2¾"), unusually heavily coated with thick brown fuzz. Flowers 6–8" wide. Habit narrow, with erect branching.

- 1950 E Blaine St: much pruned, so squat and not narrow any more

cv. **Samuel Sommer**™ Robust, upright, densely clothed. Branches ascend sharply. Leaves broad, leathery, cupped, glossy dark green above, rusty-brown fuzzy beneath; to 10½" × 5¼". Flowers 10–14" wide. Seedcones abundant.

- U.W.: Hall Health Center has one 35' tall
- 38th Ave E & E Crockett St: one 33½' tall and very wide is behind street sign
- 1400 E Boston St: two with a Portugal Laurel, taller 35'
- Magnolia Village: street-trees on W McGraw St east & west of 33rd Ave W

cv. 'St. Mary' A bushy crown yet no dwarf. Leaf 6–10" long, to 4" wide, dark and glossy above, of average rusty-red fuzz beneath, edge undulated. Flowers abundant, cupped, *ca.* 5" wide; blooms young.

− 2342 34th Ave S: one 34' tall
− 5234 Ivanhoe Pl NE

cv. 'Victoria' Pointy leaves, shiny above, rusty-red fuzzy beneath, with conspicuous red stipules. Flowers average to large (8–12" wide), markedly fragrant. Growth bushy, but not dwarf; it resists snow breakage well.

− 5660 NE Windermere Rd: two large specimens W of the house by Keswick Dr
− 23rd Ave NE & NE 117th St: SE corner: one in the front yard is *likely* this cv.
− Green Lake: 5 in the traffic circle north of the Evans Pool building

[**Hybrid Evergreen Magnolia**—*M. grandiflora* × *M. virginiana*—cv. 'Freeman' was named in 1962 for its narrow habit, cold-hardiness, and free-flowering. Leaves to 10¼" × 4½"; faint brownish felt beneath. Flowers creamy-white, slightly fragrant, *ca.* 5" wide, not floppy. Practically sterile. Known in Seattle at the Arboretum (#781-59A south of nursery in 27-5E is 43' × 2'9¾") and at the U.W. at the SE corner of Johnson Hall (27' tall).]

Fraser MAGNOLIA

M. Fraseri Walt.   Ear-leaved Umbrella-Tree
From the SE U.S.   Indian-physic

Leaves are like giant arrowheads 8–15" long, brick-red or pumpkin-pie color in fall. Flowers pale yellowish, 6–10" wide, late April into early June. It can attain 110' × 9¾'. Barely known in Seattle except at the Arboretum, where four #2601-40 and one #963-40 are all over 70' tall; the largest 79½' × 4'7½" (in 25-1E).

Galaxy MAGNOLIA

M. 'Galaxy'
(*M. liliiflora* 'Nigra' × *M. Sprengeri* 'Diva')

A hybrid released in 1980 from the U.S. National Arboretum; common here. Flowers light purple, sweet, to 10" wide, in late April. It can attain 40'+ tall.

− Arboretum: #51-83 in 26-2E is 35' × 1'2"
− U.W. one 22' tall S of Music bldg., W of an 'Iolanthe' Modern Hybrid magnolia
− 8235 Densmore Ave N: in the front yard
− 7346 51st Ave NE: an older, much pruned specimen
− 5123 NE 73rd St: a young one
− 1918 47th Ave SW: one NW of the house
− 1927 45th Ave SW: one in north part of the front yard

[*M.* '**Spectrum**'—a sister seedling of *Magnolia* 'Galaxy'. Named and released in 1984. Rare in Seattle. Compared to 'Galaxy' it has less fragrant, darker, larger (10–12" wide) flowers with narrower petals, narrower and hairier leaves, a broader habit. Examples: 17th Ave E & E Highland Drive: NE corner yard 24' tall. 400 21st Ave E: a street-tree.]

Japanese Silverleaf MAGNOLIA

M. hypoleuca S.& Z.   Whiteleaf Magnolia
=*M. obovata* Th., *non* Ait, *ex* Link, *non* Willd.   Japanese: Ho-no-ki ホオノキ
From Japan and the Kuriles.   Ho-ho

Though similar to Umbrella magnolia (far more common in Seattle than this rare Asian tree), the Japanese Silverleaf magnolia doesn't have floppy foliage, and its 8" wide white "water-lily" flowers are deliciously fragrant and more attractive than those of Umbrella magnolia. It can attain 105' × 29'.

– Arboretum: tallest of 7 is 59½' (#868-40 in 22-2E); stoutest 43' × 3'11¾" on Azalea Way (#707-51 in 29-2W); the best overall is 55½' × 3'11" on the south side of Loderi Valley (#707-51 in 28-2E)
– 1225 McGilvra Blvd E: at SE corner of house, 34' tall
– Locks bed #15 (east end by lightpost), #121 (north edge)
– 12230 9th Ave NW: low & broad; by streetlight
– U.W.: one (or a *hybrid* with *M. officinalis*) *pl.* 1997 is 23' tall S of the Music bldg.

Kobus MAGNOLIA

M. Kobus DC.   Japanese: Ko-bu-shi コブシ
=*M. præcocissima* Koidz.
From Japan, S Korea.

Kobus magnolia's pure white (or very faint pink-tinged) 4" wide flowers give it an aspect like that of our native Pacific Dogwood: the two trees often flower at the same time, are structurally similar, the same size (to 100' tall at most), and prefer the same growing conditions. It is common here.

– Zoo: 2 in the NW corner (outside the fence) by 2 handsome Japanese Red Pines; the largest is 40' × 7'6" (below forking into two)
– Arboretum: tallest of 6 #2051-41 is 54½' (in 25-1E); stoutest 4'5½" (in 26-2E)
– 7130 8th Ave S: one 35' × 5'2" × 40' wide (1988) in an industrial setting
– Volunteer Park: 2 at the Burke monument (largest 3'10"); two by the north pond; one south of the museum
– Parsons Gardens Park: by the corner entrance
– Substation landscape on 6th Ave NE, north of NE Northlake Way: 2
– U.W.: west of the SE part of McCarty Hall
– Locks bed #25 (small, shaded), 105 (44' tall), 206 (shrubby)

hybrid Kobus MAGNOLIA

M. × *Lœbneri* Kache   Löbner Magnolia
=*M. Kobus* var. *Lœbneri* (Kache) Spong.
(*M. Kobus* × *M. stellata*)

Named for German horticulturist Max Löbner (1870–1947), various cultivars exist; most are more like Kobus than Star. Flowers 4–6" (8") wide, white or pink; petals 11–15 (30). Recorded to 46' tall. Local nurseries have offered mostly 'Merrill' (common here) and 'Leonard Messel' (see under Star Magnolia).

- Arboretum: tallest is #44-54B, 32' × 2'10½" (a 'Merrill' S of the nursery in 26-5E)
- 802 33rd Ave E: right on the corner, 31' tall, with a smaller Saucer magnolia
- 2160 38th Ave E: 24½' tall, right by sidewalk
- Wallingford Ave N, N of Green Lake Dr N: 4 street-trees, west side
- 824 13th Ave: 26' tall, 5-trunked
- Zoo: Tropical Asia (Thai Village); 3; biggest one over path, by water storage shed

Lily MAGNOLIA

M. liliiflora Desr. *(liliflora)*   Purple Lily Magnolia
=*M. quinquepeta* (Buc'holz) Dandy   Chinese: Zi Yu Lan
From China.

A shrub; rarely a very small tree (34' × 5'6" × 40' wide Philadelphia, PA, 1980). Flowers slender and purplish, appearing with the leaves in mid- to late spring and early summer. Cv. **'Nigra'** has larger, especially dark purple flowers.

- 2025 23rd Ave E: one 16' tall is in the back yard and not visible
- 4181–4191 42nd Ave NE: one 13' tall very easily seen from the sidewalk
- 8810 2nd Ave NE: one at house's NW corner
- 1831 7th Ave W: 3-trunked, low wide specimen
- Locks bed #112 (by #111)

[**Hybrid Lily Magnolia**—*M. liliiflora* × *M. stellata*—Originated in 1956 as an intentional cross at the U.S. National Arboretum. In 1965, 8 clones were named and became known as "**the Girls**" (referring to their cultivar names) or "**the Kosar-DeVos hybrids**" (referring to the scientists involved). The eight cultivars are more or less shrubby; 'Ann', 'Betty' (especially), 'Ricki' and 'Susan' are the most treelike. All have late, dull fall color. All can be trained to tree form. Habit narrow. Long slender erect red purple buds, open to reddish-purple upright flowers in April. In Seattle, 6 cultivars can be viewed at the Arboretum in 28-1E, 27-1W & 24-2E. Three examples elsewhere (I do not know their cultivar names): 5514 S Orcas St. 8008 35th Ave NE. 4720 46th Ave NE.]

Modern Hybrid MAGNOLIAS

M. 'Vulcan' *et al.*

'**Vulcan**' is Campbell (*M. Campbellii* ssp. *mollicomata* 'Lanarth') × Lily *(M. liliiflora)* bred by F.M. Jury of New Zealand. Sold in North America ≤1992. Flowers *ca.* 10" wide, brilliant ruby red, of 8–10 petals. Blooms when young. 'Vulcan' is an example of a flood of brand new hybrid magnolias that have gone on sale recently in Seattle. Below are listed 8 other cultivars. Inasmuch as some mislabeling occurs in nurseries, and I have not had time to check all of these, some citations are just good *guesses.* (The same applies for the 8 *Yellow* Magnolia cultivars listed in a few pages.)

- NW 80th St, just west of 24th Ave NW: a street-tree, N side, *ca.* 12' tall
- 5430 NE Windermere Rd: next to driveway
- 530 McGilvra Blvd. E: in yard's SW corner
- 12th Ave S & S Hanford St: one 8½' tall is south of the intersection
- 100 W Olympic Pl: 4 street-trees

– Dunn Gardens: one N of the house right next to a 'Serene' (described below)

[*M.* 'Caerhays Belle'—*M. Sargentiana* var. *robusta* × *M. Sprengeri* 'Diva'—Bred in 1951 at Caerhays Castle, Cornwall, England. First flowered in 1965. Young specimens exhibit strong apical dominance. Flowers appear in February–March; *ca.* 12" wide, freely borne, nodding, clear pink, of 12 broad petals. Seedcones are ornamental. Examples: Arboretum #236-92 is 34½' × 2'3¼" in 27-1W. 5430 NE Windermere Rd has one, on the right, looking from the road.]

[*M.* 'Caerhays Surprise'—*M. Campbellii* ssp. *mollicomata* × *M. liliiflora* 'Nigra'—Bred in 1959 at Caerhays Castle, Cornwall, England. Flowers *ca.* 8" wide, pale purple, over an unusually long period. Example: 6020 34th Ave NW has a street-tree on 60th, west of a 'Kwanzan' Cherry.]

[*M.* 'Coral Lake'—*M.* 'Legend' × *M.* 'Butterflies'—Bred by D. Leach of North Madison, OH; registered in 1997. Flowers 7" wide, pink with yellow stripes. Example: Dunn Gardens.]

[*M.* 'Daybreak'—*M. brooklynensis* 'Woodsman' × *M.* 'Tina Durio'—Bred by A. Kehr of Hendersonville, NC; registered in 1991. Flowers pink, very fragrant. Example: 5126 47th Ave NE.]

[*M.* 'Iolanthe'—*M. Soulangiana* 'Lennei' × *M.* 'Mark Jury'—Raised in New Zealand in 1966; first flowered in 1970; sold in North America <1981. Flowers in (late January) April–May, 10–11" wide, cup-shaped, rosy-pink, creamy-white inside, nodding and floppy (suggesting those of Sargent magnolia); borne even at an early age. A vigorous small tree. Examples: 3027 NW 59th St. U.W.: one 18' tall S of the Music bldg., *pl.* 1997]

[*M.* 'Royal Crown'—*M. liliiflora* × *M. Veitchii*—Raised in 1955 by D. Todd Gresham of Santa Cruz, CA. Named ≤1962. Flowers crownlike, 10–12" wide, of 9–12 erect petals (the outermost reflexed); deep purplish-pink in the bud, opening paler (dark red-violet outside, white inside). Blooms when young. Examples: Arboretum #685-70 is 33' × 2'6¾" in 26-3E. 1728 11th Ave E (near E Howell St): 26½' tall (hidden by 'Bing' Cherry street-tree). Zoo Tropical Asia has several in vicinity of Elephant Forest; best one where paths to Elephant Barn and Elephant Forest diverge, east of Main Loop.]

[*M.* 'Serene'—*M. liliiflora* × *M.* 'Mark Jury'—Bred in New Zealand in 1970s; sold in North America <1991. Flowers deep rose, large, bowl-shaped. An upright small tree. Examples: Arboretum #243-92 is 15' tall in 28-3E. Dunn Gardens: one north of the house right next to a 'Vulcan'.]

[*M.* 'Star Wars'—*M. Campbellii* × *M. liliiflora*—Bred in the 1970s by O. Blumhardt of New Zealand. Named ≤1982. Sold in North America ≤1991. Flowers rich pink-purple, star-shaped, 10–12" wide. Very free-flowering over an extended season. Fertile. The original was 25' tall at 10 years. Example: Arboretum #244-92, just east of Azalea Way in 26-1W, is 25' × 1'9½".]

Oyama MAGNOLIA

M. Sieboldii K. Koch   Egg Magnolia
=*M. parviflora* S.& Z., *non* Bl.   Japanese: Oyama-renge オオヤマレンゲ
From Japan, Korea & Manchuria; and disjunctly in SE China.

A bush or small tree to 33' tall with 3–4" wide, fragrant white flowers in late spring and early summer. Rare in Seattle. The largest is in front of an Empress Tree at 10325 15th Ave NW. At the Arboretum 3 are by the visitor center; others are in 28-3E, 27-4E, 27-3E. At the Locks one is in bed #116. One is south of a redleaf Japanese maple near the sidewalk east of 4915 NE 60th St. 7743 20th Ave NW has a yard tree.

Sargent MAGNOLIA

M. Sargentiana var. *robusta* Rehd. & Wils.
From W China.

This may be the best magnolia for skeletonized leaves. Textured like tightly stretched, stiff nylon stockings, its partly rotted leaves make good additions in dried arrangements. The tree itself makes a stunning show when its 8–13" wide pink flowers bloom in earliest spring, and again when its bold seedpods (to 10" long) turn rosy red in autumn. The tree grows to 80' × 10'. It is rare here.

– Arboretum: the tallest of 6 is 80' × 4'7½" (#65-53 in Loderi Valley—30-1E), the stoutest 49½' × 5'3½" (#55-52A by two tall Katsuras in 13-7E)
– Dunn Gardens: one 44½' × 6'7"
– 1900 Shenandoah Dr E: one 48' × 7'1" × 44½' wide (1990)
– 37th Ave E & E Ward St: 45' tall, N of the Yellow Cucumber-Tree (Magnolia)
– Locks bed #7 (one 15' tall died back, yet resprouted); #29 (6' tall); #30 (by #29)
– S.U.: 27½' tall on E wall of Administration Bldg. just N of entrance

Saucer MAGNOLIA

M. × *Soulangeana* Soul.-Bod. *(Soulangiana)*   (our) Common Magnolia
(M. denudata × *M. liliiflora)*   Lily Tree / Tulip Tree

Saucer magnolias are hybrids and backcrosses between the Yulan magnolia and Lily magnolia, originating near Paris early in the 19th century. Now extremely popular, well known and by far the most abundant of magnolias. From Yulan was inherited tree size and whitish color; from Lily magnolia, shrubbier habit and purplish color; from the union of both, beauty and vigor. Many cultivars exist: some more distinctive than others. Much confusion exists in the naming: there are too many names for the number of distinct clones, and descriptions are often inconsistent and contradictory. Saucer magnolias begin life shrubby: some stay so and others form small trees, usually at least at wide as they are tall. One in Maryland is among the largest recorded: 51' × 14' × 63' wide(!) in 1972. In March and April the naked branches burst their silky buds, giving rise to lovely flowers—hence the common name Tulip Tree. The flowers are white inside and usually striped purple and white outside. Some cultivars are nearly pure white, others are deep rosy pink or burgundy. Even after the trees assume full summer foliage, sporadic flowers often appear.

In Seattle, common and well known. Other cultivars than the 7 noted below *do* exist (*e.g.*, 'Grace McDade'), but naming them confidently is beyond me.

– 7011 24th Ave NW: one 25' × 5'7" × 38' wide (1988)
– 21st Ave E & E Highland Dr: NW corner yard one N of a big Japanese Maple
– 33rd Ave S & S College St: NW corner yard has one 32' tall

cv. 'Alba' *et al.*   White Saucer Magnolia

Names given to white-flowered Saucer magnolias include: 'Alba', 'Alba Superba', 'Amabilis' and 'Lennei Alba'. They defy sorting. They tend to flower relatively early in the season, and are white or *nearly* white. They are usually treelike.

– Arboretum: 44-7E ('**Lennei Alba**' #3-48, multitrunked, 24' tall), 13-5E (*affin.* '**Alba Superba**' #X-602)
– 135 39th Ave E: one N of the house is close to 50' tall
– 24th Ave E & Interlaken Blvd E: NW corner house has one next to a big purple-leaved Japanese Maple
– Locks bed #7
– E Columbia St, north of Randolph Ave: one 30' tall

cv. 'Alexandrina'

The trees cited below are thought to be the clone originally called 'Alexandrina', with midseason flowers, dark purplish-pink; white inside. But other clones have also been called 'Alexandrina'.

– Arboretum: one 40' × 4'1" in Loderi Valley (29-2E)
– 2514 E Lynn St: one 30' tall east of the house
– Carr Pl N at N 39th St: one 25' tall southeast of the house
– 4625 Eastern Ave N: above the garage
– 6th Ave W & W Halladay St: SW corner yard has a low, broad specimen
– 1st Ave N just N of Smith St: on the W side
– 1919 Interlaken Dr E: by the driveway
– 7574 East Green Lake Dr N
– 5908 36th Ave NW
– 8323 28th Ave NW: dominating the small front yard
– 48th Ave NE & NE 103rd St: SW corner yard has a big one on the W edge
– 4th Ave NE & NE 44th St: NW corner has one east of the house
– 7512 43rd Ave NE
– 9126 8th Ave NE: in back yard, arching over the sidewalk
– 2515 51st Ave SW (@SW Waite St): one east of the house

cv. 'Brozzonii'

Tall, narrow buds open to large flowers (to 10" wide), white overall but faintly shaded with light purple at the base; late. Leaves bold, to 10" long. Growth strongly upright. Similar to *M.* × *Soulangiana* 'Picture' but flowers less purple.

– Arboretum: four; best 36½' × 4¼" #1249-47 east of Azalea Way (16-1E)
– Locks bed #109

cv. 'Lennei'   Lenné Magnolia

Flowers very large, goblet shaped; petals thick, overlapping, deep purple outside, creamy-white inside; relatively late to bloom. Leaves broad, to 11" × 6⅜". Twigs stout. Shrubby, sprawling, open, flattish. A similar treelike cultivar is 'Rustica Rubra'. Fruitful; sometimes its seedlings have been sold under the name.

– Arboretum: #892-40 in 26-3E, #2-48 in 25-3E, and #758-59 in 23-2E
– 1633 E Lynn St (at 18th Ave E): one 23' tall by a driveway (across the street on the NW corner is a regular Saucer magnolia)
– Leschi Park: one 2'3¼" around
– 3260 10th Ave W
– 4551 15th Ave S: two
– 4137 49th Ave SW (south of SW Dakota St): one behind a fence

cv. 'Lilliputian'

A charming miniature Saucer magnolia, in both habit and bloom. Flowers small, white flushed purple at base; late in the season.

– 3850 NE 96th St: an unusually broad specimen east of the house

cv. 'Picture'

From a garden in Ishikawa Prefecture, Japan. Cultivated ≤1925 by nurseryman K. Wada. In U.S. commerce <1975. Extremely rare. Red-purple buds open to *large* flowers (10–14" wide), soft pink outside, white inside; scented of violets. Blooms well when young; blooms profusely when mature. Strong, narrowly upright. Similar to 'Brozzonii' but flowers not as pale with a much larger area of purple.

– 1002 36th Ave E: 24½' tall at N end of front yard
– Children's Hospital: Whale Garage has one 17½' tall
– 20th Ave NE & NE Northgate Way: NW corner yard has one 16' tall

cv. 'Rustica Rubra'

Like 'Lennei' but a bigger shrub or real tree; flowers more rosy-red, smaller; blooms much earlier (early April), more fuzz on its leaf-undersides. Common.

– Arboretum: #533-63A S of the nursery (27-4E) is multitrunked; #X-467 in 27-4E
– 3915 48th Pl NE: one 30' tall
– Locks bed #108 (the nearby bed #109 has cultivar 'Brozzonii')
– 1737 44th Ave SW (north of SW Holgate St): one next to a plume Sawara Cypress

Sprenger MAGNOLIA

M. Sprengeri Pamp.   Chinese: Wu Dang Mu Lan
From China.

In spring before the leaves emerge, 8–10" wide pink flowers grace the best known selection of this species, called the '**Diva**' **magnolia**. White-flowered forms exist but are seldom grown. It can attain 68' × 8'. It is rare here.

- Arboretum: a '**Diva**' is 58½' × 3'7½" (#56-52A in 12-5E); a '**Diva**' seedling is 50' × 3'5½" in Loderi Valley (#394-65 in 29-1E); #489-64 in 30-1E; #285-75 in 11-5E
- 1300 Dexter Ave N (with Hollywood Juniper)
- U.W.: two S of Meany Hall (with a pink Saucer magnolia nearer the bldg.)
- 4223 NE 33rd St: 2 '**Diva**' in front; a Galaxy magnolia behind a West. Red Cedar
- 5101 NE 70th St: white and purple flowers
- Zoo: Tropical Asia (Tapir); a 2-trunked '**Diva**' beneath a prominent Red Oak

Star MAGNOLIA

M. stellata (S.& Z.) Maxim.   Starry Magnolia
=*M. tomentosa* Thunb.   Japanese: Shide-Kobushi
=*M. Kobus* var. *stellata* (S.& Z.) B.C. Blackb.   シデコブシ
From Japan.

A dense shrub, completely covered with fragrant white flowers very early in spring. The flowers can fade to a very pale pink; and some appear after the leaves emerge. At most, it may grow to 43' × 5' yet Seattle has few even half that large. Varied cultivars and hybrids—all vastly outnumbered by the regular form—one of the most abundant magnolias here. Easily told in bloom by its *numerous* 9–20 (60) and *very slender* petals. Total intermediacy exists between Star and Kobus magnolia; their hybrids (*M.* × *Læbneri* Kache) are often extremely similar to one parent or the other. In fact it is *illogical* to maintain Star and Kobus as separate species. But—that's what the Magnolia Society does and I follow it . . .

- 808 36th Ave E: 26' × 2'1" × 22' wide (1990) in front by a blue Colorado Spruce
- 9223 Matthews Ave NE: one 28½' tall
- 22nd Ave E & E Crescent Dr: SE corner has one 17½' tall
- U.W.: 2 N of Parrington Hall with 4 Peanut-Butter Trees
- 2583 7th Ave W (at Raye St): a standard street-tree
- Locks bed #119, 204 (opposite gatehouse), 326
- 6504 Ravenna Ave NE: a street-tree

f. *rosea* Veitch   Pink Star Magnolia

Some cited below are hybrids such as '**Leonard Messel**'. They can be so alike!
- Arboretum: the best '**Leonard Messel**' is #26-64C, 23½' × 1'3½" in 24-2E
- 1900 Shenandoah Dr E: one 28' × 2'5" × 25' wide (1992)
- 6551 NE Windermere Rd: one 23½' tall by the driveway
- Sand Point Way NE & NE 103rd St: NE corner has one 23½' tall
- S.U.: 19½' tall on east wall of Administration building
- 1717 13th Ave (north of E Olive St): a tall one
- U.W.: one S of Allen Library with 3 regular Star magnolias
- 4316 NE 38th St: two street-trees
- 28th Ave W & W Galer St: NE corner yard (a Saucer mag. to W; a Lily mag. to E)
- Locks bed #322 ('**Leonard Messel**')
- 4319 NE 45th St: a small street-tree
- 1822 1st Ave N

Sweet Bay (MAGNOLIA)

M. virginiana (L.) L.   White *or* Swamp Laurel
=*M. glauca* L.   Silver, White *or* Swamp Bay
From the eastern U.S.   Beaver Tree

Sweet Bay is distinct from our other magnolias in that individuals may be variously evergreen, semi-evergreen, or deciduous, according to genetic and environmental factors. Most here are more or less evergreen, though they can look anemic, sparse and unhappy by late winter. The common names note the tree's resemblance to bays and laurels; it too has been used medicinally. It can be a shrub but is usually a tree with a strong tendency to fork. It attains up to 95' × 16' and has ghostly pale leaf undersides and 2–4" wide white, rose-scented flowers from June onwards. It is uncommon here.

- Arboretum: #878-48 two in 28-2W, two in 27-2W; largest 31½' × 4'11" × 41' wide; #1402-46 in 28-3E; two #878-48 in 15-1E
- U.W. Medicinal Herb Garden: 3 under a Pin Oak in section E (*i.e.*, the east end)
- McClure School (1915 1st Ave W): one W of the N entrance, 20' tall, two-trunked
- Meany School (301 21st Ave E): a two-trunked, small tree on the east side
- 14th Ave E & E Harrison St: SW corner apartment building landscape, 24½' tall
- Locks bed #327 has two
- Boylston Ave E, north of E Aloha St: five on the east side
- 1st Ave NW & NW 95th St: SW corner has 2 small trees

var. *australis* Sarg.   Southern *or* Evergreen Sweetbay

Evergreen examples. Some cited below are clones such as '**Henry Hicks**'.

- Arboretum: at least 5, best being #390-66, 45½' × 2'9" in Loderi Valley (30-B)
- 1528 McGilvra Blvd E: at the end of the driveway
- 1667 E Boston Terrace: a cv. '**Henry Hicks**' *pl.* 2002
- 6006 Latona Ave NE
- 2100 E Thomas St: a street-tree on 21st Ave E, north of a 14' Anise magnolia
- 2019 23rd Ave E: the *variegated* cv. '**Mattie Mae Smith**' in front yard (*pl.* 2004)

[**Hybrid Sweetbay Magnolia**—*M.* × *Thompsoniana* (Loud.) de Vos *(M. virginiana* × *M. tripetala*—A shrubby tree. Leaves to 10" × 5"; sometimes partly evergreen. Flowers white, very sweet, *ca.* 6" wide, lightbulb shaped. Known in Seattle only at one private garden and at the Arboretum (#443-61 in 27-2E).]

Umbrella Tree (MAGNOLIA)

M. tripetala (L.) L.   Elkwood
=*M. Umbrella* Desr.
From the eastern U.S.

Most abundant of the really large-leaved magnolias in Seattle, this is still relatively uncommon; however, it stands out prominently wherever it may be placed. The gigantic leaves, up to 2' long and over 1' wide, are borne on stout twigs in umbrella-like whorls around vilely-scented white flowers in May–June. It can attain 85' × 10½' and is usually multitrunked.

- Arboretum: five; #2603-40 in Loderi Valley (28-1E) is tall, 62½' × 2'10"; and in 12-6E is a stout 2-trunked tree 52' × 4'1½" + 4'¾"; a third by the service road S of Rhododendron Glen (13-5E) is 56' × 3-trunked
- 1707 NW 63rd St: a stout single-trunked tree 29' × 4'11" × 35' wide (1993)
- U.W.: one by some hollies behind Hutchinson Hall
- Evergreen Park Cemetery: one 22½' × 3'2" not far from the pond
- Locks bed #29 (9' tall), 111, 119 (by #115)
- 12036 36th Ave NE: one N of house
- 12520 7th Ave NW: S of house
- 20th Ave NE & NE 73rd St: NW corner yard: one by the telephone pole
- 35th Ave & E Olive St: SE corner yard has one S of the house
- 344 McGilvra Blvd E: 34' tall

Veitch MAGNOLIA

M. × *Veitchii* auct., *emend.* Bean
(M. denudata × *M. Campbellii)*

Of English origin, an intentional 1907 hybrid between the Yulan and Campbell magnolias, much admired for its excellent constitution, rapid growth and great beauty: it has 6" wide pink flowers in spring. Capable of reaching 100' tall, its ultimate size remains to be seen. It is rare here.

- Arboretum: 5, the largest 3 are 49' × 5'1½" (#730-59A in 11-6E); 49' × 3'8¾" (#154-61 in 15-4E); 54' × 2'11" (#X-470 in 27-2E)
- 10019 48th Ave NE: 48' × 6'2" × 50½' wide (1990)
- 19th Ave NE & NE 113th St: NW corner has a 5-trunked one 47' tall
- 4625 Eastern Ave N: in the back yard, branching across the alley: 46' × 3'5"
- Locks bed #17 (east of the big oak), 328 (restricted access)
- 3504 and 3556 W McGraw St (E & W of Piedmont Pl W)
- 4205 E Highland Dr: four heavily pruned specimens
- 2343 NW 100th St: one west of the carport
- 556 N 83rd St: in yard's SW corner

Wada's Memory MAGNOLIA

M. 'Wada's Memory'
=*M.* × *kewensis* Pearce 'Wada's Memory'
=*M.* × *Proctoriana* Rehd. 'Wada's Memory'
=*M. Kobus* 'Wada's Memory'
=*M. salicifolia* 'Wada's Memory'
(M. Kobus × *M. salicifolia)*

In 1940 this was one of several seed-raised plants that the Washington Park Arboretum bought (as Kobus magnolia) from Koichiro Wada (1911–1981) of Hakoneya nursery, Numazu-shi (later of Yokohama), Japan. The flowers proved unusually large (to 7" wide) and showy, so the clone was propagated from 1952 onward. It is rare but in commerce. The name 'Wada's Memory' was chosen by Wada himself in 1957. This hybrid differs from Anise magnolia *(M. salicifolia)* in its greater size and vigor; its leaves are not so bluish beneath, and are often larger; the leafbuds are hairy.

- Arboretum: the original tree (#869-40A) is 45' × 4'10½" (in 11-6E); others exist, such as one 77' × 3'2" (#869-40 in 22-1E); #1130-57A in 10-7E is 48' × 3-trunked
- Locks bed #15
- Wallingford Ave N, just north of East Green Lake Dr N: 4 street-trees, W side

Watson MAGNOLIA

M. × *Wieseneri* Carr.   Japanese: Ukezaki-Oyama-renge
=*M.* × *Watsonii* Hook. fil.   ウケザキオオヤマレソゲ
(M. hypoleuca × *M. Sieboldii)*

From Japan, a hybrid of Japanese Silverleaf and Oyama magnolias. Shrubby, or a small tree to 28' tall, with large white *richly fragrant* flowers in (May) June–July (September), and thick, dark leaves, pale underneath. Choice. Extremely rare.

- Locks bed #324 has one two-trunked and 15' tall
- 3027 West Laurelhurst Dr NE: one in the middle of the front yard
- 9750 Marine View Dr SW: one 28' tall N of driveway—visible from 45th Ave SW

Yellow MAGNOLIA

M. 'Elizabeth' *et al.*

'Elizabeth' is Yulan *(M. denudata)* × Cucumber tree *(M. acuminata)* bred in 1956 at the Brooklyn Botanic Garden, named and patented in 1977; named after Elizabeth Scholtz (Van Brunt), then Director of the Garden. Much sold since 1986. Flowers yellow, to 7" wide, from late March into May (early July). Sterile. Two clones have circulated under the name 'Elizabeth'; the incorrect one may be the more common. In Seattle, what passes for 'Elizabeth' is not as successful as some newer yellow-flowered hybrids (7 cultivars of which are listed below). The peculiarly luminous yellow of the opening flower rapidly deteriorates into a cold, creamy or greenish white; it is also subject to *Botrytis* infestation that stains the petals dirty brown.

- Arboretum: #139-83 is 34' × 2'2" (in 12-8E)
- 2315 N 82nd St: 27' tall
- 727 N 48th St: one by the chimney is 24½' tall
- S.U.: one W of Pigott bldg. is 21½' tall
- 1127 17th Ave E: south of the stairs
- 7710 Dibble Ave NW
- 10830 11th Ave NE

[*M.* 'Butterflies'—*M. acuminata* 'Fertile Myrtle' × *M. denudata* 'Sawada's Cream'—Bred by P. Savage of Bloomfield Hills, MI. Introduced ≤1988; patented 1991. Flowers dark yellow, before the Yulan magnolia-like leaves. Examples: 6826 55th Ave NE. Broadway E & E Hamlin St: a street-tree on Hamlin of the SW corner (see 'Yellow Bird' below)]

242

[*M.* 'Gold Star'—*M. acuminata* var. *subcordata* 'Miss Honeybee' × *M. stellata*—Bred by P. Savage of Bloomfield Hills, MI. Creamy yellow starlike flowers of 14 strap-shaped petals open to 4" wide in March/early April before the foliage. Example: 6037 26th Ave NE.]

[*M.* 'Ivory Chalice'—*M. acuminata* × *M. denudata*—Bred by D. Leach of North Madison, OH; registered in 1985. Flowers 6" wide, creamy-white to yellowish-green, borne over a long period. Examples: 2 street-trees at 3323 NE 45th St, *pl.* 2005.]

[*M.* 'Sun Ray'—A colchicine-induced polyploid form of 'Sundance' from A. Kehr of Hendersonville, NC; introduced ≤1996. Example: 1424 41st Ave E (*pl.* Oct 2001)—south of a Brooklyn magnolia 'Hattie Cartham'.]

[*M.* 'Sundance'—*M. acuminata* × *M. denudata*—Bred by A. Kehr of Hendersonville, NC. Flowers to 8" wide, often making seedcones. Example: 18th Ave E & E Lynn St: NE corner (*pl. ca.* 2000).]

[*M.* 'Yellow Bird'—*M. acuminata* × *M. brooklynensis* 'Evamaria'—Originated in 1967 as an intentional cross at the Brooklyn Botanic Garden. Introduced in 1981. Flowers deep yellow, appearing with the leaves, smaller but more intense than those of *M.* × *brooklynensis* 'Evamaria', and 1–2 weeks later. The leaves recall Cucumber Tree Magnolia. A fertile tetraploid. Examples: Broadway E & E Hamlin St: a street-tree on Broadway of the SW corner (see 'Butterflies' above). 2009 E Aloha St has two.]

[*M.* 'Yellow Lantern'—*M. acuminata* var. *subcordata* × *M. Soulangiana* 'Alexandrina'—Bred by P. Savage of Bloomfield Hills, MI. Registered in 1985. Flowers tulip-shaped, clear lemon-yellow. Very hardy. Vigorous, upright with a single trunk. Example: the garden at 12th Ave S & S Hanford has one 14½' tall *pl. ca.* 1999 (inside the fence).]

Yulan (MAGNOLIA)

M. denudata Desr.   Chinese White Magnolia
=*M. heptapeta* (Buc'hoz) Dandy   Chandelier Magnolia
=*M. conspicua* Salisb.   White Yulan
=*M. Yulan* Desf.   Chinese: Yu Lan
From E China.

Most magnolias are visual feasts; but Yulan is more, being one of several East Asiatic magnolias used both in medicine and in cooking. The pickled flowerbuds are used to flavor rice. As an herbal remedy, the flowerbuds are "…one of many drugs reputed to give lightness to the body, brightness to the eye, added length of life, culminating in a green old age." (Smith, p. 254) The tree can reach 80' × 8¾' and has ivory white flowers 4–7" wide in spring before leafing out. It's uncommon in Seattle; much like a large-growing white-flowered Saucer magnolia.

– Arboretum: the largest of 4 are 46½' × 5'1½" (#27-40D in 12-4E—south of Rhododendron Glen) and 52½' × 4'2¾" (#27-40A in 14-4E—N of Rhod. Glen)
– City Light building at Interlake Ave N & N 97th St: one 28' tall on the S side; with a Callery Pear tree, east of Interlake Ave N
– 2341 11th Ave E: a 24½' tall Yulan (a 24' tall Saucer magnolia at 2339 11th)
– 1902 E Blaine St (a Saucer magnolia at 1900): one 28' tall
– 6220 25th Ave NE: one 23½' tall

– Locks bed #305 has one with a twisty trunk between two Japanese Red Pines

MAGNOLIA relatives

Three genera are related so closely to *Magnolia* in the narrow sense that some botanists now—and most botanists soon will—include them as mere sections of *Magnolia*. All are broadleaf-evergreen Asians. All have only *recently* been tested here and are *rare*. Some will die in severe winters. In addition to 8 species cited below, others must also have been planted in Seattle, as nurseries stock them.

Manglietia. The name is from a Malay or Javanese name for one of the species. Differs from *Magnolia* in having 4–6 rather than 1–2 ovules per carpel.

[*M. Chingii* Dandy—Thousand Mountain Lotus Tree—Leaves copper-red when young; at maturity to 9¼" × 2½", dark green above, pale beneath. Flowers 3" wide, fragrant, of 9–11 petals. Recorded to 65' tall in the wild. Zoo: of two in Australasia, the taller is 13½'. Arboretum #62-93A in the SE corner of 28-B is 6' tall.]

[*M. Fordiana* Oliv.—Lotus Tree—Leaves bronzy when young; at maturity to 9" × 2¾", dark green above, ghostly pale beneath. Flowers from April into July, 4"+ wide; 9 thick petals, waxy white with a pink tinge. Recorded to 100' × 15½' in the wild. Zoo: one 13' tall in Australasia. Arboretum #48-81A in 28-2E is 28½' × 1'4¼".]

[*M. insignis* (Wall.) Bl.—Red Lotus Tree—Leaves evergreen to semi-evergreen, to 8¼" (11¾") × 2⅜" (3¾"), dark glossy green above, paler beneath. Flowers in May or June; fragrant, 3–5" wide; of 9–12 petals, the outer ones pale or deep pink, or suffused purple, inner ones creamy-white. Seedcone 3–4" long, bright purple at first. Recorded to 120' tall in the wild. Zoo: at least 3 in Australasia, tallest less than 10'. Arboretum #18-98 in 28-2E is 11½' tall. 321 Boyleston Ave E (south of E Harrison St): a street-tree *pl.* in 2003. 26th Ave E & E. Miller St: SW corner yard has one *ca.* 9' tall by the driveway. Three on the S side of NE 70th St, east of 45th Ave NE.]

Michelia, named after Pier Antonio Micheli (1679–1737), botanist at Florence. Differs from *Magnolia* in having axillary rather than terminal flowers.

[*M. Doltsopa* Buch.-Ham. *ex* DC.—Sweet Michelia—Leaves to 8½" × 3", dark shiny green above, pale and dull beneath. Flowers showy, white, 4–7" wide, of 12–16 narrow petals; very fragrant, in April. Recorded to 100' tall in the wild. More cold-tender than the other species. 2040 42nd Ave E, unit 4, has one 19½' tall against the building.]

[*M. Figo* (Lour.) Spreng.—Banana Shrub. Port-Wine Magnolia—Leaves dark glossy green on top, paler and dull underneath. The largest 6" × 2½". When young, coated lightly beneath with brown hair. Flowers *intensely* fragrant, 1½" wide, of 6 petals, rich creamy yellow or maroon. *Shrubby;* to 20 tall'. I planted one in 1987 and it is still only 10½' tall.]

[*M. Maudiæ* Dunn—Smiling Forest Lily Tree—Leaves to 8" × 3¼", white beneath. Flowers pure white, fragrant, of 9 broad petals. Recorded to 60' tall in the wild. Zoo: one 9½' tall in Australasia. Arboretum #22-98 in 27-1E is 7½' tall.]
– U.W.: one by a wild madrona S of Allen Library

[*M. Wilsonii* Finet & Gagnep. (=*Magnolia Ernestii* Figlar)—Yellow Lily Tree—Leaves to 7½" × 2⅝", gray beneath. Flowers soft yellow. Recorded to 60' tall in the wild. Its leaves are borne in flatish layers. It looks apt to grow big here, and the two specimens noted have not yet bloomed: U.W.: one 16' tall S of Allen Library between a wild Madrona and 'Schwedleri' Norway Maple. Arboretum #25-98 in 25-3E is smaller, 13½' tall.]

Parakmeria, named in 1951, has scant or no credibility but is duly noted here, being used by nurseries. Differs from *Magnolia* in its androdioecious flowers.

[*P. lotungensis* (Chun & Tsoon) Y.W. Law = *Magnolia lotungensis* Chun & Tsoon—Eastern Joy Lotus Tree—Leaves dark and glossy, reddish while young, paler green beneath, to 6" long. Flowers pale yellow or whitish; petals 9–14, broad. Recorded to 100' tall in the wild. Zoo: one in Australasia. Arboretum #26-98 on the east edge of 28-3E is 4' tall. The Seattle Chinese Garden has one larger than the preceding specimens.]

MALLOTUS

Mallotus japonicus (Th. *ex* Murr.) Muell.-Arg.　　Food-wrapper Plant
EUPHORBIACEÆ　　Chinese: Qiū
From E Asia.　　Japanese: Akame Gashiwa アカメガシワ

A cold-tender extremely rare small tree with anti-ulcer compounds. Bark vaguely like that of Stripebark Maples. It can grow 50' × 5'. Young leaves reddish—like *Poinsettia* 'blosssoms"; to 10" × 6"; sometimes lobed. Yellowish male and red female flowers on seperate trees. One 20' tall at Locks bed #305, south of a Cretan Maple. Two #178-86 at the Arboretum south of the greenhouse; the taller 14'.

MAPLES in general

In quantity of individual trees (not number of different kinds) Seattle has more maples than any other tree. Three species are native, the Bigleaf being our most abundant tree. This single species can almost make or break our autumn display according to how it colors each year. It might well be called our unofficial City Tree. Five other North American species, 7 Europeans and 21 Asians are grown here: 36 species in all, out of 111–124! Others surely exist; the Arboretum has over 60 species—27 of them not known *elsewhere* in Seattle—and virtually all maples find our mild climate hospitable. In the Language of Flowers maples signify "reserve", but for Seattle a more appropriate word is "effusiveness." A great many cultivars exist; the following pages do not cite *all* that are here. Some species that have been sold in local nurseries, but for which I can cite no examples now, are: *Acer Campbellii* Hook fil. & Thoms. *ex* Hiern., *Acer distylum* S. & Z., and *Acer pentaphyllum* Diels. I have seen yards that *had* these—but then the trees died or were moved.

Bigleaf MAPLE

Acer macrophyllum Pursh　　(our) Common Maple
ACERACEÆ　　Broad- *or* Large-leaf Maple
Native here; from SW B.C. into California.　　Pacific *or* Oregon Maple

The largest-leaved maple is our most abundant tree, and a valuable "staple crop" for Seattle's squirrels. Around 1900, it was our most widely planted street-tree, but due to the ruinous effects of root-heaving on adjacent sidewalks, its use as a street-tree is now illegal by City ordinance. Many old specimens are now in poor shape, falling apart and being cut down. Everyone has favorites, in wooded parks, open lawns, or as massive street-trees. Most neighborhoods have huge landmark specimens: our thickest trunks require over 20' of tape measure. Carkeek Park has one 102' × 29'7½" × 92' wide—but an Oregon tree was 37' around in 1993! Seattle's tallest, in wooded ravines, are 120–130' or more. At Discovery Park on the Loop Trail are two very big trees: 106' × 19'10¼" × 108' wide, and 83' × 25'1" × 107' wide. The tallest in the State in 1989 measured 158' in height!

See the *Arboretum Bulletin*, Winter 1981, for more information.

cv. 'Seattle Sentinel'

Slender in form, not strictly columnar, 'Seattle Sentinel' has merit, but has been grown (via grafts) almost nowhere except at the Arboretum. The original specimen was a street-tree on 18th Ave, south of E Madison St: 60' × 6'6" × 22' wide. It was noticed and named by Brian Mulligan in 1951, and died in 2005. Grafted specimens of it remain at the Arboretum, and are larger—one in the nursery (#97-52C) is 92' × 6'3".

Box-Elder (MAPLE)

A. Negundo L. Ash-leaved Maple
=*Negundo aceroides* Moench Plains *or* Manitoba Maple
=*Negundo fraxinifolium* (Raf.) DC. Stinking Maple
From much of N America. Maple Ash / Sugar Ash

Box-Elder's *compound* leaf recalls that of the Elders (*Sambucus* spp.) and its wood was much used for making boxes—hence the name Box-Elder. Many tree enthusiasts call it a rank, plebeian tree of no particular merit. It is short-lived and often burly, crooked and ill-colored. Yet where satisfied with rich soil and plenty of room, it can attain up to 120' × 20' and spread to over 100' wide. When young or even when old, if well cared for it can make an adequate shade tree, and it tolerates trying conditions with stoic strength. But for all that, its reputation is still dirt to most people.

In Seattle, rare in parks, uncommon in old neighborhoods as a street-tree, often leaning and with a wide crown.

- S.P.U.: north of the Student Union Building was an aged, hollow hulk, its burls covered with mosses and licorice fern; at about 10½' around, it was killed in 1987; another is on the NE corner of campus is 52' × 7'7½"
- 4212 Meridian Ave N: larger of 2 street-trees under wires is 36½' × 9'4"
- 12th Ave E, south of E Prospect St: a street-tree, W side, 53' × 7'5¼"
- Arboretum: 59' × 5'8" (#233-58 in 15-3E)
- E John St, west of 30th Ave E: largest of 3 street-trees, S side, is 7'6½" around

- E Madison St & E Lee St: one at this intersection (not far from an Arizona Cypress)
- Locks bed #327 has a large leaning one

cv. 'Variegatum'   The Ghost Tree

A common female clone with whitish-variegated leaves. Eventually the branches usually *revert* to producing green foliage. In early spring it produces copious, conspicuous, dainty dangling flowers that mature into the familiar winged maple seeds, often persisting on the branches throughout the winter.

- 18th Ave E & E Prospect St: 4 street-trees on the SE corner, tallest 50'
- 8th Ave NE & NE 57th St: a broad one on the N end of the church lawn
- 43rd Ave NE & NE 38th St: one on SW corner
- 3028 Cascadia Ave S: one by the driveway
- 3829 S Burns St (west of 40th Ave S): one in the front yard

[cv. 'Flamingo' is similar but a ♂ whose young growth is partly *pinkish*. 4732 45th Ave NE has 3 street-trees. The SE corner of 11th Ave E & E Harrison St has 7.]

[cv. 'Violaceum' is a ♂ clone with handsome *red-purplish flowers;* its twigs are pleasingly pale, too. Two right by the sidewalk: 2000 26th Ave E, and 6841 40th Ave NE.]

[cv. 'Winter Lightning' is a new clone with *golden* twigs. Children's Hospital has 8 by the NW part of the building. A young street-tree at 8011 19th Ave NW.]

Canyon MAPLE

A. saccharum ssp. *grandidentatum* (Nutt. *ex* T.&G.) Desm.   Bigtooth Maple
=*A. grandidentatum* Nutt. *ex* Torr. & Gray   Western Sugar Maple
From central western N America: Montana to N Mexico.   Wasatch Maple

A small (to 68' × 8¼') cousin of Sugar maple. Only four are known in Seattle. The autumn color is yellow. Two are at the Arboretum: 23' × 1'4" (#619-64A in 35-5E—N of nursery), 21' × 1'3" (#873-58A in 35-5W—in pinetum), and a much larger one is at 8546 30th Ave NW. The clone **Rocky Mountain Glow**™ (='Schmidt') has red fall color, and may exist as a young street-tree here.

Coliseum MAPLE

A. cappadocicum Gledit.   Cappadocian Maple
=*A. lætum* C.A. Meyer   Caucasian *or* Colchican Maple
From E Asia Minor, the Caucasus, to the Himalayas in China.

A rare Asiatic counterpart to the overused Norway maple. One of very few maples that commonly has root-suckers. It has reached 91' × 11½'. In Seattle, largely at City Light substations, where it does so well that it deserves to be used more extensively. Lovely yellow fall color. Some do send up reddish root-suckers. The trunks are usually far from round.

- Arboretum: four #875-58 & 901-55 west of Japanese Garden parking lot (3S-3E), largest a 61' tall 4-trunked tree; tallest 67' (its trunk bolted); 53½' × 2'8½" (#336-54 in 1S-4E); small #506-70A & B in 40-6W

- 6525 Sunnyside Ave N: 2 street-trees, 42' × 6'1¼" (S) and 43½' × 5'4½" (N)
- Substation at 23rd Ave & E Pine St: 30 specimens *pl.* 1966; largest 5'9¾"
- Substation on Bellevue Ave E, north of E John St: 3 by the benches
- Substation at 6th Ave NW & NW 76th St: three at S end
- Stone Ave N & N 100th St: 9 street trees (+ 4 *non* street-trees) on the SW corner
- U.W.: north of tennis courts north of the I.M.A. Building is one in a row of varied trees, flanked by a Silver maple NE and a stunted Norway maple SW

Cretan MAPLE

A. sempervirens L.
=*A. orientale* auct., *non* L., =*A. creticum* auct., *non* L.
=*A. heterophyllum* Willd., =*A. virens* Thunb.
From the NE Mediterranean region.

A small-leaved, semi-evergreen bush or small tree up to 40' tall. Very confused as to nomenclature. Extremely rare in Seattle. Arboretum #443-64A is 24½' tall in the rockroses (21-3E). One 27' × 2'6" × 23' wide at the Locks in bed #305.

[*A. obtusifolium* Sibth. & Sm.—Syrian Maple—(=*A. syriacum* Boiss. & Gaill. =*A. orientale* L.) From the E Mediterranean. Like Cretan maple but fully evergreen, larger leaved. In Seattle known only as a young tree 16½' tall N of the Good Shepherd Center just west of an Evergreen Hawthorn.]

Dwarf MAPLE

A. glabrum Torr.   Rocky Mountain Maple
=*A. Douglasii* Hook.   Rock *or* Douglas Maple
Native here; from SE Alaska and to New Mexico.   Sierra Maple

A rare native here: only one specimen is known in the *wild*, on the very edge of the City limits. Few are planted; its fall color is poor here. Its leaves are much like those of Red maple, yet very long-stemmed and are sometimes trifoliate on basal suckers. It can reach 80' × 6' but is usually a true dwarf maple.

- Golden Gardens Park: 12 by a yellow metal sculpture W of the offleash dog area, all suckering from their bases, the tallest 44' and stoutest trunk 2'9½"
- Lincoln Park: 4 on the east side, SE of the wading pool; largest 2'3½" around
- Jackson Park: *ca.* 30' tall growing *wild* from the base of a chain-link fence on NE 145th St opposite 10th Ave NE (flanked west by a Western White Pine and east by Madrona); a maintenance crew will likely cut it down—but it will resprout
- Arboretum: 30½' tall (#421-61 in 46-1E); 21' tall 5-trunked (#749-65 in 36-1E)
- NW 78th St, just E of 8th Ave NW: a street-tree, N side, E of a 'Sunburst' Locust
- U.W.: one 21½' tall in Forestry courtyard
- 6241 44th Ave NE: a multitrunked one south of the house
- 2653 NW 58th St: a multitrunked specimen in the yard's NE corner

English MAPLE

A. campestre L.   (not our) Common Maple
From Europe, N Africa,   Small-leaved *or* English Cork Maple
the Near East.   Field *or* Hedge(row) Maple

The only *Acer* native in England, this is the original "Maple." Its basal suckers, and rarely its regular twigs, can be *corky*-ridged, unlike other maples, but like some elms, some sweetgums, and so forth. Autumn color is butter yellow. Its wood was highly valued for carving into large drinking-vessels called "mazers," but was also used for general cabinetry, joinery and turnery, to fashion various articles ranging from harps to snuff boxes. A dense tree; often shrubby where native, sometimes used for hedges and topiary. When left alone it reaches up to 90' × 14'. Tacoma's Wright Park has one 83' × 11'2" × 64' wide (1987).

In Seattle, common. It resembles and may be confused with Montpelier maple—a smaller, darker, glossy, less common species. The cultivar **Queen Elizabeth**™ ('Evelyn') is used as a street-tree. *Variegated* clones such as 'Carnival' are young, small and extremely rare—limited to a few gardens.

– 2018 - 2020 E Newton St: a street-tree 58' × 7'9"
– 627 35th Ave: one 59' tall
– Ravenna Blvd NE: twelve W of 15th Ave NE, the largest 6'11½" around
– Mt Baker Blvd: 10 by S McClellan St, the tallest 79½'
– Keystone Pl N & N 57th St: 16 in the triangle, the largest 57' × 7'1¾"
– Salmon Bay Park: several, the largest (on the S side to the east) is 60½' × 6'4"
– Lincoln Park: one 65' × 5'11"
– U.W.: the Denny Hall lawn has four, the tallest 58' and stoutest 5'1"
– 45th Ave SW & SW Seattle St: 6 street-trees on the SW corner
– 1st Ave W & W Prospect St: SW and SE corners
– 12th Ave S, south of S Cloverdale St: 6 **Queen Elizabeth**™ street-trees, W side

Full Moon MAPLE

A. japonicum Th. *ex* Murr.   Downy Japanese Maple
From Manchuria, Japan, Korea.   Japanese: Hauchiwa Kaede ハウチワカエ

The regular form of this species has a roundish leaf like that of Vine maple. It grows to 50' × 6½' in nature. Virtually absent in Seattle except at the Arboretum; but young examples are in some private gardens.

– Arboretum: largest are a 30' tall multi-trunked 'Ō-isami'—leaves to 7½" wide—
    (#721-66 in 32-1E), and a specimen 27½' × 1'9" (#784-66A in 32-B); in the
    Japanese Garden is a 'Vitifolium' (#98-63) 28' × 2'0"
– S.U: one 10' tall on south lawn of The Quad
– 18th Ave E & E Prospect St: NE corner, on house's SW corner
– 8238 2nd Ave NE: an 'Ō-taki' with its own sign, facing sidewalk south of the stairs

cv. 'Aconitifolium'   Cutleaf *or* Fernleaf (Full Moon) Maple

Called by the Japanese "Maiku Jaku" (マイクジャク; *i.e.* dancing peacock), this is grown for its *deeply divided* leaves that give an elegant effect and turn spectacular colors in the fall. It is shrubby and uncommon.

– 28th Ave NW & NW 65th St: SE corner yard has one on its west side
– U.W.: CUH has several in the courtyard
– 21st Ave E & E Aloha St: NE corner house has one on its NW corner
– N 47th St, just W of Woodlawn Ave N: 2 street-trees, N side
– 5112 NE 75th St: a very stout specimen

Golden Full Moon MAPLE

A. Shirasawanum Koidz. '**Aureum**'
=*A. japonicum* 'Aureum'
From Japan.

Like Full Moon maple, but with *golden*, smaller (2–5" wide), more lobed leaves (9–13), and different flowers. Though this cultivar is bushy and small in cultivation, its wild parent the Shirasawa maple (Japanese: O-itaya-meigetsu; オオイタヤメイグツ) is able to reach 65' × 8¼'. Rare here.

– 2711 33rd Ave S: an old stout tree 19½' with a redleaf Japanese maple
– 3803 NE 96th St: one in the yard's NE corner
– Volunteer Park: one 29½' tall in a bed with 6 Japanese maples between the museum and the wading pool—it's the southernmost tree there
– 814 Hillside Dr E: one with two Hinoki Cypresses
– Arboretum: in the Japanese Garden

Hornbeam MAPLE

A. carpinifolium S. & Z.   Japanese: Chidori-noki チドリノキ
From Japan.

The specific epithet is from *Carpinus*, Hornbeam tree, and Latin *folium*, a leaf. Leaves elongated, unlobed, with 18–25 pairs of parallel veins—utterly unlike those of familiar maples. The largest leaves are 8" × 3¼". Fall color usually dull golden-brown, at best yellow, orange and red. Only the seeds make it a maple. Bushy, broad, and well-suited for woodland gardens. Male and female flowers borne on separate trees. Recorded to 50' × 5' in the wild. Extremely rare here.

– Arboretum: largest is 33' × 5'4" × 43' wide (#470-53A) in 3S-3E (south of the Japanese Garden); the nursery has a multitrunked one 28' tall (#470-53C; with a smaller #37-99A)
– Locks bed #208 has a small specimen at the west end

Japanese MAPLE

A. palmatum Th. *ex* Murr.   Smooth Japanese Maple
From SW China,   Japanese: Iroha-momiji イロハモミジ
Korea, Japan.   Yama-momiji ヤマモミジ

Whole books treat the 325+ Japanese Maple cultivars: no other maple has nearly as many variations. Some are known by Japanese names (*e.g.* 'Sangokaku'), some Latinized (*e.g.* 'Atropurpureum'), or have modern English names (*e.g.* 'Burgundy Lace'). It is November's Floral Emblem in Japan, for the fall color display is almost "out of this world." Though generally shrubby in many of the cultivars, the tree can be as large as 60' × 11'. The young, unfolding leaves of many (especially purple-colored cut-leaved ones) are sorrel-flavored, excellent additions to salads. Not only superior to most other maple leaves, they're also better than those of the Sorrel Tree!

In Seattle, very common: certain kinds rare, others more common. Naming the numerous cultivars is work for specialists. Just a *few* are cited below.

- 2015 29th Ave W (at W Crockett St): one 41' tall, wider still, its trunk over 8'0"
- 601 36th Ave E: 40½' tall
- 23rd Ave E & E Newton St: 38' tall
- Lake View Cemetery: one not far from the entrance, by the road, 37½' × 7'6¼"
- Dorffel Dr E, by Maiden Lane E: a street-tree, E side, 31½' × 6'6"
- Arboretum: over 60 cultivars, mostly in 33-2E (the Woodland Garden)
- 19th Ave NE & NE 52nd St: SW corner yard has a big one W of a street-tree Beech
- Bigelow Ave N & Newton St: two in the SE corner yard, the talller 37'
- 33rd Ave S & S Dose Terrace: SE corner has one 31' tall, and wider

Redleaf *or* **purpleleaf** cultivars
- 24th Ave E & Interlaken Blvd E: NW corner house has a 37' tall one next to a 30'+ tall white-flowered Saucer Magnolia
- Fuhrman Ave E at 886 E Gwinn Pl: a huge 'Bloodgood' example 33½' tall
- 4835 Fauntleroy Way SW: a 'Bloodgood' 29' tall at yard's S edge
- Arboretum: the Japanese Garden has large 'Burgundy Lace' (and many other cvs.)
- 9412 12th Ave NE: a large example

'Butterfly'—*variegated* gray-green with much creamy white (and some pink)
- S.U.: 22' tall north of west entrance to University Services Building
- 320 Melrose Ave E: north of entrance
- 1909 E Lynn St (at E Howe St): two by front door

Green *cutleaf, threadleaf, spiderleaf, laceleaf* cultivars
- MOHAI: Heritage Tree specimen 6' tall, over 100 years old. Originally imported directly from Japan to Seattle by nurseryman Julius Bonnell, for the 1909 Alaska Yukon Pacific Exposition. On Valentine's Day of 1964 the tree was *pl.* here.
- 3403 SW Manning St

Purplish *cutleaf, threadleaf, spiderleaf, laceleaf* cultivars
- 931 11th Ave E: 12' tall
- Arboretum: an 'Ever Red' is 9' × 2'1¼" (#42-98A, N of nursery)
- 1427 36th Ave: a big one 12½' tall

- 20th Ave E & E Lynn St: SE corner has one 11' tall × 18' wide
- 2530 36th Ave W
- 4201 55th Ave NE

'**Osakazuki**'—splendid red fall color
- 1839 40th Ave E

'**Sangokaku**'—the "Coralbark Maple"
- 1223 Spring St: 2
- S.U.: 24' tall south of west entrance to University Services Building
- 2347 Rosemont Pl W: 5 street-trees
- 2912 W Blaine St
- 38th Ave SW & SW Olga St: NW corner has 5
- Woodlawn Ave N, north of N 48th St: 3 street-trees, E side

'**Seiryu**'—*upright*-growing green laceleaf
- 3034 10th Ave W: back yard
- 4207 Woodland Park Ave N
- 6216 17th Ave NE: NW corner of the yard

'**Shishigashira**'—Crested *or* Lion's Mane maple—upright; tight; wrinkly little leaves
- 2128 Park Rd NE (off Ravenna Blvd.): a street-tree 18½' tall
- 4340 NE 55th St: one 15½' tall in SE corner of the yard, visible behind the fence
- 7554 44th Ave NE: a 12' tall one west of the house

Korean MAPLE

A. pseudosieboldianum (Pax) Kom.   Purplebloom Maple
From S Siberia, E Manchuria, and Korea.

Extremely rare here. A slender small tree related closely to Siebold, Full Moon and Japanese maples. Leaves round, (7) 9–11 lobed, to 5½" wide, very downy, deeply lobed. Flowers purple. Young twigs lightly hairy. Fall color brilliant orange or red. By contrast, the leaves of its Japanese cousin Siebold maple have 9 lobes almost exclusively, are less deeply lobed, less conspicuously toothed, and have earlier fall color; the flowers are later and yellowish-white rather than purple.

- Arboretum: largest is 43½' × 3'3¼" #23-70A in 25-B
- U.W.: 5 *pl.* in early 1990s between Smith Hall & Allen Library, tallest 24'

Montpelier MAPLE

A. monspessulanum L.   Montpellier Maple
From S & central Europe, N Africa and the Near East.

In general this is much like English maple, but has darker, smaller (1½–3⅛"), less lobed, and glossier leaves. The winged seeds are borne in parallel pairs (⊂) instead of at 180° apart. Recorded to 65' × 9¼'. Rare here.

- Queen Anne Blvd: 11 old street-trees on 8th Ave W between W McGraw & W Wheeler St, the largest 48' × 7'8" × 48' wide (1988)
- 8th Ave W, north of W Fulton St—by Mt Pleasant Cemetery: one 45' × 5'8" (1988)

- Woodland Park: two NW of the soapbox derby ramp, taller 47' and stouter 4'7½"
- Lake Park Dr S, just north of S McClellan St: larger of 2 on E side is 53' × 5'5¼" (nearby, just south of S McClellan St on Mt Baker Blvd, are 10 tall English maples)
- Summit Ave, north of E Union St: a street-tree downhill from two English maples
- Zoo: one 27½' × 5'3¼" outside the south fence N of the Spanish War monument
- W Dravus St, east of 4th Ave W: a street-tree, S side, 29' × 5'4"
- U.W. Friendship Grove, representing Italy, 37' × 3'5½"

Nikko MAPLE

A. Maximowiczianum Miq. *ex* Koidz. Japanese: Megusuri-no-ki
=*A. nikoense* auct., *non* Maxim. メグスリノキ
From central China, Japan.

A tree up to 80' × 7¼', with fuzzy, trifoliate leaves. Very rare here.

- Arboretum: 46' × 2'6" (#554-65A in 25-B); 41' × 1'6" (#903-65A in 33-3E); 30' × 3'1" (#754-40B in 33-4E); it is also in the Japanese Garden
- Locks bed #16 (41' tall), 26
- U.W.: Hansee Hall's S courtyard SE corner has 1 (crowded by a West. Red Cedar)
- 15th Ave NE & NE 89th St: NW corner has one west of the driveway

[*A. triflorum* Kom.—Three-flowered *or* Rough-barked Maple—From Manchuria and Korea. Leaflets 3, with a few coarse teeth; long hairs on both sides and on the stems and twigs. Fall color brilliant. Bark curling in coils for a pleasingly rugged look. (Nikko maple is smooth-trunked, its leaflets untoothed, with short hairs.) *Acer triflorum* flushes first in spring, and begins coloring a bit earlier in fall. Recorded to 60' tall in the wild. In Seattle, Arboretum #1340-50 is 38' × 1'7" in 26-B; 8338 14th Ave NW has a youngster.]

Norway MAPLE

A. platanoides L.
From Europe, to beyond the Caspian Sea.

Similar to Bigleaf maple in bark and form; closer to Coliseum and Sugar maples in leaf, the Norway maple is barely native in Norway (where it's called Lønn or Spiss Lønn). It is extensively grown in this country, doing better in cities than most similarly-sized maples—it can attain 122' × 25¼'. Street-tree cultivars abound, all recognizable as this species by their leaf shape, though crown shape varies. They include: Cavalier™, 'Cleveland', 'Columnare', Emerald Queen™, 'Erectum', Summershade™ and 'Superform'.

In Seattle, Norway maple is abundant and naturalized weedily.

- Volunteer Park: one 88' × 12'3" on the roadside by the wading pool
- Interlaken Park: one 90' × 7'0" in the ravine below 19th Ave E & E Crescent Dr (most easily found when yellow in November)
- S.P.U.: one 49½' × 10'2¼" S of the Science Building is declining; one east of it is 75' × 9'4¼" × 85' wide
- Washelli Cemetery: best of two north of the military area is 64½' × 10'9¼"
- Green Lake: largest of 80+ is a low-forking street-tree 47' × 11'10¼" in NW part
- 36th Ave NE, between NE 55th & NE 52nd: 14 old street-trees

- U.W.: Denny Hall lawn, very near Savery hall, one 80' × 9'10" × 78½' wide
- E Columbia St, west of 34th Ave: a street-tree, N side, 41' × 11'5¼" & very wide
- 25th Ave NW & NW 73rd St: NW corner has a neighborhood landmark 56' tall
- 42nd Ave SW & SW 98th St: NW corner property has a big one on its W side
- **Cavalier**™ City street-trees: E Yesler Way, from 18th to 23rd Ave
- **'Cleveland'** City street-trees: 5th Ave, from Olive to Spring St
- **Emerald Queen**™ City street-trees: NW Market St, from 13th to 24th Ave NW
- **'Erectum'** street-trees: Oswego Place NE, north of NE 65th St, just W of I-5

cv. 'Crimson King'   Purpleleaf Norway Maple

A common, old cultivar whose leaves are *purplish* all summer. 'Royal Red' is virtually identical; 'Faassen's Black' is not such an opresively dark tree.

- Evergreen Park Cemetery: one in the SW area is 51' × 7'10" × 49' wide
- Arboretum: one of two #660-49 E of Japanese Garden parking lot is 52' × 4'8½"
- Broadway E & E Aloha St: 8 street-trees on NW corner
- U.W: near Ceramic Metal Arts

cv. **Crimson Sentry**™   Dwarf Purpleleaf Norway Maple

A common, newer cultivar of tightly *compact* habit whose leaves are *purplish* all summer—if not gray with mildew. Fall color is like soggy cornflakes.

- Wallingford Ave N & N 53rd St traffic circle has 3
- S.U.: "Championship Field" has 30 on its west side (13th Avenue)

cv. 'Drummondii'   Harlequin *or* Variegated Norway Maple

Leaves variegated white. Reverts to wholly green, bit by bit, unless the green shoots are suppressed. Most here are young.

- 2506 33rd Ave S (south of S Bayview St): two street-trees
- Seattle Center House: east entrance, 47' × 4'¾"
- N 46th St, Aurora Ave to Phinney Ave: City street-trees *pl.* 1988 (*most* now gone)
- 9052 Burke Ave N

cv. 'Faassen's Black'   Purpleleaf Norway Maple

A common, old cultivar whose leaves are *purplish* all summer. It is not as *dense* as 'Crimson King', its leaves held horizontally instead of drooping.

- 12th Ave NW & NW 116th St: NW corner house has one above driveway, 57' tall
- Kubota Garden Park: one of four by exit is 58½' × 3'8½"
- 8552 31st Ave NW: large one in yard
- 3556 NE 110th St: 43½' tall
- 50th Ave SW, just south of SW Hudson St: 2 street-trees, E side

cv. 'Globosum'   Dwarf Norway Maple

A shrub grafted on a trunk to make an inelegant squat little mushroom tree.

- Phil Smart Mercedes Benz on 600 E Pike St: 5 street-trees
- 1207-1211 26th Ave E: several jammed in front yards
- 4730 & 4734 2nd Ave NE: 4 street-trees

— 408 17th Ave E: 3 street-trees

cv. 'Green Lace'   Cutleaf Norway Maple
Leaves deeply dissected, recalling the 'Sweet Shadow' Sugar maple.
— 2000 43rd Ave E: 3 street-trees, largest 31½' × 3'½"

cv. **Princeton Gold**™ ('Prigo')   Yellow-leaf Norway Maple
A new, very rare tree. Leaves cheerful yellowish.
— 932 NW 54th St: a street-tree W of a Sweetgum & purpleleaf White Birch
— 12th Ave NW & NW 67th St: NW corner has a street-tree on 12th

cv. '**Schwedleri**'   Schwedler Norway Maple
A common, very old form whose leaves emerge red in April, then turn dark green
in summer. Big leaves; droopy aspect. A similar, new version is 'Deborah'.
— Me-kwa-mooks Park: one 64½' × 10'6¼"
— Volunteer Park: one 71' × 7'1" (drawn up by 2 Silver maples & 2 Pin Oaks)
— Kinnear Park: the largest of 6 on the upper level is 53½' × 9'1"
— Meridian Park: 1 Norway & 5 'Schwedleri' W of picnic shelter; largest 53' × 7'1¼"
— U.W.: one 47' × 6'0" between Sieg Hall and Allen Library

hybrid Norway MAPLE

A. truncatum × *A. platanoides* **Norwegian Sunset**™ ('Keithsform')
A. truncatum × *A. platanoides* **Pacific Sunset**™ ('Warrenred')

Introduced in 1989 by Schmidt nursery of Boring, OR. Common in Seattle as
street-trees. Differs from Norway maple in being smaller, with smaller leaves,
more cordate at the base, and acute seed angles. Differs from Shantung maple
in being larger, with larger leaves, the lobes toothed rather than entire, and the
base cordate instead of usually truncate; seeds *infertile* (or usually so). Pacific
Sunset™ differs from Norwegian Sunset™ in that it colors earlier and more prettily
(yellow-orange to bright red) in fall. But I cannot tell the two clones apart.
— 11th Ave NW, north of NW 80th St: a street-tree, W side, was bought as a seedling
  Shantung maple *(A. truncatum)* but *looks* intermediate; it is relatively stout
— Burke Ave N & N 47th St: NE corner
— 4100 E Highland Dr: 3 in front yard
— 18th Ave E, just north of E Prospect St: 2 street-trees, W side
— Stone Way N, near N 40th St: many street-trees
— U.W.: Husky Stadium parking-lot

Paperbark MAPLE

A. griseum (Franch.) Pax   Chinese: Xue Pi Feng
From W China.

A maple beloved for highly attractive, unusual bark—cinnamon-orange, papery and peeling. For this feature alone it is well worth growing. Moreover, it has rich red fall color. It is one of the few trifoliate maples and attains 50' × 6¼' or more. After decades, it is finally becoming common in Seattle.

- Arboretum: the largest is 41' × 3'11½" (#1233-47 on Asian Maple hillside, 25-B)
- Washelli Cemetery: one 33' × 5'½" south of the mausoleum/columbarium; another one south of the new mausoleum
- Good Shepherd Center: a pair in front of the building; largest 22½' × 2'7½"
- U.W.: two in Grieg Grove between Allen Library and Thomson Hall
- Willard Ave W & W Comstock St: SE corner has one south of the fire hydrant

Red MAPLE

A. rubrum L.   Swamp *or* Scarlet Maple
From much of central and E North America.   Shoepeg Maple

Rhode Island's State Tree. Remarkable for tolerance of moist, low-lying, even swampy ground, and for its admirable autumn display; a valued hardwood producer too. The tree shape varies from spreading mushroom-like crowns to upright narrow columns. Recorded to 145' × 26'. Fall color can be yellow, orange, shades of burgundy, or (usually) red. Street-tree cultivars differ in tree shape and leaf details as well as fall color, but scarcely enough to interest most people. Some are: 'Doric', October Glory®, Red Sunset™, and 'Shade King'.

In Seattle, old street-trees are uncommon but young ones (planted in the last 30 years) are very common, being used here recently as much as any other large shade tree. A good ornamental in any city, such strong fall color makes it especially valuable in Seattle, where it serves as strawberries for our cornflakes, making our annual feasts of autumn color much more appetizing.

- 1246 16th Ave E (south of E Galer St): a dying street-tree, 55' × 8'9½" × 78' wide
- Interlaken Park: one 92' × 5'11¼" on a hump of land east of the roadside Coast Redwood grove about where 22nd Ave E dead-ends off Boyer Ave E in Montlake
- Arboretum: #X-322 in 3-5E is 58' × 6'9¼"
- Volunteer Park: 55½' × 7'2" east of the wading pool; one across the road W of the bandstand is 62½' × 7'3½"
- 36th Ave, south of E Olive St: 4 old street-trees, E side, tallest 67½'; stoutest 8'2¼"
- **'Columnare'** Arboretum: #554-63 in 33-2W is 77½' × 3'10"
- **Doric**™ City street-trees on NE 50th St, from 15th NE to 17th NE
- **Karpick®** 10 street-trees *pl.* 1998 near 22nd Ave NE & NE 73rd St
- **October Glory®** many street-trees *pl. ca.* 1993-94 on Beacon Ave S
- **Red Sunset®** City street-trees on Fremont Ave N, from N 34th to N 50th St

hybrid Red MAPLE

A. × *Freemanii* E. Murr.   Freeman Maple
(A. rubrum × A. saccharinum)

This hybrid was first raised in 1933 at the U.S. National Arboretum by Oliver M. Freeman (1891–1969). The name commemorating Freeman was only given in 1969. Only *clones* are sold these days, but older plantings of seedling Red maples have a few chance hybrids. Often nurseries ignore the *Freemanii* name and sell cultivars as if they were *purebred* Red maples. They are common here.

– Arboretum: one 77' tall, two-trunked, S of beehives in 37-5E, has *yellow* fall color and *hairy* leaf undersides; 80' × 6'11¼" (#265-56 in 11-3E); 74' × 4'2" (#265-56A in 4-5E); an 'Armstrong' (narrow and upright) 80½' × 3'9½" (#1110-56 in 2-5E)
– NE Ravenna Blvd has a female 73' × 7'0" just W of I-5 (the *entire* blvd. tally is 62 Sycamore maples, 35 Red maples, 3 *hybrid* Red maples, and 4 Sugar maples)
– 1420 41st Ave E: one *pl. ca.* 1977 is 70½' × 6'9"
– Montlake School: 2 street-trees (largest 47' × 5'½") on 20th Ave E (+5 Red maples)
– 'Armstrong' City street-trees: Madison St, from 7th to 12th Ave, & 20th to 29th
– 'Armstrong' City street-trees: N 39th St, west of Phinney Ave N; best 66' × 5'1¼"
– U.W.: 7 'Armstrong' N of Henderson Hall; 18 **Scarlet Sentinel**™ between the HUB and Allen Library (in some years this cultivar turns yellow, not scarlet, in fall)
– Green Lake: 6 **Autumn Blaze**® trees by basketball court; 6 others elsewhere, too

Shantung MAPLE

A. *truncatum* Bge.   Purpleblow Maple
From N China.   Chinese: Yuan Bao Feng

Shantung (Shandong) is a Province of China. A tree like Norway maple but much smaller, roundish, with smaller more elegant leaves. Leaf 5- or 7-lobed, 2½–4½" (6½") wide, usually hairless or nearly so; margins untoothed; coppery or purplish when unfolding in spring. Fall color is comparatively late, usually red but can have gold, orange or yellow. Bark usually somewhat corky unlike that of the otherwise reminiscent Coliseum maple. Recorded to 75' × 7⅓'. Extremely rare here. Its hybrids with Norway maple are common.

– Arboretum: largest is 34' × 5'9¼" × 52' wide #808-53 (12-3W)
– U.W.: one 43½' × 2'0" in woods N of Medicinal Herb Garden, W of Rainier Vista
– 21st Ave NE & NE 52nd St: an 'Akikaze Nishiki' by a public stairway, 17' × 1'10¼"

[*A.* **longipes** Franch. *ex* Rehd.—From China. Seattle has *one* backyard tree 16' tall. Best at the Arboretum is #533-70 in 25-B is 25' × 1'1½". Recorded to 60' tall in the wild.]

Siebold MAPLE

A. *Sieboldianum* Miq.   Japanese: Ko-hauchiwa-kaede
From Japan.   コハウチワカエデ

Leaves (7) 9 (11) lobed, very downy when young; wonderful orange-red fall color.
Flowers yellowish-white. A slender tree to 60' × 2½'. Extremely rare here.

— Arboretum: largest of at least four is 29' × 3'2½" #769-40 (33-2E)
— Locks bed #114

Silver MAPLE

A. *saccharinum* L., *non* Wangenh.   Silverleaf *or* White Maple
=*A. dasycarpum* Ehrh.   Water Maple
=*A. eriocarpum* Michx.   River Maple
From much of central & eastern N America.   Soft Maple

A huge, fast-growing tree (to 138' × 31½'), Silver maple has deeply-cut leaves that
are unusually bright white underneath, and turn yellowish-orange in October.
No other maple of this bulky stature has such a graceful, drooping aspect. There
are some exceptionally fine cut-leaved cultivars, such as 'Wieri'.

White Poplar (see entry) is sometimes called Silver or White maple: its 'Nivea'
cultivar has maple-like leaves with vivid white undersides. Silver maple was once
commonly planted in Seattle, but has lost favor because it sometimes develops
multiple trunks with unsightly sprout-ridden burls, and often falls easy prey to
storm breakage. On the whole, it is neither better nor worse than Bigleaf maple
under cultivation: both grow rapidly and get too large to be ideal street-trees.
As they age, these trees can turn into monstrous menaces of rough appearance.
This sad situation may be forestalled by regular, intelligent pruning and care. Yet,
rather than practice preventive care in time, many people resort to brutal use of
the chainsaw late in the tree's life, thereby only worsening its condition.

Both Red and Silver maples reseed only sparingly here—the seeds ripen in late
spring or early summer when conditions are too dry for sprouting. Also, squirrels
eat Silver maple seeds—they've large moist, tasty and nutritious kernels.

— E John St, west of 20th Ave E: 3 street-trees (+Black Walnuts); best 62½' × 13'½"
— Volunteer Park: one in NE part 93½' × 8'1½"; one NE of bandstand 81½' × 8'11¾"
— Rodgers Park: six, the largest NE of restrooms, 11'10" around
— 9635 47th Ave SW: 68' tall
— S.P.U.: one 90' × 6'11¼"
— 7727 33rd Ave NW: by driveway & telephone pole
— 927 32nd Ave (south of E Spring St): *ca.* 75' tall
— U.W.: 16 south of Lander Hall, tallest 62'
— 13th Ave NW & NW 75th St: NE corner has a neighborhood landmark 70½' tall
— 28th Ave NW, north of NW 75th St: west side; a young cutleaf upright street-tree

Stripebark MAPLES in general

The Stripebark or Snakebark maple group is mainly East Asian, but has one American. They're valued as ornamentals for their distinctive bark. Woodland conditions suit them best; hot sunny sites stunt them, as can be seen if the various examples cited below are compared with reference to their locations.

The Arboretum harbors our oldest and best examples of the six species treated below—and other stripebark species as well. Identifying the various kinds is easy enough with "normal" specimens, but some odd trees prove frustratingly intermediate. The two least rare kinds are Red Stripebark and Père David's Maple.

A. capillipes Maxim.   Red Stripebark- *or* Snakebark-Maple
From Japan.   Japanese: Hoso-e-kaede ホソエカエデ

More *red* in its various parts than any other Stripebark treated here. It is the *last* species to flower in spring and its young leaves are pinkish. Its maximum recorded size is 82' × 7¼'. Though this is, along with Père David's Maple, one of the better known and most widely planted of the Stripebarks, it is still rare here.

– Arboretum: largest is 45' × 2'7¼" #9-61 in Woodland Garden (33-1E)
– Locks bed #115 (an exposed site), #110 (wild), #119 (34' × 4'1" × 42½' wide; weakly lobed leaves but otherwise true to type), #121 (quite normal)
– Dorffel Dr E, south of Maiden Lane E: a street-tree, E side, N of a Purpleleaf Plum
– U.W.: CUH courtyard entrance has two
– 15th Ave E & E Mercer St: NE corner yard has one in its SE corner
– Roanoke Park: NE corner has a youngster
– S.P.U.: N of Alexander Hall, to east
– Phinney Neighborhood Center: 2 south of the building (+ a Himalayan white pine)
– Midvale Ave N, south of N Allen Pl: a street-tree, E side
– 1510 Warren Ave N: a hacked specimen

A. cratægifolium S. & Z.   Hawthorn-leaf Maple
From Japan.   Japanese: Uri-kaede ウリカエデ

Leaves small (2–3½" long) and dark, shaped vaguely like those of Washington Hawthorn *(Cratægus Phænopyrum)* but not as glossy; finer-toothed, with delicate rusty hairs beneath. The tree is bushy, slender, with *weakly*-striped trunks. Male and female flowers borne on separate plants. Fall color can be a pale yellow, or, as E. Wilson writes, can go "from yellow to crimson or black-purple—no other maple is so dark." Recorded to 40' tall in the wild. Very rare in Seattle.

– Arboretum: largest *was* 24' × 1'2" when it died at age 40 in 1994; best now is #627-37 is in Woodland garden (33-1E) in salal, 20½' tall, multitrunked
– S.U.: a 'Veitchii' (variegated leaves) 16' tall west of the S entrance of Fine Arts bldg, next to a 'Tolleson's Blue' Rocky Mountain Juniper; a young 6½' tall tree at NE corner of Campion Hall by a stone that says In Memory of Kai Nagel
– U.W.: CUH

A. Davidii Franch. (Père) David's Maple
From China. Chinese: Qing Zha Feng

This Stripebark, though called in China "Snake's Skin Maple" or "Green Toad," was officially named after a French Jesuit who worked in China, abbè Armand David—also named after him was Dove Tree (*Davidia involucrata*). The tree has bronzy young growth and its leaves are often strongly curved and folded. It can reach 62' × 7¾' and is our least rare Stripebark.

- Arboretum: many; largest is 50½' × 5'8" in 15-3E
- Kruckeberg Botanic Garden: 54' × 4'4"
- U.W.: one S of the Padelford garage, N of the stairs (Wahkiakum Lane)
- U.W.: CUH courtyard entrance has a cv. **'Serpentine'** (elongated; slender leaves)
- 2019 E Louisa St: two street-trees
- 307 NW 84th St: a street-tree
- Good Shepherd Center: 2 in front of bldg. (+Paperbark maples), better 29' × 1'7½"
- 18th Ave NW & NW 95th St: NW corner has 2 (and a Southern-BEECH)

A. Davidii ssp. **Grosseri** (Pax) de Jong Grosser's Stripebark
= *A. Grosseri* Pax (incl. *A. Hersii* Rehd.) Chinese: Ge Luo Feng
From China.

Puzzlingly variable: different forms are united here. Grosser Stripebarks are like typical Père David's maple but have *finer-toothed* leaves with longer stalks. The form called 'Hersii' is hard to differentiate by leaf, but may grow taller. The tallest forms reach 65' in height. It is rare here.

- Arboretum: many; best on Asian Maple hillside (25-1E/26-1E), #85-48 is 58' × 2'11¼"; #1138-47 *or* 901-54 (two tags on one tree!) is 55½' × 4'10¼"
- U.W.: three NW of Benson Hall (reseeding; tallest 34½'); two in brick circles by Mercer Hall's E entrance
- 18th Ave E, south of E Galer St: a street-tree, west side, remains green late into fall
- Locks bed #26 (two young vigorous specimens, west 30' and east 36' tall); bed #205 has a 'Hersii'
- S.U.: 23½' tall NW of The Quad (east of an *A. capillipes*); 20' tall at 11th & Spring St. with a 15' tall Hiba Arborvitæ
- Seattle Center: both the E and W sides of Key Arena have examples over 30' tall

A. pensylvanicum L. Striped *or* Stripedbark Maple
From eastern N America. Goosefoot Maple / Maleberry
Moosewood / Whistlewood

The only Stripebark not native in East Asia. Recorded to 77' × 4½'. It flushes later than the similar E Asian *A. tegmentosum*. It's uncommon in Seattle.

- Arboretum: few; best S of Loderi Valley (27-B), #130-68 **'Erythrocladum'** (with *reddish* twigs) is 21' × 2'10½"; #610-44 is 25' × 1'8¼" in 26-1W
- 1913 E Blaine St
- 4026 Sunnyside Ave N, south of N 41st St: 2 street-trees
- Dunn Gardens: several young **'Erythrocladum'** in the Upper Ravine Glade
- Good Shepherd Center: a young 6' tall **'Erythrocladum'** by the exit drive

A. rufinerve S.& Z. Bat Maple / Grey-budded Snake-bark Maple
=*A. tegmentosum* ssp. Cucumber-bark Maple / Redvein Maple
rufinerve (S.& Z.) E. Murr. Japanese: Uri-hada-kaede ウリハダカエデ

From Japan, this has relatively large leaves with scattered *reddish* hairs on the undersides. It can surpass 65' × 7¼'. It is very rare here.
- Arboretum: largest in 24-B, #568-50 is 51½' × 4'6" and very wide, too
- U.W.: one 37½' × 2'7¾" with 2 smaller *A. Davidii* N of Suzzallo Library
- U.W.: CUH courtyard entrance has one
- S.P.U.: N of Alexander Hall, to west
- Locks bed #26 has a 44' tall cv. '**Albolimbatum**' (= 'Hatsuyuki') with whitish variegated leaves; two *A. Davidii* ssp. *Grosseri* are also in this bed

A. tegmentosum Maxim. Manchu *or* Manchurian Stripebark
From Korea, Manchuria.

A *big*-leaved Stripebark with leaves shaped like Red Stripebark's yet greener and more finely and sharply toothed. Flushes early. Twigs glaucous. Reported to 49' tall. Extremely rare here.
- Arboretum: largest (both #164-49) 36½' × 4'5¾" (17-4E) and 46' × 4'3¼" (16-4E)
- U.W.: CUH courtyard entrance has one
- S.P.U.: one 28½' × 1'8" at NW corner of Peterson Hall

[*A.* '**Silver Cardinal**'—Hybrid Stripebark—A new *variegated* clone, extremely rare. One at 4340 NE 55th St (invisible from street). A second variegated hybrid is '**Silver Vein**' and it *may* be here, somewhere. Ditto for non-variegated hybrids such as '**White Tigress**'.]

Sugar MAPLE

A. saccharum Marsh. Hard Maple
=*A. saccharinum* Wagenh., *non* L. Rock Maple
From much of central and eastern N America, but not far south.

This maple produces excellent hardwood, famous fall color and the best maple syrup and sugar. "Tapping the sugar bush" is an industry and seasonal way of life in upstate New York, Vermont, Wisconsin, Ohio and Ontario. Many trees other than maples may be tapped for sap, but the happy combination of Sugar maples, cold frosty nights and warm, sunny days found in the Northeast yields the richest results. New York, Vermont, Wisconsin and West Virginia have all chosen this for their State Tree. Its stylized leaf is Canada's National Symbol. (But Alex Muir's *Maple Leaf Forever* was inspired in 1866 by a Silver maple leaf!)

Regarding fall color, Thoreau eloquently gives voice to our praise:

Little did the fathers of the town anticipate this brilliant success when they caused to be imported from further in the country some straight poles with the tops cut off, which they called sugar maple trees—and a neighboring merchant's clerk, as I remember, by way of jest planted beans about them. Yet these which were then jestingly called beanpoles are these days far the most beautiful objects noticeable in our streets. They are worth all and more than they have cost—though one of the selectmen did take the cold which occasioned his death in setting them out—if only because they have filled the open eyes of children with their rich color so unstintingly so many autumns. We will not ask them to yield us sugar in the spring, while they yield us so fair a prospect in the autumn. Wealth may be the inheritance of few in the houses, but it is equally distributed on the Common. All children alike can revel in this golden harvest. These trees, throughout the street, are at least equal to an annual festival and holiday, . . . and poor indeed must be that New England village's October which has not the maple in its streets. This October festival costs no powder nor ringing of bells, but every tree is a liberty-pole on which a thousand bright flags are run up. (*Journal*, October 18th, 1858)

Sugar maple has various subspecies, such as **Black Maple**, given specific status by some botanists (*A. nigrum* Michx. fil.). The largest dimensions recorded are 151' × 22½'. In Seattle, common. The Black maple cultivar '**Greencolumn**' has been used as a street-tree here since the 1990s. Few color poorly; the best assume their bright orange glowing garb late September–October. Please, don't tap any: our climate rarely has sufficient stretches of appropriate weather.

– 17th Ave E, south of E Roy St: a street-tree, W side, 81' × 12'2" × 73' wide
– Dunn Gardens: one that colors poorly is huge, 89' × 10'9¼"
– 225 14th Ave E: two street-trees, the larger 79' × 10'4½"
– 6744 Jones Ave NW: a street-tree, 72' × 10'2"
– Hiawatha Playfield: on the N end of the east side (with a Red maple S of it)
– Columbia School street-trees: 7 on S Ferdinand St, 2 on 35th Ave S
– U.W.: one 74' × 6'11½" N of Benson Hall; one 77' × 6'10¼" E of Hansee Hall; one SE of Thomson Hall; a narrow one 64' × 5'4½" NE of the Observatory
– Waters Ave S & S Roxbury St: SW corner yard
– Green Lake: a **Black maple** 63½' × 5'6" north of the east side children's play area
– 6315 22nd Ave NE: a street-tree

cv. '**Newton Sentry**' — Sentry Sugar Maple

Pencil-slim, almost ludicrously skinny. Few ascending branches, with several competing central leaders and stubby lateral branches. Extremely rare.

– Arboretum: south of Japanese Garden (0-B), #839-55 is 58' × 2'3"
– Denny Way, east of Dexter Ave N: 15 street-trees, the tallest 42' × 2'3½" × 6' wide

cv. '**Sweet Shadow**' — Cutleaf Sugar Maple

Deeply slashed leaves make this an elegant, distinctive tree; it is rare here.

– Arboretum: 60' × 3'4½" (#253-63 in 23-4W); 53' × 3'7½" (#253-63A in 23-5W)
– Safeco plaza at Brooklyn Ave NE & NE 45th St has five, 40–50' tall
– 610 17th Ave E (south of E Roy St): a street-tree 54½' tall
– 341 NE 90th St: a stout, very wide one 53½' tall
– 1111 15th Ave (north of E Spring St): a street-tree 52' tall, north of a Norway maple
– 4120 Palatine Ave N: 43' × 4'10" × 39' wide (1993)

Sycamore MAPLE

A. Pseudoplatanus L.
(A. Pseudo-platanus)
From Europe, W Asia.

Gray *or* English Harewood
Scottish *or* Scotch Plane
Great Maple

Known as the Sycamore in England. Americans, however, call it Sycamore maple because what we call Sycamore is another tree altogether (see PLANETREE). Sycamore maple grows larger in England than in America (to 132' × 27¾') though it is not native in either place. Dark, dull, of subdued autumn color (in rare years clear yellow). Not very ornamental nor of outstanding wood quality, yet widely planted for centuries, largely because Christians thought it the Biblical "Sycamore" that Zacchæus climbed to view Jesus. It signifies "curiosity" in the Language of Flowers. Very common here, and naturalized weedily.

– Volunteer Park: one 79' × 8'10" across the road NW of the bandstand
– S.P.U.: one NW of McKinley Hall is 90' × 6'11¼"
– Green Lake: *ca.* 90; one 74½' × 9'6" NW of the wading pool; a grove of 4 on the SE side, the largest 67' × 8'9½" (with 3 Wineleaf-Sycamore and 2 Norway Maples)
– E James St, east of Broadway: a street-tree, S side, 60' × 8'6"
– E Queen Anne Playground (2nd Ave N & Howe St): surrounding it
– Hiawatha Playfield: street-trees on the east side

cv. 'Atropurpureum' — Wineleaf Maple
='Spaethii'

In spring the leaves are green or faintly bronzish beneath, then gradually turn distinctly *purple* as the season progresses. (In contrast, purpleleaf Norway maple leaves are dark on both sides.) Common here.

– Stroud Ave N & N 80th St: the SE corner has one 71' tall and very stout
– 711 21st Ave E (north of E Roy St): two street-trees, the larger 71' × 8'7¼"
– Locks bed #127

cv. 'Erectum' — Pyramidal Sycamore Maple

Extremely rare. On Roosevelt Way NE between NE 50th and 47th St, *ca.* 12 City street-trees remain of the original 1970s planting. The trees are not markedly different than ordinary, but their branches are up and out the way of traffic.

cv. 'Prinz Handjery'

Extremely rare. Growth slow; effectively a dense dwarf. Besides topgrafting this clone, at least one nursery has sold its *seedlings*, observing that they "breed true." Similar to (and sometimes sold as) *A. Pseudoplatanus* '**Brilliantissimum**' (young leaves brilliant shrimp-pink, later pale yellow-green, finally dark green). Its emerging leaves are *reddish*, it develops a wider, less dense crown, and the leaves remain yellow-dotted above, and pale purplish beneath, all summer.

– Bellevue Botanic Garden (12001 Main St *in Bellevue*) has one *ca.* 14' tall
– 8009 38th Ave NE: a young tiny specimen that eventually will be worth a look
– SSCC Arboretum: a young tree labeled cv. '**Brilliantissimum**' in the Cœnosium

Rock Garden is 6' tall (I saw it only in *winter* so cannot confirm its i.d.)

f. *variegatum* (West.) Rehd.   Variegated Sycamore Maple

Under this name are grouped various seedlings and cultivars with yellowish or whitish variegation. They are extremely rare here. One 52' × 4'8½" × 41' wide is in the south part of Mt Pleasant Cemetery. A 4-trunked tree 34' tall is at 2324 Federal Ave E.

[*A. velutinum* Boiss.—Persian Maple—From the Caucasus. Like Sycamore maple but with large buds, larger leaves (to 12" wide, shallowly five-lobed; stem to 12" long) staying green late in fall, then turning brown or burnt orange. The leaf is hairy when young, but these hairs mostly fall away except on the veins. Recorded to 131' × 12⅓' in the wild. In Seattle, extremely rare: Arboretum #21-82A in the nursery's SE corner is 41½' × 2'½"; a young heavily pruned tree on NE corner of 19th Ave NW & NW 77th St.]

Tailed MAPLE

A. caudatum Wallich
From the Himalayas into NE Asia.

Only *one* specimen is known in the city, a street-tree at 7047 24th Ave NE, north of two rare pink-berried Mountain Ashes. It is remarkable for its long slender flower clusters. A small tree; recorded to 33' in the wild.

Tatarian MAPLE

A. tataricum L.   Tartarian Maple
From SE Europe, W Asia.   Tartar Maple

A shrub or small tree rarely to 50' × 5'. Its leaves may look less like those of "regular" maples than any other kind in this guide. Nor does it look a bit like a maple when it's flowering. But its winged seeds and bright yellow fall color are at once perfectly maple-like and showy. Tatarian and Amur maples are similar. Both bear delicately scented flowers in May. The Tatarian's leaves are wider, blunter, lighter green and less shiny. The Tatarian is rare here.

– Arboretum: an old 17' tall one at SE end of the Japanese Garden parking-lot
– Interlaken Park: 2 very old shrubs in the grassy areas west of the 26th Ave E bridge (the larger broader than its 19' height)
– Meridian Ave N, north of N 50th St: 6 street-trees *pl.* in 1990s, E side; tallest 27½'
– 36th Ave NE, south of NE 52nd St: 9 street-trees

A. tataricum ssp. *Ginnala* (Maxim.) Wesm.   Amur Maple
=*A. Ginnala* Maxim.   Siberian Maple
From Turkestan, China, Manchuria, E Siberia, Korea, Japan.

Common here, overplanted since the 1990s. A small and shrubby maple. Left to itself, it becomes a suckering bushy tree, as are most of Seattle's oldest specimens. More recently, nurseries have sold it trained into tree, or standard form. In any case, it is a colorful species, attaining at most about 49' × 9¼'. It flushes green *early* in spring, is glossy all summer, and turns rich red in autumn.

- 4260 NE 113th St (at Sand Point Way NE): one 24' × 5'5½" × 45' wide (1993)
- 38th Ave E & 38th Pl E: NE corner yard has one 30' tall and much wider
- U.W.: 1320 NE Campus Parkway has 3, tallest 31½' × 2'3"
- U.W. Friendship Grove, representing Bulgaria, 21½' × 3'4½"
- Brooklyn Ave NE, by University District Safeway store: 5 trained street-trees
- Seattle Center: Exhibition Hall landscape has one
- Zoo: Family Farm has one 22' tall
- 42nd Ave SW & SW Admiral Way: SW corner (Jack in the box restaraunt) has 4

Trident MAPLE

A. Buergerianum Miq. *(Buergeranum)*   Chinese: San-chio-feng
From China, Korea, and a *var.* in Taiwan.

Relatively well known and distinctive compared to most East Asian maples. It has 1½–3½" long, glossy, trilobed leaves and *shaggy* bark. Cultivars exist. It's usually less than 50' tall in cultivation; in Chinese forests it grows to 100' × 14'—unusually large for an East Asian maple. Uncommon, if not rare here.

- 1815 NE 58th St: a huge specimen 54' tall stands east of a green garage
- Mark Spencer Apartments (727 Bellevue Ave E): two, the larger 29½' × 3'5½"
- Arboretum: the largest is 43' × 2'9¾" (#79-55 in 11-3E)
- 25th Ave E, north of E Madison St: three over 40' tall on the W side
- U.W.: SE of Smith Hall; also one east of corporation yard 3 is 24' × 2'1"
- U.W. Sand Point Housing: opposite 6047 and 6337 NE 61st St
- Locks bed #17 has one 33' tall

Vine MAPLE

A. circinatum Pursh
Native here; from SW British Columbia to N California.

A popular, common, well known maple, native in Seattle woods and widely planted here. In the *woods* it is usually a multitrunked, very characteristic "octopus" form, with slender, silvery-gray-green trunks gracefully arching and bending in all directions, the leaves turning bright yellow in fall. *Open-grown* specimens planted in sunshine, and especially if in poor soil, tend to be stunted, burned, slower growing and reddish in the fall, nor is their bark so attractive. In short, Vine maple is happiest in woodland conditions. The largest dimensions recorded are only 63' × 5½'. Eight rare cultivars exist.

- Arboretum: one at the north edge of 15-2E is 31' × 3'10¼" and wider than tall
- Seattle Center Arena: tallest of a dozen against the east wall is 46' × 1'9"
- U.W.: 2 by west entrance of Harris Hydraulics Lab.

Vineleaf MAPLE

A. cissifolium (S.& Z.) K. Koch   Japanese: Mitsude Kaede ミツデカエデ
From Japan.

A mushroom-shaped tree with trifoliate leaves, dainty flowers, and the warm fall color we expect from maples. In nature the largest specimens are over 80' × 9¾'. It is very rare here.

- Arboretum: the largest is 41½' × 4'¾" #557-63 (one of three trees in 12-3E); 41' × 3'4¼" #587-49 is on Asian Maple hillside (26-B)
- U.W.: 37' × 3'8½" by the SW corner of Raitt Hall (near a 114' × 12'9" Douglas Fir)
- Canal Substation (8th Ave NW & NW 45th): 5 SW of bldg.; 1 at bldg.'s SE corner
- 2828 Boyer Ave E: two *clipped* specimens
- 2521 West Montlake Place E: a street-tree

MAYTEN TREE

Maytenus Boaria Mol.   Chilean Mayten
=*M. chilensis* DC.   Maiten Tree
CELASTRACEÆ   Spanish: Maitén
From Chile, Argentina.   Araucarian: Huripo

One of the finest-textured broadleaf evergreens that we can grow—a graceful, desirable ornamental even though its flowers are insignificant. It can attain 100' × 10½'. In Seattle, extremely rare. Slow to moderate in its growth rate; sometimes it suckers. The Arboretum has two forms: one with long, broad, pale leaves up to 2½" × 1" wide; the other with small, narrow and dark leaves. The latter, also present at the U.W. campus, is healthier and more attractive.

- U.W.: two west of the Oceanography Teaching Building, the largest 37½' × 3'2"; two stunted trees only 19' tall by Montlake Blvd NE at the southwest corner of parking lot E-1; a **Green Showers**™ in Mercer Hall courtyard
- Arboretum: tallest 28½' × 1'7¾" (#520-48A in 11-5E); #358-78 **Green Showers**™ measures 16' × 1'1" in 5-1E
- 3910 Whitman Ave N: a 3-trunked specimen
- Good Shepherd Center: one 11½' tall NW of main parking-lot

MEDLAR TREE

Mespilus germanica L.   Open-arse
=*Pyrus germanica* (L.) Hook. fil.   Hosedoup
ROSACEÆ   Medlar
From SE Europe to central Asia.

A quaint, awkward, humble aberration related to Hawthorn and Crabapple trees, In nature Medlar is thorny and small-fruited. Select cultivars bear pretty white flowers in May, and golfball sized luscious fruits, on thornless branches of picturesque irregularity. In either case the tree tends to grow horizontally and at the most reaches 59' × 6¼'. The odd fruit is comparable to rose hips: rock hard when unripe; when ripe soft, mushy, and yielding delicious applesauce if squeezed. They are brown in color, and flattened rather than round. Detractors liken the contents to diarrhea and several European names suggest as much. In Seattle, very rare and little known. The fruit is ready to eat from late October–late December. The Arboretum tree often accentuates its singularity by being so bold as to flower again from early October through mid-November—but these little blooms are fruitless.

- Arboretum: a #559-57 cv. '**Macrocarpa**' in 11-3W grafted on Common Hawthorn rootstock is 16½' × 3'5" × 34½' wide and is propped up by two 4 × 4s
- Seattle Center Fisher Pavilion: one at each end, east & west, grafted on hawthorn
- U.W. Medicinal Herb Garden: one grafted on hawthorn is N of Cascara Circle
- Meadowbrook Park's edible arboretum has cv. '**Bredasa Reus**' (Breda Giant)
- Twin Ponds Park: several in the NE part not far from the restrooms; tallest 17'
- E Calhoun St, east of 24th Ave E: 2 street-trees, N side

MONKEY TREE

Araucaria araucana (Mol.) K. Koch   Monkey-tail Tree
=*A. imbricata* Pav.   Monkey Puzzler
=*Pinus araucana* Mol.   Monkey Puzzle
ARAUCARIACEÆ   Puzzle Monkey
From S Chile, SW Argentina.   Chilean *or* Chile Pine

Thriving in the mild Pacific Northwest better than anywhere else in North America, our most common South American tree is well known because of its distinctive appearance. Cactus-like when young, in age it's somber, dark and almost ludicrous. Ferociously sharp leaves arm slender branches and earn it the appellation Monkey Puzzle—for to climb one is to risk painful scratches. Still, raccoons and squirrels sometimes attempt it.

Some trees are male, others female; extremely few bisexual. The large round 5–8" wide female cones break up when mature in late summer or fall, releasing big edible seeds tedious to husk but worth the effort. They are (or were) a staple crop, usually roasted, for the natives in Chile and Argentina. If a male tree is not near enough to pollinate the female, most of the husks will be hollow duds.

It has been officially protected in Chile since 1976. The largest sizes on record there are 165' × 25'. In England it has reached 95' × 13' so far, but is usually seen no more than 70' × 9½' and in Seattle not quite that big yet.

- 9th Ave NW & NW 60th St: the SE corner has a ♂ 65' tall
- Martin Luther King, Jr. Way S & S Yesler Way: SE corner has a 60' tall ♂
- U.W.: Denny Hall lawn has a ♀ 56½' × 7'1"
- Calvary Cemetery: a ♀ 55½' × 7'3¾" with a ♀ 51½' × 7'9¼" right beside her and a ♂ 52' × 7'1¾" a little to the west
- Good Shepherd Center: a ♀ east of the building is 55' × 7'7¾"
- 5284 44th Ave SW: a ♀ is 56½' × 7'7"
- 16th Ave E & E Roy St: NW corner has a 55' tall ♀ by the alley
- Othello Park (43rd Ave S & S Othello St): a ♂ in the N end is 53' × 5'11"
- 902 15th Ave E: a ♂ and a ♀ both *ca.* 52' tall
- Pratt Park (19th Ave S & S Main St): a ♂ is 45' × 7'4¼"

– Bhy Kracke Park (Bigelow Ave N & Comstock Pl): a ♀

[**Bunya-Bunya**—*A. Bidwillii* Hook.—From Australia. Extremely rare here, since it will die in a cold winter. It is common in California. The substation at 812 NE 75th St has one *ca.* 6' feet tall by an extremely rare *Furcræa* plant. Recorded to 174' tall in the wild.]

[**Paraná Pine**—*A. angustifolia* (Bertol.) Ktze.—From mountains of S Brazil, NE Argentina, and Paraguay. Extremely rare here. The garden at 4025 NE 110th St has one 9 years old, 5' tall. Others doubtless exist; it may be hardier than is commonly supposed; worth a try. When young it recalls a blue China-fir. Leaves rather broad despite the Latin specific name; with a glaucous bloom that can be rubbed off. Sharp and recurved, stiff, on older twigs. Forward-pointing and soft on young growth. Recorded to 115' × 14¼' in the wild.]

MOUNTAIN ASH & kin in general

The original Mountain Ash (*Sorbus aucuparia*) is one of our most abundant trees, widely planted and naturalized here. At least 18 cousins, uncommon to rare, also occur here, some without even book-coined English names. Those few with genuine English names are known to only a handful of Seattleites, so this guide treats the genus *Sorbus* alphabetically by scientific names. As a whole they're small, from shrub-sized to (rarely) 80' tall. All are deciduous; most display rich fall color. Creamy-white flowers of April to June, give rise to berries of varied colors and sizes, mostly unpalatable raw. Ten kinds in Seattle have pinnately-compound leaves, after the fashion of regular ash trees; 5 have alder-like leaves; 3 bear intermediate shaped ones. All prefer sunshine to shade. In Seattle, besides the Common Mountain Ash, only three *Sorbus* are not downright rare: *S. americana* (Red Cascade™ Mountain Ash) *S. Aria* (Whitebeam), and *S. hupehensis* (Hupeh Mountain-Ash). The Arboretum collection is of national importance.

Sorbus alnifolia (S.& Z.) K. Koch   Korean Mountain-Ash
ROSACEÆ   Dense-head Mountain-Ash
From China, Korea, Japan.   Alder Whitebeam

This species has a leaf 1–4" long rather like a Hornbeam (*Carpinus*). It is much appreciated in the eastern U.S. as an ornamental, and the tallest can reach 70'. Though rare here, its presence in the wholesale nursery trade bodes well.

– Substation on NW Market St, west of 28th Ave NW
– Bitter Lake Park (Linden Ave N & N 130th St): 2 at E corners; best 28' × 3'2"
– 6734 Cleopatra Ave NW
– Green Lake: one on the SW strip below Woodland Park is 27½' × 1'10½"
– Arboretum: : #49-94A in nursery is 1'4½" around; #42-93 in 21-5E is smaller
– 1217 21st Ave E: two street-trees
– 11th Ave W & W Armour St: 2 in traffic circle
– U.W.: one 26' × 1'1½" west of Fluke Hall
– Martin Luther King, Jr. Park: 6 *pl.* in the north part in 1988

S. americana Marsh. American Mountain-Ash
From NE North America. Roundwood / Missey-moosey

Like Common mountain ash, but smaller, more slender in form and leaf, with tiny flowers in denser clusters, and smaller berries. The maximum sizes reported are 71' × 3'6" and 42' × 7'11". It usually turns yellow in autumn. *S. tianschanica* **Red Cascade**™ ('Dwarfcrown') of nurseries is really an American clone.

– Arboretum: 2 ordinary specimens in 25-6E; *all* others in Seattle are **Red Cascade**™
– 8318 27th Ave NW: 3 street-trees
– 37th Pl S, north of S Hanford St: many street-trees
– Montlake School: 5 street-trees on 22nd Ave E (*pl.* spring 2004)
– 929 Broadway E: a street-tree
– 7073 25th Ave NE: a street-tree

S. anglica Hedl. Anglican Whitebeam
From SW England, Wales, SW Ireland.

A small shrubby tree like a dwarf Swedish Whitebeam (*S. intermedia*). Known here as follows: two at the Arboretum in 20-4E & 21-4E (#1182-50; the larger 35' × 2'7"); on the U.W. campus one 20' × 3'1" is south of parking lot E-11.

S. Aria (L.) Crantz White Beam (Tree)
=*Cratægus Aria* L. White-leaf Tree / Lote Tree
=*Pyrus Aria* (L.) Ehrh. Sea-Ouler / (Red) Chess-Apple
From Europe, N Africa. Cumberland Haw

Whitebeam signifies "concord" in the Language of Flowers; its alder-like leaves are cottony-white on the underside. It can grow to 80' × 9'. Cultivars include: 'Lutescens', 'Magnifica' and 'Majestica'. Uncommon.

– Arboretum: #1227-50A is 1'6¾" around (22-5E); #232-59 is 49' × 4'4¼" (21-4E); f. *longifolia* #445-52B is 47' × 3'9½" (14-5E); '**Lutescens**' #83-58 is 47½' × 3'½" (20-5E); '**Salicifolia**' #72-72 is 2'6¼" around (20-4E)
– Virginia Mason Hospital (925 Seneca St): one 46' × 3'6¾" by Terry Ave & Seneca
– 32nd Ave W, from W McGraw to Smith St: 1 City street-tree of cv. 'Lutescens' on the east side, and 2 larger on the west side
– Federal Ave E & E Blaine St: SE corner has 6 street-trees
– E Yesler Way, west of 18th Ave: 2 street-trees, S side
– E Mercer St, west of 36th Ave E: s street-trees, N side
– 34th Ave E, just north of E Mercer St: a street-tree, W side
– 3617 47th Ave NE: 2 in yard
– U.W.: N of Hutchinson Hall

S. × *arnoldiana* Rehd. Pinkberry Mountain-Ash
=(?) *S. aucuparia* × *S. discolor*

Of uncertain origin, 1907. In effect, a pink-berried Common mountain ash.

– 58th Ave NE & NE 65th St: NW corner has 1 by the sidewalk by an Alaska Cedar
– Arboretum: three in 24-3E all died or were killed (as with specimens at the U.W.)

S. aucuparia L. Common *or* European Mountain-Ash

=*Pyrus aucuparia* (L.) Gaertn. Witchen Tree *or* Witchwood

From Europe, N Africa, Rowan *or* Roan / Quickbeam *or* Quicken

W Asia, Siberia. Fowler's Service Tree

Called *Mountain Ash* because it is found higher in the Scottish Highlands than any other tree, particularly the lowland-loving Common Ash (*Fraxinus excelsior*), which is similar in leaf shape and in its light-colored, medium-weight, versatile wood. Called *Rowan* for its red berries and maybe for its autumn color. In remote times it was not grown merely for ornament as it is nowadays, but for fending off evil: it's rich in superstitious lore, especially in Scotland and Wales. It signifies "prudence" in the Language of Flowers.

Note how various professions may focus on mountain ash. *Antiquaries* delve into musty archives to find out which Scottish clan used the tree as a symbol, which clan dyed plaids with its bold colors, which landmarks were named after it. *Artists* strive to capture its cherry-like bark, scarlet berries and well-proportioned foliage, to somehow create an inspiring image, or at least a recognizable impression of the tree, capable of awakening memories and touching us with their dexterous interpretation of its charms. *Botanists* describe it minutely, noting number of stamens, color of anthers, arrangement of carpels, pubescence of sepals, and serrations of margins, so as to classify it in relation to the other 80–100 (200) species of *Sorbus*. *Druggists* extract sorbitol from the berries, to use in confectionery, pharmaceuticals and such. *Ecologists* study its natural history, to find out why it grows in higher elevations than other British trees, and why its bountiful offspring are seeded by birds so far and wide. *Economists* leave no stone unturned (or leaf!), to discover practical uses, especially profitable ones, focusing primarily on its wood and berries. *Folklorists* collect, collate, digest, interpret, and present in orderly fashion all of the surviving oral traditions, myths, jokes, crafts, customs and beliefs, explaining among other things why it is supposed to repel evil. *Gardeners* clean up and prune, doing everything necessary to keep it healthy, happy and good-looking. *Geologists* think that mountain ash is something spewed forth in volcanic eruptions, and are more interested in the tree's fossilized remains than in its living contemporaries. *Herbalists* gather its potent parts, prepare remedies for diarrhea, scurvy or other such ills as can be cured by their decoctions, ointments, powders, essences and the like. *Landscape Architects* advise exactly where to plant it for optimal effect. *Lawyers* may not know the tree from an oak or a cedar, but will be available for counsel at standard rates when somebody slips on the fallen berries, or when an old tree falls on a car. *Novelists* skillfully weave words, euphoniously evoking vivid imagery, using the tree symbolically to striking effect, or in subtle suggestion if they deem it meet. *Nurserymen* supply it in any size, any quantity, wholesale or retail, in a number of select grafted cultivars, such as 'Cardinal Royal', 'Columbia Queen' and 'Black Hawk'. *Pedants* claim that it's not a "true" ash and demand that a dash be used in writing its name. *Philologists* don't care what it's called; they collect and classify all the dozens of European folk names given it, trace the roots and provenance thereof, and check to see if any Asian or African counterparts exist. *Poets* listen to what the tree has to say, reflect upon the message, then give it eloquent voice, deriving pleasure from sharing it with us, from articulating the breathing, quiet life that we call Mountain Ash. And *Witches and Warlocks* flee or revere it—depending on which tradition they follow.

In Seattle, very common. Short-lived as it is, many older ones are rotting and dying. In wooded parks, it's frequently seen multitrunked, suckering from the base and from trunk burrs. The greatest height (85') and stoutest trunk (11'2½") for this species were both recorded here in Washington.

- Washelli Cemetery: the largest is 44½' × 10'½" × 47' wide but it is dying
- Locks bed #16 (2; multitrunked), 102 (N end; multitrunked), 203 (big; 2-trunked)
- Green Lake: many; plus a large-berried (to ⅝" wide) manifestation on the NE shore
- Condon Way W & W Newton St: an old big tree
- Zoo: Rose garden's SW corner has one 56' × 7'0"
- U.W.: an old small multi-trunked tree between Hutchinson Hall and tennis courts
- U.W. Friendship Grove, representing Czechoslovakia
- Stone Ave N, south of 96th St: 6 street-trees that *may* be cv. 'Cardinal Royal'

cv. '**Fastigiata**'   Fastigiate *or* Columnar Mountain-Ash

More than one cultivar is slender and upright, especially while young. The test is how well they hold their slimness in advanced age: those that do can be called by this name if one does not limit it to a single clone.

- 6th Ave NW & NW 48th St: SE corner, in the back yard
- 5910 Latona Ave NE: one 41' tall
- 6511 5th Ave NE: one of two here is amazingly fastigiate

S. domestica L.   The True Service
=*Pyrus domestica* (L.) Sm.   Whitty Pear Tree
=*Pyrus Sorbus* Gaertn.   The Sorb Tree
From S & E Europe, N Africa, SW Asia.   Service Tree

Unlike all our other *Sorbus*, this has rough, rugged bark and relatively large (to 1½" long), somewhat pear-shaped fruit that is edible raw when half rotten and soft in texture like a ripe medlar or persimmon. It is among the largest of its genus, able to surpass 80' × 14¾'. The Arboretum has three in 36-4E raised from Yugoslavian seeds in 1949. The tallest is 79' × 5'¼" and the largest 77½' × 6'0". Sunnyside Ave N, south of Woodlawn Ave N (*i.e.* north of N 65th St), has a street-tree 46½' × 5'3½" on the east side. No others are known here.

S. Folgneri (Schneid.) Rehd. **hybrid**   Hybrid Chinese Whitebeam

Sorbus Folgneri is a Chinese species (to 60' × 6½') known here only as *hybrids* (that may not be identical). Arboretum #130-74 in 21-4E is 33' × 1'11¼" and has some viable seeds. A second is 27' × 2'7" × 31½' wide at the Locks in bed #29 (with a 5' one): it flushes very early, has long large leaves with a whitish underside, creamy-white, strongly fragrant flowers in May, *seedless* orangeish berries, and late, pretty autumn color.

S. Forrestii McAll. & Gillh.   Forrest's Whiteberry Mountain-Ash
From SW China.

A tree named in 1980; too little known to be in the *Flora of China*. Reported to 40' tall, with 11–19 leaflets, and white berries. Seattle specimens were previously confused with *S. Prattii*. Three are at the Arboretum in 24-4E (best 16' × 2'3¼" #1084-45A), and three *pl.* 1992 on Green Lake's NE shore.

S. hupehensis Schneid.   Hupeh Mountain-Ash
From China.   Chinese: Hu Bei Hua Qiu

Reported up to 50' × 5', but mostly bushy in our specimens [some of which may be the very closely related *S. oligodonta* (Cardot) Hand.-Mazz.]. Leaflets (9) 13–15 (17), berries snow white or pink, *ca.* ⅓" wide, held on the naked twigs into December. Since 1990 the cv. '**Pink Pagoda**' has been sold here; '**Coral Fire**' with darker pink berries, arrived a few years later.

– Arboretum: #519-47A in 24-4E is 31½' × 3'3½"; #63-94A in 23-4E is smaller
– Boren Ave N, north of Denny Way: 2 small yet old street-trees, E side
– Seattle Center: north of Northwest Rooms, east of Warren Ave N, 15' tall
– 2112 N 36th St: a street-tree
– E Roy St, west of 27th Ave E: 3 street-trees, south side
– Corliss Ave N & N 64th St: NW corner has 5 street-trees
– 7419 34th Ave NW
– Dunn Gardens: a tree 18' tall SW of the house may be a *hupehensis;* if not it is similar; it was raised from Chinese seeds and donated by Dan Hinkley
– U.W.: one 11' tall by Montlake Blvd NE southwest of parking lot E-1
– 1820 E Lynn St
– Locks bed #114

S. intermedia (Ehrh.) Pers.   Swedish Whitebeam
=*Pyrus intermedia* Ehrh.   Swedish: oxel
From N Europe.

A handsome tree attaining over 75' × 13'. Its leaf shape is somewhat "intermediate" (as the name indicates) between those of the Common mountain ash and Whitebeam. Red berries ½" in diameter look like tiny tomatoes, and are sweet and edible in October. The tree is rare here; it occasionally reseeds.

– 9th Ave W, south of W Barrett St: a street-tree, E side, *ca.* 25' × 7'1" (under wires)
– Lowell School Playground/parking lot (1058 E Mercer St): one 40' × 5'1"
– Arboretum: #161-60A in 22-5E is 40' × 4'1½"
– 5607 NE Keswick Dr: one 36' tall right next to the house
– U.W.: one 34' × 4'3" NE of Thomson Hall
– 13215 Linden Ave N: 4 near the sidewalk
– Fairview School (Roosevelt Way NE & NE 78th St): 26' tall on the S side

S. × *latifolia* (Lam.) Pers., s.l.　　　　　Service Tree of Fontainebleau
From Europe.　　　　　　　　　　　　　　Cornish Whitebeam

Likely a hybrid between *S. Aria* and *S. torminalis* (L.) Crantz, but its origin and affinities are cloudy. Under this broad heading can be placed dozens of "microspecies" very local in parts of Europe. One such is *S. devoniensis* E.F. Warb., from SW England and SE Ireland. Insofar as our Arboretum trees labeled *S. latifolia* and *S. devoniensis* are virtually indistinguishable, as are the few other Seattle trees that look like either, they are lumped together under the better known and older name. They make handsome, vigorous trees, and can grow to 75' × 11'. The berries are orange-brown, speckled, against golden October leaves.

– Arboretum: two "latifolia" (#1489-45 in 22-5E), the larger 54½' × 4'1"; three "devoniensis" (#565-64, 820-50, X-50), the larger 62½' × 4'8½"—all in 22-5E
– Colman Park: one 50½' × 3'4" by the roadside giant Leyland Cypress

S. pallescens Rehd.　　　　　　　　　　Chinese Whitebeam
From W China.　　　　　　　　　　　Chinese: Hui Ye Hua Qiu

A close kin of *S. Aria.* Leaves to 6¼" × 3½", both sides hairy when young. Berries to ¾" wide, white—red on sunny side with pale specks. Recorded to 52' × 6'.

– Arboretum: #550-90 in 20-4E is 23' × 11¼"; #545-90A & B are 2 street-trees on 26th Ave E by E McGraw St, the taller 15'
– U.W.: CUH has three #545-90, largest 27' × 2'6½"

S. Prattii Koehne　　　　　　　　　　Pratt's Mountain-Ash
From W China.　　　　　　　　　Chinese: Si Kang Hua Qiu

A large shrub or small tree to 25' tall, with white (a tinge of pink sometimes) ¼–⅜" wide berries. Leaf to 5½" long; leaflets 21–33; yellowish fall color. Much confused with *S. Forrestii.*

– Arboretum: #1084-45 in 36-1E is 29½' × 1'1½"; #415-90A in 25-4E is 10' tall
– 1115 41st Ave E: in front yard behind the hedge
– 7519 22nd Ave NW: back yard has one 9' tall—hard to see from the alley
– Good Shepherd Center: a youngster by the NE parking-lot

S. Rehderiana Koehne　　　　　　　　Rehder's Mountain-Ash
From W China and Tibet.　　　　　Chinese: Xi Nan Hua Qiu

A small, slender tree, late to bloom, with small long-lasting berries of various colors: pink, yellow or creamy-white. Rust-colored hairs on the buds, young shoots and leaves (of 15–19 leaflets). Berries pale with age. *S.* '**Joseph Rock**' is likely a variant of it. The trees cited below are not uniform, but similar.

– Arboretum: #542-57 in 23-4E is 35' × 1'11½"; #258-48A in 25-4E is 18' (3-trunks); 'Joseph Rock' #73-94A in 24-4E is 21' tall
– Locks bed #113 (by #112), and #121 (grafted on *S. aucuparia*)
– Dunn Gardens: a 'Joseph Rock' is 21' tall
– 1216 20th Ave E: 2 street-trees, not wholly healthy
– 7047 24th Ave NE: 2 street-trees, pink-fruited

- 3051 44th Ave W: 3 street-trees
- Good Shepherd Center: a pale yellow berried Nat'l Arboretum *"S. discolor"* seedling NE of the bldg. is either *Rehderiana* or more like it than *S. discolor*

S. Sargentiana Koehne   Sargent's Mountain-Ash
From W China.   Chinese: Wan Xiu Hua Qiu

Bold *large* leaves, to 13" long; of (7) 9–11 (13) leaflets, the largest up to 6" × 1⅞" (terminal one smallest), sharp-toothed; buds red, glossy, huge and sticky. Fall color late but spectacular (usually red). Berries tiny, in enormous clusters of sometimes over 200. A grafted, unnamed clone tends to grow slowly into a broad, low tree. Recorded to 42' × 5¼'. Known here only as follows.

- Arboretum: #258-90 on Azalea Way in 35-1W is 15' tall
- 2601 NW 59th St: one in the NE corner of the lot is 12½' tall

S. sitchensis Roem.   Sitka Mountain-Ash
From SW Alaska to California, Montana & Alberta.

A shrubby native of NW mountains. It has stout twigs and 7–11 broad leaflets. Magnuson Park's Community Garden east border has a few youngsters.

S. × *thuringiaca* (Ilse) Fritsch   Bastard Service-Tree
From W & C Europe.   Finnish Whitebeam

A hybrid between Common mountain ash and Whitebeam, with the leaves clearly intermediate. It has been recorded to 72' × 9¾'. Often confused with a species not known here except at the Arboretum, *S.* × *hybrida* L.—broader leaves, larger, rounder and redder berries.

- Calvary Cemetery: a giant old and senescent tree is 33½' × 9'6" × 41' wide
- Arboretum: cv. 'Fastigiata' is 37' × 4'5½"—#722-67 north of the nursery fence
- SW Admiral Way, south of SW Olga St: a street-tree on the east side
- Meridian Ave N, south of N 55th St: 2
- Laurelhurst School: at least 3
- NW 80th St, W of 24th Ave NW: many street-trees on the S side *pl.* 1992
- 7520 Earl Ave NW: 2 street-trees

S. tianschanica Rupr. *(tianshanica)*   Turkestan Mountain-Ash
From Kashmir, Afghanistan and Turkestan.

A small tree to 25' tall with glossy dark-green foliage. One from Hillier's nursery in England was planted at the Arboretum in 1955, but died. A grafted, unhealthy one is 19' tall at the Locks in bed #3. So called *S. tianschanica* **Red Cascade**™ really is a clone of *S. americana* (which see).

[**Hybrid Mountain-Ash**—× *Sorbaronia fallax* (Schneid.) Schneid. *(Sorbus aucuparia × Aronia melanocarpa)*—**Ivan's Beauty**™ was named and sold in the 1990s but originated decades ago. Leaves partly compound, to 5" × 3". Fruit wine-purple, blueberry sized, edible. Montlake School has one 14' tall, *pl. ca.* 1997. Meadowbrook Park's edible arboretum has one 13' tall, *pl.* 1997. The Arboretum has × *Sorbaronia hybrida* (Moench) Schneid. *(Sorbus aucuparia × Aronia arbutifolia)* **'Brilliantisssima'** 15½' × 1'5½"—#683-67 in 25-5E.]

Black MULBERRY TREE

Morus nigra L.
MORACEÆ
From central Asia.

(not our) Common Mulberry Tree
Persian Mulberry Tree

Extremely rare here: a few of us prize its berries: dark purplish-black, plump, juicy, from June into October. A rugged little tree, at most 52' × 10'. Leaves rarely lobed; 3–7" long, roundish overall, dark and glossy above, fuzzy beneath. Both examples cited below were grafted on White mulberry trunks—*not* good.

– NE 61st St, west of Brooklyn Ave NE: a 9' tall street-tree, N side
– NW 80th St, just east of 14th Ave NW: a 22' tall street-tree, N side (a Lodgepole Pine to its east)

Paper MULBERRY TREE

Broussonetia papyrifera (L.) L'Hér. *ex* Vent.
=*Morus papyrifera* L.
From China, Taiwan, Japan, the Ryukyus.

Tapa-Cloth Tree
Chinese: Gou Shu, Ch'ou Shu
Ku Shu *or* Kou Shu
Japanese: Kaji-no-ki カジノキ

Grown in parts of SE Asia for its bark, made into a kind of paper used for umbrellas, lanterns, cords, tapes, scrolls; and pounded into a cloth called *tapa*. In warm climates, it reaches 66' × 13¾'; in cold northern lands it is smaller or even shrubby. Females yield edible round fruit. Root-suckers bear deeply lobed, jagged, eye-catching leaves. In Seattle, extremely rare: all attempts—save one—to grow it have failed; it is weak here, apparently despondent in our cool climate.

– 4611 Eastern Ave N: the north edge of the yard (by the alley) has a suckering male

White MULBERRY TREE

M. alba L. s.l.
=*M. australis* Poir.
=*M. bombycis* Koidz.
From India, China, Korea, Japan, *etc.*

Silkworm Mulberry Tree
Chinese: Sang
Japanese: Kuwa *or* Guwa クワ

Largest of temperate zone mulberry trees—to 100' × 23'. It signifies "wisdom" in the Language of Flowers. The silk industry depends on it, as its leaves are the only food for the little green silkworm whose secretions we weave into luxurious, valuable fabric. A highly variable tree: different strains serve for silk production, for berry production, for resistance to cold; and ornamental selections such as weeping mop-head form, striking cut-leaved foliage, and dwarf size have also been isolated. Individual trees are usually either male or female. Non-fruiting males such as the cultivars '**Kingan**' and '**Stribling**' make fast-growing, broad spreading shade and street-trees—but they are brittle and their pollen hurts some people. All these various White mulberries turn yellow in autumn, and hate shade. Most grow fast and have at least some leaves that are conspicuously *irregularly lobed.*

The berries look like small blackberries, are sweet but bland, and when ripe may be anything from *white* through *pink* to *red* or *darkest purple*, not totally black until they shrivel up. They ripen late June through mid-September. Like mulberries in general they're notorious for leaving dark, persistent stains.

White mulberry is common here. It loves our climate but is not in turn loved by most of us. Some consider it coarse, others call it messy, and many think it strictly for the birds. In fact the berries are good for people as well as for wildlife, and the young shoots and leaves may even be steamed for greens. It makes a durable, attractive ornamental and has not been tiresomely overplanted here.

The examples cited below include the small-leaved, small-berried "Russian" or "Tatarian" forms often planted to attract birds, as well as regular seedlings.

- U.W.: a ♂ west of the old Drama/TV Building is 52' × 9'1" × 55' wide
- 15th Ave & E Olive St: NW corner lot has very large one in the back
- Jefferson Park: one on the golf course is 50' × 5'7"
- 2622 Franklin Ave E: 2 street-trees, a ♂ to the N (7'¼" around), and a ♀ to the S
- 5th Ave NW & NW 56th St: SW corner has a multitrunked 34' tall ♀
- Leary Way NW, northwest of 6th Ave NW: a 34½' × 4'½" ♀ street-tree (with Red Sunset™ Red Maples) by the #28 bus-stop, E side
- 1018 23rd Ave E: 35' tall

cv. 'Pendula'   (Teas') Weeping White Mulberry Tree

A small, top-grafted weeping mop-head. As weeping as any tree grown here; almost no horizontal or upright tendency. More common than the regular kind; our most abundant mulberry tree. 'Chaparral' is a *fruitless* version.

- Calvary Cemetery: two in the SE part, the larger 12¾' × 4'4" × 17' wide
- 8311 16th Ave NW: a 14½' tall street-tree
- 23rd Ave E & E Prospect St: a 11' tall street-tree, E side
- Kubota Garden Park: some on the east side (with Camperdown Elms)
- LDS Church at 8th Ave NE & NE 57th St
- 2544 NE 143rd St: 12' tall
- 43rd Ave NE & NE 80th St: NE corner yard has one by the driveway
- 4405 SW Holgate St: a street-tree 9' tall
- 3821 E Galer St: 4 street-trees of the fruitless 'Chaparral'

cv. 'Unryu' (Unruyu)   Twisted *or* Contorted Mulberry Tree
=*M. alba* 'Contorta' *or* 'Tortuosa'   Zig-zag Mulberry Tree
=*M. latifolia* 'Spirata'

From Japan. Uncommon. A broad shrubby tree with *zig-zag* branches. Leaf to 10" × 8¼"; stem to 2¼" long; unlobed but not flat; semi-glossy above. Spring catkins up to 1¾" long, inconspicuous. Berries few, small.

- Arboretum #120-79 is 23½' tall × 35' wide in 36-3E
- Good Shepherd Center: one west of the building is 10' tall × 19½' wide
- 4th Ave NW, north of NW 58th St: one on the E side

– 1707 S Main St

[**Hybrid Mulberry**—*M. alba* × *M. rubra* 'Illinois Everbearing' is grown rarely, not as an ornamental but for its edible black berries, available from June into September. It looks much like *M. alba;* the leaves are rarely lobed, and usually no more than 6" × 4". One is south of the house on the NW corner of 5th Ave NE & NE 90th St.]

Oregon MYRTLE

Umbellularia californica (H.& A.) Nutt.   California (Bay) Laurel
=*Laurus regia* Dougl.   California Olive *or* Sassafras
LAURACEÆ   Pepperwood / Pacific Myrtle
From SW Oregon through California.   Spice Tree / Headache Tree

A broadleaf evergreen that can attain 175' × 41¾'. In looks laurel-like, in wood myrtle-like, in odor bay-like. Possibly excepting Cascara no other Pacific Coast native tree has so many local names. No tree in a much larger area has wood so valuable as to support a sizable specialized trade in it. No tree mentioned in this guide has a stronger odor: the penetrating pungency of its bruised leaves can cause pain or dizziness if deeply inhaled. Indians harvested the large marble-sized fruit (ripe from September–October), roasting the seeds. An article on it is in the *Arboretum Bulletin,* Fall 1971. See also Bay LAUREL.

Common and reseeds weedily here. Very shade tolerant. Open-grown examples are broad and round-topped, very dense when healthy.

– Arboretum: 19-2E has #1450-37 86' × 5'3" (largest of 3 trunks), and one in 20-3E measures 9'8" around the base of a 4-trunked specimen
– one only *ca.* 65' tall yet massive-trunked is visible in the alley of the block bounded by 35th & 36th Avenues and E Olive & Pine Streets
– University Heights Center (5031 University Way NE): one 73' × 11'1" *pl. ca.* 1906
– 1728 13th Ave S (north of S Grand St): one 52½' tall
– Zoo: by N 57th St overpass at Phinney Ave
– Latona Ave NE & NE 88th St: a broad specimen 41' tall
– 2126 Dexter Ave N: in back yard
– Locks bed #17, 121 (wild), 211 (near #210; 2-trunked)

[**Orangebark** *or* **Chilean Myrtle. Temu Tree**—*Luma apiculata* (DC.) Burret = *Myrtus Luma* auct.—in the MYRTACEÆ. A Chilean/Argentinian shrub or tree to 65' tall. Lovely orange bark. Leaves evergreen, paired, aromatic, ½–1⅞" long. Puffy little white flowers give rise to shiny black edible berries in late summer/fall. Cold-sensitive but tried in Seattle since the late 1980s; rare. Good Shepherd Center: 14' tall N of the shed, 10' tall S of the garage. Zoo: 7 or more in Australasia, the tallest 11'. Arboretum #59-00A is multitrunked in Loderi Valley (28-2E); one 13½' tall is on the stairway uphill E of the stone cottage.]

California NUTMEG TREE

Torreya californica Torr.   California Torreya
= *Tumion californicum* (Torr.) Greene   Stinking Cedar
TAXACEÆ   Stinking Yew
From central California.

A little known yew-like tree highly prized for its wood. Crushing the very stiff sharp 1–2 (3½)" needles makes them "stink." The tallest ever recorded (near Mendocino) was 141' × 14'10" in 1944—it was cut down illegally in 1982 when 250 years old, for the sake of its precious wood. Neither this species nor its Japanese relative should be confused with the unrelated tropical tree that yields the spices nutmeg and mace. In Seattle, extremely rare. Youngsters (#388-78) are at the Arboretum in 40-4W, 39-4W, and N of the nursery; the tallest 22'. The U.W. Botany Greenhouse has it. Some at the Locks died in 2004. Kruckeberg Botanic Garden in Shoreline, just N of Seattle, has one 30' × 3'4" (2003).

Japanese NUTMEG TREE

T. nucifera (L.) S.& Z.   Japanese Torreya
From Japan, Korea.   Japanese: Kaya カヤ

A shade-tolerant, often shrubby conifer with dark, glossy, hard, sharp-pointed needles ¾–1¼ (1½)" long, sweet-smelling when crushed; and (if pollinated) an edible seed rich in oil. The tree can attain 115' × 24¼'. It is very rare here.

- Ashworth Ave N & N 43rd St: the SW corner has a ♂ 42' tall, over 8'0" around a basal trunk that gives rise to three 1' thick trunks, rising as high as they can before being periodically chain-sawed by the utility-line crews; it is about 95 years old; the previous owner told lineworkers she'd rather they cut the wires than the tree, but her plea was ignored; with it is are two Umbrella-Pines and a Yew-Pine
- 4625 Eastern Ave N: a slender ♂ 23' tall at the alley intersection
- Arboretum: a shaded slender small tree in 18-2E is 22½' × 1'3½"

OAKS in general

The oak, both in Europe and America, is the most majestic of forest trees. It has been represented . . . as holding the same rank among the plants of the temperate hemispheres that the lion does among the quadrupeds, and the eagle among birds; that is to say, it is the emblem of grandeur, strength, and duration; of force that resists, as the lion is of force that acts. In short, its bulk, its longevity, and the extraordinary strength and durability of its timber, attest its superiority over all other trees, for buildings that are intended to be of great duration, and for the construction of ships. In one word, it is the king of forest trees. (Loudon, p. 1717)

Oaks have been the most important trees in Western civilization. Their value in dollars and cents is now eclipsed by many other things, including fast foods and fashionable clothing, but when we realize the distinction between luxurious frills and the bare necessities of existence, it is clear that no amount of silver or gold is as valuable (*i.e.*, useful) as an oak forest. Over 500 species of *Quercus* exist. A selection of names applied to some suggests their variety: Bamboo-leaf oak, Chestnut oak, Holly oak, Laurel oak, Silverleaf oak, Willow oak. Many are evergreen. The only constant, easily seen feature is the acorn (from "ac cern" = oak corn). Many peoples used to depend on them, as countless birds and beasts still do.

Seattle is anomalous in the temperate northern hemisphere, in having only one native oak, and not an abundant one at that. But there are 49 non-natives here, not including 5 hybrids, plus *ca.* 20 more species only at the Arboretum. An article about the 5 most common oaks in Seattle (English, Pin, Red, Scarlet, and Oregon White) is in the *Arboretum Bulletin*, Summer 1983. Our future may hold Sudden Oak Death syndrome—in California and S Oregon since 1995, it is a fungal pathogen *(Phytophthora ramorum)*, recalling Dutch Elm Disease and other fatal scourges. It has killed tens of thousands of California Black oaks, California Live oaks, and Tan oaks.

Here is the geographic division of the oaks treated in this guide:

ASIAN (9)

Bamboo-leaf *(Q. myrsinæfolia)*	Chinese Cork *(Q. variabilis)*
Daimyo *(Q. dentata)*	Konara Oak *(Q. glandulifera)*
Mongolian *(Q. mongolica)*	Oriental White *(Q. aliena)*
Ring-cupped *(Q. glauca)*	Sawtooth *(Q. acutissima)*
Ubame *(Q. phillyræoides)*	

EUROPEAN (9)

Armenian *(Q. pontica)*	Cork *(Q. Suber)*
Cork *hybrid (Q. Cerris* × *Q. Suber)*	Durmast *(Q. petræa)*
English *(Q. robur)*	English *hybrid*
Holm *(Q. Ilex)*	Hungarian *(Q. Frainetto)*
Turkish *(Q. Cerris)*	

EAST NORTH AMERICAN (20)

Bartram *(Q.* × *heterophylla)*	Black *(Q. velutina)*
Bur *(Q. macrocarpa)*	Chestnut *(Q. Prinus)*
Chinquapin *(Q. Muhlenbergii)*	Laurel *(Q. laurifolia)*
Laurel *hybrid*	Live *(Q. virginiana)*
Pin *(Q. palustris)*	Post *(Q. stellata)*
Red *(Q. rubra)*	Scarlet *(Q. coccinea)*
Shingle *(Q. imbricaria)*	Shumard Red *(Q. Shumardii)*
Southern Red *(Q. falcata)*	Swamp White *(Q. bicolor)*
Water *(Q. nigra)*	White *(Q. alba)*
White *hybrid*	Willow *(Q. Phellos)*

WEST NORTH AMERICAN (17)

Arizona White *(Q. arizonica)*	Blue *(Q. Douglasii)*
California Black *(Q. Kelloggii)*	California Live *(Q. agrifolia)*
California Valley *(Q. lobata)*	Canyon Live *(Q. chrysolepis)*

Huckleberry *(Q. vacciniifolia)*
Leather *(Q. durata)*
Mexican *(Q. salicifolia)*
Mexican *(Q. obtusata)*
Oregon White *(Q. Garryana)*
Silverleaf *(Q. hypoleucoides)*

Interior Live *(Q. Wislizeni)*
Mexican *(Q. mexicana)*
Mexican *(Q. viminea)*
Netleaf *(Q. rugosa)*
Rocky Mt White *(Q. Gambelii)*

Total: 55 species and hybrids

[**Tan Oak** *(Lithocarpus densiflorus)* is with Chinquapin & kin]

[**Poison Oak** *(Rhus diversiloba)* is a native shrub or vine best seen at Seward Park, where some have crept 50' into trees]

Arizona White OAK

Quercus arizonica Sarg.
FAGACEÆ
From Arizona, New Mexico, Texas, Mexico.

Arizona Live Oak
Arizona Oak

A broadleaf evergreen, to 60' × 12½' at most. It is extremely rare here, and can be easily confused with a species known here only at the Arboretum: Gray oak (*Q. grisea* Liebm.). Sorting these two is difficult. The Arizona leaf undersides are more obviously *veiny*. The two species hybridize in parts of Texas.

– Arboretum: #518-62C in 44-2E is 29' × 1'½"; #518-62B is 21' tall 2-trunked in 35-2W; a 3rd #518-62 is 34' × 1'1" in 14-5E; (*Q. grisea* is #550-62 in the rockery 1S-4E)
– Locks bed #202 has an 18' tall leaning specimen of appealing beauty
– U.W.: one 19' × 2'0" in the shrubbery by the bicycle racks N of Kane Hall
– Good Shepherd Center: one 17' tall NW of the building is the southernmost of a row of 5 evergreen oaks, the specific identity of which remains unknown
– 46th Ave NE & NE 97th St: one in the SW corner garden

Armenian OAK

Q. pontica K. Koch
From NE Turkey to the Caucasus.

Shrubby—to 35' tall. Tardily deciduous chestnut-like leaves to 8½" × 5½".

– Arboretum: #627-60 in 43-3E is 12' tall
– Good Shepherd Center: one 11' tall is east of the building, north of the entrance

Bamboo-leaf OAK

Q. myrsinæfolia Bl. *(myrsinifolia)*
=*Cyclobalanopsis myrs.* (Bl.) Oerst.
From S China, Korea, Japan, Laos.

Japanese Live Oak
Chinese: Xiao Ye Qing Gang
Japanese: Shira-kashi シラガシ (白樫)

The Bamboo-leaf oak has long, narrow, drooping evergreen leaves to 5¾" × 1⅞" wide. It can reach 82' × 18⅓'. Though attractive, it is very rare here.

Redmond's Marymoor Park has one larger than any in Seattle, 50' × 4'0" × 36' wide (1999)—in the building courtyard.

- Arboretum: #706-40A on Foster Island is 35' × 3'4½"; #272-63A is in 44-2E; the Japanese Garden has two #80-60, 43½' × 4'1½" and 42' × 4'7"
- Locks bed #17 has one 23' tall (E of a *Castanopsis* and a *Lithocarpus edulis* Chinquapin), #205
- 3424 Wallingford Ave N has a small, weak specimen
- Zoo: one 14' tall on the Rain Forest Loop

Bartram OAK

Q. × *heterophylla* Michx. fil.   Burrier's Oak
(Q. Phellos × *Q. rubra)*

The original specimen of this cross grew on John Bartram's land on the Schuylkill River by Philadelphia. Recognized as unusual, it was described botanically in 1812. One parent was clearly Willow oak, but the other was uncertain: some said Black oak, others Red. The hybrid made acorns that were sent to people interested in trees. One such acorn was planted by Humphrey Marshall (1722–1801) at Marshalltown, Chester County, PA. His tree is now over 200 years old, and about 100' × 13½'. The Willow oak/Red oak cross also turned up elsewhere. In Seattle, ours came mixed with Willow oak nursery stock in the 1970s, used as City street-trees in the Rainier Valley as follows. Seedlings raised from our Rainier Avenue Willow oaks bear *lobed* leaves—so hybridity continues today.

- Rainier Ave S, from S Genesee St north to the intersection with Martin Luther King, Jr. (Empire) Way S: a planting—originally—of over 100 Willow oaks, but also with about 10 hybrids, and various Red, Shumard Red, and Scarlet oaks
- S Dearborn St: 2 (and 4 Willow oaks) on the south side, just west of Rainier Ave
- S Dearborn St: 8 on the south side between 7th & 8th Avenues

Black OAK

Q. velutina Lam.   Yellow Oak
=*Q. tinctoria* Michx.   Dyer's Oak
From much of central & eastern North America.   Quercitron Oak

Black oak was more often used for dying, tanning and medicine, but has been less planted than Pin, Red and Scarlet oaks (its better-known associates) as these are usually showier in autumn. It can look much like either Red or Scarlet oak. Its leaves are perplexingly variable. One clear, if trivial, difference is its *large fuzzy buds*. The largest Black oaks reach 165' × 34½'. It is rare in Seattle.

- Pacific Medical Center (1200 12th Ave S): the largest of 3 (with 4 Southern Red oaks and a Pin oak) is 75' × 9'6½"
- Green Lake: north of the Pitch n' Putt golf course, the middle oak (65½' × 7'4") N of the path, flanked on the W by a Swamp White oak, on the E by a Bur oak
- Victory Heights Playground (19th NE & NE 107th): one 62' × 7'9½" by restrooms
- U.W.: one 61' × 4'6" (with 7 Pin oaks) on the W side of Stevens Way opposite the

Mechanical Engineering bldg.

– Arboretum: many, in various locations, thriving and fast-growing; #2067-38 in 36-1W is 103' × 7'2½"; #693-57A in 36-1W is 100' × 7'3¼"

Blue OAK

Q. Douglasii H. & A.
From California's hot, dry foothills.

Leaves unlobed or bluntly, shallowly lobed, bluish, to 3½" × 2" wide, golden-brown in autumn. Recorded to 94' × 20¼'. Extremely rare here. Arboretum #590-66 in 41-1E is 17½' tall. 1130 16th Ave E has a street-tree. *pl.* 2001.

Bur OAK

Q. macrocarpa Michx.   Mossycup Oak
From central and eastern N America.   Prairie Oak

The State Tree of Illinois, Bur (Burr) oak is a huge tree with big leaves and acorns. Virgin forest trees reached sizes up to 180' × 53'! Leaves 15" × 8" wide can be found, and are easily recognized by their characteristic deep "waists." The acorns stand out both in size (up to 2½" long and wide) and in their distinctively fringed "mossy-cup" appearance. Bur oaks are uncommon here, and unhappy, needing a more continental climate to thrive.

– U.W.: right up against Denny Hall, one 78½' × 9'0"
– Arboretum: unfortunately most here are ugly if not unhealthy; some lofty specimens on Foster Island are impressive, the tallest 94' × 6'4¼"
– Green Lake: 2 on "Oak Hill" SW of the Bathhouse Theatre, the largest 65' × 6'4"; on the N side of the path north of the Pitch n' Putt golf course, the easternmost of 3 oaks (4'7½" around) is a Bur
– Zoo: 8 north of the north parking lot, the largest 59' × 5'7"
– 121 NE 57th St: a street-tree, 57' tall
– Palm Ave SW, north of SW Massachusetts St: 3 street-trees, W side—the tallest 42' and the stoutest 7'9" around
– 1205 S Lucile St: two in one yard

California Black OAK

Q. Kelloggii Newb.
= *Q. californica* (Torr.) Coop.
From central Oregon to Baja California.

A less colorful West Coast cousin of Black oak, with smaller leaves (to 10" × 6" wide), and bark that is slower to become conspicuously rough. It grows up to 130' × 33' and is well known in many parts of Oregon and California, including Yosemite Valley. Almost none are in Seattle. The Arboretum has one 94½' × 9'2¾" (#2200-40A in 37-4E); one 92½' × 6'5" (#2318-38A in 43-1W); #2318-38B is 63' × 7'4½" in 11-2W. One 46' tall is at the Locks bed #13.

California Live OAK

Q. agrifolia Née   Holly-leaved *or* Coast Live Oak
From California, Baja California.   Spanish: Encina

A massive, spreading broadleaf evergreen, common in California's central coast; Oakland was named for it. The leaves are amazingly holly-like, and *convex*. The largest dimensions recorded are 108' × 30¾' × 200' wide. It is rare here.

– 6049 NE Keswick Dr: one, *pl.* in 1956, is 45' × 6'3" × 42' wide (1989)
– Locks bed #17 (by bench; 56' × 7'1"), 29 (over bench)
– U.W.: one 46' × 4'11" on the lawn NE of 15th Ave NE & NE 42nd St
– E Highland Dr, E of 22nd Ave E: 5 (and 2 Holm oak) street-trees, N side; clipped
– Seneca St, west of Boren Ave: 20 street-trees *pl.* in April 1991 (with 6 Holm oaks)
– 2806 NW 60th St: street-tree 31½' tall

California Valley OAK

Q. lobata Née   California White Oak
From California.   Mush Oak

Among the largest of all oaks; recorded to 178' × 43½'. Its acorns are also enormous, up to 2½" long and—along with other kinds—constituted the most important food resource of California Indians. As a shade tree, it has been called "the American Elm of California." Ranchers and farmers call it Water oak since it is often by rivers or lakes. In Seattle, very rare. It grows well, but has poor fall color and makes no acorns.

– S.P.U.: in front of Crawford Music Building are two with an English oak west of them; the larger is 78' × 12'10" × 87' wide
– NE 62nd St, east of 36th Ave NE: a street-tree, S side, by alley, 70' × 10'1"
– View Ridge Playfield: one 59½' × 9'3½" and *broad* is N of the wading pool
– Arboretum: the largest of four is 89½' × 6'½" (#2198-40A in 37-4E)
– 1515 2nd Ave W: one 56' tall—until 2005

Canyon Live OAK

Q. chrysolepis Liebm.   Cañón Live Oak
From SW Oregon, California, Baja   Goldcup Oak
California, Nevada, Arizona, New Mexico, Texas.   Maul *or* Iron Oak

A broadleaf evergreen, its leaves (to 4" × 2") and acorn cups usually *gold-tinted* beneath. It can attain 110' × 36¼'. Very rare in Seattle.

– Locks bed #1, 5, 23, 29, 120, 208, 210, 323 (the best, *pl. ca.* 1956, had been 56' × 11'10" × 78' wide but broke and had to be removed in July 2005)
– U.W.: 53' × 8'6½" by Music Building's SE wall; one *pl.* 1986 W of Johnson Hall
– 8546 30th Ave NW
– Arboretum: 45' × 4'2" (#425-52A in 42-2E); 58½' × 3'4¾" (#937-52 in 14-6E)

Chestnut OAK

Q. Prinus L., *non* auct.   Rock Chestnut-Oak
=*Q. montana* Willd.   Tanbark Oak
From the eastern U.S. and S Ontario.

Despite the name, there are other oaks still more Chestnut-like in appearance, especially as regards their leaves; yet the *bark* of this species resembles that of the American Chestnut tree. The leaves are up to 11" × 5" and have 6–12 big blunt teeth per side. This is the most rugged-*looking*, but not the largest of chestnut oaks, reported only to 144' × 22⅓'. It is rare here.

- 627 36th Ave E: 104' × 12'7" × 95' wide (1990) in the back yard
- Volunteer Park: of 2 behind the bandstand, the largest is 91' × 5'10"
- Arboretum: the tallest, #79-36B in 37-2W, is 99' × 5'6¾"; the stoutest is #X-175, the largest of over a dozen on Foster Island, 87½' × 6'2½"
- View Ridge Playfield: one 59' × 5'3¼" south of the wading pool; in the NE part of the park a 49' × 4'9½" tree looks to be Chestnut oak × Swamp White oak
- U.W.: Friendship Grove, representing Gabon, 61' × 4'11¼"
- U.W.: one 3'9" around at the bottom of the stairs S of Padelford parking garage
- Locks bed #122 has a small, shaded one whose precise i.d. remains uncertain

Chinese Cork OAK

Q. variabilis Bl.   Oriental Oak
From China, Japan, Korea, Taiwan.   Chinese Oak

This looks like a *corky*-barked chestnut tree. Leaves up to 8½" × 3¼", edged by fine bristly teeth. Reported to 100' × 12½'. Only 5 known here. The Arboretum: 1 on Foster Island, 2 in 42-1E/43-1E—the largest 86½' × 5'¾" (#1980-37A). Loyal Heights Playfield has one 31½' × 2'9½" SE of the bldg. The U.W. campus has a small spreading one by the bench south of parking lot W-4.

Chinquapin OAK

Q. Muhlenbergii Engelm. *(Muehlenbergii)*   Yellow Chestnut-Oak
=*Q. acuminata* (Michx.) Sarg., *non* Roxb.   Chinkapin Oak
=*Q. prinioides* Willd. var. *acuminata* (Michx.) Gl.
From New England to northeast Mexico.

This oak with the beautiful name has slender leaves much like those of chestnut trees, often with yellowish stems. The acorns are tiny but sweet, and the tree they bring forth can attain 160' × 31½'. It's very rare here.

- Loyal Heights Playfield (22nd Ave NW & NW 75th St): the largest of 4 at the south end is 58½' × 9'9½"
- Arboretum: two #695-39 slender examples in 42-2E, 65' × 5'0" & 73' × 4'4¼"
- View Ridge Playfield: the westernmost of 3 oaks south of the SW ballfield is this species or a hybrid, 65½' × 6'11"

Cork Tree (OAK)

Q. Suber L.   Cork Oak

From the W and central Mediterranean region.

The spongy bark of this broadleaf evergreen tree is the cork used for such things as dart boards, bottle stoppers, floats, *etc.* The deeply furrowed bark seen on trees grown for ornament rather than for producing cork, is called "virginal;" only after it has been stripped away once does high-quality, smoother, fast-growing "reproduction" cork develop. Whole groves of cork trees are periodically de-barked to supply cork commercially, mostly in Spain and Portugal. The tree can attain 85' × 25' and also makes acorns used for feeding livestock. It is rare in Seattle, easily grown and handsomely rugged. None known here have been stripped yet, nor is it likely any will be, so we have only the inferior grade of cork.

– *alley* N of W Armour St, E of 44th Ave W: one N of 2846 garage is 50½' tall
– U.W.: a 3-trunked one west of the HUB is 49½' tall, its largest trunk 6'11" around
– U.W. Friendship Grove, representing Spain, 32' × 5'7½"
– Locks bed #210 has two, taller 41'
– Arboretum: #569-52 in 20-3E (larger of pair) is 38' × 4'9¼"
– S Lander St, west of 6th Ave S: one on the north side
– 7th Ave NE & NE 45th St: NE corner landscape has one
– Parking garage on 1st Ave, north of Spring St, E side: two
– 815 NW 52nd St: 2 street-trees
– 1806 S Lane St: a street-tree

[**Hybrid Cork Oak**—*Q. Suber* × *Q. Cerris* '**Lucombeana**'—Recorded to 118' × 25' in England. The Miller Botanic Garden specimen's seedlings look identical to itself; the Good Shepherd Center has such a one, 7½' tall, *pl.* 1997, at the N end of the main parking lot. Leaves dark green and shiny, semi-evergreen, to 5" × 2", ovate, coarsely and sharply toothed or shallowly lobed. Bark *somewhat* corky.]

Daimyo OAK

Q. dentata Th. *ex* J.A. Murr.   (Japanese) Emperor Oak
=*Q. Daimio* K. Koch   Japanese: Daimio カシワ
From Mongolia, China, the S Kuriles, Korea, Japan.   Chinese: Hu Shu

Thick leaves as large as 20" × 11¾" wide (which are sometimes eaten as a spring vegetable in north China) and big, bristly acorns are a feature of this boldly distinctive tree. Recorded to 98½' tall in Japan. It's extremely rare in Seattle.

– Green Lake: north of the Pitch n' Putt golf course, south of the path, the 2nd oak from the west, 82' × 11'10½"
– Woodland Park: one 73' × 8'2¼" in a grassy area, near a grove of 15 Sitka Spruces
– Arboretum: the largest of nine is 84' × 6'½" (1929-37G in 44-2E)
– Seattle Center: south of the Intiman Theatre by the Kobe Bell, is one 64' × 7'8" with Japanese Maple and Japanese Flowering Cherry; a plaque by it reads: "In memory of George Washington 1732–1799: This tree is planted by Mary Morris Chapter D.A.R. in the bicentennial year of his birth 1932"

Durmast OAK

Q. petræa (Matt.) Liebl.   Sessile Oak
=*Q. sessiliflora* Salisb.
From Europe, W Asia.

An associate of English oak, but far less known and grown than that species. It can grow as large as 150' × 36¾'. The only specimen known in Seattle is one 81½' × 10'10½" at the NE part of Garfield Playfield (23rd Ave & E Cherry St).

English OAK

Q. robur L.   (not our) Common Oak
=*Q. pedunculata* Ehrh.   British *or* Pedunculate Oak
From Europe, N Africa, the Caucasus.

The original "Oak." Its lead role in British history is indelibly memorialized not only in ink of prose and poetry, paint and pencil of artists' canvases, sturdy beams of buildings and ships—but in the national consciousness of the people, as attested by enduring proverb, song and phrase. The oak of Druids, of mistletoe, and yule logs, of Robin Hood's cudgel and King Arthur's round table; the oak that earned its proud title King of the Forest. It can grow to 150' × 40'+.

Its small, bluntly lobed leaves lack pretty fall color. Very common here. It makes many big acorns (ripe from mid-August through September); seedlings and saplings are common; it's naturalized weedily.

– Kinnear Park: an open-grown tree *pl. ca.* 1890 is 71' × 12'5" × 73' wide
– Blake Island: one 84' × 12'2" × 77½' wide—not *in* Seattle—but a boat ride away
– S.P.U.: one 65' × 11'9" × 68½' wide is west of two California Valley oaks in front of Crawford Music Building
– Jefferson Park: one 81' × 10'6" × 94½' wide
– Zoo: the S side of the Rose Garden has one 77' × 10'9¼"
– Volunteer Park: a street-tree SW of the conservatory is 82½' × 9'6"
– Arboretum: the largest of many is 9'9½" around (of 3 at N end of Azalea Way)
– Mt Baker Park: tallest of 13 is 102' × 9'9" (with 19 Turkish oaks and a Pin oak)
– E Lee St, west of McGilvra Blvd E: one on the south side
– U.W.: one 6'4¾" around N of Benson Hall; 9 (best 83½' × 6'6") east of the I.M.A. Building (with 6 Red oaks); SW of the Administration Building is a **freak form**, narrow and upright (41' × 2'10¼") with slender, deeply lobed (almost slashed) leaves (from the Arboretum; it was once labeled *Q. Haas* #225-70)
– U.W. Friendship Grove, representing The United Kingdom
– Triangle at Broadway & Spruce St: 77' × 9'10" is 1 of 2 bigleaf versions (leaves up to 8" × 4¾" wide compared to the normal maximum of 6¼" × 3½" wide)
– Locks bed #18A looks in general appearance and in leaf, exactly like regular Seattle English oaks, but its acorns being borne on very short stems or none, make it either a very unusual English oak or a hybrid
– Locks bed #19 has been called *Q. canariensis* Willd., but is not; it appears to be a bigleaf version of English oak, or maybe a hybrid of that and Hungarian oak.

*f. **fastigiata*** (Lam.) Schwarz

Columnar *or* Fastigiate English Oak
Cypress Oak / Upright English Oak

These grow narrowly upright like wavy, irregular Lombardy (Black) Poplars. The precise shape depends on the tree's age, what its growing conditions are, whether it was grown from acorn or graft and what care it receives. It is quite unmistakable, and common.

– 36th Ave E & E Valley St: the NW corner yard has one 92½' tall
– 14th Ave E, south of E Ward St: a yard on the E side has a big one 87½' tall
– Arboretum: a 78½' × 5'10" street-tree N of Madison St; one 90' × 5'6¼" in 14-3E
– U.W.: a *broad* tree 71' × 9'9¾"N of Harris Hydraulics Lab; one 69½' × 5'4¼" SE of Lewis Hall; 4 street-trees on 15th Ave NE, north of NE 40th St
– Evergreen Park Cemetery: 3 not far from the entrance (and elsewhere); tallest 83'
– Queen Anne Playfield (1st Ave W & W Howe St): about 25 at the S end
– Seattle Center: 5 at each end of the Mural Amphitheatre stage

[**Q. Crimson Spire**™ ('Crimschmidt')—said to be Fastigiate English oak × White oak. A new clone, patented in 1995. W Dravus St, by 27th Ave W, has 11 street-trees. Some are by NE Radford Dr & NE 64th St. There are 11 street-trees on *or near* 2nd Ave from Thomas to Mercer St.]

[**English Oak hybrid**: At Madison Park (43rd Ave E & E Madison St) are four regular English oaks, the largest 64½' × 8'11". In the northeast corner is a hybrid 81' × 9'9½". It flushes later in spring, has small persistent *hairs* on its twigs and leaves, and its acorns are *stalkless* and have *knobby scales*. Moreover it has larger leaves of darker color that stay healthy and unblotched all year. Likely these five oaks were all seedlings from an English oak, but the hybrid among them originated from an acorn that had resulted from cross-pollination—but what species its "father" was is unknown.]

Holm OAK

*Q. **Ilex*** L.

From the Mediterranean region to the W Himalayas.

Holly Oak
(The) Holm

The least rare of our evergreen oaks; it reseeds weedily. A dark, dense broadleaf evergreen with an ascending habit, able to reach 131' × 28¼'. "Holm" and "holly" both evolved from the Middle English *holin*, meaning prickly. The English called this tree the "Holly Oak" thus comparing the imported evergreen oak to their native holly tree, while the Romans had called holly the "sharp-leaved Ilex" *(Ilex Aquifolium)*, thus comparing holly to this evergreen oak. Follow? "Ilex" itself is of uncertain origin, but seemed to refer exclusively to this tree. Though the general appearance of the tree is holly-like, it isn't alone in this respect: other evergreen oaks can resemble hollies even more, as do many *Osmanthus*.

– 7016 28th Ave NE: 53' × 6'9½"
– Locks bed #4 (two big, two small), 210 (48' × 7'0"), 307
– 1638 Peach Ct E: one 43' tall up against the south side of the house
– 39th Ave E & E Howe St: NW corner yard, S of the house
– 5 by bus-stop at Midvale Ave N & N 45th & N 46th St
– 903 Broadway (by Marion St): a multi-trunked tree

– Arboretum: tallest is 52' × 2'10¼" (#963-58B in 21-2E)
– 52nd Ave S & S Willow St: SE corner, behind garage on 52nd, one 41' tall
– 6020 Oberlin Ave NE: one by driveway
– 5727 28th Ave NE: two street-trees

Huckleberry OAK

Q. vacciniifolia Kell.   (one of many) Scrub Oak
=*Q. chrysolepis* var. *vacciniifolia* (Kell.) Engelm.
From dry foothills of Oregon and California; also way up high in the Sierras.

Closely related to Canyon Live oak. It is a broadleaf evergreen shrub in nature; grown in Seattle it often attains *treehood*, making larger leaves and acorns than do specimens in the wild. Very few are in Seattle. One 33' tall is at 8546 30th Ave NW. Arboretum #540-66 is 15' tall in 35-2W; a 2-trunked one 18½' tall is in 14-6E; #687-55C in 1S-5E is 28½' tall. Many are at the Locks, in beds #17 (two, at the bottom of the stairs), #205, #314 (a definite tree 28' × 4'7½" × 27' wide), and #330.

Hungarian OAK

Q. Frainetto Ten. **Forest Green**® ('Schmidt')   Italian Oak
From Italy to the Black Sea.

Named *Frainetto* in 1813, an error for *Farnetto*, an Italian name. Its dark green leaves are beautifully lobed, to 9¾" × 5½", very short-stemmed, hairy on both sides. Acorns *ca.* ¾" long. A tree of handsome form, splendid foliage, impressive strength and no obvious faults—except ho-hum fall color. Recorded to 131' × 17¾'. A newcomer here, all we have is a clone.

– Children's Hospital: one *pl.* 1989 is 46' tall by 45th Ave NE & NE 47th St; a 2nd by a parking lot is 38' tall
– Wing Luke School (37th Ave S & S Kenyon St): 43' × 3'2" *pl.* 1991 by W gate
– U.W. Medicinal Herb Garden: one 32' tall in section C was *pl.* in 1995
– S Harney St, west of 12th Ave S: many
– 31st Ave E, south of E Pike St: 3 street-trees, west side
– Green Lake: 2 N of wading pool *pl. ca.* 1997

Interior Live OAK

Q. Wislizeni A. DC.   Sierra Live Oak
From California, Baja California.

A broadleaf evergreen with an open airy crown, and smooth bark. Wide, flat, shiny and variably-toothed leaves. It can attain 100' × 22⅓'. Extremely rare here.

– Arboretum: the largest is 66' × 5'4" (#2197-40A in 37-4E)
– Locks bed #24 (two shaded-stunted ones), 112 has one 51' tall
– 8546 30th Ave NW (this one looks a bit like *Q. Emoryi* Torr.)
– 8315 13th Ave NW: 39½' tall multitrunked; right by the sidewalk

Laurel OAK

Q. *laurifolia* Michx.   Swamp Laurel-Oak
=Q. *obtusa* (Willd.) Pursh   Diamond-leaf Oak
From wet heavy soils of the southeastern U.S.

A semi-evergreen tree, fully deciduous only in the latter part of our particularly harsh winters. Laurel oak is a disputed tree, divided by some botanists into two species, and by some thought to be a hybrid between Water and Willow oaks. Certainly more than a few Water oaks have been called Laurel oaks. It can reach 148' × 24½' and tolerates wet soil. The leaves are thin, blunt-tipped, widest at the middle, to 5⅓" × 2⅓". The only specimens known here are:

– Arboretum: the largest of 4 #1404-46 in 42-B/43-B are 78' × 4'3½" (**B**) and 76½' × 5'3½" (**A**); to the south a bit #534-61A is 64' × 4'6" but appears to be a Water oak or a **hybrid**—just like a bigger one (75½' × 6'6¼") at the U.W. SE of Smith Hall by Skagit Lane, with leaves to 8" long. One should also compare to these the Arboretum Water oak #607-38H in 41-1W—a clear hybrid; leaves strongly lobed
– 32nd Ave NW, from just south of NW 56th to 59th St: 4 ±evergreen street-trees, west side, plus others that are deciduous
– 508 N 78th St: by sidewalk east of steps; a weeping peach tree is west of the steps

Leather OAK

Q. *durata* Jeps.
=Q. *dumosa* Nutt. ssp. *durata* (Jeps.) A. Camus
From California, in chaparral and foothill woodlands.

Like Huckleberry oak, this is a *shrub* in nature but potentially tree-sized as grown in Seattle. It is a broadleaf evergreen rarely seen as tall as 8–12' in the wild. It has small, convex, deep green, prickly leaves. One *ca*. 12' tall is at the far east end of bed # 205 (employee parking) at the Locks.

Live OAK

Q. *virginiana* Mill.   Louisiana Live Oak
=Q. *virens* Ait.   Southern Live Oak
From the far south of the U.S.; Mexico, Cuba.

A broadleaf evergreen of much fame. Along with Evergreen Magnolia it may be considered the unofficial tree symbol of the Deep South. It is the State Tree of Georgia. In the Language of Flowers is stands for "liberty" or "first in the hearts of his countrymen." Its wood, famous for shipbuilding, is extremely stiff, hard, and heavy. It is primarily a *wide-crowned* tree: the maximum height noted is 87' and the thickest trunk over 36½' around, but the spread of its branches can approach 175'! In Seattle only the following young trees are known.

– Genesee Park: of dozens *pl. ca.* 1982, few remain—best 32' × 3'4¾" in NW corner
– S.U.: 3 street-trees on 12th Ave, east of Bellarmine Hall, N of 2 Holm oaks, 1 Coast Live oak; tallest 19½' × 1'10½"

- 8th Ave W, south of W Crockett St: 6 street-trees, west side, the tallest 32'
- Amy Lee Tennis Center (2000 Martin Luther King, Jr. Way S): 13 *pl. ca.* 1978 are with *Photinia Davidiana* shrubs west of the outdoor courts; tallest 19'
- Wallingford Ave N & N 46th St: SE corner yard
- U.W.: 4 on west side of Burke Gilman Trail (3 north of Whatcom Lane, 1 south)
- 1703 NW 67th St
- Arboretum: one #361-92 in 43-2W is only 12½' tall

Mexican OAKS

Q. mexicana Humb. & Bonpl.   In Mexico: Encino
From Mexico.

A broadleaf evergreen tree with slender leaves 2–4" long. Known only as a youngster 20' tall at the Good Shepherd Center (W of the parking lot), and one *pl.* in 2002 at 9329 Lima Terrace S. The former is already ripening acorns.

A 2nd Mexican oak even rarer is *Q. viminea* Trel. One 28' tall, *pl. ca.* 1991 in the back yard of 347 22nd Ave E. Leaves of this species average 3¼" × ¾".

A 3rd Mexican oak is *Q. salicifolia* Née. One was *pl. ca.* 2004 in the garden at 12th Ave S & S Hanford. Leaves recall Bamboo-leaf oak; up to 6¼" × 1½".

A 4th Mexican oak is *Q. obtusata* Bonpl. One less than 8' tall is at the Good Shepherd Center (S of the building). It looks *much* like Netleaf oak.

Still more very young, super-rare Mexican species almost surely exist here. Mexico has well over 100 species of *Quercus*.

Mongolian OAK

Q. mongolica Fisch. *ex* Ledeb.   Liaotung Oak
=*Q. liaotungensis* Koidz.   Chinese: Meng Gu Li
=*Q. wutaishanica* Mayr   Ch'ai Shu
From much of NE Asia.

An English oak cousin, with similar short leafstems. But extremely rare and not thriving here. The U.W. has one (#719-59) 35½' × 3'1" just north of the NE 45th St viaduct on 25th Ave NE. Younger, smaller ones at the Arboretum (#201-82C is 40' × 1'10½" in 2S-1E; #48-84A is 17' tall in 42-B, and #47-84A is 19' tall in 39-1W).

Netleaf OAK

Q. rugosa Née
=*Q. diversicolor* Trel.
=*Q. reticulata* Humb. & Bonpl.
From Arizona, New Mexico, Texas, Mexico, Guatemala.

A coarse broadleaf evergreen with rough, veiny leaves, to 8" × 5"; golden-felty on their undersides. Acorns long-stalked. It can reach 100' × 12½'. Very rare.

- Locks bed #316 (45' × 3'0" × 25' wide), 324

- Arboretum: #521-62B is 16' tall, too shaded in 44-2E; #521-62 is 23½' tall in 5-1W
- 51st Pl S & S Raymond St: a yard with one 31' tall, very broad, not far from a male 20' tall English Holly cv. 'Angustifolia'
- 2030 42nd Ave E: a 14½' tall street-tree under wires
- 2068 Interlaken Pl E: 20' tall, right by the sidewalk
- U.W.: 1320 NE Campus Parkway has one *pl. ca.* 2003

Oregon White OAK

Q. Garryana Dougl. *ex* Hook.   Garry *or* Western White Oak
Native here; from south B.C.   (our) Native Oak
to central California.   Pacific Post Oak

Every Seattle tree-enthusiast ought be acquainted with this, our only native oak. Though familiar in many Pacific Northwest locales, it is not so here, and wild saplings are exceedingly rare. Whidbey Island's Oak Harbor was named after this tree. Victoria has many grand ones, as do the Tacoma prairies. The largest dimensions on record are 150' × 25½'. Told by its *stout*, hairy twigs and buds; *dark* leaves, to 6½" × 5".

- Martha Washington Park: one centuries old, with a hollow trunk, 63' × 14'6" × 56' wide, fell in the winter of 1987–88; the largest left is only 59' × 7'6"
- 51st Ave S & S Holly St: NW corner yard has one 77' tall SW of the house
- Oak Manor Apartments, 730 Belmont Ave E: one 71½' × 11'7½"
- Seward Park: more than can be counted, but not very large
- Seward Park Uplands neighborhood once had many in yards—note road names: Oakhurst Place, Oakhurst Road, Oaklawn Place
- 5115 S Othello St (just east of Rainier Ave S)
- vicinity of 48th Ave S & S Myrtle St: big ones in back yards
- 3316 35th Ave S: one in the back yard, easily viewed from the alley
- 8604 45th Ave S (at S Cloverdale St): one 60' tall, much wider
- 42nd Ave E & E Newton St: NE corner has one 64' tall
- E Ward St, west of 28th Ave E: two street-trees N side, the larger 72' tall
- U.W.: the best (not largest) are two west of the Burke-Gilman Trail, north of Pend Oreille Rd; a larger one 60' × 5'10" is south of Benson Hall
- 29th Ave, south of E Pike St: two street-trees, E side
- 8th Ave NE, a yard on the W side, just S of NE 58th St
- yard S of 4548 33rd Ave W: one against garage
- 821 W Barrett St: back yard
- 2914 9th Ave W: back yard
- 6739 37th Ave SW: 54' tall

Oriental White OAK

Q. aliena Bl. var. *acuteserrata* Maxim *ex* Wenzig.   Chinese: Hu Li
From China, Korea, Japan.   Japanese: Nara-gashiwa ナラガシワ

Despite the name "White" oak, this is a chestnut oak. It can grow to 100' × 9½'. Its acorns are said by some to be only good for pigs, but others report their being sold in markets for human use. In Seattle, extremely rare—just as well, as the leaves are often warped, get ugly leaf-spot fungus blotches in summer, have yellow-brown fall color. Almost no acorns are made here. The leaves are up to 12⅝" × 5¼" wide; edged with (6) 9–13 (16) teeth per side; stem ¾–1⅝" long.

- U.W. Medicinal Herb Garden: one 63½' × 4'2¼" E of the Plant Lab
- Green Lake: on the S side of the path N of the Pitch n' Putt golf course, the westernmost oak (50½' × 5'11"), and the smallest, least healthy one (40½' × 3'1½")
- Seward Park: a 55' tall 4-trunked one (+Hornbeams) on the amphitheatre's W side
- Locks bed #20 has a tree previously called *Q. mongolica* var. *grosseserrata*
- Arboretum: *none;* one cut in Oct. 2003; another 60' × 1'9" was cut in July 1985

[**Konara Oak**—*Q. glandulifera* Bl. =*Q. serrata* Th. *ex* J.A. Murr.—Also E Asian; up to 82' × 9¾' in the wild. Locks bed #205 (employee parking lot) has a tree that is this—or some ally. The Arboretum has 2 old specimens (#1978-37 in 45-2E, tallest 60', stoutest 3'4") and one young tree (#524-67 in 36-2W). Leaves usually small and vaguely chestnut-like yet proportionately broader; pale beneath, usually with a light silvery sheen of fine hairs. They vary from 2–10" long × up to 5⅜" wide; edged with 6–14 gland-tipped teeth per side; stem ¼–1⅛" long.]

Pin OAK

Q. palustris Muenchh.
From the central and eastern U.S. (not in the South), and S. Ontario.

Seattle's most abundant oak. Happily named, and almost universally so called, Pin oak is *slender* in all respects: trunk, limb, branch, twig, leaf—only the tiny squat acorns belie the name. Rapidly growing, it can attain up to 135' × 23¼'. Inexperienced tree-watchers must be careful not to confuse it with Scarlet oak, which is less common, less slender, makes bigger acorns, has rougher bark and deeper fall color. Cultivars '**Crownright**' & '**Sovereign**' are used as street-trees; **Green Pillar**™ ('Pringreen') is tightly fastigiate and new (patented 1995).

- Mt Baker Park: 106½' × 9'2" by tennis courts (+19 Turkish and 13 English oaks)
- Queen Anne Blvd: on Bigelow Ave N by Comstock Pl is one 93' × 10'1¾"; on 10th Ave W, north of W Halladay St, the largest of 16 is 94' × 12'3¾" × 92' wide
- Zoo: the Family Farm pigsty has one 73½' × 11'11¼" × 102½' wide!
- N 57th St, west of Greenwood Ave N: the best of 4 street-trees is 77' × 11'3¾"
- Ravenna Park: the largest, by NE 55th St, is 78½' × 12'6¾"
- Hiawatha Playfield: the largest is 92' × 10'1"—west of the Heritage Red Oak
- Lake Washington Blvd E: one 103' × 9'4" in the hairpin curve by Lakeview Park
- Volunteer Park: the west border, towards the north end, has one 105' × 9'6"
- Broadmoor: 23 relatively small ones line E Madison St east of 33rd Ave E
- '**Sovereign**' City street-trees: 8 at SE triangle at Delridge Way SW & SW Barton St
- Children's Hospital: several **Green Pillar**™ east of the "giraffe" entrance area
- Magnuson Park: five **Green Pillar**™ on the community garden's spiral mound

Post OAK

Q. stellata Wangh.   Iron *or* Rough Oak
From the central & eastern U.S.   Box White Oak

G. Emerson explained in 1850: "In the Southern States, it is called Post oak, and is preferred to all other kinds of wood, on account of its durability, when used as posts." Called Rough oak from the roughness of its leaves. Leaves shiny and intensely dark above, hairy beneath, to 8⅜" × 6¾"; remarkably wide, boldly lobed, comparatively "cross-like" in outline with dominant middle lobes. Fall color dull yellow or brown. Recorded to 108' × 19¾'. Extremely rare here.

– Good Shepherd Center: a relatively young one in the NE area is 19' tall

Red OAK

Q. rubra L.   Common Red Oak
=*Q. maxima* (Marsh.) Ashe   Northern Red Oak
=*Q. borealis* Michx. fil.   Eastern Red Oak
From central and eastern North America.

New Jersey's State Tree proves to be Seattle's fastest-growing oak, on average. Certain odd individuals of other kinds sometimes show surprising rapidity of growth, and the Arboretum has some southern oaks (*e.g.*, Shumard Red oak) growing like there is no tomorrow. But for all that, the safest bet if you want a big oak in a hurry is to plant a Red oak—and then stand back! The adage that oaks grow slowly is chiefly true of senescent wrecks and shaded or otherwise inhibited individuals. In nature, the largest Red oaks reach 165' × 30'4"—one in Tacoma's Wright Park is 124' wide! Red oak trunks, limbs, leaves and acorns are all *stout*; compared to the skeletal Pin oak, it's a brawny tree. The largest of its leaves measure 14½" × 9" wide on 2" stems.

In Seattle, plentiful in all sizes, including wild youngsters.

– U.W.: Denny Hall lawn, towards Savery Hall, has one 91' × 15'3" × 112½' wide; 14 about 100' tall are NE of Suzzallo Library—the tallest 111½'
– Hiawatha Playfield: the largest is N of the gym, 77' × 13'10" × 110½' wide
– Volunteer Park: best of 6 NE of the museum is 105' × 13'6½"
– 921 18th Ave (south of E Spring St): a street-tree, W side, 72' × 12'6½"
– 1030 39th Ave E: 98' tall N of the house (a Shingle oak is S of the house)
– 3007 10th Ave W: a broad tree in the back yard
– 4049 Cascadia Ave S: a broad tree 60' tall is a front yard landmark
– U.W. Friendship Grove, representing Denmark (out-growing most of its 50+ companions) 69' × 8'9¾"

Ring-cupped OAK

Q. glauca Th. *ex* Murr.   Japanese Blue Oak
=*Cyclobalanopsis glauca* (Th.) Oerst.   Blue Japanese Oak
From the Himalayas & much of E Asia.   Japanese: Ara-kashi アラカシ(粗樫)

A formal looking broadleaf evergreen; to 82' × 9¾'; leaves to 6¼" × 2⅞" wide. Related to Bamboo-leaf Oak. Some were sold wrongly as Japanese Red oak (*Q. acuta* Th.). Very rare here, and slow growing.

– Locks bed #3 has two, the larger 34' × 3'4½", #23 (by the Eucalypt), #30 (21' tall)
– Arboretum: #2259-37A is 31½' × 2'6¼" in 42-2E
– 740 35th Ave: several youngsters inside the fence just N of an Evergreen Magnolia
– 1828 11th Ave: north of the bldg.; *pl.* 1987
– 1417 4th Ave W: a street-tree *pl.* in 1985 is 18½'tall

Rocky Mountain White OAK

Q. Gambelii Nutt.   Colorado *or* Utah White Oak
=*Q. utahensis* (A. DC.) Rydb.   Gambel Oak
From SW U.S. mountains, and far N Mexico.

A tree to 75' × 18¼'. Leaves bluntly lobed. Extremely rare in Seattle.

– Arboretum: only young specimens (#102-98) in the nursery
– Children's Hospital: a young specimen NE of the "giraffe" entrance
– Locks bed #21A has a tree that may be *Q. Gambelii* crossed with Chinquapin oak. Not typical *Q. Gambelii* as its leaves are too shallowly lobed, its twigs too hairy.

Sawtooth OAK

Q. acutissima Carruth.   Bristle-tipped Oak
=*Q. serrata* S.& Z., *non* Th. *ex* J.A. Murr.   Japanese Chestnut-Oak
From the Himalayas and much of E Asia.   Chinese: Ma Li

Leaves chestnut-like, to 7" × 2½", bristly-toothed. Acorns squat. Recorded to 115' × 12½'. We have old Arboretum trees and a few youngsters elsewhere.

– Arboretum: largest of three #912-48 in 44-2W are 66½' × 3'11¼" and 61' × 4'11¼"
– 35th Ave NE & NE 75th St SAFEWAY: 4 street-trees, largest *ca.* 45' × 3'5½"
– Rainier Ave S SAFEWAY: many behind on Courtland Pl S, north of S Andover St

Scarlet OAK

Q. coccinea Muenchh.
From the eastern U.S.

Scarlet oak is the District of Columbia's "State" Tree. Less common here than Pin or Red oaks, it is intermediate in texture. All three species are beautiful ornamental shade trees; this one may owe its relative scarcity to being touchier about transplanting. The largest size recorded is 181' × 20¼'.

– 38th Ave NE & NE 77th St: NE corner has one 93½' × 14'½" × 97½' wide

- Zoo: one 58½' × 12'1" × 66' wide in the south parking lot
- Arboretum: in 39-1W and NW thereof are 7 big old trees, the tallest 101½' × 8'3½" (#736-40D) and stoutest 9'2" around (in 39-3W)
- Locks bed #102 has one 86' tall that has many offspring
- Greenwood School (144 NW 80th St): largest of 26 street-trees is 69' × 12'1½"
- Roosevelt High School (built in 1922): SE corner has one *ca.* 69' × 10'10"
- Madison Park Beach (43rd Ave E & E Madison St): one 68' × 11'8¾"
- 18th Ave & E Howell St: NE corner has a landmark specimen

Shingle OAK

Q. imbricaria Michx.   Northern Laurel-Oak
From the eastern U.S.

A tree to 110' × 19' with "laurel-like" but deciduous leaves to 8" × 3"; its wood was used to make shingles. The following examples are the only ones known here.

- 1030 39th Ave E: one 105' tall south of the house (two Red oaks *growing as one* are north of the house)
- U.W.: the lawn NE of 15th Ave NE & NE 42nd St has two, the larger 94' × 8'7¼" × 74' wide; the smaller (with a conspicuous self-grafted low branch) 7'9¼" around
- Arboretum: the largest of four in 44-1E measures 94' × 5'11" (#1490-37F)
- SSCC Arboretum: one 35½' × 2'5¾"
- 320 N 110th St: east of house; south of house is a street-tree Silverbell

Shumard Red OAK

Q. Shumardii Buckl.   Leopard *or* Spotted Oak
=*Q. Schneckii* Britt.   Shumard Oak
From the central and eastern U.S., mostly in the south.

This has leaves much like Scarlet oak's but usually with conspicuous tufts of orange-brown, felty hairs in the vein-axils beneath. Moreover, it colors *late* in the fall, or often stays green well into winter. It can grow to 226' × 25'. Rare.

- Arboretum: #535-61B by the water in 50-2E is 94' × 8'1¼"; #530-61A in 31-4E is 93' × 7'5½" and just N of it in 32-4E is a smaller #588-58A
- U.W.: of the "Red Square" (Central Plaza) oaks by Gerberding Hall, the tallest is 80', stoutest 6'11¼" around
- Triangle at 6th Ave & Denny Way: 7 City street-trees
- 20th Ave NW, from Leary Ave NW to Shilshole Ave NW: City street-trees
- 22nd Ave NW, from Ballard Ave NW to Shilshole Ave NW: City street-trees
- Rainier Ave S, from S Lake Way to S Alaska St: City street-trees (mixed with Willow oaks and a smaller number of Red, Scarlet and Bartram oaks)

Silverleaf OAK

Q. hypoleucoides A. Camus   Whiteleaf Oak
=*Q. hypoleuca* Engelm., *non* Miq.
From the southwestern U.S., northern Mexico.

A broadleaf evergreen with long, narrow leaves (to 8½" × 1¾"), leathery and thick, dark green on top and cottony white underneath. It can reach 73' × 10¼' and is a splendid ornamental, but rare here.

- Locks bed #8, #316 (two, reseeding; taller 47' × 5'2"; stouter 43' × 6'5¾")
- Arboretum: in 44-2E one is 48' × 1'11" (#238-68B)
- E Highland Drive, east of Harvard Ave E: 3 street-trees (with 10 Persian Ironwoods)
- Meridian Ave N, north of N 39th St: a street-tree, west side
- 36th Ave E, 2nd house N of E John St: a street-tree, east side

Southern Red OAK

Q. falcata Michx.   Turkeyfoot Oak
=*Q. triloba* Michx.   Spanish Oak
=*Q. digitata* (Marsh.) Sudw.
=*Q. cuneata* auct., *non* Wangh.
From the southeastern U.S. with a few more northerly populations.

Another of our extremely rare oaks. The name "Spanish oak" is also used for Pin, Red, Scarlet and Shumard oaks, yet most writers use it for this species. Looking at the tree, one doesn't observe anything particularly Spanish about it, but its leaves are very distinctive. A single Southern Red oak was at once the tallest, stoutest-trunked and widest ever recorded: 135' × 28' × 141' wide (1983) in Maryland. (Usually a skinny tree in the woods holds the height record, and an open-grown one has the largest trunk and spread.)

- Pacific Medical Center (1200 12th Ave S): a row of 8 big oaks, from west to east: S.Red/ Black/ S.Red/ S.Red 85' × 9'2¾"/ Pin/ Black/ Black/ S.Red 92½' × 8'10"
- Arboretum: Foster Island has six #608-38; best 92' × 5'7¼" (**C**); 85½' × 6'1½" (**B**)

Swamp White OAK

Q. bicolor Willd.
=*Q. platanoides* Sudw.
From the N half of the central and eastern U.S., and extreme S Canada.

Swamp White oak has glossy foliage and a usually rounded head of branches; its leaves tend to be pale-felty on their undersides, to 7¾" long, shallowy lobed, and usually yellowing in autumn. Big acorns are borne on long stalks. The bark is *flaky* and the tree can reach up to 139' × 27½'. It's rare in Seattle.

- Green Lake: north of the Pitch n' Putt golf course, north of the path, the westernmost of 3 oaks, 74½' × 7'10¼"
- 2718 NE Blakeley St: two wide street-trees, pruned around wires; 45' × 5'7¼"
- U.W.: two S of the Burke Museum with Bristlecone Pines; larger 55' × 5'1½"

– Arboretum: 43-3E has the largest, #1927-37D, 79' × 5'9"; and State land south of SR-520 has 3 (largest 56' × 5'8")
– View Ridge Playfield: one W of the SW ballfield, and one S of it; neither very big

Turkish OAK

Q. Cerris L.

From central & S Europe to SW Asia.

Turkey Oak
Bitter Oak

In the southeastern U.S. *Q. lævis* Walt. is also called Turkey oak, but after the bird, not the country. The Old World Turkish oak has bark that is extra dark, deep and rough, even for an oak; its 6" × 3" leaves are usually fine-sandpaper textured on top; it can reach 141' × 26½' and its acorns boast *bristly-fringed cups*. It's uncommon and little known here. Most are on public property, are old, and have tall slender stems. Wild offspring are readily found near the parent trees.

– Queen Anne Blvd: Bigelow Ave N, by W Lee St, has 5 with Pin and Red oaks; the largest 94½' × 8'5" × 60' wide
– Mt Baker Park: 19 Turkish, 13 English, and a Pin oak street-trees; the tallest Turkish is 104' × 6'2" and the stoutest 103' × 7'4¼"
– Jefferson Park Golf Course: one 83' × 8'7" × 75' wide
– Arboretum: N of Madison St, 2 on the W side, the larger 118½' × 7'6¼" (6th tree N of the fastigiate English oak); 16 other English oaks here and 5 more on the E side
– Day School: one NW of grounds by 40th St crosswalk is 6'10¼" around; others are at the S end of the playground
– U.W. Friendship Grove, representing Turkey
– Locks bed #18

Ubame OAK

Q. phillyræoides A. Gray
(phillyreoides)
From China, Korea, Japan, the Ryukyus.

Japanese: Ubame ウバメガシ
Chinese: Wu Gang Li

A broadleaf evergreen, shrubby or up to 50' tall, with glossy, yellow-green spoon-shaped leaves. The Arboretum has it in 43-2E (31' tall #379-51A) & 21-1E (27' × 2'11" #183-59B). It is at the Locks as follows: #108 (north side), #202 (27' tall, by a Digger Pine), #308 (39½' × 5'10" × 37' wide). Bush-sized ones in private gardens are the only other specimens known in Seattle.

Water OAK

Q. nigra L.
=*Q. aquatica* Walt.
From the southeastern U.S.

'Possum Oak
Duck Oak

Tardily deciduous or essentially evergreen; in April the old leaves drop, the new leaves reddish as they unfold. Recorded to 133' × 22'9". It is often mistaken for Laurel oak, which has smaller, thicker leaves, widest at the middle (not above the middle as in Water oak) and their top-sides are relatively shiny whereas Water oak leaves (to 7½" × 3½") are shinier beneath than on top. Very rare here.

– Arboretum: eight #607-38; tallest 86' × 6'1" (**B**); stoutest 82' × 8'8½" (**I**) in 45-1E
– U.W.: one 64½' × 8'9" SW of Architecture Hall; one 63' × 8'8¼" SE of Balmer Hall; SE of the Music Building (not far E of a Canyon Live oak); a small one under power wires E of the Burke-Gilman Trail N of Pend Oreille Rd
– 1225 S Southern St: 68' tall
– 38th Ave NE & NE 100th St: NW corner has one 58½' tall

White OAK

Q. alba L.   American *or* Ridge White Oak
From the C & E U.S., S Ontario & Québec.   Stave *or* Forkleaf Oak

As English oak symbolized England, this New England counterpart came to symbolize "independence" to the transplanted colonists. No other oak in North America has as many famous and historic trees on record as does White oak. Connecticut, Maryland and Iowa all claim it as State Tree. Its wood is extraordinarily valuable and widely used. The leaves are usually pinkish as they unfold, and turn purplish-red in mid-October. By most any measure, White oak is one of the best ornamentals of its class, especially when it is several hundred years old. It can attain 182' × 32¼'. It is uncommon in Seattle.

– Arboretum: one 101' × 6'8¾" on Foster Island; 96' × 5'10¼" (#384-38A in 37-1W)
– Lincoln Park: one 85½' × 5'11" is the best of many in the central part of the park north of the horseshoe pits; tallest is 95½' × 5'¼"
– Lake Washington Blvd, opposite E Jefferson St: one 80' × 9'5¼"
– Me-kwa-mooks Park: a multitrunked one 62½' tall in the SW corner
– Interlaken Park: two with many English oaks and Black Walnuts in the meadow above where 18th Ave E dead-ends from Boyer Ave E
– Jefferson Park Golf Course: one 75' × 7'9¾" outside the fence on Beacon Ave S
– View Ridge Playfield: two, one west (62½' × 7'7"), the other north (55½' × 7'4½")
– Green Lake: north of the Pitch n' Putt golf course, south of the path, the easternmost oak, 68½' × 7'0"
– 4527 35th Ave S: an old stout tree in the back yard can be viewed from the alley

[**Hybrid White Oak**—*Q. alba* × *Q. macrocarpa*—Trees resulting from this cross can be called *Q.* × *Bebbiana* Schneid. The Arboretum has two #1938-37 in 43-2E, the larger 101' × 6'1¼". Green Lake has a tree 70' × 7'5" that *may* be one. It is just west of the White oak north of the Pitch n' Putt golf course.]

Willow OAK

Q. Phellos L.   Peach Oak.
From the southeastern U.S.   Pin Oak.

Named for its distinctively *narrow* leaves (up to 7" × 1⅝" wide) the Willow oak is easily recognized by its fine texture. Its fall color is a weak yellow, though some s[ecimens' leaves stay green into winter. It has been recorded to 158' × 25¼'. In Seattle it is rare.

- Lake Washington Blvd E & 36th Ave E: one 80' × 9'8"
- Arboretum: best are #1123-47 in 39-B; 89' × 4'11½" and 74½' × 7'1¾" × 80' wide
- U.W.: one 44' × 3'9½"by the Burke-Gilman Trail south of Wilcox Hall
- Rainier Ave S, from S Genesee St north to the intersection with Martin Luther King, Jr. (Empire) Way S: a planting—originally—of over 100 Willow oaks, but also with about 10 hybrids, and various Red, Shumard Red, and Scarlet oaks
- S Dearborn St, east of Poplar Pl S: 4 City street-trees (with 2 Bartram oaks), S side
- 515 20th Ave E: a street-tree under wires

OLIVE

Olea europæa L.   Common Olive
OLEACEÆ
From SW Asia.

A world famous tree, the long renowned emblem of peace. Cultivated since *ca.* 3,600 B.C. In the wild it is thorny, the leaves are smaller, and fruit usually ≤⅝" long. Cultivars can be thornless, with fruit 1½" long. Spaniards brought it to North America <1577. It needs dryness to thrive; it can withstand freezing winters where the temperature doesn't plunge below about 10°–0° F. It does poorly in wet-summer regions. The tree will live and serve as an ornamental well beyond its ideal zone as a commercial fruit-producer. As ornamentals, olive trees offer a long life (1,500 years), drought tolerance, gnarled trunks with handsome cavities and folds, and dusty-looking gray-green foliage. The fruit, though prized for oil, is amazingly messy, and the roots sometimes sucker. Leaves narrow, leathery, very dark green above and whitish beneath; to 3" × ¾"; in opposite pairs. Flowers yellowish-white, not showy, in the summer. Recorded to 98½' tall; trunks to 23½' around in Spain. In Seattle, rare; all date from the 1990s and onward.

- 4646 Beach Dr SW: 2, plus palms, banana, *etc.*
- 1922 E Calhoun St in Montlake: 9½' tall
- Zoo: at least 7 N of giraffes and in savanna vicinity; tallest 8½'
- 7251 27th Ave NE: a front-yard tree
- 8551 16th Ave NW: very young

[*Phillyrea latifolia* L.—Mock Privet. Jasmine Box. Sharpberry Tree. Also in the Olive family, and from the Mediterranean region. Prized for its compact habit, glistening foliage and troublefree disposition. If it sported large flowers or showy fruits, people would stampede for it. Leaves glossy, to 2" × 1⅜" but usually ≤1½" long. Flowers from March into June, tiny, greenish- or creamy-white. Berries deep purplish or slate black, dull and inconspicuous, ¼–⅓" wide, with one large seed; bitter. Slow and shrubby for many years; eventually tree sized; recorded to 46' × 7'. Very rare in Seattle. Arboretum #642-56 is 30' × 2'8" in 12-8E; best of three in 25-3W is 23' × 1'8¾". A few yards have it. A young one is at the Good Shepherd Center under the Gray Poplar.]

OSAGE ORANGE

Maclura pomifera (Raf.) Schneid.　　　　　　　　　　Hedge Apple
=*M. aurantiaca* Nutt.　　　　　　　　　　　　　　　Hedge Tree
=*Toxylon (Ioxylon) pomiferum* Raf. *ex* Sarg.　　　　　　Bow-wood
MORACEÆ　　　　　　　　　　　　　　　　　　　Bowdock
From NE Texas, SE Oklahoma, SW Arkansas.　　　　　Bowdark

Osage Orange was so named since it's native in Osage Indian territory, and makes "mock oranges." Other *Mock Orange* plants are so called because of fragrant white blossoms. In this case the name refers to green or pale-yellowish, orange-sized fruits of a brain-like appearance. In Seattle they measure up to 3¾" across when mature in October; further south they can be 5" across and more colorful. They're inedible and may be slightly toxic. Hardy under adverse conditions and usually thorny, the tree is planted far beyond its native home, for hedges. Its excellent wood—extremely hard, very durable, close-grained and heavy, has been made into bows, police clubs, tobacco pipes and wagon parts. As early as 1916, a dye extracted commercially from the fruit gave army uniforms their distinctive green color. The shiny leaves turn yellow in late October. The tree can reach 109' × 25' and has bark recalling that of Black Locust.

　　Very rare in Seattle.

– Mt Baker Blvd, south of S McClellan St: a fruitless one 78' × 5'8"
– 1309 Lake Washington Blvd S: a fruitful one 28' × 5'1"
– Arboretum: two thorny ♂ trees in 37-2E (#510-37; the larger 45½' × 3'8½")
– U.W. Medicinal Herb Garden: two on the east border of section G (the nursery area)—both thorny, one fruitful
– Kinnear Park: small, topped, thorny ones by the upper level restrooms

OSMANTHUS

Osmanthus heterophyllus (G. Don) P.S. Green　　Common Osmanthus
=*O. Aquifolium* Sieb.　　　　　　　　　　　　　Holly Olive
=*O. ilicifolius* (Hassk.) hort. *ex* Carr.　　Chinese, Sweet *or* False Holly
OLEACEÆ　　　　　　　　　　　　　　　Japanese: Hi-ira-gi ヒイラギ
From Japan, the Ryukyus, Taiwan.

Osmanthus are broadleaf evergreen shrubs and trees. The name is from Greek *osme*, fragrance or odor, and *anthos*, a flower. The flowers are tiny, but sweetly fragrant; ♂ and ♀ are mostly on separate plants. As with hollies (*Ilex* spp.) the leaves are most spiny on young or sheared specimens; unlike hollies, the leaves are *opposite*, not alternate. Osmanthus grow best in part shade. This species is common in Seattle, highly variable, and is usually considered a shrub. Its leaves are 1½–2½" (4") long, and usually prickly (as many as 5 spines per side). The tiny, white flowers perfume the air in fall. Berries ripen in June on females. A purpleleaf and several variegated cultivars exist.

– Arboretum: one 22½' is the tallest of three #542-53 in 39-3W
– 1144 21st Ave E: a tree south of the house

- 5919 49th Ave SW: a single-trunked tree 20' tall, wider still
- Children's Hospital: five *variegated* ones by a row of Incense Cedars, tallest 15½'
- Phinney Ave N & N 122nd St: a 12½' tall *variegated* specimen on the west border
- 914 N 35th St: a 11½' tall *variegated* tree

[*O.* × *Fortunei* Carr.—*O. heterophyllus* × *O. fragrans*—Hybrid Osmanthus. Japanese: Hi-ira-gi-mokusei ヒイラギモクセイ. Leaves to 3¾" long, edged with up to 12 spiny teeth per side. Flowers smell like apricots when blooming in October - December. The clone of common cultivation is ♂. 4115 Brooklyn Ave NE: 27½' × 5'9". Arboretum #78-50B is 28' tall, #78-50A is 26½' tall, both multitrunked in 25-1E. Cleopatra Ave NW, south of NW 73rd St, a west side yard: 24' tall multi-trunked. The cv. 'San José' has larger, pale orange flowers, and leaves to 4¾" long. Arboretum #932-48B is 31' tall, 3-trunked in 25-B. The SE corner of Brooklyn Ave N & N 56th St has one west of the house.]

[*O. armatus* Diels—Chinese Osmanthus. From W China. Leaves to 7" × 2¼", with up to 7–10 spiny teeth per side. In advanced age the plant makes smaller, less spiny leaves. Flowers in October or November, creamy-white. Berries ¾" long. Recorded to 30' tall; usually matures at half that height. Very rare. Arboretum #1094-38 is 20' tall in 22-2W; 8 more (with 4 *O. heterophyllus*) are in 20 4W, the tallest 23'. The garden at 4025 NE 110th St has one 14' tall. The Good Shepherd Center has one <8' tall.]

[*O. fragrans* Lour.—Tea Olive—From China & Japan. Leaves to 5¾" × 1⅞", *very finely* spiny or spineless. Flowers whitish, yellow, *or* orange. Cold-tender. Very rare. Arboretum #35-75 is 21' tall in 43-6E; #531-90A is 15½' tall in 31-2E (Woodland Garden). The garden at 12th Ave S & S Hanford has a youngster *ca.* 7' tall.]

[*O. yunnanensis* (Franch.) P.S. Green—From China. Leaves to 9½" × 2½" with up to 54 spiny teeth per side. Flowers (late January) February-March. Less cold-hardy than other osmanthus. Recorded to 45' tall in the wild. Extremely rare. Arboretum #590-56 is 16½' tall in 25-1W—once taller but cold cut it back. A smaller one is at Kubota Garden Park, and a bigger one at the Miller Botanic Garden N of Seattle.]

PALM TREE

Trachycarpus Fortunei (Hook.) Wendl.
= *T. excelsus* Wendl.
= *Chamærops excelsa* Mart., *non* Th.
= *Chamærops Fortunei* Hook.
PALMÆ / PALMACEÆ / ARECACEÆ
From China.

Windmill *or* Chinese Fan Palm
Hemp *or* Chusan Palm
Chinese: Zong *or* Tsung-lü
Japanese: Shuro シュロ
Wa-juro ワジュロ

Out of thousands of species, only this palm has been grown extensively here. It has proved consistently hardy: some are over 65 years old. So, a palm seen in Seattle is almost certain to be this one, especially if it is tree-sized. It can attain 40' or more with a trunk about a foot thick. Unlike the Date or Coconut Palms, it makes no useful fruit; but where native, is not considered a useless tree:

This is one of the coir palms, producing that useful fibre which is made into cordage, clothing, trunks, brushes, and the like. It is found in the south of China, and formerly extended as far north as the Yangtze. The tree grows to a height of more than thirty feet. The fibrous integument is annually gathered and steeped in water, to separate the fibres for use in manufactures. Excellent matting is made from the bark, combined with more or less of the fibre. The large leaves of this palm are made into fans. The young flower buds, called Tsung-yü, also called Tsung-sun, are eaten, although by some considered to be more or less deleterious. Steeped in honey and soaked in vinegar, they are used as votive offerings by the Buddhists. (Smith, p. 102)

Moreover, its wood is hard, heavy, strong and useful. Sexes are separate; females make clusters of grape-like berries. It reseeds freely here. Standing stark on lawns in otherwise conventionally landscaped yards, it's as bizarrely conspicuous and out of place as the proverbial sore thumb—yet when well integrated into a designed landscape it attracts no special notice.

– Locks: many, conspicuous, the tallest 32' × 1'3"; reseeding (beds #128, 305)
– 168 Lake Washington Blvd: one 33' tall by front door
– alley off E Denny Way, east of 14th Ave E: one 32' tall
– 5416 40th Ave SW (south of SW Brandon St): a ♀ 32' tall
– 763 S Homer St: one 31' tall
– 22nd Ave S & S Massachusetts St: NW corner yard has one 29½' tall
– 746 N 74th St (with other palms & palmlike plants): the tallest 29'
– 6909 52nd Ave S: five, the tallest 28'
– 1223 W Bothwell St: two, taller *ca.* 25'
– Arboretum: of four #108-92 south of the greenhouse, tallest is 24'
– U.W.: south of the Plant Lab., a 21' male to the east and a 22' female to the west
– 4216 3rd Ave NW: more than you will believe, and several other kinds of palms
– 3128 East Laurelhurst Dr NE: a male
– S.U.: 5 (2 female) south of 11th Ave & E Madison St
– 24th Ave E & E McGraw St: NE corner
– Azteca restaurant, 1823 Eastlake Ave E: 3
– 5817 57th Ave NE: one with a blue Colorado Spruce
– Broadway E & E Lynn St: 4 stout ones on the NE corner

[**Dwarf** *or* **Mediterranean Fan Palm**—*Chamærops humilis* Hook. fil.—From the Mediterranean region; the most northerly occurring palm species. Slow, usually multi-trunked, it can make a *small* tree. Fronds 1–3' wide, roundish, of *ca.* 20–30 segments; stem to 52" long, usually *edged with short spines.* 4216 3rd Ave NW has a 13' tall one, in back, visible from the alley. 3728 SW Ida St has one 10' tall SW of the house. 840 NW 45th St has some around a *Trachycarpus;* also *Nerium Oleander;* Tree Privets. 5215 36th Ave NE has a street-tree with a *Myrica.* 2014 E Calhoun St has a street-tree. Locks bed #8, 327.]

[**Pindo** *or* **South American Jelly Palm**—*Butia capitata* (Mart.) Becc.—From SE Brazil and Uruguay. A cold-hardy feather palm, capable of enduring 12° F. Ideally it is both sheltered from severe cold and given much summer heat. Grows slowly. Trunk short, stout. Fronds bluish, arching 6–9' long, of *ca.* 100 leaflets on each side. Flowers striking pale yellow to pinkish-maroon. Fruit yellow, orange or red, edible, 1–1½" long, in weighty clusters of 30–75 pounds; ripe from August to mid-March. 2014 E Calhoun St: 12½' tall. Zoo: 11' tall by jaguars. Leary Way NW & NW 45th St: NW corner has 2 (+3 *Trachycarpus* + some *Yucca* shrubs). Swanson's Nursery has 1 with 3 *Trachycarpus* in the N parking lot. A street-tree at 3728 SW Ida St (with other palms such as *Sabal Palmetto* 16' tall, *Chamærops humilis, Trachycarpus Fortunei* 18½' tall and *T. Wagnerianus* 8' tall). Two flank the entrance stairs at 4216 3rd Ave NW, and a larger one is uphill from them.]

[**Chilean Wine-** *or* **Syrup-Palm**—*Jubæa chilensis* (Mol.) Baill.—From Chile. A cold-hardy feather palm. Grows slowly. Trunk tall, pale, *very* stout. Fronds 6–15' long. 746 N 74th St has a 10½' tall one, as well as other palms: *Brahea edulis, Butia, Chamærops humilis, Sabal minor, S. Palmetto, Rhapidophyllum hystrix, Trachycarpus Fortunei, T. khasianus, T. Takil* and *T. Wagnerianus.* Locks bed #313 has a tiny sulking *Jubæa.*]

[**Other Palms**—*Ceroxylon, Washingtonia*—and other genera, are planted here, and I think it commendable. Virtually all are young, have partly endured severe winter cold, and we still need to experiment much before learning what kinds and conditions are most apt to result in palm success in Seattle. The SW corner of 24th Ave W & W Armour St has *Butia paraguayensis, Chamærops humilis, Sabal causiarum, S. minor, Trachycarpus Fortunei* and *T. latisectus.*]

PAWPAW

Asimina triloba (L.) Dun.   Wild Banana Tree
=*Annona triloba* L.   Michigan *or* Nebraska *or* Hoosier Banana
ANNONACEÆ   Hardy *or* Prairie *or* Indian *or* Indiana Banana
From much of the central   Custard Apple
and eastern U.S., & S Ontario.   Fetid Shrub

The Pawpaw (*or* Papaw) is a suckering shrub or small tree (at most 60' × 7'8") with weak wood. Its flowers appear before the leaves and go through a prolonged metamorphosis from small and green to large and purple, unlike any other tree. The leaves appear very late, are 6–15" long, stink when bruised (as elder or bittersweet nightshade) and fall late. The odd fruit can reach 7" × 2½" but unfortunately doesn't always ripen into edibility here (select cultivars are dependable). Pawpaw is rare in Seattle. The following praise is old fashioned, long-winded and hyperbolic, but heartfelt—perhaps it can, resurrected after 170 years of slumber, convince more of us to try growing Pawpaws.

This, in our view, is the prince of wild fruit bearing shrubs. The leaves are long, of a rich appearance, and green, considerably resembling the smaller leaves of tobacco. The stem is straight, white, and of unrivaled beauty. In fact, we have seen no cultivated shrub so ornamental and graceful as the pawpaw. The fruit closely resembles a cucumber, having a more smooth and regular appearance. When ripe, it is of a rich yellow. There are generally from two to five in a cluster. A pawpaw shrub, hanging full of fruits, of a size and weight disproportioned to the stem, and from under long and rich looking leaves of the same yellow as the ripened fruit, of an African luxuriance of growth, is to us one of the richest spectacles, that we have ever contemplated, in the array of the woods. The fruit contains from two to six seeds, like those of the tamarind, except that they are double the size. The pulp of the fruit resembles egg custard, too luscious for the relish of most people. The fruit is nutritious, and a great resource to the savages. So many whimsical and unexpected tastes are compounded in it, it is said, a person of the most hypochondriac temperament relaxes to a smile, when he tastes the pawpaw for the first time. (Flint, p. 48)

– Locks bed #203 has one 28' × 2'3" leaning and shaded
– U.W. Medicinal Herb Garden: two in the south part of section G (the nursery area), of slender habit, the taller 24'
– 5736 29th Ave NE: 3 street-trees

- 6220 28th Ave NE: 2 street-trees
- 4351 SW Willow St: 2 in front yard
- 1203 and 1207 NE 80th St. each have one
- 209 23rd Ave E: a street-tree

PEACH TREE

Prunus Persica (L.) Batsch   Common Peach
=*Amygdalus Persica* L.   Chinese: Tao
ROSACEÆ
From China.

We grow peach trees for fruit *or* lovely March-April flowers (usually pink, rarely white or dark rosy red). The fruit ripens here mid-August until late September. Some ornamental cultivars (*e.g.*, double-flowered, weeping) produce a few small greenish peaches. Nectarines are fuzzless peaches. In Seattle, peach trees are uncommon compared to apple, cherry, plum and pear trees. Most are stunted, small, diseased, short-lived and weak. But when in bloom, or laden with ripe fruit, they are exquisite. Those in warm, sunny, well-drained sites thrive if cared for—especially cultivars adapted to this area or (*e.g.*, **'Frost'**) resisting peach leaf curl disease. A California peach tree measured 57' × 6½' in 1972—*here*, one 15' × 2' is notably large. Most cited below are flowering (not fruiting) cultivars, only worth visiting when blooming.

- Interlake Ave N & N 36th St: the NE corner yard
- 4th Ave NE & NE 42nd St: NW corner yard
- 27th Ave NE, north of NE Blakeley St: a double-red street-tree, E side
- 2015 E Mercer St: two street-trees
- Meadowbrook Park's edible arboretum planting has cvs. 'Charlotte', 'Frost', 'Mary Jane' and 'Oregon Curl Free'
- 7553 27th Ave NW
- 1030 39th Ave E: a cv. 'Frost' street-tree (other fruit trees also)
- 6533 20th Ave NE: a *dwarf* street-tree, only 8½' tall but *pl. ca.* 1969

Weeping Peach Trees (most are very small, double pink-flowered trees):

- 5410 NE Windermere Rd: one by sidewalk
- 508 N 78th St: by sidewalk west of steps; a Laurel Oak east of steps
- 6807 32nd Ave NE: right by the sidewalk

PEANUT-BUTTER TREE

Clerodendrum trichotomum Th. *(Clerodendron)*   Harlequin Glory-Bower
LABIATÆ (LAMIACEÆ) *or* VERBENACEÆ   Fate Tree
From E Asia.   Chinese: Ch'ang Shan; Japanese: Kusagi クサギ

A suckering shrub/tree with fragrant white flowers and showy fruit. Though the flowers smell sweet, the bruised leaves stink of peanut butter. It leafs out late and opens white flowers from July into September. Turquoise berries against bright red backgrounds follow the flowers. It can be damaged by severe winter cold, but lack of summer heat also keeps it shrubby. In Portland, many small trees are found; in Seattle it needs training to be a small tree. When a tree (to *ca.* 26' × 3'), it is often low-forking and broad.

- 15th Ave E & E Aloha St: NW corner yard
- 2511 25th Ave E: two
- 36th Ave, south of E Denny Way: 7 street-trees, E side, and a pruned Laurel Oak
- 3853 44th Ave NE: a street-tree
- U.W.: 4 N of Parrington Hall with 2 Star Magnolias
- Parsons Gardens Park: two
- Locks bed #311
- N 61st St, just west of Corliss Ave N: a street-tree, N side

Callery PEAR TREE

Pyrus Calleryana Decne. *(Pirus)*   Flowering Pear
ROSACEÆ
From China, Japan.

A recently popular, overplanted flowering tree of healthy, troublefree habit; white flowers in March–April, good fall color, no messy fruit. Virtually all of ours are cultivars developed in the 1950s–1990s; most are planted as street-trees. They include: Aristocrat™, 'Autumn Blaze', 'Bradford', 'Capital', Chanticleer®, 'Rancho', 'Redspire', Trinity® and 'Whitehouse'.

- Arboretum: #217-73A, in 42-3E, is 45' × 4'1"; four #65-73 are in 11-2W, the tallest 48' and stoutest 4'8½" around
- U.W.: 15 at Stevens Court (west of Brooklyn Ave NE, north of NE Pacific St)
- 22nd Ave E, north of E Calhoun St: 3 street-trees, W side
- Meridian Park: children's play area has some
- 24th Ave NW, south of NW 57th St: street-trees
- E Aloha St, west of 20th Ave E: 6 **Aristocrat**™ street-trees
- 1514 NE Ravenna Blvd: 2 '**Autumn Blaze**' street-trees, N side
- NW 80th St, from 32nd Ave NW to Greenwood: 47 '**Capital**' street-trees *pl.* 1992
- Freeway Park (6th Ave & Seneca St): over 20 **Chanticleer**®—tallest 54'
- 31st & 32nd Avenues , south of E Cherry St: **Chanticleer**® City street-trees
- 19th Ave S & Davis Pl S (both), north of S Charles St: '**Rancho**' street-trees
- '**Redspire**' 125 planted in Ballard in February 1994
- 22nd Ave, S of Union St: 14 '**Redspire**' street-trees, E side
- U.W.: 30 '**Redspire**' on Campus Parkway between 15th Ave NE & University Way
- S Wheeler St, east of 20th Ave S: **Trinity**® City street-trees

[*P. Fauriei* Schneid.—Korean Flowering-Pear. Korean Pea-Pear—From Korea; used as a rootstock mostly. Differs from Callery pear as follows: leafs out before blooming; flowers appear later in spring, are smaller, fewer per cluster; tree broad, shrubby; defoliates much earlier in fall. Fruit *ca.* ½" long, first olive green with prominent beige dots; then black inside and out. Leaves small, finely hairy beneath. Fall color reddish. Recorded to 35' tall in the wild. Extremely rare here. Arboretum #224-68 in 11-1W is 23' × 2'6" × 29½' wide. Kensington Pl N & N 54th St traffic circle has a broad, low 2-trunked tree. Five **Korean Sun**™ (cv. 'Westwood') street-trees are on W Lee St between 1st & 2nd Ave W (St Anne's School); two street-trees are at 1150 17th Ave E (south of 4 larger Callery pears).]

Common PEAR TREE

P. communis L.
From Europe, W. Asia; of
unknown, partly hybrid origin.

European Pear
Domestic Pear
Orchard Pear

This familiar species has white flowers in March–early April and fruit ripe for picking late August–early November. Cultivars include 'Anjou', 'Bartlett', 'Bosc', 'Comice' and 'Flemish Beauty'. Pears stand for "affection" in the Language of Flowers, and Pear Trees symbolize "comfort"—what a happy pair! Larger than their close cousin the apple trees, they can surpass 75' × 17½' and live up to 600 years, yielding valuable wood.

- 6th Ave S & S Fidalgo St: a healthy one 60'+ × 9'6" in 1983 was killed in October 1987 to make room for a few extra parking places
- Jefferson Park Golf Course: the largest of several is 70½' × 6'2¼"
- 27th Ave & E Cherry St: NE corner yard has one 42' tall
- 8th Ave S & S Sullivan St: SE corner, in back yard; a huge tree, 55½' tall
- 5614 Brooklyn Ave NE: in back yard; an old tree, 58' tall (+ two Bigleaf Maples)
- Woodland Park: one 42½' × 5'2¼" by the top of soapbox derby ramp by N 50th
- Rainier Playfield (Rainier Ave S & S Alaska St): one 50' × 4'5¼" east of ballfields
- 30th Ave NW & NW 68th St: NE corner has one 38½' tall west of the house
- Othello Park (43rd Ave S & S Othello St)
- Peppi's Playground (32nd Ave & E Spruce St): taller of two is 33' × 3'11"
- Maplewood Playground (Corson Ave S & S Angeline St): 2 at the north end

Dancer® PEAR TREE

P. betulæfolia Bge. **Dancer®** ('Paradise')
=*P. betulæfolia* 'Southworth'
From N China.

Birchleaf Pear
Chinese: Du Li

A clone patented in 1989. The long leafstem permits "dancing in the slightest breeze." Leaves silvery with hairs in spring; coarsely and sharply toothed, bright green above, silvery-green beneath. Very late to drop in fall, some hang on into winter. Fruit sparse or none, green-brown, ≤½". Rare in Seattle.

- 6732 1st Ave NW: a street-tree
- 7021 7th Ave NW: 2 street-trees
- 11th Ave NW & NW 57th St
- 12558 12th Ave NW: 2 street-trees
- 19th Ave NW, north of NW 83rd St: 3 young street-trees
- 8324 23rd Ave NW: 3 street-trees
- 6412 30th Ave NW: 3 street-trees
- Dayton Ave N, north of N 64th St: a street-tree, E side
- 5731 31st Ave NE: 4 street-trees
- 19th Ave E & E Prospect St: SW corner yard has one east of the house

Oriental PEAR TREE

P. pyrifolia (Burm. fil.) Nakai var. **culta** (Mak.) Nakai   Japanese Pear
=*P. sinensis* auct., *non* Decne., Lindl., Poir.   Peking *or* Chinese Pear
=*P. serotina* Rehd.   Sand *or* Asian *or* Apple Pear
From China.   Chinese: Sha Li; Japanese: Nashi ヤマナシ

Of the 15–20 (30) species of *Pyrus*, only this and the Common pear tree are extensively grown for their fruit; the others are grown chiefly for ornament or are not grown at all outside of special collections. Its pears are generally roundish and of weaker flavor and crunchier texture than common pears. A dozen cultivars in Pacific Northwest nurseries now prove that its reputation as a valuable tree has spread beyond the confines of East Asian populations. The cvs. include: 'Chojuro', 'Hosui', 'Nijiseiki' and 'Shinseiki'. In Seattle they're common. It is chiefly a back yard fruit tree and the great majority are young specimens.

- Lincoln Park: one 46' × 4'6¼" N of the wading pool SW of Webster St, forms pears *ca.* 2" wide, 1½" long, inferior to those of cultivars
- Good Shepherd Center: several cultivars south of the parking lot
- 5537 26th Ave NE: a street-tree with a Prune tree
- 1118 NW 50th St: a street-tree

[*P. serrulata* Rehd., a species from central China (Ma Li), makes roundish pears ½–¾" wide, ripening brown. It is extremely rare here. The U.W. campus has one 33½' × 2'1½" by the concrete path west of Bloedel Hall.]

Weeping Willowleaf PEAR TREE

P. salicifolia Pall. '**Pendula**'   Silver Pear Tree
From SW Asia.   Silver Frost® Pear Tree

Only since the 1980s has Seattle had these. It is topgrafted and makes a small sprawling tree wider than tall. Red-tipped flowerbuds open to creamy white flowers that give rise to greenish-yellow pears *ca.* 1½" long. The leaves are silvery with hairs, and *narrow*, ca. *ca.* 3" × ⅝".

- 4223 Woodland Park Ave N
- 829 35th Ave: 2 street-trees
- 923 NW 60th St: a street-tree
- 5538 NE Penrith Rd

PERSIAN IRONWOOD

Parrotia persica (DC.) C.A. Mey.   Persian Witch-Hazel
HAMAMELIDACEÆ
From N Iran (Persia), and the Caucasus.

A wide-spreading small tree—up to 80' tall and used for telephone poles where it's native! The bark is pleasingly mottled and flaky. Tiny red flowers open in late January–March. Leaves lopsided, shortstemmed, to 7" long, wavy, shiny, with varying but always exciting fall color. It is a first-class, troublefree, mildly stimulating ornamental. Common in Seattle; becoming well known.

- 52nd Ave S & S Roxbury St: W side of substation has 3, tallest 54', stoutest 5'0"
- 34th Ave E & E Madison St: taller of a pair is 50'+ tall
- Arboretum: in 7-5E, #915-47 is 50' tall; #134-47 only 37' tall
- 1637 22nd Ave E: 45½' tall
- 7709 16th Ave SW: one 41' tall
- W. Beacon Hill substation (14th Ave S & S Angeline): 2 at the N end, the taller 40'
- Substation at 23rd Ave & E Pine St: three at the NE part
- U.W.: 5 SW of Fluke Hall; an older larger one on Pend Oreille Rd east of gate 3; 3 on SE wall of Communications bldg., tallest 37'
- Phinney Ave N & N 50th St: one 37' tall north of the SE corner building
- 1300 Dexter Ave N

[*Distylium racemosum* S.&Z.—Isu Tree—A related E Asian broadleaf evergreen shrub or small tree. Likely too heat-loving to thrive here, but promoted by nurseries. Very rare. Arboretum #387-57A in 6-4E is only 14' tall; in 6-5E a full 16' tall. An old, big one at 1225 McGilvra Blvd is hard to see. Bradner Gardens Park has one 9½' tall near the SE corner. One was *pl.* in 2004 at 3425 West Laurelhurst Drive NE: right against the house.]

[*Sycopsis sinensis* Oliv.—A Chinese broadleaf evergreen shrub or small tree. Extremely rare. Arboretum #1417-40 & 985-41 in 6-4E form a *grove*, the tallest 36½'; the stoutest trunk 1'9" around. Children's Hospital has one 23' tall by the stairs S of the "giraffe" parking garage. Some Seattle yards have young specimens.]

[× *Sycoparrotia semidecidua* Endr. & Anl. = *Sycopsis* × *Parrotia*—Half-deciduous, half tree. Leaves to 6" × 2⅝", borne in attractive tabular layers; flowers not showy. Extremely rare. Arboretum #52-72 is 33' × 2'4" in 6-4E. A young, 14' tall street-tree flanked by Serviceberry trees is on the east side of 28th Ave E, north of E Valley St.]

American PERSIMMON

Diospyros virginiana L.   Common Persimmon
EBENACEÆ   Sugar Plum Tree / Winter Plum
From the central & eastern U.S.   'Possum Wood *or* Apple *or* Plum

The Persimmon is primarily known as a wild fruit tree of individual temperament, neither comparable nor related to more familiar fruit trees. Its cherry or small plum-sized fruit is edible when it becomes soft, fragrant and orange (usually not until after frost strikes). Unripe, the fruit's astringency will dry and pucker tongue and cheek to an ungodly aching irritation. Superior fruit cultivars exist but are scarce.

Usually a slender tree of small size, at most 131' × 22', its heavy, hard, dark and elastic wood is related to ebony but not as valuable. It has rugged, checkered bark, pleasing fall color, and any uneaten fruit can also be pretty in autumn: the orange fruit against a blue sky on a clear day is adorable. Unnoticed little creamy-white flowers in late June are good bee forage; some trees are solely male or female, others are bisexual. In the Language of Flowers this eccentric tree means "bury me amidst nature's beauties."

In Seattle it is rare, exasperatingly slow, and forms few fruits worth eating (ripe late October–February, like 1"-wide, smooth, gooey, overripe apricots of their own peculiar flavor).

- Denny Park: a fruitful one 36' × 4'0" by the flagpole
- Arboretum: 3 in 12-1W, 13-1W & 12-2W, the tallest 42½' × 2'7"; plus one #786-66 cv. 'John Rick' 35½' × 1'11½" (larger leaves, and fruit up to 2" wide); four on the hillside path E of the ballfield, the largest 27' × 2'6"
- 1408 N 47th St: two ♂ street-trees, the taller 45' × 3'10¼"
- 45th Ave NE, south of NE 60th St: two street-trees, E side, the taller 30'
- 209 23rd Ave E

Date-Plum (PERSIMMON)

D. Lotus L.
From W Asia, N Iran,
N India, China, Korea.

Date of Trebizond / Italian Lignum-vitæ
Wood of Life / Bastard Menynwood
Pock Wood

Little known in the United States, the Date-Plum is a close relative of Persimmon, but smaller (to 100' × 15½'); its fruit also smaller, less colorful and usually less edible; its leaves smaller, and dull colored later in fall. In brief, an inferior tree chiefly worth growing for curiosity's sake. But it does provide a useful rootstock for the fruiting cultivars of its superior cousins. The tiny fruits, likened to date-flavored plums, have been (along with other contenders, *e.g.* those of European Hackberry) put forth as the "Lotus" of Homer. In China, "they ward off evil influence, and when eaten for some time, give a pleasing appearance to the countenance, and strength and lightness to the body." (Smith, p. 153)
Date-Plum trees are extremely rare here.

- U.W.: until cut down in autumn 1986, one was 50' × 5'9"
- Kinnear Park: upper level, NW of the restrooms, overhanging a path, is one 37½' × 4'9½" × 42' wide; it makes seedless but sweet fruit yearly
- Locks bed #203 has a slender one 46' × 1'10", right next to a 58' tall Sweetgum

Kaki PERSIMMON

D. Kaki L. fil.
From NE India,
Burma, China, Korea.

Chinese *or* Oriental *or* Japanese Persimmon
Tomato Tree / Chinese Fig
Chinese: Shi

This yields the persimmon fruit of store and market—differing from the American in being larger (up to 3½"), thick-skinned, less piquantly flavored and varying widely in shape. The national fruit of Japan, it is as well known in much of east Asia as apples are here. "Kaki" (カキ) is its Japanese name. The tree can grow 60' tall and is usually grafted on Date-Plum rootstock. It's been cultivated for eons in many improved forms. California orchards now produce commercial quantities, and more of us grow our own but the tree is still uncommon here. The tree is as attractive as it is useful and is easily grown.

- 10th Ave S, N of S Thistle St: 3 street-trees, E side, the tallest 35½'; stoutest 2'11½"

- Arboretum: 'Fuyu' seedlings (#X-372) are in 12-3W (27½' × 1'7¼") and uphill east of the stone cottage; also in the Japanese Garden
- 41st Ave NE & NE 75th St: the NW corner yard has one
- Brooklyn Ave NE & NE 50th St: one next to an apple tree south of the house
- S.U.: 8' tall SW of the Quad's fountain
- 3740 E John St: a street-tree (a Corkscrew Hazel west of it)
- 38th Ave E & E Newton St: SE lot (1936) has one
- Broadway E & E Edgar St: NE corner has one south of the housse
- 9634 15th Ave NW (across from Swanson's Nursery)
- U.W.: two shade-suppressed saplings in a grove of mixed trees west of Bloedel Hall

Chinese PHELLODENDRON

Phellodendron chinense Schneid. var. *glabriusculum* Schneid.

RUTACEÆ

From China.

These broad-spreading trees, rarely to 60' tall, thrive in continental climates. Though the name is similar to *Philodendron*, they are not related to the well-known houseplants. According to most authorities there are 3–10 species of *Phellodendron*—but as these "species" freely intergrade and the differences between them are slight, dissidents logically maintain that there is only one species, of baffling variability. Nurseries in the U.S. have sold various kinds, generally under the name **Amur Cork Tree** (*P. amurense* Rupr.)—in 1993 Robert Van Pelt measured a real Amur specimen, in Broadmoor, 41' × 5'8"× 54' wide.

In Seattle, extremely rare. They are slow-growing, look stunted and show little inclination to grow. They have smooth, gray, somewhat cherry-like bark; ash-like leaves of (usually) 11–15 leaflets turning yellow in autumn; and tiny yellow-green flowers (June–July) giving rise to juicy black berries of unknown edibility, ⅓" wide, tasting like too strongly-flavored licorice jelly beans.

- S Jackson St, from 5th to 8th: a couple dozen City street-trees, the tallest 36'
- Zoo: 1 by African wild dog, and 3 by the Hippopotamus pond; tallest 15'
- Children's Hospital: one *pl.* in the late 1980s

Sakhalin PHELLODENDRON

P. sachalinense (Fr. Schmidt) Sarg.

=*P. amurense* Rupr. var. *sachalinense* Fr. Schmidt

From W China, Sakhalin, Korea, N Japan.

Similar—like all *Phellodendrons!*—to the preceding but possibly not such a failure in Seattle: it seems to do better. Also extremely rare here. At the Arboretum in 48-2E & 48-3E, the largest are 58½' × 5'1" (#316-75), and 57' × 4'5½" (#18-73A); #354-59 in 14-B is small. One 24½' tall is at 11326 15th Ave NE.

PHŒNIX TREE

Firmiana simplex (L.) W.F. Wight   Chinese Parasol Tree
=F. platanifolia (L. fil.) Marsili   Japanese Varnish Tree / Bottle Tree
STERCULIACEÆ   Chinese: Wu Tong
From E Asia.   Japanese: Ao-giri アオギリ

"Phœnix Tree" was so named because the Chinese say that bird prefers to perch on this slender tree of smooth greenish snakelike bark. Since 3 specimens survived the Hiroshima A-bomb explosion, all the more appropriate a name. The bold leaves are lobed like those of Fig trees, to 15¾" long and wide. In July or August, large clusters of lightly fragrant, creamy, star-shaped flowers open; they are not very pretty. The seedpods, to 4–5" long, make cute *little parasols*. The name Varnish Tree refers to brownish fluid released by the opening seedpods. Recorded to 72' × 7¼'. Though a weedy ornamental in the SE United States, in Seattle, only a *few youngsters* are known.

- Arboretum: #1533-56A is 22½' × 1'8¼" north of the greenhouse; #5-91A is on the south side of Rhododendron Glen (11-6E)
- 5428 49th Ave SW: the garden here has a youngster *ca.* 8' tall

Chinese PHOTINIA

Photinia serratifolia (Desf.) Kalkman   Chinese: Shi Nan
=P. serrulata Lindl.
ROSACEÆ
From S India, China, Taiwan, the Philippines.

A broadleaf evergreen shrub or small tree up to about 50' × 5'. It is common here in older yards as a foundation planting that grew into a tree, arching out from the house. In March–April very conspicuous bronzy new foliage emerges; flat-clustered white flowers (March) April–May give rise to little red berries. Chinese photinia has been superseded by its hybrid offspring the Fraser photinia.

- 8912 Fauntleroy Way SW: one way in the back yard is *ca.* 50' tall
- Locks bed #24 (44' tall, at top of the stairs), 26 (by 28), 28 (33' tall), 210 (bushy)
- 3933 46th Ave S: 43' tall
- south of 4919 Phinney Ave N: one 41½' tall
- 1400 37th Ave E: immense, in NW corner of yard, 37' tall
- 4th Ave N, north of Newton St: a yard, W side, one 35½' tall
- U.W.: one 34' tall with 2 main trunks by a Ponderosa Pine east of Lewis Hall; two S of Lander Hall, tallest 30½'
- Epiphany School (3710 E Howell): 33' tall by a double-flowered Weeping Cherry
- (Old) Beacon Hill School (16th Ave S & S Lander St): tallest of 3 by entrance is 33'
- Arboretum: the best is 32' × 1'¼" (#275-51A in 20-2E)
- Meridian Ave N & N 42nd St: NE corner has one 30' tall
- Volunteer Park: one 31' × 4'8" across the road opposite the service area gate
- 9121 Fauntleroy Way SW (at SW Wildwood Pl): a '**Nova Lineata**' 26' tall; wider

Fraser PHOTINIA

P. × *Fraseri* Dress   Common or Hybrid Photinia
(*P. serratifolia* × *P. glabra* [Thunb.] Maxim.)   Redtip

This hybrid originated in 1940. Cultivars include '**Birmingham**', '**Red Robin**' and '**Robusta**'. It's a shrub or small tree with bright fire-engine red, very glossy new foliage, relatively sparing in flower and fruit. Being so colorful, neat and new, it skyrocketed to popularity and became a major landscape feature here in the 1980s. Nurseries sell it shrub-sized for hedges, and as standard trees that can be expected to slowly reach about 20' × 3'. It's overplanted, yet it is a desirable, attractive asset—disagreement centers on how often and where to plant it. A brand new *variegated* clone is called **Pink Marble**™ ('Cassini'), but citing tree examples of it is not yet possible.

– U.W.: 34½' tall, + a blue Atlas Cedar on SE corner of 11th Ave NE & NE 41st St
– 3500 27th Pl W: 34' tall south of bldg. 6
– 1408 Orange Place N (north of Lee St): 32' tall in yard
– Arboretum: the largest specimens are #171-59 in 16-3E (best 30' × 4'2¼")
– 8052 15th Ave NE: two, the taller 27½'
– Broadway E, north of E Lynn St: 8 street-trees
– Boylston Ave E & E Harrison St: only 6 left of 35 street-trees *pl.* in early 1980s
– 35th Ave NE, north of NE 55th St: 5 street-trees, W side

[*P. Beauverdiana* var. *notabilis* (Schneid.) Rehd. & Wils.—is from E Asia and extremely rare here. Deciduous, with November fall color and splendid orange-red ⅓" long berries. Leaves to 7⅜" × 3¼". White flowers in May. Arboretum #293-60 is a pair in 47-2E; larger 40' × 2'3¼"; one SE of the pinetum in 33-5W is 37' × 1'10½". At the Good Shepherd Center a young example by the garage is 11' tall.]

PINES in general

Loosely used, "Pine" may refer to various kinds of trees. In books it usually refers to species of *Pinus*, all of them evergreens with needle-like leaves and woody cones. Other non-*Pinus* pines treated in this guide are:

Chile Pine—see MONKEY TREE *(Araucaria)*
Paraná Pine—see under MONKEY TREE *(Araucaria)*
Umbrella Pine—see UMBRELLA PINE *(Sciadopitys)*
Yew Pine—see YEW PINE *(Podocarpus)*

In Seattle 45 species are known outside of the Arboretum, only two of them native (Lodgepole and Western White). Our ten most common, in approximate order from most abundant to least common, are: Mugo (shrubby), Austrian, Western White, Lodgepole, Ponderosa, Scots, Japanese Red, Eastern White, Japanese Black, and Jack. The U.W. has 29 species, Locks 18, Volunteer Park 11.

Here is the geographic division of the pine species treated in this guide:

Chinese (*P. tabulæformis*)
Japanese Black (*P. Thunbergiana*)
Japanese White (*P. parviflora*)
Kwantung (*P. kwantungensis*)
Yunnan (*P. yunnanensis*)

Himalayan White (*P. Wallichiana*)
Japanese Red (*P. densiflora*)
Korean (*P. koraiensis*)
Lacebark (*P. Bungeana*)

EUROPEAN (9)

Aleppo (*P. halepensis*)
Bosnian (*P. Heldreichii*)
Macedonian (*P. Peuce*)
Scots (*P. sylvestris*)
Swiss Stone (*P. Cembra*)

Austrian Black (*P. nigra*)
Cluster (*P. Pinaster*)
Mountain & Mugo (*P. Mugo*)
Stone (*P. Pinea*)

EAST NORTH AMERICAN (8)

Eastern White (*P. Strobus*)
Loblolly (*P. Tæda*)
Red (*P. resinosa*)
Table Mountain (*P. pungens*)

Jack (*P. Banksiana*)
Pitch (*P. rigida*)
Shortleaf (*P. echinata*)
Virginia (*P. virginiana*)

WEST NORTH AMERICAN (19)

Bigcone (*P. Coulteri*)
Bristlecone (*P. longæva*)
Gregg (*P. Greggii*)
Jelecote (*P. patula*)
Limber (*P. flexilis*)
Mexican White (*P. strobiformis*)
Montezuma (*P. Montezumæ*)
Piñon (*P. edulis*)
Sugar (*P. Lambertiana*)
Whitebark (*P. albicaulis*)

Bristlecone (*P. aristata*)
Digger (*P. Sabineana*)
Jeffrey (*P. Jeffreyi*)
Knobcone (*P. attenuata*)
Lodgepole (*P. contorta*)
Monterey (*P. radiata*)
Piñón (*P. cembroides*)
Ponderosa (*P. ponderosa*)
Western White (*P. monticola*)

Total: 44 species.

Pines grouped by needles per bundle:

2 needles per bundle (16)

Aleppo (*P. halepensis*)
Bosnian (*P. Heldreichii*)
Cluster (*P. Pinaster*)
Japanese Black (*P. Thunbergiana*)
Lodgepole (*P. contorta*)
Piñón (*P. edulis*)
Scots (*P. sylvestris*)
Stone (*P. Pinea*)
Virginia (*P. virginiana*)

Austrian Black (*P. nigra*)
Chinese (*P. tabulæformis*)
Jack (*P. Banksiana*)
Japanese Red (*P. densiflora*)
Mountain & Mugo (*P. Mugo*)
Red (*P. resinosa*)
Shortleaf (*P. echinata*)
Table Mountain (*P. pungens*)

Bigcone (*P. Coulteri*)
Gregg (*P. Greggii*)
Jelecote (*P. patula*)
Lacebark (*P. Bungeana*)
Monterey (*P. radiata*)
Pitch (*P. rigida*)
Yunnan (*P. yunnanensis*)

Gray (*P. Sabineana*)
Jeffrey (*P. Jeffreyi*)
Knobcone (*P. attenuata*)
Loblolly (*P. Tæda*)
Piñón (*P. cembroides*)
Ponderosa (*P. ponderosa*)

Bristlecone (*P. aristata*)
Eastern White (*P. Strobus*)
Japanese White (*P. parviflora*)
Kwantung (*P. kwantungensis*)
Macedonian White (*P. Peuce*)
Montezuma (*P. Montezumæ*)
Swiss Stone (*P. Cembra*)
Whitebark (*P. albicaulis*)

Bristlecone (*P. longæva*)
Himalayan White (*P. Wallichiana*)
Korean (*P. koraiensis*)
Limber (*P. flexilis*)
Mexican White (*P. strobiformis*)
Sugar (*P. Lambertiana*)
Western White (*P. monticola*)

Aleppo PINE

Pinus halepensis Mill.   Jerusalem Pine
PINACEÆ
From the Mediterranean region.

Needles 2 (3) per bundle, 2½–5¼" long; *cones* 2–4¾" long, backward turned and long persisting on the branches; *tree* usually 50–60' tall but in California to 144' × 12'.

Aleppo Pine is extremely rare in Seattle. One 37' tall is with 2 Sweetgums and varied maples on N 38th St west of Stone Way N. Arboretum: #119-93A (from Spain) and #230-94B (from Turkey)—both 16' tall and on Foster Island.

Austrian Black PINE

P. nigra Arn.   Austrian Pine
=*P. austriaca* Hoess   European Black Pine
=*P. nigricans* Host   Common Black Pine
=*P. Laricio* Poir. var. *austriaca* (Hoess) Loud.
Various subspecies of *P. nigra* range from Spain to the Black Sea;
the Austrian one extends from E Austria to N Italy and NE Greece.

Needles 2 per bundle, 3–5½" long; *cones* borne singly or in groups of up to 6 in a whorl, 2–4" long; *tree* to 150' × 21'.

Dark, massive, rugged. Plain and rather uninteresting compared to many other pines, it is still widely planted here for historic rather than rational or esthetic reasons. There are many prettier pines, including its subspecific kin the Corsican, Crimean, and Pyrenean Black pines. In Seattle, too common.

- Washelli Cemetery: largest is 95' × 11'7" (+6 Doug. Fir) 180' N of 1921 mausoleum
- Volunteer Park: best of 4 across the road south of the wading pool is 106' × 10'0"
- U.W.: a street-tree by Hall Health, 74' × 8'½"; S of new law building, 67' × 7'2¼"
- Martha Washington Park: SW part has one 80' × 9'2¾"
- Dunlap School (8621 46th Ave S): one 64' × 9'8"
- 2504 S Ferdinand St: a handsome, broad tree 46' tall
- Locks bed #23, 205 (eight), 208 (three), 302 (60' tall)

ssp. *Laricio* (Poir.) Maire   Corsican (Black) Pine
=var. *Poiretiana* (Ant.) Aschers. & Graebn.   Calabrian Pine
=var. *calabria* (Loud.) Schneid.
=var. *maritima* (Ait. fil.) Melv.
=var. *corsicana* (Loud.) Hyl.
From Calabria (*i.e.* S Italy), Sicily, Corsica.

Corsican pine's needles are longer (4–6¾") than those of Austrian pine, the cones shorter, and the tree is narrower, with slender branches forming a lighter crown, to 180' × 23'. It is rare in Seattle compared to Austrian pine.

- Volunteer Park: on the E border, near Prospect St, one by a Beech is 104' × 8'8¼"
- Arboretum: the tallest of 2 #419-37 in the pinetum (35-5W) is 84', stoutest 7'¼"
- U.W.: 3 northeast of Clark Hall, the largest 83' × 7'7½"

ssp. *Pallasiana* (D. Don) Holmboe   Crimean (Black) Pine
=var. *caramanica* (Loud.) Rehd.
From SE Europe and the Asia Minor area.

This race has longer needles like those of Corsican pine, and the cones are a bit longer than Austrian pine's. The trunk tends to fork candelabrum fashion, making a broad-crowned tree. Specimens planted in the British Isles have reached 135' × 17½'. It is extremely rare in Seattle.

- Laurelhurst Playfield: of 9 by the tennis courts, the stoutest is 80' × 11'2¼" (26 Ponderosa Pines are N of the tennis courts)
- View Ridge Playfield: the tallest of 16 is 77' (also there are 5 Scots pines)
- Arboretum: #375-58A in the crabapple meadow (33-7E) is 70' × 6'7"

Bigcone PINE

P. Coulteri D. Don   Coulter Pine
From S California, NW Mexico.

Needles 3 per bundle, 6–14" long; *cones* 8–14 (20)" long, weighing to 5–7 (8) pounds, fiercely clawed; *seeds* large and edible; *tree* to 144' × 17¼'.

A bold, striking tree with the most massive cones of any pine, and the longest needles of any grown here. The cones usually cling unopened to the branches, dropping only in storms. This Goliath of the pine tribe is too huge for average yards. It can only be mistaken for Gray (Digger) pine. It is uncommon in Seattle though very conspicuous.

- U.W.: one in front of Winkenwerder Hall is 96' × 10'11½"; the tallest of 9 west of

McMahon Hall and by Gardeners' Vista is 109½' × 7'2"
- Arboretum: pinetum grove of 7 (in 38-5W), the largest 84' × 9'9¾" (#2135-40B)
- 9228 Wallingford Ave N: one 85' tall
- Locks bed #118A

Bosnian PINE

P. Heldreichii H. Christ   Balkan *or* Bosnian Redcone Pine
=*P. leucodermis* Ant.   Snakeskin *or* Graybark Pine
From SE European mountains.   Herzegovinian Pine

Needles 2 per bundle, 2⅜–3½" (4¼") long; *cones* 2–4" long, dark purple-red when young; *tree* to 100' × 18¾'.

A dark, bolt upright, medium-sized tree. Young trunks and the branches retain smooth light gray bark (*leucodermis* means white skin, from Greek *leukos* and *derma*) for a long time; the shoots upon losing their needles are similar to snakeskin due to closely spaced leaf cushions. The Arboretum has 4 old trees, including #1105-49A in 32-7E that is 52' × 3'10". Youngsters are uncommon in Seattle, such as many at SSCC Arboretum, one 32' tall on the SE corner of 45th Ave SW & SW Dawson St, and one 20' tall at Kinnear Park.

Bristlecone PINE

P. aristata Engelm. *ex* Parry & Engelm.   Rocky Mt. Bristlecone Pine
From high, arid mountains in   Foxtail *or* Hickory Pine
W Colorado, N New Mexico, N Arizona.   Pricklecone Pine

Needles (1,2,3,4) 5 per bundle, 1–2" long, bearing conspicuous drops of whitish pitch jocularly called dandruff; *cones* 1½–3½ (4½)" long, with fragile, short needlelike bristles; *tree* to 76' × 12¾'.

Well publicized as capable of living to 2,435 years where conditions are favorable, namely, in bone dry, harsh alpine wasteland. Venerable age, unkind to the health of the stubborn trees, weathers them into photogenic, inspiring wrecks. In Seattle, youngsters are common; older, cone-bearing specimens are not. In any case the trees are remarkably densely foliated, dark and slow-growing.

- Volunteer Park: one 33½' × 2'8" west of the water tower
- U.W.: the NW corner of parking lot E-2 has a pair, coning, the largest 20' × 2'5½"
- Locks bed #101 (two by west lightpost), 214 (3' tall), 316 (two, very small)
- 3941 NE Surber Dr: 23' tall
- Orca at Columbia School (3528 S Ferdinand St): a small one E of entrance, by dwarf Alberta (White) Spruce, rosemary, *etc.*

[**Intermountain, Great Basin** *or* **Western Bristlecone-Pine**—*P. longæva* D.K. Bailey =*P. aristata* var. *longæva* (D.K. Bailey) Little—From central Utah, S Nevada, and E California's White Mountains. Needles (3,4) 5 per bundle, 1–1¼" long. Cones 2⅜–4" long. One aged 4,700+ years is called "Methuselah;" the oldest was 4,995 years when cut down. Exceedingly rare in cultivation. It needs alkaline soil to get established, is finicky and slow. Recorded to 94' × 39⅓'. A youngster is at 9043 Dibble Ave NW.]

Chinese PINE

P. tabulæformis Carr. *(tabuliformis)* — Chinese Hard Pine
=*P. sinensis* Mayr, *non* Lamb. — Chinese Red Pine
From China, Korea. — Chinese: You Song

Needles 2 (3) per bundle, 3½–7" long; *cones* 1½–2½" long; *tree* to 80' × 10'.

In China, a valuable timber tree known as "Red" or "Horsetail" pine. As grown here, an uncommon pine that usually develops a broad crown of wide spreading branches, decorated by persistent little cones. Trunk thickness increases slowly. It most resembles Japanese Black pine. Possibly *some* Seattle specimens are really *P. densata* Mast., from the Tibetan Plateau, that originated as a hybrid involving Chinese pine and Yunnan pine.

– Arboretum: the largest (#2404-37D in pinetum, 35-5W) is 78' × 5'0"; #464-40A is 54½' × 3'4½" on Foster Island (hurt by Red Oaks; leaning)
– Seward Park: several NE of stove #6, the largest 73' × 3'10"; one by the park entrance is 57' × 6'4"
– Woodland Park: the largest of a number by the cobblestone mound in the N end (very close to Aurora Ave) is 3'11" around, the tallest over 70'
– Volunteer Park: one NE of the reservoir is 49½' × 4'10¼"
– Zoo: S of the fence at the SW corner is one 53' × 3'7½"
– Locks bed #207 has a younster (near bed #208)
– 4814 Purdue Ave NE: one 41' tall, near the street light
– 7510 30th Ave NE: one uphill east of a Douglas Fir

Cluster PINE

P. Pinaster Soland. — Landes' *or* Sea *or* Mediterranean Pine
=*P. maritima* Poir., *non* Lamb. — Bordeaux *or* Maritime *or* Bournemouth Pine
From SW Europe, NW Africa. — Dill-seed Tree / Pinaster (Pine)

Needles 2 (3) per bundle, 5–10" long; *cones* 4–10" long; *tree* to 120' × 18½'.

The *Pinaster* might well be called the Star pine, for its cones are often in star-like whorls or clusters, conspicuous due to their large size. Cluster pine is the main pine of Portugal and of southern France, and is used extensively for seaside erosion control, for timber and for naval stores (*i.e.* pitch, tar, resin and turpentine) production. In Seattle it is uncommon. It stands out in age with a long, often leaning, red, bare trunk of deeply plated bark, surmounted by a romantically irregular crown of branches bearing very long, thick needles, and large cones which squirrels eagerly destroy as they go for the seeds.

– Zoo: by Phinney Ave N are 20, the tallest 80', the stoutest 7'10"
– Arboretum: the largest of several is 91' × 8'10" (#1465-37A in the pinetum, 36-5W)
– Volunteer Park: by NE area of wading pool, flanked by 2 Austrian pines, one 78½' × 6'5½" wears a sign that says NO DOGS OR BICYCLES ALLOWED IN POOL
– Matthews Beach Park: tallest of 5 E of parking lot is 55'; stoutest 6'11¼"
– Pritchard Island Beach Park (55th Ave S & S Grattan St): one in the S end
– Soundview Playfield (15th Ave NW & NW 90th St): 3 W of the children's play area

(+other pines such as Japanese Black and Western White); best 45' × 7'3½"
- Lincoln Park: the area NE of the wading pool had a big one that died; 13 wild offspring are *ca.* 10 years old
- 4510 NE Tulane Pl: one of few yards that has a specimen

Eastern White PINE

P. Strobus L.   Northern White Pine
From the central and eastern   Weymouth Pine
U.S., SE Canada; a disjunct   Pumpkin Pine
var. in Mexico and Guatemala.   Soft Pine

Needles 5 per bundle, 3–5½" long; *cones* slender and pitchy, 4–8 (10)" long; *tree* to 270' × 37½'.

The original and foremost "White pine," this played a leading role in the drama of early European history in the New World—above all other trees, White pine exerted more influence and had the greatest impact. It is a world-class tree whose significance in nature and stupendous size place it at the forefront of its kin. The State Tree of Maine and Michigan, it was the most important constituent of the northeastern forest, and the most valuable material resource for early settlers. A symbol of lofty patriotism, its image has flown on flags and graced postage stamps; masts and figureheads of its wood sailed the seas. Its exalted dimensions and stately beauty have astonished and bewildered onlookers for centuries. Not stiff or rigid, it forgoes brute strength to be instead lax, airy, soft and cheerful in color, form, wood and influence.

In Seattle, common; its cousin Western White pine is native here.
- Arboretum: many, largest 110' × 9'3" in 30-5W
- Interlaken Park: one in the middle of native woods is 115½' × 5'10¼"
- Volunteer Park: the largest of many is 88' × 8'12", by the SE corner bus-stop
- Golden Gardens Park: one 101' × 6'5" near upper level restrooms
- U.W.: various specimens, such as 1 west of the flagpole, 2 east (plus 2 Western White pines and 1 Austrian Black pine)
- U.W. Friendship Grove, representing Guatemala

cv. 'Fastigiata'   Columnar White Pine

Slender, its branches grow upward making a very narrow tree. Uncommon.
- Arboretum: 34-6E has #494-57A, 65' × 5'7¼" (by a smaller fastigiate Scots pine); it is also in the Japanese Garden's extreme SW corner
- U.W.: 55' × 4'7" NW of the HUB
- 208 30th Ave (at E Spruce St): 3 in yard
- 6523 38th Ave NE: three
- 5242 35th Ave NE: two

f. *nana* (Hornibrook) Welch   Dwarf White Pine

Dwarf, bushy cultivars under this name in some cases eventually shoot their bolts and compact, broad form to become small trees. Likewise with cultivars

'Radiata' and 'Umbraculifera'. Such trees bear cones to 3" and needles only to 2¾" long. These are very rare tree-sized in Seattle.

 – U.W.: one 47½' tall SE of Husky Stadium (north of a Scots pine)
 – 6208 36th Ave NW: one 20' tall by alley

cv. 'Pendula'   Weeping White Pine

A gracefully floppy semi-dwarf mound, very distinctive. Uncommon here.

 – 2510 29th Ave W (2nd yard north of W Smith St, on E side): 26' tall
 – 10715 38th Ave NE: one 26' tall with a 38' tall weeping Sierra Redwood
 – Arboretum: #495-57 is 15½' × 2'10½" in 13-4E
 – Kubota Gardens Park: several; one being 22' × 2'3½"
 – 334 Erie Ave: one by garage; a larger Japanese Red pine to the south
 – 13308 10th Ave NE: one 22½' tall
 – Volunteer Park: 13' tall, on lawn east of the water tower

cv. 'Torulosa' ('Tortuosa')   Twisted *or* Contorted White Pine

Conspicuously twisted needles and to a lesser degree the branches. It looks diseased. (Cultivar name invalid, being Latin yet post-1959.) Uncommon.

 – 8318 Meridian Ave N
 – 6052 52nd Ave NE
 – 62nd Ave S & S Prentice St: SE corner has one 29' tall (+ a Japanese White pine)
 – SSCC Arboretum: one 23½' tall in the Milton Sutton conifer garden

Gray *or* Gray-needle PINE

P. Sabineana Dougl. *ex* D. Don *(Sabiniana)*   Ghost *or* Foothill Pine
From California.   Digger Pine

Needles 3 per bundle, drooping, 7–14" long; *cones* massive, heavily clawed, 5–10½" long; *tree* to 161' × 18½'.

Sparsely foliated, grayish and weepy, this species is often multitrunked candelabrum fashion, with squat, dark, conspicuous and very persistent cones. It owes its historic English name—Digger pine—to the fact that many Californian Indians, derogatorily designated Diggers by white settlers, ate its large seeds. It is rare in Seattle, and likely to be confused only with Bigcone Pine—a greener, denser tree, with larger, yellowish cones.

 – U.W.: the largest of two N of the Undergraduate Library is 90' × 10'4¼"
 – Leschi boat moorage area (Lake Washington Blvd south of E Jefferson St) had 5, the largest 7'10" around in 1983—now there are 2, the largest 67' × 9'2½"
 – Rodgers Park: one 70' × 9'4½" near 1st Ave W & W Armour St
 – 814 McGilvra Blvd E has one down by the lake 86' × 9'9" (1990)
 – 5612 1st Ave NW: 57' tall
 – Locks bed #327 had one 7'7" around in 1985, but it broke up in June 1987; smaller ones remain in beds #23 (67' tall), 202 (63' tall), 327 (with a smaller Jeffrey pine)
 – Arboretum: the largest is #1499-56A in pinetum 33-4W, 56' × 3'0"

Gregg PINE

P. Greggii Engelm. *ex* Parl.
From mountains of E Mexico.

Needles 3 per bundle, 3–5" (6") long, bright yellow-green, delicate; *cones* 2½–5" (6") long, curving back on the branches, in clusters; spineless; often warped; *tree* to 100' × 8'.

Named after Josiah Gregg (1806–1850), trader, writer, and botanical explorer, who discovered it in 1847. Exceedingly rare. Arboretum #688-60A in 33-5E is 43' × 4'2¾". Locks bed #205 (employee parking) has a youngster.

Himalayan White PINE

P. Wallichiana A.B. Jacks.   Himalaya Pine
=*P. Griffithii* McClelland, *non* Parl.   Bhutan Pine
=*P. excelsa* Wall. *ex* D. Don, *non* Lamb.   Blue Pine
=*P. nepalensis* de Chambr., non J. Forbes
From the Himalayas, E Afghanistan to N Burma.

Needles 5 per bundle, 4–8" long, droopy; *cones* slender, 6–13" long; *tree* to 165' × 17'.

A companion of Deodar Cedar in the mighty Himalayan valleys. Quite like Eastern White pine but wider, with larger cones and longer, droopy needles. Old examples are rare here, young ones uncommon.

- 5563 S Holly St: 80' × 9'5", *pl. ca.* 1939
- Arboretum: 85' × 4'5" (#177-51 east of Azalea Way in 21-1W); 83' × 6'2½" (#382-55 in 6S-9E); 70½' × 5'6¼" (#382-55B N of crabapple meadow 34-5E)
- U.W.: 51' × 5'4¼" +a blue Atlas cedar between Fisheries center & S Campus center
- 54th Ave NE & NE 55th St: SE corner has three, the tallest 80'
- 5th Ave W & W Raye St: NE corner has one E of house
- Zoo: by the Snow Leopard exhibit; tallest 40'+
- S.U.: 52½' × 4'9¼" not far from the pond below Campion Hall, in company with Japanese Black & Red pines, blue Colorado Spruce, *etc.*
- Locks bed #201 (by #203; 76' tall), 205, 304
- Highline Mental Health (2600 SW Holden St): 4 west of a bldg.; the tallest 67'
- 8415 8th Ave NE: a cv. 'Zebrina' (striped needles) 26' tall
- Twin Ponds Park: a cv. 'Zebrina' (striped needles) 16' tall W of the tennis courts

[**Hybrid White Pine**—*P.* × *Schwerinii* Fitsch. *(P. Wallichiana* × *P. Strobus)*—It inherits blister rust resistance from *P. Wallichiana*. Individual specimens vary but in general look intermediate. Needles 5 per bundle, 3½–7⅝" long. Cones 3–7½" long. Extremely rare. U.W.: 85' × 7'7" by Communications bldg. Arboretum #138-54 is 76' × 6'5¼" in 6S-9E and #138-54A is 62' × 5'1½" in 34-6E. One 42' × 2'8" at Green Lake N of the theater looks like it is dying.]

[**Hybrid White Pine**—*P.* 'Mercury'. *(P. Wallichiana* × *P. parviflora)*—Needles 5 per bundle, 2¼–6¼" long. Cones 3½–6" long, relatively persistent. Extremely rare. Arboretum #138-63 is 69' × 4'¼" in 23-1W, and a 2nd is 56½' × 3'3½" in 1S-5E. One *pl. ca.* 1994 is 23' tall is just north of the city at Twin Ponds Park, W of the tennis courts; near it are a Japanese White pine and a 'Zebrina' Himalayan White pine.]

Jack PINE

P. Banksiana Lamb.
=*P. divaricata* (Ait.) Dum.-Cours.
From much of Canada, and the
Great Lakes region to New England.

Gray *or* (Northern) Scrub Pine
Hudson Bay Pine
Horncone Pine
Princess Pine

Needles 2 per bundle, ¾–1¾" long, yellowish-green; *cones* persistent, bent, strongly curved, often dented, 1–3" long; *tree* to 100' × 9½'.

Slender branched, and of a sickly hue, Jack pine is commonly planted as a no-maintenance small pine, tolerant of conditions wherein most of its cousins refuse to grow. It looks like a gaunt, starving Lodgepole pine.

– Arboretum: the taller of 2 on Foster Island is 69' × 3'5¼" (#1111-45B)
– U.W.: 54' × 2'5" dying in a grove W of Anderson Hall; 45' × 2'11½" N of the Burke Museum; 45½' × 2'2¾" east of the Art Building (crowded by Bay Laurel)
– Lake View Cemetery: one 37' × 3'8" × 28½' wide, by 84' × 21'10" Sierra Redwood
– Stone Way N & N 36th St (Bank of America)
– Zoo: 9 west of the Fremont (south) parking lot; largest trunk 3'1¼" around

Japanese Black PINE

P. Thunbergii Parl. *ex* DC., *non* Lamb.
=*P. Thunbergiana* Franco
From Japan, South Korea.

Japanese: Kuro-matsu クロマシ
O-matsu

Needles 2 per bundle, 3–5¾" long; *cones* 1½–3" long, sometimes dozens per cluster; *tree* to 130' × 20½'.

Japanese Black pine is a large, valuable forest tree in nature. Cultivated in the West it is usually irregular in form and slow to moderate in growth. Slender white buds and spring "candles" contrast strongly with its rich dark green foliage. More than any other pine it has the odd habit of sometimes producing excessive clusters of dozens of tightly packed cones per shoot. It is common here; few are over 30' × 3'. It most resembles the far less common Chinese pine.

– Ravenna Park: one 75½' × 5'6" is best of 10 (+5 Eastern White pines, 2 Ponderosa pines,2 Mountain pines) at the S end of the 20th Avenue bridge on the W side
– 4401 52nd Ave NE: by steps in front of house
– Bagley Ave N & N 77th St: NW corner has one 59' tall
– 32nd Ave NE & NE 90th St: one 52' tall with a Japanese Maple on the SW corner
– University Bridge: NE end, 2 by stairway with Sumach, Aspens, Madrona and Pear
– U.W.: across Stevens Way opposite the front of Architecture Hall, by the stairs
– Soundview Playfield (15th Ave NW & NW 90th St): by tennis courts and play area
– S.U.: 2 flank west entrance of Lemieux Library, N-most 34½'
– 808 W Etruria St

Japanese Red PINE

P. densiflora S.& Z.   Japanese: Aka-matsu アカマツ
From NE China, E Korea, Japan.   Me-matsu

Needles 2 per bundle, 3–5" long; *cones* 1¼–3" long; *tree* to 164' × 20½'.

The most common Japanese pine in nature and here. Remarkably *reddish* in trunk and limb, much like Scots pine, with which it is easily confused. Both species are very common in Seattle.

– Arboretum: #1754-37 in the pinetum (36-4W), 70' × 7'0" & 74' × 4'11½"
– Seward Park: tallest of three is 76' × 4'9"
– Ravenna Park: the largest of 10 N of the lower tennis courts is 75' × 4'10½"
– Locks bed #108 has 11 *pl.* in 1927, the largest 33' × 5'2"; #109 has 3, the largest 48' × 4'11"; others are in beds #27 (three), 28 (61' tall), 305 (two at bldg. corners)
– U.W.: 53' × 6'5" at SE corner of Balmer Hall; NE corner of Meany Hall
– S.U.: 37' tall E of Pigott bldg., N of entrance, mingled with a Vine Maple and 7' tall purple weeping Beech
– West Seattle Golf Course: the largest is 38' × 5'4"
– Lincoln Park: a grove W of the horseshoes
– 60th Ave NE & NE 55th St: NW corner

cv. 'Pendula'   Weeping Japanese Red Pine

A rare dwarf, called by the Japanese "Shidare-Aka-Matsu." Usually it is a *groundcover;* even the largest specimens known here scarcely qualify as trees.

– 2nd Ave NW & NW 62nd St: NE corner has 3 facing W at retaining wall's N end
– Kubota Garden Park: below Overlook
– 807 NE 84th St: a street-tree

cv. 'Umbraculifera'   Tanyosho Pine
='Tanyo-sho' タギョウツョウ   Japanese Table Pine
='Tagyo-sho'   Umbrella Pine

A common mushroom-head tree often seen as a dwarf rockery shrub.

– Kubota Garden Park: the largest of a few old ones is 34' × 7'1"
– S.U.: one 25½' × 7'4¼" is NW of 10th Ave & E Jefferson St, by Campion Hall
– E Highland Dr, west of 19th Ave E: a street-tree, N side, 22½' × 5'1½"
– Hawthorne Hills Vet. Hospital 4020 NE 55th St: 22' tall
– Green Lake: 8 on the SE shore between 66th and Sunnyside, the tallest 18½'
– King County Administration bldg. (5th Ave between James & Jefferson Sts): two

Japanese White PINE

P. parviflora S.& Z.   Japanese: Hime-ko-matsu ゴヨウマツ
=*P. pentaphylla* Mayr   Goyo-matsu
From Japan.

Needles 5 per bundle, ¾–3½" long; *cones* 1½–4" long; *tree* to 100' × 11½'.

As grown in Seattle, Japanese White pines are represented by slow, small, cute, distinctly bluish specimens with needles 2" or less long. Sometimes the name cv. 'Glauca' is used for these. The only pines likely to be mistaken for it would be either relatively rare Kwantung pine or *dwarf* Eastern White pines. It is less common here than Japanese Black or Red pines.

– F.A. McDonald School (144 NE 54th St): larger of two is 32' × 2'9"
– 2223 E Howe St: 27' tall in back yard by garage; visible from E Blaine St
– Arboretum: #796-41 south of the Japanese Garden (1S-1E) is 47½' × 3'6½" and
  shows the *wild* form of this species; #92-48 ('Glauca') in 0-5E is 36' tall and *gaunt;*
  #506-55A ('Glauca') in the conifer meadow (43-6W) is 23' × 1'7"
– 12th Ave S & S Washington St: SW corner has one 24' tall near the telephone pole
– Broadview-Thomson School (13052 Greenwood Ave N): NW corner, with two
  larger Lodgepole pines
– Substation on Bellevue Ave E, north of E John St: 2 by sidewalk, a Shore pine to N
– U.W.: tallest of 3 west of the HUB is 20'; 6 between Miller and Smith Halls
– Locks bed #205A with a Jeffrey pine

Jeffrey PINE

P. Jeffreyi Balf. *ex* A. Murr.
From SW Oregon, California, a bit of Nevada, NW Mexico.

Needles 3 per bundle, 5–13" long; *cones* 5–12" long; *tree* to 230' × 25'.

Long-needled, large-coned, dense, dark in foliage and bark—the big black wolf of our pines. This refers only to Seattle specimens, for in California mountains it can be orange-barked, blue-needled, open and altogether different in appearance! A very few youngsters in Seattle may grow up resembling the colorful Californian kind. Jeffrey Pine is common here, and resembles Ponderosa Pine, but is darker in all respects, denser, stouter, with larger cones and needles.

– 43rd Ave NE & NE 38th St: SW corner has one 91½' tall
– Volunteer Park: one 93½' × 11'1½" NE of the reservoir
– U.W.: largest of many is 79½' × 9'6¼", by the tennis courts west of Lewis Hall
– Arboretum: #202-54B in 33-7E is 85' × 7'2"; #1717-56B in 35-6E is 68' × 7'3¼"
– Locks bed #28 (two, taller 81' + a Japanese Red pine), 205A, 327 (+ a Digger pine)

Jelecote PINE

P. patula Schiede *ex* Schlecht. & Cham.   Mexican Weeping Pine
From mountains of E Mexico.   Mexican Yellow Pine

Needles 3–4 (5) per bundle, 4–12" long, strongly weeping, very slender and shining; *cones* 2½–5¾" long; *tree* to 140' × 11¼'.

The slender, graceful, weeping habit of Jelecote pine is unique in our pines, utterly unmistakable and supremely attractive. Severe winter cold can brown the shiny grass-green needles somewhat or even kill the tree. It's very rare here; few cones have been produced so far.

– Locks bed #211, 304 (40' tall behind the flagpole)
– 5829 16th Ave S: four in the front yard, the tallest 27'
– Good Shepherd Center: one NW of main parking lot is 25' tall
– 26th Ave E & E Aloha St: NE corner; N of the house

Knobcone PINE

P. attenuata Lemm.
=*P. tuberculata* Gord., *non* D. Don
From SW Oregon, California, NW Mexico.

Needles (2) 3 per bundle, 3–7½" long; *cones* curved, very hard and knobby, long persisting unopened, 4–6"+ long; *tree* to 117' × 11¼'; bark relatively smooth.

Rare in Seattle, Knobcone pine is distinctly conspicuous with its whorls of rock-hard, curved cones, never opening here. In nature they open only after forest fires. One can pry cones off the trees and open them by heating in an oven, thereby revealing their beautiful rich-red inside color.

– Arboretum: the tallest (#200-54D in pinetum, 37-6W) is 81½' × 7'3¼"; the stoutest are E of crabapple meadow in 34-7E, #200-54B being 68' × 7'½"; A 8'3"
– 8546 30th Ave NW: one 64' tall
– U.W.: 2 by the overpass to the Health Sciences complex (with Bristlecone and Pitch pines); two behind Bloedel Hall by the Burke-Gilman trail, both 50' × 5'3"
– Happy Medium School (620 20th Ave S): two in front with a Japanese Maple
– 16th Ave & E Olive St: NE corner has 6
– 1674 E Boston Terrace has one *ca.* 56' tall uphill behind the house
– NW Market St, just west of 2nd Ave NW: 12 (also two Scots pines)

[**Hybrid Knobcone Pine**—*P. attenuata* × *P. Coulteri?*—With the two U.W. Knobcone pines behind Bloedel Hall is an apparent hybrid 45' × 4'11", with rough bark and a kinked trunk. No record of it seems to exist. Its parentage is in doubt.]

Korean PINE

P. koraiensis S.& Z.   Korean Nut-Pine
From E Korea, Manchuria, the Russian Far East, Japan.

Needles 5 per bundle, 2½–5" long, prettily blue-green; *cones* 3½–6" long; *tree* to 150' × 15½', with relatively long branches making a broad-crowned specimen.

Korean pine is distinguished from other white pines in that its cones *don't open* to release their very large, edible seeds. It is very rare here, but highly ornamental, especially when laden with its heavy cones.

– Arboretum: the tallest is 49½' × 2'9¼" (#105-58 east of Azalea Way in 23-1W); #222-68A is 34' × 3'4" in conifer meadow (43-5W)
– 12 are west of Aurora Ave N by Woodland Pl N, at N 64th, the largest 46½' × 3'8½" (with many Nikko Firs and Norway Spruces)
– Locks bed #16 has one 31' tall, reaching out over the lawn

Kwantung PINE

P. kwangtungensis Chun *ex* Tsiang   Guangdon(g) Pine
From SE China, Vietnam.   Chinese: Hua Nan Wu Zhen Song

Needles 5 per bundle, 1½–3" (5") long; *cones* 1½–4" (6⅝) long; *tree* to 100' × 15¾'.

Its habit recalls Swiss Stone pine, its foliage the 'Glauca' Japanese White pine but stouter, with needles longer, stiffer, pointier and thicker. Twigs glaucous, hairless or extremely minutely pubescent. The Arboretum has old trees such as #1943-40 that is 30½' × 2'2" (in 22-1W) and 42' × 3'5" (in 0-5E). Youngsters are extremely rare in Seattle, such as one 11' tall at Evergreen Park Cemetery, south of Memory Glen.

Lacebark PINE

P. Bungeana Zucc. *ex* Endl.
From mountains of N China.

Needles 3 (5) per bundle; 2–5½" long; *cones* 1½–3" long; *tree* to 120' × 21'.

At least in advanced age, Lacebark pine lives up to its name, with beautifully mottled trunks. A Chinese name, "Pai P'i Sung," means Whitebark pine. It is rare and slow-growing in Seattle.

– Arboretum: the best of 3 (#237-48) in 23-1W are 44' × 2'1½" and 37' × 3'4"; a smaller #807-76 in 43-6W
– Locks beds #16 (by stairs, 27' × 2'2½"), #17 (shade stunted), 214 (by lightpost)
– Good Shepherd Center: one 12' tall N of the summerhouse
– Seattle Center: west of Key Arena, with a fastigiate Eastern White pine
– S.U.: 2 S of Sullivan Hall/school of law bldg., W of the basalt sculpture

Limber PINE

P. flexilis James   Rocky Mountain White Pine
From the Rocky Mts, Canada to Mexico.   Squirrel Pine

Needles (3,4) 5 (6) per bundle, 1⅝–2¼" (3") long; *cones* 2¾–6" long; *tree* to 85' × 29½'.

A timberline tree throughout the West, often living over 1,000 years. In Seattle Limber pine is an uncommon, dark-needled tree. Many cultivars exist; some of them are technically selections of the var. *reflexa* noted below.

– Arboretum: the pinetum (36-4 and 5W) has three #396-37; best 71' × 5'1¾"
– U.W. Friendship Grove, representing Honduras, 44' × 3'2"
– 2222 NE 82nd St: a broad, prominent tree 34½' tall
– Woodland Park: two NW of Woodland Park Ave N & N 50th St; taller 35'
– Shilshole Bay Marina (7001 Seaview Ave NW): 6 (with other pine species) bordering the N end parking lot; the largest 25½' × 3'3¼"
– Meany School (301 21st Ave E): one 23' tall on the east side
– U.W.: a cv. '**Glenmore Dwarf**' 20' × 2'11½" by 11th Ave NE & NE 41st

var. *reflexa* Engelm.   Southern Limber-Pine
=*P. Ayacahuite* Ehrenb. var. *reflexa* (Engelm.) Voss
From Arizona, New Mexico, SW Texas, Mexico.

A southern variant of *greater vigor;* its needles are bluer, thinner and longer—(2") 2⅜–3½" long. Its seeds are bigger. It looks intermediate between Limber pine and Mexican White pine. Cv. '**Vanderwolf's Pyramid**' has been common here since the 1990s, and most of the following are likely it.

– Arboretum: #433-51 cv. '**Glenmore Silver**' is 66' × 4'9½" in 23-1W
– SSCC Arboretum: one 33' tall in the Milton Sutton conifer garden
– Green Lake has 2 youngsters thriving south of the NW tennis courts; taller 29½'
– 3513 W Howe St: one near the house is 32½' tall
– 13536 Densmore Ave N: one in the yard's SW corner is 28½' tall
– Rite Aid 8500 35th Ave NE: 11 on the E border

Loblolly PINE

P. Tæda L.   North Carolina *or* Old Field Pine
From the SE United States.   Frankincense Pine

Needles (2) 3 per bundle, 5–10" long; *cones* 2–6" long; *tree* to 182' × 21½'.

The epithet *Tæda* is from an ancient Latin name for a resinous pine tree or pine *torches* in general—for which it is well suited and was much used. One of the first trees to occupy ground exhausted by cultivation. Tolerates wetter conditions than do most pines. Loblolly refers to the moist depressions on which the tree is usually found in the wild. Handsome bright green, but extremely rare here.

– U.W.: one 72' × 4'2" in the grove of mixed conifers west of Anderson Hall
– 4508 Purdue Ave NE: one 47' tall in the back yardbehind a 31½' Stone pine
– 1600 18th Ave: two, the northern tree 40' tall, and southern 46½' tall

Lodgepole PINE

P. contorta Dougl. *ex* Loud. var. *contorta*   Shore, Coast *or* Beach Pine
=*P. inops* Bong., *non* Ait., *non* Soland.   Scrub *or* Knotty Pine
Native here; from much of western North America.   Screw *or* Prickly Pine

var. *latifolia* Engelm. *ex* S. Wats.   Common *or* Rocky Mt. Lodgepole-Pine
From the Rockies—mostly.   Tamarack Pine

var. *Murryana* (Balf.) Engelm. *ex* S. Wats.   Sierra Lodgepole-Pine
From SW Oregon thru Californa into Baja.

Needles 2 per bundle, 1–3 (4)" long; *cones* ¾–2½" long, prickly; *tree* to 200' × 21'.

A weathercock species, vacillating in appearance according to its environment to such a degree that 4 variants are usually given botanic status, and Seattle has three as noted above. Most of the wild natives and planted Seattle trees better fit descriptions of the **Shore** than the **Lodgepole** races—the two best known. Shore is thick-barked, Lodgepole thin-barked. However ideal and convenient it may seem to divide the species into races, individual trees can look intermediate. "Lodgepole pine" refers to Indian usage of slender trees for building lodges (not to be confused with tepees). To distinguish *any* form of this variable species from Jack, Mountain or Mugo pines, look for the cones' *prickles*.

– Lincoln Park: 86' × 6'8" by main west path intersection in the middle of the park
– Kubota Garden Park: largest are 81½' × 6'4¼" and 69' × 6'4"
– U.W.: SW of the Waterfront Activities Center is one 62' × 5'5½"; one SE of the salmon homing pond, 42½' × 3'3½" (both are var. Murrayana)
– 46th Ave S & S Warsaw St: 6 in the SE corner yard; tallest 65'
– Locks bed #206 (two)
– Volunteer Park: one 55' tall × 3-trunked east of the north part of the eastern path
– 42nd Ave W & W Barrett St: SW corner yard has one 51' tall
– U.W. Friendship Grove, representing Malagasy, 43' × 3'1"
– Big (Wedgwood) Rock: 28th Ave NE at NE 72nd St: three
– North Transfer Station (Dump): Carr Pl N & N 34th St: many
– 28th Ave NW & NW 86th St: NE corner yard has a big one
– 6501 31st Ave NE: a cv. '**Taylor's Sunburst**' (needles *gold* in early summer) <5' tall
– 40th Ave W & W Emerson St: SE corner has a cv. '**Taylor's Sunburst**' <5' tall south of a larger 'Vanderwolf's Pyramid' Limber pine
– Dunn Gardens: a young 4' tall cv. '**Chief Joseph**' N of the house is *gold* in winter
– SSCC Arboretum: a young cv. '**Chief Joseph**' in the Cœnosium Rock Garden

Macedonian White PINE

P. Peuce Griseb. *(P. Peuke)*   Yugoslav Pine
From the Balkan Mountains.   Balkan Pine

Needles 5 per bundle, 3–4½" long; *cones* 3–7" long; *tree* to 130' × 13½'.

Extremely rare in Seattle. The Arboretum has four east of Azalea Way (22-1W & 23-1W), the largest 78' × 4'7¼" (#328-47). One 42' × 4'0" represents Rumania at the U.W. Friendship Grove; 22' east of the Limber pine.

Mexican White PINE

P. strobiformis Engelm.   Southwestern White Pine
=*P. Ayacahuite* Ehrenb. *ex* Schlecht.   Border White Pine
var. *brachyptera* Shaw
From SE Arizona, SW New Mexico, Trans-Pecos Texas, N Mexico.

Needles (2,3,4) 5 (6) per bundle, (2") 2¾–4⅜" (4¾") long; *cones* 4¾–11¾" (23½") long; *tree* to 111' × 15½'.

Closely related to Limber pine, yet relatively tall and slender, with larger cones. "Mexican White pine" is also used for *P. Ayacahuite* (not known in Seattle). Extremely rare—but resisting blister rust disease, it may become common. At the Arboretum, tallest is 79½' (#392-37C in pinetum 38-4W), the stoutest trunk 3'11¾" (#392-37A in pinetum 35-5W). The SE corner of Brooklyn Ave NE & NE Pacific St has one 41' × 3'7¼". The U.W. has a grove of 7 south of McCarty Hall, largest 75½' × 6'3".

Monterey PINE

P. radiata D. Don   Insignis Pine
=*P. insignis* Dougl. *ex* Loud.   Radiata Pine
From a few isolated groves of California's
central coast; and Guadalupe Islands, Mexico.

Needles (2) 3 (4) per bundle, 2½–5 (7)" long, shiny grass-green; *cones* 3–7" long (usually 3½–4" here), stay unopened on the tree indefinitely; *tree* to 211½' × 29'; bark thick.

World famous for rapidity of growth, this rare pine has become New Zealand's foremost commercial tree, outproducing all others, growing larger there than in nature. One reached 211' in 41 years; growth rings 1½" wide have been found! By some accounts also an admirable *ornamental* species, planted widely for its bright greenery. In Seattle, uncommon. When young, hurt or killed by exceptional winter cold.

– U.W.: 7 around the forestry buildings; best 72½' × 7'5½"
– 2011 E Lynn St: one 78' tall
– across the street from 3816 SW 108th St: a yard has one 67' tall
– 5116 SW Hudson St: by the garage
– 1821 41st Ave E: 56' tall

- Nob Hill Ave N & Galer St: NE corner, one 45½' tall, S of an Austrian Black pine
- Arboretum: #183-94 in 7S-9E is already 45' tall; a 2nd is in the pinetum (34-4W)

Montezuma PINE

P. Montezuma Lamb.   Rough-barked Mexican Pine
From Mexico, S Guatemala.

Needles (3,4) 5 (6) per bundle—in Seattle usually 5 per bundle and 9–12" long; *cones*
3–6" (8") long (not made here yet); *tree* to 157' × 15¾'; bark deep and chunky.

Rapid-growing, stout and bold, an exuberant species unhappy with some of
our colder winters, but apparently tolerating them. Alas, the following are the
only ones known here. Arboretum #560-65A is 73' × 7'3" in 34-6E; one 57½'
× 6'5¼" representing Mexico in the U.W. Friendship Grove.

Mountain PINE *and* Mugo PINE

P. Mugo Turra   Dwarf *or* Swiss Mountain Pine
=*P. Mughus* Scop.   Mugo *or* Mugho Pine
=*P. montana* Mill.

P. Mugo ssp. **uncinata** (DC.) Domin   Giant Mugo Pine
=*P. montana* var. *rostrata* Ant.   Mountain Pine
=*P. Mugo* var. *rostrata* (Ant.) Gord.
=*P. uncinata* DC.

(Both) From mountains in parts of Europe.

Needles 2 per bundle, 1–3" long; *cones* ¾–2¾" long; *tree* shrubby or to 80' × 9¾'.

Mountain and Mugo pines intergrade and hybridize to a bewildering extent. If
Seattle had only the two extremes (shrubby Mugo and tree-like Mountain pine)
our task would be easy. But some of our specimens are intermediate enough
to be called either name. The following is an oversimplification: Mugo Pine in
Seattle is a common shrub, many-stemmed, 1–6' tall, usually wider, with cones
¾–1½" long. Mountain pine in Seattle is an uncommon tree, 10–40' tall, with
cones 1½–2¾" long having markedly thicker, knobbier scales. Large Mugo
pines and any size of Mountain pines can be confused with Lodgepole/Shore
pines—they differ in all technical characters, but their general appearance and
roles in Seattle landscapes are amazingly similar.

- Volunteer Park: one 58½' × 3'10½" is the larger of 2 Mountain pines on the bank
  above the road NW of the reservoir
- 6526 34th Ave NE: 3-trunked Mountain pine 46' tall by a telephone pole
- Interlaken Blvd E: east of 24th Ave E, on the north side of the road just beyond a
  30' tall Irish Yew and English Holly, is a 39½' × 3'2" Mountain pine
- Discovery Park: chapel S632 has a Mountain pine 33½' × 2'11" × 25' wide *pl.* 1942
- Laurelhurst Playfield: a Mountain pine 40' × 2'3" + 1'8½"
- U.W.: shrubby Mountain Pine (or a big Mugo) between Denny & Balmer Halls
- Green Lake: Pitch n' Putt golf course has a Mugo pine 22' × 4'9¼" × 42½' wide

- Mt Pleasant Cemetery: in the middle is a Mugo pine 24' × 6'0" × 34½' wide
- S.U.: of 3 Mugo pines at 10th Ave & Columbia St, tallest are 26' and 25'
- 5811 28th Ave NW: a Mugo pine 24½' tall
- Locks bed #118 (a big Mugo pine), 202 (8½' tall Mugo pine)

Piñón (PINE)

P. cembroides Zucc. *ex* K. Bayer	Pinyon (Pine)
P. edulis Zucc. *ex* K. Bayer	Nut Pine
From SW North America.	

Needles (2) 3 (4,5) per bundle in *cembroides* and (1) 2 (3) per bundle in *edulis;* ¾–2 (2¾)" long; *cones* 1–3" long & wide; *tree* to 75' × 17¾'.

Whole books detail the human and natural history of these little trees. "Piñón pine" is a common tautology. Four kinds (species or subspecies depending on the botanist's opinion) are in the United States; most are in Mexico; at least 8 species are called piñón. All are important for their large, edible seeds, and are similar in size, rarely over 30' × 6'. *Any* pine seed (nut) is edible if big enough, and all have much the same flavor and texture. Piñón seeds are especially big, easy to harvest and shell, and are borne in significant quantities.

In Seattle, rare. Likely most of ours are *P. cembroides* rather than *P. edulis*. Harvest time is September–October, but many trees produce few cones if any, and many cones have few filled seeds or none.

- Jefferson Park: largest of 3 west of the clubhouse is 31' × 3'3½" × 26' wide
- S.U.: one 32' × 2'4" at SE corner of Loyola Hall (10th Ave & Columbia St)
- 21st Ave SW & SW Andover St: 4 behind fence on NW corner, the tallest 31½'
- Cal Anderson Park: two in the NE corner, the taller about 20½' × 2'0"
- Acacia Cemetery: one near a building is 24½' × 1'6½"
- 2209 - 2211 11th Ave W: one 22' tall
- Ivanhoe Pl NE & NE 52nd St: NW corner, one 13' tall (+ a Mountain Hemlock)
- W Seattle Golf Course: 2, shaded by maples by NE restrooms; a tiny one farther S
- Locks bed #214 has two small specimens

Pitch PINE

P. rigida Mill.	Northern Pitch Pine
From the eastern U.S., but not far	Torch Pine
south; and extreme S Ontario & Québec.	Sap Pine

Needles 3 per bundle, 2–5½" long, tough; *cones* 1¼–4" long, persistent and prickly; *tree* to 135' × 12½'.

This tree's abundant presence suggested the name "Pine Barrens" for great areas of Cape Cod, Long Island and New Jersey. Though not looking especially pitchy, despite its name, it is unusual in that the trunk is often besprouted with needle tufts, like no other pine here except the extremely rare Shortleaf pine. Its persistent cones adorn an irregular, yellowish-green crown. It's rare in Seattle and virtually all are on public property.

- Arboretum: 36-5W (the pinetum) has 3 #212-45, the largest 71½' × 5'10½"
- Seward Park: one north of the entrance circle with blue Atlas Cedar & Chinese pine, is 55' × 5'11¼"
- Beacon Ave S & S Alaska St: NW corner has 25 Scots and 5 Pitch pines, the tallest of the latter 58½' and the stoutest 4'11½" around
- Hiawatha Playfield: 2 in NE part, the larger 53' × 4'0"
- Substation on Bellevue Ave E, north of E John St: two on the S side
- U.W.: many—one 44' × 5'6½" by Cyclotron; 2 on the W side of Bagley Hall (with a larger Scots pine); 1 west of the Faculty Center; 4 west of the overpass to the Health Sciences complex (with Bristlecone & 2 Knobcone pines); 2 north of Chemistry Library; NE of the Waterfront Activities Center; near Mercer Hall
- Volunteer Park: 3 (+5 other pine species) in a grove NE of reservoir; 45' × 4'7¼"

Ponderosa PINE

P. ponderosa Dougl. *ex* Laws.
From much of the western half of
N America; the native stand closest
to Seattle is near Ft. Lewis.

Bull *or* (Western) Yellow Pine
Heavy *or* Sierra Brownbark Pine
Big *or* Western Red Pine
Blackjack Pine

Needles (2) 3 per bundle, 5–11¼" long; *cones* 3–6 (8)" long; *tree* to 300' × 47'!

The State Tree of Montana, this giant and highly valued timber tree is the most far-ranging and best known of western North American pines; it's also the most important. Washington's largest may be one three miles north of Trout Lake (Klickitat County), measuring 213' × 22' (1995). It is common in Seattle.

- 1524 24th Ave E: a forked-trunk specimen 126½' × 10'9"; *pl. ca.* 1930
- Washelli Cemetery: one 117' × 12'0" NE of the old (1921) mausoleum
- Lincoln Park: many; largest 107½' × 8'3¼"
- Arboretum: largest is 105½' × 7'5", one of 7 north of ballfield restrooms
- Zoo: one 74½' × 11'1½" (below forking) by Evanston Ave N & N 59th St
- 8th Ave NW & NW 122nd St: NW corner has one 95½' tall
- 8034 Wallingford Ave N: one about 100' tall
- Dayton Ave N, north of N 87th St: a yard, E side, has a stout specimen
- U.W.: one 98' × 8'1¼" in the grove of mixed conifers west of Anderson Hall; one north of Parking Division building on Stevens Way
- S.U.: five NW of the Garrand Building, the tallest 98½'
- 4620 49th Ave S: one 87' tall
- Discovery Park: some by the old army buildings are naturalized
- Ravenna Park: fair-sized ones in the far south part, the stoutest 100' × 8'10½"

Red PINE

P. resinosa Ait.   Norway Pine
From the Great Lakes region to beyond Maine.

Needles 2 (3) per bundle, 4–7" long, brittle; *cones* 1–2½" long; *tree* to 154' × 15½'.

The State Tree of Minnesota, called "Norway pine" because early exporters of its wood desired to compare it with the Norway Spruce. "Red pine" is well explained by its bark. It is rare here—though many people call Japanese Red pine simply "Red pine."

- Hiawatha Playfield: 9 in the NE part (with 2 Pitch, 2 Eastern White and 2 Western White pines), the tallest is 73' and largest 69½' × 4'5½"
- Arboretum: the largest of 4 in the pinetum (36-5W) are 63' × 3'1¼" (#389-37C) and 59' × 3'8¼" (#1753-37A); one on Foster Island is 65' × 2'7¾"
- Green Lake: one 58' × 4'9" east of the stone bridge south of the wading pool

Scots PINE

P. sylvestris L.   Northern Pine

From much of the Old World tem-   Scotch Pine

perate zone, Atlantic to Pacific oceans.   Scotch *or* Scots Fir

Needles 2 per bundle, 1–4½" long; *cones* 1–3" long; *tree* to 157' × 19'.

This is the original "Fir." Furthermore, a Scot will thank us to say "Scots" or "Scottish" (not "Scotch") whether calling it Pine or Fir. Among all pines, or firs, this has the widest geographic range: in fact its range is equaled or exceeded by few trees of any kind. To dwellers in the chilly far north of Eurasia, it proved a lifesaver of a tree: aside from many everyday uses, it afforded famine food by way of its ground-up inner bark. The tree is still valuable in commercial forestry.

Common in Seattle, its bark color is similiar to the Japanese Red Pine's, though often more of a yellow-orange. Its foliage is *gray-green* while that of the Japanese is a conventional dark yellow-green.

- Seward Park: slender ones in a grove at the peninsula tip; tallest 106½' × 4'2½"
- Golden Gardens Park: the largest is 75' × 6'10" while the tallest is 91'
- Arboretum: the largest of 3 in the pinetum (36-6W) is 75' × 4'11½" (#1471-37A)
- U.W.: 87' × 2'6" by McMahon Hall; 4 on the lawn west of Meany Hall (2 smaller Japanese Red pines N of them); 8 with 5 Katsuras in front of Padelford Hall
- U.W. Friendship Grove, representing Sweden
- Locks bed #23 (four), 101 (by east lightpost)
- 18th Ave S & S Lander St: the NE corner has a twin-trunked street-tree 54' tall
- Renton Ave S & S Oregon St: a broad, leaning specimen 40½' × 8'6½"
- 8607 28th Ave NW: a young 'Aurea' (winter needles bright gold) *ca.* 6' tall
- SSCC Arboretum: a young cv. 'Aurea' 5' tall in the Cœnosium Rock Garden

cv. 'Fastigiata'   Columnar Scots Pine

A rare, tight column like Lombardy (Black) Poplar. Slower-growing than the regular kind, but no dwarf. Seattle's largest may be Arboretum #491-57A in the crabapple meadow (34-6E): 37½' × 2'3" (near a larger fastigiate Eastern White pine). On Lake Washington Blvd. S, above I-90, the tallest of four is 29'.

Shortleaf PINE

P. echinata Mill.
=*P. mitis* Michx.
From the southeastern U.S.

Common Yellow Pine
Arkansas *or* North Carolina Pine
Rosemary Pine

Needles 2 (3) per bundle, 2¼–5" long; *cones* 1½–2½" long; *tree* to 146' × 14'.

Extremely rare here, it is like a dwarf, coneless (so far) Pitch Pine.

– Discovery Park: 2 by SW intersection of Washington Ave & Iowa Way, best 40' × 3'6½" (+2 Ponderosa pines and 4 Paper Birches); a 3rd Shortleaf to the S 30' × 2'4"
– Arboretum: one 27½' × 1'2½" on Foster Island (#552-48B)

Stone PINE

P. Pinea L.
From the Mediterranean.

Italian *or* Mediterranean Stone Pine
The Pine of Rome / Parasol *or* Umbrella Pine

Needles 2 (3) per bundle, 3–5 (8)" long; *cones* massive, 3¼–6" long; *seeds* large, hard-shelled and edible; *tree* to 120' × 21⅓'.

Characteristic of many Mediterranean landscapes, this mushroom shaped tree is beloved for its picturesque appearance and for its large edible seeds (nuts), borne in the original "pine apples." In Seattle, old examples are rare. Seedlings, baby blue by nature, are sold as "Blue pines" at supermarkets during the Christmas season. While young and potted they're sensitive to severe cold, but plant them in Mother Earth and soon, Dr. Jekyll & Mr. Hyde-like, they outgrow their sensitivity and juvenile cuteness to wax strong, dark green and long needled.

– Arboretum: one 50' × 8'10"in the crabapple meadow (#X-66 in 34-5E)
– Broadmoor golf course: one 50' × 8'5" × 41' wide in 1992
– Laurelhurst Playfield: one with two Azara trees by the footbridge overpass
– 9539 Sand Point Way NE
– Locks bed #23 (two, near #26), 101 (in the middle)
– 10th Ave E & E Miller St: NW corner has two, the taller 40½'
– 910 NW 62nd St: one west of the house

Sugar PINE

P. Lambertiana Dougl. *ex* Taylor & Phillips
From SW Oregon to NW Mexico.

Great Sugar Pine
Big *or* Gigantic Pine

Needles 5 per bundle, 3–4½" long; *cones* (7) 10–30" long!; *tree* to 300' × 46¾'.

The largest pine, with the longest cones, this is truly a fitting California companion for the awesome redwoods. It's very rare here.

– Lincoln Park: one (near Eastern White pines) by a main path south of the tennis courts is 111½' × 7'5", coneless so far(?); a Grand Fir east & Douglas Fir west of it
– U.W.: the lawn by 15th Ave NE & NE 42nd St has one 96' × 11'½"
– Arboretum: #1327-46 in 22-1W: 82' × 5'2"; Foster Island #1327-46E: 69' × 3'½"

Swiss Stone PINE

P. Cembra L.   Arolla Pine
From the Alps of Central Europe,   Russian Cedar
into central Asia in the Carpathians.

Needles 5 per bundle, 2–3½" (5") long; *cones* 2–3½" long, purple-blue, never opening; *tree* to 130' × 22'.

Slow growing, dense and tidy of crown. Perfect size for small urban lots. Resists blister rust. The seeds are large and sold in Europe for food and for oil. It is rare in Seattle and most are young.

- Arboretum: two #231-61 in 1S-5E, the taller 42' and stouter 3'4"
- one *ca.* 28' tall on E side of 3300 block of West Laurelhurst Drive NE: across the street opposite a yellow fire hydrant; a larger Japanese Cedar stands N of it
- Children's Hospital: near north end of parking lot 4

Table Mountain PINE

P. pungens Lamb. *ex* Michx. fil.   Poverty *or* Hickory Pine
From the eastern U.S., mainly in the Appalachians.   Prickly *or* Pine

Needles 2 (3) per bundle, 1½–3" long; *cones* cruelly prickly and tenaciously persistent, 1¼–4" long; *tree* to 97' × 9½'.

Condemned as a worthless ornamental by some writers, Table Mountain pine admittedly lacks well-proportioned, inspiring beauty—but it is picturesque and doesn't get too big for the average yard. Its showy, persistent cones neither drop messily nor attract squirrels, and being relatively rare, the tree's novel aspect delights the eye. It is uncommon here, and most are in more expensive neighborhoods; the largest are about 25–45' tall, the stoutest trunks over 5' around.

- 32nd Ave W & W Raye St: NE corner has a 41' tall 3-trunked one with an Eastern White and a Chinese pine
- Arboretum: #1126-49 east of Azalea Way in 20-1W is 58½' × 2'8½"
- 6806 54th Ave NE: big
- 43rd Ave NE & NE 60th St: the NW corner yard has one 30' tall and far wider
- 9313 Fauntleroy Way SW *and* 9369
- Wallingford Playground (Wallingford Ave N & N 43rd St): one 26' × 5'1¼"
- U.W.: 26½' × 3'5½" at Stevens Way & Pend Oreille Rd intersection; one by the Burke-Gilman Trail near the overpass to Hitchcock Hall
- 3539 NE 96th St: a big one NE of the house
- 4204 47th Ave S (just south of S Adams St): one 30' tall at the yard's far SW corner
- 3921 15th Ave S: one at each end of this building

Virginia PINE

P. virginiana Mill.
From the eastern U.S., Long Island,
New York, to NE Mississippi.

Scrub *or* Poverty Pine
Jersey Pine

Needles 2 per bundle, 1½–3" long; *cones* 1½–3" long, prickly; *tree* to 120' × 9½'.

Usually scraggly, and seldom grown. Exceedingly rare. Cv. 'Wate's Golden' has needles *gold* in winter, and a specimen of it 13' tall is on the west side of the SSCC Arboretum's Cœnosium Rock Garden.

Western White PINE

P. monticola Dougl. *ex* D. Don
Native here; from B.C.
to W Montana and S California.

Idaho *or* California White Pine
Mountain White Pine
Fingercone *or* Soft *or* Silver Pine

Needles 5 per bundle, 2½–5½" long; *cones* 5–15 (18)" long; *tree* to 290' × 34½'.

Our native white pine has a dark silver, straight and slender trunk that holds close whorls of dark, dense bluish-green branches. The State Tree of Idaho, this beautiful tree is a peer of the famous Eastern White and Sugar pines. The graceful habit of these three is very appealing—and when combined with the noble size of aged specimens, sublime.

In Seattle, plentiful; most *wild* ones are north of the canal. In many parks and neighborhoods it's seen with its Eastern cousin. The two achieve similar maximum sizes both in nature and as grown here. People often need a few years of observation before they can tell these two apart at a glance. The native is darker, denser and usually narrower.

- U.W.: Denny Hall lawn has a forking specimen 106' × 11'7"
- Lincoln Park: one at extreme N end is 109' × 8'1¼"
- Washelli Cemetery: one 108' × 11'5½" N of the military area
- Evergreen Park Cemetery: largest of over a dozen 82½' × 11'7¾" SE of 117th St gate
- Me-Kwa-Mooks Park: one 84' × 8'3¾" is the largest of three
- Cowen Park: 101½' × 7'2"
- Arboretum: the largest of 7 in the pinetum (35-6W) is 96½' × 7'6" (#418-37B)

Whitebark PINE

P. albicaulis Engelm.
From high mountains of western North America.

Alpine Whitebark Pine
Northern Nut-Pine

Needles 5 per bundle, 1⅓–3¼" long; *cones* 1⅓–3½" long, dark chocolate or purple, not opening, but disintegrating after ripe; *tree* to 90' × 27'.

Closely related to Limber pine but extremely rare—difficult to establish, slow growing. Aged specimens in the wild often have handsome pale bark. The only one known here is a specimen 19' × 1'5" with a Mountain Hemlock at Acacia Cemetery, near where the first left turn is possible as you drive in.

Yunnan PINE

P. yunnanensis Franch.   Chinese: Yu Nan Song
From SW China.

Needles 3 per bundle, 7–10" (12") long; *cones* 3–4½" long; *tree* to 100' × 6'.

This recalls Montezuma pine in its bold foliage. Extremely rare; *two* known here:
Arboretum #136-92 is 18½' tall in the pinetum (35-5W). A taller one at Locks
bed #205 (employee parking)—likely var. *tenuifolia* W.C. Cheng & Y.W. Law.

Chinese PISTACHIO

Pistacia chinensis Bge.   Chinese Pistache / Gitterwort
ANACARDIACEÆ   Chinese: Huang Lien Shu
From China, Taiwan, the Philippines.   Kai Shu

The pistachio nuts of commerce are borne by a related tree unknown in Seattle—it
will probably grow here if somebody will just try it! The *Chinese* pistachio tree
is an important timber producer, growing as large as 100' × 16'. The male trees
grow larger than the females. The rather inconspicuous flowers begin in April
before the leaves emerge, continue into May, giving rise to thin-fleshed, hard,
inedible berries about ¼" wide, first green, then yellow, next red and finally
metallic blue when fully ripe. The leaves are compound, borne alternately on the
twigs, each compound leaf usually having 8, 10 or 12 leaflets, strongly odorous
when crushed, smelling resinous like Smoke Tree and Sweetgum leaves. The
young shoots are cooked as a potherb in China (called Huang Lien Ya), despite
their powerful odor.

In Seattle, extremely rare, small, slow-growing and variably spectacular in its
fall color: in effect, it is a daintier version of Sumach. Judging by the performance
of those in Seattle we may surmise that our stock is sub par, or that the species
simply doesn't do as well here as in a continental climate—though it doesn't
have to be large to be attractive, which ours are. For more information about
Chinese pistachio, see *Arnoldia*, Sept./Oct. 1978, pp. 165–169.

– University Bridge: the NW end (Sadako Sasaki Peace Park) has *ca.* 10 of mixed sizes
  and sexes (most ♂), the tallest 37', the largest 35' × 3'3"
– Locks bed #205 has a 30' tall ♂
– 2052 23rd Ave E: a ♀ 33½' tall
– a 27' tall ♂ in street right-of-way south of 7064 35th Ave NE
– Good Shepherd Center: east of bldg, near the N end, a ♂ 18½' tall
– 6520 Jones Ave NW: 2 young street-trees
– 6th Ave W, south of W Raye St, north of Smith St: 12 street-trees on E, 4 on W

PITTOSPORUM

Pittosporum tenuifolium Gaertn.   Maori: Kohuhu
PITTOSPORACEÆ
From New Zealand.

Northwest nurseries have offered at least 17 Kohuhu cultivars. Most of them feature variegated or colored foliage, such as 'Irene Paterson': pale green marbled white. In Seattle, it and other *Pittosporum* are uncommon at most, and usually rare, cold-tender broadleaf evergreens. But we plant them, and until a cold winter kills them, shall enjoy them. Kohuhu is a shrub or tree (recorded to 60' × 6¼'). It has *wavy-edged, thin* leaves, to *ca.* 3" × 1" borne on *blackish twigs*. In April it makes one little flower per leaf, the petals dark purple to nearly black; sweet scented in the evenings.

- Locks bed #313 has one 25' tall at the east end
- Arboretum: #364-89D is 23' tall (in 9-3E)
- 4025 NE 110th St: the garden here has one 16' tall—not visible from the street
- 8540 18th Ave NW: 15½' tall
- Good Shepherd Center: near the exit driveway is one 12½' tall
- 4340 NE 55th St: the fenced garden's SE corner has an 'Irene Paterson' 14' tall

[Australian Pittosporum—*P. bicolor* Hook.—is from SE Australia and Tasmania. It is *narrow* and *bolt upright*. Its leaves recall those of the Labrador tea bog shrub: to *ca.* 2" × ⅓", *felty* beneath. Locks bed #313 has one 23' tall.]

[Mountain Pittosporum *or* Black Mapou—*P. Colensoi* Hook. fil.—is from New Zealand. *Shrubby*, it can reach 30' tall. Leaves *thick*, to *ca.* 7" × 2". Flowers in April, dark red, *few but big* in trios or pairs. The Good Shepherd Center has one 5' tall west of the bldg.]

[Lemonwood *or* Tarata—*P. eugenioides* A. Cunn.—is from New Zealand. It is *robust*, to 50' tall, with big glossy leaves, to *ca.* 6⅛" × 2¼". The April flowers are creamy yellow, fragrant, *densely clustered* in bunches up to 70 or more. The U.W. has two 19' tall N of the bldg. on the SW corner of Brooklyn Ave NE & NE 40th St. Arboretum #363-89A is 18' tall, very wide, in 9-3E. Locks bed #313 has one.]

[Hybrid Pittosporum—*P.* 'Garnettii'—is *P. tenuifolium* × *P. Ralphii*. Gray-green, white-edged leaves; +some pink. One 12' tall is by a *Stewartia monadelpha* N of the house at 7544 44th Ave NE. One is kept shrubby under the eaves at the Dunn Gardens.]

[Karo *or* Ralph's Kohuhu—*P. Ralphii* Kirk—is from New Zealand. Shrubby, it can reach 30' tall. Leaves *silky at first*, can be wavy-edged, to *ca.* 3" × 1". Flowers in April, one per leaf or as many as 5 together, pale green-white urns capped with deep purple corollas. Arboretum has three #84-97 in 9-3E, tallest 18½'. Private gardens have smaller ones.]

[Tobira *or* Japanese Pittosporum—*P. Tobira* (Th.) Ait.—is from E Asia. It is more cold-hardy and has been grown in Seattle for decades, but is slow to attain treehood. Bushy cultivars exist. Leaves, thick, glossy, to *ca.* 4" × 1½". The April-May flowers are *showy, big, white*, and sweet. Colorful *orange seeds in fall*. At S.P.U. the taller of a pair W of McKinley Hall is 21½'. At the U.W. the taller of a pair *pl.* 1986 W of Bagley Hall is 16' × 1'9".]

London PLANE

Platanus × *hispanica* Mill. *ex* Münchh.   Hybrid Plane (Tree)
=*P.* × *intermedia* hort.
=*P.* × *hybrida* Brot.
=*P.* × *acerifolia* (Ait.) Willd.
=*P. orientalis* hort., in part, *non* L.
=*P. orientalis* var. *acerifolia* auct.
(*P. orientalis* × *P. occidentalis*)

PLATANACEÆ

"London" plane achieved its particular English name as well as much fame, by easily tolerating adverse city conditions. Even in industrial London's stifling black soot, it grew fast, broad and lofty, was little hurt by pollarding, and cast plentiful shade—all in such foulness that many trees couldn't survive at all! So London plane became the best known and most widely grown of the Oriental plane/American sycamore hybrids, that first arose in Europe during the late 1600s. Writers should make clear whether their "London plane" refers only to the real thing as cloned in London, or to any such sycamore / plane hybrid, including inferior strains. Like most, this guide takes the latter position for simplicity's sake, but the truth suffers if we note that Seattle's commonest strain is *not* the original London plane. Moreover, many Seattleites call all of these trees "sycamore." Whatever their name, these mighty trees are common here. Our most abundant kind (technically called cv. 'Pyramidalis') has a short and massive trunk that soon divides into widely spreading, stout forks. The lower bole of older trees is swollen, burly and knurly, and the bark is easily flaked away. Distinctive seed-balls dangle (1) 2 (3) per string from twigs. As few other trees here so readily burst sidewalks and invade sewers, it ought to be planted only where ample space is available for it to grow into a giant. Both parental species are famous on their respective continents for gigantic size, so the ultimate potential of their hybrid children is wonderous to contemplate—the largest dimensions so far exceed 160' × 29'!

– 4123 12th Ave NE: a street-tree 85' × 18'2¼"
– Interlaken Park: one 96½' × 10'10" is our tallest 'Pyramidalis'
– 6000 NE Windermere: the real London plane, 96½' tall
– Ballard Playground: southernmost of two on the east is 82' × 16'7½"
– triangle at Belmont Ave E & Bellevue Pl E has one 81' × 16'7½" × 100'+ wide
– B.F. Day School Playground: the largest of four on the west side is 16'7" around
– Zoo: the largest of six S of the south parking lot is 15'1½" around
– Adams School (2637 NW 62nd St): 67½' × 14'11½"
– Salmon Bay Park: the largest, on the south side, is 72½' × 14'6½"
– Mt. Baker Blvd: 80½' × 13'11" by 36th Ave S; one S of McClellan St is 75' × 13'10"
– Georgetown Playground (Corson Ave S & S Homer St): 33
– W Seattle High School (4075 SW Stevens St): 30
– Madrona Playground (34th Ave & E Spring St): 16, the largest 12'10" around
– Green Lake: 29 in rows leading to the Evans Pool building, largest 12'6½" around
– U.W.: lining Memorial Way, *pl.* 1920, 48 on the E, 53 on the W

- Monorail route and at the Seattle Center: many
- Pioneer Square and Occidental Park: about 60 were *pl. ca.* 1972

Oriental PLANE

P. orientalis L.
From the Balkan Peninsula and Asia
Minor; widely planted further east and west.

Oriental Planetree
Persian: Chinar
Dulb

Probably the most beloved and certainly the most enormous shade tree of southeastern Europe and Asia Minor. Greek philosophers, Roman statesmen, Persian princes, Alexander the Great and untold thousands of ordinary people all enjoyed its refreshing shade, heartening amplitude and long-lived, tough and rugged beauty. In the Language of Flowers it means "genius." One measured 164' tall with a trunk circumference of about 103'! Many specimens famed for size, beauty or association have earned a place in history.

In Seattle, uncommon; almost solely represented by old trees on public property. Such trees may be backcross London plane hybrids that have inherited nearly all of their superficial characteristics from the oriental rather than the occidental species. It is also possible that Seattle's are genuine Orientals. It is neither easy to determine nor particularly pressing to do so. The trees thrive and are attractive here—their technical identity is curious but of secondary importance compared to this happy fact. To distinguish them from our London planes: the Oriental's seed-balls frequently number 3 per string and are smaller, their leaves are deeply lobed like those our our native Bigleaf Maple.

- Lake Washington Blvd E, by E Republican St: one by a driveway is 81' × 11'9¼"
- Salmon Bay Park: the SE corner has one 71' × 12'¼"
- Volunteer Park: one 66' × 10'7¾" is by 12th Ave E & E Prospect St
- Arboretum: boulevard N of Madison St has 8 London planes and 3 Orientals, the largest of the latter (3rd plane from the S, in 3S-7E) is 88½' × 9'5½"; further N on the Blvd is one 73½' × 9'¾" in 38-2W south of the viaduct footbridge; 14-3W has 3, largest 70' × 8'2½" (#31-54C); 6-1E has one (#31-54A) 72' × 7'9" grown from seeds from wild trees in Turkey
- Lake Washington Blvd E & E Harrison St: the triangle has one 7'9" around
- U.W.: one 6'2" around E of the Burke-Gilman Trail, N of Pend Oreille Rd

American Sycamore (PLANE)

P. occidentalis L.
From the central and eastern U.S.,
far S Ontario, and parts of Mexico.

American Plane (Tree)
Buttonball Tree
Buttonwood

The most massive tree east of the Rocky Mountains. The following measurements speak for themselves:

129' × 48'6" Ohio (1982)
176' × 33'4" Lower Wabash Valley (pre-1921)
161' × 24'4" Michigan (1979)

Named "sycamore" by European immigrants reminded by its broad maple-like leaves of their sycamore (see Sycamore MAPLE), this tree came to symbolize "woodland beauty" or "independence" in the Language of Flowers. In general it's a forest denizen, and does not thrive in cities as do its hybrid offspring. It is uncommon in Seattle compared to London plane but is occasionally found growing with it in parks or (more commonly) as a street-tree. It leafs out more slowly and much later than London plane; its bark is dark gray and finely checkered rather than flaky or forming large crusty plates. The trunk is neither swollen nor burled, nor does it fork into the crown as low as does London plane. It is less vigorous and greatly suffers from anthracnose fungal disease. In winter, those specimens that are healthy enough produce large seed-balls, borne singly rather than in twos or threes. Some cited below may be hybrids that merely *look* like their American parent. Most in Seattle are too ugly and unhealthy to be cited. The few listed below are worth visiting and the first two are of the foremost grandeur.

- 30th Ave, north of E Yesler Way: a street-tree, E side, 91½' × 12'5½"
- Woodlawn Ave N, north of N 34th St: a street-tree 78' × 11'4¼"
- 18th Ave E, north of E Prospect St: a street-tree, 86' × 10'5"
- 35th Ave NE & NE 50th St: 4 street-trees on the NE corner
- S Irving St, just east of 31st Ave S: a street-tree, N side

Cherry PLUM TREE

Prunus cerasifera Ehrh.	Myrobalan (Plum Tree)
=*P. Myrobalana* (L.) Loisel.	Flowering Plum Tree
=*P. domestica* var. *myrobalan* L.	

ROSACEÆ

This is an ancient Eurasian hybrid race, not known wild except as escaped from cultivation. It stands for "privation" in the Language of Flowers. Occurring in several forms, it's usually grown for floral or foliage display or as a rootstock rather than for its fruit. The leaves are green, bronze, red or purple; the flowers are white or pink, in late February–March; the plums are yellow, red or purple, up to 1¼" long, ripe late July to mid-September. Unlike most fruit, they're quite good even when nowhere near fully ripe. The tree can grow as large as 50' × 9½'.

In Seattle, we have mostly purpleleaf kinds grown for ornament, called Flowering plum trees. Immediately below are cited greenleaf examples, next *purpleleaf* cultivars, finally *hybrids*. The hybrids are only *part* Cherry plum, so their parentage and proper names are supplied.

- I-90 Plaza vicinity (SE of the tunnel's east end): the larger of two (yellow-fruited) is 38' × 6-trunked × 51½' wide
- Zoo: 37' × 7'5" northeast of N-most restrooms; a slender 40' 'Pissardii' to E
- Ravenna Park: the far south end, by hollies and Scots Pines has one 31½' × 6'10¼" (red-skinned, yellow-fleshed plums)
- 22nd Ave E, east of Boyer Ave E: a street-tree, (small, very juicy yellow plums)
- U.W.: between Sieg Hall and Allen Library is an old tree 30½' × 4'9½" of

handsome form that bears very few yellow plums
- Lake View Cemetery: two yellow-fruited trees by 15th Ave E, N of the entrance
- E Queen Anne Playground (2nd Ave W & Howe St): east of the building are a yellow-fruited one and a 'Pissardii' purpleleaf
- 36th Ave SW, north of SW Manning St: two red-fruited street-trees, E side
- 1421 15th Ave: 3 red-fruited street-trees
- 14th Ave & E Union St: SE corner has a red-fruited specimen
- 26th Ave E, just S of E John St: 2 street-trees, red-fruited, W side
- alley S of NW 59th St, E of 26th Ave NW: 2 *big* ones, on 2 different properties

cv. **'Krauter's Vesuvius'**   Krauter's Vesuvius Plum Tree

Introduced *ca.* 1956 by Carl Krauter of Bakersfield, California. Burbank's very different older clone 'Vesuvius', gets confused, of course. In Seattle, it's hard to tell 'Krauter's Vesuvius' from 'Thundercloud', so none are cited (see 'Thundercloud' examples). 'Krauter's Vesuvius' has darker leaves than 'Thundercloud' and is more strongly upright, less spreading. It is relatively heat- and drought-tolerant and so is the most widely sold purpleleaf plum tree in the Southwest. A 'Krauter's Vesuvius' seedling from California, (Dwarf) **Purple Pony**®, has been sold here only since 1988. It is a dwarf, sparing in bloom, and fruitless, thus differs from its parent, though identical in an individual flower or leaf.

cv. **'Nigra'**   Nigra Plum Tree

The name 'Nigra' was first used by in 1916 to refer to a 'Pissardii' selection with "very dark purple leaves." The 'Nigra' of today's nursery trade is mostly offered by British and Canadian nurseries, also Australian, Dutch, *etc.*—but few American ones. It is indeed a dark leaved tree, yet also differs from 'Pissardii' in being smaller and more compact and in having *pink* flowers, later in spring. 'Nigra' is very rare here. The Fred Meyer store on N 85th street in Greenwood has four south of its parking lot; east of the parking lot are 'Pissardii'.

cv. **'Pissardii'**   Pissard's Plum Tree
='Atropurpurea'

The original purpleleaf plum tree, found in Persia, by M. Pissard, the French head gardener to the Shah. About 1880 it was sent to France. It was widely grown; some of its seedlings (especially its hybrid offspring) have in turn been named and propagated. The flowers are pale pink in their bud stage, opening white. The foliage emerges reddish but becomes dark bronzy-purplish or even somewhat green in the summer—there is variation because the original clone has been propagated by cuttings, grafts and seed. The red-purple plums are roundish, 1–1¼" wide and usually have yellow flesh.

It is very common here. Our largest plum trees of all are 'Pissardii' and only a few of our very oldest 'Thundercloud' approach it in size.
- 32nd Ave NW & NW 85th St: one was 47' × 7'4" × 57' wide in 1987; *declining*
- 26th Ave E & E Lynn St: NW corner yard, by the garage, 32' tall and very stout
- U.W.: four between Gowen and Savery Halls

- Locks bed #29 (behind the fence)
- Triangle at 8th Ave W & W Fulton St has 2 old specimens
- Zoo: northeast of N-most restrooms, a slender 40' one is W of a greenleaf Cherry plum 37' × 7'5"
- 1518 22nd Ave S (south of S Atlantic St): 2 large old street-trees
- Lincoln Park: the larger of two by the south restrooms is 41½' × 4'4¾"

cv. 'Thundercloud'   Thundercloud Plum Tree

Luther Burbank introduced an ornamental darkleaf 'Pissardii' seedling in 1919 under this name. It's unknown whether the cultivar sold by the tens of thousands these days is Burbank's or another clone given his name. The tree sold under this name has an aspect and size like 'Pissardii' but *pink* flowers opening later in spring, and darker foliage than most 'Pissardii' trees. It shares these features with 'Krauter's Vesuvius' and 'Nigra' and cannot be told from the former, but is a larger, more open tree than 'Nigra' and not as dark in summer. The plums are the size and shape of those of 'Pissardii' but dark-skinned *and* fleshed, really hiding well in the foliage because they are the same color as the leaves.

In Seattle, most are street-trees planted during the 1970s and 1980s, virtually impossible to tell from 'Krauter's Vesuvius'. Below are mixed examples.

- 16th Ave E & E McGraw St: a large old one in the NW corner yard
- 18th Ave E & E McGraw St: SW corner yard has an old specimen
- Boyer Ave E, east of 22nd Ave E: a 37' tall street-tree, N side
- Arboretum: one 38' × 4'4" in 6S-9E has been labeled 'Vesuvius' for decades—NOT Burbank's clone of that name, it was acquired by the Arboretum long before 'Krauter's Vesuvius' was heard of
- Locks bed #28 has *sprouts*, and 10 street-trees are N of the facility on NW 54th St
- 135-143 Madrona Pl E (north of E Denny Way): one (117-123 has a big 'Pissardii')
- 45th Ave SW, north of SW Lander St: 5 street-trees

P. 'Blireiana'   Blireiana Plum Tree
=P. × *blireiana* André
(*P. cerasifera* 'Pissardii' × *P. Mume* 'Alphandii')

A popular, widely planted hybrid of a purpleleaf Cherry plum and a Japanese Apricot. Its flowers are hot-pink, doubled, and fragrant, in late February–March. The leaves emerge reddish but become muddy green-bronze by mid-summer; they are wider than other purpleleaf plum tree leaves (except those of 'Moseri') because of the Apricot influence. Plums are almost never borne. 'Blireiana' is a natural dwarf tree, rarely seen even 15' tall, its warty little trunk practically never a foot thick. In full bloom it's like an enchanting Easter miracle, cute and irresistible—a filthy and impoverished street urchin transformed by a smile and heavenly halo. But then the flowers fade and it returns to its fruitlessness, mud color and congested twiggyness.

- NE 74th St, east of 42nd Ave NE: more than 40 street-trees
- 36th Ave NE, north of NE 65th St: 9 street-trees
- Palm Ave SW, south of SW Massachusetts St: 5 street-trees, E side

– 2211 E Newton St: two street-trees

P. 'Cistena' — Cistena Plum Tree

=*P.* × *cistena* (Hansen) Koehne

Shortly after 1895 when he joined the South Dakota State Agricultural Experiment Station at Brookings, Dr. N.E. Hansen began hybridizing the native Sand Cherry (*P. Besseyi* Bailey), a bush with tiny fruit. In spite of the small size of the cherries, the Sioux and other Great Plains Indians valued the plant. Hansen selected superior Sand Cherry seedlings and crossed them with other kinds of cherries, plums and apricots. From the purpleleaf plum 'Pissardii' cross the best outcome was named 'Cistena' (Sioux for "baby") and released in 1910. It is a bushy dwarf, not naturally treelike, with the smallest leaves of all purpleleaf plums. The flowers, slightly pink in the bud stage, open white, late in the season (with those of 'Newport'), about late March into the first week of May.

In Seattle, 'Cistena' suffers and does poorly unless pruned annually and sprayed to control scale. Its patented sport '**Big Cis**' may do better.

– 1802 23rd Ave E: a 10' street-tree north of a 'Blireiana'
– NE 61st St, east of Roosevelt Way: two street-bushes, S side
– 1229 W Bothwell St: above garage
– Dayton Ave N, just north of N 39th St: east side
– 2801 NW 63rd St: a street-bush on 28th Ave NW

P. 'Hollywood' — Hollywood Plum Tree

A hybrid, ('Pissardii' × 'Duarte') discovered *ca.* 1932 in Modesto, California. The 'Duarte' ancestry has 3 involved species (an American and 2 separate east Asians). Its white flowers are like those of 'Pissardii' but give a fuller effect as they're slightly larger and a great many have several extra petals. They're also fragrant. The leaves are largest of all purpleleaf plums, greenish by midsummer and often blotched on top, purplish beneath—like 'Trailblazer' in this respect. The plums are roundish, wine-red colored, 1¼–2½", ripening late June to mid-July, earliest of all. The real 'Hollywood' is very rare in Seattle. Most if not all of trees sold under this name are actually 'Spencer Hollywood' or 'Trailblazer'. Seattle's best specimen of 'Hollywood' is at the U.W. Medicinal Herb Garden, north of section G (nursery area): 42' × 4'9".

P. 'Moseri' — Moser Plum Tree

=*P.* × *blireiana* cv. 'Moseri'

Named for M. Moser, a nurseryman at Versailles, this is like 'Blireiana' but larger, a more open tree with paler flowers of only 15 petals, opening a bit later. It's common in Seattle, though almost no one knows its name. It has disappeared from the local nursery trade, too.

– 11th Ave E, north of E Edgar St: a street-tree, E side, 19' × 4'2" by fire hydrant
– Fuhrman Ave E, south of Broadway E: 2 street-trees, W side; stouter 3'8" around
– Volunteer Park: one 17½' × 3'4½" × 26' wide SE of the museum

343

- Lake View Cemetery: one 21½' × 3'1" SW of flagpole
- S.U.: one 19' × 3'2¼"across the street east of the N end of Administration bldg.
- Green Lake: has 4 by Ravenna Blvd.; best 21' × 2'6½"
- W Dravus St, east and west of 12th Ave W: street-trees on both sides
- Zoo: one 17' × 2'1" west of the Seattle Zoological Society Headquarters Building
- 2602 NW 63rd St: a street-tree

P. 'Newport'   Newport Plum Tree

A Minnesota cross made in 1913 of the complex hybrid 'Omaha' × 'Pissardii', it was christened 'Newport' and distributed under that name in spring of 1923. It is common in Seattle. 'Newport' is distinctly wide-spreading and rarely over 15' tall. The last purpleleaf plum to bloom in spring and (except for Burbank's 'Vesuvius') the least valuable as a flowering tree: the flowers simply are so small and pale that, appearing as they do with the emerging bronzy-red leaves, they are less showy than most. They are more showy if heavy pruning is done in winter or spring, thereby making the tree produce strong summer shoots—but the winter silhouette of trees so pruned is ugly. Left alone, 'Newport' naturally has the most attractive branching habit of all the cultivars. The summer foliage is dark reddish-purple. An improved, patented sport of 'Newport' recently offered in our local nurseries is '**Mt. St. Helens**'—it came from Oregon in 1981.

- Evergreen Park Cemetery: several, possibly *pl.* 1927, largest 30' × 4'7¾" × 40' wide
- 31st Ave E & E Harrison St: many street-trees
- 22nd Ave E, north of E Louisa St: E side has 3 street-trees N of 2 'Thundercloud'
- 1811 N 95th St: one with a bench built around it
- 164 Lynn St: 3 old. tired street-trees
- W Ruffner St, east of 13th Ave W: a large street-tree on the S side

P. 'Spencer Hollywood'   Spencer Hollywood Plum Tree

A very fruitful, naturally dwarf clone named and introduced *ca.* 1960 by S.J. Rich nursery of Oregon. Flowers pale pink, fragrant. Leaves dark glossy green on top, purplish beneath. Plums in July and August, red inside and out. Sold without exception incorrectly as "Hollywood."

- Taylor Ave N & Roy St: 8 street-trees on Roy, 6 on Taylor, and 3 on 6th Ave N
- 5721 27th Ave NE: a street-tree *pl.* in 1988
- 17th Ave NW & NW 73rd St: a street-tree on SW corner
- 2nd Ave NE, just north of 43rd St: a street-tree, W side
- E Pine St, just east of 19th Ave: a street-tree, S side, west of a 'Blireiana'
- 7229 28th Ave NE: two street-trees
- 6657 58th Ave NE: one at the corner
- 3552 NE 86th St: a large front yard specimen
- 8225 17th Ave NE: one NE of the house
- W McGraw St, between Morely Pl W & Eastmont Pl W: S side yard, by sidewalk
- 3566 SW Admiral Way: a street-tree

P. 'Trailblazer'   Trailblazer Plum Tree

From Portland; sold since 1954–55. 'Pissardii' × 'Shiro' is its parentage. ('Shiro' is a hybrid with four species in its background). 'Trailblazer' was first 'Oregon Trail' until someone pointed out that name belonged to a green-leaf Japanese plum. It is often confused with 'Hollywood'. The summer foliage is similar, as are the plum pits. But both flowers and fruit are very distinctive, and 'Hollywood' is a stronger, bigger tree. The flowers are pink in the bud stage, opening nearly white, ⅝–1" wide, at the time of 'Thundercloud' (*i.e.* after 'Pissardii). The leaves unfold green then quickly turn dark and finally are like those of 'Hollywood': semi-glossy and blotched green on top, purplish beneath, but smaller. The plums are egg shaped, to 2" long, bright cherry-red when rubbed, with pale yellowish-pink flesh and a relatively big pit. They ripen late July into September. In Seattle, uncommon; scarcely sold any more.

– Woodlawn Ave N, south of N 53rd St: 3 street-trees, W side
– 1417 15th Ave: 2 street-trees; to N 3 green Cherry plums then 2 smaller 'Trailblazer'
– Arboretum: #560-57 in 7S-9E is small, suffering from shade; only 15' tall
– 303 Lake Washington Blvd (north of E Alder St): a street-tree, N of 2 'Newport'
– 342 22nd Ave: 2 street-trees
– 55th Ave SW opposite SW Orleans St
– 3905 NE 51st St: 2 street-trees
– 6534 17th Ave NE: by driveway
– 6537 32nd Ave NE: in yard's NE corner
– 636 NW 79th St: a street-tree

P. 'Vesuvius'   Vesuvius Plum Tree
='Stribling Thundercloud'

Luther Burbank originated this hybrid and offered it in 1907. Named after the Italian volcano whose eruption destroyed the Roman cities of Herculaneum and Pompeii. It shows practically no 'Pissardii' influence and may have none. Its peach-like foliage aspect, and scant flowers are all most unlike 'Pissardii'. It certainly has *Prunus salicina* or *P. Simonii* genes in it. It is arching, with a short slender trunk. The pure white flowers are too few to be effective ornamentally. If they are cross pollinated they can bear deep purplish-red plums with yellow flesh and small pits. The leaves are distinctly narrow, often puckered and curled up on their sides. They are dark and uniformly colored throughout the summer. It can attain up to 30' in height, eventually. In Seattle, rare; many younger specimens are very slow and small, and may be grafted on Peach rootstocks. Most trees sold under the Vesuvius name are 'Krauter's Vesuvius'—utterly different.

– N 43rd St, east of Woodlawn Ave N: 3 street-trees, N side (and a 'Thundercloud')
– E Miller St, west of 25th Ave E: 2 street-trees, N side (and 4 'Blireiana')
– N 36th St, west of Densmore Ave N: 2 street-trees, S side
– 7310 17th Ave NW: 2 street-trees—a greenleaf Cherry plum and 2 'Blireiana' to N
– 38th Ave NE, north of NE 70th: 6 street-trees (+15 'Thundercloud', 5 'Pissardii')
– 4532 47th Ave NE
– 4829 36th Ave NE: one by the carport

- 1918 41st Ave SW: a heavliy pruned small tree in yard's NW corner
- 1215 W Armour St
- S.P.U.: one 33' tall SE of Crawford Music bldg

[**Citation** "**Plum**" is a patented purpleleaf peach × plum cross, used as a *rootstock*. Its bright pink 1" flowers in March-April are short-stalked and sterile. Slender leaves are *ca.* 4½" × 1½". A specimen 19' tall grows north of the Good Shepherd Center.]

[**Mystery Plum** #1 is a purpleleaf plum hybrid street-tree at 17 W Raye St that I have found nowhere else. It has double white flowers, yet can set some plums.]

[**Mystery Plum** #2 is a purpleleaf plum hybrid found here and there in Seattle, of unknown i.d. It *may* be 'Kankakee Newport'. It is relatively late to bloom, is not very pretty, has sharply toothed leaves, and is malcontent in Seattle—all suggestive of native American plum genes. Yet its plums have *big* pits suggesting E Asian genes. 27th Ave NW, just south of NW 80th St: a street-tree, E side. 8209 42nd Ave NE: 2 street-trees. 7703 36th Ave NE: a street-tree.]

Common PLUM TREES

Cultivated Plum / Fruiting Plum

P. × *domestica* L.   European Plum Tree
=*P. communis* Huds., *non* Arcang.   Prune
=*P. sativa* Rouy & Camus
From Eurasia; of complex hybrid origin, likely *(P. cerasifera* × *P. spinosa* L.)
Sample cvs.: 'Damson', 'Green Gage', 'Italian Prune', 'Stanley', 'Yellow Egg'.

Fruiting plum trees of garden and orchard consist of numerous mongrels rather than pure un-hybridized species selections. Incongruously, plum tree stands for "fidelity" in the Language of Flowers. In Seattle they're common. We have many cultivars; the most abundant is a European hereabouts called the Italian Prune tree. This kind is relatively long-lived, strong, and can root-sucker rampantly to form extensive thickets. White flowers late March–early April give rise to plums available (early July) late July–late September (late October). Most of the trees are less than 20' × 5' yet their maximum dimensions are likely 45' × 8'. Cited below are chiefly Italian Prune trees.

- Othello Park (43rd Ave S & S Othello St)
- Plum Tree Park (26th Ave between E Howell & E Olive Streets)
- Good Shepherd Center: 4 south of the outdoor restrooms
- Magnuson Park: a row N of swimming area
- Peppi's Playground (32nd Ave & E Spruce St): a 5-trunked tree in the NW corner
- Maplewood Playground (Corson Ave S & S Angeline St): 3 SW of ballfields
- 44th Ave NE & NE 50th St: SW corner has some (Children's Hospital grounds)

346

P. salicina Lindl.   Oriental *or* Japanese Plum Tree
=*P. triflora* Roxb.   Salicine
From China (Li), but long grown in Japan (Sumomo スモモ).
Sample cvs.: 'Beauty', 'Burbank', 'Methley', 'Santa Rosa', 'Satsuma', 'Shiro'.

Compared to Europeans, these bloom *earlier*, have *slenderer* leaves, and can have
pretty fall color, too. Cultivars classed as "Japanese Plums" can be hybrids of
several species including Cherry Plum. As for size, a 'Shiro' in Ballard was 34'
× 6'7" × 47' wide in 1995—and larger still when cut down in 2000.

- Gasworks Park (N end of Lake Union): 4 nearly fruitless specimens on a mound in
  park's NE part, largest 25' × 3'11"; fruit red-skinned & yellow-fleshed
- 8010 13th Ave NW: a street-tree 'Weeping Santa Rosa'
- 5635 3rd Ave NW: a street-tree 'Weeping Santa Rosa'
- 8221 40th Ave NE: a 'Weeping Santa Rosa' in yard's NE corner
- 2826 11th Ave E: a street-tree, early-ripening dark, blue-skinned
- 3214 NW 72nd St: red-fruited
- 3112 Fuhrman Ave E: a yard tree
- 3130 Fuhrman Ave E: a street-tree: early-ripening dark, blue-skinned
- 4319 Wallingford Ave N
- U.W.: an early-ripening dark, blue-skinned one is S of Lander Hall, but in ill health
- 1520 41st Ave E: 2 street-trees
- 1125 N 77th St: a street-tree west of a small Apple tree
- 1737 NW 63rd St: a broad specimen
- *south of* 7312 Dibble Ave NW: a street-tree
- 2008 33rd Ave S: a street-tree

[As they do poorly in Seattle's climate, **native American hybrid plum trees** are scarcely
grown here, but cultivars such as the following offered in mail-order catalogs have at
times been planted: 'Sapa', 'Superior', 'Tecumseh', 'Underwood' & 'Waneta'.]

[**American Plum** (*P. americana* Marsh.) from central & east N America hates Seattle,
needing a continental climate to thrive. Flowers tiny, white, and later in spring than
those of most plums. Leaves finely, sharply toothed. Rarely if ever fruits here. It is rare.
A street-tree 12½' tall is on 2nd Ave W, north of W Galer St, W side, shaded by the huge
Hybrid Catalpa. 1414 E Cherry St has 2 tiny street-trees with yellowtwig *Cornus*, weeping
Redwood. The U.W. Medicinal Herb Garden has a youngster NW of Cascara Circle.]

[**Apricot Plum** (*P. Simonii* Carr.) is from N China. Closely related to Japanese Plum.
Known here only as two very old trees, too shaded to fruit, on Lake Washington Blvd.
E, north of E Madison St, E of the ballfields. The taller is 33½' and stouter 3'11".]

[**Mexican Plum** (*P. mexicana* S. Wats.) is from the south-central U.S. and NE Mexico.
Closely related to Cherry plum but has less vertical, more wavy branching habit, higher
gloss leaves, and more meaty, less watery, plums. 1416 N 53rd St has one *ca.* 25' × 3'0".
A few smaller specimens are known in other Seattle yards.]

Aspen (POPLAR)

Populus tremuloides Michx.
SALICACEÆ
From most parts of the continent:
the widest range of any tree species
in North America.

Quaking *or* Trembling Aspen
Canadian *or* American Aspen
Golden *or* Mountain Aspen
Quiver-leaf
Aspe

The aspen is a choice source of food and shelter for beavers and other wildlife. We use its wood for many things, including clothespins, matches, pulp and veneer. A graceful tree, its trembling leaves are fascinating to watch on a windy day, and its brilliant autumn yellow seems to light up its surroundings. Most literary allusions to the aspen's quivering leaves celebrate its European cousin. For example in *The Faery Queen* Spenser has a bewitched knight whose

> "hand did quake,
> And tremble like a leafe of Aspin greene,
> And troubled bloud through his pale face was seene"

In the Language of Flowers, aspen signifies either "lamentation" or "excess of sensibility." Aspen *was* a rare native in Seattle bogs. It's been commonly planted here since the 1970s. The notably slender, gray-green, smooth-barked trunks grow rapidly to 30–40' tall, thereafter more slowly to 60'. Trunks are rarely found a full 1' in diameter. (Maximum aspen dimensions on record are 126' × 14'.) Many specimens tend to sucker from the roots.

– Matthews Beach Sewage Plant: some by the the creek and Sand Point Way NE
– 3804 E Crockett St: a ♀ is immense, its trunk more than 6½" around
– Lake City Way NE & NE 98th St: *ca.* 2 dozen; tallest 80'+
– Evergreen Park Cemetery: 68½' tall (multitunked) near offices
– Benefit Park (9320 38th Ave S): 16 at the N end
– U.W.: one 64' × 3'9½" east of McMahon Hall; NE end of University Bridge; by Burke-Gilman Trail from Brooklyn Ave NE to 15th Ave NE
– Sacajawea Playground (NE 94th St between 17th & 20th): 6 by the fence on the N side, the largest 61½' × 6'0"
– 39th Ave & E Olive St: NW corner has 20 ♀ street-trees, largest *ca.* 4'0" around
– 3407 42nd Ave SW: a *weeping* street-tree, under wires, by telephone pole

[The **European Aspen** (*P. tremula* L.) is known here only in its cv. '**Erecta**', the "Swedish Columnar Aspen," a distinctly columnar ♂. Uncommon; our oldest date from *ca.* 1990. U.W.: 52½' × 2'2" is tallest of 7 east of the canoe house. One south of Meany School is 41' × 2'0". 1632 E McGraw St has 10 in a row, tallest 41½'. 1st Ave NW, south of NW 73rd St: a street-tree, east side. 5815 7th Ave NW.]

Black POPLAR

P. nigra L.

From the far NW of Africa, through Europe to W Siberia and the Caucasus.

Likely the first tree called "poplar" by the English—prefixed *Black* to distinguish it from White poplar. It signifies "courage" in the Language of Flowers. In its typical state it attains at most 135' × 46'. Its typical form is extremely rare in Seattle; its cultivars and hybrids common. A female 73' × 7'10" is with 12 Ghost poplars (see below) by the "Montlake Cut" on the U.W. campus. Arboretum #129-99 in 43-2W is the only other known.

cv. 'Italica'	Lombardy Poplar
=var. *italica* (Muenchh.) Koehne	Pyramidal Poplar
=var. *pyramidalis* (Borkh.) Spach	Mormon Tree
=*P. fastigiata* Desf.	
=*P. italica* (Muenchh.) Moench	
=*P. dilatata* Ait.	

A mutant thought to have originated from a Black poplar in Italy during the late 1600s or early 1700s, and widely grown throughout Europe from the second half of the 18th century onwards. A male clone, now world famous as the ubiquitous exclamation point (!) of trees. Its wood is essentially worthless due to extreme knottiness, but the tree is often planted as a huge living fence or windbreak. The fluttering leaves create a pleasant effect, especially when yellow in autumn. Perhaps its most serious fault is the habit of sending unsightly suckers from its burly bole and far-ranging roots—yet this is the only way it can reproduce, since it cannot set seed. It's very common and well known here. To many it is THE poplar. As far as is known, Seattle has the largest recorded Lombardy poplars outside of New Zealand, where dimensions up to 157½' × 36'1½" have been recorded.

- Lake Washington Blvd S, by S Atlantic St: 141' × 30'4"
- South Park Playground (8th Ave S & S Thistle St): one 128½' × 26'5¼"
- Jefferson Park Golf Course: largest of some near the north end is 120' × 21'11"
- Volunteer Park: one W of lower tennis courts is 130' × 20'0"
- U.W.: of some along Stevens Way by Architecture Hall, best is 110' × 18'1½"
- Lake Washington Ship Canal, west of Fremont: many
- Evergreen Park / Washelli Cemetery: a long landmark row on Aurora Ave N, 35 trees on the east and 66 on the west
- 1st Ave W, north of W Highland Dr: 9 old street-trees, E side
- Ravenna Ave NE, north of NE 86th St: tallest of 8 on W side is 125'

cv. 'Afghanica'   Ghost Poplar
=cv. 'Thevestina' *or* var. *thevestina* (Dode) Bean   Tebessa Poplar
=var. *afghanica* Aitch.& Hemsl.   Afghan Poplar
=*P. usbekistanica* Kom. 'Afghanica'   Algerian Black Poplar

A Black poplar mutant widely planted in central Asia, SE Europe and N Africa, the Ghost poplar is slender and upright in form like Lombardy poplar—for which it is often mistaken. But form aside, it differs in every detail: the bole is round rather than fluted and clean rather than besprouted; the bark is whitish-gray rather than yellowish-brown; the leaves are not heart-shaped and have poorer fall color; it is smaller in stature and a female rather than a male clone, so it releases cottony seeds in the summer. It is common here, mostly on public property.

- U.W.: by the "Montlake Cut" canal are 13 poplars in a row: 12 are Ghost and 1 is typical Black poplar (not far away is a circle of 9 smaller Lombardy poplars); the largest Ghost poplar is 105½' × 11'2"
- W Seattle Golf Course: a large number; one in the creek ravine is 132' × 7'7"
- Arboretum: one S of pinetum in 32-7W is 125½' × 8'3¼"; of six (+ 6 Bolleana White poplars) on Lake Wash. Blvd, N of E Roanoke St, the tallest is 124' × 6'9¾"
- Jefferson Park: hundreds; many stand sentinel on the ridge; tallest 124½' × 7'5"
- Leschi Park: tallest of a pair in the SE corner is 121½' × 9'5"
- Seward Park: dozens, with a few Lombardy and Bolleana White poplars
- Ravenna Park: 6 near the south end restrooms are almost 100' tall
- Volunteer Park: four SW of the reservoir
- Woodland Park: by the 3 footbridges over Aurora Ave N

[A **Hybrid Mystery Poplar** that *must be* part Black poplar is 64½' tall, right by the street at 11014 15th Ave NE. No other tree in Seattle matches it. It has *hairy* twigs, leaf stems, margins and undersides. Leaves are *ca.* 4" × 2⅜", the small ones *crinkly.* ♂]

Cathay POPLAR

P. cathayana Rehd.   Mongolian Poplar
=*P. suaveolens* auct., *non* Fisch.   Chinese: Qing Yang
From NW China to Manchuria and Korea.

Commonly planted by tombs and temples near Peking, this is almost unknown in the West. It flushes early in spring, and has been reported up to 100' × 10'.

- Arboretum: two ♀ #473-71 in 14-2E and 15-1E; largest 62½' × 4'3½"
- Camp Long: five ♀ east of the south pond; largest 54' × 4'1"

Certines POPLAR

P. × *berolinensis* (K. Koch) Dipp. '**Certinensis**'

The male clone known by this name since at least 1893 is a cross of the Asian *Populus laurifolia* Ledeb. and Black poplar. Likely it arose in France, as Certines is a town about 35 miles NW of Lyon. The original Berlin poplar is female and less desirable. In the Great Plains and prairie regions of the U.S. and Canada,

Certines poplar has been grown for decades under both names. It's extremely rare in Seattle, flushes early in spring and has dark, handsome foliage.

– U.W.; the largest of 6 west of the Oceanography Teaching bldg. is 95½' × 5'6"; also present at N-8 parking lot
– (the ♀ *P.* × *berolinensis* is at the Arboretum (#390-60); best 93½' × 7'2" in 15-1W

Black Cottonwood (POPLAR)

P. balsamifera L. ssp. *trichocarpa* (T.&G.) Braysh.	(our) Native Cottonwood
=*P. trichocarpa* T.&G. *ex* Hook.	Oregon *or* Western Balsam Poplar
Native here; from S Alaska	Black Balsam Poplar
to northwestern Mexico.	Balm / Rottenwood

Our native cottonwood is so massive that it outgrows not only all of its kin, but nearly every other deciduous broadleaf tree as well. Given plenty of moisture and full sunshine it can grow to 230' × 32½'!—but it has a short lifespan, reaching maturity at 60–100 years and decrepitude or death in 100–250 years. Males, mostly larger than females, make colorful catkins 4–5" long in March–April; females form pea-sized seedpods in grape-like clusters, which when ripe from mid-May through June release millions of tiny seeds borne on cottony tufts (hence the name cottonwood). In November these huge trees become beacons of yellow foliage.

The stately grandeur of a mature specimen draws our admiration, and most people savor the spring air redolent with its balmy perfume. But the cottonwood's suckering habit, heaving roots, brittle limbs and the messiness of sticky bud-scales, twig and leaf debris and drifts of cottony seeds make it unbearable for most yards—quite aside from its disproportionate size. As often as not it dies violently: the roots don't yield an inch, but an aged trunk may snap in a raging storm, taking neighboring trees or structures with it in its mighty crash. Not surprisingly, then, most cottonwoods in Seattle are in woods or parks. Beavers often gnaw on our lakeshore examples.

– O.O. Denny Park: tallest is 162½' × 13'6"; largest is 115' × 16'0"
– Boren Park: a ♂ 150' × 24'4½" around its *forked* trunk
– Madrona Park: a landmark ♂ tree 146' × 22'9"
– Lakeridge Park: a roadside tree 146½' × 11'6½"
– Arboretum: many, such as one labeled #S-0008-A in 13-B, a ♂ 140' × 16'1"
– Colman Park Beach: burry beach landmark ♂ is 115½' × 21'0"+

[A **Hybrid Cottonwood** that *looks like* it is our native crossed with a NE Asian (*P. Maximowiczii* Henry) is known here only as a 73½' tall ♀ at the Zoo, *pl.* 1996, 47' N of Orangutan Research Station on the Trail of Vines (a tall rare willow and a Chinese Chestnut hybrid near it). Its seed catkins are about 12" long when dropping in June.]

[**Aurora Poplar**—called variously *P.* 'Candicans Aurora', *P.* × *candicans* 'Variegata', *P. balsamifera* 'Aurora', *P.* × *Jackii* 'Aurora'—is a clone named in 1954 in England. A ♀. Leaves hairy, toothed, *when young splashed creamy-white and pink*. Known here only as one *pl.* 1993 at Golden Gardens Park E of the train tracks, S of the underpass.]

Gray POPLAR

P. × *canescens* (Ait.) Sm.   Grey Poplar
=*P. alba* var. *canescens* Ait.

A hybrid from Europe and W Asia of White poplar and European aspen *(P. tremula)*. It is usually grown as a male clone that can reach as large as 125' × 18½'. The weeping cultivar '**Pendula**' is also male. Extremely rare in Seattle.

– Good Shepherd Center: the SE corner of the building has 3 '**Pendula**' with a 100' Lombardy poplar, the largest 50' × 9'10¼" & tallest 83½' × 8'8"
– Arboretum: #92-62 in 15-B is 78' × 6'3"

Hybrid Black POPLARS

P. × *canadensis* Moench., *non* Michx. fil.
=*P.* × *euramericana* (Dode) Guinier

Most of the well known and widely planted hybrid Black poplars originated in Europe during the 18th and 19th centuries, the result of accidental crosses between an eastern North American cottonwood (*P. deltoides* Bartr. *ex* Marsh.) and Black poplar. Others are wholly American hybrids and distinctive cloned cultivars. All are tough and possess proverbial hybrid vigor, together forming a group of great variety, complexity and value. They are widely planted for wood production in some parts of the world, and for ornament in others. Most of these hybrids are male (even though they may have feminine names), generally achieving heights of 100–150' or more. They are distinguished not so much by leaf characteristics as by overall form, rate of growth and time of flushing, making exact i.d. in the field depend on keen observation. Their many shapes and sizes suit a variety of particular needs. Aspen-like when young, these hybrids soon grow into dramatic, picturesque giants, reaching truly awe-inspiring proportions with advanced age. Some bear long colorful catkins in spring; others have new leaves unfolding a bright red-orange at the same time.

In Seattle, common in a collective sense. They were once often planted but now scarcely ever are. Five different hybrid clones are known here, as follows:

cv. '**Eugenei**'   Prince Eugene's Poplar
=*P.* × *Eugenei* Sim.-Louis *ex* K. Koch   Carolina Poplar
=*P. deltoides Eugenei* hort.   Norway Poplar
=*P. carolinensis* hort.   Sudden Sawlog

By far the most common cultivar of the group in North America. Over the decades millions have been planted. But because its roots can readily heave pavement or invade sewer lines, and its branches are prone to storm breakage, 'Eugenei' has been banned from streetside planting in many cities. It originated about 1832 in France, from 'Regenerata' pollinated by Lombardy poplar. By 1913 the original specimen measured 150' × 25'! It is a male clone.

In Seattle, uncommon, though it outnumbers the other four cultivars put together. (Further study may reveal that 'Eugenei' in the strict sense is separate from and superior to the more common clone "Carolina Poplar.")

- Arboretum: best of 7 on Lake Wash. Blvd, south of E Roanoke St, is 123' × 15'1"
- NE 110th St, east of 35th Ave NE: 6 street-trees, N side; largest 101' × 9'9"
- U.W.: one 93' × 10'9" NW of stadium is the sole specimen (many were cut down)
- Myrtle Edwards & Elliott Bay Parks: *ca.* 30, +*ca.* 100 Lombardy poplars
- 4523 W Raye St: 6 west of a Lombardy poplar

cv. 'Marilandica'   Maryland Poplar

Female, this clone was a seedling of a Black poplar pollinated by 'Serotina' about 1800, probably in Holland. Its maximum recorded dimensions are 131' × 19⅓'. Apparently much energy it could otherwise use for growth is channeled into making seedpods. Because of its cottony seeds in June, 'Marilandica' is less valued as an ornamental tree than are the other clones. Known only as follows.

- Arboretum: 2 on Lake Wash. Blvd, north of Boyer Ave (20-5W), 108½' × 10'10½" × 74' wide & 109½' × 10'4½" × 76' wide; 2 west of the ballfield, 94' × 7'7¾" & 97' × 7'0"

cv. 'Regenerata'   Railway Poplar

A female, likely a seedling of 'Marilandica' pollinated by 'Serotina'. It arose in 1814 or earlier in France, and was much planted beside English railways. The largest dimensions recorded are 131' × 15'. Compared to 'Marilandica' it is a taller, narrower tree with redder leaves in spring and it produces less cotton since most of its flower catkins drop well before ripening. Known only as follows.

- Mt Baker Blvd S, by 33rd Ave S: the largest of two is 103' × 14'2"

cv. 'Robusta'   Giant Poplar

A male that arose in France *ca.* 1885–1895 as a seedling of an eastern U.S. cottonwood pollinated by *P. nigra* 'Plantierensis'. From its father it inherited the *hairy* twigs that distinguish it from the other hybrid Black poplars. Its leaves unfold early in spring and are a bright orange-red before greening. The leafstalks are often galled. Recorded to 136' × 16'. It's uncommon here.

- Magnolia Playfield (34th Ave W & W Smith St): tallest of 11 at the S end is 85' and the stoutest is 14'2¼" around (a low-forking specimen)
- Magnolia School (28th Ave W & W Smith St): best of 3 E of bldg. is 79' × 10'16"
- Green Lake: 6 were S of Evans Pool (best 9'0" around when cut down in 1989); 17 new trees *pl.* by Gaines Point in 1997 to replace the cottonwood grove felled there
- Jefferson Park Golf Course: 54 on the west side of Beacon Ave S at the SE part

cv. 'Serotina'   Black Italian Poplar

The oldest of these hybrid clones, this is a male that originated *ca.* 1700, likely in France, from an eastern U.S. cottonwood pollinated by a Black poplar. It was planted in Switzerland, then Italy, finally England where it was called the Black

Italian poplar. "Serotina" refers to its very late leafing-out in spring. It is a huge tree, to 151' × 22½' or more. In Seattle, extremely rare. (The handsome goldleaf variant '**Aurea**' is found in Portland, Tacoma and Vancouver but not here.)

– Alki Beach Park: one 98' × 11'4" × 72' wide by 64th Pl SW, fell in 1990 but *resprouted;* a second (89' × 10'11" × 79' wide in 1992) stood east of 62nd Ave SW until the Parks Department cut it down, and suppressed all the suckers of the other, so now Seattle has none of this fine clone.

[*Cottonless* **Cottonwood**, *P. deltoides* cv. 'Siouxland', is a ♂ clone from South Dakota <1965, known here only as 6 *pl.* in 2000 on Interlaken Blvd. E, east of 26th Ave. The tallest is already 33'. I have not verified the accuracy of their identity. But if they are in fact the real 'Siouxland' then that clone is not *P. deltoides*, but rather a hybrid.]

Weeping POPLARS

P. Simonii Carr. cv. '**Pendula**' Simon Weeping-Poplar
From China, Korea.

P. tristis Fisch. Tristis Weeping-Poplar
From central Asia or Siberia. Brown-twig Poplar

In the 1930s Seattle's Park Dep't. obtained two Asiatic poplars, then called *P. chinensis* and *P. sinensis.* These names have been corrected as cited above.

The more common of the pair, *P. Simonii* 'Pendula', was widely planted around town in various parks, golf courses, playgrounds and other places both private and public. It is a male clone that makes a large, elegantly pendulous tree. It is unlikely that any other North American city has as many as Seattle does. Only five locations are cited below—we might easily list fifteen.

– Arboretum: Lake Washington Blvd by E Roanoke St has a row of 24, the tallest 94' and the stoutest trunk 13'6" around
– Green Lake: almost 30, the largest 75' × 10'7½"
– Delridge Playfield (Delridge Way SW & SW Alaska St): about a dozen
– Golden Gardens Park: 15 by the beach
– Rodgers Park: 5 by tennis courts; 4 north of Queen Anne Bowl

P. tristis is a mystery tree, introduced to the West from St. Petersburg, Russia, about 1841. It has not been recorded wild, yet is hardy enough to grow in some places north of the Arctic Circle. Also a male clone, it differs from the Simon Weeping poplar in every detail. In brief, it is a smaller, darker, less markedly pendulous tree. Extremely rare in Seattle; only two specimens left:

– Arboretum: #827-58 in 14-B is 39½' × 3'2¾"; an old leaning specimen 53½' × 5'1" at the SE end of the row of 25 Simon Weeping poplars

[*Fastigiate* **Simon Poplar**, cv. '**Fastigiata**', is a ♂ clone known here only in Interbay by 17th Ave W & W Dravus St. Its branches ascend strongly but it is not columnar like Lombardy and Ghost poplars; in age it really sprawls out.]

White POPLAR

P. alba L.   Abele / Woolly Poplar
From N Africa, west-central Asia.   White Aspen

White poplar is as appropriately named as Bald Eagle, Black Panther, Blueberry, Greyhound, and Redwood. The dark green top side of its leaves, in stark contrast to the cottony white underside—as different as night and day—prompted its association with "time" in the Language of Flowers, and the leaves' perpetual fluttering evoked "perseverance." No other very common tree in Seattle has such bright snow-white leaf undersides. After turning yellow in autumn the dropped leaves lie brown on the ground, their whitish color slowly fading to silvery gray. The tree is similar in hardiness, rate of growth and toughness to Siberian Elm, Black Locust, Silver Maple, Russian Olive and Tree of Heaven. It suckers frequently from both bole and roots. Recorded to 140' × 22'. In Seattle, it exists solely in two clones *very* unlike one another.

cv. 'Nivea'   Silver *or* Snowy Poplar

A female, leaning, suckering and often making maple-shaped leaves that lead people to call it "Silver Maple." This is the kind with the snow-white leaves.
  – Van Asselt Playground: 16 in a row, the tallest 73' × 9'3"
  – Licton Springs Park (Ashworth Ave N & N 97th St): one 63½' × 10'2" in NW part
  – Ravenna Park: by NE 61st St, west of 21st Ave NE, a rotting tree 7'7½" around
  – Lake Washington Blvd S: 3 near Lakewood, tallest 53' and stoutest 6'8½" around
  – Crown Hill Cemetery: 67' × 8'9" with Oregon Ashes in NE corner outside fence
  – Lake View Cemetery: one by 15th Ave E, north of the entrance, is 60' × 6'10"
  – 1014 NE 88th St: one 60' tall
  – Woodland Park: larger of two is 55' × 7'2"

cv. 'Pyramidalis'   Bolleana (White) Poplar
=var. *pyramidalis* Bge.   Pyramidal White Poplar
=var. *Bolleana* (Lauche) Otto   Bolle Poplar

A male clone grown for its strongly *upright habit* and attractively light-colored bark. It can surpass 125' × 21½'. The leaves are not so white beneath, nor so maple-like (except on root-suckers) as those of 'Nivea'; in fact they far more resemble those of Gray poplar.
  – Arboretum: one 127½' × 8'9½" × 33' wide on Lake Washington Blvd, north of E Roanoke St (it's one of 6 along with 6 'Afghanica' Black poplars)
  – S.P.U.: one 101' × 18'6" × 88' wide is prominent in the main lawn
  – Fremont Ave N, south of N 38th St: two street-trees, W side, larger 81½' × 20'2"
  – NW 77th St, west of 25th Ave NW: 5 street-trees, S side, largest 80½' × 18'1¼"
  – 115 18th Ave E (south of E John St): two street-trees, larger 15½" around
  – Seattle Center: 3 SE of the exhibition hall
  – S.U.: 15 flanking E James St
  – Froula Park (12th Ave NE & NE 72nd St): 5 on S side (11 Lombardy poplars to E)
  – Pacific Medical Center (1200 12th Ave S): 13

Tree PRIVET

Ligustrum lucidum Ait. fil.
OLEACEÆ
From China, Korea.

Glossy *or* Shining *or* Chinese Privet
White-Wax Tree
Woa Tree

A broadleaf evergreen shrub or tree to 95' × 16' with creamy-white fragrant flowers August–September, against dark glossy leaves 3–6" long. In China, it is an emblem of chastity and is used as the chief producer of white or insect wax—a large scale-insect (called Pe-La) is encouraged to "make itself at home" in the tree, and the wax it secretes in turn is widely employed for candle-making, polishing, and in medicine. In Seattle, common. Of our various privets only this kind is consistently tree-sized; it is usually sold and planted as a tree. One 44' × 4'2" in 1993 was cut down *ca.* 1999. Beware—heavy snow breaks it badly. Other kinds of privet here are usually kept as clipped hedges or unclipped shrubs and only rarely trained into tree form.

– U.W.: one 37½' tall N of Benson Hall; 31' tall W of Bagley Hall
– 1310 Lake Washington Blvd.: 29' tall
– 941 Broadway E (south of E Prospect St): 2 street-trees, larger 27' × 3'1"
– 1134 Lakeside Ave S (north of S Judkins St): 2 street-trees
– Arboretum: the best is 23' tall, #156-63, shaded by Oregon Ashes in 43-5E
– 2944 NW Esplanade St: several outside the fence, under power wires

[The **Chinese Privet** (*L. sinense* Lour.) is a shrub here, but a tree 29' × 3'10¼" × 35½' wide is at Parsons Gardens Park. One 24' × 2'7" is by the bus stop on the SE corner of 4th Ave S & S Brandon St. It blooms around the 4th of July. Leaves semi-evergreen, narrow, only 1–3" long.]

Chinese QUINCE TREE

Pseudocydonia sinensis (Thouin.) Schneid.
=*Chænomeles sinensis* (Thouin) Koehne
=*Cydonia sinensis* Thouin
=*Pyrus cathayensis* Hemsl., in part
ROSACEÆ
From China.

Perfume Quince
Chinese: Mu Kua

Though deciduous, Chinese quince may keep some of its leaves through most of the winter in our mild climate. In form it is a large shrub or small tree to 50' × 6¼', with attractively mottled flaky bark. Pretty, very pale pink flowers (late March) April–May give rise to enormous eye-catching greenish-yellow fruit 3–7" × 2–4" wide, weighing ½–1½ pounds. These fruits are fragrant, waxy or oily-textured, with hard, dry, semi-woody flesh that boldly defies anyone to eat it. Even if brought inside and put near a sunny window to ripen completely, the fruit still makes at best a mediocre jelly. In Seattle, Chinese quince is rare.

– U.W. Medicinal Herb Garden: one 29' × 2'5½" north of section F; another 18½' tall is south of the Plant Lab. at its west end
– U.W.: two small ones west of Bloedel Hall, overshadowed by 2 Monterey Pines

- Arboretum: several, mostly shrubby, #264-59B is 27½' tall in 32-5W
- Franklin High School Playfield: a shrubby one on the east hillside
- Locks bed #304A

Common QUINCE TREE

Cydonia oblonga Mill.   Fruiting Quince Tree
=*C. vulgaris* Pers.   Golden-Apple Tree
=*Pyrus Cydonia* L.
From the Near East to central Asia.

This is the original "Quince," grown more for its edible fruit than ornamental beauty. It is a small, spreading, crooked tree rarely reaching 25' × 5½'. Palest-pink 2" wide flowers appear late April–May with the pale green, ever so soft young foliage. The fuzzy, yellow-gold fruit is variously shaped, somewhat apple- or pear-like with asymmetric bulges. When unripe it's like a lemony bar of soap. When ripe it is usually eaten only cooked, or preserved in confections such as marmalade. In ancient Greece the fruit was called the "golden apple" and symbolized love and matrimony. It came to mean "temptation" in the Language of Flowers—perhaps in association with the serpent's apple in Eden, or with the apple of Aphrodite.

It's uncommon in Seattle, and little known. (Our abundant quince shrub, "Flowering" or "Japanese" quince, is a red-flowered *spiny* bush, making golfball sized fruit.) Nurseries offer quince cultivars such as 'Champion', 'Cooke's Jumbo', 'Orange' (='Apple'), 'Pineapple', 'Smyrna' and 'Van Deman'. Few are known on public property: it is chiefly a back yard fruit tree.

- Othello Park: one *ca.* 50' NW of children's play area is 15' × 3'9" × 24' wide
- 1820 Federal Ave E
- Meadowbrook Park's edible arboretum planting has cv. 'Aromatnaya' *pl.* 1998
- 24th Ave E & E Roy St: NW corner has a street-tree
- 107 NE 60th St: two street-trees
- 1848 40th Ave E: one south of the house
- 2410 E Galer St: one by the sidewalk

REDBUD

Cercis canadensis L.   Common *or* Eastern Redbud
LEGUMINOSÆ (FABACEÆ)   American Judas-Tree
From the central and eastern   Junebud Tree
U.S., S Ontario and parts of N Mexico.   Redbird Tree

"Redbud" is an American name for this species; many descendants of European settlers in North America still call the tree by the name of its Old World cousin: Judas Tree. In foliage the tree looks more like a lilac than like anything else (except the rare shrub *Disanthus*). It can be shrubby or a tree to 66' × 10½'. Its 2–7" long leaves are *heart-shaped* and turn yellow in autumn. But redbud is grown for neither foliage nor form—it's prized for floral effect, which ranges from a pale

357

purple haze to a clear, bright rosy-pink spectacle (April into early June). Both flowers and tender young seedpods are edible, making colorful, flavorful salad garnishes. Common in Seattle; it amply outnumbers the original Judas Tree.

– E Mercer St, just east of 34th Ave E: two street-trees, S side
– 414 14th Ave (just south of E Remington Ct): 2 street-trees; taller 28'
– 5260 12th Ave NE: relatively large-trunked
– U.W.: two youngsters east of Center on Human Development and Disability
– 7536 24th Ave NE: a street-tree, large—but with a conk on its trunk
– Arboretum: several are by Graham Visitor Center

f. *alba* Rehd.   Whiteflower Redbud

Flowers *white*. More than one clone exists. Uncommon; all are young.

– S.U.: 17' tall, in border below Madison St, west of the Administration Bldg.
– Federal Ave E & E Aloha St: NW corner
– 2316 Warren Ave N: 2 street-trees
– 1120 N 76th St: a street-tree flanked by two Mountain Ashes
– 7334 50th Ave NE: a street-tree

cv. 'Forest Pansy'   Purpleleaf Redbud

Leaves *purple* in spring, bronzy in ssummer, turning several colors in the fall. Common.

– 6109 / 6115 32nd Ave NW: a street-tree under power lines, 21½' × 3'4¼"
– 20th Ave E & E Calhoun St: NE corner house has 2 street-trees on Calhoun
– 5th Ave NE, north of NE 65th St: a street-tree

var. *texana* (S. Wats.) Hopkins   Mexican Redbud
=*C. canadensis* var. *mexicana* (Rose) Hopkins   Texas Redbud
=*C. occidentalis* var. *texensis* S. Wats.
=*C. reniformis* Engelm. *ex* S. Wats.
=*C. texensis* (S. Wats.) Sarg.
=*C. mexicana* Rose

From the Arbuckle Mountains of S Oklahoma to N Mexico. It is Oklahoma's State Tree. Much grown in the Southwest; usually shrubby. Rare in Seattle compared to typical Redbud, but choice. Differs in its leaves being "wet look" glossy, often ruffled or undulate; thicker; hairless to densely hairy; rounded and notched at the apex (not pointed); the base deeply cordate; the stem short.

– 1222 20th Ave E: 2 street-trees south of a big Black Locust
– 2510 E Lynn St: a street-tree 11½' tall
– 4330 NE 58th St: up in the yard, growing into telephone wires

California REDBUD

C. occidentalis Torr. *ex* Gray   Western Redbud
From S Oregon, California, Utah, Nevada, Arizona.

Usually a bush; very rarely over 30' tall or tree-like. Rather than being pointed like other redbud leaves, its leaves are rounded like those of the Judas Tree, but are thicker, smaller and bluer, almost a metallic or jade-green effect sometimes. It commonly flowers not only in spring but also in late summer–autumn. This advantage is offset by its nonexistent fall leaf color (here). Very rare in Seattle.

- Arboretum: #254-57 is 23½' tall in 21-3E
- U.W.: taller of two *pl.* W of the HUB in 1990 is 2-trunked, 16' tall, by lightpost
- U.W.: CUH has #55-87, a shrubby one labeled *C. Siliquastrum* (Judas Tree)
- Minor Ave E, south of E Roanoke St: 7½' tall street-tree south of a ♂ Oregon Ash; north of a cutleaf White Birch
- 12th Ave NE & NE 106th St: NE corner has one by fire hydrant; severely pruned
- 7912 35th Ave SW: one NW of the house is barely visible from the sidewalk

Chinese REDBUD

C. chinensis Bge.
From China.

Chinese redbud is either a tree up to 50' × 4' or—usually in Western gardens—a bush rarely to 16' tall. Leaves like common redbud's, but thicker, glossier, and have three instead of five main veins; they tend to be larger too. The flowers are *spicy* in flavor unlike those of the other species. Uncommon here. Since the 1990s the main cultivar has been '**Avondale**'; as are most of the following.

- Arboretum: #384-53A south of nursery (22-4E) is largest of at least four, 10' × 2'0"
- S.U.: shrubby; at SW corner of the Pigott building
- 733 16th Ave: a street-tree
- 706 N 65th St: a street-tree, W of a 'Shirotae' Cherry, E of a Washington Hawthorn
- 7014 2nd Ave NW: a stout street-tree
- 1811 E Calhoun St: a street-tree
- 1st Ave N, just north of Howe St: a street-tree, east side
- near or at 825 NE 58th St: a street-tree
- 1409 NW 64th St: a street-tree
- 706 N 65th St: a street-tree west of a larger cherry tree

Judas Tree (REDBUD)

C. Siliquastrum L.   European Redbud
From SW Europe to W Asia.   Love Tree

In southern Europe many believe this was the tree upon which Judas Iscariot hanged himself after betraying Jesus. But Northern Europeans think Elder was the tree. We'll never know—this is all stuff of legend, not Scripture. In the Language of Flowers, Judas Tree means either "unbelief" or "betrayal." It grows to 65' × 10½' and has larger, darker flowers than those of the common redbud, and round-tipped rather than pointed leaves. It is usually stronger and more showy in bloom. The flowers and tender young seedpods are also edible, tasting subtly different from those of the common redbud. Like the California redbud, it sometimes flowers again in autumn. In Seattle, it's rare.

- Cal Anderson Park (Broadway reservoir): one 39' × 7'2¼" on the west side
- 5525 35th Ave NE: one 27' × 4'5" × 39' wide (1993)
- 4925 Stanford Ave NE: one 36' × 5'8" (1989)
- 8th Ave NE & NE 83rd St: NE corner yard has one E of the house
- 4549 West Laurel Dr NE: between the driveway and steps
- U.W.: a shrubby specimen by a Scots Pine east of Kincaid Hall
- Locks bed #313 has a shrubby pair against the wall
- N 38th St, west of Carr Place: a street-tree, N side
- Arboretum: #563-39C is a 21½' tall leaning, shaded slender tree in 2-5E; #284-90 'Alba' is NE of Rhododendron Glen (15-5E); #44-90 is in 20-3E
- 1928 NW Milford Way: 22' tall
- 20th Ave NW & NW 67th St: NE corner yard has one 20' tall
- Bradner Gardens Park: one north the salmon bench east of the windmill

[*C. racemosa* Oliv.—From China. Extremely rare in its native China; equally rare in cultivation; at least one Seattle garden has a youngster, and it is now in local nurseries. Leaf hairy beneath, pointed at apex, rounded at the base. Flowers pale pink, borne in 3–5" long racemes of 10–40. Recorded to 39' × 6½' in the wild.]

Coast REDWOOD

Sequoia sempervirens (D. Don) Endl.   California Redwood
CUPRESSACEÆ (TAXODIACEÆ)   Common Redwood
From coastal SW Oregon and N California.   Coastal Redwood

On the foggy coast of northern California grow the world's tallest trees, the renowned and awesome redwoods, with trunks like mammoth reddish-brown pillars. The tallest known currently are about 370'. Authentic records exist of even taller individual Eucalypts and Douglas Firs—but as a general rule, and as far as is known *now*, redwoods are the tallest standing trees. Big specimens have sent up mere suckers as high as 150 feet! The trunks can be as much as 100' around—32' in diameter! One that had its rings counted proved to be 2,200 years old; some may approach 4,000. The wood is reddish, soft, very durable and highly valued. The Save-the-Redwoods League co-operates with State and National authorities to preserve many of the best remaining tracts of old-growth forest.

Coast redwoods thrive in Seattle and are common: our tallest non-native trees. They're perfect conifers to plant in wet, shady ravines, but poor choices for average yards. Sometimes basal suckers are present, and reseeding is common. Though 4 cultivars are treated below, other less distinctive ones exist here.

- Interlaken Park: Seattle's tallest non-native tree, once topped, is 165½' × 16'3" × 64½' wide (in a grove of 12 on the boulevard section closed to vehicles)
- Seward Park: the largest at the peninsula tip is 159' (dead top) × 13'5½"
- Lake Wash. Blvd E: one 157' × 16'3" at the sharp curve below Lakeview Park
- Ravenna Park: the tallest of 11 in the ravine W of 20th Ave NE bridge is 155' × 11'5"
- Madrona Park: one 153' × 18'2¼" right by the boulevard

- Lincoln Park: the largest of many is 146' × 14'10" SE of the service yard
- Viretta Park (39th Ave E & Evergreen Place): one 135' × 16'5"
- U.W.: one by the Waterfront Activities Center is 120½' × 21'3" around its base before it forks into 4 trunks; one by Winkenwerder Hall is 107' × 15'4½"
- Franklin High School: one 116' × 16'8½" is a Heritage Tree
- 3156 East Laurelhurst Dr NE: one *pl.* 1918 is 115½' × 19'2"
- Volunteer Park: one on the east border is 112½' × 16'1½"
- Green Lake: the largest in the golf course is 103½' × 15'4½"
- Locks bed #122, 201 (99' tall), 203 (91' tall; by #204), 205 (four)

cv. 'Adpressa'   Shortleaf Redwood

Tree dense, pyramidal, wispy-looking. Shoots much narrower and slenderer; young tips creamy-white (it's also called 'Albo-spica'). Needles much smaller than typical, bluer, and uniformly directed forward (*adpressa* means pressed against or on). Growth slow. Often kept as a shrub by pruning. Rare.

- 108 NW 41st St: one by the steps is about 32' × 3'0"
- Arboretum: #522-79B in the conifer meadow (41-6W) is 10½' tall

cv. 'Cantab'   Cambridge Redwood

Named 'Cantab' ≤1953 (abbreviation of *Cantabrigia*, the Latinized name of Cambridge). Varies from a congested shrub (called 'Prostrata') to fully treelike, albeit denser in habit and slower-growing than typical. Needles broad, short (*ca.* ½" long × almost ¼" wide), very glaucous. Rare.

- Arboretum: 59½' × 3'10¾" (#420-60 in 40-4W); 55' × 2'9¼" (#532-69 in 37-1W)
- 1230 NE 88th St: 32' tall
- 2533 8th Ave W: 19' tall, right by the sidewalk

cv. 'Glauca'   Blue Redwood

Needles notably glaucous or bluish-gray rather than green. More than one clone has been so called. The Arboretum 'Aptos Blue' in 39-6W & 40-6W are plain green, but 'Henderson Blue' in 41-6W is powder-blue.

- Arboretum: two of four old trees S of 26th Ave E & E Lynn St play area; tallest 103'
- 1068 24th Ave E

cv. 'Loma Prieta Spike'   Weeping Redwood

A newer clone that grows tall but whose branches flop down to create a very tall, beanpole oddity. The only one known in Seattle is north of the garage at 3048 NW 74th St.

Dawn REDWOOD

Metasequoia glyptostroboides Hu & Cheng   Chinese Redwood
From China.   Chinese: Shui Hsa / Shui Shan

Perhaps the first tree to be subjected to modern sensational publicity, Dawn redwood was bally-hooed as a "living fossil" again and again in the late 1940s and onwards, for it had been thought extinct, but was then found growing wild. Specimens in China have measured as much as 200' × 34½' and are estimated to live as long as 450 years. Peasants use its carrot-flavored foliage for cattle feed, though wild stands are protected by the government. In December 1947 seeds were distributed to public gardens all over earth. Seattle's oldest specimens were seedlings in April 1948; now they bear cones themselves, even fertile seeds. It is common in Seattle. A first-class ornamental, it resembles Bald Cypress more than any other tree. Despite its recent introduction it's far more widely distributed here than is Bald Cypress. It differs from the cypress in that it has a fluted trunk with flaky coppery bark, and comparatively coarse foliage that flushes earlier in spring, drops earlier in autumn, and is borne on opposite rather than alternate shoots. In places *warmer* than Seattle it grows faster; some elsewhere just as old as ours are over 125' tall; the thickest trunks are over 19' around.

- Arboretum: largest of four in (13-5E / 13-6E) Rododendron Glen is 107½' × 11'3¼" (#64-48B in 13-5E)
- U.W.: one 88' × 9'1" NW of Guggenheim Hall
- Seattle Center: north of Key Arena / the Coliseum (by a 2-trunked Coast redwood)
- Green Lake: 3 east of the Aqua Theater, tallest *ca.* 70'
- Locks bed #12, 202 (three), 212 (two at south end; 85' tall)
- Harvard Ave E & E Gwinn Pl: 4 on the SE corner with 5 Italian Cypresses
- west of Tashkent Park (on Belmont Ave E south of E Mercer St) is one 91' tall
- 39th Ave NE & NE 140th St: NE corner has one 58½' tall
- Loyal Heights School: many young street-trees on 26th Ave NW

Sierra REDWOOD

Sequoiadendron giganteum (Lindl.) Buchh.   Giant Sequoia
=*Sequoia gigantea* (Lindl.) Decne., *non* Endl.   Mammoth Tree
=*Wellingtonia gigantea* Lindl.   Bigtree
From high-elevation W slopes of California's Sierra Nevada Mts.

The Sierra redwood is the most massive of all trees, and among the tallest. Some have lived over 3,000 years. The *bark* can be 2' thick! The maximum sizes ever recorded, exaggerations aside, were *at least* 347' tall, and trunks nearly 125' around. As of now the largest in wood volume is the "General Sherman Tree" at 274' × 85'0" (over 55,000 cubic feet). The "Boole Tree" trunk is 92'7" around but has far less wood volume. There is currently one or more 312' tall. In New Zealand a planted one is 44' around; in Great Britain several are 170' tall or more and one is 36½' around. Both Washington and British Columbia have specimens over 150' in height. It is common in Seattle. Many have dead or rounded tops.

- 1523 Madrona Drive: once topped, a 155' tall tree has several competing leaders
- Arboretum: #90-43A in 19-4E towers 144' × 20'2"; the pinetum (38-7W and 37-7W) has a grove of 8 (#101-48), the tallest 139' × 13'11"
- Lincoln Park: tallest is 128' × 15'5" a bit SE of the tall Coast redwood
- Leschi Park: one *pl.* in 1892 is 126' × 22'2½"
- E Harrison St by Lake Wash. Blvd E has one 124½' tall (by an Eastern White Pine)
- U.W. Medicinal Herb Garden: one 123½' × 18'11"
- U.W.: one 120½' × 17'7¼" by the Waterfront Activities Center
- Green Lake: here and there; the tallest 114' and largest 22'11" around
- Volunteer Park: on the lawn directly east of the museum, 112' × 26'2"
- 6531 40th Ave SW: a very *broad*, stout tree *pl. ca.* 1926 is 100½' × 26'3"
- Acacia Cemetery: the largest of several are a pair, each about 106' × 27'0"
- 17th Ave E & E Prospect St: a street-tree leans like the Tower of Pisa, 103' × 20'4"
- Locks bed #14 (100' tall); 201 (five; tallest 103'), 202 (two; by #201 & #203), 203 (seven), 204 (two)

cv. 'Pendulum'   Weeping Redwood *or* Sequoia

The *weeping* Sierra redwood cultivar is far smaller and less common here. It is every bit as striking in its own way. Some in Europe are over 100' tall.

- 4518 SW Wildwood Pl, opposite 46th Ave SW: one 33' tall; very stout and wide
- Evergreen Park Cemetery: best of 2 by the entrance is 50½' × 3'9¾" × 17' wide
- S.U.: Connolly Center has one 40' tall north of the parking lot
- 10715 38th Ave NE: one 38' tall with a 26' tall weeping Eastern White Pine
- 10th Ave E & E Howe St: NW corner yard has an old stout one 32' tall
- Fauntleroy Way SW & SW Findlay St: NW corner yard has one 27' tall
- U.W.: CUH Soundscape Garden has one 24' tall

REHDER TREE

Rehderodendron macrocarpum H.H. Hu   Chinese: Mu Gua Hong
STYRACACEÆ
From China—at 7–10,000' on Mt Omei only, a sacred
mountain in the west of Szechuan Province.

A slender tree, rare both in nature and in cultivation. It bears pretty, fragrant 1" white flowers in May and can grow over 60' tall. The leaves are up to 8" × 2¾" with red stems. Performing best in woodland conditions, it is unlikely to make its way into average landscapes. Its seedpods, up to 3¼" long, are more curious than lovely. Five are at the Arboretum, the three largest: in 36-B (37' × 1'10¼"—#950-55A), 33-B (37' × 2'3½"—#950-55B), & 13-6E (45½' × 3'7"). The U.W. has one behind Winkenwerder Hall by the Burke-Gilman Trail, next to a Western Red Cedar. It is in bad shape, likely because of the shock it was subjected to during transplanting, but turns a pretty red in mid-October.

RUSSIAN OLIVE

Elæagnus angustifolia L. Wild Olive / Silver Tree / Bohemian Oleaster
=*E. hortensis* Bieb. Trebizond Grape *or* Date / Zakkoum-oil Plant
ELÆAGNACEÆ Oleaster / Jerusalem Willow
From west-central Asia.

Despite its many names the Russian Olive tree is uniform in its appearance and is not readily mistaken for other kinds. It thrives in sun and tolerates hot, dry conditions and poor soils. Silvery-gray, delicate foliage presents a willowy aspect of much beauty, in pleasing contrast to its dark, shaggy bark. Tiny, fragrant, silver-yellow flowers in June give rise to "olives" edible if they ever ripen fully—which they appear not to do in Seattle. It attains at most 65' × 12½'. Several European languages have names Russian Olive for that translate "Paradise Tree." In Seattle it is uncommon but conspicuous. Most are less than 25' × 5'; some are kept as clipped hedges; some are spiny; it's often semi-evergreen (we might say ever-gray). Always a nice change for eyes tired of green, yellowish, and bluish trees.

– A yard by the alley N of intersection of 25th Ave E & E Roanoke St: 3; tallest 29'
– Sycamore Ave NW, just south of NW 73rd: a street-tree, W side
– U.W.: between the Medicinal Herb Garden and Benson Hall
– 27th Ave NE, just south of NE 68th St: a street-tree, W side
– 30th Ave NE & NE 70th St: NE corner, one N of the house
– 5100 NE 54th St
– 4219 Corliss Ave N: a street-tree 38' tall by the driveway
– 8248 Meridian Ave N
– 4212 S Angeline St
– 320 NW 48th St: 36½' tall
– 12510 7th Ave NW
– 2445 Magnolia Blvd W: much pruned; not far from the road
– Genesee Park: far northeastern corner has seven, the tallest 26'
– 1602 Palm Ave SW

[*E. macrophylla, E. multiflora* and *E. umbellata*—are three shrubs in Seattle that, rarely, are pruned into tree shape *via* sucker removal. All have silvery leaf undersides and fragrant flowers, but their leaves are larger than Russian Olive's, and they make *red* berries. The largest such tree known is an *E. umbellata* 19' tall, wider still, at 2233 40th Ave E.]

SASSAFRAS

Sassafras albidum (Nutt.) Nees Mittenleaf / Smelling-stick
=*S. officinale* Nees & Eberm. Tea Tree / Cinnamon-wood
=*S. variifolium* Ktze. Saloop / Ague Tree
LAURACEÆ
From the central and eastern U.S. and extreme S Ontario.

Few American trees have so rich and romantic a history. The very *name* suggests exotic oddity and arouses interest: in effect it's flavored like the tree, tangy, spicy, delicious. Spaniards named it, possibly after an Indian name. It can attain 130'

× 19' and live nearly 1,000 years, yet is often no more than a slender, suckering, thicket-forming tree. The leaves are often lobed in unequal mitten-like fashion, such as is seen (here) in some mulberry tree leaves. The rubbery twigs are easily bent in circles or tied in knots. The bark is rough and handsomely rugged. Tiny flowers, yellow-green, appear from mid-April into early June.

Voluminous medicinal, herbal, toxic and culinary lore has accumulated since Europeans first learned of this species in 1560. In brief: its essential constituent, causing its characteristic flavor, is safrole (found also in oils of Oregon Myrtle, Camphor Laurel, Cinnamon leaf, Nutmeg, *etc.*). Until the F.D.A. learned that vermin (actually laboratory rats) could get liver cancer from it, safrole was used to scent or flavor medicines, candies, soaps, perfumes, tobacco, soft drinks, gum drops, ice cream and whatnot. In kitchens of rural America, root beer was brewed and "gumbo filé" made, using sassafras. From infancy to the grave, countless people sipped sassafras tea and nibbled the tasty twigs. Drug stores and health-food stores sold it. Now it's officially banned as unsafe (except in a processed state with the safrole removed), though many people still use it, confident its good effects outweigh any possible bad ones.

In Seattle it's rare. Considering how troublefree, attractive and interesting it is, perhaps the difficulty of propagation and transplanting is to blame.

– 34th Ave S & S McClellan St: NW corner yard has one 51' × 6'11" (1989)
– Seward Park: about two dozen scattered, slender ones—most are near the trail-head at the tip of the peninsula; the tallest 88' × 2'8"; stoutest 3'4" around
– 5764 28th Ave NE: once a large tree; now suckers becoming trees
– U.W.: one 50' × 4'4" by Denny Hall was cut down in 1993 but its *suckers* remain
– 1716 NW 63rd St: a street-tree 31½' × 5'9¾" east of an English Laurel
– Arboretum: the tallest is 62' × 2'9" (#2201-37 on the north edge of 18-3E)
– 5133 S Willow St: five

[*Lindera obtusiloba* Bl.—From China, Japan, and Korea; related to sassafras. Very rare in Seattle but being promoted as a "Great Plant Pick," it may become common. Leaves vary from unlobed to one- or tri-lobed, 3–7" long; brilliant bronzy-red when young; gold in fall; spicily fragrant when crushed. Tiny yellow flowers in early March are studded along the slender bare branches. Females make berries ⅓" long, first green, next red, then deep wine-red, finally shining black in October. Since the handsome horizontally layered foliage and springtime flowers are the most attractive features, and females grow smaller, males might well be preferred where trees rather than shrubs are desired. In the Arboretum's Woodland Garden (33-1E), the tallest ♂ is 23' × 1'11¼", and ♀ is 19½' × 2'1"—both wider than tall. They were raised from seeds in 1955 and planted in 1961. Three more trees from this batch are in the Japanese Garden, the tallest only 14'.]

SEA BUCKTHORN

Hippophaë rhamnoides L. Willow Thorn
ELÆAGNACEÆ Sallow Thorn
From Eurasia.

Related to Russian Olive, this also has silvery willowlike foliage and subtle flowers, but the flower sexes are borne on separate trees, and females make ornamental juicy bright orange berries. Leaves ¾–3½" long, very slender, dark green and speckled silvery above; silvery beneath. It can root sucker, and can be a mere shrub or a tree to 59' × 4½'. Capable of fixing nitrogen symbiotically, it thrives on poor soils—such as near the sea.

– Arboretum: ssp. *yunnanensis* Rousi is 34½' × 3'11¼" (#284-48B in 50-2E)
– Good Shepherd Center: a male 19' tall on the south wall of the annex; a female is S of the main building and E of the Children's Garden
– 208 NE 42nd St: 2 female street-trees flank a male
– Meadowbrook Park's edible arboretum planting has it
– 4015 NE 70th St

SERVICEBERRY

Amelanchier arborea (Michx. fil.) Fern. Downy Serviceberry
(often misidentified as *A. canadensis* (L.) Med.) Juneberry
ROSACEÆ Shadbush
From eastern North America. Sarvice

A shrub or tree to 76' × 9' with a smooth beech-like trunk. The young unfolding foliage is whitish-hairy over green, soon followed by erect clusters of pure white narrow-petalled flowers in late March–April. Relatively dryish berries sometimes follow. In Seattle, these beautiful small trees were rare until the 1990s. Autumn color is usually showy and bright, not plain yellow like that of our native Western serviceberry.

– Arboretum: 43' tall multitrunked #365-59 on Asian Maple hillside; 11-1E & 12-1E
– Kubota Garden Park: one 34½' multitrunked near SE corner
– 300 NW 78th St: 2 stout street-trees, the taller 26'
– Canal Substation (8th Ave NW & NW 45th St): 11 street-trees, 7 on 8th, 4 on 45th
– S.U.: E Columbia St, N side, just west of 10th Ave: 3 street-trees
– 4549 18th Ave NE (Chi Omega sorority): just south of front door; 23' tall
– NE 46th St, east of 40th Ave NE: 4 front yard trees *pl.* 1990
– 2011 E Pine St: a street-tree *pl.* 1990
– U.W.: 5 of this *or hybrids* were *pl. ca.* 1990 in Grieg Garden (NE of the HUB lawn)
– 543 N 75th St: 2 street-trees
– 5744 26th Ave NE: two very fruitful street-trees
– 7322 Jones Ave NW: a larger yard-specimen; likely a hybrid
– Green Lake: one *pl.* 1991 on the NE shore, not far from Meridian Ave N

Alleghany SERVICEBERRY

A. lævis Wieg.   Smooth-leaved Serviceberry
=*A. arborea* ssp. *lævis* (Wieg.) S. MacKay *ex* Landry
From eastern N America.

Differs from *A. arborea* in having nearly or totally hairless leaves, strongly tinted red or coppery while young; larger flowers in drooping clusters; berries delicious. In Latin, *lævis* means smooth; not rough, in reference to the leaves not being hairy. Recorded to 101' × 7½'. Clones sold under this name—rightly or wrongly—include **Lustre**®, 'Majestic' and 'Prince Charles'. **Cumulus**® was patented in 1972 and has been sold under various names including *A. lævis*. Dozens of **Cumulus**® were planted in Ballard in 1993 and exhibit great vigor and lovely flowers, but often if not usually get discolored leaves, and are fruitless.

– Arboretum: 47½' tall multitrunked (#821-57 on Yew Hill 30-4W); 47' tall multitrunked, largest trunk 1'8½" around (#180-47 on Asian Maple hillside 27-B); 10-1E, 11-1E & 12-1E
– 921 NW 105th St: a yard tree
– 42nd Ave SW & SW Genesee St traffic circle has one
– 812 S Rose St: a street-tree
– 1154 20th Ave E: 3 **Cumulus**® street-trees
– 7704-7702 16th Ave NW: 6 **Cumulus**® street-trees
– 7022 23rd Ave NW: **Cumulus**® street-tree
– 6511 23rd Ave NW: 2 **Cumulus**® street-trees
– 7720 32nd Ave NW: 2 **Cumulus**® street-trees
– NW 73rd St, east of 28th Ave NW: 4 **Cumulus**® street-trees, S side

Hybrid SERVICEBERRY

A. × grandiflora (Zabel) Rehd.   Apple Serviceberry
(*A. arborea* × *A. lævis*)
From eastern N America.

Midway between its parents, and better than either for ornamental purposes. More floriferous than its parents, with leaves unfolding bronze or purplish; large and succulent berries. Common, sold under varied names. At present, usually only cultivars are planted, such as '**Autumna Brilliance**' (the most sold). In the examples cited below, cultivars are named only if known. '**Robin Hill (Pink)**' has flowerbuds bright pink, gradually fading white after opening. Both '**Ballerina**' and '**Cole's Select**' make superb crops of edible berries.

– 6525 2nd Ave NE: 2 '**Autumn Brilliance**' *pl.* in 1993
– 2518 1st Ave W: 2 '**Autumn Brilliance**' street-trees
– 2209 N 42nd St: 2 '**Autumn Brilliance**' street-trees +a larger '**Robin Hill**' yard tree
– 920 22nd Ave E: two '**Autumn Brilliance**' yard trees
– 4702 46th Ave NE: a big one SW of the house
– Good Shepherd Center: N wall of shed has '**Ballerina**' 21½' × 1'3" and one 16' tall N of the summerhouse; '**Cole's Select**' is 19' tall NW of the gym
– 7322 Jones Ave NW

- 3047 NW 62nd St: one grafted on Mountain Ash *(Sorbus aucuparia)*
- Arboretum: one labeled *A.* × *Lamarckii* 'Robin Hill' #90-60 is 55' × 2'2¼" in 32-B
- 16th Ave S between S College & Bayview: 'Robin Hill' street-trees
- 10002 Dibble Ave NW: 6 'Robin Hill' street-trees
- Ballard Community Center: at both entrances; 6 'Robin Hill'
- 3120 12th Ave S (@ S Hanford St): 3 'Princess Diana' in the front yard; tallest 16'

Western SERVICEBERRY

A. alnifolia (Nutt.) Nutt.   Saskatoon Serviceberry *or* Berry
(incl. *A. florida* Lindl.)   (our) Native Serviceberry
Native here; from much of north–   Pacific Serviceberry
west & north-central N America.

Usually a shrub, our native serviceberry is rarely a tree to 42' × 5'. Compared to the preceding cultivated species, it has leaves of rounder outline (to 2½" × 2¼"), much coarser teeth and inferior fall color (usually plain yellow, not warm reddish-orange). Also its flowers are in compact clusters, later—late April–early May. The berries are large, edible from June through mid-August, and several cultivars have been selected specifically for fruit production such as 'Smoky' which was introduced to the nursery trade in 1952. Birds or other wildlife eat most of the local berry crop while humans, waiting for fully ripened fruit, are lucky to get any at all. In Seattle this is an inconspicuous but fairly common shrub. It would be excluded from this guide but that there was a real *tree* 36' × 2'4¼" × 38' wide at the U.W., killed in 2003. No others known in the city are anywhere near as large.

- Carkeek Park: 34' × 1'3¾" (2004), another 33' tall
- Arboretum: *ca.* six on hillside 10-1E, 11-B, 11-1E, 11-2E & 12-1E; tallest over 30' but still shrubby, while the tallest of 19 East North American kinds *with* them is 44'
- Locks bed #25 (shrubby), 108 (shrubby), 120 (25' tall), 122 (shrubby; W end)
- Bagley Ave N & N 42nd St: the church on SW corner has 3 street-trees E, 3 N
- Burke Ave N & N 43rd St: the house on SW corner has 3 street-trees on 43rd
- Good Shepherd Center: 'Smoky' in Seattle Tilth garden
- 5725 27th Ave NE: a young small street-tree north of an older European Plum tree
- Lenora Pl N & Roosevelt Way N: a shrubby wild one by the utility pole

SILK TREE

Albizia Julibrissin Durazz. *(Albizzia)*   Pink *or* Persian Acacia
=*Acacia Julibrissin* (Durazz.) Willd.   Japanese Silk Tree
LEGUMINOSÆ (FABACEÆ)   Mimosa Tree
From the Near East, Ethiopia, India,   Pink Siris
China, Taiwan, Japan and Okinawa(!)   Nemu

This well-known tree of delicate, tropical luxuriance aptly signifies "elegance" in the Language of Flowers. It leafs out very late with dainty, frond-like foliage that "goes to sleep" by folding up at night. People prize the tree for the beautiful foliage alone, but its fragrant flowers, showy pink or reddish "powder puffs" opening late July–late September are even more delightful. These are followed by flat seedpods 3–6" long. The tree may grow to 60' × 12', usually in a natural umbrella shape (to 90' wide or more) unless it is forced by shading to grow straight up in search of the full sunshine it desperately needs. In a warm sunny place it grows rapidly, but in shade is stunted, growing at a snail's pace. In either case it is often short-lived. Despite its name, "Silk Tree" should not be confused with the tree that feeds the silkworm—the very different White Mulberry.

It's common here, reaching about 45' × 6½' at best, then usually dying—or being chain-sawed into such ugliness as ought to be illegal. After a frost or two in November, Silk Tree becomes "sulk tree," appearing forlorn and bedraggled, like a fancy new hairstyle caught in a thundershower. While other trees exult in vibrant autumn color, it pouts, limp and miserable, drably aching for its more tropical homeland.

The brand new '**Summer Chocolate**' was first sold in 2005 locally. Found in Japan in 1990, it was patented in 2003, and features *burgundy* foliage.

– Arboretum: 21-3E has the best on public land, to 50' × 3'7" (#683-49)
– Bagley Ave N, south of N 39th St: a street-tree, W side, 41' × 6'8" × 67' wide
– 1807 E Calhoun St: larger of 2 street-trees is 43½' × 5'6½" × 55½' wide
– Kubota Garden Park: a slender shaded specimen is 55' tall
– 2932 Fuhrman Ave E: two behind an English Laurel hedge; taller 34½'
– 332 NW 79th St: a street-tree
– Locks bed #17 (two by bottom of stairs), 114 (by 115)
– Zoo: here and there, near the primates, gorillas, and so on
– Green Lake: youngsters, that may someday be impressively large
– U.W.: SE of Sieg Hall
– 4925 Stanford Ave NE
– 8234 Corliss Ave N
– 44th Ave SW & SW Morgan/Fauntleroy Way SW: SE corner has 4 street-trees
– 4909 2nd Ave NW: a big street-tree
– 2523 34th Ave S (north of S Lander St): two
– 1908 34th Ave S (at S Plum St)

SILVERBELL TREE

Halesia carolina L.
=*H. tetraptera* Ellis
=*H. monticola* (Rehd.) Sarg.
=*Mohrodendron carolinum* Britt.
STYRACACEÆ
From the southeastern U.S.

Carolina Silverbell
Opossum-wood
Snowdrop Tree
Calico-wood
Tiss-wood
Bell Tree

Shrubby to medium-sized trees, every twig strung with pretty white (rarely pink) "bells" in late April–May, that give rise to sharply angled large dry seeds. The Carolina species (one of 3 total) is notably variable, ranging from a shrub to a tree 100' × 13½'. The name Silverbell may be confused with its cousin Snowbell Tree. Silverbells are uncommon in Seattle. Little known or grown, most are small trees suckering from their bases. Were the optimal form of this variable assemblage identified and put into the nursery trade, it would surely be a welcome addition to our ornamental flowering tree population. Too many spring flowering trees here (*e.g.*, cherries, crabapples and the like) are relatively unhealthy, fussy, short-lived, pest-ridden, diseased, high-maintenance, or are boring in their ubiquity. Silverbells are low-maintenance trees deserving wider use. They thrive as long as they are not planted in a shady or dry site. Their mere yellow fall color, and dry brown seedpods in winter are strikes against them.

– Arboretum: many and varied, the tallest 62½' × 3'6¼" (#117-49 in 21-1W, east of Azalea Way; cabled; 2-trunked); 59' × 3'1¼" (#X-267A in beehive area); 11-8E (by Camellia parking lot) has 53' × 4'6" (#231-41B) and 52½' × 5'5½" (#231-41A)
– Zoo: one 40' × 3'9¾" on Phinney Ave N opposite N 52nd/53rd streets
– 20th Ave NE, east side, at NE 124th St: 45' tall between utility pole & Douglas Fir
– U.W.: one 16' × 1'10½" NW of Parrington Hall
– McClure School (1915 1st Ave W): one 32' × 3'11¾" on E side, 60' S of the N end
– Locks bed #4 (a shrubby one), 328
– 5754 26th Ave NE: several youngsters
– 2111 22nd Ave E: 2 young street-trees on E Newton St

[*Melliodendron xylocarpum* Hand.-Mazz.—From China. Recorded to 65' tall. Leaves to 8" × 3", densely hairy when young. Flowers short-stemmed, white-pink, to 2" wide, in April-May, making plump, hairy seed capsules up to 2¾" long. In recent years local nurseries have offered this—but I am unable to cite any specimens in Seattle.]

SMOKE TREE

Cotinus Coggygria Scop.
=*Rhus Cotinus* L.
ANACARDIACEÆ
From Eurasia.

Common *or* European Smoke-Tree
Venus *or* Venetian Sumach
Smoke Plant / Cloud Tree
Wig *or* Periwig Tree
Purple Fringe-Tree

A small and spreading, usually multitrunked shrub or tree to 40' tall. Bees are greatly attracted to its blossoms in late May. But it isn't until after it blooms that the spent flower-clusters justify the puzzling names Smoke Tree or Periwig Tree, when they give it a blurry, hazy aspect with an indescribable airy, feathery charm. The strongly odorous leaves were used as a famine food in China. Its twigs and bark yield a valuable yellow-golden dye. In the Language of Flowers it means "splendour" or "intellectual excellence."

In Seattle, common. Purpleleaf forms (both seedlings and named cultivars) outnumber green ones, and it is more commonly kept bushy by pruning than allowed to attain tree stature. It colors prettily in November like a miniature Sugar Maple, particularly if growing on a relatively dry, sterile, sunny site.

GREEN:
– 46th Ave S & S Holly St: NE corner has a heavily pruned tree
– 32nd Ave NW, just N of NW 56th St: a street-tree, W side 17' × 2'1½" × 25' wide—leaves bronzy while young, then green; flowers red

- 13511 36th Ave NE: 14' and much wider
- 1335 California Ave SW (north of SW Atlantic St): one 12' tall in yard's NE corner
- Children's Hospital: one good sized green is along with many purple examples

GOLD:—the relatively *new* patented **Golden Spirit**™ ('Ancot')
- Broadway E & E Hamlin St: a street-tree on SW corner, *pl.* 2004

PURPLE:
- U.W.: SW corner of Suzzallo Library; N of the Burke-Gilman Trail just west of 15th Ave NE, 2 flank a Sweetgum by the substation
- 31st Ave W, north of W McGraw St: a street-tree (N of Eastern Dogwood), east side
- 7514 13th Ave NW: pretty; two-trunked
- 6406 14th Ave NW: SW corner of yard
- courtyard E of Lincoln High School (off Woodlawn Ave N & N 44th St)
- 4215 Linden Ave N (with a Vine Maple)
- 8004 42nd Ave NE: one 21½' tall south of the house
- 8214 22nd Ave NE
- U.W. Medicinal Herb Garden: 2 in section B

American SMOKE TREE

C. obovatus Raf.
=*C. americanus* Nutt.
=*Rhus cotinoides* Nutt.
From a few disjunct locales in the southeastern U.S.

A larger tree than the preceding (to 54' × 8') but less showy in summer, though fully as spectacular in autumn. Its leaves are larger (up to 7" × 5"), not so round in outline and are finely downy on the undersides. It is rare here.
- Arboretum: #309-55, best of trio is 40' × 1'9" S of boxwoods in 5-1E
- 3306 NW 71st St: 30'+ tall; west of a large Black Walnut
- S Findlay St, east of 48th Ave S: 2nd yard from corner, N side, has one 25½' tall
- 3222 45th Ave SW: 28' tall
- U.W.: one 23' tall east of Chemistry building is shaded by two basswood (Lindens)

[**Hybrid Smoke-Tree**—*C. Coggygria* × *C. obovatus*—In recent years local nurseries have offered '**Grace**' and some have been planted here. Also people can get '**Flame**' from mail-order sources. It is a bit early to cite any as *trees* in Seattle, but six street-trees are on the NE corner of 47th Ave NE & NE 68th St.]

SNOWBELL TREE

Styrax japonicus S.&Z. *(japonica)* Japanese Snowbell- *or* Snowdrop-Tree
STYRACACEÆ   Japanese Storax
From Japan, Korea, the Ryukyus,   Japanese: Ego-no-ki エゴノキ
China, Taiwan, the Philippines.   Chinese: Mo Ch'u / Ye Mo Li

A tree to 50' × 8' covered with small white (or pink) flowers late May–late June. The fruit is an acrid, hard, felty little berry used to make fish poison. The leaves are small (*ca.* 3" long), dark, glossy, and yellow in fall. It's overplanted here and easy to grow—but ought not be planted in dry sunny sites. It reseeds freely. A few cultivars have been sold recently, such as 'Carillon' and 'Emerald Pagoda'.

– 10723 24th Ave NE: 49' × 2'9" (1990)
– 32nd Ave NE & NE 88th St: NE corner house has a multitunked one 37' tall
– 2311 Broadway E: one 34½' tall
– Arboretum: the best is 31½' × 4'8" (below fork) × 37½' wide, on Azalea Way (#1028-39 in 19-1W)
– 1119 37th Ave E: one 31' tall at yard's NE corner by sidewalk
– 18th Ave E & E Galer St: SW corner house has one *ca.* 30' tall +a larger Hemlock
– U.W.: the largest of many are NW of Anderson Hall (24½' × 2'9¾") and SE of Benson Hall (29' × 2'10½")
– Zoo: Rose Garden
– Locks bed #5, 111, 202, 209 (by 210), 214
– Belvedere Park (SW Admiral Way & SW Olga St): 4 in SW and 2 in NW corner
– 26th Ave E near E Galer St: some young street-trees of '**Pink Chimes**'

Bigleaf SNOWBELL TREE

S. Obassia S.&Z. *(Obassis)*
From N China, Manchuria,
Korea, Japan.

Fragrant Snowbell-Tree
Japanese: Haku-unboku ハクウンボク
Chinese: Yu Ling Hua

This doesn't look at all like *S. japonicus*. Its leaves are many times larger (up to 10½" × 9" wide on stalks 1½" long), duller, rounder and fuzzier. It flowers somewhat before the other, beginning in early May, in drooping clusters 4–8" long. It is more slender, a woodland-lover that can surpass 56' × 3½'. (It must be noted that the closely related *Styrax grandifolius* Ait. of the southeastern U.S., literally means "bigleaf" and is so called in books as is *S. Obassia*. But this American bush has relatively small leaves and is not grown *here*.)

In Seattle, uncommon.

– Arboretum: the tallest of several is 47' × 2-trunked (#645-41 in 36-B)
– Lincoln Park: two over 40' tall SE of the service yard, east of the road
– Locks bed #211 has one 31' tall and a smaller one is at the S end of #102
– U.W. Medicinal Herb Garden: one with rosemary between sections E & F
– 4316 NE 38th St: a small specimen south of a common snowbell tree
– 1527 NE 76th St: one at house's NE corner

[*Sinojackia xylocarpa* Hu—Jack Tree. Weight Tree—From SE China (Cheng Chui Shu). A shrubby little tree sold here only in recent years. The leaves are thin, shiny beneath, finely toothed, 1–4" long. In March or April it has dangling white flowers that give rise to odd, sharp-tipped brown fruits *ca.* ¾" long. A dense, floppy street-tree is at 7038 24th Ave NE.]

SORREL TREE

Oxydendrum arboreum (L.) DC. *(Oxydendron)*   Lily-of-the-Valley Tree
=*Andromeda arborea* L.   Sorrelwood
ERICACEÆ   Sourwood
From the eastern U.S.

A seemingly faultless little tree recently planted extensively here. Slender and well-proportioned, with elegant, drooping and glossy leaves to 9" long, it is highly ornamental and deservedly popular. The young spring leaves taste like sorrel, and so have gained repute as delicious thirst-quenchers and salad garnishes. But they cannot compete in this respect with those of our common purple cutleaved Japanese Maples. In autumn Sorrel trees turn breathtaking deep crimson, reddish-purple—fairly screaming for attention. The beautiful urnlike, waxy-white flowers, tiny yet very numerous, from late July onwards, are excellent for bees. The tree may attain up to 118' × 8½' yet is usually regarded as a small species.

In Seattle, common in yards and other private landscapes, rarer in parks.

– Arboretum: the tallest of 20 are 50' × 2'4½" (in grove of 8 on 31-2E hill south of Woodland Garden); 49½' × 3'9½" (#1550-45 roadside by Rhododendron Glen)
– Phinney Ave N & N 90th St: SW corner house's SE corner has one
– S.U.: 28' tall @NW corner of Lemieux Library, with a 13' tall *dwarf* Norway Spruce

SPINDLE TREE

Euonymus europæus L   Common *or* European Spindle-Tree
=*E. vulgaris* Mill.   European Burning-bush
CELASTRACEÆ   Skewerwood / Prickwood
From Europe, SW Asia, and the Caucasus.   Gatteridge Tree

A truly spindly and irregularly tangled shrub-tree with an intricately twisted crown usually broader than tall. Twigs dull gray-green. Flowers from late April into June, inconspicuous. Fruit a decorative seed-capsule: pink-red, bursting open in fall to reveal colorful poisonous orange seeds, contrasting with the late, bright, autumn leaf color: burnt orange or red to dark purplish. Leaves 1–3½" long; opposite. Uncommon in Seattle.

– Zoo: the tallest of 5 on the Family Farm west border is 39' × 2'6½"
– Arboretum: 4 north of pinetum (38-5W); 5 east of pinetum (39-4W & 38-3W) with 8 *E. Hamiltonianus*
– 141 Dorffel Dr E: a street-tree touching a beauty bush *(Kolkwitzia)* on the rockery
– 2342 34th Ave S: one 22' tall N of the house
– Roanoke Park: 14½' tall on the E border; its fallen trunk was 3'10" around in 1992
– 7320 45th Ave NE: one atop the rockery south of the driveway
– 3814 NE 75th St: one with Aspens and Yellow Buckeyes
– 6337 40th Ave SW: one by a Douglas Fir at the yard's south fence

[*E. Hamiltonianus* Wall.—a rare, semi-evergreen, big shrub or small tree. Like *E. europæus* but has purple anthers, not yellow, its leaves average larger, it blooms a bit later. Kubota Garden Park has three, the stoutest 21' × 3'9½" and the taller middle one 24'.]

[*E. japonicus* Thunb.—an evergreen, common shrub in Seattle, rarely pruned into tree shape. A tree 18' × 2'2" × 22' wide is N of the main entrance of 7727 63rd Ave NE.]

SPRUCES in general

Sharp, pointed, prickly, harsh, scaly, pitchy pulp trees, they're spruce in youth but ragged in age. Most have needles ¾–1¾" long. Their delicate, dangling cones are mostly 2–4" long. Older twigs are rough with pegs and the bark is thin, flaky and scaly. Climb an old spruce and get pitchy, scratched and very dusty; in contrast climb an old Fir and get sweetly pitchy and only a bit dusty.

In Seattle there are three abundant species: **Norway** (most common and largest), **Colorado** (its bluish forms are most popular and well known), and **Sitka** (native here). Four more uncommon but not rare kinds are Engelmann, Oriental, Serbian and White. Nine rarer species complete our population—except for many more at the Arboretum, where the spruce collection is outstanding in diversity, good health and accurate labeling. It must be mentioned, however, that spruces do better in climates colder than Seattle's.

Black SPRUCE

Picea mariana (Mill.) B.S.P.   Swamp *or* Double Spruce
=*P. nigra* (Ait.) Link   Bog *or* Gum Spruce
PINACEÆ   Lash-horn
From Alaska, Canada, and the NE U.S.

Vermont was named ("Verd mont" = Green Mountain) because Black Spruces covered its hills so thickly. Pioneers often used the springy boughs for mattresses, and brewed a well-known beer from the twigs. It attains 100' × 12½' at most and is recognized by its very short needles and unusually persistent ½–1½" cones.

Black Spruces are very rare here. There are two forms: the "dwarf Alaska fir" of nurseries, of yellowish-green cast, and the far more attractive bluish forms from back East.

– Arboretum: two 9' apart in the Japanese Garden are E of a prominent 27' tall Paperbark Maple, the larger is 55½' × 2'2¾"; the dwarf cv. 'Doumetii' is 23' tall (#192-59 in 28-4E)
– 12504 Phinney Ave N: 42' tall, 3-trunked, by driveway, leaning from a White Birch
– 824 33rd Ave E: in back by alley 38' tall
– 4404 NE 106th St: two, tallest 23½'
– Zoo: some with more White spruces in the Northern Trail exhibit

Colorado SPRUCE

P. pungens Engelm.   Colorado Blue Spruce
=*P. Parryana* Sarg.   Blue Colorado Spruce
From the Rocky Mountains.   Blue *or* Silver Spruce

The State Tree of Colorado and Utah. It attains up to 159' × 16' and varies in color from olive green to bright silvery-bluish. The latter are highly valued as ornamentals and widely planted. Bluish forms include chance seedlings as well as many named, grafted cultivars such as 'Fat Albert', 'Glauca', 'Hoopsii', 'Koster', 'Moerheimii' and 'Thomsen'. The 2–5" long cones are similar in their light color and flaky texture to cornflakes. When compared to most spruces, both its twigs and needles are relatively *stout*. In Seattle, the multifarious *bluish* kinds are abundant and familiar. Engelmann, White, and Dragon spruces share similar color yet differ in twigs and cones, nor are they as stout, coarse, large and common as the Colorado. Insects ruin many specimens to an extent not fully comprehended until one compares trees sprayed each year with those left to the bugs. The plain greenish Colorado spruces are less attractive, smaller, never so narrow or weepy, and are only useful for occasionally planting side by side with their blue brothers, to remind us how much more handsome the latter are.

BLUISH:
- 36th Ave & E Pine St: SE corner has one 89' tall behind an English Maple
- 3302 East Laurelhurst Dr NE: one 87½' tall (same yard has a Noble Fir)
- Volunteer Park: one 79½' × 6'8½" is east of the museum
- 48th Ave NE & NE 39th St: one 76½' tall on the SE corner
- 32nd Ave S & S College St: NW corner has one 71' tall
- U.W.: one 71' × 5'4" is south of Thomson Hall
- Viewlands School: SW of bldg. is a large 67' tall twin-trunked specimen
- Acacia Cemetery: one 61' × 8'¾"
- S.U.: a 46' tall beauty by the pond below Campion Hall
- Kubota Garden Park
- 3306 NE 70th St
- Locks bed #101

GREENISH:
- U.W. Medicinal Herb Garden: by Rainier Vista are a blue and green one flanking a 'Zebrina' (variegated) Western Red Cedar
- 5409 NE 65th St: a narrow one 54½' tall
- G.A.R. Cemetery/Park
- Green Lake and Woodland Park
- Rodgers Park
- Kinnear Park

Dragon SPRUCE

P. asperata Mast.   Chinese Spruce
From China.   Chinese: Yun Shan

In its native land this is a very variable and common species, the east Asian equivalent of Norway spruce. It attains up to 150' × 13' and has cones 3–5 (7)" long. The smaller cones and stouter, sharper needles distinguish it from Norway spruce. It's very rare here and virtually all are on public property.

- Arboretum: at least 10 (received as the typical species and vars. *aurantiaca*, *ponderosa* and *retroflexa*), in 25-5E, 25-4E, 24-4E, 24-2E, 23-5E, and 9-1E; the

largest (both #570-47 in 24-2E) 85' × 4'11¾" and 79' × 5'4"; but also the several trees labeled *P. likiangensis* var. *montigena* are suspiciously similar and at least one accession may really be a Dragon spruce
- Volunteer Park: one east of the museum was 51' × 3'10" until felled in fall 2005
- Van Asselt Playground (Beacon Ave S & S Myrtle St): 3 with 2 smaller mystery spruces SE of the bldg.; a 4th by a little Japanese Maple S of the wading pool
- Bagley Ave N & N 140th St: NE corner yard has two W of the house, the taller 40'; a larger Norway spruce is south of them
- U.W. Friendship Grove: Yugoslavia's "Serbian spruce" is actually a 39½' × 1'10¼" Dragon spruce

Engelmann SPRUCE

P. Engelmannii Parry *ex* Engelm.　　　Rocky Mountain White Spruce
From the Cascades and Rockies
(and 3 small groves in the NE Olympic Mts.).

Like Colorado spruce, the foliage of Engelmann spruce ranges in color from green to blue. But both botanically and ornamentally it's closer to White spruce, though its cones (1½–3" long) more resemble those of Sitka spruce. It has been recorded to 223' × 25' and yields valuable wood. Together with Alpine Fir, it characterizes the alpine forests of most of the Rocky Mountains from Mexico well into British Columbia. It's uncommon in Seattle. Even small coneless specimens can be identified by their finely *hairy* twigs.

- Arboretum: the largest is 63' × 3'11½" (#1012-49)—one of three in 19-5E & 20-5E; one 59' × 4'2" is NE of a fastigiate blue Atlas Cedar in 43-4E
- Mt Baker Park: one at the N end by a Momi Fir and Bigleaf Linden is 59' × 2'3¾"
- 14027 27th Ave NE: one 45½' tall
- U.W. Friendship Grove, representing Uruguay, 30½' × 1'2¾" (shaded by an Oak)
- 5613 44th Ave SW (south of SW Findlay St): two street-trees (with 2 'Boulevard' moss Sawara Cypresses)

Himalayan SPRUCE

P. Smithiana (Wall.) Boiss.　　　Morinda *or* Weeping Spruce
=*P. Morinda* (Loud.) Link.　　　　West Himalaya Spruce
From the W and central Himalayas.　　　Indian Spruce

A distinctive spruce easily recognized by its unusually long needles (up to 2¼"), larger cones (4–7⅞" long), and droopy habit. It can grow to 230' × 24'. Extremely rare here. One 47' × 3'2" represents Nepal at the U.W. Friendship Grove; the Arboretum's largest (47' × 4'4½") is #860-58A in 26-5E.

Meyer SPRUCE

P. Meyeri Rehd. & Wils.　　　Chinese Blue Spruce
From NW China.　　　　　　　Meyer Blue Spruce

Extremely rare here, our specimens are viciously sharp, dark bluish, and ungainly in habit: without question the ugliest spruce—which is quite an achievement! Frank Meyer, for whom it was named, deserves far better: he was a *great* plant explorer who sent many valuable plants from China to the U.S., including seeds of this spruce in 1908.

The Arboretum has two #121-64 in 32-6W; the larger 42' × 2'1¼" In 1988 a specimen was planted by Rainier Vista east of parking lot C-10; it is 39' × 1'10" and stands 9' from a Shagbark Hickory. For all three of these trees, the *accuracy* of their i.d. is in doubt, as is that of the U.W. Friendship Grove Dragon spruce.

Norway SPRUCE

P. Abies (L.) Karst.   Norwegian Spruce
=*P. excelsa* (Lam. & DC.) Link   Common Spruce
=*P. vulgaris* Link   Spruce Fir
=*Abies excelsa* Lam. & DC.
From Europe, east to the Urals.

The original "Spruce," although "spruce" was really only one of the prefatory adjectives used to qualify "fir" in simpler times when Silver Fir, Scots Fir and Spruce Fir were northern Europe's three big evergreen forest trees. Hence, semantically, calling this tree "spruce" without the "fir" is equivalent to calling it "Norway" without the "spruce"! However, modern English usage is uniform in this respect. This was also the original Christmas tree, the tree that made the Black Forest so dark, and the main timber tree of most of Europe for centuries. Its wood is fashioned into sonorous sound-boards for pianos and bellies for stringed instruments, including the famous ones made by Stradivari. Of other conifers, only Lawson Cypress has more cultivars.

Norway spruce is one of the darkest, most somber of trees. Beautiful in youth, it loses most of its charm if not vigor to become grim and haggard in age, attaining maximum dimensions of 226' × 20½'. The cones are larger than those of other spruces (except the Himalayan's), 4–9" long and up to 2½" wide when fully open. Squirrels often rip them to shreds in their eagerness to eat the young seeds from late June into early July. In the Language of Flowers, it means "hope in adversity." Killed by the millions from acid rain in Europe, it needs such assurance and more.

This is Seattle's most abundant and largest spruce. It rarely reseeds here. Most of its many cultivars are shrubby, so do not belong in a tree guide.

— Seward Park: the tallest, in the fish hatchery area, is 120'
— Golden Gardens Park: one 113' × 5'0" near upper level restrooms
— Acacia Cemetery: the largest is 84' × 11'1¾" × 55½' wide
— Belvedere Park (SW Admiral Way & SW Olga St): one 89' × 9'3"
— Volunteer Park: the largest is 89' × 8'11"
— Hiawatha Playfield: the largest is 80' × 8'4" (between swing set & wading pool)
— Lake View Cemetery: the largest is 79' × 8'5½" × 53½' wide
— Interlaken Park: the largest of over 120 is 91½' × 8'1"

– Ravenna Park: the tallest of 29 in the ravine east of 20th is 110'; largest 7'6" around
– U.W.: one 75½' × 6'5" NW of the HUB; one 66' × 7'1" east of the Medicinal Herb Garden section G (nursery)

cv. 'Aurea' — Golden Norway Spruce

Young needles bright yellow in late March into April, aging to soft yellow-green. Less vigorous than ordinary seedlings. Can scorch in full sun. Very rare.
– U.W.: one 42' × 1'11" on the east side of Rainer Vista south of Stevens Way

cv. 'Cupressina' — Cypress Norway Spruce

A dense broad column with tightly ascending branches. Needles shorter and cones smaller than typical. Rare.
– Arboretum: #203-65A is in 26-4E, 60' × 3'5¼"; #96-65A is 34' tall in 32-6W
– U.W.: some east of Hughes Penthouse Theatre

cv. 'Inversa' — Weeping Norway Spruce

A very pendulous small tree, both branches and twigs hanging down the stem. Very dense. Uncommon. Nureries sell it—and *other* clones— as 'Pendula'.
– Kubota Garden Park: one many decades old is 32' × 2'9"

f. *virgata* (Jacques) Rehd. — Snakebranch Spruce

A twigless freak of striking appearance, known in Seattle *only* as follows (we once had 3 more). It has generally been miscalled "Tigertail spruce" hereabouts.
– Volunteer Park: one 78½' × 5'6" NW of the bandstand

Oriental SPRUCE

P. orientalis (L.) Link — Caucasian Spruce
From the Caucasus and Asia Minor — Eastern Spruce
—*i.e.* the original "Orient."

In appearance, and for all practical purposes, this is a refined, dainty, more compact version of Norway spruce. Most people agree it's more attractive. It has short dark needles, ¼–½" long and cones 2–4" long. The tree reaches at most 210' × 20½'. It is uncommon here.

– Lakeview Park: one 88½' × 10'4"
– Arboretum: 75½' × 4'5" #831-47B in the pinetum
– Volunteer Park: 68½' × 4'3¼" and 60' × 6'3" N of bandstand
– Green Lake: 63' × 6'8¼" on SE shore between 66th and Sunnyside; 6 N of theater
– Cal Anderson Park / Broadway Reservoir: 2 at N end, taller 59' (two-trunked)
– Cowen Park: the largest of several is by the NW corner sign
– Locks bed #102 has a small specimen
– S.U.: 40½' tall at SE corner of Pigott Bldg. (3-topped)
– 12239 8th Ave NW: a *yellowish* cv. (maybe '**Skylands**'), young
– 13500 Northshire Road NW: a *yellowish* cv., very young, *ca.* 5' tall

– 1510 18th Ave: one 71½' tall

Red SPRUCE

P. rubens Sarg.
=*P. rubra* (Du Roi) Link, *non* A. Dietr.
From eastern North America.

Yellow Spruce
He Balsam

A valuable lumber tree that grows as large as 162' × 15' and makes cones 1–2½" long. Known here as follows: at the Arboretum 47' (tallest); 2'11¾" (stoutest) (#150-54 in 22-5W); and representing Liberia at the U.W. Friendship Grove, 38' × 1'6½".

Sakhalin SPRUCE

P. Glehnii (Fr. Schmidt) Mast.
From S Sakhalin, N Japan.

Saghalin Spruce
Japanese: Aka-ezo-matsu アカエゾマツ

Up to 130' × 15½' with cones 1½–3½" long. Sakhalin spruce is known here only at the Arboretum (largest of three is 64½' × 5'2" #220-59A in 24-4E), one 14½' × 1'1" at the U.W. Friendship Grove, representing Vietnam, one 14½' tall at SSCC Cœnosium Rock Garden, and one in the back yard of 6851 40th Ave NE. The Japanese Garden also has a small #201-52.

Serbian SPRUCE

P. Omorika (Panc.) Purk.
From Yugoslavia (SW Serbia).

Servian Spruce

Distinctly narrow, droopy, and scarcely spiny—and due to these features judged one of the most ornamental spruces, Serbian spruce is becoming increasingly common in our landscapes; most are young. It can grow up to 164' tall and makes cones 1¼–2½" long.

– Arboretum: in the Japanese Garden, #782-49 is 60' × 3'½"; elsewhere, the tallest of 7 is 53½' × 2'5¾" (#782-49B in 26-5E); the stoutest is 2'8¼"
– Substation on 35th Ave NE opposite the post office: 6, the tallest over 50'
– Fairview School (Roosevelt Way NE & NE 78th St): one on the S side, 47' tall
– W Barrett St, east of 22nd Ave W: a yard, S side, has 2, the taller 46'
– Greenwood Ave N & N 120th St: NW corner has one 45½' tall
– Martin Lauther King, Jr. Way & E Thomas St: NW corner: 45½' tall
– U.W.: 10 south of the Henry Gallery
– 5565 NE Windermere Rd: a cv. '**Nana**' (dwarf) 11½' tall
– 8038 20th Ave NW: cv. '**Nana**' S of the entry walk is 8½' tall (*pl. ca.* 1975)
– SSCC Arboretum: a 7½' tall very wide cv. '**Nana**' in Milton Sutton conifer garden
– NOT the U.W. Friendship Grove—a tree so labeled is Dragon spruce

Siskiyou SPRUCE

P. Breweriana S. Wats. *(Brewerana)*
From SW Oregon, NW California.

Weeping Spruce
Brewer Spruce

An extremely rare, very *weepy* tree, to 200' × 19' with cones 2½–5½" long. It can live 2,100 years. Rare here. Two are at the Arboretum in 25-2E, the larger 32½' × 1'3¼" (#2133-40). One is 22' × 1'8" near the driveway of 815 NW 116th St. One 15½' tall on the south border of 1108 NW 80th St. At S.U., one 11½' tall is west of the Garrand building, flanked by Japanese Snowball Trees and a *purpleleaf* Black Elder. Locks bed #210 has one 11' tall.

Sitka SPRUCE

P. sitchensis (Bong.) Carr.
=*P. Menziesii* Carr.
Native here; from S Alaska to N California.

Airplane *or* Western Spruce
Coastal *or* Tideland Spruce
Silver Spruce

One of the world's largest trees: the biggest individuals recorded are so huge as to almost embarrass the redwoods: 317' tall, up to 81½' around, and nearly 100' wide! It is the State Tree of Alaska, and has been an important lumber source since loggers discovered it. In World War I thousands of "spruce soldiers" roamed coastal forests in search of choice timber to use in making æroplanes—the antique biplane models with sleek spruce bodies and tough black walnut wood propellers that flew up to 165 m.p.h. *The Spirit of St Louis* was such a plane. Sitka spruce wood combines high strength and light weight to an extraordinary degree. Indians used the roots to weave tight, strong, pliable, attractive and elaborate basketry and hats.

In Seattle, native here around 1900, but now only a few *wild* youngsters are known. Nearby Blake Island has an old tree 136'× 13'6". Planted specimens are common, yet galled, very wide-crowned and usually ugly. The 2–4" cones look much like those of the Colorado spruce, and the foliage looks like that of the extremely rare Yeddo spruce but is more prickly.

– Lake View Cemetery: one, 85½' × 9'4" × 67' wide
– U.W.: one NW of the Montlake Bridge is 85' × 8'9"
– Arboretum: over 40—tallest 97' × 3'5¾" in 31-5W; the stoutest 89' × 5'8" in 15-B
– Woodland Park: picnic/lawn area E of Aurora has a grove of 14, largest 96' × 7'5"
– Green Lake: the largest of 6 is south of the NW parking lot, 88' × 5'2½"
– N 57th St, east of Latona Ave N: a street-tree, S side
– Volunteer Park: about a dozen in the NW corner
– Victory Heights Playground (19th Ave NE & NE 107th): one 62' × 7'5½" by wires
– 2nd Ave NW & NW 125th St: NW corner has one 89' tall by the driveway

Tigertail SPRUCE

P. polita (S. & Z.) Carr. Japanese: Hari-momi ハリモミ
=*P. Torano* (Sieb. *ex* Koch) Koehne Bara-momi
From Japan.

The Latin name *polita* (polished or adorned) probably refers to the lustrous smoothness of the needles and buds. The vernacular is said to refer to the habit of very old trees having shoots curved in the shape of a tiger's tail. Needles dark, sharpest of all, like nails—rigid, stout and fiercely sharp, ½–1" long. Cones 2–5" long. Habit usually gaunt, stiff-branched and wholly graceless, but the tree is fascinating (the same way a shark might be). Recorded to 150' × 12½' in the wild. Extremely rare in Seattle. Arboretum #38-44 (in 23-1E) is 40' × 2'2¼". One 12½' tall is at the SSCC Arboretum's Cœnosium Rock Garden.

White SPRUCE

P. glauca (Moench) Voss Alberta White Spruce
=*P. canadensis* (Mill.) B.S.P., *non* (Michx.) Link Cat *or* Skunk Spruce
=*P. alba* (Ait.) Link Black Hills Spuce
From a vast range: Alaska through Canadian Spruce
Canada and the far northern U.S. Single Spruce

Indians preferred White spruce roots for sewing their birchbark canoes together. It is a variable species. The Black Hills version, small growing, is South Dakota's State Tree. The Alberta race grows largest, to 184' × 12½'. White spruce is much like Engelmann spruce but has *hairless* twigs, and makes cones only 1–2¾" long. It is uncommon in Seattle and usually seen small, slender and grayish.

– Arboretum: the tallest of many is 75½' × 3'6½" (in 30-6W); the stoutest 72' × 4'6¾" (in 35-3W); both are tagged #X-48A; one 53½' × 2'10" is by a Ginkgo across the lake east of the tea house in the Japanese Garden
– Kubota Garden Park: the tallest is 47' × 2'3"
– 4512 47th Ave SW: a street-tree
– 1500 E McGraw St: 35' tall
– 8th Ave NE & NE 59th St: NE corner has one 26½' tall
– SSCC Arboretum: a young cv. '**Pendula**' in the Cœnosium Rock Garden is 6' tall

cv. '**Conica**' Dwarf Alberta (White) Spruce

This looks nothing like its parent; it is a bushy little dwarf conifer, common and familiar: totally dense, conical, and *pure green*. The largest here, after many decades of growth, are *small* trees.

– Calvary Cemetery: 20' × 3'2¼"
– Wahelli Cemetery: 18½' × 2'3¾"—50' SE of "pyramid" at N end
– 1600 E Boston Terrace: 17¼' tall, one of a pair by the front door

Yeddo SPRUCE

P. jezoensis (S.& Z.) Carr.
From Manchuria, Korea,
Kamchatka, Sakhalin, N Japan.

Jezzo Spruce
Yezo Spruce
Japanese: Ezo-matsu エゾマツ

Yeddo spruce looks like Sitka spruce, but has shorter needles (½–¾" long) that are not as fiercely sharp; its cones are smaller, only 1½–2½" (3¼)" long. It can reach 230' × 20'. Almost nonexistent in Seattle. A large old one 58½' tall is at 9733 Arrowsmith Ave S, south of S Perry St.

var. *hondoensis* (Mayr) Rehd.

Hondo Spruce

From central Japan, this is a smaller tree with darker twigs, slightly smaller cones, shorter needles duller above yet brighter white beneath. It too is extremely rare here: a tree 48½' × 5'1" × 39' wide is in Evergreen Park Cemetery.

STEWARTIA

Stewartia spp. *(Stuartia)*
THEACEÆ

These are trees related to Camellias, yet with one exception they're deciduous. All seven deciduous species bear pretty white flowers in summer and have showy fall color; three have highly attractive flaky peeling bark. In Seattle, only one is common. The rest are largely collectors' items, rarely seen despite their merits. Besides the species treated below, the genus includes:

> *S. Malacodendron* L.—(at the Arboretum)
> *S. pteriopetiolata* W.-C. Cheng—(evergreen)
> *S. sinensis* Rehd. & Wils.—(with splendid bark)

The following are treated alphabetically by their scientific names.

S. × *Henryæ* Li
(S. monadelpha × *S. Pseudocamellia)*

Hybrid Stewartia

This hybrid of the two most commonly grown species is no better-looking than either parent, and lacks any special advantages. Some nurseries offer it anyway. Extremely rare in Seattle: two #1112-57 at the Arboretum in 10-4E were once mislabeled *S. sinensis;* the largest 35' × 1'8". The Locks has one 30' × 2'2" in bed #327 (with a smaller *S. monadelpha*).

S. monadelpha S.& Z.
From Japan, S Korea.

Orangebark *or* Tall Stewartia
Japanese: Hime-shara ヒメシャラ

The largest species (to 80' × 9½') but with the smallest flowers (1–1½" wide). Bark showy cinnamon-orange, very uplifting when viewed in winter, especially against a backdrop of glossy deep evergreen foliage. It is uncommon in Seattle.

– Arboretum: the largest 41' × 3'8½" below forking (#5-48C, in 10-4E)
– Locks bed #204 (tiny), 211 (two), 214, 304A, 327 (with a bigger *S.* × *Henryæ*)

- 5727 64th Ave NE: one more than 35' tall is visible from the alley
- S.U.: SE corner of 10th & Spring St has one with a Purple Oakleaf Beech

S. ovata (Cav.) Weatherby f.   Alleghany Stewartia
grandiflora (Bean) Kobuski   Mountain Camellia
From the southeastern U.S.   Summer Dogwood

Shrubby, or a small tree of floppy, heavy habit to 27' tall, without showy bark. It is the last of the clan to bloom in summer, from late July into August—after the other species are done; flowers to 4½" wide. Leaves noticeably larger and wider than those of other species, to 9" × 4". Fall color purplish-bronze to golden, bright orange or red. It is very rare in Seattle.

- Arboretum: the tallest 25' × 1'3¼" #850-41 (14-8E); 14' × 2'2½" #850-41C (12-7E)
- 6208 51st Ave NE: 2-trunked; hacked; by sidewalk & driveway; a *S. monadelpha* is NW of the house

S. Pseudocamellia Maxim.   Deciduous Camellia
(incl. *S. koreana* Rehd.)   Common Stewartia
From Japan, S Korea.   Japanese Stewartia

Its flowers are small balls of cotton in the bud stage, opening to "silk" camellia-like blossoms 2½–3" wide (or more). Leaves 1⅓–4" long. Fall color orange-red to deep burgundy. Bark handsomely mottled and flaking. The Japanese race, called in Japan "Natsu-tsubaki" (ナツツバキ), grows larger (to 60' tall) and is more commonly cultivated. Korean stewartia is smaller, narrower, has wider-opened flowers and oranger fall color.

In Seattle, common. Seen in yards, cemeteries, school and hospital land-scapes—just about everywhere, but few in parks. It is often grown from cuttings and can be bushy or tree-like.

- Arboretum: 11-5E has one (with two trunks) 42' × 2'8" (#1547-45A)
- Evergreen Park Cemetery: 36½' tall, by fastigiate English Oaks by the entrance
- S.U.: 31½' tall on 10th Ave, N of stairs leading down to The Green
- Locks bed #204 (by S end), 206 (by iron gate), 214 (two), 323
- Kubota Garden Park: 30' tall
- U.W.: SE of Lewis Hall
- Substation on the NE corner of 34th Ave SW & SW Roxbury St

S. rostrata Spong.   Roughbark Stewartia
From E China.

An extremely rare, little known species. Its bark is rough and gray, not showy, but it has attractive flowers and leaves—to 6" × 2½", rubbery-feeling; wet glossy looking, very short-stemmed. It can grow to be 40' tall.

- Locks bed #211 (27' × 1'10" × 26' wide), 205
- Dunn Gardens: a 4-trunked one 21' tall in the nursery area by the garage
- Arboretum: #29-88 is 4-trunked, shrub-sized, in 11-5E
- 3915 NE Surber Dr: two partly *pink*-flowered street-trees

S. serrata Maxim. — Early-blooming Stewartia

From S Japan. — Japanese: Hikosan-hime-shara ヒコサソヒメシャラ

The first stewartia to flush in spring, and to bloom (in early May): red sepals against creamy swelling balloon-like petals; done by early June. A small tree recorded to 40' tall; dark green foliage; abundant 2–2½" flowers. Leaves to 3¾" × 1⅛", dull above, shiny beneath; stem red. Bark plain brown. Extremely rare in Seattle: Arboretum #257-54A is 31' × 1'11" in 11-5E. Locks bed #210 (by 211).

[*Eurya japonica* Thunb.—An E Asian broadleaf evergreen shrub or small tree. Our only unambiguous *tree* of it is 18' tall, on the east side of the house at 4025 NE 110th St.]

Potanin SUMACH

Rhus Potaninii Maxim. — Chinese Varnish-Tree

ANACARDIACEÆ — Chinese: Qing Fu Yang / Ching Fu Yang

From China.

A tree to 80' × 8' with 5–11 leaflets. Flowers showy in handsome whitish clusters, May through early July. Fruit red, hairy, tiny. Extremely rare in Seattle, only the following specimen is known: Cowen Park has one 29' × 3'1½" in the SE part; the Arboretum had a much smaller #1034-52 that died from shade. [Related is *R. verniciflua* Stokes (flowers greenish-white, in modest drooping clusters, May into July. Fruit yellow, shiny, hairless. Sap poisonous.); the Arboretum's finest stands 49' × 1'8½" in shady woods of 4-2E.]

Smooth SUMACH

R. glabra L. — Scarlet Sumach

From at least a part of every one of the 48 — Sleek Sumach

lower States, and parts of Canada and Mexico! — Vinegar Tree

In effect, a small, *fuzzless* Staghorn sumach. Its maximum recorded size is 45' × 3¼'. It is a common shrub here, rarely tree-sized, is weedy on Harbor Island—and short-lived to boot.

– U.W.: until cut in 1987, one 25'+ × 2'11½" (1986) stood against MacKenzie Hall—its stump and suckers remain—27½' × 1'7" now. At the NE end of the University Bridge two are notable: 29' × 1'4½" and 27½' × 2'3¼"
– Seattle City Light South Service Center (4th Ave S & S Spokane St): visitor parking lot had one 17' × 3'0" × 23' wide that was cut down in 1988
– Zoo: of five at Sloth Bear, tallest is 29'

Staghorn SUMACH

R. typhina L.
=*R. hirta* (L.) Sudw., *non* Engelm.
From eastern N America.

Fuzzy, Velvet *or* Hairy Sumach
Virginian Sumach
Staghorn

A shrub, or a (generally leaning) tree recorded to 61' × 4¼' with pithy, stout, velvety twigs and strong root-suckers that easily burst through asphalt. Every October, the bold, compound leaves of 11–31 leaflets turn brilliant red—rarely yellow. Greenish, tiny flowers in congested clusters during the summer give rise (on female specimens) to prominent red and furry seed-cones (sometimes called "bobs"). Its appearance from top to toe justifies the meaning "splendour" in the Language of Flowers. The chief historic use of most sumachs was as a tannin source: their bark yielded significant amounts of high quality tannin to use for leather tanning. "Sumach" (or Sumac or Shoomac, *etc.*) is derived from an Arabic name *summâq*. "Staghorn" is an old American name, because the branches are like velvety new antlers.

In its native area, Staghorn is the largest sumach. Its lightweight wood was used for inlay work and to craft souvenirs, walking-sticks, napkin rings, sock-darning balls, and tabourets. Its hollowed twigs served, like those of Elder, as "sap quills" to tap maples in syrup season. Like Smooth sumach (to which most of these remarks also apply) its ripe red seed-clusters can be taken in their prime in late summer or early autumn (before they are too leached by rain), soaked in water, which when strained and sweetened makes a refreshing pink lemonade-like beverage, as sweetly acidic as thimbleberries. [*Poison* sumach doesn't grow here.]

Most of the foregoing are antiquated practices. Now sumach's chief value is ornamental: it's widely grown for stout, bold branching patterns, tropical exuberance of foliage, and unbeatable autumn displays. Its ability to thrive even in poor soils and to act as a soil-stabilizer on banks makes it ecologically valuable.

Nearly all of Seattle's tree-sized sumachs are this species. A common cultivar is the Cutleaf, Fernleaf or Shreddedleaf sumach (whichever you prefer; '**Dissecta**'), similar yet wider, smaller and with foliage as described.

- Seattle City Light South Service Center (4th Ave S & S Spokane St): visitor parking lot had one 31' × 3'11" × 33' wide east of the building—it died
- 10th Ave & E Fir St: NW corner bldg. has a large stout tree 33' tall
- U.W.: by the Center on Human Development and Disability, the largest are 26½' × 1'7" and 23' × 2'2½"; by the Oceanography Teaching Building, the tallest is 31½'; N of Fluke Hall one is 28½' tall; one 20' × 3'4¼" by the Burke Gilman Trail
- 36th Ave NE & NE 43rd St: NW corner yard has a **cutleaf** tree 9' tall × 25½' wide
- 48th Ave S & S Alaska St: NW corner yard has a **cutleaf** tree with the rhodies
- 2212 N 46th St: a **cutleaf** tree in the front yard

[At the Locks bed #17 is a tiny 5' specimen of *R. chinensis* Mill.—the only other example known in Seattle is the Arboretum (#37-56) 12' × 1'0" by the Japanese Garden parking lot. In 1990, another #37-56 nearby, 24' × 1'11", fell down.]

[The largest **Shining Sumach** (*R. copallina* L.) known here was at 3355 47th Ave NE, 25' south of the bus stop, hanging too low over the sidewalk so that it was *cut*, but has resprouted. This species is very rare in Seattle.]

[**African** *or* **Willow Sumach** (*R. lancea* L. fil.), from S Africa, has evergreen slender trifoliate leaves. Planted in Seattle, it languishes from lack of summer heat, or dies in cold winters. A youngster 6½' tall is at the Zoo southwest of the Day & Night exhibits.]

SWEETGUM

Liquidambar Styraciflua L.
HAMAMELIDACEÆ
From the southern and eastern U.S.
and parts of central America.

Red *or* Starleaf Gum
Alligator or Opossum Tree
Bilsted / Gum Tree

The common Sweet Gum in its forest haunts is a mighty tree (to 200' × 44') producing wood that has been used for many things, from cigar boxes to sewing-machine cabinets. Its maple-like, star-shaped leaves turn crimson, orange, yellow or purple in autumn—or remarkably, sometimes persist, enduring green even into the New Year. When bruised or ripped apart or tossed onto a compost heap, they exude a pleasant fragrance that earned the name *Sweet* gum tree. The twigs can be corky-ridged, sometimes very heavily so. Some bright hawkers used to gather such twigs to sell as "alligator plants" during winter in big Northeast cities. Prickly seed-balls ½–1½" wide are borne singly on little stalks or are now and then fused together in groups of 2–8. The sweetgum is very common in Seattle, being one of our overused urban trees. It shows *much* variation in twig corkiness, bark roughness, fall color and leaf retention.

– 24th Ave E, north of Boyer Ave E: 5 street-trees, E side, the tallest 99' × 8'½" and the stoutest trunk 8'8½" around
– one in Broadmoor was 83' × 9'0" × 75' wide in 1993—much bigger now
– Arboretum: the tallest is 98' × 7'5" (#2334-37A in 6-5E)
– E Aloha St, west of 15th Ave E: two street-strees, S side, the larger 9'3½" around
– Boylston Ave E, near Bellevue Pl E: 3 street-trees, largest 8'5½" around, tallest 83'
– Dorffel Dr E, north of E Howell St: a street-tree, E side 85½' × 8'1"
– 34th Ave S & S McClellan: NW corner yard (with Seattle's largest Sassafras)
– Loyal Heights School (2511 NW 80th St): 13 street-trees
– U.W.: one 5'2" around SW of the Chemistry Library; 9 between the Art Bldg. and MacKenzie Hall
– Stewart St, from 6th Ave to Eastlake Ave: City street-trees
– Locks bed #203 (58' tall), 213 (75' tall)
– U.W. Friendship Grove, representing Haiti
– 4th Ave, from Yesler Way to Virginia St: City street-trees

cv. 'Variegata'   Gold Dust® *or* Variegated Sweetgum

Uncommon. Yellow-variegated. Ours are less than about 40 years old. Similar clones that may come to be grown here are 'Golden Treasure' and 'Aurora'.

- View Ridge School (50th Ave NE at NE 73rd St): 3 on the east side, tallest 72'
- Meany School (301 21st Ave E): 5 on the E side
- NE 60th St, west of 65th NE: a street-tree, N side (with two normal Sweetgums)
- Fauntleroy Way SW & SW Morgan: City street-trees, both variegated and normal
- 18th Ave S, north of S Raymond St: street-trees, E side, 2 variegated and 3 normal
- 19th Ave NE, north of NE 82nd St: a street-tree, W side
- 2nd Ave W & W Thomas St: street-trees on the NE corner

Chinese SWEETGUM

L. formosana Hance   Formosan Sweetgum
From E Asia.   Chinese: Feng Hsiang Shu

An overweight version of the American sweetgum, with a stouter, heavier form of growth and leaves. The Chinese name means "Fragrant Maple." It can grow to 130' × 15' and its seed-balls resemble burdock burs. Extremely rare here.

- 12th Ave E, between E Boston & E Lynn streets: a street-tree, W side, 34' × 4'11¼"—under power lines, so often cut back
- Arboretum: 4-5E has two #617-48, the larger 57½' × 3'1"

[*L. acalycina* H.T. Chang—From China; extremely like Chinese sweetgum, yet more cold-hardy; maybe narrower. The Arboretum has one 29' × 1'3" (#85-90 in 44-6E). Nurseries have had it recently so youngsters are apt to exist in Seattle.]

TALLOW TREE

Sapium sebiferum (L.) Roxb.   Chinese Tallow-tree
EUPHORBIACEÆ   Chinese Candlenut-tree
From China.   Popcorn Tree

In China the seeds' whitish waxy coat is used to obtain vegetable tallow used for candles and soaps. Heat-loving; drought-tolerant, it is naturalized in parts of the southern U.S. from North Carolina to SE Texas. Performs well on any soil. Young growth red tinged. Leaves heart-shaped, 1–3", suggestive of those of aspens; sap white. Flowers catkin-like, in July, delicate yellow. Sterile specimens are often preferred for ornamentals. Fall color orange-yellow, glowing red or maroon-purple in November. Tree usually small. Recorded to 80' × 12' in the wild. Very rare in Seattle and should only be planted in hot spots—*unlike* the following pair.

- Arboretum: #243-89 (in 9-2E) is 20½' × 11½" and still wan green into November
- 3102 NW 85th St: a street-tree on 31st Ave NW, with some lilacs and a Stone Pine

TAMARISKS

Shrubs or small trees, distinctive in appearance and attributes. They're widely planted in salty soils, desert areas and along seacoasts. Camel saddles are made of tamarisk wood, and one species produces a manna when insects feed on it. They have shredding cedar-like bark, delicate, minute foliage and pinkish flowers.

In Seattle, one kind is common, others rare. Few on public property, and young specimens are seldom seen at all because in recent years they've been scarce or nonexistent at local nurseries.

Spring-Flowering TAMARISK

Tamarix parviflora DC.   Smallflower Tamarisk
=*T. tetrandra* hort., *non* Pall.
TAMARICACEÆ
From SE Europe; possibly also native in Spain and Algeria.

A graceful shrub or small tree to 44' × 5¾' with tiny but abundant fluffy pink flowers (March) late April–May (June). It is Seattle's common tamarisk.

- 4433 50th Ave S (@S Oregon St): one in the back yard is 24' tall
- 41st Ave E & E Garfield St: SE corner, poking through the fence: 19½' tall
- 1226 41st Ave E (south of E Lee St): 20½' tall
- 4925 Stanford Ave NE: 16' tall, N of driveway
- 4103 37th Ave S: one 20' tall
- 2817 East Park Drive E (by E Hamlin St): 20½' tall in yard's SE corner
- 4736 44th Ave NE

Summer-Flowering TAMARISK

T. chinensis Lour.   Salt Cedar
=*T. ramosissima* Ledeb.   Salt Shrub
=*T. æstivalis* hort. or *T. hispida æstivalis* hort.
=*T. pentandra* hort., *non* Pall.
From China and temperate E Asia.

A larger, more tree-like species than *T. parviflora* (up to 44' × 12½' and wider than tall). In Seattle there are two quite dissimilar forms. The first is quickly dismissed because it is the shrubbiest tamarisk we grow, and even the largest noted in Seattle (at 1230 Federal Ave E) is hardly tree-like, though 26' tall. One 24½' tall grows with a Silk Tree on the SE corner of 33rd Ave S & S Hinds St. This form has pink flowers from late June into early August.

The second form is very rare, but grows larger than our other kinds. Its flowers appear from April through October but don't compare with the showy displays of the other tamarisks here. However, its foliage and trunk make it an equally valuable ornamental—in fact, disregarding floral merit, this beats the others hands down. Its proper name is likely cv. '**Plumosa**'. The largest known here is at 11th Ave E & E Roy St: 20' × 5'7" × 29' wide. One 18½' tall is on the NE corner of 47th Ave SW & SW Dawson St.

TREE OF HEAVEN

Ailanthus altissima (Mill.) Swing. *(Ailantus)*
=*A. glandulosa* Desf.
=*A. cacodendron* (Ehrh.) Schinz & Thell.
=*A. japonica* hort. *ex* Rehd.
=*Toxicodendron altissimum* Mill.
SIMAROUBACEÆ
From China and Taiwan.

Tree of Brooklyn
Chinese Sumach
Stinking Chun
Heavenwood
Ghetto Palm
Paradise Tree

Delicacy and daintiness are not this creature's forte. Whatever its name, this tree of heaven manifests an undeniably strong, even immoderately predominant presence here on earth. It insists on making itself not only noticed, but felt—as has no other tree brought from China to America: it arrived here over 200 years ago, in 1784, and now is *wild* in cities such as New York, Cleveland, Boston, Baltimore and Philadelphia. A joke goes that it grows better in these unnatural concrete forests than in the country.

Its appearance is bold and tropical. Growing vigorously, it can reach 102' × 20' with an open branching pattern of stout, lustrous, rich-colored twigs. The leaves are compound, up to 6' long on suckers. It flowers in July, the male trees stinking. Winged seeds, often colored a bright orange-red in August, persist on female trees through winter, making a musical rattling noise in the wind.

Although the Tree of Heaven spreads in much of America both by reseeding and root-suckering, in Seattle it root-suckers and reseeds sparingly.

– Arboretum: the "swimming hole" vicinity (by SR 520 ramps) has two ♀ 1967 accessions, planted in 1972, the larger 60' × 11'8" × 81' wide
– Volunteer Park: one 71½' × 8'5¼" between the museum and wading pool
– Lincoln Park: tallest of 5 south of the tennis courts is 82'; the stoutest 6'3" around
– 38th Ave SW & SW Lander St: SW corner has a street-tree 11'9" around, but short (43') because of overhead power lines
– E Howell St, west of 19th Ave: a ♂ street-tree, N side, 70½' × 8'9½"
– 13th Ave S, south of S Judkins St: a ♂ street-tree, E side, 64½' × 10'9¼"
– Meridian Ave N & N 35th St: SW corner yard (with English Elm)
– 47th Ave S & S Adams St: NW corner yard ♀
– near Condon Way W & W Newton St
– 32nd Ave NE & NE 115th St: NW corner yard
– U.W.: SW corner of Mary Gates Hall, and many by Padelford garage
– 5116 27th Ave NE: a tall ♂ in the back yard

TULIP TREE

Liriodendron Tulipifera L.
MAGNOLIACEÆ
From the eastern U.S. and extreme S Ontario.

Yellow *or* Tulip Poplar
Saddle(leaf) Tree
Whitewood

This is the "Tulip tree" proper, probably a loose translation of its specific scientific name. Its odd truncate leaf shape is like a tulip flower silhouette, and its flowers (mid-June into early July) are passably similar to those of tulips when viewed close-up without botanical prejudice. However, for all that, it doesn't deserve the name Tulip tree as much as Saucer Magnolia does. Moreover, most people who live where it grows wild don't call it Tulip tree, but Yellow Poplar, because the tree has yellowish foliage leafing out in March, yellow-golden color in November, leaves that flutter in the wind, and lightweight and whitish wood like that of poplars.

Above all it is characterized by its towering growth and unique leaves. The tallest currently known is 178' (one was 198' in 1930), and trunks have been noted 38' around! It stands for "fame" in the Language of Flowers and its flowers mean "rural happiness." Indiana and Tennessee (formerly Kentucky too) made it their State Tree. The wood is valued for many purposes.

It thrives in Seattle, is common here, and we have great examples.

– 700 McGilvra Blvd E: a front yard landmark specimen 122' × 15'9½"
– Leschi Park: one 109' × 12'10¼"
– Park Rd NE & NE Park Rd: the larger of two old street-trees is 92½' × 13'11"
– U.W.: one east of Hansee Hall is 83' × 12'6½"
– Volunteer Park: five 100' to 115' tall in the NE area; the stoutest trunk 10'1½"
– 7341 Seward Park Ave S: 102' tall
– 1634 Palm Ave SW: a beautiful tree despite having been topped, 85' × 14'5½"
– 3217 36th Ave S: one that forks into two trunks is 101½' tall
– 2569 4th Ave W (in back yard): *ca.* 100' tall
– Green Lake Pitch n' Putt golf course: the largest of three is 98' × 13'3"
– 2nd Ave NE, south of NE 50th St: 3 street-trees, W side, the tallest 95½'
– 16th Ave E & E Aloha St: SW corner curb-bulging Heritage Tree: 90' × 10'10¼"

cv. 'Fastigiatum'   Fastigiate Tuliptree

Narrow form, upright branches. Also called 'Pyramidalis' and 'Arnold'. Rare.

– Arboretum: 28-4E has two: 64' × 2'6" (#95-56) and 72½' × 3'9¼" (#212-67)
– Children's Hospital: one 29' tall above stairway NE of "giraffe" entrance
– Broad St, east of 1st Ave: 3 street-trees; Eagle St, east of 1st Ave: 2 street-trees
– 5th Ave downtown by Key Tower: 6 street-trees
– University Way NE: a few street-trees *pl.* 2004 north of NE 41st St

[*L. chinense* (Hemsl.) Sarg.—From China, N Vietnam. Very rare in Seattle but offered at local nurseries. Not as large or dense as its American relative. Leaves orange to brown as they unfold in spring; at maturity very pale beneath, wholly hairless, and quite narrow-waisted. Bark smooth, very pale. The Arboretum's is 63½' × 3'6¼" (#94-56 in 27-2E).]

TUPELO

Nyssa sylvatica Marsh.
=*N. biflora* Walt.
=*N. villosa* Michx.
=*N. multiflora* Wangh.
CORNACEÆ (NYSSACEÆ)
From the eastern U.S., far S Ontario,
and parts of Mexico.

Tupelo *or* Black *or* Sour *or* Bee Gum
Black Tupelo / Upland Yellow-Gum
Snag *or* Umbrella Tree
Swamp Hornbeam
Beetle Bung
Pepperidge
Hornpipe

Tupelo is a shiny-leaved tree with exciting color in October (yellow-apricot to flaming scarlet or bright crimson), and deeply rugged bark. Females bear small, bluish, thin-fleshed, edible sour fruit (November–January). It's a valuable timber producer (to 141' × 27'). Some are over 600 years old. It tolerates either wet muck or drier sites.

Long little-known here, tupelo is no longer rare in nurseries. Once it is firmly established it proves troublefree and a pretty ornamental, looking somewhat like a Persimmon tree but with glossier foliage and better fall color.

– 14th Ave E, north of E Roy St: a ♀ street-tree, (with 3 Sweetgums) 64½' × 6'6½"
– Arboretum: tallest of 15 is 73½' (#140-48K, a ♂ in 44-B); the stoutest trunk 4'2½" (#140-48H in 37-4E; ♀)
– Locks bed #107 (♂), 212 (three), 213 (63' tall)
– Beacon Ave S & S Webster St: SE corner yard has one 47½' tall by a White Birch
– U.W.: a ♂ 40' × 3'4½" east of the salmon homing pond

[*Nyssa sinensis* Oliv.—Chinese tupelo—from China and Vietnam. Its Chinese name is Lan Guo Shu. Planted in Seattle since the 1990s; rare. More thirsty. Less glossy, larger leaves (to 10½" × 3¼"). Example street-trees: 4002 NE 72nd St (5); 6032 Vassar Ave NE (2); Broadway E, just S of E Hamlin St, on the W side; 2722 33rd Ave S; 6239 26th Ave NE.]

UMBRELLA PINE

Sciadopitys verticillata (Th.) S.&Z.
SCIADOPITYACEÆ (TAXODIACEÆ s.l.)
From Japan.

Japanese Umbrella-Pine
Parasol Pine
Japanese: Koya-maki コウヤマキ

As one Seattleite put it: "it's a pine but it's not a Pine." The Umbrella Pine has wide, flat, grooved needles 3–6¼" long, borne in umbrella-like whorls. Its pliable cones are egg-shaped, 2–4 (5)" long. Dark red-brown, fibrous bark resembles that of our native cedar more than it does that of any other pine.

In Japan it has reached 150' × 15½' but in our climate it proves *slow*, the very largest 75' × 11' and the vast majority rarely seen more than 35' × 5'—yet rich green and pleasingly billowy in either case. It is common here.

– 23rd Ave & E Spruce St: SE corner church parking lot has Seattle's first Heritage Tree, dedicated in October 1996; 41' × 7'7"
– Evergreen Park Cemetery: the largest of several is on the W side, by a road, south of the middle; 58½' × 9'11½" (below forking into 4)

- 20th Ave E & E Prospect St: NW corner, 50' tall
- Brooklyn Ave NE & NE 62nd St: NE corner: 44½' tall
- 13th Ave S & S Atlantic St: SE corner has one 40' tall
- Locks bed #302—immediately left of the visitor center entrance; 36' tall
- Nob Hill Ave N & Garfield St: NW corner has one 32½' tall at W side of yard
- U.W. Medicinal Herb Garden: 3-trunked, 28' tall by the large blue Atlas Cedar

VIBURNUM

Viburnum spp.
CAPRIFOLIACEÆ

Usually shrubs, deciduous or evergreen, this genus has few tree-like species. They would be left out of this book but that some nurseries recently have sold a few *trained* as single-trunk trees. Below are citations of varied *Viburnum*.

- *V. Lentago* L.—Nannyberry. Sheepberry. Wild Raisin—From C & E North America. Arboretum: the tallest of 14 #X-126 in 24-4W is 27½' and stoutest 2'0". Calvary Cemetery has a young trained one 9' tall in the NW part. S.U. has a young trained one 11½' tall NE of Arrupe Jesuit Residence
- *V. odoratissimum* Ker-Gawl. & var. *Awabuki* (K. Koch) Zabel—Bigleaf Viburnum— From E Asia. Arboretum #1404-56 in 12-8E is 23½' tall. Locks bed #209
- *V. prunifolium* L.—Blackhaw. Stagbush—From the E United States. Arboretum #96-46B in 25-5W is 28½' × 1'5"

Black WALNUT

Juglans nigra L.
JUGLANDACEÆ
From the eastern U.S. and far S Ontario.

Common Black Walnut
Eastern Black Walnut
American Walnut

Tree to 165' × 28¼'; *leaflets* 13–27; *husks* 1½–2¾" wide, usually dull & rough; *nuts* 1⅛–1¾" wide, usually rough and deeply grooved, even sharply jagged, usually very dark.

Called "black" because its nuts and bark are very dark, this species is more prized for wood than for nuts, though the latter are delicious. The dark, heavy wood is so sought after that many a stately tree gets logged before reaching maturity. At least one sold for $30,000! Prior to World War I, German agents tried to buy supplies in Pennsylvania, for few woods (or none) are so ideal for gunstocks and airplane propellers. While the war was being fought, a slogan was "Fight with your walnut trees!" Nowadays, the tree is grown extensively in parts of Europe, not for nuts or ornament, but for wood.

The nuts are messy to husk, hard to crack and only of moderate size. But they are delectable. Cultivars feature larger, easier-to-crack and sometimes even better-flavored nuts. Certain reward attends its use in growing for timber-production. The tree is handsome enough to be grown for ornament alone—however, many plants dislike growing underneath walnut trees: a kind of baneful influence pervades the soil there.

In Seattle, common. Reseeding. Probably 90% of our walnut trees are of this species; 9% are English and 1% may be another kind. The nuts are ready for gathering mid-September onwards. Veteran's Day proves a consistently good time for harvesting them. Beware the husk stains if persistent brown spots bother you. Stores sell the shelled nut-pieces at exorbitant prices.

– 5100 46th Ave S: an old giant 95' × 13'1¼"
– 1537 Palm Ave SW: a specimen of landmark magnitude
– Orange Pl N & Lee St: NE corner: 56' × 11'6½" × 83'
– 32nd Ave S & S Day St: one 58' tall
– U.W.: the larger of two on the Denny Hall lawn is 79½' × 9'0"
– Roosevelt High School: one 71½' × 9'3½" on the SE corner
– Volunteer Park: several scattered in the south half of the park; best 87' × 9'11¼"
– Denny Park: several
– Arboretum: 2 in the "swimming hole" vicinity—with California and Texas Black Walnuts and 3 English Elms; a smaller one (#319-42) in 36-5E is 61½' × 4'7"
– Ravenna and Cowen parks: on both sides of 15th Avenue NE
– 1624 7th Ave W (south of W Blaine St): a street-tree 69' × 8'11½" × 80'+ wide
– 5th Ave W & W Garfield St: 4 street-trees on the SE corner; best 61' × 7'10"
– West Green Lake Way N: 70' street-trees (+ 5 English Walnuts to the northwest)
– Davis Pl S & S Dearborn St: SW corner

Arizona Black WALNUT

J. major (Torr. *ex* Sitsgr.) Heller
From southwestern N America.

Tree to 85' × 18'9"; *leaflets* 9–15 (25); *husks* (1) 1¼–1½ (2⅛)" wide, semi-smooth, dull or glossy green; *nuts* (¾) 1–1⅜" wide, medium to deeply rough-grooved.

In effect a smaller version of the common Black walnut that retains its foliage green later into autumn. It's extremely rare in Seattle.

– U.W. Friendship Grove, representing Cameroon (mislabeled Texas black walnut), 42½' × 3'4¼"

California Black WALNUT

J. Hindsii (Jeps. *ex* R.E. Smith) Rehd.   Northern California Walnut
=*J. californica* Wats. var. *Hindsii* Jeps.
From S Oregon to central California.

Tree to 115' × 24¼'; *leaflets* (9) 11–19 (23); *husks* (1¼) 1½–1¾ (2)" wide, smooth, semi-glossy, light yellow-green; *nuts* (⅞) 1–1⅜ (1½)" wide, smooth, faintly grooved if at all.

A tree with dark bluish-green foliage which stays green long into autumn, and rather big husks enclosing small nuts. It is extremely rare in Seattle. A two-trunked one in the Arboretum "swimming hole" vicinity (east of Roanoke St) is 50' tall, its larger trunk 6'8" around. It is south of the Texas Black walnut and north of the 2 common Black walnuts.

Hybrid Black WALNUT

J. nigra × *J. Hindsii*

Tree to 130' × 23½'; *leaflets* (11) 17–19 (23); *husks* 1½–2 (2¼)" wide; *nuts* (¾) 1–1¼ (1⅞)" wide, weakly to moderately grooved.

In 1879 Luther Burbank took pollen of the northern California Black walnut (*J. Hindsii*) and fertilized an eastern Black walnut (*J. nigra*) to see what would result. He called the offspring 'Royal' and it proved very fast-growing and productive of nuts. Now there is a whole swarm of hybrid Black walnuts; they vary greatly in appearance and value and are more common on the Pacific Coast than tree books tend to indicate. In general, their nuts are the size of the Californian, but rougher-shelled due to the influence of the East Coast parent. Their foliage stays green on the trees when the East Coast trees are yellow or naked in autumn, and the leaflets are usually more slender and less hairy. These hybrids are rare in Seattle; the specimens cited show much variation.

- 22nd Ave & E James St: one 77' × 14'5½" × 81' wide (the house was built in 1903)
- 18th Ave E, south of E Galer St: a street-tree, W side, 64' × 11'5¼"
- Louisa Boren Lookout (15th Ave E & E Garfield St): one 5'11" around
- Arboretum: one 37' × 3'1" (#X-16 in 31-2W)
- W of the Burke-Gilman Trail, north of NE 65th St: two that produce better nuts than any of the preceding
- Hiawatha Pl S & S Bush Pl: NW corner has an old dying tree 40' × 9'9½"

Texas Black WALNUT

J. microcarpa Berl.

=*J. rupestris* Engelm. *ex* Torr.

From southwestern N America.

Little Walnut
River Walnut

Tree to 59' × 14' or shrubby; *leaflets* 11–25; *husks* ¾–1¼" wide, smooth, unpocked; *nuts* ⅝–⅞" wide, moderately grooved.

A handsome tree with tiny yet abundant and well-flavored nuts. It is extremely rare here. In the vicinity of the Arboretum "swimming hole" (east of Roanoke St) is one 45' × 8'6" × 64' wide; 29-2W has #149-63, 18' × 2'1". The tree at the U.W. friendship Grove representing Cameroon is mislabeled *Texas* but is an *Arizona* Black walnut.

Butternut (WALNUT)

J. cinerea L.

From eastern North America.

White Walnut
Oilnut

Tree to 125' × 20½'; *leaflets* (9) 11–15 (17); *husks* 1½–3⅜" long, felty sticky; *nuts* 1⅜–2½" long, very deeply grooved and jagged.

Compared to its native associate Black walnut, this is shorter-lived, makes lighter and less valuable wood, has smoother and grayer bark, spreads its branches wider, and produces nuts entirely different in shape, and buttery flavor. It is usually regarded as an inferior ornamental. As with many of its kin, its immature nuts are sometimes pickled, and its sap may be made into syrup. Confederate soldiers wore uniforms dyed with butternut husks. It is uncommon in Seattle; compared to other walnuts here it tends to produce fewer nuts.

- 9530 14th Ave NW: one 78' tall
- 4408 S Ferdinand St: one 64' tall
- U.W.: two N of Parrington Hall (by a Pin Oak & Shingle Oak); larger 59' × 6'4¼"
- 1st Ave NW, south of NW 62nd St: a street-tree, E side (with an English walnut)
- 7618 Linden Ave N: a street-tree 38½' tall (N of a Mountain Ash)
- N 82nd St, west of Greenwood Ave N: a street-tree, N side, 46' tall

Cathay WALNUT

J. cathayensis Dode
=(?) *J. formosana* Hay.
From W & C China, Taiwan.

Chinese Butternut
Chinese Walnut

Tree to 92' × 17¾'; *leaflets* (9) 11–17; *husks* 1¼–2¾" long, felty sticky; *nuts* (as made in Seattle) 1¾–2⅜" long × 1⅝" wide, very jagged and spiny, much like butternuts.

A strong and tropical-looking tree with compound leaves as much as 3½' long, with 10" leaflets. Though its nuts can pass for common butternuts, its foliage is far more like that of Japanese walnut. Only two are known in Seattle: a 6-trunked one 53' tall at Frink Park, on the west side, by the sidewalk of 31st Ave S, north of S Jackson St (with a smaller 2-trunked 65½' tall Black walnut); and one 40' tall in the 2nd yard north of W Emerson St on 36th Ave W.

In *The Flora of China* this species is made a synonym of *J. mandshurica* Maxim. But Cathay flushes later, has much longer flower spikes, and spiny nuts.

English WALNUT

J. regia L.
From much of Asia
(and likely the Balkans).

Circassian *or* Carpathian Walnut
Common *or* European Walnut
Royal *or* Persian Walnut

Tree to 120' × 28'; *leaflets* (5) 7–9 (13), blunt, wide and untoothed; *husks* 1½–3" wide, smooth and glossy; *nuts* the familiar store and market kind.

The original "Walnut Tree" and most important. More of its nuts are produced agriculturally than any other kind of nut, period. The wood is also highly desirable, used to make costly furniture, gunstocks, musical instruments and many other articles.

In Seattle, common—especially in parts of southeast Seattle, and from Wallingford to Ravenna. More distinctive in appearance than any other kind of walnut tree here, its smooth gray bark, short broad crown and wide, blunt leaflets make it unmistakable. Trunks 7' around or more are rare.

- 5846 22nd Ave S: a Heritage Tree in the back yard is 51' × 10'1" × 79' wide

- Volunteer Park: one 72' × 5'7¾" in a grove of mixed trees SE of the water tower; one on the hillside W of the reservoir, above the asphalt path
- 4140 20th Ave SW: a broad specimen 44½' tall
- 17th Ave NE: a street-tree 34' N of Ravenna Blvd fire hydrant is 35½' × 6'1¼"
- N 43rd St, west of Burke Ave N: a street-tree, N side (E of a larger Black walnut)
- 1522 N 107th St: a huge specimen in the back yard
- 6512 & 6516 41st Ave SW (south of SW Morgan St): two street-treees

Japanese WALNUT

J. ailantifolia Carr. *(ailanthifolia)*   Japanese: Onigurumi オニグルミ
=*J. Sieboldiana* Maxim., *non* Goepp.
=*J. mandshurica* Maxim. ssp. *Sieboldiana* (Maxim.) Kit.
=*J. cordiformis* Dode var. *ailantifolia* (Carr.) Rehd.
From Japan, Sakhalin.

Tree to 111' × 37¾'; *leaflets* (9) 11–17 (21); *husks* vary from about 1¼–1½" wide and roundish, to about 2" long × 1½" wide, felty sticky; *nuts* 1¼–1⅝" long, smoothish or weakly bumpy and pocked.

This tree has bark and form like that of Butternut, which is to say it is a gray-barked, broad-spreading tree. Its foliage, however, is bolder, with the compound leaves as long as 2½' or more. The nuts vary in shape far more than butternuts, and are weakly flavored. It is rare in Seattle.

- 13th Ave S & S Andover St: SE corner yard has one 47' × 6'7" × 66' wide (1989), that makes small rounded nuts
- 5549 55th Ave NE: the back yard has an immense tree. This Windermere / Sand Point area has many that make longer nuts, *e.g.*, @ 57th Ave NE & NE 61st St
- Arboretum: 29-2W has a 40' tall, multitrunked specimen (#1701-56); two #969-57 are in 31-3W & 31-2W, the larger 29' × 2'1¾"
- Interlaken Park: some youngsters, on the bluff west and north of 20th Ave E
- 32nd Ave NE & NE 62nd St: NW corner (with a Japanese Maple)
- 17th Ave NW & NW 62nd St: NE corner
- 1822 30th Ave (south of E Denny Way)

var. *cordiformis* (Maxim.) Rehd.   Flat Walnut *or* Heartnut
=*J. cordiformis* Maxim., *non* Wangenh.   Japanese: Himegurumi ヒメグルミ

A strange race not known wild but much cultivated; a percentage of its nuts give rise to regular Japanese walnut trees, and the remainder make Heartnut trees—in leaf and tree form indistinguishable from the regular kind, but with smooth, more or less heart-shaped and sharp-pointed nuts 1¼–1½" long, borne on dangling clusters long as 17". It is rare in Seattle.

- 2810 NE 115th St: a multitrunked tree S of the house, topped in 2005
- 6015 NE Windermere Rd (also a big one next door, close to the house)
- 3203 - 3207 Franklin Ave E: 36' tall (an English Laurel at its base)

396

WHEEL TREE

Trochodendron aralioides S.& Z.
TROCHODENDRACEÆ
From Japan, the Ryukyus, S Korea, Taiwan.

Pinwheel Tree / Bird-lime Tree
Japanese: Yama-guruma ヤマグルマ

A broadleaf evergreen, slender tree at most 80' × 20½'. Known as Wheel Tree because it makes little greenish wheel-like flowers from late March into June. Its whorled, dark leaves are reminiscent of those of the Mountain Laurel (*Kalmia latifolia* L.); to 6¼" × 2¾". It's rare in Seattle.

– Arboretum: many (the tallest, 32' multitrunked, is one of four #581-41 in 30-2E); the Japanese Garden also has some, the tallest 30'
– Locks bed #115 (bushy), 305 (29' × 1'6"), 327 (two)
– Kruckeberg Botanic Garden: 34' tall
– 3317 West Laurelhurst Dr NE: one 20' tall under a plume Sawara Cypress
– U.W.: youngsters S of Allen Library

WILLOWS in general

Many willows exist besides the well known pussy willows and weeping willows. Most are shrubs or small trees, loving sunshine and plentiful moisture. The light, tough wood of some kinds is useful, but more importantly willows are employed as ornamentals, as erosion-controls, and as basketry and wickerware materials. Seattle has over 20 kinds altogether, excluding invariably shrubby ones. Two more shrubby native species exist besides the five treated in this guide:

Salix Geyeriana Anderss. var. *meleina* Henry—Geyer Willow
S. eriocephala ssp. *mackenzieana* (Hook.) Dorn—Mackenzie Willow
(=*S. rigida* Muhl. var. *macrogemma* (Ball) Cronq.)

The above two species are only known here as large shrubs. Four non-native willows presently known in Seattle only as large shrubs, *may* reach tree size:

S. exigua Nutt.—Coyote Willow. (U.W. Medicinal Herb Garden has one)
S. magnifica Hemsl.—Magnolia-leaf Willow. (Locks bed #304A has a ♀ 17' tall)
S. 'Melanostachys'—Black Pussy-Willow. (S.U.: 11' tall on E wall of Admin. Bldg.)
S. sachalinensis Fr. Schmidt cv. 'Sekka'—Dragon, Sekka or Setsuka Willow

Bay WILLOW

Salix pentandra L.
=*S. laurifolia* Wesm.
SALICACEÆ
From N & C Europe, W Asia.

Laurel-leaved Willow
Bay-leaved Willow
Sweet Bay Willow
Laurel Willow

Bay willow leaves are reminiscent of those of Bay Laurel in general appearance, not in odor—except in some strains, it is said. As a shrub or at its greatest size of 70' × 23' it handsomely exhibits dark, glossy, full foliage. Male specimens are preferred as ornamentals because of their bright yellow catkins in May or June. It is extremely rare in Seattle.

- Arboretum: a somewhat weepy ♂ 26' × 2'7" (#148-60A in 47-4E)
- U.W.: a bushy 30' ♀ with 9 trunks SE of the basketball court east of the Center on Human Development and Disability

Corkscrew WILLOW

S. *Matsudana* Koidz. cv. 'Tortuosa'   Contorted *or* Curly Willow
=S. *babylonica* var. *pekinensis* 'Tortuosa'   Twisted Hankow Willow
The species from China, Manchuria,   Dragon's-Claw Willow
E Siberia, and Korea; the cv. from China   Rattlesnake Willow
was introduced to the West in 1923.   Twisted Willow

Strikingly twisted, bent and curled branches, twigs and leaves make this common female clone distinctive. Corkscrew willow has attained 75' × 16' but most are cut down while much smaller.

- U.W.: one 59' × 5'6½" S of Plant Services; one 52' × 3'6" NW of McMahon Hall
- 346 16th Ave E (S of E Harrison St): 2 street-trees, taller 52'
- 223 NW 56th St: stout
- 29th Ave W & W Garfield St: NW corner has a stout one 44½' tall
- Museum of History & Industry (2700 24th Ave E): S side
- 4th Ave NE & NE 44th St: NW corner has 3 street-trees

S. **'Golden Curls'**   Golden Corkscrew-Willow
(S. *Matsudana* 'Tortuosa' × S. *sepulcralis* 'Chrysocoma')
= S. × *sepulcralis* 'Erythroflexuosa'

Originated in 1961 in Argentina; in N American commerce by 1972; in Seattle by the 1990s. Weeping, with *golden*, twisted twigs. With some reddish in the twigs is S. **Scarlet Curls**°—extremely similar and undifferentiated below.

- 6731 19th Ave NW: a street-tree
- 4401 Williams Ave W: in back yard (a 'Shogetsu' Cherry is in front)
- 3rd Ave NW & NW 56th St: SE corner yard (uphill is a typical Corksrew willow)

[The only non-contorted **Peking** *or* **Hankow Willow** (S. *Matsudana* Koidz. = S. *babylonica* var. *pekinensis* Henry) known here are: 1) an old ♀ tree (catkins ½–1¼") at Madrona Park, S of the bldg: 49½' × 8'9" × 65' wide (likely the Globe willow, cv. 'Umbraculifera'). 2) 4038 Dayton Ave N: a 24' × 1'3¾" street-tree (of possibly cv. 'Navajo'). Some botanists lump *Salix Matsudana* under S. *babylonica*, but *The Flora of China* does not.]

Crack WILLOW

S. *fragilis* L.   Brittle *or* Snap Willow
From central Europe and SW Asia.   Redwood Willow

Twigs an unexciting greenish-brown, very brittle (but no more so than some of its hybrids or certain other species). You can flick your finger and snap off twigs with the lightest pressure, or let strong winds make a mess of them for you. Leaves turn dirty golden-green and drop earlier in fall than those of White willow or its hybrid. Growth slower than for its hybrids or White willow. Trunk

short, crown broad. In Seattle, extremely rare. Arboretum #80-73 in 49-3E, is a
♀ 28½' × 4'10¼". The U.W. campus has the same clone 32½' tall, on the east
side of the slough, N of the footbridge to the E-5 parking lot.

Dappled WILLOW

S. integra Thunb. '**Hakuro-nishiki**'
= 'Nishiki' *or* 'Albomaculatra'

A Japanese clone with most of its leaves *speckled white and pink*. Since the 1990s
it has been sold here, usually topgrafted on a straight French Pink Pussy-willow
trunk. Common, but though tree shaped, it is not tree sized. Leaves up to 3⅝"
× 1" wide, hairless, subtly toothed, and often opposite or whorled in trios.

– NE 58th St, east of 43rd Ave NE: a street-tree, N side (with pampas grass)
– 510 18th Ave E
– 30th Ave NE & NE 54th St: SW corner yard has a street-tree
– 7324 17th Ave NE

Darkleaf WILLOW

S. myrsinifolia Salisb.
=*S. nigricans* Sm.
From C & N Europe, W Siberia, Asia Minor.

Shrubby or a small tree with dark fuzzy twigs, deep green, glossy, *roundish* leaves,
and catkins of only average ornamental value. Likely none exist here but the
following: the Arboretum has #403-65 in 21-4W, 22½' tall, and by the water
27' tall 48-4E. On the U.W. campus, one *pl.* 1968 is 24' tall, 380' south of the
footbridge to the E-5 parking lot, on the west side of the slough. On the east
side of the slough, N of the bridge, several grow; the tallest 24½'.

Pacific Black WILLOW

S. lucida Muhl. ssp. *lasiandra* (Benth.) E. Murr.   Western Black Willow
=*S. lasiandra* Benth.   Pacific Willow
Native here; from much of western N America.

Our largest native willow species, reaching 85' × 9½'; its leaves at their longest
can be 14" × 2½" wide or more! The eastern North American Black willow (*S.
nigra* Marsh.) grows far larger, up to 140' × 28¼'. The name Black willow may
refer to the *relative* darkness of the species, but the bark is brown and the leaves
are green. It is common in moist, open, deciduous woods and by lakes and
streams. It grows rapidly but doesn't live long. Trunks more than 50 years old
are rare—those that exist are rotten.

– Arboretum: a ♀ by the stream in 25-7W was 76' × 6'3" but died; just south of the
  520 freeway on Foster Island is a broad, squat ♀
– Rodgers Park: SW part has ♂ and ♀ (with blackberries and horsetails); tallest 60'

– Green Lake: some at the S end, but many goldtwig White willows as well

Purple Osier (WILLOW)

S. purpurea L.
From Eurasia.

Usually a slender shrub but recorded up to 37' × 1¼'. Its winter twigs are often purplish on the sunny side. The leaves are bluish-green; unlike most willows some are *opposite* rather than all being alternate. In Seattle the dwarf cv. 'Nana' is common. The also shrub-sized weeper 'Pendula' is rare—one is N of the driveway of the NE corner of Broadway E & E Boston St. The treelike ♂ cv. 'Streamco' (released in 1976 from New York) is seen here and there such as dozens in Carkeek Park; 24' tall at the Zoo, and so on. The ♀ cv. 'Nancy Saunders' is 22' tall on the east wall of the Good Shepherd Center, towards the N end.

French Pink Pussy WILLOW

S. caprea L.
=*S. præcox* Salisb.
From Europe, Asia.

Goat Willow
Great Sallow
Sally

The original "Pussy Willow." Some writers use the name Pussy willow only for a far North American species (*S. discolor* Muhl.) not even grown in Seattle. The common name Pussy willow is chiefly applied to male trees of various species both wild and cultivated. Their claim to fame is humble and fleeting, but beloved: early spring "pussies" (catkin buds) open reddish-gray and turn (in males) bright yellow with fragrant pollen, then whiten, becoming bloated, ugly, and ruined by rain.

Salix caprea—or more likely a ♂ hybrid clone of it—is Seattle's common non-native cultivated Pussy willow species, found in yards, as a street-tree and in planted landscapes only: not wild. It has been recorded up to 75' × 11¾' in Europe. Its leaves are midsize, moderately hairy, very short-stemmed, and have crinkly edges. Galls are unknown on Seattle specimens.

– Interlaken Park: one *pl.* 1981 is 70' × 3'1¼"
– Colman Park: at least 6, tallest 58' and stoutest 4'2"
– Zoo: Family Farm has examples, tallest *ca.* 35½'
– Myrtle Edwards / Elliot Bay Park: many
– Peppi's Playground (32nd Ave & E Spruce St): some on the mound S of the play area, while the slope E of the play area has wild Scouler Pussy willow
– Diagonal Ave S public shore Duwamish River access
– Sand Point / Magnuson Park

cv. '**Kilmarnock**'
='Pendula' (for the most part)

Weeping Goat-Willow
Kilmarnock Willow

An absolutely pendulous male form that arose in Scotland before 1850. It is grafted at about 3–6' up on a straight trunk wherefrom it flops in dangling mop-head fashion. Thus it is a bush-sized tree that needs decades to attain 20' × 6¼'. In full summer foliage it looks more like a dense, strongly weeping crabapple tree than like a familiar weeping willow. Once extremely rare here, now common.

– 9th Ave NW & NW 61st St: NE corner
– 8513 8th Ave NW
– 8339 20th Ave NW: a street-tree
– 2637 NW 59th St

cv. '**Weeping Sally**'

Like 'Kilmarnock' but female, hence with less showy catkins. Extremely rare. The north-central part of Calvary Cemetery has one 11½' × 4'10½" × 12' wide.

Hooker Pussy WILLOW

*S. **Hookeriana** Barratt (Hookerana)*
=*S. amplifolia* Cov.
Native here; from E Siberia & S Alaska to NW California.

Beach *or* Shore Willow
Coast Willow

Noteworthy for its relatively big leaves, and for preferring to grow not far from salt water. It can be shrubby or a tree to 50' × 9¾'. Stout, fuzzy twigs bear leaves larger, on average, than any of our other willows (2½–7" × 1¼–3" wide). They are a dark glossy green on top, whitish and densely fuzzy underneath. They almost invariably lack *stipules* (that occur on all other willows here). Galls are rarely observed on Seattle specimens. The male catkins are as much as 4" long, supremely showy as pussies in February. Hooker willow is extremely rare *wild* in Seattle, uncommon planted here, and short-lived—75% of specimens cited in this book's first edition died.

– U.W.: some on E side of the slough, N of the E-5 parking lot bridge, tallest 31½'
– 31st Ave E & E Thomas St: NE corner has two, the taller 30'
– Locks (*south* side of the waterway): a wild 22' tall ♀ just W of the fish ladder
– Swift Ave S: on the E side, north of where 23rd Ave S intersects is a ♂ (one of the very few specimens found in the city that has stipules)
– 31st Ave NW, north of NW 80th St: small street-trees
– NW 85th St, just W of Jones Ave NW: N side, behind fence; E of an Apricot tree
– 10th Ave W & W Ruffner St: SW corner has one on the E side (+Hybrid P. willow)
– 107 Garfield St
– Fremont Ave N & N 76th St: NE corner behind laurel hedge
– Loyal Heights School: SE corner has one
– 45th Ave NE & NE 60th St: SE corner yard has one right by sidewalk intersection

Hybrid Pussy WILLOW

S. × ***sericans*** Tausch *ex* A. Kern.   Broad-leaved Osier
=*S.* × *Smithiana* auct., *non* Willd.
=*S. rugosa* hort., non Sér.
(*S. caprea* × *S. viminalis* L.)

This is a strong, handsome tree with early, large and showy male catkins. Its leaves are distinctly long, slender and pointed (generally 3–7" × 1–1½" wide), and do not get galled or discolored by disease. British botanists alone seem to have understood this hybrid correctly. American and European writers confuse a related hybrid (*S. cinerea* × *S. viminalis*) with this one, which means in practice that the decorative hybrid pussy willow male clone usually called *Salix* × *Smithiana* is more often than not the one noted here. In Seattle few are known.

– 2519 E Highland Dr: 3 by alley uphill west of house, tallest 37'
– 10th Ave W & W Ruffner St: SW corner (with a Hooker pussy willow)
– 2803 Magnolia Blvd W has one visible behind a clipped hedge
– [1928 5th Ave W (in back yard by alley): one started as a twig in a 1958 Valentine's Day bouquet, and by 1988 was 35' tall, its trunk over 8'0" around! Cut in 1990.]

Piper Pussy WILLOW

S. Piperi Bebb.
Native here; from NW Washington to 40 miles N of San Francisco.

In spring of 1889, a 22 year old botanist, Charles Piper, collected herbarium specimens of a Seattle willow. He did not think it anything special and identified it with the books he had available as *Salix lasiolepis* Benth. var. *Bigelovii* (Torr.) Bebb. But botanist Michael Bebb, specializing in sorting willows, decided that the tree Piper found was a species new to science, so published in *Garden and Forest* (1895, the year Bebb died) the name *Salix Piperi*. Though some botanists today do not regard Piper willow as specifically distinct from Hooker willow, others think it far more similar to *S. lasiolepis* and amply differentiated in both appearance and ecology from Hooker willow.

In Seattle, Piper's willow is common by wet lakeside areas and the like. Its leaves are scarcely hairy when young then *hairless;* dark, glossy green on top, pale bluish-white beneath, of above average size. Most specimens have conspicuous red "apple" galls, usually by the midrib near the top of the leaf. In its bloom stage it looks much like the Scouler Pussy willow, but that species tolerates less boggy sites and grows far larger.

– Arboretum: hundreds on the Marsh Island and Waterfront Trail connecting Foster Island with mainland Seattle (the largest is a ♂ 29' × 4'0" × much wider)
– Andrews Bay and around Bailey Peninsula (Seward Park)
– Union Bay by the U.W. campus
– wetlands north and east of North Seattle Community College
– 7th Ave NW & NW 58th St: NW corner yard by gate in Leyland Cypress hedge

402

Scouler Pussy WILLOW

S. Scouleriana Barratt *ex* Hook. *(Scoulerana)*   (our) Common Pussy Willow
=*S. flavescens* Nutt., *non* Host   Western Pussy Willow
=*S. brachystachys* Benth.   Mountain Willow
=*S. Nuttallii* Sarg.   Fire Willow
Native here; from much of western N America.

By far our most abundant and widespread willow: found in wet places, woods,
hillsides, meadows, parks and yards. Also the most variable, it is guaranteed to
vex beginning botanists. Ornamentally it's the least valuable, often being downright ugly. Its chief distinction is size: dimensions up to 82' × 21' make it the
largest of all Pussy willows. The catkins or "pussies" appear January–April. The
leaves are mostly midsized, smaller than those of the Hooker and Piper Pussy
willows, but larger than those of the French Pink or Sitka Pussy willows—yet
some Scoulers (var. *Thompsonii* Ball) have very small leaves. They tend by late
summer to be bronzy or brownish on the undersides and often orange spotted
above, taking on an unsightly rusty aspect. Saplings usually hold their leaves
green until January. The stipules are relatively large. Fuzzy little "felt" galls in
horn or triangular shape, caused by *Acarina* mites, sometimes occur along the
midrib from the middle to the leaf tip.

   In Seattle, extremely common, ranging from shrubs to trees over 60' tall.
 – W Commodore Way, SE of Lockhaven Apts @3100: a ♂ 37' × 8'11½" × 35' wide
 – Carkeek Park: one in the woods is 60' × 3'7"
 – Camp Long: many, at least one trunk *ca.* 8'0" around
 – Lincoln Park: many
 – 21st Ave E & E Highland Dr: SW corner has one next to a Grand Fir
 – Volunteer Park: a lone specimen is south of the reservoir
 – S.U.: 23' tall ♂ var. *Thompsonii* SW of Casey Bldg.
 – 24th Ave NW & NW 75th St: SW corner yard has var. *Thompsonii* in the shadow
   of a purpleleaf Plum tree
 – Locks bed #120 (by light)

Sitka Pussy WILLOW

S. sitchensis Sanson *ex* Bong.   Velvet Pussy Willow
Native here; from most of the   Silky Pussy Willow
Pacific NW, and S to central California.   Satin Pussy Willow

A usually shrubby species, at most 40' × 5¾'. Like Piper Pussy willow, it thrives
in soggy, sunny sites, though in every botanic detail the two are distinct. Sitka's
dark, persistently felty twigs give rise to markedly *slender* catkins. Its leaves are
slender, small, *dark matt and veiny* on top, vividly, luxuriously shining satin-
hairy beneath, with tiny stipules. "Apple" galls by the midrib at the leaf base are
occasional but not numerous. Even less common are the very inconspicuous
swollen leafstalk galls caused by a *Euura* sawfly.

In Seattle, almost all are on very wet sites, are shrubby, and are late to drop their leaves in fall.

– Montlake Playfield (16th Ave E & E Calhoun St): highly concentrated, with only very few Piper but more Scouler and Pacific Black willows
– Arboretum: many along the Waterfront Trail and on Marsh Island
– Coulon Park (off Lake Wash. Blvd N *in Renton*): a ♀ 35' × 2'8" × 37' wide (1998)
– Green Lake: the chief pussy willow species here—tallest 26½'
– Discovery Park's West Point sewage plant: many planted ♀; only one ♂ noted
– Seward Park: many along the lake edge by the fish hatchery

Rosemary WILLOW

S. Elæagnos Scop.   Eleagnus Willow
=*S. rosmarinifolia* Host, *non* L.   Hoary Willow
=*S. incana* Schrank, *non* Michx.   Sage Willow
From C & S Europe, western N Africa to W Asia.

A shrub or tree as much as 52½' tall, with the slenderest leaves on any of our willows, gray-green on top, white-woolly on their undersides. With leaves like these, the name Rosemary willow is well applied. In Seattle, Rosemary willow is extremely rare, but choice. Ours are the ssp. *angustifolia* (Cariot) Rech. fil. from S France and Spain; their leaves are up to *ca.* 4¾" × ½". The Arboretum, in 49-3E, has a 6' tall shrub (#373-92A). One at the U.W. west of the salmon homing pond (by a bench and a bed of Lavender Cotton) is 19' × 7'3" × 31½' wide. Children's hospital has youngsters.

Violet WILLOW

S. daphnoides Vill.   European Violet-Willow
From Europe to N Scandinavia, also the Himalayas and central Asia.

Though in July the shoots are green—by autumn/early winter the twigs are attractively violet-bluish bloomed. Leaves 2–6" long, to 1" wide, glossy green above, dusty blue below. Attractive catkins. Recorded to 60' tall. Likely none exist here but the following: the Arboretum has #146-60B in 47-4E, a ♀ 44½' × 9'3". The U.W. campus, south of the footbridge to the E-5 parking lot, on the west side of the slough, has a ♂ 30' tall. On the east side of the slough, N of the bridge, three #146-60 ♀ grow; the tallest 40'.

Babylon Weeping WILLOW

S. babylonica L.
From W China—not Babylon.

No trees so important as ornamentals, so abundant, so large, so well known, are so confused in the minds of tree experts trying to name and classify them. What the average person calls Weeping willow is any of at least 6 different clones, nearly all of hybrid origin. Authoritative tree books differ in their application of names. No single account adequately deals with *all* the clones, giving their full descriptions, synonymy, and illustrations. The clones differ in size, rate of growth and vigor, twig color, sex, degree of weeping, leaf retention in autumn, hardiness and relative abundance. The largest dimensions on record for weeping willows are 134' × 28¾' and trees fully as wide as tall are known. These monstrous specimens are invariably *hybrids*.

Weeping willows symbolize melancholy, mourning and forsaken lovers. Napoleon loved the weeping willow(s) he had on St. Helena, so when a storm shattered his particular favorite in 1821, cuttings of it were replanted on his grave. Nurserymen as well as devotees have since filled the world with so-called Napoleon willows: these again consist of varied kinds, although the original, authentic clone was a non-hybridized *Salix babylonica*.

In Seattle, does the pure, original Babylon Weeping willow exist, or are all our forms hybrids? The writer is uncertain but thinks we *had a few*—but may no longer. Purebred trees will differ from the common hybrids by being slower-growing, smaller in stature and more weepy. It does not matter in Seattle—but in most northern places pure Babylon stock is simply too tender for cold winters and so is nonexistent. Whether the leaves (on average) are smaller or larger and hairier than those of the hybrids, is disputed by experts.

| cv. **'Crispa'** | Ringleaf, Screwleaf, *or* Hoopleaf Willow |
| ='Annularis' | Ram's-Horn Willow |

This cultivar, a female, has her leaves curled in strong rings and spirals, and is not as strongly weeping. In our coldest winters all the ends of the twigs freeze and die. Known only as follows here:

– Green Lake: the largest of five at the north end is 40' × 7'8½" and wuder than tall
– Arboretum: one (#812-60B) 56' × 5'¼" by the bridge to Foster Island
– Queen Anne Blvd: one 90' north of 8th Ave W & W Lee St, 38½' × 4'2¼"
– Madison Park's *unamed park* on 43rd Ave E near E Lynn St has one 31½' tall
– Good Shepherd Center: a youngster 11' tall is north of the bldg.

Golden Weeping WILLOW

| *S.* × *sepulcralis* Simonk. cv. **'Chrysocoma'** | Niobe Weeping Willow |

≠*S. alba* cv. 'Tristis'
≠*S. alba* var. *tristis* (Sér.) Koch
=*S. alba* cv. 'Vitellina Pendula Nova'
=*S.* × *chrysocoma* Dode
(*S. babylonica* × *S. alba* var. *vitellina* cv. 'Tristis')
From Europe, where it originated in the 1880s.

This is our common weeping willow, the one so strongly prominent in winter because of its long, bright, drooping yellow-gold twigs. Broad and dense, it is not as tall (in Seattle at least) as the Sepulchral hybrid. Its leaves average a bit larger than those of the Sepulchral, up to 7" × 1" wide on stems sometimes over ½" long; they also color yellow and drop earlier in the fall. In late March its charteuse brightens a largely bare lakeside landscape. A very uplifting spectacle. The clone is essentially male, with conspicuous 1½–2" long catkins in April or May, but female flowers occasionally appear. [Though nurseries and some books commonly call this tree 'Tristis', that name strictly belongs to a less weepy, female goldtwig weeper that may not occur here—one *may* be south of 2035-2037 Fairview Ave E (Wandesfordes Dock); it is a partly weepy ♀, 60'+ tall.]

In Seattle, very common.

- Dahl Playfield (25th Ave NE & NE 77th St): one 57½' × 14'7¼" × 79' wide
- 9220 Wallingford Ave N: one *pl. ca.* 1907 63' × 13'1½" × 80' wide (2000)
- Matthews Beach Park
- Boyer Ave E & E Lynn St intersection has one 55½' tall
- Dunlap School (8621 46th Ave S): two, the larger 45' × 11'4"

Sepulchral Weeping WILLOW

S. × *sepulcralis* Simonk.   Salamon Weeping Willow
=*S.* × *Salamonii* Carr. *ex* Henry
(*S. babylonica* × *S. alba*)

From France <1964, this is a female (rarely androgynous), with catkins about 1¼–2" long. It grows tall, with olive-green twigs, leaves 3–6½" long and less than 1" inch wide, on very short stems, staying green on the trees into December and January. In Seattle, uncommon and outnumbered by the golden weeper. At its best as old specimens in parks, as cited below:

- Colman Park Beach: by the lake was one 12'0"around in 1983, but it fell in December 1986; smaller specimens remain, the largest 80½' × 10'1¼"
- Madrona Park: 3 south of the parking lot, the largest 73½' × 14'0"
- Green Lake: one 51½' × 8'10¼" east of NW tennis courts; one 61' × 8'5½" is the larger of two by the boat rental dock

[Less important hybrid weeping willows exist in Seattle. Anyone much interested in them should study the Arboretum specimens labeled *S.* × *elegantissima* K. Koch (Thurlow Weeping Willow; #22-65—both ♂ & ♀ clones are so labeled; unlabeled trees also exist). These are thought to be *S. babylonica* × *S. fragilis*. Also, the U.W. has strange hybrids; on San Juan Road and eastward are 13 (some ♂, most ♀)—the largest 30' × 9'0".]

White WILLOW

S. alba L.   European White Willow
From Europe, NW Africa, W Asia.   Huntingdon Willow

An important timber tree, to 135' × 30½'. Its wood has been used for many things, including cricket bats, artificial limbs, flooring, charcoal for artists and gunpowder, toys and so forth. Various botanic and garden varieties and hybrids exist. In Seattle, one may safely assume that all our planted non-native willows that are very big and tall trees are White willow or its hybrids (of course this includes the Golden and Sepulchral Weeping willows).

var. *cærulea* (Sm.) Sm.   Cricketbat Willow
=var. *calva* G.F.W. Meyer   Blue Willow

This name covers the White willows known in Seattle besides the silverleaf or goldtwig variants treated below. These trees are uncommon here, which is just as well as they're prone to disfiguring anthracnose in late spring. All are female and make short catkins ½–1¼" long.

– Lake View Cemetery: one on the W side is 67' × 7'11¼"
– Green Lake: several in SW area

var. *sericea* Gaud.   Silverleaf Willow
=f. *argentea* Wimm.   Royal Willow

Foliage densely and persistently silvery-hairy, making the tree distinctively silvery, looking like an enormous Russian Olive tree. Wonderful but extremely rare here. All noted are female and make catkins to 2½" long.

– 31st Ave & E Arlington Pl: NE corner has a back yard colossus 56' tall
– 12th Ave NW & NW 130th St: NW corner has one 51' tall west of mailboxes,
  under wires, in gully with Western Red Cedar and Bigleaf Maple
– Arboretum: giants were cut down in 45-5E; #444-54A in 22-5W is 80' × 5'11½"

var. *vitellina* (L.) Stokes   Goldtwig *or* Golden Willow
                                                       (Russian) Yellow Willow

This var. has winter twigs that are lemon-yellow, golden, or red. It is our only common manifestation of *Salix alba*. We even have it naturalized around lakes. It is a huge tree, golden twigged, and doesn't weep, except sometimes a little bit. Most of ours are male, with catkins 2½–4⅜" long in April-May, but females do exist, with catkins 2–5" long. The leaves are not very hairy.

– Arboretum: S of the SR-520 onramp are over a dozen, the tallest 90'
– U.W. Friendship Grove, representing Ireland, 51½' × 8'5½"
– Green Lake: many, most of them female
– Magnuson Park
– S of 2035-2037 Fairview Ave E (Wandesfordes Dock): a partly weepy ♀, 60'+ tall
  that may be *S. × sepulcralis* 'Tristis'

Hybrid White WILLOW

S. × rubens Schrank   Rochester Willow
(*S. alba* × *S. fragilis* L.)

White willow crossed with Crack willow produces these trees. They vary greatly and we once had several clones. Hybrids are distinguished from White willows by their *usually* larger leaves and catkins, more brittle twigs, and a resistance to the blight often attacking the Whites in spring. In Seattle they're rare and ignored. All that are left are two old females: on Lake Washington Blvd. in the Arboretum, by the stream, S of the viaduct footbridge (38-3W); the larger 79' × 10'3¼". Its average leaves are 5" × 1" wide, glossy dark green above, dull blue-green beneath; some leaves reach 10" × 2". Catkins 1¾" long in bloom, lengthen to 2½" long in seed.

WINGNUT TREE

Pterocarya fraxinifolia (Lam. *ex* Poir.) Spach   Caucasian Wingnut
=*P. caucasica* C.A. Meyer
JUGLANDACEÆ
From SW Asia.

A vigorous, strong and bold species with compound leaves after the fashion of walnut trees; leaflets (7) 15–27 (41). The little "winged nuts" that grow in showy, dangling chains, are inedible. It is fast-growing and has reached up to 125' × 21½' in cultivation. Like poplars, it thrives in rich, moist soil, and needs full sunshine; the powerful roots can cause trouble to manmade structures. But it lacks the lovely fall color of poplars. It is extremely rare in Seattle.

– Arboretum: #664-57 is in 31-3W, 64½' × 6'6½"
– 24th Ave NW, from NW Market St to NW 65th St: *ca.* 90 City street-trees were planted. Many were removed in 1988 or later because they were disruptive—they simply need more room and ought not be planted in confined quarters surrounded by concrete. Now, the street has pruned Wingnuts, Callery Pears, Red Oaks and Zelkovas. From 57th to 64th, only 27 Wingnuts remain, the stoutest 6'4¾"

[*P.* × *Rehderiana* Schneid. is *P. fraxinifolia* × *P. stenoptera*. The only one known in Seattle is at the Zoo: a youngster 7' tall just outside the jaguar exhibit. It bears 18–24 leaflets on a slightly *winged* common stem.]

[*P. rhoifolia* S.&Z.—Japanese wingnut—From Japan; Sawa-gurumi (サワグルミ). It bears 11–21 leaflets on an unwinged common stem; the buds bear *scales* unlike the other species. Known in Seattle as: two youngsters at the Zoo just inside the jaguar exhibit. Arboretum #333-84 is 10' from the road in 17-3W, 39½' × 2'3½".]

[*P. stenoptera* C. DC.—Chinese wingnut—From China; Feng Yang. It bears 11–25 leaflets on a *strongly winged* common stem. Though it's been for sale at local nurseries since the 1980s, I can cite only 4 old Arboretum trees: #561-69**A** in 48-3E is 77½' × 7'11" while **B** is 68½' × 8'10¾" (making seedlings); #762-51A in 29-2W is 7'6¾" below its low fork; #762-51 in 8-6E is 56' × 5'9".]

[*Platycarya strobilacea* S.&Z. is another Walnut family tree that bears no nuts. From E Asia. Leaves of 7–17 sharply toothed leaflets; green late into November, finally yellow. Flowers yellowish, from late June to mid-July. Fruits woody, conelike and suggestive of those of teasel; 1–1½" long. Bark rough, gray, fissured. A large shrub or elegant small tree. Recorded to 80' × 8¼' in the wild. Extremely rare here. 4547 S Lucile St has one 17' tall, *pl. ca.* 1995. Arboretum #46-94 is in 30-3W.]

WINTER'S BARK

Drimys Winteri Forst.
WINTERACEÆ
From S America.

A cold-tender, broadleaf evergreen, slender tree at most 100' × 10'. Named either after Captain John Winter who found its bark both spicy and medicinal while on the famous 1578-79 voyage with Sir Francis Drake—*or* after Sir William Winter who was an investor in the expedition. Its leaves vary much in size, up to *ca.* 7½" × 2¾" and are notably pale beneath. White flowers appear in May or June. Very rare in Seattle.

– 12th Ave S & S Hanford St: the garden here has one 19' tall inside the fence
– Good Shepherd Center: 11' tall against the east wall towards the north end

YELLOW-HORN

Xanthoceras sorbifolia Bge.   Shinyleaf Yellow-horn
SAPINDACEÆ   Chinese Flowering Chestnut
From N China.   Popcorn shrub / Hyacinth Shrub

Prized for its flowers and elegant bright green foliage. Usually a spindly shrub, rarely a small tree; can form colonies by root suckering. Leaves, flowers, seeds are all edible. Leaves recall mountain ash, being pinnately compound, 5–12" long, of 9–17 shiny leaflets. Flowers in April and May, the 6–10" tall clusters like those of horse chestnut, white, first with yellowish-green, then red centers. The fruit is an easily-cracked capsule to 2½", containing edible ½" nuts. Bark like black locust. Heat-loving; very cold-hardy and drought tolerant. Often short-lived. It can bloom the third year raised from seed. Recorded to 26' × 3'.

– 4625 Eastern Ave N: an old one not visible from the road, is 15½' × 9"
– 2009 E Aloha St: young
– 12224 Densmore Ave N: one *pl.* in 2004 along the long driveway

YELLOW-WOOD

Cladrastis kentukea (Dum.-Cours.) E. Rudd   Yellow Locust *or* Ash
=*C. lutea* (Michx. fil.) K. Koch   Gopherwood
=*C. tinctoria* Raf.
=*Virgilia lutea* Michx. fil.
LEGUMINOSÆ (FABACEÆ)
From the southeastern U.S.

In nature this is an uncommon, even endangered species. It has been recorded to 87' × 23' × 96' wide, and has reliable bright yellow or even yellow-orange fall color. Its heartwood is also deep yellow. Uncommon in Seattle, Yellow-woods are unreliable as flowering trees: their white flowers appear full force in some Junes, but are absent or weak in most years. They have no other faults except a branching habit prone to breaking up; careful pruning can help with this.

- U.W.: 44½' × 8'3¼" W of Anderson Hall; 51' × 7'5¾" N of Benson Hall right next to a Sugar Maple
- Lincoln Park: 6 SE of tennis courts (best 60' × 8'2¼"); at least a dozen by and N/NE of the wading pool (largest 57' × 6'1")
- Zoo: Phinney Avenue side or west entrance has many youngsters; further south opposite N 53rd St is an older tree 32' × 4'0"
- First Hill mini-park (Minor Ave & University St): 8 youngsters
- S.U.: one 23' tall W of Loyola Hall
- Locks bed #202 (44' tall; by #203), 205

[**Chinese yellow-wood**—*C. Delavayi* (Franch.) Prain = *C. sinensis* Hemsl.—Flushes *very* late in spring, and is finer textured; leaflets 9–17 rather than 7–11. It is found 35' × 4'2¼" at the Arboretum (#1258-45 in 18-5E). A 25' tall street-tree at 8538 30th Ave NW. A young tree by the driveway of 5710 26th Ave NW (Westwind Apts.).]

English YEW

Taxus baccata L.   Common Yew
TAXACEÆ
From Europe, SW Asia, N Africa.

Yew, dark symbol of death, yielded wood for the great longbows wielded with deadly accuracy by Old England's famed archers against their Norman foes. Long associated with mystery, mourning, immortality and dread, it endures longer than trees with more cheerful associations—sometimes more than 1,500 years. Slow-growing, dark, dense and patient, it may reach 106' × 65' (no misprint, that calculates to a 20' trunk diameter!).

This is the original "Yew" and is rightly called English yew since the Britons of old revered it, planting it in nearly all of their graveyards. Its wood is heavy, strong, dark, hard, fine-grained, useful and durable.

Modern Englishmen turned from bending longbows to clipping yew topiary and hedges. They now smile at their ancestral belief in the toxic shadow cast by yew, nor is it any longer a living symbol of sorrow, penitence, or infidelity. In short, the yew hath seen better days and is currently out of fashion. Its attractive red berries, ripe and available from late July into mid-November, are sweet, slimy and edible, but their hard little hearts are bitter and lethal: spit out these seeds as you value your life! Only female and bisexual specimens produce berries; male trees merely diffuse dusty clouds of yellow pollen anytime from February to April.

In Seattle, English Yew is common and reseeding.

- Cowen Park: a ♂ is 60' × 7'4" × 52½' wide near NE 62nd St; a ♀ west of it
- Arboretum: a ♀ 55½' × 8'0" (#X-70A) is the larger of two by the road in 45-3E
- Volunteer Park: a ♀ 51' × 10'5" in the SE corner
- Zoo: the Rose Garden has a ♀ 47' × 10'5" × 60' wide
- Lakeview Park: NW corner
- Broadway E & E Republican St: NE corner (churchyard): a 42' tall ♀
- Me-kwa-mooks Park

– Locks bed #113 (wild), 203A, 209 (four), 212 (wild); bed #206 has Hybrid Yew

cv. 'Adpressa'   Shortleaf Yew

With short, densely set, dark bluish-green needles. Though usually bushy it can be a 36' tree. Two females as large as any known here (it's rare) are about 15' tall under Deodar Cedars on the south side of W Galer St at 28th Ave W.

f. *aurea* (Nels) Pilg.   Golden Yew

A collective name for seedlings or cultivars in which the foliage is more or less *yellowish*. Color is usually most developed at needle tips and margins. Often the spring growth is bright golden, but gradually fades to green. Usually a dense shrub, sometimes a small tree. Seedlings vary considerably in habit. Both male and female forms exist. Kubota Garden Park has many. Volunteer Park has one 21½' tall in the SW corner, and 5 by the water tower.

cv. 'Fastigiata'   Irish Yew
= 'Hibernica'

This famous, abundantly grown yew arose at Florence Court, Ireland, about 1750. It is female and holds its branches close, vertical and parallel, making a *dense column*. Old specimens can flop and splay out at the top. The largest recorded are over 63½' × 10¾' but it tends to be very slow-growing and is often no more than a bush. Gold-colored mutants have been cloned; our prevalent old clone is 'Fastigiata Aureovariegata'—a male with the young needles edged bright golden. Irish Yews are common here, mostly as bushes 10–20' tall rather than obvious trees.

– 2507 1st Ave W: two enormous specimens, the taller 31'
– Mt Pleasant Cemetery: well over a dozen, the tallest 29'
– one 29¼' tall on 35th Ave at E James St, by the telephone pole
– 16th Ave E & E Aloha St: NE corner yard has one 26' tall
– Broadway E, north of E Edgar St: two big old trees, E side
– U.W. Medicinal Herb Garden: a sheared pair *with* two Golden Irish yews
– Mt Pleasant Cemetery: several Golden Irish yews, the tallest 27'
– 3027 NW 67th St: a prominent Golden Irish yew 28½' tall

Hybrid YEW

T. × *media* Rehd.
(*T. baccata* × *T. cuspidata* S.&Z.)

Hybrid offspring of English and Japanese yews first appeared about 1903; now many cultivars exist. The largest-growing are trees to 40' tall after decades, but in general they are shrubs, ideal for hedges or wherever shade-tolerant evergreens are desired. In Seattle, many of our bushy yews are hybrids. Few here can be called *trees* unequivocally, for they are variously clipped, sheared or otherwise kept small, or are too young, or are gigantic unpruned shrubs. When untouched by gardeners' tools, they tend to make multiple trunks and act shrubby by spreading widely. In general, heights of 17' and trunks of 7" thickness are unusually large. One in in the north part of Lincoln Park is 34' tall. S.P.U. has a 31½' tall male west of McKinley Hall.

Pacific YEW

T. brevifolia Nutt. (our) Native Yew
Native here; from Alaska Western Yew
to central California. Oregon Yew

Seattle's slowest-growing native tree: our largest may be 175–425 years old. It can grow to 90' × 20' but is often an ill-formed, sparse, floppy shrub. The wood of this species was long valued by natives and settlers alike. A bow of Pacific yew once shot an arrow 453 yards and 4 inches—over a quarter of a mile! By 1998 *taxol* was a billion-dollar drug obtained from its bark; now it is synthesized.

It's common in Seattle's shaded native woods. Virtually none are seen in formal landscapes of any sort. Beginning tree students have trouble trying to tell it from English yew. The experienced eye notes that the two differ slightly, yet sufficiently, in all aspects. Pacific yew needles are dark bluish-green, ½–1½" long and *abruptly* pointed; English yew needles are gradually tapered, are often glossy, and tend to hang many more years on the twigs.

– Seward Park: largest was 64' × 7'1" × 43' wide but died; a living ♀ is 38½' × 6'11"
– 2222 70th Ave SE (on Mercer Island): a ♀ is 50' × 13'1" × 46½' wide
– Lincoln Park: NE of the south restrooms an atypical ♂ specimen (in full sunshine, on a lawn), is 38' × 10'11½" × 57½' wide
– Schmitz Park: several by the gate; the largest is 39½' × 5'9"
– Ravenna Park: many; the tallest is 42' × 4'1¼"; stoutest 29½' × 6'7"
– Golden Gardens park: the largest is a ♂ 45½' × 5'11½"
– Interlaken Park: the largest are 50½' × 4'9" and 40' × 5'2¾"
– Arboretum: Japanese Garden parking lot has a 2-trunked ♂ 34' × 2'1¼" + 1'10" W of a 2-trunked ♂ English yew 55' × 4'8¼" + 4'1½" (both likely the same age)
– Matthews Beach Park: largest of 2 uphill from the play area is a ♀ 40' × 5'5¼"

Plum YEW

Cephalotaxus Harringtonii (Knight *ex* Forbes) K. Koch Cow's-tail Pine
=*C. pedunculata* S.&Z. *(Harringtonia)*
CEPHALOTAXACEÆ
From E Asia.

Plum yews bear robust yew-like foliage and plum-like fruit (in appearance, not flavor). The needles are 1¼–3" long; the plums ripen in October at up to 1¼" long—pine-flavored, juicy, chewy, not gratifying. Some plants are male, some female, others mixed. They're uncommon here. Very few *trees* are known: most specimens are shrubby. However, Plum yews are a standard entry in tree guides and our largest shrubs eventually reach tree size. [Technical note: the name *C.*

Harringtonii in its narrow sense applies to a male garden clone from Japan, unknown wild; the variable *wild* plants are var. ***drupacea*** (S.&Z.) Koidz.]

- U.W. Medicinal Herb Garden: one S of section B is 6-trunked, 25½' tall; fruitful
- Volunteer Park: two very *wide* ones behind the museum are sparingly fruitful
- 3832 Ashworth Ave N: a ♂ 24½' tall N of the driveway
- 2300 7th Ave: two males, taller 23'
- 1483 NW 77th St: one 17½' tall at the house's NE corner
- 3450 NW 59th St: a short two-trunked ♂ overhangs the sidewalk
- 8724 2nd Ave NW: one 19½' tall but sickly, NW of the house

cv. '**Fastigiata**'   Fastigiate *or* Spiral Plum-Yew

This is like a big-needled Irish yew except completely shrubby and a fruitless male. Needles are 1½–2½" long, whorled on stout green twigs. One west of Bagley Hall on the U.W. campus is as large as any known in Seattle, 19' tall.

Plum-fruited YEW

Prumnopitys andina (Poepp. *ex* Endl.) De Laub.   Spanish: Uva de Cordillera
=*Podocarpus andinus* Poepp. *ex* Endl.   Mapuche: Lleuque
=*Prumnopitys elegans* Phil.
=*Prumnopitys spicata* (Poepp.) Molloy & Muñoz-Schick
PODOCARPACEÆ
From SW Argentina, S Chile.

This looks much like English yew but is brighter, lighter green and more drooping. It can surpass 70' in height and makes a plum- or grape-like fruit. It is known in Seattle only as follows and is fruitless so far: the U.W. Medicinal Herb Garden has one from the Arboretum (#305-57) that is 19' × 1'1½" north of section F. The Arboretum has two youngsters (#62-89**B** in 1S-5E, and **A** in 1S-6E).

YEW PINE

Podocarpus macrophyllus (Th. *ex* Mur.) Sw.   Japanese Podocarp
=*P. longifolius* hort. *ex* Sieb.   Longleaf Podocarp
=*P. chinensis* hort.   Yew Podocarp
PODOCARPACEÆ   Chinese: Lo-han-sung
From E Asia.   Japanese: Inu-maki イヌマキ

A tree to 82' × 12½' called in China "Disciples-of-Buddha Pine." Yew Pine combines the realms of fine-textured conifers such as pines, with the bolder look of broad-leaved evergreens such as evergreen oaks. Its warm, red-brown bark contrasts pleasingly with its greenery. For all practical purposes it is a mere shrub that slowly reaches 20' × 2' at most. Leaves 3–8" long, up to ½" wide. Fruit pea-sized, powder-blue, egg-shaped, borne sparingly here; possibly poisonous but its ripe red swollen stalk is edible though insipid.

   In Seattle, uncommon. Often confused with the absolutely shrubby *P. chinensis* Sw. (= *P. macrophyllus* var. ***Maki*** Sieb. *ex* Endl.), that has leaves only 1½–3½" long and proportionately narrower. It should not be confused with houseplant members of its genus not hardy outdoors here. Other *Podocarpus* that may prove cold-hardy and tree-sized here, and are being tested as young plants in a few gardens, include the New Zealand *P. Cunninghamii* Colenso and *P. Totara* G. Benn *ex* D. Don. Both bear petite needles.

- 4830 54th Ave S: one 23½ tall at the house's SW corner
- McGilvra Blvd E & E Highland Dr: SE corner has two 20'+ tall ones W of house
- U.W.: 7 in Stevens Court courtyard; tallest ♂ 19½' and ♀ 19¼'
- 17th Ave E & E Mercer St: SW corner has a 2-trunked ♀ 17½' tall × 17' wide
- Arboretum: a 12½' tall ♀ #802-51 among barberries in 20-B
- S.P.U.: 13' tall west of Alexander Hall; 12' tall west of McKinley Hall
- 5th Ave & University St: 2, heavily pruned, by Benihana Sushi in the plaza
- Ashworth Ave N & N 43rd St: SW corner yard has one (with two Umbrella Pines and a Japanese Nutmeg Tree)
- 11265 Marine View Dr SW: one 13' tall under the huge Southern Catalpa

[**Prince Albert's Yew**—*Saxegothæa conspicua* Lindl.—From S Chile and Argentina. The 1851 epithet *conspicua* remarkable (the tree being notable for its yew-like habit, juniper-like fruit, podocarp male flowers, *etc.*). Exceedingly rare; it offers nothing particularly outstanding. Foliage yew-like, the wide needles to 1⅛" long, hard and curved, dark green above, pale bluish beneath. Fruit ⅓–¾" wide, rounded, vaguely like a juniper berry but with prickly blue-green scales. Recorded to 131' tall in the wild. Arboretum #281-91B in 40-4W is <4' tall, and weak. The Good Shepherd Center has one 2' tall N of the summerhouse with hellebores and *Lonicera fragrantissima*.]

ZANTHOXYLUM

Zanthoxylum simulans Hance   Chinese Prickly-Ash / Szechwan Pepper
=*Z. Bungei* Planch.   Chinese: Ch'uan Chiao / Ye Hua Jao
RUTACEÆ   Japanese: Kashou カショウ
From China, Japan.   Terihazanshou テリハザンショウ

A shrubby small tree, its trunk armed by odd horn-like spines. Leaves highly pungent, hairless, compound, 3–5" (9") long, consisting of 5–11 leaflets ¾–2" long. Inconspicuous May flowers beloved by bees give rise to tiny red fruits with shiny black seeds. One whiff of the spicy odor of this tree goes a long way. The dried fruit is used as a condiment in Chinese cooking.

- Arboretum: two #348-69 are in 9-6E, the largest 28' × 1'7¼" and notably broad; 60' west of these, #369-89 in 9-5E is 11' tall
- 7519 22nd Ave NW has a youngster 9½' tall in the back
- Zoo: a youngster <6' tall is on the Main Loop in the SE area

[**Japan Pepper**—*Z. piperitum* (L.) DC.—From E Asia; Japanese: Sanshou サンショウ(山椒). Exceedingly rare; often its name is applied wrongly to *Z. simulans* or *Z. schinifolium* S.&Z. The real McCoy is a mere shrub, with leaves 3–6" long bearing 11–23 *tiny* leaflets, its spines in *pairs*. The Arboretum has #733-58 in 4-1E, about 8' tall.]

ZELKOVA

Zelkova serrata (Th.) Mak.
=*Z. acuminata* (Lindl.) Planch.
ULMACEÆ
From China, Taiwan, Japan, Korea.

Common *or* Sawleaf Zelkova
Chinese: Chü Shu / Ju Shu
Japanese: Keaki / Keyaki ケヤキ

Of no floral beauty, yielding no useful fruit, Zelkova is, at least while young, decidedly plain. Its most interesting credit may be a name beginning with Z. Where native, it is valued as a timber producer (it grows to 164' × 31½'), and sometimes people cook its young leaves as a (rather insipid) potherb. It is not ugly even if not showy; it is troublefree, too. In great age it can be majestic. The bark and winter form is pleasing, and its fall color can be an attractive yellow, orange or rusty red. Cultivars such as 'Halka', Green Vase® and Village Green™ exist. Zelkovas are uncommon in Seattle. Some cited below are wider than tall.

– Arboretum: the tallest #799-54 is 64' × 4'1" in 36-3E; the largest is 5'6" in 11-4W
– Seattle Center: Fisher Pavilion lawn has one 53' × 7'4"
– 15th Ave E & E John St: 6 *pl.* 1967 (+Oshima cherry trees); the largest 44½' × 6'4"
– U.W.: one 39' × 6'0" is south of the Chemistry Library; over 100 street-trees line NE Pacific Street east of the University Bridge
– Green Lake: 11 near the Evans Pool building and beach
– between I-5 freeway and Melrose Ave, from Olive Way to Denny Way: 10
– 'Village Green' City street-trees: 16th Ave SW, from SW Findlay St to SW Morgan

APPENDIX

Outline of Scientific Nomenclature

Below, ranked from broader categories to narrower, are the six levels of scientific plant-classification used in this book, and the proper technical terms for each. All are employ×ed with differing degrees of emphasis by various botanists: usage is a subjective matter, not an absolute rule.

FAMILY (plural *families*)
A group of related genera.
Always capitalized in this book (e.g. ACERACEÆ); 71 families are in this book.

GENUS (plural *genera*)
A group of related species.
191 in this book.

SPECIES (plural *species*; abbreviated *sp.* in the singular and *spp.* in the plural)
The basic unit of classification. For example, *Juniperus communis* is one of the species of the genus *Juniperus*.
Traditionally, *hybrids* (indicated by ×) are treated as equal in rank to species and are included in lists of species. This book has well over 800 species and hybrids.

SUBSPECIES (plural *subspecies*; abbreviated *subsp.* or *ssp.*)
A geographic race. Just over a dozen are mentioned in this book.

VARIETAS (plural *varietates*; abbreviated *var.*)
A minor race not deserving subspecies status; or by some botanists considered interchangeable with that category. This book indicates over 30.

FORMA (plural *formæ*; abbreviated *f.*)
A seedling variation: a percentage of seedlings tend to exhibit a distinctive characteristic worth naming. 27 *formæ* are cited in this book.

If we add on the horticultural *cultivars*, then all told, over 1,400 different kinds or "taxa" of trees are treated in this book. Living examples are cited of 550 different cultivars in Seattle. In addition, 47 cultivars are mentioned by name though no exact location is supplied. If that was not enough, dozens of other cultivars are known to have been sold at local nurseries recently—though did not get included in this edition for one reason or another. Seattle has an immense diversity of trees; cataloging this diversity is a major challenge.

Hybrid ALMOND;
Prunus × persicoides.
Blooming in March.

Japanese ANGELICA
TREE; *Aralia elata.*
Late July flowers.

Red ALDER; *Alnus rubra.*
Showing its red.

Japanese APRICOT; *Prunus Mume* 'Dawn'. Blooming in March.

ARBORVITÆ; *Thuja occidentalis* 'Fastigiata'. Greek Orthodox Church.

European ASH; *Fraxinus excelsior* 'Jaspidea'. Yellow in late September.

Manna ASH; *Fraxinus Ornus*. Blooming in May.

European BEECH; *Fagus sylvatica* f. *purpurea*. Lake View Cemetery.

European BEECH; *Fagus sylvatica* f. *purpurea*. U.W. Art building; mid-May.

Paper BIRCH; *Betula papyrifera*. Calvary Cemetery; mid-March.

New Zealand CABBAGE TREE;
Cordyline australis. Flowering in late May.

CASCARA; *Rhamnus Purshiana*.
An old large trunk

White BIRCH; *Betula pendula*.
Interlaken Park; 110½' tall.

Yellow BIRCH; *Betula alleghaniensis*. U.W.

Atlas CEDAR; *Cedrus atlantica* 'Glauca'.
Lake View Cemetery.

Northern CATALPA; *Catalpa speciosa*. 37th
Ave E, south of E Madison St; early July.

Incense CEDAR; *Calocedrus decurrens*.
Lincoln Park.

Deodar CEDAR; *Cedrus Deodara.*. Leschi Park.

Birchbark CHERRY; *Prunus serrula.*
35th Ave.

Bitter CHERRY; *Prunus emarginata.* Early May
flowers.

Japanese CEDAR; *Cryptomeria japonica.*
Denny Blaine Park.

Western Red CEDAR; *Thuja plicata*
'Zebrina'. Locks bed #123.

Weeping CHERRY; *Prunus pendula* 'Pendula Rubra'. Lake View Cemetery.

Yoshino CHERRY; *Prunus ×yedoensis*. U.W. Liberal Arts Quad; late March.

Korean Hill-CHERRY; *Prunus verecunda*. Ravenna Park; late October fall color. Cut down in 2005.

Japanese Hill-CHERRY; *Prunus Jamasakura*. Early March

'Amanogawa' Japanese Flowering CHERRY. 1916 E Blaine St; April.

'Kwanzan' Japanese Flowering CHERRY. Showing Mazzard rootstock; April.

'Tanko-shinju' Japanese Flowering CHERRY. Green Lake.

Weeping CHERRY; *Prunus pendula*. 6820 Phinney Ave N; mid-March.

CRABAPPLE; *Malus × atrosanguinea.*
U.W. late March.

CHINA-FIR; *Cunninghamia lanceolata.*
2218 32nd Ave S.

CRABAPPLE; *Malus* 'Hopa'. U.W.;
late March flower display.

CRABAPPLE; *Malus* 'Golden Hornet'.
Fruit in mid-October.

CRABAPPLE; *Malus ioensis* 'Plena'. Early May flowers.

CRABAPPLE; *Malus* 'Pink Beauty'. U.W. late March flower display.

CRABAPPLE; *Malus* 'Dolgo'. U.W. early April flowers.

CRABAPPLE; *Malus × purpurea* 'Lemoinei'. Late March flower display.

Bald CYPRESS; *Taxodium distichum.*
Green Lake; early November color.

Lawson CYPRESS; *Chamæcyparis Lawsoniana* 'Ellwoodii', 1743 26th Ave E.

CYPRESS; *Chamæcyparis Lawsoniana*
'Erecta Viridis'. Calvary Cemetery.

CRAPE-MYRTLE; *Lagerstrœmia indica.*
Flowers in mid-September.

EMPRESS TREE; *Paulownia tomentosa* 'Lilacina'. Arboretum; early May flowers.

LAWSON CYPRESS

'Westermannii'. Calvary Cemetery.

'Fraseri'. 2158 E Shelby St.

'Wisselii'. Sunnyside Ave N & N 40th St.

Sawara CYPRESS; *Chamæcyparis pisifera* f. *squarrosa* 'Boulevard'. 4548 NE Tulane PL.

Hybrid Pacific DOGWOOD; *Cornus* 'Eddie's White Wonder'. Flowers in late April.

Sawara CYPRESS; *Chamæcyparis pisifera* 'Plumosa Aurescens'. Lake View Cemetery.

Pacific DOGWOOD; *Cornus Nuttallii*. April flowers

American ELM;
Ulmus americana. 25th Ave &
E Columbia St.

FIG TREE; *Ficus Carica.*
Seattle's largest; January.

Snow Gum EUCALYPT; *Eucalyptus pauciflora* ssp. *niphophila.*

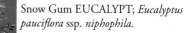

Eastern DOGWOOD; *Cornus
florida* f. *rubra.* Calvary Cemetery;
late April bloom.

Douglas FIR; *Pseudotsuga Menziesii*. O.O. Denny Park; 255' tall before it snapped.

Douglas FIR; *Pseudotsuga Menziesii* 'Pendula'. NE 155th St. opposite 9th Ave NE.

Grand FIR; *Abies grandis*. Arboretum.

Noble FIR; *Abies procera*. Late October cones.

Chilean FIRE-TREE; *Embothrium coccineum.*
Scarlet flowers in June.

GINKGO; *Ginkgo biloba.*
Early November fall color.

White FIR; *Abies concolor.*
Pretty bluish foliage.

Hybrid GOLDENCHAIN; *Laburnum
× Watereri.* Arboretum; mid-May.

Downy HAWTHORN; *Cratægus mollis*. Fall color in early October.

Common HAWTHORN; *Cratægus monogyna* 'Pendula'. With a 'Paul's Scarlet'; mid-May.

Eastern HEMLOCK; *Tsuga canadensis*. Calvary Cemetery.

English HOLLY; *Ilex Aquifolium*. Red berries in winter.

California Buckeye (HORSE-CHESTNUT); *Æ. californica*. Locks #126; mid-July full bloom.

Chinese JUNIPER; *Juniperus chinensis* 'Oblonga'. U.W.

Eastern Red Cedar (JUNIPER); *Juniperus virginiana* f. *glauca*. Brooklyn Ave NE & NE 52nd St.

Himalaya HORSE-CHESTNUT; *Æsculus indica*. Locks #11; early June full bloom.

KATSURA; *Cercidiphyllum japonicum.*
Late October fall color.

Black LOCUST; *Robinia Pseudoacacia.* An old
rotting trunk 13½ feet around.

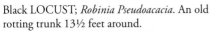

Tree LILAC; *Syringa reticulata* ssp. *pekinensis*
Summer Charm®. Early June.

LOQUAT; *Eriobotrya japonica.*
Late October flowers.

Galaxy MAGNOLIA; *Magnolia* 'Galaxy'.
Early April.

Sargent MAGNOLIA; *Magnolia Sargentiana*. 37th Ave E & E Ward St; mid-March.

Japanese Silverleaf MAGNOLIA;
M. hypoleuca. Late May.

MADRONA; *Arbutus Menziesii.*
Our most colorful native species.

Japanese MAPLE; *Acer palmatum* 'Sango Kaku'.
A young tree in winter.

Paperbark MAPLE; *Acer griseum*. Washelli
Cemetery.

Stripebark MAPLE; *Acer tegmentosum*.
Several species bear such bark.

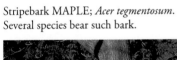

Sugar MAPLE; *Acer saccharum*.
Fall color in mid-October.

MONKEY TREE; *Araucaria Araucana*.
A male specimen.

White MULBERRY; *Morus alba*.
U.W. campus; mid-November.

MOUNTAIN ASH; *Sorbus Forrestii*.
Early October white berries.

MOUNTAIN ASH; *Sorbus americana*
Red Cascade™. Early October red berries.

California Valley OAK; *Quercus lobata*.
S.P.U.; late April.

Daimyo OAK; *Quercus dentata*.
Green Lake; early Novenber.

English OAK; *Quercus robur*.
Kinnear Park; early fall.

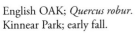

Oregon White OAK; *Quercus Garryana*.
Capitol Hill; late April.

Canyon Live OAK; *Quercus chrysolepis*. Locks bed #1; July 2005.

PALM; *Trachycarpus Fortunei*. Berries on a female tree.

Callery PEAR; *Pyrus Calleryana*. 22nd Ave E; mid-November.

Scarlet OAK; *Quercus coccinea*. Zoo; early October.

Japanese Red PINE; *Pinus densiflora.*
Ravenna Park.

Cluster PINE; *Pinus Pinaster.*
Zoo, on Phinney Ave N.

Montezuma PINE; *Pinus Montezumæ.*
U.W. Friendship Grove.

PERSIAN IRONWOOD; *Parrotia persica.* 1637
22nd Ave E; early November.

Hybrid PLANE; *Platanus × hispanica.*
Green Lake; mid-November.

Cherry PLUM; *Prunus cerasifera* 'Pissardii'.
26th Ave E; mid-March.

Sugar PINE; *Pinus
Lambertiana.* U.W.

Stone PINE; *Pinus Pinea.*
Arboretum.

Aspen (POPLAR); *Populus tremuloides.*
Flushing in late April.

Ghost (Black) POPLAR; *Populus nigra* 'Afghanica'. U.W.; winter.

Hybrid Black POPLAR; *Populus × canadensis* 'Robusta'. Magnolia Playfield; early November.

Weeping Simon POPLAR; *Populus Simonii* 'Pendula'. Lake Wash. Blvd. E; early April.

SILK TREE;
Albizia Julibrissin.
Bagley Ave N;
early August.

SERVICE-
BERRY;
Amelanchier
spp. Arbo-
retum; late
October.

Cottonwood
(POPLAR);
Populus balsam-ifera ssp.
trichocarpa.
Boren Park;
over 150' tall;
winter.

SMOKE TREE;
Cotinus Cog-gygria. 32nd Ave
NW; early July.

Tree PRIVET; *Ligustrum lucidum*.
U.W.; early August.

Judas Tree (RED-BUD); *Cercis Siliquastrum*.
Cal Anderson Park; early May.

Coast REDWOOD; *Sequoia sempervirens*.
Interlaken Park; 165½ feet tall.

REDBUD; *Cercis canadensis* 'Forest Pansy'. 32nd Ave NW.

Colorado SPRUCE; *Picea pungens* f. *glauca*.
Kubota Garden Park.

Sierra REDWOOD; *Sequoiadendron giganteum*.
Green Lake; the tallest is 114'.

SASSAFRAS; *Sassafras albidum*. Arboretum;
late October (by a 144' tall Sierra Redwood).

SORREL TREE; *Oxydendrum arboreum*. U.W.;
early November.

Sitka SPRUCE; *Picea sitchensis.*
Lake View Cemetery; 85½ feet tall.

Common STEWARTIA; *Stewartia Pseudocamellia.* Arboretum.

TULIP TREE; *Liriodendron Tulipifera.*
Green Lake; early November.

TUPELO; *Nyssa sylvatica.* 14th Ave E,
north of E Roy St; early November.

Corkscrew WILLOW; *Salix Matsudana* 'Tortuosa'. Montlake Playfield; late March.

Hooker Pussy-WILLOW; *Salix Hookeriana.* U.W.; late February.

Pacific YEW; *Taxus brevifolia*. Lincoln Park.

YEW-PINE; *Podocarpus macrophyllus.* 17th Ave E & E Harrison St.

Native Trees, Naturalized Trees

A "native" has a natural range covering our area and is currently growing wild in Seattle, in a natural setting. A "former native" is on record as wild here once, but now seems only to exist as planted. A "possible native" has not been recorded wild here but may exist, since it is a native in similar localities. Below are listed 33 trees treated in this guide which WERE, ARE, or MAY BE native in Seattle.

Red ALDER	*Alnus rubra*
Sitka ALDER	*Alnus sinuata*
Oregon ASH	*Fraxinus latifolia*
Paper BIRCH	*Betula papyrifera*
CASCARA	*Rhamnus Purshiana*
Western Red CEDAR	*Thuja plicata*
Bitter CHERRY	*Prunus emarginata*
Pacific CRABAPPLE	*Malus fusca*
Pacific DOGWOOD	*Cornus Nuttallii*
Douglas FIR	*Pseudotsuga Menziesii*
Grand FIR	*Abies grandis*
Black HAWTHORN	*Cratægus Douglasii*
Shortspine Black HAWTHORN	*Cratægus Suksdorfii*
Western HEMLOCK	*Tsuga heterophylla*
MADRONA	*Arbutus Menziesii*
Bigleaf MAPLE	*Acer macrophyllum*
Dwarf MAPLE	*Acer glabrum*
Vine MAPLE	*Acer circinatum*
Oregon White OAK	*Quercus Garryana*
Lodgepole/Shore PINE	*Pinus contorta*
Western White PINE	*Pinus monticola*
Aspen (POPLAR)	*Populus tremuloides*
Black Cottonwood (POPLAR)	*Populus balsamifera* ssp. *trichocarpa*
Western SERVICEBERRY	*Amelanchier alnifolia*
Sitka SPRUCE	*Picea sitchensis*
Geyer WILLOW	*Salix Geyeriana* var. *meleina*
Mackenzie WILLOW	*Salix eriocephala* ssp. *mackenzieana*
Pacific Black WILLOW	*Salix lucida* ssp. *lasiandra*
Hooker Pussy-WILLOW	*Salix Hookeriana*
Piper Pussy-WILLOW	*Salix Piperi*
Scouler Pussy-WILLOW	*Salix Scouleriana*
Sitka Pussy-WILLOW	*Salix sitchensis*
Pacific YEW	*Taxus brevifolia*

Naturalized trees are not natives but grow *wild* here, reproducing side by side in a natural state with our natives. A non-native species that reseeds or tosses up some persistent root-suckers is not considered a naturalized tree. Strictly speaking, "naturalized" means "reproducing in the wild": second-generation offspring must be produced.

When a tree has reseeded on a large scale, but none of its offspring are mature enough to reseed themselves, it may be described as "apparently becoming naturalized." When a naturalized tree either coexists with natives or out-competes them, it is called "thoroughly" or "fully" or even "rampantly" naturalized.

Another way of looking at it is to call some trees *original* natives, and to call the naturalized kinds *new* (or recent) natives. Even so, we cannot consider a wild acorn-grown English Oak in a Seattle park, a "Seattle native" quite as justly as its cousin the Oregon White Oak, whose parents and ancestors have lived here for thousands of years. And certainly precision and convenience argue well for maintaining separate lists of native and naturalized plants.

1) Naturalized on a city-wide scale, and spreading. Except for the birch and oak, which thrive only in sunshine, these can be found in natural woods, including our old-growth forests:

White BIRCH	Norway MAPLE
Mazzard CHERRY	Sycamore MAPLE
Common HAWTHORN	MOUNTAIN ASH
English HOLLY	English OAK
English LAUREL	English YEW

2) Here to stay, and even spreading, due primarily to powerful, persistent root-sucker regeneration:

English ELM	Lombardy (Black) POPLAR
Black LOCUST	White POPLAR
Common European PLUM	TREE OF HEAVEN

3) Locally well-established, but overall of secondary importance. These all reseed successfully except for Bigleaf Linden which is reproducing primarily from root-suckers.

APPLE	GOLDENCHAIN TREE
Black CHERRY	Portugal LAUREL
European CHESTNUT	Bigleaf LINDEN
European HORNBEAM	Black WALNUT
Common HORSE CHESTNUT	English WALNUT

Scores of other trees reseed here on a minor scale.

Shrubs that can be Trees...

The closer a person looks, the more arbitrary the everyday distinction between "trees" and "shrubs" seems to be. In Nature there is no clear division, but a continuum of diverse forms ranging in size from tiny to immense. Size and form vary greatly not only with the plant's genetic heritage but also with its location, its age, and its history—especially its history of human interference in transplanting, grafting, pruning, fertilizing, *etc.* Even *vines* such as wisteria are sometimes forced into tree form.

Because most Seattle yards are too small for large trees, this book makes a special effort to present information about very small trees as well as the usual large ones. Specifically, some rather shrubby representatives of tree genera have been included as a matter of interest and for the sake of completeness, as well as some kinds so rare or so recently introduced in Seattle that their ultimate size here remains to be seen. Meanwhile the examples cited may hardly look like trees in the everyday sense. Some plants that routinely assume tree form in other climates may be left out, however, if they are only seen in a shrubby state in Seattle with no likelihood of assuming tree form here.

Finally, some plants that are commonly thought of as shrubs may actually be trees in their own right but are usually pruned into a shrubby state: English Laurel is an outstanding example. As long as the question of shrub or tree is recognized as a problem of terminology rather than a matter of scientific accuracy, the reader should be able to enjoy the guide untroubled.

There are many species that are shrubby in Seattle except for a few quite treelike specimens. Eight genera are singled out here:

Box (*Buxus sempervirens* L.) BUXACEÆ is from Europe, N Africa & W Asia. It tolerates deepest shade, close shearing, and symbolizes stoicism. It is common; many cultivars exist. Baker Park (8347 14th Ave NW) has one 23' tall on the west side of the park. 6008 50th Ave NE has one 19½' by the street light.

Camellia. THEACEÆ are varied E Asian species and hybrids. Some are very familiar here. The U.W. has a *C. reticulata* 26½' × 1'10¼" west of Winkenwerder Hall. The SW corner of 5234 Brooklyn Ave NE has a 24' tall *C. Sasanqua* tree with fragrant pink flowers in winter. A treelike common *C. japonica* is 22' tall at 3521 Woodlawn Ave N.

Cornel. Bloodtwig Dogwood (*Cornus sanguinea* L.) CORNACEÆ is from Europe. In the early 1900s it was planted much in Seattle; now it runs wild. The U.W. has one 29' × 1'9½" near the top of Island Lane, and a 2nd SE of Guggenheim Hall is 16' × 1'11".

Cotoneaster. ROSACEÆ mostly E Asian, are broadleaf evergreen or deciduous, and prized for their profuse red berries. Volunteer Park's south border has one 30½' × 1'1¼"—it is a *C. frigidus* hybrid.

Elder *(Sambucus)* CAPRIFOLIACEÆ are widespread and two species are native in Seattle. In 1993 a European Black Elder *(S. nigra)* in Ballard was 28' × 4'2" but was cut. A 2nd Black Elder 30½' × 1'7½" in Volunteer Park was cut down in 2005. The Zoo has a planted example of our native Blue Elder *(S. cerulea)* 25' tall—*not yet* cut down.

Oldwood (*Leucosidea sericea* Eckl. & Zeyh.) ROSACEÆ is from S Africa. About 1986 it was planted planted in bed #8 at the Locks, where it is now 18' tall. It has attractive pale yellow flowers, silky compound leaves, and shreddy red-brown bark.

Rhododendron. ERICACEÆ is a large diverse genus. Well known; overplanted here. The tallest I've measured is one in the Arboretum (23-1E) labeled "#?1273-40 *R. Fortunei* hybrid" that is 40' × 2'3¼". Mt. Pleasant Cemetery has a *Rhododendron catawbiense* hybrid in the SE part, south of the forested middle border; it is 20' × 3'11½" × 23' wide.

Pacific WAX-MYRTLE or Bayberry (*Myrica californica* Cham. & Schlecht.) MYRICACEÆ is a broadleaf evergreen from the coastal strip of SW Washington to S California. It tolerates any sunlight level or soil, and is useful as a shrub or small tree. One on the NE corner of Peterson Hall at S.P.U. is 30' × 3'4½" × 30' wide.

Calendar of Tree Features in Seattle

Calendars such as this are only approximate since trees vary in flowering and fruiting times according to the year and other factors such as their exact location. Specimens of our native Bitter Cherry have been found flowering in Seattle from mid-March into early June—but in the calendar only May is given as its period because the majority of specimens are in full bloom in that month. Rare and common trees are included, as well as both showy and inconspicuous flowers. However, it is far from a *complete* account.

January

Little worth observing happens in early January, but in years when the latter part of the month has a warm spell, some tree flowers begin opening: Japanese Apricot (white to pink or red); Cornelian-Cherry Dogwood (yellow); Hazel (catkins); Persian Ironwood (red); and most reliably of all, the autumn–winter blooming Higan Cherry (pale pink). A few crabapple trees still have lovely fruits, such as Ormiston Roy and Red Jewell.

February

The same trees that began flowering in January are now even more advanced and showier. Other trees displaying flowers or catkins include: Alder (catkins); Almond (white or palest pink); Apricots (palest pink); Azara (tiny, vanilla-scented); the earliest cherries such as the 'Hally Jolivette' (white), 'Whitcomb' Higan (pink), and Okamé (pink); American Elm (tiny); Japanese Cedar (pollen); Campbell Magnolia (dark pink, or white); Silver Maple (tiny, red); the earliest plums, namely the Cherry Plum (white), 'Blireiana' (dark pink) and 'Pissardii' (white or palest pink); Coast Redwood (pollen); Pussy Willow (catkins); Yew (pollen).

March

Mid-March to mid-April is a very busy time for our spring-flowering trees. Showy flowers: Almond (white or palest pink); Apricot (palest pink); many cherries: 'Hally Jolivette' (white), single-flowered weeping Higan (pale pink), 'Whitcomb' Higan (pink), 'Shirotae' Japanese (pure white), Sargent (pink), 'Accolade' (pink) and Yoshino (pale pink); Cornelian-Cherry Dogwood (yellow); Campbell, Galaxy, Sargent, Star, Yulan & Veitch Magnolias (pure white through deep pink); Callery Pear (white); Persian Ironwood (red); all sorts of plums (whites and pinks); non-native Serviceberries begin (white); Pussy Willows continue.

Less showy flowers: pollen of Japanese Cedar, Lawson Cypress, Western Hemlock, Coast & Sierra Redwoods, English Yew; catkins of Alders, Hornbeams and Poplars; tiny flowers of Elms, the Box-elder and Red Maples. Deodar Cedar is shedding needles; its new shoots are flushing. Larches, Tulip Tree and others green up. Cottonwood (Poplar) bud scales drop and are sticky and fragrant.

April

April is even more floriferous than March. Orchard apple begins (white); many cherries: Goldbark (white), Japanese (white, yellow, pinks), Mazzard (white), 'Akebono' Yoshino (pink); most Crabapples (white, pink or red); our native Dogwood (white); Dove Tree begins (white); Empress Tree (lavender); the common Goldenchain begins (yellow); Horse Chestnut begins (white); Bay & English Laurels (yellow & white); Madrona (white); Kobus (white) and various cultivars of Saucer Magnolia (white to deep rose); Bigleaf Maple (yellow); Mountain Ash (creamy white); Peach (pink to red); Pear (white); Chinese Photinia (white); Pittosporum (varies); 'Newport' Plum is the last purpleleaf plum to bloom (palest pink); Quince (palest pink); Redbud (pink); our native Serviceberry begins (white); Silverbell (white); Tamarisk (pink).

Less showy flowers: Beech; Hackberry; Holly; Hornbeam (catkins); Vine Maple (red & white); Oregon Myrtle (yellow); pine pollen; poplar catkins; weeping willow (catkins); elm seeds start scattering everywhere.

May

Many trees that began blooming in April are still displaying in May. Manna Ash (white); New Zealand Cabbage Tree (white); Cascara (tiny, dull); Bird Cherry, Bitter Cherry, Black Cherry & 'Shogetsu' Japanese Cherry (all white); the native crabapple comes into full bloom (white) as continue many non-native kinds; Eastern Dogwood (white or pink); Giant Dogwood (creamy white); Pacific Dogwood (slackening its white pace); Dove Tree (white); elm seeds everywhere; Empress Tree (lavender); Epaulette Tree (white); Spinning-Gum Eucalypt (white); Chilean Fire-Tree (scarlet); Ginkgo (look now if you wish to tell male from female); Goldenchain (yellow); Hawthorns (white or pink or red); English Holly (tiny, white); Horse Chestnut, and Red & Yellow Buckeyes (white, red, and yellow); English Laurel continues (white); Black Locust and its hybrids (white or pink); Madrona (white); Cucumber-Tree Magnolia (green); Japanese-Silverleaf Magnolia and Umbrella-Tree Magnolia (both white); Medlar (white); Mountain Ash (creamy white); White Mulberry (green); Palm (yellow); Pawpaw (purplish); pine pollen; cottonwood and poplar cotton litter; Rehder Tree (white); Sassafras (yellow, tiny); Silverbell continues (white); Smoke Tree in late May (beige); Bigleaf Snowbell (white); Tamarisk (pink); Tulip Tree (green); Wheel Tree (green).

June

The frantic pace of May slackens in June to a level not so overwhelming. By the last week the first edible fruits are to be expected: cherries, hazelnuts (the bushy native species) and serviceberries; loquats may be ready too.

Manna Ash (white); Mount Ætna Broom (yellow); Northern Catalpa (white); Chilean Fire-Tree (scarlet); Kousa Dogwood (white tinged with pink in age); Washington is the last hawthorn to bloom (white); Hop Tree (greenish-white); Himalayan Horsechestnut (white); Portugal Laurel (white); Tree Lilacs (white); Bigleaf Linden is the first of its clan to flower (yellow, tiny); Black Locust and its hybrids continue (white to pink and rosy-purple); Cucumber-Tree, (green); Evergreen, Sweet-Bay, Umbrella-Tree, and Watson Magnolia (all white); Osage Orange; Persimmon (tiny, whitish-yellow); Phellodendron (dull); cottonwood and poplar cotton litter continues; Russian Olive (tiny, yellow, fragrant); Japanese Snowbell (white); Stewartias begin (white); Yellow-wood (white).

July

More fruit ripens: cherries, Japanese apricots, Black Hawthorn berries, native (shrubby) hazelnuts, loquats, mulberries, plums and serviceberries. Madronas are shedding slippery leaves.

Flowers: all catalpas (white and one rare yellow kind); chestnuts (white); Tanbark-Oak Chinquapin (fragrant creamy-white spikes); Chitalpa (white or pink); Crinodendron begins (white); Kousa Dogwood still (white fading pinkish); Eucryphia begins (white); Euodia (white); Golden Rain Tree (yellow); California-Buckeye Horse Chestnut (white); lindens (yellow); Maackia (white); white magnolia flowers: Bigleaf, Evergreen, Umbrella-Tree, Sweet-Bay, and Watson; Silk Tree (rosy); Sorrel Tree (white); Stewartias continue (white); Summer-blooming Tamarisk (bushy) is pink; Tree of Heaven stinks with its greenish-white flowers.

August

The ripening fruit list grows very long. Not all of these are edible; some are merely showy: almonds, apples, apricots, Cascara berries, Black cherries, Cornelian-Cherry Dogwood fruit; fir cones are now conspicuous; Turkish hazelnuts; mountain ash berries are bright; mulberries; acorns begin to ripen; Osage oranges swell up large; peaches, pears, plums; Tree of Heaven seeds are yellow-green or often bright reddish; Heartnut walnuts are first of their group to ripen; yew berries redden. The native hemlock sheds its needles. The Smoke Tree is striking now.

Flowers: Angelica Tree (creamy white); catalpas continue; Chinese Scholar-Tree (white); Chitalpa continues (white or pink); Crinodendron (white); Pacific Dogwood's 2nd bloom begins; Eucryphia carries on (white); Euodia continues (white); Golden Rain Tree (yellow); Maackia (white); Yellow Cucumber-Tree Magnolia has a 2nd bloom (yellow); Saucer magnolias have had sporadic flowers all along, but add most in August (pink to white-striped purple); Peanut Butter Tree (white); Tree Privet (creamy white); California Redbud commences its 2nd bloom (deep pink); Silk Tree (rosy).

September

The fruit list stays long, the flower list shrinks, and certain trees start showing autumn color—a little bit of everything for tree lovers. Fruits: almonds, apples, Cascara berries, Atlas Cedar pollen cones, chestnuts, Cornelian-Cherry Dogwood fruit, Kousa Dogwood fruit, Pacific Dogwood fruit, figs, Ginkgo fruit, hawthorn berries, hickory nuts begin in late September, Honey Locust pods, Monkey Tree cones start disintegrating, mulberries, acorns, peaches, pears, plums, quinces, Butternut & Heartnut walnuts, yew berries.

Flowers: Angelica Tree continues (berries ripening too); Chinese Scholar-Tree continues (white); Chitalpa continues (white or pink); Crinodendron continues (white); Crape-Myrtle (white, pink or red); Pacific Dogwood's 2nd bloom continues (white); some Kousa Dogwoods also have a 2nd bloom; Chinese & September Elms have tiny flowers; the bushy Franklin Tree is gorgeous (white); the bushy Strawberry-Tree Madrona has white flowers and red berries; Medlar's 2nd bloom; Peanut Butter Tree continues (white); Tree Privet (creamy white); California Redbud's 2nd bloom is strong (deep pink); Silk Tree (rosy).

White pines, Coast and Sierra Redwoods are shedding now.

422

October

Few flowers are left: some Crape-Myrtle, Pacific Dogwood, the bushy Franklin Tree, and California Redbud.

Many fruits: apples and crabapples, Cascara berries, Deodar Cedar cones are showy; Euodia seed-clusters are worth a look; figs, hawthorns, hickories, hollies, Honey Locust pods, Madrona & Strawberry Tree berries; medlars are beginning to ripen; mountain ash, acorns, Osage oranges, pawpaws begin to approach ripeness; pears, persimmons, Piñon Pine seeds are ready; walnuts in increasing numbers; yew & Plum-Yew.

The Deodar Cedar pollen is shed, the native Western Red Cedar is dropping its old brown parts.

Fall color is everywhere—a select list is: 'Flame' Narrowleaf Ash (burgundy), Green & Oregon Ashes (yellow); Beeches (yellow-brown); Sweet & Yellow Birches (yellow); Sargent Cherry (red); American Elm (yellow); Ginkgo (yellow); Hickory (yellow); Horse Chestnut (yellow-brown); Katsura (rainbow of yellows & reds); Maples (all colors); White Mulberry (yellow); Pin, White & other oaks (bright reds); Smoke Tree (a riot); Sorrel Tree (crimson); Stewartia (pastel reds, oranges, yellow); Sumach (screaming red, orange or yellow); Sweetgum (variable from pure yellow or red to a mixture—or still green); Tulip Tree (yellow); Tupelo (scarlet); Yellow-wood (yellow); Zelkova (yellow to rusty-red).

See the fall color lists on pp. 429-31 for more information.

November

About the only tree flowering in November is the autumn Higan Cherry. Fruit still showy or edible: apples and crabapples, Madrona berries, medlars, pears, persimmons, walnuts, and yew berries.

Trees still quite colorful include: European Ash (weak yellow); Manna Ash (yellow to orange); Mazzard Cherry (yellow to red); Bald Cypress (bronzy-purple); Ginkgo (yellow); Hornbeam (yellow); Osage Orange (yellow); Callery Pear (red tints); Persian Ironwood (yellow to orange or red); Chinese Pistachio (yellows, red); Aspen & Cottonwood Poplars (yellow); Dawn Redwood (red-brown); Smoke Tree (as in October); Sweet Gum; Tulip Tree (yellow-gold); Tupelo (red).

December

Again, only the autumn Higan Cherry can be expected to flower bravely. The fruits still left to see or eat are few: crabapples, holly berries, Madrona berries, medlars, mountain ash berries. A few alders are still green, and some Cottonwood Poplars are still full of yellow leaves. In some wooded parks, sapling willows and Cascaras act evergreen. If we don't experience a very sharp cold, some deciduous trees will stubbornly hold many of their leaves.

Miscellaneous Lists

These lists categorize trees according to form and appearance, so can be useful in identifying trees. Only those trees mentioned in the guide are included.

1. **Bark** especially showy
2. **Broadleaf evergreen** trees
3. **Contorted** branches, twigs or leaves
4. **Corky**-ridged branches or twigs
5. **Deciduous conifers**
6. **Galls**
7. **Leaves** big, bold, coarse effect
8. **Leaves** compound palmately
9. **Leaves** compound pinnately
10. **Leaves** compound bipinnately
11. **Leaves** cutleaf, dissected variants
12. **Leaves** fall color
13. **Leaves** fragrant
14. **Leaves** late/slow to appear in spring
15. **Leaves** late/slow to drop in fall or winter
16. **Leaves** persisting brown and dead on the twigs
17. **Leaves** purplish-reddish
18. **Leaves** silvery, bluish, grayish
19. **Leaves** stinking
20. **Leaves** tiny and dainty
21. **Leaves** variegated
22. **Leaves** yellowish-golden
23. **Narrow** form: columnar variants
24. **Suckers** from the roots commonly
25. **Tender**, semi-hardy here
26. **Thorny**, prickly or bristly
27. **Weeping** form

1. **Bark** especially showy, eye-catching and conspicuous: not merely beautiful or interesting, but such that people will often notice or plant these trees largely for the bark.

BIRCH (most *Betula*)
Birchbark CHERRY (*Prunus serrula*)
Goldbark CHERRY (*Prunus Maackii*)
CRAPE-MYRTLE (*Lagerstrœmia indica*)
Arizona CYPRESS (*Cupressus arizonica glabra*)
Chinese ELM (*Ulmus parvifolia*)
EUCALYPT (most *Eucalyptus*)
Corkbark (Alpine) FIR (*Abies lasiocarpa arizonica*)
Shagbark HICKORY (*Carya ovata*)
California Buckeye (HORSE CHESTNUT) (*Æsculus californica*)
MADRONA (*Arbutus*)
Box-elder MAPLE (*Acer Negundo* 'Violaceum', 'Winter Lightning')
Paperbark MAPLE (*Acer griseum*)
Stripebark MAPLES (*Acer capillipes, Davidii, pensylvanicum, rufinerve, tegmentosum*)

Cork Tree (OAK) (*Quercus Suber*)
PERSIAN IRONWOOD (*Parrotia persica*)
PHŒNIX TREE (*Firmiana simplex*)
Lacebark PINE (*Pinus Bungeana*)
Bolleana (White) POPLAR (*Populus alba* 'Pyramidalis')
Chinese QUINCE (*Pseudocydonia sinensis*)
STEWARTIA (*Stewartia monadelpha, Pseudocamellia*)
Corkscrew WILLOW (*Salix* 'Golden Curls' / Scarlet Curls®)
Violet WILLOW (*Salix daphnoides*)

2. Broadleaf evergreen trees. The following are definitely, consistently evergreen here. For less consistently evergreen kinds see list 15.

ACACIA (*Acacia*)
AZARA (*Azara*)
Southern-BEECH (*Nothofagus Cunninghamii, Dombeyi, Solandri*)
Italian BUCKTHORN (*Rhamnus Alaternus*)
CABBAGE TREE (*Cordyline*)
Hollyleaf CHERRY (*Prunus ilicifolia* and hybrids)
CHINQUAPIN & kin (*Castanopsis cuspidata, Chrysolepis chrysophylla, Lithocarpus densiflorus, Lithocarpus edulis, Lithocarpus Henryi*)
CRINODENDRON (*Crinodendron Patagua*)
EUCALYPT (*Eucalyptus*)
EUCRYPHIA (all *Eucryphia* except *E. glutinosa*)
EURYA (*Eurya japonica*)
Chilean HAZEL (*Gevuina Avellana*)
HOHERIA (*Hoheria*)
HOLLY (*Ilex*)
Summer HOLLY (*Comarostaphylis diversifolia*)
HOP BUSH (*Dodonæa viscosa*)
Catalina IRONWOOD (*Lyonothamnus floribundus* f. *aspleniifolius*)
ISU TREE (*Distylium racemosum*)
JAPANESE BLUEBERRY TREE (*Elæocarpus sylvestris*)
KŌWHAI (*Sophora microphylla, tetraptera*)
Canary Island LAUREL (*Apollonias Barbujana*)
Bay LAUREL (*Laurus nobilis*)
Camphor LAUREL (*Cinnamomum Camphora, japonicum*)
English LAUREL (*Prunus Laurocerasus*)
Portugal LAUREL (*Prunus lusitanica*)
Silky LAUREL (*Neolitsea sericea*)
Yunnan LAUREL (*Machilus yunnanensis*)
LOQUAT (*Eriobotrya* and hybrids)
MADRONA and STRAWBERRY TREE (*Arbutus*)
Evergreen MAGNOLIA (*Magnolia grandiflora*)
Sweetbay MAGNOLIA (*Magnolia virginiana* var. *australis*)
MAGNOLIA relatives (*Manglietia, Michelia, Parakmeria*)
Syrian MAPLE (*Acer obtusifolium*)
MAYTEN (*Maytenus Boaria*)
Chilean MYRTLE (*Luma apiculata*)
Oregon MYRTLE (*Umbellularia californica*)
OAK (18 of 55 *Quercus*)

OLIVE (*Olea europæa*)
OSMANTHUS (*Osmanthus*)
PALM TREE (*Trachycarpus Fortunei*)—*all* palms
PHILLYREA (*Phillyrea*)
PHOTINIA (*Photinia* × *Fraseri, P. serratifolia*)
PITTOSPORUM (*Pittosporum*)
Japanese SPINDLE TREE (*Euonymus japonicus*)
African SUMACH (*Rhus lancea*)
SYCOPSIS (*Sycopsis sinensis*)
Tree PRIVET (*Ligustrum lucidum*)
WAX-MYRTLE (*Myrica californica*)
WHEEL TREE (*Trochodendron aralioides*)
WINTER'S BARK (*Drimys Winteri*)

3. Contorted branches, twigs or leaves: these twisted cultivars appear quite freakish when compared to regular specimens.

Japanese CEDAR (*Cryptomeria japonica* 'Cristata')
Hinoki CYPRESS (*Chamæcyparis obtusa* 'Coralliformis')
Leyland CYPRESS (*Cupressus* × *Leylandii* 'Picturesque')
Pink HAWTHORN (*Cratægus lævigata* 'Pink Corkscrew')
English LAUREL (*Prunus Laurocerasus* 'Camelliæfolia')
Black LOCUST (*Robinia Pseudoacacia* 'Tortuosa' and Twisty Baby™ / 'Lace Lady')
White MULBERRY TREE (*Morus alba* 'Unryu')
Eastern White PINE (*Pinus Strobus* 'Torulosa')
Corkscrew WILLOW (*Salix Matsudana* 'Tortuosa' and *S.* 'Golden Curls' / Scarlet Curls®)
Ringleaf WILLOW (*Salix babylonica* 'Crispa')

4. Corky-ridged branches or twigs sometimes present.

Largeleaf EHRETIA (*Ehretia Dicksonii*)
English ELM (*Ulmus minor* var. *vulgaris*)
Hybrid ELM (*Ulmus* × *hollandica*)
Winged ELM (*Ulmus alata*)
English MAPLE (*Acer campestre*)
Bur OAK (*Quercus macrocarpa*)
SWEETGUM (*Liquidambar Styraciflua*)

5. Deciduous conifers.

Bald CYPRESS (*Taxodium distichum*)
LARCH & Tamarack (*Larix, Pseudolarix*)
Dawn REDWOOD (*Metasequoia glyptostroboides*)

6. Galls—a selective list of some commoner galls; many other kinds exist.

Alpine FIR (*Abies lasiocarpa*) twigs
Bigleaf LINDEN (*Tilia platyphyllos*) leaves
Oregon White OAK (*Quercus Garryana*) twigs and leaves
Black Cottonwood (POPLAR) (*Populus balsamifera* ssp. *trichocarpa*) twigs and leaves
Lombardy (Black) POPLAR (*Populus nigra* 'Italica') leafstalks
Norway SPRUCE (*Picea Abies*) twigs
Sitka SPRUCE (*Picea sitchensis*) twigs
WILLOW (all native *Salix* except *S. Hookeriana*) twigs and leaves

7. **Leaves** Big and bold; a coarse effect, often affording an aspect of tropical luxuriance.

Castor ARALIA (*Kalopanax septemlobus*)
CABBAGE TREE (*Cordyline*)
CATALPA (*Catalpa*)
Largeleaf EHRETIA (*Ehretia Dicksonii*)
EMMENOPTERYS (*Emmenopterys Henryi*)
EMPRESS TREE (*Paulownia tomentosa*)
FIG (*Ficus Carica*)
Chilean HAZEL (*Gevuina Avellana*)
HICKORY (*Carya*)
IDESIA (*Idesia polycarpa*)
Basswood (LINDEN) (*Tilia americana, heterophylla*)
LOQUAT (*Eriobotrya japonica*)
MAGNOLIA (*Magnolia acuminata, hypoleuca, macrophylla, tripetala*)
MALLOTUS (*Mallotus japonicus*)
Bigleaf MAPLE (*Acer macrophyllum*)
Persian MAPLE (*Acer velutinum*)
Sargent MOUNTAIN-ASH (*Sorbus Sargentiana*)
Paper MULBERRY (*Broussonetia papyrifera*)
Bur OAK (*Quercus macrocarpa*)
Daimyo OAK (*Quercus dentata*)
Red OAK (*Quercus rubra*)
PALM (*Trachycarpus Fortunei*)—and other kinds
PAWPAW (*Asimina triloba*)
PHŒNIX TREE (*Firmiana simplex*)
Bigcone PINE (*Pinus Coulteri*)
Montezuma PINE (*Pinus Montezumæ*)
PLANE (*Platanus*)
Black Cottonwood (POPLAR) (*Populus balsamifera* ssp. *trichocarpa*)
Bigleaf SNOWBELL TREE (*Styrax Obassia*)
SUMACH (*Rhus*)
TREE OF HEAVEN (*Ailanthus altissima*)
TULIP TREE (*Liriodendron tulipifera*)
WALNUT, Heartnut & Butternut (*Juglans*)
WINGNUT (*Pterocarya*)
YELLOW-WOOD (*Cladrastis kentukea*)

8. **Leaves** compound palmately or digitately, including "pinnately trifoliate" (hand-shaped) leaves.

   A) Opposite-budded:
EUCRYPHIA (*Eucryphia × nymansensis*)
HORSE CHESTNUT & Buckeye (*Æsculus*)
Nikko MAPLE (*Acer Maximowiczianum*)
Paperbark MAPLE (*Acer griseum*)
Roughbarked MAPLE (*Acer triflorum*)
Vineleaf MAPLE (*Acer cissifolium*)

   B) Alternate-budded:
GOLDENCHAIN TREE (*Laburnum*)
HOP TREE (*Ptelea trifoliata*)
PALM (*Trachycarpus Fortunei*)
African SUMACH (*Rhus lancea*)

9. **Leaves** compound pinnately.

   A) Opposite-budded:
ASH (*Fraxinus*)
EUCRYPHIA (*Eucryphia glutinosa*)
EUODIA (*Tetradium*)
Box-Elder MAPLE (*Acer Negundo*)
PHELLODENDRON (*Phellodendron*)

   B) Alternate-budded (*abuptly* or *evenly* pinnate):
Honey LOCUST (*Gleditsia triacanthos*)
KŌWHAI (*Sophora microphylla, tetraptera*)
Chinese PISTACHIO (*Pistacia chinensis*)
Chinese TOON (*Toona sinensis*)

   C) Alternate-budded (*oddly* pinnate):
CHINESE SCHOLAR-TREE (*Sophora japonica*)
HICKORY & Pecan (*Carya*)
LOCUST (*Gleditsia* & *Robinia*)
MAACKIA (*Maackia*)
MOUNTAIN ASH (*Sorbus*)
PLATYCARYA (*Platycarya strobilacea*)
SUMACH (*Rhus*)
TREE OF HEAVEN (*Ailanthus altissima*)
WALNUT, Heartnut & Butternut (*Juglans*)
WINGNUT (*Pterocarya*)
WISTERIA—a common vine sometimes trained into tree form
YELLOW-HORN (*Xanthoceras sorbifolia*)
YELLOW-WOOD (*Cladrastis kentukea*)
ZANTHOXYLUM (*Zanthoxylum*)

10. Leaves compound bipinnately or "doubly pinnate" or "twice pinnate."

ACACIA (*Acacia Baileyana, A. dealbata*)
ANGELICA TREE (*Aralia elata, A. spinosa*)
CHINABERRY (*Melia Azedarach*)
GOLDEN RAIN TREE (*Koelreuteria*)
Chilean HAZEL (*Gevuina Avellana*)
KENTUCKY COFFEE-TREE (*Gymnocladus dioicus*)
Honey LOCUST (*Gleditsia triacanthos*)—partly
SILK TREE (*Albizia Julibrissin*)

11. Leaves cutleaf, dissected variants.

Red ALDER (*Alnus rubra* f. *pinnatisecta*)
European BEECH (*Fagus sylvatica* 'Asplenifolia')
White BIRCH (*Betula pendula* 'Crispa')
Alder BUCKTHORN (*Rhamnus Frangula* 'Asplenifolia')
CHINQUAPIN & kin (*Lithocarpus densiflorus* f. *attenuato-dentatus*)
European HORNBEAM (*Carpinus Betulus* 'Incisa')
Catalina IRONWOOD (*Lyonothamnus floribundus* f. *aspleniifolius*)
Full Moon MAPLE (*Acer japonicum* 'Aconitifolium')
Japanese MAPLE (*Acer palmatum*)—several cultivars
Norway MAPLE (*Acer platanoides* 'Green Lace')
Sugar MAPLE (*Acer saccharum* 'Sweet Shadow')
Staghorn SUMACH (*Rhus typhina* 'Dissecta')

12. Leaves fall color (categories adapted from Wilson Flagg).

A) Little or no color, at best weakly yellow:
ALDER (*Alnus*)
Castor ARALIA (*Kalopanax septemlobus*)
European ASH (*Fraxinus excelsior*)
CHITALPA (× *Chitalpa*)
CHINESE SCHOLAR-TREE (*Sophora japonica*)
EMPRESS TREE (*Paulownia tomentosa*)
FIG (*Ficus Carica*)
GOLDENCHAIN TREE (*Laburnum*)
HARDY RUBBER-TREE (*Eucommia ulmoides*)
Silver LINDEN (*Tilia tomentosa*)
Black LOCUST & its hybrids (*Robinia*)
MAACKIA (*Maackia*)
MAGNOLIA (*Magnolia*)
English OAK (*Quercus robur*)
PAWPAW (*Asimina triloba*)
White POPLAR (*Populus alba*)
RUSSIAN OLIVE (*Elæagnus angustifolia*)
SILK TREE (*Albizia Julibrissin*)
SNOWBELL TREE (*Styrax japonicus*)
SPUR LEAF (*Tetracentron sinense*)
TAMARISK (*Tamarix*)
WILLOW (*Salix*)

B) Varying shades of purple, crimson, scarlet, orange & yellow:

European BEECH (*Fagus sylvatica*)
CHERRY (*Prunus avium*) cultivars & hybrids
Pacific CrabAPPLE (*Malus fusca*)
Washington HAWTHORN (*Cratægus Phænopyrum*)
Yellow Buckeye (HORSE CHESTNUT) (*Æsculus octandra*)
KATSURA (*Cercidiphyllum japonicum*)
Red MAPLE (*Acer rubrum*)
Sugar MAPLE (*Acer saccharum*)
Vine MAPLE (*Acer circinatum*)
MOUNTAIN ASH (*Sorbus aucuparia*)
PERSIAN IRONWOOD (*Parrotia persica*)
Chinese PISTACHIO (*Pistacia chinensis*)
SASSAFRAS (*Sassafras albidum*)
SERVICEBERRY (*Amelanchier*)—most; not our native species
SMOKE TREE (*Cotinus*)
STEWARTIA (*Stewartia*)

C) Green, with mixtures of red, purple, or yellow:

APPLE (*Malus domestica*)
APRICOT (*Prunus Armeniaca*)
DOGWOOD (most *Cornus*)
HAWTHORN (most *Cratægus*)
PEACH (*Prunus Persica*)
PEAR (*Pyrus*)
PERSIMMON (*Diospyros*)
PLUM (*Prunus domestica*)
QUINCE (*Cydonia* & *Pseudocydonia*)
SWEETGUM (*Liquidambar Styraciflua*)

D) Reddish, purplish, scarlet, crimson; very little yellow:

'Flame' Narrowleaf ASH (*Fraxinus angustifolia* 'Flame')
Sargent CHERRY (*Prunus Sargentii*)
Bald CYPRESS (*Taxodium distichum*)
FRANKLIN TREE (*Franklinia alatamaha*)
Pin OAK (*Quercus palustris*)
Red OAK (*Quercus rubra*)
Scarlet OAK (*Quercus coccinea*)
White OAK (*Quercus alba*)
SORREL TREE (*Oxydendrum arboreum*)
SUMACH (*Rhus*)
TUPELO (*Nyssa sylvatica*)

E) Yellow, essentially:

Green ASH (*Fraxinus pennsylvanica*)
Oregon ASH (*Fraxinus latifolia*)
American BEECH (*Fagus grandifolia*)
BIRCH (*Betula*)
CASCARA (*Rhamnus Purshiana*)—in woods; not in the open
CATALPA (*Catalpa*)
Bitter CHERRY (*Prunus emarginata*)

Black CHERRY (*Prunus serotina*)
CHESTNUT (*Castanea*)
ELM (*Ulmus*)
GINKGO (*Ginkgo biloba*)
Downy HAWTHORN (*Cratægus mollis*)
HAZEL (*Corylus*)
HICKORY (*Carya*)
European HORNBEAM (*Carpinus Betulus*)
HORSE CHESTNUT (*Æsculus Hippocastanum*)
KENTUCKY COFFEE-TREE (*Gymnocladus dioicus*)
LARCH & Tamarack (*Larix, Pseudolarix*)
LINDEN (most *Tilia*)
Honey LOCUST (*Gleditsia triacanthos*)
Bigleaf MAPLE (*Acer macrophyllum*)
Box-Elder MAPLE (*Acer Negundo*)
English MAPLE (*Acer campestre*)
Norway MAPLE (*Acer platanoides*)
Silver MAPLE (*Acer saccharinum*)
Vine MAPLE (*Acer circinatum*)—in the woods; not in the open
White MULBERRY (*Morus alba*)
OSAGE ORANGE (*Maclura pomifera*)
PHELLODENDRON (*Phellodendron*)
PLANE (*Platanus*)
POPLAR, Aspen & Cottonwood (*Populus*)
REDBUD (*Cercis*)
SERVICEBERRY (*Amelanchier alnifolia*)
SILVERBELL (*Halesia carolina*)
TULIP TREE (*Liriodendron Tulipifera*)
WALNUT, Heartnut & Butternut (*Juglans*)
WINGNUT (*Pterocarya*)
YELLOW-WOOD (*Cladrastis*)

13. **Leaves** fragrant (excluding conifers).

EUCALYPT (*Eucalyptus*)
EUODIA (*Tetradium*)
HOP TREE (*Ptelea trifoliata*)
Bay LAUREL (*Laurus nobilis*)
Camphor LAUREL (*Cinnamomum Camphora*)
LINDERA (*Lindera obtusiloba*)
Anise MAGNOLIA (*Magnolia salicifolia*)
Chilean MYRTLE (*Luma apiculata*)
Oregon MYRTLE (*Umbellularia californica*)
Chinese PISTACHIO (*Pistacia chinensis*)
PITTOSPORUM (*Pittosporum*)
SASSAFRAS (*Sassafras albidum*)
SWEETGUM (*Liquidambar*)
Chinese TOON (*Toona sinensis*)
WAX-MYRTLE (*Myrica californica*)
WINTER'S BARK (*Drimys Winteri*)
ZANTHOXYLUM (*Zanthoxylum*)

14. **Leaves** late/slow to appear in spring (sometimes preceded by flowers).

ASH (some *Fraxinus*)
CATALPA (*Catalpa*)
CHINESE SCHOLAR-TREE (*Sophora japonica*)
CRAPE-MYRTLE (*Lagerstrœmia indica*)
Bald CYPRESS (*Taxodium distichum*)
English ELM (*Ulmus minor* var. *vulgaris*)
EMPRESS TREE (*Paulownia tomentosa*)
FIG (*Ficus Carica*)
HACKBERRY (*Celtis occidentalis*)
HICKORY (*Carya*)
KENTUCKY COFFEE-TREE (*Gymnocladus dioicus*)
Honey LOCUST (*Gleditsia triacanthos*)
Cucumber Tree (MAGNOLIA) (*Magnolia acuminata*)
MULBERRY (*Morus*)
OSAGE ORANGE (*Maclura pomifera*)
PAWPAW (*Asimina triloba*)
PERSIMMON (*Diospyros*)
American Sycamore (PLANE) (*Platanus occidentalis*)
REDBUD (*Cercis*)
SILK TREE (*Albizia Julibrissin*)
TREE OF HEAVEN (*Ailanthus altissima*)
TUPELO (*Nyssa sylvatica*)
WALNUT, Heartnut & Butternut (*Juglans*)

15. **Leaves** late/slow to drop in fall or winter—sometimes actually evergreen.

ALDER (*Alnus*)
APPLE (*Malus domestica*)—saplings
CASCARA (*Rhamnus Purshiana)*—seedlings and saplings
Bald CYPRESS (*Taxodium distichum*)
Eastern DOGWOOD (*Cornus florida*)—some
Evergreen DOGWOOD (*Cornus capitata*)
Chinese ELM (*Ulmus parvifolia*)
Cornish ELM (*Ulmus minor* var. *cornubiensis*)
English ELM (*Ulmus minor* var. *vulgaris*)
September ELM (*Ulmus serotina*)
Chilean FIRE-TREE (*Embothrium coccineum*)
GOLDENCHAIN TREE (*Laburnum*)—some
Chinese HACKBERRY (*Celtis labilis*)
Carrière HAWTHORN (*Cratægus × Lavallei*)
Evergreen HAWTHORN (*Cratægus × grignonensis*)
Shining HAWTHORN (*Cratægus × nitida*)
Cretan MAPLE (*Acer sempervirens*)
English OAK (*Quercus robur*)—especially saplings
Laurel OAK (*Quercus laurifolia*)
Water OAK (*Quercus nigra*)
Dancer® PEAR (*Pyrus betulæfolia* Dancer®)
Cottonwood (POPLAR) (*Populus balsamifera* ssp. *trichocarpa*)
Chinese QUINCE (*Pseudocydonia sinensis*)

RUSSIAN OLIVE (*Elæagnus angustifolia*)
SYCOPARROTIA (× *Sycoparrotia semidecidua*)
SWEETGUM (*Liquidambar Styraciflua*)—many
WILLOW (*Salix*)—many, especially weeping ones

16. **Leaves** persisting brown and dead on twigs sometimes nearly until spring, especially on younger specimens in sheltered, unpolluted locations.

American BEECH (*Fagus grandifolia*)
European BEECH (*Fagus sylvatica*)
European HORNBEAM (*Carpinus Betulus*)
Pin OAK (*Quercus palustris*)
Scarlet OAK (*Quercus coccinea*)

17. **Leaves** purplish-reddish.

European BEECH (*Fagus sylvatica* f. *purpurea*) and its cultivars
White BIRCH (*Betula pendula* 'Purpurea')
Hybrid CATALPA (*Catalpa* × *erubescens* 'Purpurea')
Choke CHERRY (*Prunus virginiana* 'Schubert')
Japanese Flw. CHERRY (*Prunus serrulata* 'Royal Burgundy')
CRABAPPLE (*Malus*)—several kinds, notably 'Royalty'
HOP BUSH (*Dodonæa viscosa*)
Japanese MAPLE (*Acer palmatum* cultivars)
Norway MAPLE (*Acer platanoides* cultivars)
Sycamore MAPLE (*Acer Pseudoplatanus* 'Atropurpureum')
Cherry PLUM (*Prunus cerasifera*) and its cultivars & hybrids
SILK TREE (*Albizia Julibrissin* 'Summer Chocolate')
European SMOKE TREE (*Cotinus Coggygria*)

18. **Leaves** silvery, bluish, grayish, or whitish, either on the undersides only or on both surfaces; sometimes only or chiefly in spring (excluding conifers).

ACACIA (*Acacia Baileyana, A. dealbata*)
EUCALYPT (*Eucalyptus*)
Silver LINDEN (*Tilia tomentosa*)
Sweet-Bay (MAGNOLIA) (*Magnolia virginiana*)
Whitebeam (MOUNTAIN ASH) (*Sorbus Aria, Folgneri* hybrid, *pallescens*)
Silverleaf OAK (*Quercus hypoleucoides*)
OLIVE (*Olea europæa*)
Dancer® PEAR (*Pyrus betulæfolia* Dancer®)
Weeping Willowleaf PEAR (*Pyrus salicifolia* 'Pendula')
Gray POPLAR (*Populus* × *canescens*)
White POPLAR (*Populus alba*)
RUSSIAN OLIVE (*Elæagnus angustifolia*)—and other spp.
Rosemary WILLOW (*Salix Elæagnos*)

19. Leaves stinking, strongly fetid (see also list 13).

CATALPA (*Catalpa*)—some
Black CHERRY (*Prunus serotina*)
English LAUREL (*Prunus Laurocerasus*)
California NUTMEG-TREE (*Torreya californica*)
PAWPAW (*Asimina triloba*)
PEANUT-BUTTER TREE (*Clerodendrum trichotomum*)
TREE OF HEAVEN (*Ailanthus altissima*)

20. Leaves tiny; dainty, fine-textured effect; see also list 11 for some cutleaved variants which produce the same elegant look in the landscape.

ACACIA (*Acacia pravissima*)
Boxleaf AZARA (*Azara microphylla*)
Southern-BEECH (*Nothofagus* spp. other than *N. obliqua* & *N. procera*)
Mount Ætna BROOM (*Genista ætnensis*)
Bald CYPRESS (*Taxodium distichum*)
EUCALYPTUS (*Eucalyptus Nicholii*)
Japanese HOLLY (*Ilex crenata*)
KŌWHAI (*Sophora microphylla, tetraptera*)
Honey LOCUST (*Gleditsia triacanthos*)
Chilean MYRTLE (*Luma apiculata*)
SILK TREE (*Albizia Julibrissin*)
African SUMACH (*Rhus lancea*)
TAMARISK (*Tamarix*)
Rosemary WILLOW (*Salix Elæagnos*)

21. Leaves variegated markedly (excluding conifers).

ANGELICA TREE (*Aralia elata*) cultivars
Boxleaf AZARA (*Azara microphylla* 'Variegata')
European BEECH (*Fagus sylvatica* 'Purpurea Tricolor')
Italian BUCKTHORN (*Rhamnus Alaternus* 'Argenteo-variegata')
Cornelian Cherry DOGWOOD (*Cornus mas* 'Variegata')
Eastern DOGWOOD (*Cornus florida* 'First Lady', Rainbow' & 'Welchii')
Giant DOGWOOD (*Cornus controversa* 'Variegata')
Kousa DOGWOOD (*Cornus Kousa* 'Wolf Eyes')
Pacific DOGWOOD (*Cornus Nuttallii* 'Eddiei')
Pagoda DOGWOOD (*Cornus alternifolia* 'Argentea')
Sunrise HORSE CHESTNUT (*Æsculus* × *neglecta* 'Erythroblastos')
English HOLLY and its hybrids (*Ilex Aquifolium, I.* × *altaclerensis* cvs.)
Portugal LAUREL (*Prunus lusitanica* 'Variegata')
Box-Elder MAPLE (*Acer Negundo*) cultivars
English MAPLE (*Acer campestre* 'Carnival')
Norway MAPLE (*Acer platanoides* 'Drummondii')
Stripebark MAPLE (*Acer rufinerve* f. *albolimbatum*)
Sycamore MAPLE (*Acer Pseudoplatanus*) cultivars
Common OSMANTHUS (*Osmanthus heterophyllus*) cultivars
PITTOSPORUM (*Pittosporum* 'Garnettii', 'Irene Patterson')
Aurora POPLAR (*Populus* 'Candicans Aurora')
SWEETGUM (*Liquidambar Styraciflua*) cultivars

Dappled WILLOW (*Salix integra* 'Hakuro-nishiki')

22. **Leaves** yellowish-golden, especially in spring or early summer, and in sunny exposures (excluding conifers).

European ASH (*Fraxinus excelsior* 'Jaspidea')
Southern CATALPA (*Catalpa bignonioides* 'Aurea')
European BEECH (*Fagus sylvatica* 'Zlatia')
Bay LAUREL (*Laurus nobilis* 'Aurea')
Black LOCUST (*Robinia Pseudoacacia* 'Frisia')
Honey LOCUST (*Gleditsia triacanthos* 'Sunburst')
Golden Full Moon MAPLE (*Acer Shirasawanum* 'Aureum')
Norway MAPLE (*Acer platanoides* Princeton Gold™)
SMOKE TREE (*Cotinus Coggygria* Golden Spirit™)

23. **Narrow** form: columnar variants; very slender, cylindrical or narrow flame-shape (excluding conifers).

European BEECH (*Fagus sylvatica* 'Dawyck' & 'Dawyck Purple')
White BIRCH (*Betula pendula* 'Fastigiata')
Japanese Flw. CHERRY (*Prunus serrulata* 'Amanogawa')
Sargent CHERRY (*Prunus Sargentii* 'Columnaris')
Spire CHERRY (*Prunus* 'Spire')
CRABAPPLE (*Malus Tschonoskii*)
Guernsey ELM (*Ulmus* 'Sarniensis')
EUCRYPHIA (*Eucryphia*)
GINKGO (*Ginkgo biloba* f. *fastigiata*)
Common HAWTHORN (*Cratægus monogyna* f. *stricta*)—when young
Japanese HOLLY (*Ilex crenata* 'Mariesii')
European HORNBEAM (*Carpinus Betulus* 'Frans Fontaine')
Black LOCUST (*Robinia Pseudoacacia* 'Fastigiata')
Bigleaf MAPLE (*Acer macrophyllum* 'Seattle Sentinel')
Norway MAPLE (*Acer platanoides*) cultivars
Red MAPLE (*Acer rubrum*) cultivars
Sugar MAPLE (*Acer saccharum* 'Newton Sentry')
MOUNTAIN ASH (*Sorbus aucuparia* 'Fastigiata')
Crimson Spire™ OAK (*Quercus robur* f. *fastigiata* × *Q. alba*)
English OAK (*Quercus robur* f. *fastigiata*)
Pin OAK (*Quercus palustris* Green Pillar™)
PITTOSPORUM (*Pittosporum bicolor*)
Bolleana (White) POPLAR (*Populus alba* 'Pyramidalis')
Ghost (Black) POPLAR (*Populus nigra* 'Thevestina')
Lombardy (Black) POPLAR (*Populus nigra* 'Italica')
Simon POPLAR (*Populus Simonii* 'Fastigiata')

24. **Suckers** from the roots commonly.

ANGELICA TREE (*Aralia elata*)
American BEECH (*Fagus grandifolia*)
English ELM (*Ulmus minor* var. *vulgaris*)
Bigleaf LINDEN (*Tilia platyphyllos*)
Black LOCUST (*Robinia Pseudoacacia*)
Bristly LOCUST (*Robina hispida*)
Coliseum MAPLE (*Acer cappadocicum*)
Paper MULBERRY (*Broussonetia papyrifera*)
PAWPAW (*Asimina triloba*)
PEANUT-BUTTER TREE (*Clerodendrum trichotomum*)
Common PLUM (*Prunus domestica*)
POPLAR & Aspen (most *Populus*)
SASSAFRAS (*Sassafras albidum*)
Smooth SUMACH (*Rhus glabra*)
Staghorn SUMACH (*Rhus typhina*)
TREE OF HEAVEN (*Ailanthus altissima*)

25. **Tender**, semi-hardy here: prone to winter damage (or even death) or, simply touchy when young or when in less than ideal locations.

ACACIA (*Acacia*)
AZARA (*Azara*)
Southern-BEECH (*Nothofagus Cunninghamii, N. Solandri*)
Italian BUCKTHORN (*Rhamnus Alaternus*)
BUNYA-BUNYA (*Araucaria Bidwillii*)
CABBAGE TREE (*Cordyline*)
CRAPE-MYRTLE (*Lagerstrœmia indica*)
CRINODENDRON (*Crinodendron Patagua*)
Monterey CYPRESS (*Cupressus macrocarpa*)—especially yellow juvenile cultivars
Evergreen DOGWOOD (*Cornus capitata*)
EUCALYPT (most kinds of *Eucalyptus*)
EUCRYPHIA (most kinds of *Eucryphia*)
Chilean FIRE-TREE (*Embothrium coccineum*)
Chilean HAZEL (*Gevuina Avellana*)
Summer HOLLY (*Comarostaphylis diversifolia*)
HOHERIA (*Hoheria*)
HOP BUSH (*Dodonæa viscosa*)
Catalina IRONWOOD (*Lyonothamnus floribundus* f. *aspleniifolius*)
JAPANESE BLUEBERRY TREE (*Elæocarpus sylvestris*)
KŌWHAI (*Sophora microphylla, tetraptera*)
Camphor LAUREL (*Cinnamomum Camphora*)
Canary Island LAUREL (*Apollonias Barbujana*)
LOQUAT (*Eriobotrya* and hybrids)
MAGNOLIA relatives (*Manglietia, Michelia, Parakmeria*)
MALLOTUS (*Mallotus japonicus*)
MAYTEN (*Maytenus Boaria*)
Chilean MYRTLE (*Luma apiculata*)
OAK (some SW North American evergreen *Quercus*, such as *Q. arizonica*)
PALM—most kinds, but notably *Washingtonia*

Jelecote PINE (*Pinus patula*)
Monterey PINE (*Pinus radiata*)
Montezuma PINE (*Pinus Montezumæ*)
Paraná PINE (*Araucaria angustifolia*)
PITTOSPORUM (*Pittosporum*)
African SUMACH (*Rhus lancea*)
WINTER'S BARK (*Drimys Winteri*)

26. Thorny, prickly or bristly, to varying degrees (excluding conifers).

ANGELICA TREE (*Aralia elata, A. spinosa*)
Castor ARALIA (*Kalopanax septemlobus*)
HAWTHORN (most *Cratægus*)
HOLLY (most *Ilex*)
Black LOCUST (*Robinia Pseudoacacia*)
Bristly LOCUST (*Robinia hispida*)
Honey LOCUST (*Gleditsia triacanthos*)
OAK (*Quercus agrifolia, arizonica, chrysolepis, durata, Ilex, vaccinifolia, Wislizenii*)
OSAGE ORANGE (*Maclura pomifera*)
OSMANTHUS (*Osmanthus*)
PEAR (*Pyrus communis*)
Cherry PLUM (*Prunus cerasifera*)
Common PLUM (*Prunus domestica*)
RUSSIAN OLIVE (*Elæagnus angustifolia*)
SEA BUCKTHORN (*Hippophaë*)
ZANTHOXYLUM (*Zanthoxylum*)

27. Weeping form: mostly named variants—not *naturally* weeping types.

A) Conifers:
Alaska CEDAR (*Cupressus nootkatensis*)
Atlas CEDAR (*Cedrus atlantica* 'Glauca Pendula')
weeping Deodar CEDAR (*Cedrus Deodara*)—two cultivars
Lawson CYPRESS (*Chamæcyparis Lawsoniana* 'Lutea', 'Pendula')
Sawara CYPRESS (*Chamæcyparis pisifera* f. *filifera*)
Douglas FIR (*Pseudotsuga Menziesii* 'Pendula')
Eastern HEMLOCK (*Tsuga canadensis*)—several cultivars
Chinese JUNIPER (one form of *Juniperus chinensis*)
Drooping JUNIPER (*Juniperus recurva*)
Needle JUNIPER (*Juniperus rigida*)
Weeping JUNIPER (*Juniperus squamata Fargesii*)
European LARCH (*Larix decidua* f. *pendula*)
Eastern White PINE (*Pinus Strobus* 'Pendula')
Japanese Red PINE (*Pinus densiflora* 'Pendula')
Sierra REDWOOD (*Sequoiadendron giganteum* 'Pendulum')
Colorado SPRUCE (*Picea pungens* 'Koster')
Himalayan SPRUCE (*Picea Smithiana*)
Norway SPRUCE (*Picea Abies* 'Inversa', 'Reflexa' & 'Pendula')
Serbian SPRUCE (*Picea Omorika*)
Siskiyou SPRUCE (*Picea Breweriana*)
White SPRUCE (*Picea glauca* 'Pendula')

B) Broadleaf trees:

European BEECH (*Fagus sylvatica* 'Purple Fountain', f. *pendula*, & 'Purpurea Pendula')
White BIRCH (*Betula pendula* 'Crispa', 'Tristis', 'Youngii')
Weeping CHERRY (*Prunus pendula*)—not all the cultivars weep
Japanese CHERRY (*Prunus serrulata* 'Kiku-shidare-zakura')
Snow Fountains CHERRY (*Prunus* Snow Fountains®)
Yoshino CHERRY (*Prunus × yedoensis* f. *perpendens*)
CHINESE SCHOLAR-TREE (*Sophora japonica* 'Pendula')
CRABAPPLE (*Malus* 'Echtermeyer', 'Louisa', 'Red Jade' Weeping Candied Apple®)
Camperdown ELM (*Ulmus glabra* 'Camperdownii')
EUCALYPTUS (*Eucalyptus lacrimans*)
Common HAWTHORN (*Cratægus monogyna* f. *pendula*)
Alpine GOLDENCHAIN TREE (*Laburnum alpinum* 'Pendulum')
MAYTEN (*Maytenus Boaria* Green Showers™)
White MULBERRY (*Morus alba* 'Chapparal' & 'Pendula')
PEACH (*Prunus Persica*)—several cultivars
Weeping Willowleaf PEAR (*Pyrus salicifolia* 'Pendula')
Japanese PLUM (*Prunus salicina* 'Weeping Santa Rosa')
Gray POPLAR (*Populus × canescens* 'Pendula')
Weeping POPLAR (*Populus tristis* and *P. Simonii* 'Pendula')
WILLOW (*Salix*)—various kinds

GLOSSARY

The explanations and definitions of terms refer to the senses intended in this book: other writers sometimes use the words differently. All capitalized words are glossary entries.

ALTERNATE (of leaves): The way leaves are arranged in relation to one another on twigs is called alternate unless the leaves are OPPOSITE one another (as in Maples for example) or whorled around the twigs (as in most conifers).

ANTHERS: The pollen-bearing tips of STAMENS; the male floral organs.

ARBORESCENT: Tree-like. A little-used synonym is *dendroid*.

AROUND (of trunks): The circumference or girth of a trunk, equivalent to someone's waist measurement. Measurements are generally taken at 4½' above the average soil level at the base of the trunk. In Great Britain and parts of Canada at 5 feet = about 1½ meters.

BACKCROSS (of hybrids): When an offspring from a cross (*i.e.* hybridization) is in turn crossed with one of *its parents*, the action and the resulting "incestuous" progeny is called a backcross. The result is a HYBRID with significantly more of its genetic background coming from one parent than from the other.

BISEXUAL: Producing both female and male reproductive organs. Most trees are bisexual. The term in *this* book is usually employed if specific individual trees, in being bisexual, are anomalous compared to the majority of their kind. For example, most individual Osage Orange trees are either male or female; few are bisexual. *Hermaphroditic* is a synonym.

BLOOM: 1) A thin, powdery or waxy layer on the skin of a fruit, or other plant part; easily rubbed off, making the surface shiny instead of dull. 2) The flower, or period of flowering.

BOTANIST: One who seriously studies plants, usually with a scientific approach. One who particularly studies or deals with trees may be called a dendrologist or an arborist. See also HORTICULTURAL.

BRACT: A reduced or modified leaf, which can be PETAL-like and showy, or utterly inconspicuous.

BROADLEAF EVERGREEN: An evergreen tree or shrub other than those known as CONIFERS. For example, Holly, Laurel, Madrona.

BUDDING: A form of GRAFTING.

CALYX: A collective term for the SEPALS.

CATKIN: An elongated, usually slender, limp, drooping, fleeting floral organ. Most catkin-bearing trees produce conspicuous male catkins whose role is releasing pollen to fertilize separate female floral organs. Technical terms for catkins are *strobile* or *ament*. An English name for some is *lamb's tail*. Common trees producing them include: Alder, Birch, Hazel, Walnut, Willow.

CLONE: A reproduction genetically identical to its source, having been reproduced/propagated vegetatively rather than sexually. A person desirous of a 'Gravenstein' Apple tree doesn't plant a *seed* to get one—it won't work—but instead grows the cloned CULTIVAR 'Gravenstein' via grafting or other asexual reproductive methods.

COMPOUND (of leaves): Most leaves are simple. Compound ones consist of a number of LEAFLETS sharing one central stalk that arises from one leafbud. See lists 8, 9 and 10 (pages 428–29), and LEAFLETS.

CONIFER: A generally cone-bearing, needled or scalelike-foliaged evergreen tree or shrub. For example: Cedars, Firs, Pines, Spruces; also the berry-bearing Junipers and Yews; and some are deciduous, as Bald Cypress, Larch, and Dawn Redwood.

CORDATE: Heart-shaped. Usually in reference to leaf bases.

CULTIVAR: See the Introduction, p.12.

CUTTINGS: A cutting is an example of clonal (= asexual or vegetative) propagation (see CLONE). For example, nurserymen snip off twigs of Leyland Cypresses, root them, and sell them—as Leyland Cypress trees, not as "rooted cuttings." *Root*-cuttings as well as *twig*-cuttings are sometimes used to propagate certain trees, such as White Poplar.

DOUBLE (of flowers): Double(d) flowers have extra petals, sometimes just a few, sometimes dozens, and appear fuller, fluffier and showier than the "single" or normal ones. They usually set less fruit than normal plants, or none. Common Roses are doubled, as are many Japanese Flw. cherry trees, and plenty of others. "Semi-double" is a stage recognized intermediate between single and fully double.

DOWNY: Softly hairy.

FASTIGIATE: Unusually slender and compact HABIT, being narrower than a typical tree-form. Useful for planting where space is severely limited or where strong vertical accent is sought.

FOUNDATION-PLANTING: Trees or shrubs planted near a house foundation—that is, by the walls—to mollify the transition from flat earth to vertical walls, to hide an ugly foundation or otherwise to beautify or accent the house.

GALLS: Swellings of various kinds, caused by certain insects. Galls can be found on virtually any parts of susceptible trees: bud, leaf, twig, flowerbud, fruit... They vary so much that generalizing about them must be minimal. Entire books are devoted to galls. See list 6 (page 426).

GLAND: Tiny secreting cells. A glandular plant part is often sticky or resinous, sometimes only microscopically so.

GLAUCOUS: Covered with a pale BLOOM, usually appearing dull powdery blue.

GRAFTING: A method of propagating plants by attaching one kind of plant onto another closely related kind. There are varied motives for grafting and different ways of doing it. Plant-propagation books go into much detail about it. See CLONE, ROOTSTOCK.

HABIT: Characteristic manner of growth. For example, narrow, broad, weeping, upswept, horizontal.

HARDY: More or less tolerant of cold, trying winters. Every place has certain hardy plants. Virtually any plant that consistently makes it through the winter outdoors without suffering significant injury, is called hardy. Those that do not are called "semi-hardy" or TENDER.

HORTICULTURAL: Horticulture is a fancy word for gardening. Horticultural has to do with growing, caring for, studying and teaching about plants. See also BOTANIST. The abbreviation *hort.* found after some names in this book, indicates names used by gardeners and nurserymen but not officially sanctioned by science.

HYBRID: A mule, a cross. When two closely related but *separate species* of plants or animals interbreed (in nature or in cultivation), their progeny is called hybrid. Among the commonly grown hybrid trees hereabouts are: most Japanese Fkowering Cherries, Redflower Horse Chestnut, Saucer Magnolia, Fraser Photinia, London Plane, virtually all plum trees, almost all of our weeping willows. Scientific names of hybrids are frequently but by no means invariably marked with an x or the multiplication sign ×).

JUVENILE: An immature stage noticeably different from the adult phase. Certain CONIFERS especially, exhibit significant juvenile foliage. Eucalypts and a few other non-conifers do too.

LANGUAGE OF FLOWERS: A "code" of symbolic meanings given to plants. It was a great fad in Victorian times, then fell into disfavor and is now largely forgotten and little known. Hundreds of plants, from mosses and mushrooms to flowers, fruits and trees, were given more or less appropriate meanings, affectations, keywords, sentiments. A bouquet of flowers could thus convey a complicated message.

LAYERING: A method of vegetative or asexual plant propagation wherein a *branch* is made to root by being placed in contact with soil or some other rooting-medium such as peat moss.

440

LEADER: The tip twig of a tree.

LEAFLETS: A bumpy little dot that serves as a breathing pore on a twig. The relative abundance and shape of lenticels help identify some trees in winter.

LENTICEL: "Little leaves" borne together forming one COMPOUND leaf. See also PALMATELY COMPOUND and PINNATELY COMPOUND.

MIDRIB: The main vein of a leaf, running down the middle. The leafstem or petiole is a continuation of the midrib.

NATURALIZED: A species not native in a given locale, but growing wild there, reproducing side by side with the natives.

OLD-GROWTH: Unlogged old trees being left or ignored or preserved—as opposed to second- or third-growth trees that follow logging, forest fires or slides.

OPEN-GROWN: A tree having full "elbow room" with plenty of sunlight and exposure to wind, as opposed to growing tall and skinny due to competition as in a forest or in a densely-planted landscape.

OPPOSITE (of leaves): When leaves are opposite one another on the twigs, rather than ALTERNATE or whorled. Maple is a good example of a tree with such arrangement.

ORIGINAL (of English names): Tree names sometimes come to signify other trees, related or unrelated. Sometimes a different tree has nearly usurped the usage of an old name. For example, modern tree-writers often ignore the fact that the "Scots Pine" was originally *the* "Fir" tree. Now the name "Fir" is applied to other trees. Hence, any tree mentioned as original in this book is the tree first known under a particular name, whether or not it is still called by that name.

OVARY: The female floral part that consists of the future fruit and seeds in embryonic form. Usually a tiny swollen bulb in the middle of the flower, with a protruding beak (STYLE) that terminates in the stigma. The POLLEN from the male floral organs (STAMENS) must come in contact with the ovary's stigma for fertilization to take place.

PALMATELY COMPOUND (of leaves): A kind of COMPOUND leaf with the main leafstalk radiating its LEAFLETS from one point. See list 8 (page 428).

PETAL: Attractive and usually colorful winglike floral appendages that delight our eyes.

PINETUM: A collection of pines and pine-like trees, as an arboretum is a general collection of trees, and a palmetum a collection of palms.

PINNATELY COMPOUND (of leaves): A kind of COMPOUND leaf with the main leafstalk lined by two rows of LEAFLETS. See list 9 (page 428). Ash and Walnut trees are good examples of trees bearing such leaves.

POLLEN: Yellowish, sporelike dust produced on ANTHERS that sit atop the STAMENS of the flowers. Pollen serves as the male portion in reproduction. *Pollination* is the process by which pollen is transferred by bees or some other source to the stigma. For *fertilization* to occur, the pollen must make its way down through the style or beak to the OVARY's inner recesses.

REVERT: When a plant with some kind of abnormality—such as VARIEGATION, or dwarfish stature or weeping habit—wholly or partly returns to producing normal or typical growth.

ROOTSTOCK: The roots used by plant propagators for BUDDING or GRAFTING cultivars. For example, an Apple tree can be obtained in dwarf, semi-dwarf, or standard sizes depending on what kind of rootstock is used.

SEMI-EVERGREEN: Also called sub-evergreen or partial-evergreen. A tree retaining its leaves, or many of them, very late in autumn or even well into winter, yet not fully evergreen as Holly is for example. See list 15 (page 432).

SEPAL: Green or occasionally reddish PETAL equivalents that are comparatively inconspicuous, hidden beneath the showy petals on the outside of the flower. Instead of being very delicate-textured, colorful, and broad like petals, sepals are usually narrow, small and plain. A collective term for the sepals is CALYX.

STAMENS: The male floral organs, each consisting of a threadlike filament topped by ANTHERS that bear the POLLEN.

STANDARD: Two meanings: 1) Relating to trees that are routinely offered by nurseries in several sizes, "standard" refers to normal or average size, as opposed to dwarf or semi-dwarf size. 2) Fraser Photinia, Bay Laurel, Serviceberry, and such plants routinely sold by nurseries either in shrub form or tree form, are called "standards" when grown in tree form: a single trunk with a definite crown.

STIPULE: Tiny leaf-like appendages at the junction of the leafstalk and the twig. Every kind of willow in Seattle has stipules, except the Hooker Pussy Willow—and even it sometimes does. Planetrees or sycamores bear prominent stipules.

STREET-TREE: A tree planted alongside a street, usually in a planting strip of lawn between the street and sidewalk. The term is also used for trees planted in traffic-diverting circles or triangles.

STYLE: The beak of the OVARY; the tapering neck between the ovary proper and the stigma.

SUCKER: Usually vertical, fast-growing, strong shoots that pop up variously from roots, trunks or branches of (usually heavily- pruned) trees. They commonly have extra-large leaves, and at least to begin with do not bear flowers or fruit. As a general rule they are considered undesirable eyesores. They are minimized by pruning in the growing season as opposed to dormant-season pruning. Also called water shoots.

TENDER: Prone to being hurt or killed in a given climate's winter. We usually tend to call tender those trees that have a reasonable chance of growing here, but that are certainly not HARDY. Tender can also apply to plants that don't have a prayer of being grown here except in a greenhouse.

TOPPED: A tree is topped when its top is decapitated by wind, lightning, or humans. Legitimate reasons for tree-topping exist in certain cases, but in general it is a practice too often abused, done poorly or for the wrong reasons, and is often cited as an abominable crime by extremists on the conservative end of the spectrum.

TOPIARY: The art of vegetative sculpture. Just as people shave poodles, or brush, comb, and curl their own hair into various artificial forms, so clippers and shears can be used

442

to shape trees and shrubs.

TRIFOLIATE: Three LEAFLETS, as a three-leaf clover.

VARIEGATION: Two or more colors appearing together in a leaf, such as green and yellow, or green and white and pink. See list 21 (page 434).

WITCHES'-BROOMS: Abnormally congested, twiggy masses growing in tree crowns like cancerous mutations. There are various causes. Some kinds of trees never get them, others frequently do. When plant enthusiasts propagate them the result is often a dwarfed version of the normal tree, quite suitable in small-scale gardens or rockeries.

GAZETTEER

Arboretum: see this book's Introduction, page *20*
Ballard Playground: 28th Ave NW & NW 60th St
Benefit Park: 9320 38th Ave S—at S Benefit St
Bradner Gardens Park: 29th Ave S & S Grand St
Burke-Gilman Trail: a long former railroad, now pedestrian / cyclist trail in N Seattle
Cal Anderson Park (Broadway Reservoir): 11th Ave & E Denny Way
Camp Long: 35th Ave SW & SW Dawson St
Carkeek Park: Go west on NW 110th St, from 3rd Ave NW
Children's Hospital: 45th Ave NE & NE 45th St
Colman Park: Intersection of 36th Ave S & Lakeside Ave S
Cowen Park: University Way NE & NE Ravenna Blvd (west of Ravenna Park)
Day School & Playground: Fremont Ave N & N 39th St
Denny Park: Dexter Ave N & Denny Way
Denny-Blaine Park: Lake Washington Blvd E & 40th Ave E
Discovery Park: 36th Ave W & W Government Way
Dunn Gardens: 13531 Northshire Rd NW (open by appointment only; 362–0933)
Franklin High School & Playfield: 3013 S Mt Baker Blvd
Frink Park: Lake Washington Blvd S & S Jackson St
Genesee Park: 45th Ave S & S Genesee St
Golden Gardens Park: North end of Seaview Ave NW
Good Shepherd Center: 4649 Sunnyside Ave N
Hiawatha Playfield: California Ave SW & SW Lander St
Ingraham High School: 1819 N 135th St
Interlaken Park & Blvd: Interlaken Blvd E, mainly west of 24th Ave E
Jefferson Park Golf Course: Beacon Ave S & S Spokane St
Kinnear Park: 7th Ave W & W Olympic Pl
Kruckeberg Botanic Garden: 20066 15th Ave NW, in Shoreline—N of Seattle
Kubota Garden Park: 55th Ave S & Renton Ave S
Lakeridge Park (Dead-horse Canyon): Holyoke Way S and Holyoke Place S
Lakeview Park: Lake Washington Blvd E & E Harrison St
Laurelhurst Playfield: 48th Ave NE & NE 45th St
Leschi Park: Lakeside Ave S between Lake Washington Blvd & S Main St
Lincoln Park: Fauntleroy Way SW & SW Holden St
Locks: see this book's Introduction, page *16*
Loyal Heights CC and Playfield: 22nd Ave NW & NW 75th St
Loyal Heights School: 2511 NW 80th St
Madrona Park: Lake Washington Blvd & E Columbia St

Magnuson Park: Sand Point Way NE between NE 65th and 74th St
Mapleleaf Playground: Roosevelt Way NE & NE 82nd St
Martha Washington Park: 6612 57th Ave S
Martin Luther King, Jr. Park: Martin Luther King, Jr. Way S & S Walker St
Matthews Beach Park: Sand Point Way NE & NE 93rd St
McClure School: 1st Ave W & W Crockett St
Meadowbrook Park's edible arboretum: by 32nd Ave NE & NE 105th St
Me-kwa-mooks Park: Beach Dr SW & SW Oregon St
Meridian Park: Meridian Ave N & N 50th St
Miller Community Center and playground: 19th Ave E & E John St
MOHAI: Museum of History & Industry; 2700 24th Ave E
Montlake School: 22nd Ave E & E McGraw St
Mt Baker Park & Blvd: S Mt Baker Blvd & S McClellan St
Nordic Heritage Museum: 3014 NW 67th St
NSCC: North Seattle Community College; 9600 College Way N
O.O. Denny Park: (A City of Seattle park, east of Lake Washington) Holmes Point Dr NE & NE 124th St
Pacific Medical Center: 1200 12th Ave S (by S Judkins St)
Paramount Park: north of Seattle at 10th Ave NE & NE 152nd St
Parsons Gardens Park: 7th Ave W & W Highland Dr
Phinney Neighborhood Center: 6532 Phinney Ave N
Queen Anne Blvd: An unofficial yet very real system of mostly tree-lined streets going around the top of Queen Anne Hill. Indicated only on the *better* maps of Seattle.
Rainier Beach High School: 8815 Seward Park Ave S
Ravenna Park: 20th Ave NE & NE 58th St (east of Cowen Park)
Roanoke Park: 10th Ave E & E Roanoke St
Rodgers Park: 1st Ave W & W Raye St
Roosevelt High School: 15th Ave NE & NE 66th St
Ross Playground: 3rd Ave NW & NW 43rd St
Salmon Bay Park: NW 70th St between 19th Ave NW & 21st Ave NW
Schmitz Park (Preserve): SW Admiral Way & SW Stevens St
Seattle Buddhist Church Wisteria Plaza: 16th Ave S & S Washington St
Seattle Center: Between Denny Way & Mercer St, west of 5th Ave N
Seattle Chinese Garden: adjacent to the Arboretum at SSCC
Seward Park: Lake Washington Blvd S & S Juneau St
Seward School & Playground: Eastlake Ave E & E Roanoke St
SSCC: South Seattle Community College; 6000 16th Ave SW
S.P.U.: Seattle Pacific University: 3rd Ave W & W Nickerson St
S.U.: Seattle University: Broadway & E Madison St
Swanson's Nursery: 9701 15th Ave NW
Twin Ponds Park: just north of Seattle at 1st Ave NE & N 155th St
U.W.: University of Washington: between NE 45th St and Portage Bay–Union Bay, mostly east of 15th Ave NE
Viewlands School: 3rd Ave NW & NW 105th St
View Ridge Playfield: 45th Ave NE & NE 70th St
Volunteer Park: 15th Ave E & E Prospect St
W Seattle Golf Course (& stadium): 35th Ave SW & SW Snoqualmie St
Woodland Park: North of N 50th St, Phinney Ave N to Green Lake Way N

SOURCES CITED
Books

Bean, W.J. and Blanche Henrey. *Trees and Shrubs Throughout the Year*. London: Lindsay Drummond, 1944.

Cartier, Jacques. *A shorte and briefe narration of the two Navigations and Discoveries to the Northwest partes called NEWE FRAUNCE*. Translated by John Florio from the Italian translation by G.B. Ramutius, from the original French. London: H. Bynneman, 1580.

Cobbett, William. *The Woodlands*. London: W. Cobbett, 1825.

Faux, William. *Memorable Days in America, November 27, 1819 – July 21, 1820*. London, 1823. Vol. 11–12 of *Early Western Travels, 1748–1846*. Edited by R.G. Thwaite. Cleveland, Ohio, 1905.

Flint, Timothy. *The History and Geography of the Mississippi Valley*. 2nd ed. Cincinnati: E.H. Flint and L. R. Lincoln, 1832.

Loudon, John C. *Arboretum et Fruticetum Britannicum; or, the Trees and Shrubs of Britain, native and foreign*. 2nd ed. 8 volumes. London: Henry G. Bohn, 1854.

Smith, Frederick Porter and G.A. Stuart. *Chinese Materia Medica; Vegetable Kingdom*. Shanghai: American Presbyterian Mission Press, 1911.

Thoreau, Henry David. *Writings of Henry David Thoreau*. 20 vols. [Walden ed.] Boston and New York: Houghton, Mifflin and Co., 1906.

Periodicals

American Forests. (monthly until Nov. 1986; bimonthly since) Washington, D.C.: American Forestry Association.

Washington Park Arboretum Bulletin. (quarterly) Seattle: Arboretum Foundation.

Arnoldia. (bimonthly until 1982; quarterly since) Jamaica Plains, Mass.: Arnold Arboretum, Harvard University.

Journal of Arboriculture. (monthly) Urbana, IL: International Society of Arboriculture.

SUGGESTED READING

There are bewildering numbers of books about trees. Below are some of a general nature deemed the best of their kind by this writer. Specialized works are omitted (*e.g.*: on conifers or on nut trees), as are forbiddingly technical manuals, foreign language writings, and books long out of print and unlikely to be found.

1) Pocket-sized tree-identification guides:
The Trees of Britain and Northern Europe
by Alan Mitchell and John Wilkinson
London: Collins, 1982 (288pp.)

A Field Guide to the Trees of Britain and Northern Europe
by Alan Mitchell
London: Collins, 1974 (415pp.)

2) Mid-sized tree-identification guides:
The Collins Tree Guide
by Owen Johnson, illustrated by David More
London: Collins, 2004 (464pp.)

Trees and Bushes of Europe
by Oleg Polunin and B. Everard
London: Oxford University Press, 1976 (208pp.)

The Oxford Book of Trees
by A.R. Clapham and B.E. Nicholson
London: Oxford University Press, 1975 (216pp.)

3) Large-sized coffeetable volumes:
Hugh Johnson's Encyclopædia of Trees
by Hugh Johnson
London: Mitchell Beazley, 1984 (336pp.)
(The 2nd edition of *The International Book of Trees*, originally published in 1973)

The Illustrated Encyclopædia of Trees
by John White; illustrated by David More
Portland: Timber Press, 2nd edition 2005 (832pp.)

4) Comprehensive tomes standard in library reference collections:
Trees and Shrubs Hardy in the British Isles
by W.J. Bean. 8th edition, revised.
London: John Murray, 1976 (4 volumes—plus a 1988 Supplement of 616pp.)

Manual of Cultivated Broad-leaved Trees and Shrubs; Manual of Cultivated Conifers
by Gerd Krüssmann, the German original; translated into English by M.E. Epp
Portland: Timber Press, 1984–86 (4 volumes)

North American Landscape Trees
by Arthur Lee Jacobson
Berkeley: Ten Speed Press, 1996 (798pp.)

5) On trees native to North America:
A Natural History of Trees of Eastern and Central North America
by Donald C. Peattie
Boston: Houghton Mifflin, 1950 (606pp.)

A Natural History of Western Trees
by Donald C. Peattie
Boston: Houghton Mifflin, 1953 (751pp.)

Textbook of Dendrology
by William M. Harlow and Ellwood S. Harrar
New York: McGraw-Hill, 5th edition 1969 (512pp.)
(An inferior 6th edition came out in 1979)

6) On trees native to the Pacific Northwest:
Northwest Trees
by Stephen F. Arno and Ramona P. Hammerly
Seattle: The Mountaineers, 1977 (222pp.)

7) On ornamental and landscape roles of trees in the Pacific Northwest:
Trees and Shrubs for Pacific Northwest Gardens
by John A. & Carol L. Grant; revised by M, Black, B, Mulligan, Jean & Joe Witt
Portland: Timber Press, 2nd edition 1990 (456pp.)

8) On big or champion-size trees:
Champion Trees of Washington State
by Robert Van Pelt
Seattle: University of Washington Press, 1996 (136pp.)

Forest Giants of the Pacific Coast
by Robert Van Pelt
Seattle: University of Washington Press, 2001 (224pp.)

Forest Giants of the World, Past and Present
by Al C. Carder
Markham, Ontario: Fitzhenry & Whiteside, 1995 (224pp.)

Giant Trees of Western America and the World
by Al C. Carder
Madeira Park, B.C.: Harbour, 2005 (152pp.)

9) Miscellaneous popular books of merit:
Aristocrats of the Trees
by Ernest H. Wilson
Boston: Stratford, 1930 (279pp.)

Knowing Your Trees
by G.H. Collingwood and Warren D. Brush, revised by Devereux Butcher
Washington: The American Forestry Association, 1979 (389pp.)

Meetings With Remarkable Trees
by Thomas Pakenham
London: George Weidenfeld & Nicholson, Ltd., 1996 (191pp.)

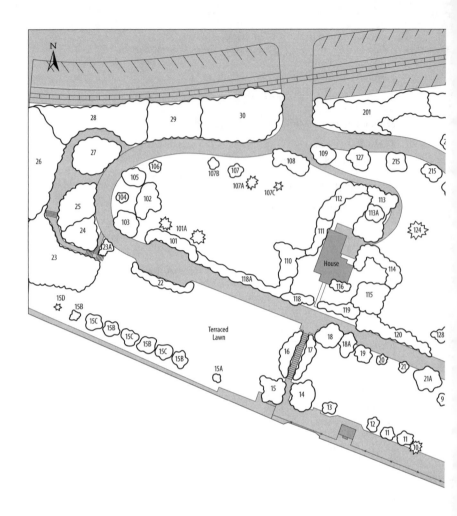

A MAP OF PLANTING BEDS AT THE LOCKS

The next six pages contain a **bed-by-bed list** of trees at the Locks, many of which are treated in this guide.

(A few trees *and shrubs* not treated in the guide are indicated by an *)

This map, supplied originally in the 1980s through the courtesy of the Seattle district Corps of Engineers, was updated in 2004 by Arthur Lee Jacobson and Keala Hagmann.

448

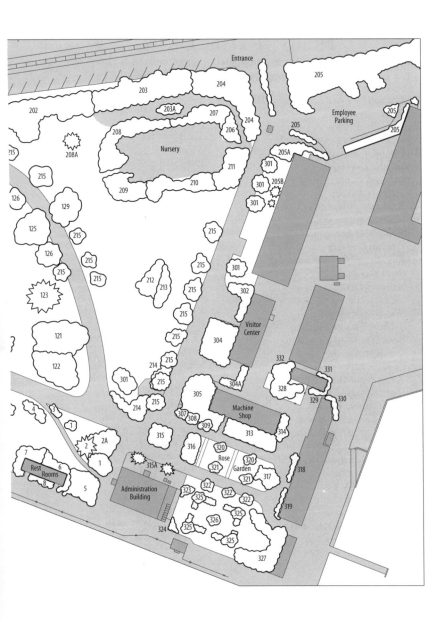

TREES AT THE LOCKS

A bed-by-bed list of those trees at the locks that are treated in this guide (a few trees *and shrubs* not treated in the guide are indicated by an *):

1 Canyon Live OAK (cut in July '05)
2 Atlas CEDAR
2A Dawn REDWOOD
3 MOUNTAIN ASH: *S. tianschanica*
   Ring-cupped OAK (two)
4 Manna ASH (wild)
   Mazzard CHERRY (wild)
   Holm OAK (four)
   SILVERBELL (shrubby)
5 Japanese CEDAR (four)
   *Enkianthus campanulatus**
   Canyon Live OAK (shrub sized)
   English OAK (wild; behind sign)
   SNOWBELL TREE
6 Incense CEDAR
   Yellow Buckeye (HORSECHESTNUT)
7 *Æsculus parviflora**
   Tanbark-Oak CHINQUAPIN
   Sargent MAGNOLIA (sprouts)
   Saucer MAGNOLIA (white)
   Chinese WITCH-HAZEL*
8 Forest CABBAGE TREE (two)
   Silverleaf OAK
   South African OLDWOOD
   PALM: *Chamærops humilis*
9 CRABAPPLE: *M. yunnanensis*
10 Plume Sawara CYPRESS
11 Himalayan HORSECHESTNUT (two)
12 Dawn REDWOOD
13 California Black OAK
14 Sierra REDWOOD
   Pacific WAX-MYRTLE
15 Manna ASH (several, wild)
   Japanese Silverleaf MAGNOLIA
   Wada's Memory MAGNOLIA
   Pacific WAX-MYRTLE (tree-sized)
15A PERSIAN IRONWOOD
15B CRABAPPLE: *M. hupehensis* (four)
15C CRABAPPLE: *M. × robusta* (three)
16 Cornelian-cherry (DOGWOOD)
   Golden LARCH
   Anise MAGNOLIA
   Evergreen MAGNOLIA
   Sprenger MAGNOLIA
   Nikko MAPLE
   MOUNTAIN ASH: *S. aucuparia* (two)

   California Live OAK
   English OAK (wild; shrubby)
   Korean PINE
   Lacebark PINE
17 Manna ASH (wild)
   CHINQUAPIN: *Castanopsis cuspidata*
   CHINQUAPIN: *Lithocarpus edulis*
   Strawberry Tree (MADRONA)
   Yellow Cucumber-Tree MAGNOLIA
   Veitch MAGNOLIA (E of big oak)
   Japanese MAPLE (by top of stairs)
   Trident MAPLE
   Oregon MYRTLE
   Bamboo-leaf OAK
   California Live OAK (big)
   Huckleberry OAK (two)
   Lacebark PINE (shade stunted)
   SILK TREE (two)
   Chinese SUMACH (tiny specimen)
18 Turkish OAK
18A English OAK variation
19 English OAK variation
20 Oriental White OAK
21 American BEECH
21A Rocky-Mt. White OAK
22 Japanese CEDAR
   CHINQUAPIN: Tanbark-Oak (two)
   Japanese MAPLE
23 Italian ALDER
   Downy BIRCH (two)
   White BIRCH (three)
   Lebanon CEDAR (small)
   Western Red CEDAR (wild; small)
   CHINQUAPIN: Tanbark-Oak (two)
   Eucalyptus sp.
   European LARCH
   Black LOCUST
   MADRONA (wild)
   Bigleaf MAPLE
   Japanese MAPLE (five)
   Sycamore MAPLE (wild)
   Canyon Live OAK (two)
   Ring-cupped OAK (by *Eucalyptus*)
   Gray *or* Digger PINE
   Austrian PINE
   Scots PINE (four)

Stone PINE (two; by #26)
23A CHINQUAPIN: Tanbark-Oak
24 CHINQUAPIN: Tanbark-Oak
Kousa DOGWOOD
EMPRESS TREE
Manchurian FIR
Turkish HAZEL
European LARCH
Japanese MAPLE (four)
Interior Live OAK (two; small)
Chinese PHOTINIA
25 Western Red CEDAR (three)
CHINQUAPIN: Tanbark-Oak (three)
Manchurian FIR
Downy HAWTHORN
Mountain HEMLOCK
Western HEMLOCK (two)
KATSURA (small)
Kobus MAGNOLIA (small)
Japanese MAPLE
Scarlet OAK (two)
Western SERVICEBERRY (shrubby)
26 Deodar CEDAR
Western Red CEDAR
CRABAPPLE: *M. Sargentii* (young)
Manchurian FIR (two)
Nikko MAPLE
Grosser's Stripebark MAPLE (two)
Redvein Stripebark MAPLE (varieg.)
Red OAK
Chinese PHOTINIA
HIBISCUS (near #28)
SPUR LEAF (young; 3-trunked)
27 Western Red CEDAR (four)
'Shogetsu' Japanese Flw. CHERRY
Sakhalin FIR (tiny)
Red OAK
Japanese Red PINE (three)
28 Oregon ASH (wild)
Deodar CEDAR
CRABAPPLE (*Malus fusca* hybrid)
Deodar CEDAR (two)
Douglas FIR (outside the fence)
Greek FIR
Manchurian FIR (three)
Common GOLDENCHAIN
Chinese PHOTINIA
Japanese Red PINE
Jeffrey PINE (two)
'Thundercloud' Cherry PLUM

SPINDLE TREE
29 Incense CEDAR
Western Red CEDAR (four)
Common GOLDENCHAIN
Western HEMLOCK
Sargent MAGNOLIA (6' tall)
Umbrella-Tree (MAGNOLIA)
MOUNTAIN ASH: *S. Folgneri* hybrid
California Live OAK (over bench)
Canyon Live OAK (by lightpost)
'Pissard' Cherry PLUM (E of fence)
30 Manna ASH
Chilean Incense CEDAR
Netleaf HACKBERRY (young)
Strawberry Tree (MADRONA)
Anhwei MAGNOLIA (2-trunked)
Sargent MAGNOLIA (by #29)
Ring-cupped OAK
Cherry PLUM (sprouts)
101 Alaska CEDAR (three)
CHINQUAPIN: Tanbark-Oak (wild)
Strawberry Tree (MADRONA)
Bristlecone PINE (two)
Scots PINE (by E lightpost)
Stone PINE (in the middle)
Colorado SPRUCE (blue)
101A Lawson CYPRESS (two)
102 CHINQUAPIN: Tanbark-Oak (wild)
Mountain HEMLOCK
MOUNTAIN ASH: *S. aucuparia*
Scarlet OAK (huge)
Bigleaf SNOWBELL TREE (sickly)
Oriental SPRUCE
103 Bigleaf LINDEN
104 double Weeping CHERRY
105 Kobus MAGNOLIA
106 'Autumnalis Rosea' Higan CHERRY
107 TUPELO
107A White FIR
107B 'Kwanzan' Japanese Flw. CHERRY
107C Sitka SPRUCE
108 White BIRCH (wild)
MADRONA (wild)
'Rustica Rubra' Saucer MAGNOLIA
Ubame OAK (on north side)
Japanese Red PINE (eleven)
Western SERVICEBERRY (shrubby)
109 'Brozzonii' Saucer MAGNOLIA
Sycamore MAPLE (wild)
Japanese Red PINE (three)

451

110 'Whitcomb' Higan CHERRY (two)
CHINQUAPIN: *Lithocarpus Henryi*
Red Stripebark MAPLE (wild)
MOUNTAIN ASH: *S. aucuparia*
Pacific WAX-MYRTLE

111 'Shirofugen' Japanese Flw. CHERRY
'Ukon' Japanese Flw. CHERRY
Umbrella-Tree (MAGNOLIA)
SNOWBELL TREE

112 'Shogetsu' Japanese Flw. CHERRY
Weeping CHERRY (big)
double Weeping CHERRY (by #113)
Yoshino CHERRY (several)
CRABAPPLE: *M. affin.* 'Almey'
Cornelian-cherry (DOGWOOD)
Lily MAGNOLIA (by #111)
Interior Live OAK
Scarlet OAK

113 Downy BIRCH
'Shiro-fugen' Japanese Flw. CHERRY
Eastern DOGWOOD
FRINGE TREE
MOUNTAIN ASH: *S. Rehderiana*
English YEW (wild)

113A Downy BIRCH

114 Japanese ANGELICA TREE (bushy)
Yoshino CHERRY
'Akebono' Yoshino CHERRY
CHINQUAPIN: *cutleaf* Tanbark-Oak
Siebold MAPLE
Red Stripebark MAPLE
MOUNTAIN ASH: *S. hupehensis*
SILK TREE (by #115)

115 Deodar CEDAR
CRABAPPLE: *M. Halliana* 'Parkm.'
Red Stripebark MAPLE
WHEEL TREE

116 Oyama MAGNOLIA

118 *Elæagnus multiflora*
Mountain HEMLOCK
Mugo PINE

118A HAZEL: *Corylus heterophylla**
Redflower HORSECHESTNUT (four)
Bigcone PINE

119 *Elæagnus pungens**
Mountain HEMLOCK
Asiatic HOLLY: *I. crenata* (by gate)
Asiatic HOLLY: *Ilex pedunculosa*
Star MAGNOLIA
Umbrella Tree (MAGNOLIA) by #115

Red Stripebark MAPLE
*Osmanthus × Burkwoodii**
Osmanthus heterophyllus

120 'Shiro-fugen' Japanese Flw. CHERRY
Kousa DOGWOOD
Portugal LAUREL
Japanese MAPLE (larger, green)
Japanese MAPLE (red laceleaf)
MOUNTAIN ASH: *S. aucuparia*
Canyon Live OAK (small)
Holm OAK (tall; wild)
PALM (wild)
*Photinia Davidiana**
Western SERVICEBERRY (shrubby)
Scouler Pussy-WILLOW (by light)

121 CRABAPPLE: *M. baccata himalaica*
Mazzard CHERRY
Sawara CYPRESS
Moss Sawara CYPRESS
Plume Sawara CYPRESS
Redberry ELDER*
Japan Silverleaf MAGNOLIA
Red Stripebark MAPLE
MOUNTAIN ASH: *S. aucuparia*
MOUNTAIN ASH: *S. Rehderiana*
Oregon MYRTLE

122 Japanese CEDAR
'Zebrina' Western Red CEDAR
Sawara CYPRESS
Moss Sawara CYPRESS (two)
Plume Sawara CYPRESS
EMPRESS TREE
GINKGO (slender; bent)
GOLDEN RAIN TREE
Chestnut OAK
Coast REDWOOD
Western SERVICEBERRY (shrubby)
Chinese WITCH-HAZEL*

123 'Zebrina' Western Red CEDAR
124 Sawara CYPRESS
125 Norway MAPLE
126 Calif. Buckeye (HORSECHESTNUT)
127 wineleaf Sycamore MAPLE
128 PALM (five)
129 Norway MAPLE
130 Sargent CHERRY
131 Yoshino CHERRY
201 Manna ASH
Roblé Southern-BEECH
'Shogetsu' Japanese Flw. CHERRY

452

Yoshino CHERRY (large)
Eastern DOGWOOD (by lightpost)
Taiwan Douglas FIR (*pl.* 1988)
Common GOLDENCHAIN
English HOLLY
Illicium anisatum *
Himalayan White PINE (by #202)
Coast REDWOOD
Sierra REDWOOD (five)
Staghorn SUMACH (at west end)
202 Japanese CEDAR (by #203)
Western Red CEDAR (three)
'Kwanzan' Japanese Flw. CHERRY
'Shiro-fugen' Japanese Flw. CHERRY
'Shirotae' Japanese Flw. CHERRY
Douglas FIR
Pindrow FIR (in Doug. Fir shade)
GINKGO (slender; in shade)
Arizona White OAK
Ubame OAK (by Gray Pine)
Gray *or* Digger PINE
Mugo PINE
Dawn REDWOOD (three)
Sierra REDWOOD (two)
SNOWBELL TREE
Smooth SUMACH (tiny, in shade)
YELLOW-WOOD (by #203)
203 European BEECH (small)
Northern CATALPA
Western Red CEDAR
'Kwanzan' Japanese Flw. CHERRY
'Ukon' Japanese Flw. CHERRY
Pacific DOGWOOD
Yellow Buckeye (HORSECHESTNUT)
MOUNTAIN ASH: *S. aucuparia*
PALM (wild)
PAWPAW
Date-Plum (PERSIMMON)
Coast REDWOOD (by #204)
Sierra REDWOOD (seven)
SWEETGUM
203A Moss Sawara CYPRESS (two)
English YEW
204 *Æsculus parviflora* *
Narrowleaf AZARA
dwarf CEDAR of Lebanon
Western Red CEDAR
'Shiro-fugen' Japanese Flw. CHERRY
'Shirotae' Japanese Flw. CHERRY
CHINESE SCHOLAR TREE

Douglas FIR
KATSURA (two)
Basswood (LINDEN) (by #203)
Star MAGNOLIA (opp. gatehouse)
Vine MAPLE (leaning)
MOUNTAIN ASH: *S. aucuparia* (wild)
Coast REDWOOD
Sierra REDWOOD (two)
Stewartia monadelpha (tiny)
Stewartia Pseudocamellia (S end)
205 APRICOT TREE
Callistemon citrinus * (two, large)
Callistemon pallidus * (two, small)
Combretum erythrophyllum * (two)
Incense CEDAR (three)
'Ukon' Japanese Flw. CHERRY
Okamé CHERRY
Lawson CYPRESS (four)
Kousa DOGWOOD
GINKGO
Portugal LAUREL
Strawberry Tree (MADRONA)
Grosser's Stripebark MAPLE
Bamboo-leaf OAK
Huckleberry OAK
Konara OAK (or allied sp.)
Leather OAK
Netleaf OAK
Red OAK
Ring-cupped OAK
Osmanthus armatus
'Aristocrat' Callery PEAR
Austrian PINE (eight)
Gregg PINE
Himalayan White PINE
Yunnan PINE
Chinese PISTACHIO
Coast REDWOOD (four)
SPINDLETREE (several)
Norway SPRUCE
Stewartia rostrata
WHEEL TREE
YELLOW-WOOD
205A Lawson CYPRESS
Leyland CYPRESS
Grevillea victoriæ *
MOUNTAIN ASH: *S. hupehensis*
PEANUT-BUTTER TREE
Japanese White PINE
Jeffrey PINE

453

205B Lawson CYPRESS (two)
206 'Shiro-fugen' Japanese Flw. CHERRY
'Ukon' Japanese Flw. CHERRY
Asiatic HOLLY: *I. Pernyi* (shrubby)
Strawberry Tree (MADRONA)
Kobus MAGNOLIA (shrubby)
Lodgepole PINE (two)
Stewartia Pseudocamellia (by gate)
Hybrid YEW
207 Deodar CEDAR (large)
Cornelian-cherry (DOGWOOD)
Kousa DOGWOOD
Chinese PINE (young; by #208)
208 *Camellia Sasanqua* (two tree-sized)
Deodar CEDAR (two)
CRABAPPLE: *M. baccata himalaica*
CRABAPPLE: *M. ×Eleyi* (two)
Common HAWTHORN (wild)
Strawberry Tree (MADRONA)
Hornbeam MAPLE (at west end)
Canyon Live OAK (large)
Austrian PINE (three)
209 'Shogetsu' Japanese Flw. CHERRY
Red Buckeye (HORSECHESTNUT)
SNOWBELL TREE (by #210)
Viburnum odoratissimum
English YEW (four)
210 CRABAPPLE: *M. ×floribunda* (big)
CRABAPPLE: *M. ×purpurea* 'Alden.'
Canyon Live OAK (the largest tree)
Cork Tree (OAK)
Holm OAK
Chinese PHOTINIA (bushy)
Siskiyou SPRUCE
Stewartia serrata (by #211)
211 Alaska CEDAR (four)
'Fugenzo' Japanese Flw. CHERRY
FILBERT (wild; by lightpost)
Asiatic HOLLY: *I. Pernyi* (three)
KATSURA (young)
hybrid Loquat/Rhaphiolepis
Amur MAPLE (young; at south end)
laceleaf Japanese MAPLE
MOUNTAIN ASH: *S. aucuparia*
Bamboo-leaf OAK (young)
Oregon MYRTLE (by #210)
*Osmanthus × Burkwoodii**
PAWPAW (north of Jelecote Pine)
PEANUT-BUTTER TREE
*Petteria ramentacea**

Jelecote PINE
SNOWBELL TREE (by lightpost)
Bigleaf SNOWBELL TREE
Stewartia monadelpha (two)
Stewartia rostrata
212 CRABAPPLE: *M. baccata himalaica*
Bald CYPRESS (five)
HORSECHESTNUT (at north end)
Dawn REDWOOD (two at S end)
TUPELO (three)
English YEW (wild)
213 Manna ASH (wild)
SWEETGUM
TULIP TREE (at S end)
TUPELO (three)
Pacific WAX-MYRTLE (shrubby)
214 'Peggy Clarke' Japanese APRICOT
thread Sawara CYPRESS
Cornelian-cherry (DOGWOOD) (3)
KATSURA (young)
Kousa DOGWOOD
Smoothbark EPAULETTE TREE
KATSURA
laceleaf Japanese MAPLE
Bristlecone PINE
Lacebark PINE (by lightpost)
Piñon PINE (two)
Pittosporum Tobira 'Variegatum'
SNOWBELL TREE
SPINDLETREE (two)
Stewartia Pseudocamellia (two)
Stewartia monadelpha
215 Redflower HORSECHESTNUT (lots)
301 Red OAK
302 Kousa DOGWOOD (3-stemmed)
GINKGO (hidden in corner)
Austrian PINE (large)
UMBRELLA PINE (by front door)
304 Narrowleaf AZARA
Naden CHERRY (by *Eucryphia*)
Eucryphia × intermedia
HIBISCUS (north of flagpole)
Himalayan White PINE (large)
Jelecote PINE (behind flagpole)
304A KATSURA
Chinese QUINCE
Stewartia monadelpha
Magnolialeaf WILLOW: *S. magnifica*
305 Japanese ANGELICA TREE (hidden)
Boxleaf or Common AZARA

454

Narrowleaf AZARA
*Ceanothus thyrsiflorus**
Ceanothus thyrsiflorus 'M. White'*
*Fatsia japonica**
IDESIA (two)
Yulan MAGNOLIA (between pines)
MALLOTUS
Cretan MAPLE (S of Cretan MAPLE)
Japanese MAPLE
PALM
*Parrotiopsis Jacquemontiana**
Japanese Red PINE (two)
WHEEL TREE (four)

307 Holm OAK
308 Ubame OAK
309 'Fukubana' Weeping CHERRY
313 *Bursaria spinosa**
*Callistemon viridiflorus**
'Kwanzan' Japanese Flw. CHERRY
Mazzard CHERRY (wild)
Sargent CHERRY
CRINODENDRON
DOGWOOD: *Cornus sessilis*
Eucalyptus camaldulensis (small)
Eucalyptus Gunnii (large)
Eucalyptus pauciflora (small)
*Fremontodendron californicum**
KŌWHAI: *Sophora microphylla*
Bay LAUREL
*Leptospermum lanigerum**
Pittosporum bicolor (narrow)
Pittosporum eugenioides (big leaves)
Pittosporum tenuifolium (east end)
PALM (west end of bed)
PALM: *Jubæa chilensis* (small)
Judas Tree (REDBUD)—two shrubs
*Vitex Agnus-castus** (SE corner)
314 Manna ASH
Campbell MAGNOLIA
Huckleberry OAK
315 *Enkianthus campanulatus** (two)
315A Alaska CEDAR
316 Korean FIR (tiny)
Netleaf OAK
Silverleaf OAK (two)
Bristlecone PINE (two)
317 'Akebono' Yoshino CHERRY
Hinoki CYPRESS
*Fatsia japonica**
318 *Camellia reticulata*

Common GOLDENCHAIN
Evergreen MAGNOLIA
PALM
Japanese WITCH-HAZEL*
319 *Cotoneaster lacteus**
Summer HOLLY
*Leptospermum lanigerum**
Evergreen MAGNOLIA
*Viburnum × bodnantense**
Black WALNUT (small)
320 'Kwanzan' Japanese Flw. CHERRY
321 Yoshino CHERRY
322 'Kwanzan' Japanese Flw. CHERRY
323 Canyon Live OAK (a shrub)
Netleaf OAK (tiny)
Stewartia Pseudocamellia
324 Watson MAGNOLIA
Netleaf OAK
325 'Whitcomb' Higan CHERRY
'Shiro-fugen' Japanese CHERRY
Yoshino CHERRY (SW)
326 Star MAGNOLIA
327 Largeleaf EHRETIA
Eucryphia glutinosa
FILBERT (wild)
Common GOLDENCHAIN
Yellow Buckeye (HORSECHESTNUT)
Texas MADRONA
pink-flower Star MAGNOLIA
Sweet Bay (MAGNOLIA)
Box-Elder (MAPLE)
PALM (SW corner)
PALM: *Chamærops humilis* (SE)
Gray *or* Digger PINE
Jeffrey PINE
Stewartia × Henryæ (bigger)
Stewartia monadelpha (smaller)
Black WALNUT (by lightpost)
WHEEL TREE (two)
328 GOLDEN RAIN TREE
Veitch MAGNOLIA
Scarlet OAK
SILVERBELL
329 *Camellia Sasanqua*
Netleaf HACKBERRY
330 FIG
Huckleberry OAK
PALM
Jack PINE

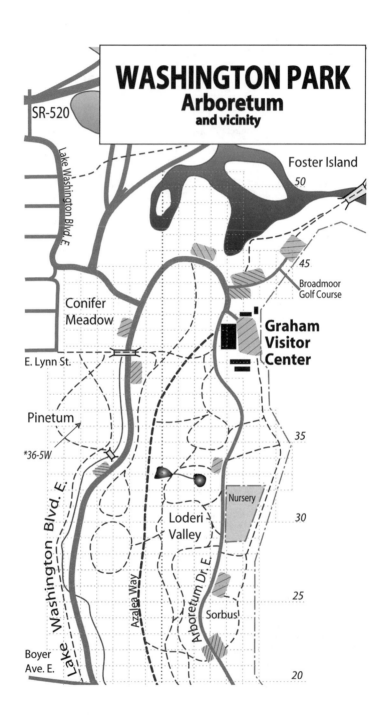

WASHINGTON PARK
Arboretum
and vicinity

SR-520

Lake Washington Blvd. E.

Foster Island

50

45

Broadmoor
Golf Course

Conifer
Meadow

**Graham
Visitor
Center**

E. Lynn St.

Pinetum

*36-5W

35

Washington Blvd. E.

Lake Washington Blvd. E.

Azalea Way

Arboretum Dr. E.

Nursery

Loderi
Valley

30

25

Sorbus

Boyer
Ave. E.

20

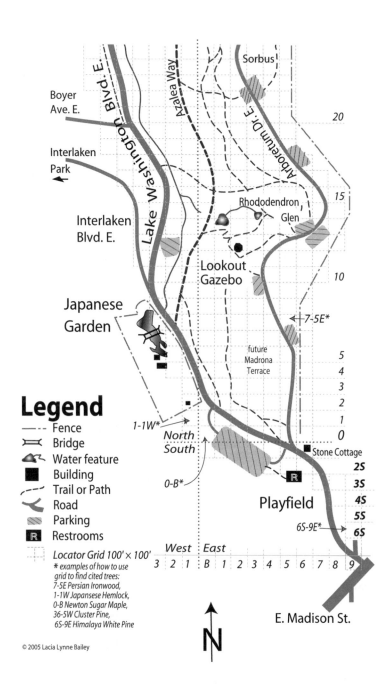

Boyer
Ave. E.

Interlaken
Park ◄

Interlaken
Blvd. E.

Japanese
Garden

Sorbus

Arboretum Dr. E.

20

Rhododendron
Glen

15

Lookout
Gazebo

10

←—7-5E*

future
Madrona
Terrace

5
4
3
2
1
0

Legend
- – – **Fence**
- ⋊–⋉ **Bridge**
- ⛰ **Water feature**
- ■ **Building**
- – – – **Trail or Path**
- ⤝ **Road**
- ▨ **Parking**
- Ⓡ **Restrooms**

— ·· — *Locator Grid 100' × 100'*
  *∗ examples of how to use
  grid to find cited trees:
  7-5E Persian Ironwood,
  1-1W Japansese Hemlock,
  0-B Newton Sugar Maple,
  36-5W Cluster Pine,
  6S-9E Himalaya White Pine*

© 2005 Lacia Lynne Bailey

1-1W* —→

North
South

0-B* —→

Stone Cottage

Ⓡ

Playfield

6S-9E* —→

2S
3S
4S
5S
6S

West East
3 ⋮ 2 ⋮ 1 ⋮ B ⋮ 1 ⋮ 2 ⋮ 3 ⋮ 4 ⋮ 5 ⋮ 6 ⋮ 7 ⋮ 8 ⋮ 9

E. Madison St.

N

458

483

486

490

X

Y

Z

NOTES

NOTES

NOTES

NOTES